2005

Radio and the Struggle for Civil Rights in the South

NEW PERSPECTIVES ON THE HISTORY OF THE SOUTH

UNIVERSITY PRESS OF FLORIDA / STATE UNIVERSITY SYSTEM

Florida A&M University, Tallahassee
Florida Atlantic University, Boca Raton
Florida Gulf Coast University, Ft. Myers
Florida International University, Miami
Florida State University, Tallahassee
University of Central Florida, Orlando
University of Florida, Gainesville
University of North Florida, Jacksonville
University of South Florida, Tampa
University of West Florida, Pensacola

University Press of Florida

Gainesville

Tallahassee

Tampa

Boca Raton

Pensacola

Orlando

Miami

Jacksonville

Ft. Myers

Brian Ward

RADIO

and the Struggle

for Civil Rights

in the South

09 08 07 06 05 04   6 5 4 3 2 1

Library of Congress Cataloging-in-Publication Data
Ward, Brian, 1961–
Radio and the struggle for civil rights in the South / by Brian Ward.
p. cm.—(New perspectives on the history of the South)
Includes bibliographical references (p.) and index.
ISBN 0-8130-2729-2 (acid-free paper)
1. African Americans in radio broadcasting—Southern States
—History—20th century. 2. African American radio stations—
Southern States—History—20th century. 3. African Americans—
Civil rights—Southern States—History—20th century. 4. Civil rights
movements—Southern States—History—20th century. 5. Southern
States—Race relations. I. Title. II. Series.
PN1991.8.A35W37 2004
384.54'089'96073075—DC22
2004043736

The University Press of Florida is the scholarly publishing agency
for the State University System of Florida, comprising Florida A&M
University, Florida Atlantic University, Florida Gulf Coast University,
Florida International University, Florida State University, University
of Central Florida, University of Florida, University of North Florida,
University of South Florida, and University of West Florida.

University Press of Florida
15 Northwest 15th Street
Gainesville, FL 32611-2079
http://www.upf.com

Contents

Figures

Foreword

Brian Ward's deeply researched and gracefully written *Radio and the Struggle for Civil Rights in the South* is one of the most important recent contributions to the history of the civil rights movement in the 1950s and 1960s. Ward employs radio as an analytical device to examine the origins, structure, and development of the civil rights movement. In his opinion, "radio was often the most important mass medium operating within southern black communities during the zenith of the civil rights struggles." Radio, Ward argues, "played an important role in laying the foundations for those struggles and was occasionally decisive in determining their outcome." His extraordinary research identifies a direct correlation between black-oriented radio and southern black identity, self-respect, protest, community formation, consumerism, and commercial enterprise.

Though radio stations first appeared in the South in the 1920s, the region did not experience an explosion of black-oriented broadcasting until the post–World War II years contemporaneous with the start of the modern civil rights movement. In the late 1940s and 1950s southern radio stations disseminated much-needed news and entertainment to the African American population. Influential facilities such as WDIA in Memphis, WOOK in Washington, D.C., WERD and WAOK in Atlanta, and WLAC in Nashville broadcast African American music, especially blues, gospel, and rhythm and blues, to listeners of both races throughout the region. By the 1960s "black radio" was ubiquitous in black homes—a powerful voice in defining, shaping, reflecting, and representing African American life. By 1963 there were more than 800 black-oriented radio stations, many of them located in the South.

Ward's great contribution is in establishing radio's central role in the African American freedom struggle. Radio exposed the injustices of Jim Crow, and civil rights activists used the airwaves to report its destruction. A colorblind medium, radio provided a platform for African Americans to demand equal, fair, and respectful treatment from whites and to establish group solidarity among themselves. Radio, Ward explains, encouraged black participation in civil rights protests, in fund raising, and in urging popular and government opinion to support African American demands.

Before black radio could succeed in improving race relations, however, it had to gain legitimacy with and respect from white listeners and sponsors. Ward explains that contrary to popular misconceptions, many early black deejays were college-educated men and women who took pains to use standard American English on air. Early black radio programs underscored traditional middle class values and gender roles, especially positive images of African American females. Indeed, Ward identifies a long tradition of southern black institutions, including colleges and churches, that utilized radiocasts for self-promotion and racial advancement.

In 1949 *Ebony* magazine asserted that African American radio preachers collectively had a weekly audience of approximately seven million listeners. While some activist black preachers used the airwaves to challenge Jim Crow, Ward correctly cautions against drawing unwarranted conclusions. "It is important," he says, "not to exaggerate either the extent of this practice, or the radicalism of those who dared to speak out against the operation of Jim Crow in the South on radio. Just as the degree of formal political engagement in the struggle for desegregation among pulpit-bound black preachers ranged from negligible to zealous, so there was a great deal of variation in the extent to which individual radio preachers espoused social and political equality in the South." Moreover, Ward suggests that "many southern whites appear to have seen African American religious broadcasts as a relatively harmless means to foster better race relations within the context of segregation through an emphasis on Christian love, brotherhood, and understanding." At best those who employed black radio to combat Jim Crow sought "to persuade, shame, or cajole significant elements in the white community to support—or at least acquiesce—to their demands. If and when it came, that acquiescence was often tardy and grudging. Moreover, it tended to be piecemeal, accompanied by a whole host of white provisos designed to diminish the impact of any black gains on white privileges."

Examining black radio in several specific locations, including Birmingham, Alabama, Charlotte, North Carolina, and the state of Mississippi, Ward underscores the complex links between local radio and emerging patterns of protest politics and race relations. Throughout the South he discovered "few unalloyed heroes." Rather, "contingency, chance, and commercial calculations often explained as much about the extent of a station's support for the movement as did any principled commitment to racial equality."

Birmingham, for example, which in 1957 had several important black-oriented stations, was an ideal radio market because the average annual black family income ranked the highest in the region. The stations, Ward writes, "served as electronic clearinghouses, simultaneously reflecting local needs and showcasing local talent, while linking Birmingham's African American community to broader regional and national trends in culture and politics." In Charlotte, two stations—WBT and WGIV—advanced gradualism, negotiation, and, less strongly, litigation to promote racial change. Significantly, Ward explains, the stations' "restraint and emphasis on interracial goodwill worked to establish the limits of publicly sanctioned techniques that whites could use to resist desegregation or otherwise constrain black progress." In the early 1960s Mississippi, where racial change occurred notoriously at glacial speed, had only five radio stations that catered to black audiences. "By contrast," Ward concludes, "many Mississippi radio stations proudly aligned themselves with the forces of white supremacy." It was not until 1969 that the launch of Hattiesburg's WORV established the first black-owned station in the state, illustrating a lack of black economic power in the radio industry. The quest for a greater black proprietorial, executive, and editorial presence in southern radio forms another important theme in Ward's book.

Merging entertainment and education, resistance and recreation, pleasure and politics, black radio played many roles in the post–World War II South. Unquestionably it helped fashion the black consciousness and purpose that spirited the civil rights movement. This is an arresting story, one Ward tells with precision, clarity, and compassion.

John David Smith
Series Editor

Acknowledgments

Although my name appears on the cover of this book and I take full responsibility for all the conclusions contained within in it, numerous individuals, organizations, and institutions have helped bring it to fruition. I am grateful to each of them. The research and writing were supported by grants from the Arts and Humanities Research Board and from the University of Newcastle upon Tyne, an Archie K. Davis Fellowship from the North Caroliniana Society, and a scholarship enhancement award from the College of Liberal Arts and Sciences at the University of Florida. The manuscript was read by Susan Douglas and Ted Ownby, whose constructive criticisms have much improved the final book. John Dittmer and Bob Zieger also read portions of the text and managed to head off at least some oversimplifications. Important leads, information, questions, advice, encouragement, support, lodgings, ale, and opportunities to speak on this topic came from Tony Badger, Julian Bond, Jane Dailey, Brian Dooley, Bob Friedman, Gary Frost, Susan Glisson, Adam Green, Maureen Hackett, Tom Hanchett, Ben Houston, John Kirk, Sheryl Kroen, George Lewis, Peter Ling, Neil McMillen, Dan Puckett, and Clive Webb.

Many archivists have provided invaluable assistance with my research, but I would especially like to recognize the help of Jim Baggett at the Birmingham Public Library Department of Archives and History, Jennifer Ford at the Department of Archives and Special Collections, University of Mississippi, Macia Richardson and Brenda Nelson-Strauss at the Archives of African American Music and Culture, Indiana University, Ray Bonis at the Special Collections and Archives, Virginia Commonwealth University, Cynthia Wilson at the Tuskegee University Archives, Alma Fisher at the L. Zenobia Coleman Library, Tougaloo College, and Jack Sutters at the AFSC Archives in Philadelphia. I would also like to thank all those people who consented to interviews with me. Meredith Morris-Babb has supported me and championed this project within the University Press of Florida while waiting patiently for me to complete it.

The book also owes much to Stephen Roy James Walsh who, back in the days when Leeds United were a top Premiership soccer club (and West Ham were actually still in the Premiership), was going to collaborate with me on a book not unlike this one, if rather less "southern." Under what passed for my supervision, in 1997 Walshie completed a Ph.D. at the University of Newcastle upon Tyne on black-oriented radio after World War II—a topic I had researched intermittently and written about in my first book, but about which I was eager to learn more. Shortly after completing his doctorate, Walshie decided to spurn the fame and fortune of an academic career in order to work in the nonprofit sector. My point here is to acknowledge that parts of this work, especially the parts relating to the early NAACP and Washington, D.C., benefit from our discussions and some of his research and insights—well, at least the ones where he was right! Steve has generously allowed me access to his interviews and various research materials in completing this work. Thanks, mate. Now, about that advance . . .

Finally, there are the personal debts that every author is pleased to acknowledge. Nobody could wish for more supportive parents, and I am wrapping up this book as my mum and dad, Mary and Gerald Ward, prepare to celebrate their diamond wedding anniversary. This book took some writing, but *that* is a real achievement. It will be a while before Jenny and I reach that particular landmark—and if I ask for her help in compiling one more bibliography, it will be touch and go whether we even make it to next week. One way or another, Jen has spent a long time in the company of this book, so it is only fitting that I should dedicate it to her, with thanks, much love, and a public acknowledgment that it really is my turn to do the ironing.

Abbreviations

ACMHR	Alabama Christian Movement for Human Rights
AFL	American Federation of Labor
AFSC	American Friends Service Committee
ANVL	Atlanta Negro Voters League
ASWPL	Association of Southern Women for the Prevention of Lynching
BCC	Black Community Coalition
BEST	Black Efforts for Soul in Television
CCB	Community Coalition on Broadcasting
CCPA	Citizens' Committee for Political Action
CIC	Commission on Interracial Cooperation
CIO	Congress of Industrial Organizations
COFO	Council of Federated Organizations
CORE	Congress of Racial Equality
CPA	Concerned Parents Association
CPB	Corporation for Public Broadcasting
CRIS	Civil Rights Information Service
EEOC	Equal Employment Opportunity Commission
FCC	Federal Communications Commission
FOR	Fellowship of Reconciliation
FPC	Fair Play Committee
IBEW	International Brotherhood of Electrical Workers
IUMMSW	International Union of Mine, Mill and Smelter Workers
MBN	Mutual Black Network
MESBIC	Minority Enterprise Small Business Investment Company
MFDP	Mississippi Freedom Democratic Party
MIA	Montgomery Improvement Association
MTCC	Middle Tennessee Coalition for Communications
NAACP	National Association for the Advancement of Colored People
NAB	National Association of Broadcasters
NATRA	National Association of Television and Radio Announcers
NBMC	National Black Media Coalition

NBN	National Black Network
NCC	National Council of Churches
NLC	Negro Labor Committee
NNN	National Negro Network
NRA	Negro Radio Association
NUL	National Urban League
OWI	Office of War Information
RCCC	Richland County Citizens Committee
RTA	Radio Tougaloo Association
SARGU	Southern Association for Racial Goodwill and Understanding
SCEF	Southern Conference Education Fund
SCHW	Southern Conference for Human Welfare
SCLC	Southern Christian Leadership Conference
SISS	Senate Internal Security Subcommittee
SNCC	Student Nonviolent Coordinating Committee
SRC	Southern Regional Council
SSC	State Sovereignty Commission
STFU	Southern Tenant Farmers Union
UCC	United Church of Christ
UDL	United Defense League
USWA	United Steel Workers of America
VCHR	Virginia Council on Human Relations
VEP	Voter Education Project
WCBC	Washington Community Broadcast Company

Introduction

Dials Set to Freedom

Saturday was dedication day on WRAP—Rrrap Radio—and we put the radios on in the living room and our bedrooms. The colored station was nonstop, rapid-fire jokes, plus a lot of commentary from the DJs on why they were great. On Sundays, though, we listened to the white stations because WRAP did church from can-do to can't. That involved a lot of dial flipping because the other stations only played r&b every tenth song. Every Sunday I counted to see if they would ever play more than two an hour, twice in a row.

Thulani Davis, 1959

Chester Laborde was the first African American to open a radio repair and sales shop in Baton Rouge, Louisiana. On June 19, 1953, Laborde drove Rev. Theodore Jemison, pastor of the city's Mt. Zion Baptist Church, to radio station WLCS, where they met up with two other African Americans, Raymond Scott and Willis Reed.[1] All of the men were members of the United Defense League, a new civil rights organization formed by local black activists the previous evening. The UDL's primary purpose was to remedy the poor service, lack of courtesy, and occasional physical abuse that was meted out to African American customers by white drivers on the city's buses. Rigid Jim Crow laws also meant that black passengers often had to stand, even when the buses were only half full, since they were forbidden to take empty seats in the "whites only" section at the front. The city's passage of Ordinance 222 earlier in the year had failed to end these practices, and white drivers had even gone on strike rather than comply with the new guidelines. The UDL decided that the only way to compel the city authorities and the bus company to address its grievances was to organize a mass boycott by Baton Rouge's black community. And the UDL decided that the quickest way to mobilize the black community in such an unprecedented mass protest was to announce the boycott on WLCS, a station that since its inception in 1947 had included in its schedule a growing number of "programs of special interest to colored groups."[2]

Thanks in part to WLCS, which announced mass meetings in local schools, churches, and stadiums and helped to coordinate volunteer car pools, the Baton Rouge bus boycott was remarkably solid, if short-lived. The protest lasted only four full days and ended in an awkward compromise when the city passed Ordinance 251. This called for more respectful treatment of black passengers and designated the rear two rows of the buses for black use, the front two rows for whites, with the middle rows available to members of both races on a first-come-first-served basis—although black passengers were still obliged to fill up from the back.[3] This represented a relatively minor tweak in the operation of Jim Crow in Louisiana, where fifty-seven years earlier another transportation case, *Plessy v. Ferguson*, had yielded the Supreme Court's famous decision legitimizing southern segregation provided that the separate provisions for each race were equal. In the intervening years racial separation had been a much more conspicuous feature of southern life than racial equality.

The Baton Rouge protest provided an important template for another bus boycott that started in Montgomery, Alabama, in December 1955. Indeed, the man who emerged as leader of that campaign, Martin Luther King Jr., would contact his fellow preacher-activist Jemison for advice on how to organize an effective mass protest. More important from the perspective of this book, the Baton Rouge bus boycott and the UDL's instinctive decision to use WLCS hinted at the extraordinary influence black-oriented radio could have among African Americans in the South at precisely the moment when the long struggle against segregation, disenfranchisement, and other forms of racial injustice began to intensify.

In the pages that follow, it will be suggested that radio was often the most important mass medium operating within southern black communities during the zenith of the civil rights struggles of the 1950s and 1960s; that it played an important role in laying the foundations for those struggles and was occasionally decisive in determining their outcome; and that it continued to articulate and reflect changing African American identity, consciousness, and protest agendas in the decade that followed the hard-won legislative victories of the mid-1960s. The argument here is not that the southern civil rights movement would not have happened without radio. Rather, it is that since the movement happened in a place where, at a time when, and among a people to whom radio was an integral part of everyday life, closer attention to the medium can help historians to explain why the southern freedom struggle unfolded in the way it did, at the times it did, in the places it did, and with the consequences it had. At the heart of this book is the complex story of how various individuals and organizations struggled to utilize the potential of radio to unite, inform, educate, mobilize, and entertain listeners in order to improve race relations and expand African American rights and opportunities in the South.

To date, radio has received relatively little scrutiny from historians of the modern African American freedom struggle. Not that they are especially noteworthy in this regard. As media scholar Michele Hilmes has explained, the serious study of radio and its impact on American politics and culture "had virtually dropped from academic sight in the United States by the late 1970s"—which was just about the time that the first important and durable histories of the civil rights movement began to appear. According to Hilmes, radio remained largely understudied until the mid-1990s, when there was renewed scholarly interest in the medium from a variety of disciplinary perspectives. Despite this general revival, radio has continued to be peripheral, if not invisible, in most historical accounts of the civil rights and black power movements. There are, however, often exceptions that serve to prove a rule.[4]

The only putatively "movement" historian to have probed the role of radio with any real sophistication is Barbara Dianne Savage, whose exemplary *Broadcasting Freedom* focused on the ways in which radio—mostly northern-based, network radio—dealt with racial issues during the era of World War II. Savage's densely textured, almost forensic account revealed that the nature and significances of the racial messages carried on radio were often bitterly contested at the points of production, dissemination, and consumption. This book rests on a similar understanding: radio's racial politics were always squeezed out from the diverse, sometimes hostile, sometimes sympathetic, sometimes aligned, sometimes adversarial agendas of civil rights organizations, advertisers, politicians, government bureaucrats, lawyers, scriptwriters, performers, station owners, network executives, and audiences. In fact, both the author and the readers of this book owe a large debt of thanks to Savage. Not only has she raised the standards of scholarship in this historical subfield, but by covering the story of network radio and race relations so ably for the period 1938–48 she has also helped to prevent this already lengthy book from becoming still longer.[5]

Savage aside, the greatest sensitivity to the role of radio in the southern freedom struggle has come from three distinct, although not wholly separate, sources. The first comprises the writings of journalists like Taylor Branch and Diane McWhorter, both of whom glimpsed the significance of black-oriented radio in the Birmingham civil rights protests of 1963 by actually talking to the people involved in that campaign.[6] The second category includes the published memoirs of African American deejays like Hal Jackson and Shelley Stewart, the work of music-oriented journalists like Nelson George and Wes Smith, and the writings of radio historians like William Barlow, Mark Newman, Gilbert Williams, and—in a somewhat different vein—the chronicler of WDIA-Memphis, Louis Cantor.[7] For all their many differences, this group of writers has relied heavily on the testimony of pioneering black deejays. Their works are largely celebratory and often rather nostalgic, rarely passing up an opportunity to boast of radio's long-neglected contribution to the movement. Of course, there are many occasions when this book does much the same thing. Nevertheless, it is worth stating that there are certain perils in relying too uncritically on the witness of men and women whose entire careers were built on a formidable talent for self-promotion. Put another way, understatement and modesty were seldom the strong suits of the announcers and entrepreneurs involved in radio. Some have been a little too zealous in asserting their own importance, not just as arbiters of styles and shapers of opinion within the African American community, but as ideological architects and practical leaders of the southern freedom struggle. That caveat aside, however, one goal of this book is to acknowledge the contribution of many African Americans and some whites working within the radio industry to the campaign for racial justice in the South.

The final category of writing that has recognized the reciprocal relationship between radio and the black freedom struggle comes from scholars working primarily within a communications or media studies tradition, including Susan Douglas, Michele Hilmes, and Susan Smulyan.[8] Each of these scholars has contributed much in empirical and theoretical terms to our understanding of how radio worked as both a capitalist business enterprise and a powerful communications medium, replete with multiple interlocking social, political, economic, educational, and recreational significances. In particular, many of these writers have demonstrated a laudable interest in how commercial, gender, and class issues have intersected with racial ones in shaping the internal dynamics of the radio industry and the style and content of its programming. Most of them have placed the broadcasting industry, its owners, employees, sponsors, regulators, and—most innovatively—its listeners at the center of their stories, focusing especially on how radio contributed to the construction of black and white racial identities in twentieth-century America. Theirs is important and illuminating work. However, this book is fundamentally different in that it places the southern freedom struggle at the center of the story and uses radio to cast new light on its origins, structure, and development.

Notwithstanding their general indifference toward radio, the movement's historians have hardly been unaware of the broader significance of the mass media in the battle against segregation and disenfranchisement. There is, for example, widespread agreement that print and especially television coverage of the violence directed against nonviolent civil rights protesters by die-hard segregationists in the late 1950s and early 1960s had a decisive influence on white attitudes to the movement at local and national, popular and governmental, levels. This is an important matter since it ultimately helps to explain the trajectory of the freedom struggle, its choice of tactics, and the ways in which the early movement managed to move influential sections of white opinion toward support for basic black civil and voting rights in the South. Conversely, the often hostile and sometimes willfully distorted mainstream media depictions of black power militancy in the late 1960s and early 1970s help to explain the unraveling of white support for more thoroughgoing efforts to secure genuine equality of black opportunity in America once statutory discrimination had been outlawed.[9]

This book, however, turns on a rather different fulcrum. At its center is the simple insight that for much of the period from roughly the mid-1920s to the mid-1970s, radio was far more consistently important as a source of news and information, not to mention education and entertainment, for the mass of *black* Americans in the South—and arguably nationally—than either television or the print press. Hordes of broadcasters, advertising executives, and record company salesmen as well as grassroots activists and civil rights leaders recognized this basic fact of black life only too well. African Americans, Martin Luther King explained with some rhetorical license in 1967, were "almost totally dependent on radio as their means of relating to society at large. They do not read newspapers. . . . Television speaks not to their needs but to upper-middle-class America." In these circumstances, King had "come to appreciate the role which the radio announcer plays in the lives of our people; for better or for worse you are opinion makers in the community. And it is important that you remain aware of the power which is potential in your vocation."[10]

Other contemporary voices also confirmed the profound influence of radio, especially of programming specifically directed at black audiences, in African American communities. Noting that the weekly or even monthly publication schedules of most black newspapers and magazines made them unsuitable vehicles for the rapid dissemination of breaking news, Julian Bond—the first communications director of the Student Nonviolent Coordinating Committee (SNCC)—remembered: "If you wanted to get to the large mass of people, you had to go to radio. Radio was what they listened to and radio was where they got their information."[11] In 1971 the media analyst Anthony Meyer concluded his study of radio with the simple observation that "black-oriented radio may well be the single most powerful mass medium for reaching the black population of this country." Perhaps not surprisingly, most African American broadcasters concurred. "Black radio was God-directed for the salvation of this nation and the world," insisted the indomitable Memphis deejay and later Detroit station owner Martha Jean "the Queen" Steinberg. If the claims of this book are a little more modest than Steinberg's, they nonetheless echo her insistence that the history of black-oriented radio was inextricably bound up with the story of the African American freedom struggle.[12]

Beyond this kind of personal testimonial there is also abundant statistical evidence that the rising tide of southern black protest in the mid-twentieth century coincided with the emergence of black-oriented radio as one of the most vital, popular, and influential institutions within the African American community. Black singers and musicians had featured on the air since the earliest days of commercial radio and the dawn of network broadcasting in the mid-1920s. It was not until the following decade, however, that there was really any inkling that African Americans might one day constitute a significant audience for radio broadcasters and their sponsors. In 1930 an enterprising advertising salesman called H. A. Haring suggested, "It would appear that a large market for radio sets might here be developed by someone who thinks out the proper appeal to the Negro mind."[13] In the Depression-era South, however, that African American market was predictably slow to materialize. In the early to middle 1930s, for example, only 0.5 percent of black sharecropping households in Mississippi and Georgia had a radio, while in South Carolina between 2 and 5 percent of African American households owned one. Even in urban centers like New Orleans and Atlanta, black radio ownership hovered around 3 percent for much of the decade. These low ownership levels gave rise to a tradition of communal listening in black neighborhoods that helped to cement radio's place near the heart of black social life.[14]

As with so much else in southern and African American history, the era around World War II represented a watershed in the story of what was known then as Negro-appeal broadcasting. Black-oriented radio programming throughout the American South—as in the nation as a whole—blossomed during the war years and even more so in the decade that followed. In 1946 the media expert Judith Waller noted, "There are frequent programs on both network and local commercial stations appealing to minority groups of listeners." Waller warned, however, that "the popularity of any commercial station would be short lived indeed should it build its entire program with only these groups in mind." That same year two southern stations, WDIA in Memphis and WOOK in Washington, D.C., ignored Waller's advice and began to shift their programming exclusively toward black listeners. Nine years later there were twenty-eight stations in America with wholly black-oriented formats. Twenty-two of those stations were located in the deep or rim South, alongside hundreds more that dedicated a substantial portion of their airtime to black audiences. So much for the wisdom of experts.[15]

In part, the postwar expansion of black-oriented programming was a consequence of the growing need for radio broadcasters to find new niche markets as television eroded their core white audiences and siphoned off ever more advertising revenue. Primarily, however, the black-oriented radio boom was stimulated by the discovery of an increasingly affluent and concentrated market of black consumers who—although still severely disadvantaged compared with their white counterparts—had an annual collective income of some $15 billion by 1953. Radio offered the best means for advertisers to reach this money. In North Carolina, for example, the proportion of African American families with radio sets leapt from 1 percent in 1930 to 33 percent just over a decade later. The urban South saw even greater increases. By the early 1950s there was an average of 1.8 sets per black household in Atlanta, while a few years later it was estimated that 93 percent of black households in Memphis had radios.[16] Even in the rural South, black radio ownership levels had reached 75–85 percent by the late 1950s. Market researchers assured sponsors, advertisers, and station owners that more than 60 percent of black southerners over twelve years of age tuned in to radio every day, with 90 percent of all African Americans listening to some radio every week. Moreover, their recall of advertisements and all other forms of information was much higher when listening to black-oriented programs than to general-market radio.[17] The message from this copious research was clear: southern black audiences listened often and closely to their radios, but they listened even more often and more closely to broadcasts specifically directed toward black listeners.

As the 1960s and an era of genuinely mass black activism in the South dawned, black-oriented radio continued to provide a uniquely effective means to penetrate a black consumer market that was worth $27 billion by 1963. In 1964 the trade magazine *Sponsor* reported that 71 percent of blacks, as opposed to 57 percent of whites, responded to the question "What do you do quite a bit in your free time?" with the reply "Listen to the radio." Only 56 percent of African Americans, compared with 67 percent of whites, answered that they read daily newspapers. This pattern was especially marked in the South, where for many years black radio ownership levels far outstripped those for television, and where literacy levels were notoriously low. In the region as a whole in 1960, just over 63 percent of black homes had a television set, while nearly 79 percent of households had a radio. Moreover, these figures for household ownership actually underrepresented the ubiquity of radio broadcasts in the African American community, where many people listened in their cars, at their workplaces, in local bars, or while shopping.[18]

The fact that African Americans listened to radio broadcasts in various ways, in a variety of locations, with varying degrees of attentiveness, raises a methodological and interpretative problem that stalks this book and, if truth be told, all attempts to use popular culture and the mass media to probe the consciousness and explain the actions of particular individuals or social groups. While it is hard enough to plot the political, economic, technical, and racial coordinates of radio program production and dissemination, it is harder still to calibrate with any precision the ways in which listeners heard, interpreted, and responded to those broadcasts. Of course, all credible historians need to be sensitive to the limitations of their evidence and wary of how much interpretative weight they place upon their source material. Still, it does no harm to confess at the outset that determining the impact of individual radio programs or types of programming on listeners is far from an exact science.

Often the evidence for how audiences reacted to radio shows is either circumstantial or simply nonexistent. Indeed, Susan Douglas has rather wistfully noted, "Radio historians struggle with one of the spottiest, most ephemeral historical records in all of the mass media." Many shows were never recorded, while regular changes of station ownership meant that any recordings that were made, as well as much in the way of historically invaluable paperwork, were often unceremoniously dumped as soon as new proprietors moved in. Moreover, as Douglas explains, the rating services that so eagerly tried to find out who was listening to what when, rarely bothered to ask people exactly *why* they listened to particular shows, and even more rarely *how* they listened to them and with what consequences.[19] As a result, there are times when it is necessary to deploy a variant of what advertising historian Roland Marchand has dubbed "plausible inference" to make the link between the content and form of particular radio broadcasts and specific attitudes and actions among their listeners.[20] The case for such a linkage is, however, made much more plausible by the many concrete examples in this book of when radio—often, but not always, in conjunction with other influences—clearly did encourage black and white Americans to act and think in certain ways in certain places at certain times.

In trying to assess the effect of radio broadcasts on their listeners, it is important to appreciate the extraordinary authority that the medium exercised within many American households at least until the 1960s and arguably much longer among African Americans. Radio personalities and writers, in collaboration with sponsors and advertisers, worked hard to preserve the wondrous mystique and reputation for integrity that the medium had enjoyed when it first brought a galaxy of entertainment, education, and up-to-the-minute news and opinion into American homes. For a long time radio was viewed as both a technical marvel and an unimpeachable source of accurate information. It was, according to Susan Smulyan, "magical and trustworthy."[21] To be sure, some of that early luster had become tarnished over the years. The powerful commercial imperatives enshrined and protected in the 1934 Communications Act became increasingly dominant in the broadcasting industry, eclipsing the visions that had accompanied the birth of mass broadcasting in the 1920s—visions of a medium that would democratize American culture and create a more educated, informed, and virtuous citizenry. Nevertheless, as Michael Kammen has argued, not only did radio generally resist the urge to "dumb down" its "programs for a mass, undifferentiated audience" more successfully than did television—its even more mass, even more commercially fueled postwar rival—but the unique bond of trust between radio and its audiences was actually strengthened by "the sheer number of local radio stations along with stations that targeted particular clienteles compared with the severely limited number of dominant, national television networks."[22]

Certainly by the time of the Montgomery bus boycott there was still enough of this sense of integrity attached to at least one local southern station for a churchgoing black activist to take more notice of a radio announcement than of her own pastor. In late January 1956, Rev. William H. Kinds of Jackson Street Baptist Church was one of three black ministers invited to a meeting with the Montgomery city commissioners. Although Kinds was not a member of the Montgomery Improvement Association, which was running the protest, the white authorities persuaded or duped or, according to some, paid Kinds to claim that the boycott had been enforced only by the use of black goon squads to terrorize would-be passengers. Kinds was also implicated in a false statement, issued by the commissioners and picked up by the Associated Press, announcing that an acceptable agreement had been reached between the city and black leaders and urging African Americans to return to the buses. The Montgomery Improvement Association immediately issued a counterstatement, carried first on the local black-oriented station WRMA and subsequently in the local press. "I'm a member of Reverend Kinds' church and I felt bad when I heard it," Mrs. Allean Wright told sociologist Willie Mae Lee, who rendered the conversation phonetically. "Dey said on the radio dat he wuz paid and you have to tell the truth on the radio cause people can sue you for lying on 'em, so it must be true." Trusting their radios not to tell lies, Wright and the other boycotters stayed off the buses.[23]

Given this kind of influence and audience penetration, it was not surprising that various individuals and groups should try to use radio to further the struggle for black freedom and equality in the South. The story of how local, regional, and national organizations, as well as a number of individual announcers and executives, used the airwaves to challenge the operation of Jim Crow and increase black political, economic, and social power forms the first of four major overlapping themes in this book. Occasionally these efforts took the form of explicit attempts to use radio to mobilize southern blacks in direct action protests or voter registration drives. However, such broadcasts were quite rare before the mid-1960s. Indeed, for a combination of economic, ideological, bureaucratic, and technical reasons that form an important subtheme in the book, radio's record of public support for specific civil rights activities in the South was for many years decidedly patchy. The very real prospect of losing lucrative white sponsorship and advertising revenue, having a broadcasting license revoked, or having Klansmen hack down a transmission tower tended to make even the most racially progressive southern station owners, managers, and announcers wary about broadcasting pro–civil rights messages.

As a consequence, much of radio's initial support for the freedom struggle involved airing programs intended to expose racial injustice, eradicate ignorance about the moral and intellectual character of African Americans, and celebrate the black contribution to American history and culture. Such programs had two main goals. First, they were designed to stimulate black pride and foster a determination, not only to endure the indignities of Jim Crow, but also to transcend and resist them whenever possible. Second, they were designed to dramatize the yawning gap between the nation's much-vaunted democratic ideals and its racial practices. Since southern blacks did not need much reminding that this disjuncture existed, many of these broadcasts were designed with white, often northern, and sometimes federal government opinion in mind. Consequently, the book also addresses the ways in which civil rights advocates repeatedly used radio to turn segregation and disenfranchisement into matters of national concern.

This introduces the second major theme of the book. Although it focuses primarily on radio programming directed at southern black audiences, it also considers how radio programs aimed at white audiences in the South—and at audiences of both races far beyond Dixie—affected the development of the freedom struggle. Clearly the burdens of both Jim Crow and the extraordinary movement that destroyed it were borne principally by African Americans, and they should occupy center stage in that story. But whites in the South and beyond, whether friendly or hostile to black aspirations, also played a crucial role in determining the timing and the tactics, as well as the successes and the limitations, of the southern freedom struggle. They, too, need to be factored into any authoritative account of the movement. They certainly played a key role in defining the relationship between radio and the freedom struggle. Indeed, the sheer paucity of African American radio station owners and managers—there were still barely a dozen black-owned radio stations in 1970—meant that many of the most successful attempts to use radio to support the southern movement were a consequence of actions or sometimes inactions by whites.

By examining how some of the southern whites involved in the radio industry responded to the mounting challenges of the civil rights and black power movements, this book also offers a modest contribution to a long-overdue trend within recent histories of the movement. While historians have generally portrayed the African American community in the South with ever more subtlety and sophistication, recognizing the diversity born of generational, gender, class, status, and geographical differences, southern whites have not been nearly so well served.[24] There has been a tendency in civil rights histories to reduce the white South to stock stereotypes: either saints who rushed to support the movement or sinners who swarmed to the Klan and the White Citizens' Councils, or who actively resisted the campaign for desegregation and voting rights in other ways. Most whites did neither, and this simple Manichean vision has produced a void in the historical literature exactly where the mass of southern whites should be. Most white southerners were profoundly concerned about the implications of black insurgency and federal civil rights legislation for their way of life and the privileges that were traditionally attached to their skin color. But most were also decent, law-abiding, and often God-fearing folk, some of whom had long harbored grave doubts about the way Jim Crow operated, without necessarily wishing to see it abandoned. While few easily shook the pernicious legacy of centuries of racism and racial privilege, many recognized that the tide of national and international opinion was surging against the South's peculiar racial arrangements and did their best to adjust to the new realities of a world in flux. Radio had a part to play in this process of imperfect adjustment. Movement sympathizers used the medium to try to persuade this vast middle ground of white southerners to accept racial change and ultimately to help fashion a new, more racially tolerant southern white identity.

Although it is beyond the scope of this book to devote much space to segregationists' uses of radio, it is worth noting that the Klan, the White Citizens' Councils, and other "massive resisters" also made considerable efforts to recruit and proselytize via the radio. In Henderson, Kentucky, for example, the Citizens' Council of Kentucky went on WSON in late September 1956, when vicious local race-baiter Jerry Waller did his best to rouse local whites to boycott Henderson's newly desegregated Weaverton High School. An alliance of liberal Henderson ministers responded by using fifteen-minute radio slots on WSON to denounce the Citizens' Council, correct "Waller's lurid distortions about the National Association of Colored People," and encourage parents of pupils at Weaverton to remain steadfast in the face of the Council's threats. "Do not be intimidated by announcements of a mass meeting so timed and located as to instill fear in parents' hearts," one broadcast urged. "Uphold constitutional law and order! End the interruption to your children's education." This strategy was at least partially successful. Even on the day the Council had set for a complete school boycott, 241 of Weaverton's 863 pupils—including five black students—braved the mob and attended classes while ministers continued to broadcast reassuring announcements throughout the day. Thereafter school attendance began to rise rapidly, and the Council's resistance in the town was pretty much broken. "We are told that our ministerial association was the first organized opposition in the south to a white citizens council," boasted Revs. C. Sumpter Logan and Theodore A. Braun.[25]

It was no coincidence that both sides in the Henderson school crisis considered radio an effective means to influence and mobilize rank-and-file white southerners. Radio, as vividly described in *Redeeming the Dial*, Tona Hangen's study of early radio evangelists, and in *Like a Family*, the marvelous collaborative account of life in a cotton mill town, had long been a vital part of southern white life, helping to fashion a sense of shared local and regional identity.[26] Certainly the Henderson vignette reminds us that the racially progressive, pro–civil rights broadcasts that form the main subject of this book should be seen as part of a competitive dialogue with other reactionary, prosegregation broadcasts that urged whites to rally to defend Jim Crow.

Radio programs that attempted to persuade black or white southerners to support, or at least acquiesce to, campaigns to end segregation and other discriminatory practices represented the most conventionally "political" uses of radio as a propaganda tool of the movement. Yet by broadening this rather narrow definition of "politics" it is possible to see other ways in which the story of radio might help illuminate important aspects of the southern freedom struggle. The cultural work of community and morale building cannot be overestimated, and what might be called the cultural politics of radio forms the third major theme in this book.

Stories of African Americans gathering together to listen to radio broadcasts of heavyweight boxing champion Joe Louis's fights in the late 1930s and 1940s are now part of African American folklore. Maya Angelou recalled black farmers from around Stamps, Arkansas, streaming into her grandmother's general store to hear the radio as Louis carried the weight of black hopes and pride into the ring. Angelou and the assembled crowd shared in a collective and creative demonstration of black unity as radio commentary on Louis's unparalleled string of victories "proved that we were the strongest people in the world."[27] Broadly similar scenes were reenacted whenever African Americans or their culture were featured on the southern airwaves. When bluesman Sonny Boy Williamson began to appear daily at 12:15 p.m. on KFFA-Helena, Arkansas, in the early 1940s, simultaneously advertising his own live appearances and a new brand of flour on *King Biscuit Time,* the African American community in Phillips County responded enthusiastically. "We never heard blacks on the radio 'cause Sonny Boy was the first," recalled mill worker J. C. Danley. Although no great fan of the blues, Danley still joined the rush to hear a black voice on the air: "When Sonny Boy came on, we would turn that on because he was black." In Houston, gospel singer James Singleterry recalled that the Kings of Harmony gospel group "used to come on air every Thursday morning at 2:15 a.m. You could walk up and down the street, I guarantee you could hear the Kings of Harmony. It's incredible. People would set their alarms to get up."[28]

Whether they listened alone or in the company of others, this kind of black-oriented radio programming helped to weld African Americans together as a community. Indeed, without wishing to minimize the significance of important gender, class, and geographical differences within the black community, radio helped to conjure up a real sense of African American identity organized around shared historical experiences and distinctive patterns of leisure, pleasure, and style. By airing African American music, preaching, drama, and comedy, by re-

FIGURE I. Sonny Boy Williamson's appearances on KFFA-Helena's *King Biscuit Time* offered some of the first regular black-oriented radio programming in the South. Courtesy of Southern Media Archive, Special Collections, University of Mississippi Libraries.

porting on the achievements of local and national black leaders, athletes, and celebrities, and by carrying news, documentaries, and public service announcements of particular interest to the black community, black-oriented radio helped to define what was unique about African American culture and to legitimize it as something valuable and worthy of respect. This was vital both to the medium's popular appeal and to its contribution to the southern freedom struggle. Even when eschewing explicit references to the black social, economic, and political predicament, the distinctive content and tenor of radio programming featuring African Americans helped to create the kinds of psychological, ideological, and organizational resources that were mobilized in the movement. Indeed, black-oriented radio often worked in ways analogous to the institutions (black churches, colleges, fraternal organizations, Highlander Folk School, labor unions, the NAACP) that sociologist Aldon Morris identified as crucial to the emergence of mass activism in the South.[29] Moreover, long after the zenith of mass protest in the South had passed, black-oriented radio continued to offer an emotional and cultural rallying point for the black community, as well as a forum for the expression of black political, social, and economic aspirations and earnest debates about how best to fulfill them.

Two other aspects of the cultural politics of black-oriented radio merit attention here. Some of the most innovative and perceptive recent scholarship on the nature of democracy in twentieth-century America has stressed the role of consumerism in determining which social groups have been welcomed into what David Hollinger has called the "circle of the we"—as in "We, the People"—and accorded the protections and responsibilities of full citizenship.[30] Especially after World War II, consumption became virtually a civic and patriotic duty, as well as a means to satisfy more personal desires. This was, according to historian Lizabeth Cohen, a period in which the "consumer-citizen" and the ideology of a "Consumers' Republic" triumphed, creating a society in which "consumption and democratic citizenship became increasingly intertwined in official and popular ideologies." In this context, notwithstanding obdurate racism and resistance in the South, the growing significance of African Americans as a powerful consumer bloc increased their prospects of finally securing full citizenship rights.[31]

Although it serves more as a theoretical underpinning than as a narrative focus for this book, it is useful to keep the political significance of consumerism in mind when considering the relationship between radio and the African American freedom struggle. Commercial broadcasting developed primarily as a tool to create or exploit consumer markets, and radio was demonstrably one of the most effective means of selling goods and services to the mass of African Americans. Moreover, this kind of increased black consumerism, simultaneously facilitated and exploited by radio, helped to integrate African Americans into the "Consumers' Republic" at precisely the moment when they were also ratcheting up demands for the citizenship rights that were supposed to accrue to loyal consumers in America. Having established their credentials as consumers of consequence by the 1950s, southern blacks were keenly aware that one of the most potent weapons in their struggle for civil and voting rights was to withhold their dollars and refuse to consume any goods and services that were clearly tainted by racial discrimination. Indeed, part of the genius of the movement was to use the threat of massive nonconsumption to force powerful southern and national business interests to end the denial of citizenship rights to an increasingly important, but disaffected, group of consumers. While a proper investigation of the synergy between the southern freedom struggle, consumerism, and nonconsumerism is beyond the scope of this book, radio was important to all three phenomena and sometimes linked them.[32]

One other aspect of the relationship between consumption, citizenship, democracy, and radio is critical to understanding the medium's role in the transformation of race relations and racial identities in the South. It was impossible to segregate the airwaves. Once radio programs were sent out into the ether, anyone with a receiver who was within reach of the signal—and, in the case of young white southerners secretly listening to the latest rhythm and blues hits on black-oriented stations in the 1950s, anyone who could escape the disapproving scrutiny of their parents—could listen in. In truth, southern whites had never been entirely successful in their efforts to secure the borders between the races; they could only imperfectly police the color line by a mixture of legal, economic, political, and terrorist tactics. In the twentieth century, radio—like other new technologies of mass consumption—frequently made a mockery of the spatial segregation that was supposed to be the foundation of the Jim Crow system by exposing each race to the culture, especially the musical culture, of the other race. As Grace Elizabeth Hale suggests in *Making Whiteness,* her study of the culture of segregation in the South before World War II, "an expanding culture of consumption . . . multiplied the sites in which racial difference could break down." Writing more specifically about radio in the 1950s, Susan Douglas argues that "this technology had particular qualities at the time that made it an agent of desegregation. Radio—more than films, television, advertising, or magazines in the 1950s—was *the* media outlet where cultural and industrial battles over how much influence black culture was going to have on white culture were staged and fought." Those battles were particularly intense in the South, where they intersected with mounting black challenges to segregation and feverish white efforts to preserve it.[33]

What was especially beguiling about this kind of cultural miscegenation via the airwaves—aside from the fact that it gave rise to the glories of rock and roll and saved America's youth from Rosemary Clooney—was its fundamentally democratic and equalitarian nature at the point of consumption. To be sure, the discriminatory politics and economics of record and radio program production continued to influence what songs were recorded and in what styles, what programs were aired, and who was paid what money for their efforts. But at the point of listening, southern black and white audiences often consumed much the same cultural materials and imbibed many of the same social values. Until the mid-1960s, this biracial musical consumption invariably occurred in segregated settings, yet it still represented a challenge to the tyranny of Jim Crow. Without wishing to romanticize or exaggerate the frequently tenuous links between white admiration for African American music and white support for black civil rights, the emergence of a biracial audience for rock and roll, rhythm and blues, and later soul music in the South created at least the potential for more enlightened racial attitudes based on the recognition of a common humanity—vividly expressed in the music and passionately proclaimed by many movement leaders—across racial lines.

The last of the four major themes in this book is the long struggle for more African American power and influence within the actual business of southern radio. As in most areas of the American economy, African Americans were woefully underrepresented and generally underpaid within the radio industry. This was especially galling given that black-oriented radio had effectively rescued the entire industry from its doldrums in the late 1940s and early 1950s by showcasing black talent both in front of the microphone and on record. Although in 1949 the Atlanta entrepreneur Jesse Blayton had become proprietor of WERD, thereby creating the nation's first black-owned station, the number of black owners did not reach double figures for another twenty years. Nevertheless, efforts to increase the number of black station owners and executives, as well as to improve the remuneration and conditions for all African Americans working in the radio industry, were a constant feature of the struggle for equal opportunity in the South. This quest became even more intense once the battle for statutory equality had been won and the focus of black protest in the South shifted toward expanding black economic opportunities and political power. As a remarkable array of local, regional, and national organizations mobilized in pursuit of black proprietorial and executive power in radio, it became one of the defining characteristics of the black power phase of the freedom struggle in the late 1960s and early 1970s.

Much of this activism was predicated on the assumption that an increase in the number of African American station owners and managers would automatically generate more socially engaged, politically committed black-oriented broadcasting. In fact, entertainment—most notably soul music—continued to overshadow educational, current affairs, and news programming on most commercial black-oriented radio stations in the South, irrespective of the race of the owners. This is not to suggest that entertainment and empowerment were ever mutually exclusive goals or outcomes on black-oriented radio; rather, this book repeatedly demonstrates that the boundaries between these nominally distinct modes of radio programming were always rather porous. It is, however, indicative of the fact that African Americans in positions of genuine influence and power within the southern radio industry tended to behave very much like their white counterparts in terms of programming choices and basic economic priorities. Moreover, most successful black radio entrepreneurs, executives, and deejays figured their own victories over pervasive racial discrimination as both a symbol of and an inspiration for black economic progress. Their hard-won success thus affirmed the basic soundness of a capitalist system within which a powerful rhetoric of equal opportunity had long served to obscure the persistence of systemic and habitual racial inequalities.

Painfully aware of this dichotomy, most pioneering African American radio entrepreneurs, executives, and deejays juggled their avid pursuit of personal economic interests with genuine concerns about how best to use radio to empower their black listeners and enhance the general well-being of the black community. Some were rather better than others at reconciling these twin agendas.

All, however, were ultimately constrained by the fact that African American audiences had very clear ideas about why they listened to radio and what they expected to hear when they did. Black audiences generally set a premium on being entertained as well as enlightened, and the most successful efforts to use radio to inform and mobilize the black community usually conformed to this criterion. Put another way, style was often just as important as substance—and as who owned the license documents or sponsored the programming—in explaining the relationship between radio, black audiences, and the southern freedom struggle. How radio reflected and helped to shape the contours of that struggle and the related transformations in racial consciousness in the South during the middle fifty years of the twentieth century forms the subject of this book.

The book is organized into three broadly chronological sections. The chapters in part 1 deal with radio's role in laying the foundations of a mass southern civil rights movement between the 1920s and mid-1950s. They describe how various organizations and individuals committed to a range of nominally progressive racial policies tried to use network and local radio to improve southern race relations and sustain a strong sense of community pride, identity, and purposefulness among African Americans. The chapters in part 2 focus on the peak years of activism in the South from the late 1950s to the mid-1960s. While acknowledging the formidable obstacles faced by those who hoped to use radio to support the civil rights movement, these chapters reveal a hidden history of how the medium encouraged black participation in civil rights protests, raised funds, and moved popular and governmental opinion toward support for black demands. Recognizing that the story of the civil rights movement unfolded somewhat differently in every southern town, city, and state, the final three chapters in part 2 examine the connections between particular radio stations, civil rights activities, and the transformation of race relations in three very different locales: Birmingham, Charlotte, and the state of Mississippi. Part 3 deals with the story of radio and race relations between the late 1960s and the mid-1970s when southerners of both races dealt with the realities of a region rid of statutory segregation and disenfranchisement. In particular, these chapters concentrate on efforts to increase African American economic opportunities within the broadcasting industry, and on attempts to increase both the quality and the quantity of political and educational programming for the southern black community.

PART I

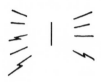

An Uphill Battle

Network Radio, Local Radio, and the Roots of Racial Change

For many years the Negro minority in this country has been fighting an uphill battle to get its story on the radio; and to get misrepresentations, distortions, and stereotypes about it off the radio.
Roy Wilkins, NAACP, 1950

Signing On

In February 1950 the African American magazine *Our World* ran a story about the proliferation of black-oriented radio programming in the South. Paying due deference to the region's traditional paranoia about outside interference in its racial affairs, the magazine declared that "many southern civic leaders are of the opinion that Negroes on the air have done more to better racial understanding in one year than hundreds of orators from 'up north' in the last decade."[1] Just three years after WDIA-Memphis and WOOK-Washington had begun to transform themselves into the first stations in the United States devoted entirely to black-oriented programming, and less than a year after Jesse Blayton had bought WERD-Atlanta to establish the nation's first black-owned station, *Our World* clearly set much store by radio's capacity to foster better race relations in the region. By the mid-1950s there were twenty-two southern stations wholly devoted to black audiences, with a further twenty-four airing more than thirty hours a week of black-oriented programming. Many other general-market stations in the region also featured a smattering of dedicated black programming, mostly comprising religious broadcasts and the odd musical showcase. With much of this black-oriented fare—especially the rhythm and blues and rock and roll programs—attracting an increasingly avid young white southern audience, by 1955 *Our World* was able to declare even more enthusiastically, if a little simplistically, that radio was "bringing the races closer."[2]

Taken together, the three chapters in part 1 explore the reasons for *Our World*'s optimism. Why had that magazine, along with many African American activists, their white allies, and even some of the more racially progressive forces operating within the federal government, come to believe that radio might be an important instrument of racial change in the South before the rise of mass black protest in the region? And precisely what sorts of changes were being advocated, in what sorts of programs, and on what sorts of stations, by the various groups and individuals who turned to radio to further their cause? As we shall see, a diverse group of racially progressive broadcasters working on both general-market and black-oriented stations used radio to stimulate black pride, challenge white racial stereotypes, encourage interracial dialogue, and assert the right of African Americans to enjoy the full benefits of American citizenship. From the 1940s onward the medium was important in thrusting the issues of segregation and disenfranchisement to the forefront of the national consciousness. Occasionally radio was used to encourage concerted action against the continued denial of those rights in the South, while a number of black and white preachers used their radio ministries to help acquaint both races with the philosophy of nonviolent protest that the movement would later employ so effectively. In sum, although many radio shows casually reiterated the prevailing racial wisdoms of the day, other programs challenged and helped to change the nation's attitudes toward African Americans and southern racial practices. This was no small achievement.

It is important to acknowledge at the outset, however, that there were very real limitations to what radio was able to contribute to the practical struggle against Jim Crow in the 1930s, 1940s, and early 1950s. Many of these limitations derived from the racial and economic agendas of those in positions of economic power and managerial authority in the radio industry. Most of the white owners and executives involved in black radio in the South were considerably more interested in dollars than in racial justice. In Memphis, black announcer Nat Williams fully appreciated that WDIA's white owners Bert Ferguson and John Pepper were not moved by racial enlightenment in switching their station to an all-black format. "They are businessmen. They don't necessarily love Negroes, they make that clear," Williams explained. "But they do love progress and they are willing to pay the price for that progress."[3]

Not only did these owners and managers depend heavily on white advertisers and sponsors for their livelihood, but they were acutely vulnerable to threats of social ostracism and much worse at the hands of other whites if they appeared to question Jim Crow or allowed any form of racial militancy on air. Bert Ferguson himself recalled the trepidation with which he and his partner moved WDIA toward an all-black format in a city run by Edward Crump's notorious political machine. "The atmosphere was such, with Crump running everything . . . we could see him saying: 'Look, we don't want any nigger radio station in town.'" There was also a fear that since WDIA's white audiences might reject products they knew were also being advertised for black consumption, sponsorship and advertising would dry up.[4]

Often the mere specter of white reprisals was enough to dissuade stations from airing programs that even touched on civil rights issues. Consequently, when white entrepreneurs catered to black audiences in the South, they usually took care to stress their economic motivations and distance themselves and their facilities from any support for black social or political aspirations. In Birmingham, for example, where local segregationists attacked black-oriented WEDR's transmitter even before the station went on air in 1949, owner J. Edward Reynolds had tried to allay local white fears about the station by announcing its intention to "stay completely out of politics."[5] At KVET-Houston, the very fact that the station's black-oriented programming was consigned to the late night schedules, safely hidden away from most white listeners, militated against broadcasts relating to racial politics. Deejay Lavarda Durst (Dr. Hepcat) wanted to interview black educator-activist Mary McLeod Bethune when she was visiting the city in the late 1940s. His plans were thwarted when he was told that he "couldn't take her to the station to interview her in the daytime. . . . you had to be on the night show and it was too late for her."[6]

Black broadcasters bristled under these kinds of constraints. Occasionally they evaded them or else found covert ways to critique racism and ridicule the southern white power structure despite them. In the mid-1930s an African American agent working for the North Carolina state agriculture department used airtime on WGTM-Wilson that should have been devoted to agricultural information to comment on the farcical southern justice meted out to the Scottsboro Boys. Typically, however, after discovering this transgression, the station carefully screened out everything to do with racial politics. Nearby WMFD-Wilmington rationalized a similar censorship policy in the name of avoiding anything "that tended to stir up ill-will, animosity and hatred."[7] Retribution for any signs of "uppityness" by black broadcasters could be very quick. In 1951 Maurice "Hot Rod" Hulbert used his time as stand-in host of WDIA's premier public affairs show *Brown America Speaks* to launch an impassioned plea for racial justice from the "ruling powers of this country" for those who "helped fell your lumber . . . , breast fed your babies, cooked your food . . . , helped you build your railroads . . . , helped you fight your wars." A flurry of white complaints saw Hulbert immediately pulled from the show.[8]

Clearly, social order and solid sales rather than racial justice and black empowerment were the paramount considerations for most southern radio stations. It was partly as a consequence of this hostility to racially progressive broadcasting in the South that many leading civil rights organizations, notably the

National Association for the Advancement of Colored People (NAACP) and the National Urban League (NUL), often turned to the national radio networks in an effort to rouse public and federal opposition to Jim Crow and racial discrimination more broadly. Those efforts form the major focus of this chapter.

"A Far Reaching Instrument": The National Urban League and the Necessary Networks

In 1928 the NUL announced that radio might become a "far reaching instrument of interracial understanding and enlightenment" and resolved to make a concerted effort to realize the fledgling mass medium's potential in this area.[9] Nearly two decades later, however, the organization was deeply disappointed with radio's accomplishments, feeling that the medium had failed to respond adequately to the needs of African American listeners or to the challenge of helping eradicate racial prejudice and discrimination throughout the nation. A 1947 NUL report complained that "since radio, the business, depends very little upon the Negro minority for support it barely gives it recognition, either in terms of jobs or treatment in its scripts." While the League felt that the medium "strives not to offend," it described it as racially conservative, a supporter not of racial change but of the status quo. "It wages no crusades," the report complained, "it remains steadfastly conscious of the prejudices of its majority audience and is careful to avoid taking liberties with them." Although the League acknowledged a postwar upsurge of "vigorous protests by national organizations of radio's treatment of minorities" and noted that other civil rights groups such as the left-wing National Negro Congress and the NAACP had recently formed special committees to investigate the potential of radio, it remained dubious about the effectiveness of these initiatives. While on one hand the NUL cautiously admitted that changes "in the Negro's role in radio, and what that medium can do for the advancement of democracy in America," were "not unlikely," on the other hand it "conceded, if somewhat reluctantly, that despite hope and fervent prayer, not very much more is likely to happen in the foreseeable future."[10]

There were a number of reasons for the gloomy nature of the NUL's 1947 report on radio and race relations, which appears so at odds with the buoyant optimism of *Our World*'s analysis written just two years later. First, the NUL account was written on the eve of the "discovery" by radio station owners, advertisers, and sponsors of what *Sponsor* magazine dubbed "the forgotten 15,000,000."[11] This was an increasingly concentrated black consumer market worth more than $12 billion annually, which listened avidly to radio and even more avidly to black-oriented programming on radio. The discovery of an African American audience that, as the NUL report recognized, had previously been fairly peripheral to the overwhelmingly white economic interests controlling the radio industry meant that, in the next decade, black spending power provided new leverage for those seeking better-quality broadcasting for and about African Americans.[12]

Second, the 1947 report betrayed the NUL's lingering disillusionment with the results of its own attempts to use radio to promote racial enlightenment and practical reforms during the era of World War II. This was part of a much broader pattern of black anger and frustration as America, in particular the Jim Crow South, seemed willing to return to racial business as usual following a war effort to which African Americans had contributed mightily and which was linked to a patriotic rhetoric of freedom and democracy. Moreover, the League's special interest in improving employment opportunities and vocational training for African Americans only accentuated its despondency about the medium. From its inception radio had relied on live and recorded black entertainment for some of its most popular programming. Nevertheless, permanent jobs in the broadcasting industry after the war remained largely the preserve of whites. NUL executive secretary Lester Granger lambasted the discriminatory barriers within the industry that curtailed black employment opportunities, especially in skilled, technical, and supervisory capacities. His complaints were well merited. In 1947 there were still only sixteen African American deejays working regularly in the entire nation, together with a handful of engineers and program directors. African Americans held only 200 of 30,000 white-collar jobs in the industry, and there were no black station owners.[13]

Postwar disillusionment notwithstanding, there was something vaguely ironic in the NUL's complaints about radio's innate racial conservatism. The League's own plans for radio had always been rather modest. Indeed, the League was itself complicit in establishing the patterns of deference and moderation that dominated early radio's approach to America's racial inequalities, particularly in their most egregious form in the South. The NUL of the 1930s and 1940s was less a civil rights protest group than a black social services organization, primarily dedicated to supporting African American economic and educational development in the urban North. When it did turn its gaze and resources southward, it was usually willing to work within the confines of a segregated society. Until the 1950s the League seldom challenged the existence of Jim Crow, even as it sought to ameliorate some of its worst material and psychological effects on black southerners. This moderation had certain rewards. Partly as a consequence of its perennial caution, the League was the most consistently successful of all the major organizations dedicated to black progress in securing airtime on southern—and, indeed, national—radio.

This was especially true during World War II. As Barbara Savage has explained, "The crisis of war enabled the organization for the first time to spread a message of equal opportunity in jobs and military service."[14] Other groups, notably the labor leader A. Philip Randolph's March on Washington movement, had pursued similar objectives. Yet the NUL's appeals for national unity and expanded black employment opportunities in the midst of the wartime emergency seemed far less threatening, both to the powerful national radio networks (CBS, NBC, and Mutual) and to local southern stations, than Randolph's plans for a massive protest in the nation's capital to demand the immediate desegregation of the war industries and armed forces. Whereas in 1941 NBC had refused the socialist Randolph's request for a program to be called *The Negro in National Defense*, CBS happily granted the far-from-socialist NUL an hour of free airtime for a variety program entitled *The Negro and National Defense* on much the same topic. In what was a typical formula for programs dealing with racial issues at this time, the NUL show mixed speeches, musical performances, dramatic vignettes, and comedy skits to produce a polite and patriotic reminder of the black desire to contribute to the country's war effort in civilian and military roles.[15]

The NUL's *Negro and National Defense* broadcast was part of the publicity campaign for a vocational opportunity program directed by Ann Tanneyhill between 1931 and 1946. Tanneyhill was an important innovator in the systematic use of radio to promote racial advance. By 1939 she was already publicizing the League's vocational programs on twenty-two local stations in cities where the League had strong chapters. Her radio efforts culminated in the "Heroines in Bronze" episode she scripted for CBS's *Spirit of '43* series. Capitalizing on the wartime push for unity across gender, racial, and ethnic lines, the show dramatized the historical and contemporary importance of black women in American, rather than exclusively African American, life.[16]

The fact that many of Tanneyhill's pioneering programs failed to air on local southern outlets only increased the League's desire for exposure on the national radio networks that dominated American broadcasting. In the early 1930s it was estimated that roughly 70 percent of American broadcasting output was accounted for by NBC and CBS. By mid-decade those networks provided around 97 percent of the nation's radio entertainment after dark, when many smaller stations with sunup-to-sundown licenses fell silent. As late as 1947, 97 percent of the nation's AM stations were network affiliates, dependent on NBC, CBS, Mutual, and the newcomer ABC for substantial amounts of their broadcasting fare.[17]

The NUL found two network shows especially useful as conduits to the South, with League representatives appearing regularly on both the popular *Southernaires* and *Wings Over Jordan* syndicated programs.[18] Inaugurated in the late 1930s by Rev. Glenn Settle as *Negro Hour* on WGAR-Cleveland, CBS's *Wings Over Jordan* was particularly influential. The show mixed gospel music from its eponymous choir with talks by guest speakers that were carefully "prepared and

FIGURE 2. Between the wars, attempts to smuggle racially progressive messages onto NBC's popular *Southernaires* gospel program led to the cancellation of the show's guest spots. Courtesy of Library of American Broadcasting, University of Maryland, College Park.

presented with the idea of furthering interracial understanding."[19] *Wings Over Jordan* was a perfect complement to, and sometimes vehicle for, the NUL's gradualist approach to racial uplift. In Atlanta—admittedly the home of a notoriously conservative NUL branch—even the state-sponsored WGST happily carried the show each Sunday.[20] In October 1940, for example, the station broadcast an edition featuring Jesse O. Thomas, the NUL's field director, who used the occasion of the League's thirtieth anniversary to talk about its past achievements and plans for improving black employment and business opportunities within the segregated South.[21]

Other featured speakers on *Wings Over Jordan* echoed the League's emphasis on black economic empowerment as both instrument and evidence of African American progress in the South. When Dr. J. E. Walker, president of both the Universal Life Insurance Company—the biggest black-owned business in Memphis—and the National Negro Business League, appeared in the summer of 1940, he acknowledged that "economic opportunity for the Negro is far below that of any other race in America" and that "the correction of this condition is largely in the power of the dominant race." Yet, he insisted, "our economic freedom lies for the most part in our own hands." Walker urged African Americans to work harder and save more: "We must cease spending more than we make! We must learn how to manage money!"[22] With its generally moderate, conciliatory tone, emphasis on black accomplishments, and Washingtonian appeals to black thrift, probity, and respectability while seeking expanded educational and economic opportunities, *Wings Over Jordan* raised few alarms among whites and provided a model for much black-oriented public affairs and political broadcasting for the next two decades.

Network programs like *Wings Over Jordan* enjoyed the sort of market penetration that organizations like the NUL coveted. However, the networks themselves were hardly hotbeds of racial enlightenment or civil rights zeal. Although NBC purported to have a nondiscriminatory hiring policy from its inception and the other networks paid lip service to the same ideals, in practice the networks pursued a highly discriminatory policy toward the employment of African Americans and helped to perpetuate some of the worst racial stereotypes of the age.[23] Two vignettes from NBC suffice to illustrate the racial views of some of those whites in positions of power at the networks.

In 1935, after a number of complaints from black organizations, NBC vice president John Royal grudgingly accepted that the word "nigger" should be eliminated from songs aired on the network "wherever possible." Royal insisted, however, that "there are certain songs where the word 'nigger' must be used" and moaned that "these darkies put a lot of pressure on us and they are sometimes too exacting."[24] By the end of the decade a campaign to rid the airwaves of the "N-word" orchestrated by the NAACP had still produced only incremental and equivocal changes in the network's policy. An interdepartmental memorandum from Edna Turner of NBC's program department reminded staff that "songs containing the words 'nigger,' 'darkey,' and 'coon,' etc. in the title and lyrics should not be programmed," not because they were intrinsically demeaning, but because they "always bring complaining letters from Negro listeners."[25] Senior executive William Burke Miller responded by insisting that Turner's memo was "too all-encompassing and arbitrary." Miller felt that "despite the complaint from Negro Advancement Societies," NBC should continue to play songs like "My Old Kentucky Home" and "Way Down upon the Swanee River." He admitted that many of these songs included the "words 'darky,' 'coon,' etc." but maintained that they "are not deliberate slaps at the Negro race and they are too well-known and too well-loved to be stricken from our networks because of an isolated group." Adding patronizing insult to racist injury, Miller felt "sure all intelligent Negroes do not resent these words which are used affectionately in such songs."[26] Edna Turner quickly backtracked. Although she remained keen to "discourage the use of such songs as 'That's Why Darkies Were Born,'" she admitted that Miller was "quite right." Irrespective of any offense given to what was still a relatively minor—and therefore commercially negligible—black radio audience, Turner agreed that "it would be unthinkable . . . to consider any of the Stephen Foster songs as being taboo."[27]

Similar racial attitudes were evident in the efforts of NBC executives to exclude race relations from the agenda of its two major public affairs shows, the *University of Chicago Round Table* and the New York–based *America's Town Meeting of the Air.*[28] In 1939, after nearly a decade of scrupulously avoiding any discussion of racial problems, the University of Chicago's director of radio Sherman Dryer proposed a *Round Table* broadcast that would deal with the question "Is the Negro Oppressed?" The idea for the show was quickly quashed, mostly at the urging of John Royal, who advised the network's president, Niles Trammell, that "you, as a Southerner, know more than anyone else that you cannot *discuss* the nigger question." Royal even suggested canceling NBC's entire agreement to broadcast *Round Table* if the university insisted on making the program.[29] While the network's other nationally syndicated discussion show, *Town Meeting*, was a little more daring, prior to the war it too broached the subject of race relations only indirectly. For example, it ran two shows on the poll tax—a device that, although it was in large measure designed to disenfranchise southern blacks, also affected poor whites and was not, therefore, exclusively a racial matter.[30]

Despite reservations about the reactionary racial attitudes evident within the network bureaucracies, the NUL initially saw network programs as a useful means both to educate northerners about racial injustice and to smuggle similar messages into the South. As John Lash explained in the NUL's journal *Opportunity*, some "local stations carry network programs which can and do express convictions which would be controversial storm centers if they originated with the stations themselves." Lash suggested that this provided a healthy antidote to the "narrowness of local viewpoints," allowing "the imposition of the national attitude over sectional prejudices." Of course, southern network affiliates could always choose not to take shows that discussed racial issues, or they could excise sections of programs that were considered too radical on the subject. "Local executives have cut special expressions of a liberal character regarding race relations," Lash admitted. But he maintained that such acts of crude censorship often backfired because "liberal sentiment gained wider circulation" as a result of such "sensational action."[31]

There was no blanket southern rejection of the growing number of network shows about race, many of them government sponsored or supported, that peppered the radio schedules during World War II. For example, between seventy and eighty-five southern affiliates took the first show in the NBC series on African Americans, *Freedom's People.*[32] During 1941 and 1942, the thirteen episodes in this series, sponsored by the federal Office of Education and conceived by black educator Ambrose Caliver, proudly affirmed the black contribution to the ongoing war effort while pointing out African Americans' historic role in shaping American life and culture. Combining music and song from black stars like Josh White and Paul Robeson with editorial comment and guest interviews with a variety of eminent black and white public figures, the show attempted to undermine white contempt for the race and highlight the injustice of continuing to deny full equality to loyal, productive, and respectable citizens of color. Inevitably, the show wrestled with how to avoid offending white station owners, sponsors, and audiences by attacking white racism head-on while at the same time trying to register the intensity of black grievances and the urgent need for reform. In fact, *Freedom's People* erred on the side of caution and barely mentioned segregation at all, preferring to tiptoe around the issue with innuendo and insinuation. Half a dozen years before Jackie Robinson integrated major league baseball, one of white America's greatest sporting icons, Joe DiMaggio, appeared on an installment of *Freedom's People* devoted to black athletic achievement. After DiMaggio had lavished praise on black pitching genius Satchel Paige, the narrator pointedly bemoaned the fact that Paige was unable to play in "the big leagues," yet never explicitly invoked the Jim Crow system that consigned Paige to the segregated Negro Leagues.[33]

This circumspection was typical. Nevertheless, at its most militant, in episodes that focused on African American achievements despite a lack of equal opportunity in education and the military and the ranks of labor, *Freedom's People* even managed to condemn the government for its role in perpetuating racial inequalities in those areas. This was no mean achievement for a federally sponsored program. In large measure, such forthrightness was a tribute to the pressure exerted by members of the show's advisory board, among them black leaders like Mary McLeod Bethune, W.E.B. Du Bois, Roy Wilkins, historian Carter G. Woodson, and southern white liberals Will Alexander and Guy Johnson.[34]

The federal government became even more eager to use the airwaves to promote a sense of cohesion and common purpose among America's diverse racial, religious, and ethnic groups in the wake of serious race riots in Los Angeles and Detroit in the summer of 1943. These conflagrations exposed the tinderbox state of race relations behind the façade of national unity in wartime America. As a result, government agencies either directly sponsored or otherwise supported a number of network series like the Office of War Information's *My People* on Mutual and one-off specials like CBS's "An Open Letter on Race Hatred."[35]

These wartime network programs on racial themes were significant in many respects. From the earliest days of radio, but especially from the birth of the networks in the mid-1920s, many commentators had enthused about radio's potential for strengthening the bonds of national unity. Yet, as radio historian Susan Douglas has pointed out, what this usually represented was "a class-bound wish, articulated by . . . white, middle-class men, that somehow radio would instill the 'Anglo-Conformity' they clearly thought would bring about social order or peace."[36] No doubt these predictions exaggerated the potential for conformity or even harmony within a nation that was riven by powerful racial, ethnic, class, gender, and regional divisions. Indeed, in some respects, the conspicuous presence of African Americans and members of other ethnic groups on radio served as a constant reminder of the stubborn diversity that foiled campaigns for WASP-ish conformity. During the war years, however, network radio's unifying, nationalizing mission was quite deliberately extended to embrace non-whites to a much greater extent than ever before. Under pressure from the federal government and various civil rights groups—and as a consequence of their own sense of patriotic duty—the networks began to promote a far more inclusive yet heterogeneous vision of a nation that needed uniting behind the war effort.

This shift of emphasis to include African Americans in public discussions of America's wartime goals and core civic ideals was certainly apparent at NBC. In April and July of 1943 two *Round Table* discussions finally dealt with the subject of racial discrimination. The network's continued sensitivity to southern ratings and lobbyists was reflected in the fact that there were no African American panelists on the first of these shows and southern white views were represented by the moderate *Atlanta Constitution* editor Ralph McGill and the conservative historian Avery Craven. Thus, while it was an achievement simply to get the show aired at all, its tone and conclusions remained predictably tentative. Yes, the panelists all agreed, racial discrimination was an evil that cast a dark shadow across America's democratic ideals. Moreover, the problem clearly warranted urgent attention—provided, that is, that any attempt to adjust the racial status quo did not stir up white resentment and reactionary violence. That proviso, of course, just about ruled out any meaningful initiatives in the South and certainly precluded any concerted federal action to dismantle Jim Crow.[37]

The second *Round Table* "race" show, in July, promised to be a little bolder, not least because it was to be integrated. Eminent black sociologist E. Franklin Frazier had agreed to appear. As airtime neared, however, there were fears that NBC's southern affiliates might reject the broadcast. Partly as a result, it was agreed to avoid any real discussion of what to do about Jim Crow. Aside from some expressions of support for the work of the Federal Employment Practices Commission in expanding black opportunities in the defense industries, the show yielded nothing more substantial than a bland agreement that the problems of racial inequality needed solving. One of the problems here was that the black and white representatives on the show had completely different sets of priorities. For Frazier and most African Americans, demolishing Jim Crow in the South was as good a place as any to start dealing with racial inequality in the United States. By contrast, dismantling segregation was nowhere to be found on the agendas of most white southerners. Even the region's self-professed racial moderates, like Howard Odum, who appeared on the July *Round Table* broadcast, balked at the idea of a precipitous end to Jim Crow.[38]

NBC's *Town Meeting* sometimes allowed a little more forthright discussion of racial matters than its network stablemate. In May 1942 an all-black lineup including philosopher-critic Alain Locke and Howard president Mordecai Johnson appeared on the show. Although briefed to debate the prospects for spiritual unity in the world and instructed to avoid mentioning America's racial problems, the guests subverted the show to address the ethical dimensions of global racism.[39] In February 1944, the African American poet-activist Langston Hughes used the same show to issue a powerful call for federal action to end racial inequality and disenfranchisement. A May 1945 *Town Meeting* featured an even more passionate denunciation of American racism and southern-style segregation from writer and left-wing activist Richard Wright, who also called for blacks to rise up and take the initiative in protesting their situation and forcing change. Wright even dared to broach the most taboo of all subjects in the southern white universe: miscegenation. He demanded the abolition of southern laws against interracial marriage, arguing that the ubiquity of mulattoes in the region clearly demonstrated the worthlessness of such laws as instruments for preserving racial purity.[40]

What was especially revealing about Wright's controversial appearance on *Town Meeting* was the way in which his candor and rejection of gradualism contrasted with the steadfast moderation of one of his fellow panelists, the NUL's Elmer Carter. A former editor of *Opportunity* magazine, Carter had always been a keen proponent of radio's potential to advance the NUL's programs. He was also acutely aware of the need to tread cautiously in order to preserve any meaningful discussion of racial matters on nervous networks like NBC. Carter doggedly insisted that substantial progress had already been made on the racial front and that the treatment of African Americans in World War II was far better than it had been in World War I. While this all smacked of quiescence and accommodation—and was certainly at odds with the indignation and impatience expressed by Wright—it was much more acceptable to the network. Thus, while Wright's words had an electrifying impact on many black listeners, there was a deluge of white complaints, by no means always from southerners, directed at both the defiant Wright and NBC. Chastened by the hostile white reaction to Wright's appearance, once the special imperatives of the war had passed, NBC's premier discussion programs again chose to ignore the contentious race issue for several years.[41]

Compared with the relatively bold fare that sometimes appeared on wartime network broadcasts, or on local shows made by northern NUL branches like

Minority Opinion on WJW-Cleveland, the few programs produced by the League in the South or featuring its representatives were extremely cautious in order to pass through the mesh of southern censorship.[42] Restrictions were slightly less onerous in the border South where, for example, KWK–St. Louis aired the local NUL's *Let's Talk It Over* show throughout the 1940s. Although these programs tended to be resolutely conciliatory in tone, guests occasionally took advantage of the extra latitude for more trenchant racial commentary outside deepest Dixie. In 1946 the League's public relations committee chairman J. Hutton Hyde went on *Let's Talk It Over* and launched a scathing attack on America's present and past relationship with Africa. Harking back to the horrors of the slave trade, Hyde explained that "the story of our dealings with Africa is such a record of guilt on our part that we can never make full atonement for the wrongs we have done." He suggested, however, that "partial atonement is always possible" and urged increased levels of U.S. aid to Africa. In the postwar era, as a succession of independent African states emerged from colonial rule and pondered whether to align themselves with the Soviet or the American bloc, such appeals carried considerable weight. More generally, civil rights activists adroitly exploited the Cold War rhetoric of freedom and democracy and growing federal concern about America's international image in order to exert pressure on those who defended the formal structures of racial oppression and discrimination at home.[43]

Further south, there was little scope for such independent program production by the League. Rather, the NUL's steady, if by no means unlimited or unfettered, presence on southern radio after World War II continued to depend largely on the networks, which welcomed the League's commitment to gradualism and interracial goodwill as instruments of racial progress. Indeed, as the networks tightened the restrictions about discussing race relations that had been temporarily relaxed during the war years, the League tended, in Barbara Savage's phrase, to "bridle its rhetoric in deference to the industry's implied political boundaries."[44] Not only did this reflect an enduring conservatism that would subsequently marginalize the League when the legal and direct-action campaign against Jim Crow gathered momentum, it also helps to explain the frustration with radio as an instrument of social change that colored its gloomy 1947 report. In the decade before *Brown v. Board of Education,* the League continued to enjoy reasonably good access to the southern airwaves. Yet this access depended largely on its willingness to espouse a political caution and sometimes a racial deference that, while it accorded with the views of many self-styled racial moderates among the South's whites, began to appear increasingly anachronistic, if not downright retrogressive, to African American activists and their bolder white allies.

From Horse and Buggy to the Age of Airplanes: The NAACP on the Radio

Although it was not unknown for NAACP representatives to be heard in the South on network shows like *Wings Over Jordan,* the nation's senior civil rights organization consistently found it harder to find exposure for its views on southern airwaves than did the NUL. Traditionally vilified as disruptive outside agitators or—especially in the Cold War—as agents of international communism, the NAACP's increasingly bold legal and propaganda assault on Jim Crow ensured widespread southern white opposition to any effort to use radio to promote its work or recruit members. In 1939, for example, the Association had sponsored a special show on WCAO-Baltimore, only to have it pulled from the schedules when management discovered that segregation at the University of Maryland was one of the topics slated for discussion. Shortly afterwards, when NAACP national president Arthur Spingarn used his guest slot on the *Southernaires* gospel music show to denounce racial discrimination, the southern white outcry was sufficient to see the slot canceled.[45] Southern white station owners, managers, and sales representatives were usually fearful of white reprisals should their facilities grant exposure to the NAACP. Many were personally hostile to the black cause. "For some of the white station owners you could not do a PSA [public service announcement] for the NAACP. . . . They didn't want you to do an announcement on voter registration . . . 'cause that would empower coloreds," recalled African American deejay Shelley "the Playboy" Stewart, who joined WEDR-Birmingham in the late 1940s.[46]

Confronted by considerable difficulties in reaching southern audiences of either race via the airwaves during the interwar years, the NAACP had initially followed much the same path as the NUL. The Association sought to persuade the general public and legislators beyond Dixie not only that racial discrimination anywhere was morally wrong and a blight on American democracy but also that southern-style segregation and disenfranchisement were particularly heinous. To this end, in 1938 and 1939 several of the Association's leading members, including W.E.B. Du Bois, Roy Wilkins, George Murphy, and Walter White, had acted as unpaid consultants for the "black" episode in the twenty-six-week series *Americans All, Immigrants All,* produced for CBS by the federal government's Office of Education. This show sought to integrate African Americans into a historical narrative that celebrated America's diverse heritage, while stressing how America's avowed commitment to freedom, democracy, and opportunity worked to unify its disparate peoples.[47]

Like the NUL, the NAACP quickly recognized that World War II offered a unique opportunity to drive home messages about racial tolerance and black citizenship rights via the airwaves. Just a few weeks after Pearl Harbor, Roy Wilkins appeared on WINX-Washington, D.C., where the local NAACP branch had a weekly Sunday evening slot. He stressed black determination to play a full part in the war effort while also urging "that the democracy which our country is fighting to save for the world might be extended in the fullest degree to all minorities within our own borders." Wilkins captured the essential thrust of much of the Association's wartime radio effort when he insisted that "in carrying on its present campaign for full opportunity in our country's war effort, and in pushing for its great objective of equal and full citizenship rights for Negro Americans, the National Association for the Advancement of Colored People is serving the highest ends of patriotism for America and for the new world which must come out of this war."[48]

With opportunities for independent program production relatively rare, the Association endorsed many of the shows produced by, or with the assistance of, those federal agencies charged with fostering greater national unity. Thus the NAACP provided advisory committee members and editorial input for a number of the wartime racial propaganda shows carried by the major networks. Du Bois and Wilkins were both advisors for NBC's *Freedom's People*, while Wilkins was part of the CBS Emergency Committee of the Entertainment Industry that pushed through his idea for "An Open Letter on Race Hatred," broadcast in the aftermath of the 1943 Detroit race riot. Perhaps even more influential in defining the Association's attitude toward using the airwaves, however, was Theodore Berry, an NAACP board member and lawyer in the government's Office of Emergency Management. Berry was one of the first to appreciate fully that the most effective use of radio to promote racial change was to focus on white racial attitudes and practices rather than simply to celebrate black achievements. Although the two approaches were not mutually exclusive, Berry insisted that since white racial prejudice was the primary source of discriminatory practices, this was where the Association should concentrate its major media efforts.[49]

Berry's agenda just about survived the protracted debates surrounding the Mutual network's series *My People*. Indeed, in many regards the story of *My People* was emblematic of the sorts of editorial battles from which all of these wartime broadcasts emerged, battered, bruised, and usually bowdlerized. By mid-1942 both the Department of War and the Office of War Information (OWI) hankered after a radio program that would boost black morale and enthusiasm for the war by enveloping African Americans in the outpouring of patriotism and democratic rhetoric that characterized domestic propaganda. Terrified of offending the senior southern congressmen who dominated many federal agencies and congressional appropriations committees, and not especially noted as bastions of racial enlightenment themselves, neither the Department of War nor the OWI had much desire to endorse the sorts of racial reforms that black leaders were pursuing under the umbrella of a Double Victory campaign to defeat racist totalitarianism abroad and racial discrimination at home. For example,

Milton Starr of the OWI, who was given responsibility for the show, favored focusing wholly on the heroism of black fighting men, believing that this would inspire even more patriotism and sacrifice among African Americans. Theodore Berry, however, pointed out that levels of black morale and commitment to the war effort were inextricably linked to evidence that the federal government was genuinely committed to eradicating prejudice and discrimination in American civilian and military life. In other words, whereas Starr sought primarily to target and inspire an African American community that he described as "rabid radio listeners," Berry wanted to expose and denounce white racism in a show aimed largely at the general population. In retrospect, Berry was mapping out the scope of many future debates among civil rights activists about whether black social, economic, and political aspirations were better served by focusing on specifically black-oriented radio programming or by fighting to get black personalities and racial themes on general-market stations.[50]

As the format and scripts for *My People* were written, critiqued, and endlessly rewritten, new voices, perspectives, and concerns were constantly stirred into the creative and economic mix. OWI director Elmer Davis encouraged Starr to deliver a "direct and powerful Negro propaganda effort as distinct from a crusade for Negro rights."[51] The Mutual network began to get anxious, lest Berry's more radical agenda win out. The network had little desire to become associated with trenchant demands for civil rights reform, with all that might entail in lost audiences and revenue in the South. Mutual's fears intensified when the OWI began to distance itself from the series, which was now designated as made not "by" but "in cooperation with" the OWI. These concerns were ratcheted up a notch further when G. Lake Imes, a former Tuskegee and Lincoln University administrator whose black-produced *My People* broadcast in Baltimore in 1942 had served as the original template for the OWI-Mutual series, joined Berry in pushing for more militant scripts. Eventually the OWI felt compelled to reassure Mutual that it would remain the final arbiter of the shows' contents and that it would "in no way undertake to discuss controversial subjects or present material of a controversial nature."[52]

After a year of this thrust and counterthrust, Mutual finally aired four programs in the *My People* series in February and March of 1943 at 7 p.m. on Saturday evenings. Mixing music, interviews, and dramatic interludes, the first show featured Eleanor Roosevelt, North Carolina white liberal Frank Porter Graham, and Mordecai Johnson, president of Howard University and an early African American proponent of Gandhian protest tactics. Even at the last minute, signs of incipient militancy were suppressed, including Johnson's plan to denounce the practice of segregating Red Cross blood supplies. He had also wanted to point out growing black skepticism about the merits of fighting a war for liberty abroad while discrimination against citizens of color flourished at home. Instead his comments were reworked into a vague statement of black support for the democratic aims of the war. Such pruning still did not satisfy all Mutual's affiliates. Its flagship outlet, WOR in New York, declined to drop a fifteen-minute commercial program from its schedules in order to make way for the debut of *My People* or to air a transcription of the show at a later time. The *Pittsburgh Courier* detected the hand of "the Southern bloc within the WOR setup" in the station's decision to pass on the show until it could be sure of its moderate tone.[53]

Each of the subsequent *My People* programs, indeed all of the government-sponsored racial propaganda shows of the war and immediate postwar era, underwent a similar process of cutting and compromise. To a greater or lesser extent, all bore the hallmarks of the tortuous negotiations and power struggles among local radio station and network executives, sponsors and advertisers, black and white civil rights activists, southern segregationists, and federal officials. Yet, although the NAACP was frustrated by the constant tempering of bold antidiscrimination messages in government-sponsored wartime broadcasts, it still recognized them as important expressions of federal concern about racial problems at home and as potentially useful vehicles for raising popular consciousness about racial injustice.

Timidity on the part of federal agencies was not the only impediment to airing more probing discussions and radical visions of how to end southern segregation and disenfranchisement. In 1945 the War Department hoped to use the CBS series *Assignment Home* as a forum for a specially commissioned drama called "The Glass." The show was intended to address the question of how African Americans would be treated after the war. As scripted, "The Glass" featured one black and one white soldier, veterans of the Battle of the Bulge where military necessity had forced the impromptu integration of segregated combat troops. The two men had fought side by side, sharing the risk of death in the service of their country. Yet they were not allowed to share a drink in the southern bar where the drama was set. The previous year CBS had allowed a generally optimistic discussion entitled "Is the South Solving Its Race Problem?" on its prestigious *People's Platform* show, thereby neatly quarantining America's racial problems in the Southland at a time when there was actually a good deal of recognition that racial inequalities were a national, not a regional, problem. "The Glass," however, represented a much more direct critique of Jim Crow. It certainly proved far too controversial for CBS, which refused to air the show despite protests from the NAACP and other organizations.[54]

Revealingly, CBS felt rather more secure in allowing singing sensation Frank Sinatra to weave a similar message into his weekly syndicated *Songs by Sinatra* show. In 1945 Sinatra had featured in a highly acclaimed short movie celebrating racial and ethnic diversity in American life called *The House That I Live In*.

Shortly after the film's release singer-dancer Gene Kelly joined Sinatra on his radio show to add his congratulations. "That short will make a big contribution to the cause of tolerance," Kelly remarked, prompting Sinatra to deliver a monologue straight out of the wartime Double Victory playbook. "Speaking of tolerance, neighbors," Sinatra began, drawing his listeners into an ethereal community of right-minded, God-fearing Americans, "every one of us knows this: God never meant for any man to fight for freedom and have any part of that freedom denied him by the country for which he fought."[55] This sentiment was really not very far removed from the moral thrust of the rejected "The Glass" show. Yet by integrating the message of tolerance and equality into a variety show, CBS avoided some of the controversy and southern resentment that a program specifically dedicated to the continuing problem of racial discrimination in the region might have aroused.

After the war, the NAACP worked harder than ever to exploit the full potential of radio—a potential that the organization was adamant existed, but that it still struggled to define and harness. In September 1945 the Association's publicity committee made several recommendations designed to improve the effectiveness of the NAACP's public relations activities. The foremost of these recommendations was that the NAACP should buy much more airtime for its own broadcasts. This reflected the belief that the Association's traditional status, as either a "guest" on radio or as one of countless behind-the-scenes advisory voices influencing commercial and government-sponsored broadcasts, compromised its ability to use the medium effectively. "It is a crying shame that the leading organization fighting for Negro rights is so far behind the times in this respect," the report concluded. To neglect "the buying of radio time and the competent preparation of scripts, is to neglect our opportunities completely. . . . It means we are plodding along at a horse and buggy pace in an airplane age so far as publicity techniques are concerned."[56] In the aftermath of this report, Arthur Spingarn and executive secretary Walter White headed a radio committee to investigate ways of improving the Association's use of the airwaves.[57]

Under the guidance of this new committee, the NAACP extended Theodore Berry's wartime approach to radio. Although it continued to seek opportunities to broadcast to southern audiences of both races either on network shows or on the occasional locally produced show, the Association appreciated that such opportunities would remain sorely limited for the foreseeable future. Consequently it concentrated on two distinct but interrelated radio strategies. The first involved courting white, primarily northern support for its legal campaign against southern segregation; the second focused on challenging the sorts of white conceptions of African Americans that allowed racial prejudice and discrimination to flourish throughout the nation. During the decade or so after

World War II, these twin agendas found expression in a variety of NAACP broadcasts.

In 1947 the NAACP enjoyed two important radio coups. After years of unsuccessful pleas to one of the early masters of radio politics, President Franklin Delano Roosevelt, to speak out against racial discrimination on radio, his successor Harry Truman agreed to address the NAACP's annual convention live on air. The Association coordinated a nationwide relay of the president's speech on all four networks and numerous independent stations. It even arranged for 125 special "listening-in" meetings around the nation to ensure the widest possible audience for Truman's declaration: "There is no justifiable reason for discrimination because of ancestry, or religion, or race or color."[58]

The second coup came three months later when executive secretary Walter White participated in an October edition of NBC's *Town Meeting* devoted to improving racial and religious understanding. The show marked *Town Meeting*'s return to the subject of race relations after several years' silence on the matter. A month later White was back on the same network, this time as a participant in a discussion called "Civil Rights and Loyalty" that marked the revival of *Round Table*'s interest in the race question. The main catalyst for NBC's change of heart here was the publication of "To Secure These Rights," the report of Truman's Commission on Civil Rights. Once again it was apparent that the networks would rarely initiate discussion of America's racial dilemmas; they moved only when they felt compelled by some kind of national crisis or were confident of government sanction for what might be seen as controversial programming decisions.

This pattern of cause and effect became even clearer in 1948. In the midst of growing Cold War anxieties about the damage Jim Crow was doing to America's image abroad, Truman had issued an executive order to desegregate the military, delivered a powerful speech on civil rights to Congress, and endorsed a strong civil rights plank in the Democratic Party's election campaign, thereby unleashing the Dixiecrat revolt of disaffected southern Democrats. In the wake of these developments, both *Round Table* and *Town Meeting* began to host discussions of racial matters on a more regular basis. In so doing they reflected and helped to intensify and define a growing national preoccupation with solving the southern race problem. It was only after Truman's public expressions of support for civil rights reform that NBC risked featuring guests who were certain to issue outspoken condemnations of both the immorality and the unconstitutionality of segregation and disenfranchisement.[59]

While southern opposition to such broadcasts remained a constant headache, the growing number of southern racial progressives on these programs, alongside northern liberals and black activists, reflected a shift toward partisan neutrality on racial matters at NBC. Paradoxically, however, the network's new acceptance of the need to resolve the most visible example of systematic racial discrimination in America was best reflected by the regular appearance on NBC discussion shows of die-hard southern segregationists like Senators John Sparkman of Alabama and Allen Ellender of Louisiana. While the presence of these hard-core bigots defused complaints that "traditional" southern viewpoints were not being represented, these men also proved ideal whipping boys for the voices of reform that began to dominate network public affairs shows. By contrast, moderate southern segregationists made rather poor foils for black or white civil rights proponents; they were prone to sudden outbursts of reasonableness and even sympathy for the black predicament, even if they usually believed that an immediate end to Jim Crow would be premature and result in an orgy of reactionary violence. As the civil rights activists of the 1960s would discover when they confronted the likes of Eugene "Bull" Connor and Jim Clark in the streets of the South, last-ditch segregationists spewing race hatred and embracing violence made the best opponents with which to dramatize the evils of Jim Crow. Similarly, it was when the most intemperate racists were featured on air that the legitimacy of black demands became most obvious. Appeals for civil and voting rights could be vividly contrasted with the desperate self-interest and racist vitriol of men like Ellender, with his shrill warning of a black descent into what he described on *Round Table* as "barbaric lunacy" if white supremacy in the South was ever displaced. While some southern whites—and no doubt a fair few northern ones—may have agreed with Ellender, the NBC discussion programs of the late 1940s and early 1950s were usually carefully orchestrated to depict such views as unacceptable and embarrassing to decent, democratically minded Americans.[60]

At one level, the increasing focus on the South in these shows represented a retreat from what had been a growing recognition during the war years that racial discrimination was a national phenomenon. It was as if, after the war, the networks—again following the lead of the federal government—sought to quarantine racial inequities in the aberrant South, with its peculiarly anachronistic system of legal segregation and its penchant for racist demagoguery. Certainly *Round Table* and *Town Meeting* generally avoided confronting the issue of racism in the country at large. Moreover, the overwhelming desire to find consensus on the southern race issue and minimize the likelihood of interracial violence continued to straitjacket discussions of the precise mechanisms for ending Jim Crow. This meant that the most progressive southern white voices heard on national or local radio usually belonged to moderates like Harry Ashmore and James McBride Dabbs, people who in the late 1940s and early 1950s were often still groping for a way to modify rather than end Jim Crow. For many African Americans the time for such accommodation to a pernicious system was rapidly receding into history. Yet the configuration of power within the radio industry regularly impaired their capacity to speak out on air as forthrightly as they might have liked.

Immediately following the announcement of Truman's support for civil rights reform, Arthur Gaith and Raymond Walsh of the NAACP had prepared a special brief on how the Association should capitalize on growing federal and popular unease at Jim Crow practices by soliciting airtime from radio stations and sponsors. The NAACP should "try to ascertain who, working for the station, is liberal in viewpoint [and] work through him or her." Meanwhile sympathetic merchants were to be encouraged to buy airtime during which brief NAACP announcements and recruitment plugs might be made. Such spots should stress the Association's nonprofit, nonpolitical credentials and the patriotic fact that it was "dedicated to the president's own civil rights program." One twenty-second slot captured the NAACP's basic approach at the height of the Cold War by appealing to America's democratic ideals: "The equality of men of all races is guaranteed by the Constitution. If you believe in equality and equal opportunity, you can help establish this cause. Join the NAACP and work for a really *United States*."[61]

In the South this strategy of Gaith and Walsh foundered simply because very few businessmen, programmers, or station owners had any interest in allowing the Association access to the airways. Occasionally, however, individual announcers went out on a limb and made airtime available for NAACP news or representatives. In Washington, D.C., in the mid-to-late 1940s, pioneering black deejay Hal Jackson used his enormous popularity in the black community to raise funds for the local NAACP chapter through all-star benefit concerts. He participated in a series of demonstrations against the stores on Connecticut Avenue that accepted black dollars for merchandise but did not allow African Americans to use store restrooms or lunch counters and never hired them. He also featured Walter White and other NAACP representatives on *The House That Jack Built*, his show on WOOK. White station owner Richard Eaton threatened to fire Jackson if he continued this kind of political activity. The economic bottom line, however, meant that Jackson remained at WOOK until 1949, when he moved to WLIB–New York. "I was too valuable for him to make good on his threat," Jackson recalled. It was a basic fiscal calculation that would have enormous influence on the story of both black-oriented radio and the southern freedom struggle.[62]

Hal Jackson's level of public, on-air commitment to the NAACP and other local activists was unusual among southern broadcasters in the 1940s and early 1950s. Beyond Dixie, however, local Association branches were much more successful in cultivating sympathetic sponsors and radio executives. After the war, the NAACP had even contemplated the idea of a regular radio show. In 1946 it solicited opinions from a wide range of civic, religious, and labor organizations about how best to produce and disseminate a nationally networked program that would reach "those listeners not already convinced on minority problems."[63] By the early 1950s, however, nothing much had happened along these lines, and the Association continued to work on a rather unsatisfactory ad hoc basis with the networks and a variety of friendly local stations mostly located outside the South. *The Walter White Show* was an outgrowth of one of those liaisons. It marked the culmination of the NAACP's efforts to use the airwaves to expose the injustice of segregation and explain the moral, constitutional, and psychological rationale for the legal campaign against it. Produced by WLIB in New York, the show ran for fifteen minutes each week from 1952 until White's death in 1955 and was eventually heard far beyond the perimeter of that city.[64]

The Walter White Show was actually the brainchild of WLIB's white liberal owners, Morris and Harry Novik, whose station boasted some of the hottest rhythm and blues music and several of the most charismatic black deejays to be heard in New York, including Jack Walker "the Pear-Shaped Talker" and Phil Gordon as well as Hal Jackson.[65] Since they bought the station from *New York Post* proprietor Dorothy Schiff in 1949, switching it to an all-black format and relocating to studios in the Hotel Theresa deep in the heart of Harlem, WLIB had assumed a major political, cultural, and social function within the black community.[66] This was a consequence, in part, of the fact that it so proudly featured the cream of black musical talent. However, it was also a consequence of WLIB's close relationship with various local black organizations and leaders, like the Negro Labor Committee's Frank Crosswaith, who appeared regularly on the station to discuss employment and housing issues affecting African Americans in the city.[67]

More important still were the station's ties to the NAACP. In the early 1950s the Noviks helped to stage, publicize, and report on local NAACP fundraising events and membership drives. Their station also relayed coverage of the Association's annual conventions to New Yorkers from wherever in the country the meetings were held. In 1953 the NAACP's publicity director Henry Lee Moon wrote to Harry Novik thanking him for granting free airtime for a February recruitment campaign and in the process acknowledging the unique capacity of radio to reach certain sections of the black community: "This enabled us to get the NAACP message to thousands of your listeners many of whom we may have otherwise been unable to reach."[68] A year later the Association presented Novik with a special award—the first time it had ever honored a radio station—for WLIB's "development of interracial understanding" and "consistent support of the program of the National Association for the Advancement of Colored People through generous reporting of the Association's activities."[69]

Invaluable though it was, much of WLIB's early support for the NAACP was of a typically informal and sporadic nature. The Novik brothers simply responded as and when the Association called for help with fundraising, recruitment, or specific local campaigns. In January 1951, however, Harry Novik proposed formalizing the relationship by means of a weekly show. "Just carrying music, even if it's good music, is not enough," Novik wrote to Walter White. The Noviks were clearly not content simply to make a good living off black talent and consumer dollars. Even his characterization of the music played on WLIB as "good" set Harry Novik apart from many of the white radio entrepreneurs and program directors who swooped on the burgeoning black market after the war. Many, if by no means all, of these people had little understanding of, or respect for, the music that drew their audiences and swelled their bank accounts. Mort Silverman, station manager at WMRY–New Orleans, was typical enough, stressing the commercial considerations that prompted his shift from "good music" to black-oriented programming: "Before 1950 we were featuring good music and failing, May twenty-eight of that year we switched to a solid Negro format. In a month we paid our way."[70] Late in his career Egmont Sonderling, who eventually acquired a chain of black-oriented stations throughout the nation, made a similar comment about his own 1950 decision to change the format of his failing classical music station WOPA–Oak Park, Illinois: "I used to have a station I enjoyed listening to but it was going broke. Now I have six stations I can't listen to but I make a lot of money."[71] The Noviks were hardly opposed to making money, but they did seek to put something back into the community from which they derived their wealth. "We would like to have a weekly forum program, and the NAACP is number one on our list!" Harry Novik wrote to Walter White. While not immediately convinced that this was a good idea, White was eventually persuaded. The first show aired on June 2, 1952.[72]

Although the show was produced in New York, White used much of his airtime to keep listeners apprised of the legal assaults on southern segregation that culminated in the NAACP's victory in the Supreme Court's *Brown* decision of 1954. He emphasized not only the justness of that campaign but also the inevitability of ultimate victory. In a December 1953 program, for example, White reviewed four days of testimony before the Supreme Court from the various school desegregation cases consolidated as *Brown*. Although he mentioned the arguments advanced by both sides, he left WLIB's listeners in no doubt about who occupied the moral and constitutional high ground. The "shocking statement[s]" and "questionable taste" of the segregationists were contrasted with the "immense amount of preparation" and "unequivocal argument" of NAACP chief counsel Thurgood Marshall. White dismissed the segregationists' claim that the passage of time had somehow legitimized the concept of "separate but equal" as analogous to saying that "because a man has been suffering from tuberculosis or cancer for many years, nothing should be done to rid him of those maladies."[73]

On another occasion White even suggested that important elements within the white South were already reconciled to the inevitability of school desegregation. While not denying the possibility of segregationist "protests," he was optimistic that "there does seem to be a growing willingness of enlightened Southerners of both races to accept peacefully the inevitable democratization of public education."[74] At a time when memories of the 1948 Dixiecrat revolt were still fresh, this seemed overly optimistic to some. Nonetheless, it was a common theme in black-produced radio shows devoted to the "race question" during the 1940s and early 1950s. Roi Ottley's long-running *New World A-Coming* show on WMCA–New York, for example, regularly praised the contribution of white racial progressives to the struggle for black equality, not least in the South. In the aftermath of the 1944 *Smith v. Allwright* decision outlawing the white primary and rekindling a small measure of southern black political participation, the show's narrator, black actor Canada Lee, had insisted that "the solid South is cracking. More and more there are white people in the South who are raising the banner of democracy in the South."[75] Such statements came from a fluid, ill-defined, but nonetheless psychologically important space somewhere between wishful thinking and a practical desire to encourage timid and tiny pockets of white support for the gathering assault on Jim Crow. They helped to fuel guarded optimism among blacks and with it a determination to keep up the pressure for change.

Unlike *New World A-Coming*, which remained essentially a New York phenomenon, *The Walter White Show* was eventually syndicated to many stations in the North and West. This established an important precedent, marking the first time that a major civil rights organization had created its own regular show designed for nationwide distribution. The goal was to reach as many people as possible with the NAACP's analysis of the racial situation and appeals for an end to discrimination. Yet, paradoxically, this ambitious ecumenical brief sometimes reduced the audience ratings and, therefore, the effectiveness of the broadcasts. The problem stemmed from the determination of the staunchly integrationist NAACP to avoid having the show pigeonholed as an exclusively black-oriented affair. This meant that it was often carried on general-market facilities with a limited black clientele and a primary white audience that had little interest in hearing discussions of civil rights issues.[76] As a result, audience ratings for *The Walter White Show* were frequently disappointing. More than once, White had to write to NAACP branches in cities where the program was due to air in an attempt to increase local awareness of the broadcasts and raise the listenership to a level that would persuade commercially driven stations to keep the show on their schedules.[77]

FIGURE 3. In 1949 Atlanta businessman Jesse Blayton became the first African American to own a radio station when he purchased WERD. In 1951 he refused to air the NAACP's *Walter White Show* without a sponsor, highlighting a tension between economic considerations and public service that would characterize his twenty years in charge at WERD. Courtesy of Archives of African American Music and Culture, Indiana University.

Whatever difficulties the NAACP encountered in trying to maximize the audience for and impact of *The Walter White Show* in the North and West, they paled when compared to the problems it faced in the South. The show failed to find a single outlet in the Deep South; even at the edges of Dixie, only KWK in St. Louis and, very briefly, WWDC and WOL in Washington took the show.[78] The closest the NAACP came to finding a permanent southern home for White's show was with the black-owned WERD in Atlanta. Negotiations broke down, however, when a sponsorship deal with the Atlanta Life Insurance Company did not materialize and station owner Jesse Blayton—himself an NUL stalwart suspicious of the NAACP's comparatively militant agenda—declined to carry the broadcasts for free as a "sustaining" public service feature.[79]

Although WERD's situation as a black-owned outlet was unusual, most southern radio stations were extremely wary of accepting any NAACP broadcasts. This reluctance became still more pronounced during the decade or so after World War II as the Association won a succession of impressive Supreme Court victories against segregation on interstate transportation, in professional and graduate schools, and in real estate practices. Although implementation of these rulings in the South remained virtually nonexistent, they suggested that time was running out for Jim Crow and raised the level of anxiety among southern whites. Every courtroom victory made NAACP access to the southern air-waves more elusive than ever. Even on the rare occasions when the Association did manage to get southern airtime in the early 1950s, there was often a catch. Walter White was invited by the black Howard High School in Chattanooga to give a speech on "any subject you wish," which would be broadcast on local station WDOD. Yet station manager Frank Hubbs warned him that this apparently open brief did not include any discussion of "intolerance, religious strife or racial prejudice."[80]

This equivocation regarding the NAACP and what it stood for was common-place, even at some of the least reactionary southern outlets. Black-oriented WSOK-Nashville was one of a handful of southern stations in the early 1950s that did allow the local NAACP branch a weekly slot. Yet owner H. Calvin Young Jr. insisted that each broadcast be prefaced with a disclaimer formally disassoci-ating his station from any of the ideas expressed on the show. The station's per-spective on racial change was made even clearer in December 1952 when Young fired black announcer Ed Cook. Cook's position at the station had been in peril ever since he urged his listeners to boycott a segregated "Passion Play" at the Ryman Auditorium, insisting that "Christianity didn't and doesn't segregate." Shortly afterwards he compounded this heresy by concluding a newscast about the exclusion of African Americans from the city's municipal golf courses with the sarcastic reminder that "America is a democracy." Calvin Young saw a clear distinction between allowing airtime for the NAACP and having his own station and staff implicated in any kind of opposition to segregation. Not for the first or last time, rumors abounded that "white supremacists and southern apologists" were forcing Young's already wavering hand and insisting that he take a stand against the racial treachery on his station.[81]

The WSOK affair had far-reaching repercussions. It highlighted several gnawing concerns about the way that the NAACP appeared to be dealing with the rising popularity of black-oriented broadcasting. On one hand, the Associa-tion was grateful for any radio exposure, especially in the South. On the other hand, Calvin Young's grudging acceptance of the NAACP's broadcasts and evi-dent hostility to the Association's goals, coupled with his cavalier treatment of Ed Cook and his steadfast refusal to allow the unionization of his station—and thus to provide a minimal level of job security for his staff—meant that it was hard not to see WSOK as part of a paternalistic and exploitative Jim Crow system. For a month the Nashville NAACP branch agonized over what to do. In mid-January it chose to sever its relationship with Young and WSOK, thereby depriving the Association of an important broadcasting foothold in Tennessee. At the same time, it sent a formal protest about the station's racial policies to the Federal Communications Commission (FCC).[82] If there was a certain irony in the deci-sion to target one of the few southern stations that actually allowed the NAACP any regular airtime, it was nonetheless in keeping with the Association's strategy of seeking redress for racial injustices through legal initiatives and federal intervention.

Beyond the NAACP, the WSOK case inspired heated debate about the merits of black-oriented radio. It was a backhanded tribute to the growing significance of the medium among African Americans that several black newspapers used the Nashville controversy to launch envious attacks on the whole radio boom. The *Cleveland Call and Post,* for example, depicted black radio as little more than an exploitative and ego-gratifying snare for black consumers' dollars. "Throughout this nation, North and South, East and West, Negroes have spent thousands of dollars with radio stations, just to cater to their egos," it railed. "The novelty of being on the air has outweighed all sane considerations of what they were getting for their money." Joseph LaCour, general manager of Associated Publishers, Inc., sent clippings like these to Roy Wilkins, confessing that the rapid expansion of black-oriented radio was making him, as a publisher of black print journals, "unhappy." LaCour even expressed the hope that there would be more controversies like the one between the NAACP and WSOK, since it had cast the upstart radio medium in such an unfavorable light. "If there is anything more in the way of a little 'hatchet work' the NAACP can do, I shall be grateful," he admitted.[83]

Roy Wilkins recognized that the criticisms of black-oriented radio from LaCour and others in the black print media were largely self-serving. They reflected, as Wilkins put it, concerns about "the diversion of advertising revenue that might go into the Negro press."[84] Nevertheless, within the NAACP leadership the WSOK affair had rekindled debate about the desirability of using exclusively black-oriented stations rather than general-market outlets. Among the most vocal critics of the former strategy was the director of the Association's Washington bureau, Clarence Mitchell, who questioned the wisdom of pursuing the fight for an integrated America on radio stations that were essentially segregated. "We certainly do not want to even appear to support the idea of a station 'serving the Negro community,'" he cautioned. Mitchell actually urged Walter White to petition the FCC to outlaw such facilities, believing that they were an expression of precisely the kind of Jim Crow mentality and separate social and economic structures that the Association wished to destroy.[85]

Mitchell's dissenting voice was ultimately drowned out. Most of the NAACP leadership, including White, Wilkins, and publicity director Consuelo Young, appreciated that no matter how hard the Association might strive to gain exposure on the national radio networks or on local general-market stations, it was stations with a sizeable chunk of black-oriented fare on their schedules that were most likely to take NAACP programs and announcements, and to welcome its representatives. To some extent this was simply a matter of economics. The owners and program managers of black-oriented stations naturally tended to schedule shows they felt would appeal to their primary demographic, and that could include NAACP broadcasts. Of course, in the South of the 1940s and 1950s, white racial anxieties frequently trumped such crude fiscal calculations and placed any shows that addressed race relations out of bounds. Perhaps the most telling rebuttal to Mitchell's argument, however, came from those who appreciated the vital role that local black-oriented programming had come to play within black communities around the nation. As Roy Wilkins explained in 1950, "The reaching of great radio chains represents difficulties which cannot always be overcome. Thus the smaller stations, which play such a part in community living and community thought, offer a chance for minority groups to tell their story to their fellow citizens."[86]

The second, related strand in the NAACP's postwar radio strategy depended on the belief that white ignorance and superstition about the character of African Americans lay behind much racial intolerance and discrimination. The NAACP therefore rededicated itself to eradicating racial stereotypes on the radio and replacing them with more positive images of African Americans as respectable and responsible citizens. The Association had begun efforts in this direction in the early 1930s when it joined the influential Chicago clergyman Bishop W. J. Walls and the *Pittsburgh Courier* in an unsuccessful campaign against the popular *Amos 'n' Andy* show on which black-voiced white comedians, Charles Correll and Freeman Gosden, presented caricatures of two southern black migrants in the Windy City. In fact, there were many similar neo–minstrel shows on air during radio's formative decades. Several of these programs emanated from the South, including *Two Black Crows* on mighty WBT in Charlotte and *Rufus and Roberta,* the creation of Curt Smith and Lois Hobbs at WRBL-Columbus, Georgia. Although many African American listeners loved these programs—being perfectly able to distinguish between the realities of African American life and the shows' broad-brush stereotypes—their updated minstrelsy presented precisely the sorts of images of blacks that the NAACP wanted removed from the airwaves and from American consciousness.[87]

Generally speaking, the peculiar circumstances of the war years saw a decline in the most demeaning black portrayals on air amid the clamor for national unity. In the summer of 1944, black educator-activist Lawrence Reddick acknowledged recent improvements in the depictions of African Americans on radio and favorably contrasted them with the pejorative treatment of blacks in motion pictures. Nevertheless, he still complained that radio routinely cast blacks as superstitious or childlike, unable to perform any music other than folk songs or spirituals or jazz, while avoiding serious discussions of black rights and grievances.[88] After the war, racial stereotyping on air threatened to intensify again and, in the spring of 1948, a meeting of the NAACP's radio committee agreed to target the problem.[89] In June, Walter White compiled for broadcasters a list of "the words which are objectionable to Negroes." He sought to abolish "concepts of the Negro as being any more lazy, amoral or immoral than other persons or any more addicted perpetually to the use of dialect and the eating exclusively of water melon and chicken."[90] Eight months later, while such images still plagued American radio, White felt able to tell a meeting of the Radio Executive Club that "broadcasting has done more to depict the Negro as a human being and an integral part of American life than motion pictures or the stage."[91]

The NAACP was not alone in waging war on derogatory racial stereotypes in America's media and culture industries. In March 1947 an installment of *New World A-Coming* entitled "The Mammy Legend" condemned that durable icon of black docility and compliance as a relic of "the Old South . . . largely a fiction, a museum piece of slavery days." The show concluded with the proud declaration "Mammy doesn't live here anymore."[92] Sometimes individuals within the industry also offered morale-boosting support to the campaign for black respect on radio. An influential ally in this regard was Canadian-born broadcaster Art Linkletter, the popular host of both NBC's *People Are Funny* and CBS's *House Party*, which by 1950 was syndicated to 165 stations across the nation. A pioneer of audience participation programs and quiz shows from the mid-1930s, Linkletter had become sensitive to the black predicament early in his radio career. When he was working in Dallas, an ill-judged joke that turned on stereotypes about black ignorance had brought him "dozens of letters . . . in protest from Negro listeners who were hurt." Shamed by his racist gaffe, Linkletter next found himself in trouble with white Texans. He had apparently violated southern racial etiquette by publicly shaking hands with a black choral director who was visiting the station. "Next day and all next week I was taken aside and severely criticized," he recalled.[93]

Thereafter Linkletter became a steady champion of the black right to respectful treatment on air, especially in the South. "Down there, the prejudice got me so mad I fought it. I did a program from there which I sold to CBS. It was called 'Music of the South,' an all-Negro program. I traced the folk songs and work songs of the Negro workers, went to the mines, the farms, the quarries and the railroads and brought Negroes onto the program each week, to sing their songs and to explain their culture which in large measure is the South's only culture." It is difficult to quantify the impact that this kind of sympathetic showcase for southern black cultural achievements might have had upon a national white audience, yet it both exemplified and encouraged the postwar drift within the radio industry toward more gracious and courteous treatment of African Americans. In a similar vein, Linkletter made a point of publicly admonishing and correcting those guests who used the word "nigger" on air. "Such offenders are mostly southerners," he admitted, although he also maintained that usually "It's not contemptuous with them—merely habit." On those occasions when a guest was unwilling to stand corrected, Linkletter immediately terminated the interview and apologized to his listeners for his guest's rudeness.[94]

The support of important white broadcasters like Art Linkletter was undoubtedly welcome. Yet African Americans sought more systematic ways to harness the power of radio to promote positive black images both to the nation at large and to the black community itself, where a revolution in consciousness and self-esteem was a necessary prerequisite for organized mass protest. In what would become a recurring complaint, many black activists felt that problems with the unflattering portrayal of blacks on air stemmed from the dearth of African Americans working in radio on either side of the microphone. At its first conference on radio and television in July 1949, the Committee for the Negro in the Arts bemoaned the lack of black employment opportunities in the industry. Actor Canada Lee saw this situation as symptomatic of a more general pattern of "abuse and slander suffered by the Negro" in all areas of the entertainment industry. Condemning "*Amos 'n' Andy, Beulah,* and other programs which falsify and distort the realities of Negro life," the committee resolved to attack discrimination in hiring and promotion practices and to utilize the power of black consumers to force radio stations to eradicate racial stereotyping on air. "The radio industry," the Committee felt, "is highly susceptible to pressure and can therefore be forced to abandon such injurious programs" by threats of withdrawn black patronage.[95]

The Committee was on to something important here. As in the broader freedom struggle, the growing economic leverage available to the black community promised to be a potent weapon in the broadcasting arena. In the face of blossoming racial pride, radio advertisers wishing to penetrate the increasingly lucrative black market felt compelled to curtail their use of degrading language and imagery. As has occasionally happened in the history of broadcasting, commercial priorities and the interests of racial progress coincided here, assisting efforts to promote more respectful attitudes toward African Americans as both consumers and subjects of radio programs. When African American listeners were polled about the most important noneconomic factors that motivated them to buy particular goods or services advertised on air, by far the most important criterion was that those products should contribute to the quest for self-improvement.[96] Black-oriented broadcasters across the nation duly took note. "The most important factor in approaching the Negro through air advertising," a representative of WLIB–New York explained to *Sponsor* magazine, "is considering the Negro consumer a being of dignity and self-respect." A Gulf Coast bakery's advertisement that had used the tune of "Shortnin' Bread" to sell its wares was consequently rejected, while a supermarket ad for "Pig Knuckles. Ham Hocks.

Chitlins. Plate Beef. Kidneys. And other meat cuts in the lowest price bracket," described in a faux-black voice as "good ol' Southern eating" drew a chorus of African American protest.[97]

Programmers with a sizeable black audience to cultivate also tended to avoid the sort of pitches for hair straighteners and skin bleaching agents that filled African American print journals like *Jet* and *Ebony*. There were exceptions, such as at WDXB-Chattanooga, where deejay Ted Bryant counted Silky Straight hair-dressing among his sponsors. Nevertheless, as *Sponsor* observed in 1949, "on programs aimed directly at Negro audiences by local stations there is virtually no advertising of hair-straightening or skin-blanching products, despite the tremendous sale of such products to Negroes."[98] *Sponsor* explained the difference in the amount of space devoted to "whitening" cosmetics in the black print media and on black-oriented radio in terms of African American embarrassment at the use of such products coupled with the racial discreteness of each medium. Unlike the bespoke black press, by the late 1940s and early 1950s black-oriented radio was often attracting a substantial, if furtive, young white audience. "Negroes are sensitive about their use of this kind of 'beauty' aid, and while mention of skin-whiteners and hair-straighteners is all right in printed media seen only by members of the colored race, Negroes would be embarrassed to think that whites might also be listening to a radio program plugging them." Certainly no black-oriented station accepted the advertisement that hawked its hair product with the crass slogan "Attention Negro women! Now you can have hair that's just as attractive as that of white women."[99]

Thanks to the campaigns of the NAACP and others, coupled with the refusal of African American listeners to be patronized or demeaned, the success of black-oriented radio programming and advertising after World War II increasingly depended on the respect with which African American consumers were treated and represented. Ben Hooks, Memphis minister, NAACP veteran, and eventually the first African American to serve as an FCC commissioner, recalled the enormous psychological impact of WDIA's courteous treatment of blacks on air. "For the first time in the lifetime of black Memphians we were called Mr. or Mrs., doctor, lawyer, whatever. . . . Never in the history of Memphis had black folk . . . [been] treated to respectful treatment."[100] In some ways, the civil rights movement of the 1950s and 1960s would be an effort to produce legal and practical manifestations of the kind of respect that black audiences had sought from radio broadcasters.

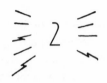

Goodwill Radio

Labor, Liberals, and the Search for Interracial Understanding

*In offering solutions to the present racial problems it is necessary
to analyze the situation and determine what undesirable factors
exist that make understanding impossible, and then create
better conditions by a process of elimination.*
Nora Allison Barber, Commission on Interracial Cooperation, c. 1936

Goodwill Hunting, North and South

During the three decades before the emergence of a mass civil rights movement in the South, the NAACP and the NUL were not the only organizations to use radio in an effort to improve race relations in the region and beyond. A diverse range of racially progressive groups—some southern-based, some national in scope and membership, some predominantly white, and some proudly biracial—also recognized the potential of the medium to promote racial justice in the South. Exactly what "racial justice" might mean in practical terms, however, remained a matter of intense and shifting debate among groups such as the Commission on Interracial Cooperation (CIC), the Southern Regional Council (SRC), the American Friends Service Committee (AFSC), and the various labor organizations that experimented with radio from the 1920s to the 1950s.

The radio experiences of these groups had much in common with those of the NAACP and the NUL. After some initial overoptimism about the extent and nature of radio's potential to influence its listeners, it became clear that the success of racially progressive radio programming would not be measured by the number of bigots miraculously converted to a life of tolerance and interracial brotherhood. Even among African Americans and those southern whites broadly sympathetic to their plight, there was little evidence that radio shows dramatizing the shame of Jim Crow ever induced apolitical or apathetic southerners to join the organized struggle against racial discrimination. Instead these broadcasts worked in more subtle ways. They formed part of a broader web of publicity, protest, and petition that helped to create a new climate of opinion in which the possibility—and occasionally even the desirability—of ending segregation and disenfranchisement became a more common feature of public and political discourse.

As with the NAACP and the NUL, there was an underlying assumption among many racially progressive organizations that white Americans should be the primary targets for any concerted radio strategy dedicated to the amelioration of black suffering in the South. This perspective undoubtedly smacked of white paternalism, especially among southern white racial progressives who clung to the notion that whites of good conscience—whites remarkably like themselves, in fact—should control the pace and substance of racial change in the region. Yet it also reflected the fact that African Americans, by and large, did not need to be educated about the iniquities of Jim Crow. Thus, while representatives of these progressive organizations did sometimes appear on black-oriented radio programs in the South, they were actually more interested in finding time on general-market stations, where they hoped to play upon the consciences, patriotism, and pocketbooks of primarily white audiences. The consensus was that since southern white prejudice, which was usually conceptualized as a by-product of the chronic economic underdevelopment that bedeviled the region, was the tumor responsible for the South's racial sickness, it was the factor in most urgent need of radio therapy.

Within this broad consensus, however, there were important differences of opinion about which sections of southern white society were most in need of racial enlightenment. There were even more intense debates about precisely what forms of social and racial reconstruction should be advocated on air. Moreover, some of these racially progressive groups spent relatively little time trying to influence the hearts and minds of white southerners at all. Before the mid-1950s, for example, the Congress of Industrial Organizations (CIO) and the AFSC—whose members were not primarily southern—used radio principally to educate northern whites about the southern racial situation. In part, this was a simple matter of practicalities. Although these organizations were eager to seize any opportunity to educate white southerners about the moral evils and economic disadvantages of segregation, such opportunities on southern radio remained tightly controlled, especially for those reviled as "outside agitators." In part, however, the focus on radio audiences beyond the South also reflected the recognition, shared by both the NAACP and the NUL, that northern public opinion and the federal government would have a key role to play in finally ending segregation. Radio broadcasts could help ensure that national opposition to Jim Crow became part of a broader public debate about the health of American democratic ideals.

By contrast with these nationally prominent, often northern-based groups, southern progressive organizations like the CIC and its successor the SRC tended to concentrate their radio efforts on reaching predominantly white audiences within their own region. In so doing, they often displayed and helped to perpetuate a fear of federal intervention and northern influence that hamstrung much progressive thought on racial matters in the South. Ironically, this inability to break out of a regional mentality and accept that federal assistance might be needed to produce anything resembling meaningful racial change in the region yoked southern racial progressives to their much more racially conservative and reactionary brethren. For at least a quarter of a century, the tone and content of radio appearances by southern racial liberals reflected their desperation to promote a southern solution to what they had at least come to recognize was a genuine social problem. At the heart of this home rule agenda—and the defining characteristic of radio broadcasts by southern white racial progressives—was the promotion of something usually characterized as either interracial understanding or interracial goodwill. Even when the definition of southern racial liberalism shifted in the late 1940s and early 1950s from a desire to ameliorate the worst effects of Jim Crow toward a rejection of segregation itself, many whites still searched forlornly for these elusive social panaceas. Almost every individual, organization, and radio station that used the airways to promote better race relations in the South repeated pleas for interracial understanding and goodwill like a mantra.

Radio, Labor, and Race Relations: Uniting Workers, Uniting Regions

Given the traditional hostility of southern planters and factory owners to organized labor, opportunities for union representatives on southern radio were always scarce. They were scarcer still whenever labor organizers threatened to broach the subject of interracial cooperation among black and white workers who were united in the fact, if not always the extent or manner, of their exploitation by southern landowners, industrialists, merchants, and bankers. In these circumstances, it made sense that organized labor's first explorations of the medium's potential for encouraging interracial cooperation among workers took place in the North. Indeed, some of the labor movement's most trenchant radio commentary on the South's racial affairs throughout the 1930s and 1940s originated and aired beyond Dixie, helping to stimulate and shape emerging national debates about race relations.

There was nothing preordained about the labor movement's attempt to use radio to advance interracial understanding and cooperation. Most of the older American Federation of Labor (AFL) craft unions of the early twentieth century enshrined the racial and ethnic prejudices of the day and jealously protected white interests in—and access to—certain trades and professions. Labor on the radio in the 1920s rarely escaped these same confines, even in the North. In Chicago, for example, the Chicago Federation of Labor's pioneering station WCFL initially offered a variety of programs geared toward specific groups of workers, defined by their jobs, their racial and ethnic identities, and their geographic location within Chicago. As such, the station tended to reinforce, rather than dismantle or bridge, the ethnic and racial distinctions that often separated workers.[1]

During the 1930s, however, the economic impact of the Depression and the triumph of the radio networks combined to reduce the significance of local ethnically oriented broadcasting. By mid-decade even WCFL had become a commercially driven affiliate of NBC and depended as much as any other station in Chicago on a mix of local and corporate advertising revenue. According to Lizabeth Cohen, the rise of standardized network programming in the 1930s helped to create a common mass culture among workers of diverse ethnic and racial backgrounds. This shared mass consumption, she contends, provided an important, if hardly the only, basis for an invigorated working-class consciousness. It promoted a sense of interracial and interethnic unity that was vital to the growth of industrial unionization and the success of the new CIO after 1935. In this era, labor became bolder in its efforts to use the airways to encourage working-class cohesion across racial and ethnic lines. Veteran communist labor organizer William Z. Foster, for example, argued that radio would be especially useful for this purpose in "an industry such as steel where the company maintains terrorism to prevent the workers from attending open meetings, [as] the radio takes the union message directly into the workers' homes."[2]

One of the most innovative of the early radio initiatives dedicated to the CIO's biracial ideals were the broadcasts of the Negro Labor Committee (NLC) on WEVD–New York, a station whose call letters honored socialist leader and union booster Eugene V. Debs. In the summer of 1935 the NLC had replaced the old Harlem Labor Committee as a coordinating agency for the activities of primarily, but not exclusively, black unionists in the city. From the start the NLC's founder and chairman, Frank R. Crosswaith, had been interested in using radio to reach New York's black and white workers. In December 1935 he appeared on WEVD alongside Walter White and A. Philip Randolph, with whom Crosswaith had previously founded the AFL-affiliated Brotherhood of Sleeping Car Porters. Crosswaith announced the opening of the NLC's Harlem Labor Center premises on 125th Street, and each of the speakers stressed the importance of unionism in the struggle for black economic opportunity and racial justice. Crosswaith, however, also went out of his way to emphasize the NLC's commitment to securing equal rights and representation for African Americans within the American labor movement. The NLC, he explained, would "look to the labor movement and to those liberal and enlightened elements among the American people who place justice and fair play above the narrow limits of color."[3]

By the early 1940s the NLC had grown into an important, if perpetually impecunious, fixture in the black labor movement in New York. The organization could claim at least partial credit for increasing union membership in Harlem from eight thousand in 1930 to more than seventy thousand a decade later. Eager to regularize the NLC's access to the airways, in December 1940 Crosswaith approached WEVD's program director George Field to ask if the station would carry a monthly NLC show as part of its free public-service scheduling. The first show aired on February 1, 1941.[4] Over the next eight months the NLC's broadcasts featured dramatic reenactments of workers' travails, stirring union anthems, local news reports, interviews, and round-table discussions. The centerpiece was an editorial, usually delivered by Crosswaith, whose mixture of Scottish and Caribbean (St. Croix) parentage lent his diction a mildly exotic lilt. Indeed, during his time with the Brotherhood of Sleeping Car Porters, Randolph had hailed Crosswaith as the "best orator not only in the union, but . . . in the country."[5]

For Crosswaith and the NLC, justice for African Americans ultimately depended on the success of a wider labor movement against exploitative capitalists who deliberately exacerbated racial friction among workers.[6] This commitment to interracial unionism and interracial cooperation more generally also provided the theme for many NLC radio shows. In February 1941, for example, listeners were told that the NLC emblem was "the hand of a Negro and white worker clasped in unity as symbolizes one of its aims, that is to organize and guide Negro workers into bona fide trade unions and to fight for the solidarity of Negro and white labor on a basis of absolute equality and justice."[7]

Although he briefly dabbled in Popular Front activities with Harlem communists in the late 1930s, Crosswaith, much like Randolph, was staunchly anticommunist. He used his time on WEVD to attack the evils of Stalinism and Hitlerism with equal gusto, always yoking his international concerns to a critique of domestic racial attitudes and practices. "The belief is still generally held, that the Negro is destined to remain the 'inferior' of all other members of the human race," Crosswaith told his listeners before quickly discrediting such views: "The last international maniac to voice this claim is Adolf Hitler."[8] The NLC kept the same global perspective when turning its attention to the peculiar circumstances of the American South. In the autumn of 1941, Crosswaith took aim at Georgia's governor Eugene Talmadge, who he claimed had stoked the fires of both racism and anti-Semitism in America by attacking the work of the Rosenwald Fund, an important sponsor of racially progressive groups and programs in the South.[9] NLC vice-chairman Thomas Young subsequently took up the attack on Talmadge. "Home-grown prejudices and perversities, that foster racial and religious discrimination, can be as powerful a force against national unity as any foreign brand," Young warned WEVD listeners. "Certainly there is little difference between the Nazi version of racial supremacy and the learned rantings on that subject by our Dixie Fuehrer governor, Eugene Talmadge of Georgia."[10]

The NLC's denunciations of Talmadge reflected a much broader interest in southern racial and union matters. Crosswaith was particularly supportive of the Southern Tenant Farmers Union (STFU), which he declared "one of the few rays of hope for the exploited and tyrannized Southern agricultural workers."[11] In 1936 Crosswaith had wired the governor of Illinois protesting the extradition of STFU organizer Sam Bennett to face criminal charges in Arkansas. In addition to making various ad hoc contributions to the union, the NLC also promoted the STFU's National Sharecroppers Week each spring.[12] In a March 1941 broadcast on the evils of southern sharecropping that coincided with this annual fundraising drive, Crosswaith once more lavished praise upon the STFU, a union that "has been able in its area to end the antagonism so often started up by the planters between white and colored sharecroppers and has united them in a joint struggle for better conditions."[13]

It was hardly surprising that the STFU was Crosswaith's pet southern union. At the core of his vision for racial progress was the kind of interracial working-class solidarity that the STFU had tried to forge amid the paranoia, prejudice, and racialized self-interest of the Jim Crow South. This sort of interracialism was exactly what the NLC consistently tried to encourage over the airwaves. Moreover, Crosswaith had stumbled across precisely the sort of ideological terrain where the agendas of radio broadcasters and civil rights advocates could most comfortably coexist. Despite perennial anxieties about airing any programs that touched on the sensitive issue of race relations—particularly programs produced by socialist-leaning labor organizers—station owners, managers, and sponsors were somewhat less alarmed by shows that put generalized messages of interracial tolerance and understanding to the fore.

In October 1941 the NLC's run of regular shows on WEVD came to an abrupt end when George Field told Crosswaith that his station could no longer provide free spots. The NLC had enjoyed nine months of free airtime, Field explained, and there were other equally worthy organizations demanding a turn on the station's crowded sustaining program schedule. Field hoped to be able to grant more free time in the future and pointed out that the NLC was always welcome to buy airtime at the station.[14] Unfortunately, this really was not an option. Since most of its affiliated unions were permanently delinquent about paying their dues, the NLC teetered forever on the brink of bankruptcy. It could never afford to pay for its own series and thereafter relied upon occasional guest spots on stations like WEVD, WLIB, and WWRL, the last of which continued to feature announcements from the ailing NLC into the mid-1950s.[15]

While the NLC fractured and foundered during the decade after the war, Crosswaith occasionally revisited the idea of a regular radio show. Like many others in the mid-1940s, he saw the emergence of FM radio as a means to rekindle the vision of those who had originally greeted radio in the 1920s as, in the words of southern liberal lawyer and FCC commissioner Clifford Durr, a major "contribution toward fulfilling Jefferson's dream of an informed democracy." Such aspirations were related to the hopes shared by Crosswaith and others, including such left-wing organizations as Eugene Konecky's Provisional Committee for Democracy in Radio, that public control of FM might enable the medium to break the shackles of commerce and become a more potent instrument of public education and enlightenment. It was in this spirit that Crosswaith supported the failed 1945 application by the NLC-affiliated International Ladies Garment Workers Union (ILGWU) for a license to operate four FM stations, including a southern outlet in Chattanooga.[16]

Labor organizers working in the South predictably struggled to get more than sincere, but ultimately vague and often platitudinous, calls for greater racial understanding onto southern stations during the 1940s and early 1950s. With a few notable exceptions, these broadcasts were usually devoid of any mention of a coherent or at least timely strategy for converting such "understanding" into a genuine challenge to segregation and disenfranchisement. In 1945, for example, CIO organizer Harry Daniels appeared on WMAL in Washington, D.C., urging an end to the local recreation board's policy of segregating the city's parks and entertainment venues. Even here, however, Daniels stepped quite gingerly. He made no attempt to link his opposition to Jim Crow in municipally operated leisure facilities to a broader demand for the end of segregation throughout the nation's capital. Instead he characterized the integration of the city's recreational facilities as a catalyst for the sort of racial tolerance and understanding that, at some undisclosed point in the future, would create an environment more conducive to the dismantling of Jim Crow. "One of the first things we learned was the value of recreation in breaking down segregation and racial prejudices," Daniels explained. "Recreation does away with racial antagonism, games of skill and athletic ability smooth the rough water of prejudice because a man or woman is recognized by what he or she can do."[17]

Rather bolder were the broadcasts made over WDIA during the Memphis United Furniture Workers Association (UFWA) strike of 1949. In January the predominantly black female membership of UFWA Local 282 walked out in protest at the firing of union organizer Emma Lou Johnson and the generally low pay and poor conditions at the Memphis Furniture Company. Initially the protest had the support of the local CIO, the NAACP, and the NUL, but a mixture of red-baiting, police harassment, and the refusal of white women stitchers at the plant to join their black colleagues undermined this early solidarity, as did the importation of replacement workers from Arkansas. As the protest threatened to collapse, strike leaders secured airtime on WDIA. They used the station's public service slots to call for financial, material, and moral support from the local black community and sympathetic unionists in the region. In one broadcast aimed at promoting interunion solidarity, Ed McCrea of the local Food, Tobacco and Agricultural and Allied Workers' Union of America described the poor conditions and meager wages at the Furniture Company as "a shame and disgrace to Memphis." Partly because of this unusually audacious use of radio to rally the Memphis community behind a specific political action, the strikers were able to stay out for eight months, long after effective CIO support had evaporated.[18]

The collapse of CIO support for the Memphis furniture workers strike—and with it the ultimate failure of the protest—was largely a result of the kind of bitter internal wrangling between left- and right-wing factions that constantly stymied effective organizing efforts at the height of Cold War anxieties and rampant anticommunism. In the South the region's peculiar racial situation often exacerbated fratricidal tensions within the CIO. For a variety of reasons ranging from a genuine moral and philosophical belief in racial equality to simple opportunism, left-wing elements among the CIO's southern organizers were the most likely to court black workers, encourage interracial unionism, and even on occasion mount early challenges to Jim Crow. Conservative elements within the CIO found this tendency troubling on three counts. First, there was serious ideological and principled resistance to Stalinist influences at work within the CIO. Second, the conspicuous presence of left-wing factions made the whole labor movement more vulnerable to anticommunist accusations. Third, any sign of untoward commitment to black civil and voting rights in the South enabled southern employers and their political allies to demonize the CIO as an instrument of integration, making it much more difficult to recruit rank-and-file white workers. Equally important was the fact that the racial views of many southern white union organizers were not especially progressive; they tended to be hostile to any policies that might jeopardize white privileges in the workplace.

These overlapping racial, ideological, and tactical concerns shaped the CIO's use of radio in the postwar South. Indeed, in one tragic incident in April 1949, they actually came to a violent public crescendo at WJLD, a pioneering black-oriented radio station in Bessemer, Alabama. For several years there had been a bitter struggle between the local affiliates of the International Union of Mine, Mill and Smelter Workers (IUMMSW) and the United Steel Workers of America (USWA) for the loyalties of iron and steel workers in Birmingham and nearby Bessemer. The CIO had opted to support the claims of the conservative, white-dominated USWA rather than those of the left-wing and avowedly biracial IUMMSW, thereby endorsing a campaign that enjoyed the full support of the local Ku Klux Klan. Indeed, the USWA had openly sought to lure white members away from the IUMMSW with explicitly racist appeals. One white IUMMSW member who refused to bolt explained that "they told us we ought to get out of Mine, Mill and make a real white man's union." In an attempt to end this feud a referendum was scheduled for April 21, 1949, at which time workers at the Tennessee Coal & Iron Company could choose which union they wanted to represent them.[19]

On the eve of the referendum, with the Klan and USWA unionists stepping up their intimidation of both black and liberal white workers, representatives of the rival unions agreed to debate the issues on air at WJLD. The primarily African American audience for this station was naturally very interested in the outcome of a labor dispute with such powerful racial overtones. Precisely what happened in the WJLD studios is a matter of some conjecture. After a fawning speech on behalf of the USWA-CIO position by dissident IUMMSW member George Elliott, the Mine, Mill's communist secretary-treasurer Maurice Travis apparently impugned Elliott's manhood and implied a toadying subservience to the Tennessee Coal & Iron Company by calling him a "Popsicle." Irrespective of whether this slur was the catalyst, an incensed Elliott slugged Travis. According to some witnesses, the assault was then taken up by thugs from the USWA who "proceeded to kick in his face and jump on him" while calling him "a 'N———r lover.'" Maurice Travis eventually lost an eye as a result of his beating. The CIO chose to ignore the racist dimensions of the USWA's recruitment activities in Alabama and elsewhere in the South. President Philip Murray implausibly accused Travis and the IUMMSW of fomenting racial tensions by fabricating links between the USWA and the Klan. In fact, flagrant appeals to white solidarity and racial supremacy had played a major part in securing a referendum victory for the USWA-CIO over the more racially progressive IUMMSW.[20]

In peculiarly dramatic and extreme form, the WJLD incident highlighted the difficulties faced by CIO organizers who went South after the war and sought to use radio as part of their Operation Dixie recruitment drive. Even racially progressive unionists often found themselves deferring to southern segregationist mores and beliefs while they encouraged black and white workers to recognize their shared economic interests and join the union movement. In October 1946, George Baldanzi, a Textile Workers Union organizer who was also assistant director—and later director—of the CIO's National Organizing Committee, initiated a series of weekly broadcasts on the powerful WBT station in Charlotte. Baldanzi eloquently stated the CIO's basic goals of "decent wages and job security . . . , improved health and safety conditions . . . [and] insurance to help the worker pay his doctor and hospital bills." He presented a vivid description of the poor wages and wretched working conditions in the region that made the unionization of southern workers imperative. Yet when it came to the racial implications of Operation Dixie, Baldanzi was more evasive. Without ever explicitly mentioning segregation, he euphemistically assured his listeners that the CIO was not "plotting to upset established social relations," as many of its opponents had charged. Indeed, while he defended the legal right of all workers to "band together . . . into organizations that will protect and advance their economic interests," Baldanzi insisted: "It is neither our intention nor desire to force a change in the long-established social relations of a large section of our people."[21]

Regardless of what the CIO hoped its biracial organizing drive might do to undermine racial prejudices and southern-style apartheid in the long term, in the short term those involved with Operation Dixie publicly accepted the existence of Jim Crow and carried on their work within a discriminatory racial framework that mocked the CIO's best principles. Caught between a racist rock and an organizational hard place, the CIO never really resolved its essential southern dilemma of how to involve black workers—potentially its most dynamic and enthusiastic constituency—on an equal basis without alienating rank-and-file white workers. As labor historian Robert Zieger has explained, the CIO "generally avoided overt and provocative statements on civil rights . . . , condemned communism and broadly endorsed civic equality in language that carefully avoided specific criticisms of southern racial attitudes and customs." By the late 1940s and early 1950s, Baldanzi's program was airing weekly across six states—including at least thirty-one stations in Tennessee, South Carolina, and Georgia. Yet, committed to this gradualist approach to improving racial matters, the best he and the CIO could muster on southern airways were earnest but vague appeals for all mankind to "work and dwell together in unity." Much the same sentiments dominated John Vandercook's nationally syndicated weekly CIO shows, heard on some 155 stations in forty-one states and the District of Columbia during the early 1950s, when new CIO president Walter Reuther began to encourage greater use of the airways.[22]

The CIO's reluctance to attack Jim Crow head-on in the South meant that it sometimes found itself estranged from some of the most racially progressive forces in the region. At times this included the influential Highlander Folk School, based at Monteagle in Tennessee. Highlander was one of the staunchest supporters of labor organizing in the region. Founded by Myles Horton in 1932 and committed from its inception to an integrationist ideal, the School had nonetheless initially declined to invite African American workers to its summer workshops for fear of inciting hostility among local whites. In 1934, however, black Knoxville College professor J. H. Davies had joined discussions at the School about the need for interracial cooperation in the labor movement. Although this inaugural biracial session was conducted under the threat of a dynamite attack from local white supremacists, thereafter Highlander's racial practices slowly moved into alignment with its racial ideals. The first fully integrated summer residential program took place in 1942 on behalf of the United Automobile Workers, and four years later the School's faculty and facilities became completely integrated.[23]

Highlander served as an important training ground for black and white labor organizers and civil rights activists. After the war, it spread the principles of grassroots democracy among workers of all colors and creeds despite constant red-baiting and harassment from southern authorities. Horton and his wife, Highlander's music director Zilphia Horton, were seldom equivocal on the subject of segregation: they were adamant that Jim Crow was an abomination, regularly spoke out boldly against it, and worked ceaselessly to destroy it. Yet when they appeared on radio in the late 1940s, even the Hortons felt obliged to temper their racial radicalism, concealing something of the passion and militancy of their opposition to Jim Crow beneath a reassuringly familiar rhetoric of democratic idealism, interracial cooperation, and universal goodwill.

In early 1947 Myles Horton was invited to appear on a special edition of CBS's *Cross Section, USA* show devoted to a discussion of George Washington's legacy in America. Required to submit a copy of his remarks to CBS in advance of the broadcast, Horton used much of his brief airtime to publicize a southern campaign called Ballots for All Americans. Cleverly couching his plea for the extension of voting rights to all American citizens in the language of the democratic ideals promulgated by the nation's Founding Fathers, Horton insisted: "The whole idea of democracy rests on the people's vote. There can't be too much democracy, and there can't be too many people voting." Without actually mentioning the racial coordinates of southern disenfranchisement, he argued that "the most important single thing we as Americans can do in 1947, to carry on the ideals of George Washington, is to fight for a free and unrestricted ballot." Horton pointedly told a national radio audience that there were nationwide implications to the campaign for electoral rights in the South. "Unless voting is encouraged, I don't think a prosperous, healthy and educated South is possible. And the country as a whole cannot prosper unless the people of the South prosper."[24]

Still carefully sidestepping direct references to segregation, Horton also used his appearance on *Cross Section, USA* to suggest what could be achieved by fostering constructive dialogue among all southerners of goodwill. Recounting the outcome of a recent meeting of southern farmers' union leaders at Highlander, he quoted one Tennessee delegate as saying, "We came together as strangers but because we are working to make life better for all people, we will leave as friends." During the course of the weeklong conference, Horton recalled, "[t]he traditional attitude toward organized labor, toward minorities, underwent a marked change."[25]

Zilphia Horton also emphasized the importance of education and dialogue in solving the South's entwined economic and racial problems when she undertook a series of radio talks as part of a nationwide fund-raising tour. Appearing on WQQW in Washington, D.C., Zilphia restated that Highlander's "work in the South is of vital concern to people all over the country. So long as the South is a fertile field for such organizations as the Columbians and the Ku Klux Klan, the rest of the nation can't rest easy." Encouraged to discuss the School's approach to combating racial prejudice, Horton reiterated the value of greater contact, education, and reasoned discussion among southerners in order to change the racial attitudes that retarded the region's moral and economic development. When southern unionists—"Democrats and Republicans, white and Negro"—came to Highlander, she explained, they arrived "with the prejudices common to such a group. But as they discussed the problems that were close to each of them, something happened. They found that what they had in common was bigger than what separated them."[26]

At this point in what was obviously a carefully scripted exchange, the WQQW moderator intervened to draw out the full implications of what Horton had rather casually described. "Do you mean to say that you have Negroes and white people studying together in a school in the Deep South?" he asked. "Haven't you had trouble with such organizations as the Klan?" Significantly, Horton used the opportunity not to excoriate the prejudices represented by the Klan but to conjure up an alternative vision of decent white southerners groping for a way to act upon their best instincts and escape the shadow of Jim Crow and racial antagonism. "Of course, we've been threatened," she conceded. But, she proudly noted, "when a vigilante group threatened to raid the school . . . the people of our little mountain community—yes, real Southerners though they are—came up with their shotguns and the raid never came off." In retrospect, given the years of persecution that lay ahead of Highlander, the conclusion Zilphia Horton drew from this episode appears hopelessly optimistic. "Now we know," she said, "that our own neighbors agree with our program and will protect us again if it ever should become necessary." Nonetheless, this sentiment was indicative of a moment when many southern white racial progressives still believed in a Silent South of like-minded whites and were desperate to highlight and encourage whatever pockets of racial liberalism they could find in the region.[27] Ultimately, however, the demands of the medium coupled with the ever-present fear of retaliation from local whites meant that the Hortons rarely felt free to articulate the full extent of their opposition to Jim Crow on air until the later 1950s and 1960s when Highlander developed a close relationship with the independent Pacifica radio network.

Hard-Core Moderates: Southern Racial Liberals on the Air

Highlander Folk School occupied a place toward the radical fringe of progressive white racial thought in the South before the 1950s. Until then relatively few of the other white southerners who thought of themselves variously as racial liberals or moderates or progressives supported the end of segregation at all, even if some had serious misgivings about its operation. Such views dominated the efforts of the Commission on Interracial Cooperation to use radio. Formed in response to the race riots that exploded in the South at the end of World War I, the CIC was arguably the foremost expression of organized racial progressivism in the South between the two world wars. By the end of its first decade of operation, however, the Commission had done little more than dabble in the new medium of radio. "We have not been insensible to the possibilities offered by the radio in the effort to promote better interracial attitudes," explained publicity director Robert Eleazer in 1929. The CIC had simply "been awaiting a favorable opportunity to look into the matter."[28]

Later that year just such an opportunity appeared to beckon, as the Commission considered sponsoring a series of broadcasts by the Utica Jubilee Singers. During the 1920s this choral group, which hailed from the Utica Normal and Industrial Institute in Mississippi, had secured a regular berth on NBC's WJZ and WEAF New York outlets, with hookups to stations as far apart as KWK in St. Louis, WJR in Detroit, WBAL in Baltimore, and WREN in Kansas. In December 1929 the group's manager, C. W. Hyne, wrote to CIC president Will Alexander suggesting that the group might be a useful vehicle for the Commission's message of interracial reconciliation and cooperation. Hyne enclosed a compendium of press clippings from around the nation and Europe that lauded the Jubilee Singers' prowess. It was less the quality of their vocal harmonies, however, than their potential to promote southern racial harmony that caught the Commission's attention. Indeed, Hyne was careful to emphasize the positive influence the singers had exerted upon radio audiences of both races. "Very frequently listeners to the broadcast programs . . . have written in stating their conviction of the vast amount of good their work has been in creating better feeling between the races," Hyne told Alexander. "Whites write that it gives them a higher appreciation of Negroes and Negroes write that it has given them great pride in their race."[29]

In the end, the Commission never actually took up the option to sponsor shows by the singers—the group left for a world tour early in 1930 while the CIC was still debating whether it could afford the fees. Nevertheless, the episode appears to have stimulated greater interest in radio, and during the 1930s the CIC began to promote its resolutely gradualist agenda through a series of radio talks. Typically these brief slots aimed, as the CIC's Nora Allison Barber put it in one such broadcast, to find "ways to promote better understanding between the races." Barber assured her listeners that racial "misunderstandings are not real but merely superficial based upon each nationality's own personal ego. Love for one's own group often leads to enmity towards other groups. . . . We harbor prejudices just because we don't know any better and because we hold to worn-out conventions set up before and during the Civil War." Broadcasting at the end of a Christian Brotherhood Week, Barber asked: "How can we have a complete brotherhood if we continue to misunderstand and hate those whom Christ said were our brothers?" The key to change, according to Barber, was education. This was "the medium through which we will tear down prejudices, false conventions, and misunderstanding, and set up in their stead complete understanding, brotherhood, and goodwill."[30]

In the CIC's world it was assumed that this improved, progressive education would still be segregated. Barber enthusiastically read out a statement from a conference of Tennessee public school administrators: "There should be taught in both white and colored schools those things that will build up in both races such knowledge and mutual understanding as will promote good will, fair play, and a spirit of cooperation that will enable us all to work together for a safer, saner, and more fruitful civilization." The irony was that by using radio to make this and other appeals to racial understanding, the CIC was using a medium that could actually defy the strict spatial segregation of southern public education. Radio could spread messages of racial enlightenment and Christian fellowship simultaneously to audiences of both races. That irony was compounded by the fact that the Commission itself was still a long way from condoning, let alone initiating, any systematic challenge to the operation of Jim Crow. In this case the medium was intrinsically more radical than the messages it carried.[31]

Other CIC broadcasts in the 1930s covered similar ground. Many sought to dispel white stereotypes of black indolence and ignorance. Barber, for example, gave another talk on the achievements of notable black leaders, while Marjorie Stanford delivered a "Contributions of the Negro" address that predated the sort of encomium to black accomplishments that became commonplace during World War II. Anxious to overturn images of African Americans as either "a semi-savage slave, or as an illiterate, dangerous freeman," Stanford described important black contributions to science, industry, commerce, and the arts in America. Moreover, she carefully noted, "The Negro has an unblemished record of faithful, intelligent, and courageous service in the Revolutionary and Civil Wars, the War of 1812, the Spanish-American War, and the World War."[32]

Very occasionally, the CIC used its slots on southern radio to edge toward more forthright condemnations of white prejudices and the social, political, and legal mechanisms that constrained African Americans. "Thoughtful consideration reveals that the greater number of problems which confront the American negro today are the direct results of jealousy, superstition, and absolute ignorance on the part of white people," white CIC member George Connor told his listeners. Affirming the shadowy existence of a corpus of southern whites who objected to the workings of Jim Crow, Connor claimed that most of the region's racial problems were the responsibility of a handful of loud, influential, and psychotic southern bigots. "It is obvious that the eagerly desired progress of the colored race is being hindered by a minority of narrow-minded white people," he declared.[33]

For Connor the abomination of lynching—"one of the most merciless, uncivilized institutions ever directed at any race"—illustrated just how far below civilized values those in the extremist vanguard of southern white supremacist politics had fallen. Jessie Daniel Ames, a fellow CIC activist, founder of the Association of Southern Women for the Prevention of Lynching (ASWPL), and subsequently a founding mother of the SRC, felt much the same. Although the ASWPL made limited headway on southern radio, it did find some national exposure in the mid-1930s through a couple of important news services. Mrs. Alma Chestnut included press releases from the ASWPL on the syndicated "News for Women" programs that she prepared for the Transradio Press Service. Leland Bickford of the Yankee Network wrote to Ames to commend the ASWPL's "valiant effort to eradicate this type of lawlessness." In May 1936 Bickford also editorialized in support of the latest in a long line of doomed federal antilynching bills before Congress. Taking aim at the South, but implicating the whole nation in its bloody shame, Bickford told listeners: "Nothing can be more contemptible in the eyes of the law-abiding citizen than the all-too-frequent lynchings which are permitted to be carried out in various parts of the country."[34]

It was daring enough that George Connor should go on air to urge southern whites to reject racial demagoguery and lynch law. It was another thing altogether that he should also call for them to support the reenfranchisement of southern blacks. "Unless he can exercise the privileges of a democracy," Connor warned, "the negro cannot be a good citizen." Echoing the NAACP's legal assault on disenfranchisement, Connor noted that, contrary to the provisions of the Fifteenth Amendment, discriminatory electoral procedures in the South meant that "the most intelligent negro in the community may be denied this fundamental American right simply because the election officer does not choose to let him vote." He concluded his broadcast with a rousing call for southern whites to accept their responsibility for making democracy a reality in their region. "If we are to maintain an ideal democracy," he exhorted, "we, the white people, must unite our efforts to stamp out the prejudice and ignorance which has caused the colored race to be subordinated to those who are no better or wiser than they."[35]

Connor's basic humility and his recognition of white culpability for racial oppression were about as good as it got among southern white racial progressives on air in the 1930s. But even Connor failed to escape entirely the lingering sense of African American inferiority, or at least of arrested social, political, and cultural development, that characterized much white racial progressive thought. Certainly he did not believe that all African Americans were ready for the rights and responsibilities of full citizenship. His proposals to end lynching and remove voting restrictions were designed to "give deserving negroes a substantial start toward cultural development and useful citizenship." Connor believed that southern whites needed to act in accordance with the dictates of their upright, patriotic, and God-fearing hearts so that they could help to put the "right" sort of southern blacks on a path toward cultural maturity and responsible civic behavior. There was nothing in this agenda resembling a timetable for ending Jim Crow. In fact, there was rarely any mention of desegregation at all, let alone the still more dreaded specter of social equality.

In a climate where direct attacks on Jim Crow were so rare, some southern white racial progressives chose to focus on remedying social injustices where race was only one among many salient factors. The poll tax, for example, excluded many poor whites as well as many poor blacks from the political process in the South. In theory, therefore, it could be attacked with some impunity in a bid to increase democratic practices in the region, not merely as a means to increase black power. The campaign to abolish the poll tax became closely associated with the Southern Conference for Human Welfare (SCHW), which was formed in 1938 by a wide spectrum of southern liberals and radicals. In part, the SCHW reflected growing dissatisfaction with the CIC's excessive caution and inability to rally—or even find—the fabled Silent South in support of economically, politically, and socially enlightened policies in the region, including those relating to race.

The story of the SCHW's first meeting in Birmingham in September 1938 is often repeated in histories of the region's fragile racial liberalism. Since the meeting was held in the city's municipal auditorium, Public Safety Commissioner Eugene "Bull" Connor insisted on separating the black and white delegates. A visiting Eleanor Roosevelt defiantly sat between the black and white sections, physically bridging the gap between the races. After this incident, the SCHW issued a statement to the effect that it would never again meet in a segregated forum. Segregationists seized on this announcement as proof that the Conference was pro-integration. Although, for most white SCHW members, this was simply untrue, the integrationist tag stuck. Combined with the presence of many communists and fellow travelers, the stigma of being labeled an integrationist organization helped to make the SCHW an easy target for race-baiters and red-baiters alike throughout a troubled decade of campaigning against the poll tax and for various other progressive social and economic causes.[36]

The double blow of being seen as both too red and too ready to integrate meant that the SCHW and its more durable offspring, the Southern Conference Education Fund (SCEF), often struggled to find exposure on southern radio. Nevertheless, there were some efforts to use network and even southern radio stations, prompting historian Linda Reed to describe a series of SCHW and SCEF radio talk shows as "one of the most widely used methods of publicity of the time."[37] Certainly there was radio coverage of both the birth pains and the death rattle of the SCHW. At the time of the inaugural 1938 meeting, before the SCHW's "true" colors became clear, "radio stations generously gave time to speakers in all large southern cities," according to Conference chair Judge Louise O. Charlton. A decade later WNOE–New Orleans covered the SCHW's final meeting as anticommunist slurs, segregationist harassment, and near insolvency combined to bring it down.[38] In the intervening years, however, the SCHW did have its fleeting moments of radio glory. For example, the Conference used radio as part of its patriotic Win the War campaign, hoping to deflect some of the anticommunist barbs hurled in its direction with a zealous affirmation of its patriotic commitment to American democratic values. Similarly, in 1947 some 175 stations across the country participated in an Americanism Radio Contest devised by the Washington branch of the SCHW to promote awareness of democratic principles and practices.[39]

Ironically, the SCHW's greatest radio coup was a direct consequence of some particularly vicious and intemperate race-baiting and red-smearing by Mississippi senator Theodore Bilbo. A paragon of segregationist sentiment, in July 1946 Bilbo had easily won his fourth Democratic Party primary and with it the certainty of being returned to his seat in Washington. This, however, was his first campaign since the Supreme Court's *Smith v. Allwright* decision of 1944 had outlawed a traditional bulwark of white supremacy, the all-white primary election. Bilbo was undaunted by such legal inconveniences. He practiced his usual blend of fraud and intimidation to ensure that barely half of the paltry five thousand black voters registered in Mississippi—a state that had a potential black voting population of some 350,000—were able to cast ballots. In the aftermath of the election, a raft of civil rights groups and other concerned individuals protested these flagrant electoral abuses. In September 1946 their protests culminated in a formal complaint to the U.S. Senate and a series of local and national hearings on Bilbo's conduct. These investigations became moot in January 1947 when an ailing Bilbo agreed to vacate his Senate seat temporarily and then died from throat cancer later that year. In the period between the controversial July 1946 election and the commencement of the official investigation into his conduct, however, Bilbo appeared on the Mutual Broadcasting System's *Meet the*

Press program. He used the opportunity to vilify one of the chief sources of criticism, the SCHW, as a bastion of communism dedicated to the mongrelization of the South. Cognizant of the FCC's rulings about granting equal airtime to both sides in controversial issues, Mutual offered the SCHW the right of rebuttal in two programs aired on August 22 and August 29. These were probably the most important broadcasts of the SCHW's life, helping to foment national revulsion against the kind of unalloyed southern-style racism personified by Bilbo.[40]

The first "Answer to Bilbo" program, chaired by columnist Lowell Mellett, was carried on 212 stations in the Mutual network, including southern outlets like WOL-Washington. Mellett's integrated panel included the SCHW's white president Dr. Clark Foreman and Dr. Joseph Johnson, black president of the Washington SCHW branch and dean of the medical school at Howard University. The show offered a marvelous window on the SCHW's beliefs and agenda. Forman began by briefly outlining the mission of the Conference. "At Birmingham," he explained, "we decided that only by uniting *all* the people of the South, regardless of race, creed, or color, could the southern states regain their place of cultural, economic, and political equality with the rest of the country." In answering Bilbo's charges that the SCHW was "head of the Communist Party of the South," Forman courteously begged his sympathetic host's leave to mimic the Mississippian's own "loose" language before boldly declaring that "the senator lied! If the senator had any evidence to substantiate his claim, he would have turned us over to the various committees of Congress which are spending so much time and money investigating those things." Referring to the electoral success of two other segregationist leaders, John Rankin of Mississippi and Harry Byrd of Virginia, Forman announced, "We are probably the greatest threat to Bilboism in the South. The Southern Conference is working to rid the South of the conditions that make it possible for Bilbos, Byrds, and Rankins to be elected."[41]

Joseph Johnson echoed the tone of Forman's remarks. He defined the SCHW's goal as "building vigorously for a more democratic and prosperous South" and justified the emphasis on outlawing the poll tax because it was "one of the ways in which democratic representation is denied citizens of the South" by Bilbo and his like. It was also left to Johnson to answer Mellett's invitation to "tell how the Negro fits into the program of the Southern Conference." Refuting Bilbo's "rantings" about innate black inferiority, Johnson pointedly charged that "men like Senator Bilbo and Adolf Hitler do not recognize science" and that consequently "the Negro in the South is denied equal opportunity in practically every field." Particularly distressing, illegal, and un-American, Johnson continued, was the denial of black voting rights in the region. In his radio address Bilbo had boasted that the Mississippi legislature was still working on ways to circumvent the *Smith v. Allwright* decision. If such legal maneuvers should fail to keep blacks from the polls, however, Bilbo was willing to resort to what he termed "persuasion." He added ominously that "if you don't know what this means, you are just not up on your persuasive measures."[42]

Revealingly, Johnson and Forman were both careful to parade the SCHW's impeccable southern credentials on air. "People speak constantly of the 'Negro problem,' and the 'race problem,'" Johnson noted. "There is no 'Negro problem' as such. It is all part of the same problem—the Southern problem." He also stressed that solving the South's problems required interracial cooperation. "It is only by working together with other forward-looking Southerners that Southern Negroes can help themselves. The so-called 'Negro problem' is also a 'white problem,' and all men of good will should attack it together." Forman returned to this theme when pointing out that although "the South *is* the nation's problem and we of the Southern Conference aren't isolationists . . . [a]s the name implies, we are an organization of Southerners. . . . only Southerners may be voting members."[43]

The second "Answer to Bilbo" show aired on Mutual a week later. It followed much the same pattern as the first but was notable in having an entirely black lineup. Joseph Johnson was back, this time as moderator. NAACP lawyer Charles Houston, Max Yergin, executive director of the National Negro Congress, and Thomas Richardson, a union leader who at the time was vice president of the United Public Workers of America, joined him. If anything, the assault on Bilbo's fitness to serve the people of America or Mississippi was even more intense this time round. Yergin again raised the specter of Nazi Germany, hoping to sway public opinion by arguing that "the Negro serves the same function for Senator Bilbo and the reactionary forces which are using him that the Jews in Germany served for Hitler." Houston called upon "[a]ll groups of Americans [to] take a lesson from history and join in the fight against Bilboism while it is still concentrated on the Negro, and not wait until the senator levels an attack directly at them." Richardson noted that "for its own survival organized labor is committed irrevocably to the fight against Bilboism, and all other forms of native fascism." Houston, who was a major architect of the NAACP's legal assault on the constitutionality of segregation and disenfranchisement, added that the SCHW was "a good illustration of a group made up of predominantly white Southerners who are fighting Senator Bilbo and all he stands for right in his own state of Mississippi." This kind of white help, Houston insisted, was indispensable if the South was ever to escape the curse of Jim Crow and economic backwardness. "The most significant development is the ever-growing number of white Southerners who are fighting Bilboism because they realize the South can never achieve its possibilities and rise except on the basis of prosperity, happiness, and full citizenship rights for all its people, black as well as white."[44]

Charles Houston overestimated the numerical strength, political influence, and moral commitment of southern white racial liberals and certainly misjudged the practical capacity of the SCHW to withstand the buffeting of Bil-boesque assaults in the mid-to-late 1940s. Nevertheless, his comments on radio in 1946 did reflect a moment of cautious optimism about the prospects for more support for black rights and aspirations from sections of the white South. During World War II and the period immediately afterwards, many southern racial progressives had shifted slowly, unevenly, but inexorably toward a more thoroughgoing critique of Jim Crow. The main catalyst here was the quickening pace of African American protest against segregation and disenfranchisement during the war years. In 1942 some of the South's foremost black leaders had issued the Durham Manifesto, announcing their opposition to "the principle and practice of compulsory segregation in American society." Although it stopped short of a call for immediate desegregation, the Manifesto articulated rising black impatience with second-class citizenship by demanding the equalization of educational facilities in the South, a federal antilynching law, and the abolition of the white primary and the poll tax. The CIC was unable to respond to this new black insurgency, and in 1944 southern black leaders and white racial progressives incorporated a new organization: the Southern Regional Council.[45]

Despite its biracial origins and continuing black membership, the SRC quickly developed into the region's leading vehicle for white racial progressives. Committed to "research and action," the Council acted mainly as a sort of clearinghouse for economic and sociological information on the operation and generally disastrous effects of Jim Crow in the region. Like its predecessor, the SRC initially eschewed any direct challenge to segregation itself. In the late 1940s and early 1950s, however, the Council began to express its opposition to segregation, effectively establishing a new litmus test for southern racial liberalism. In late 1949 an editorial in the SRC's *New South* journal endorsed the view that legally enforced segregation "in and of itself constitutes inequality" and dismissed the idea of "separate but equal" facilities and rights as "a negation of the full and complete possession of privileges and immunities of citizenship." Two years later the SRC formally confirmed its new integrationist position by condemning segregation as "a cruel and needless penalty on the human spirit."[46] A bona fide southern white racial liberal was now required to accept the inevitable end of racial apartheid in the region. A few brave souls even began to work to hasten that demise, while others sought to prepare the region to undergo this monumental transformation in a peaceful manner. Other erstwhile progressives, however, simply found this new agenda too radical and promptly left the SRC, unable to abandon their basic commitment to a segregated South.

Even among those white progressives who did publicly oppose Jim Crow, there was still much disagreement about precisely how segregation should be ended and exactly when this might happen. Few outside a radical cabal advocated immediate desegregation and fewer still were willing to risk the bloody consequences they felt sure would follow if desegregation were mandated and enforced by the federal government. Equally vexing was the question of the extent to which southern blacks should be involved in planning the region's racial future. Most white racial progressives still assumed that they would determine the timing and extent of any changes in the region's racial arrangements. Nevertheless, they did continue to seek dialogue and cooperation with moderate, responsible southern black leaders who shared their foreboding about the perils of precipitate change. Stressing the need for careful education and patience on both sides of the racial divide, moderate black and white civil rights advocates agreed that radio could provide an important instrument with which to prepare the South for its future.

In the decade or so after World War II, southern white racial progressives used radio to stage a carefully controlled dialogue about possible scenarios for racial change in the region and, rather more often, to continue the assault on some of the worst stereotypes about African Americans that underwrote white hostility to desegregation. In one striking example of this sort of preparatory work, Anna Kelly of the Charleston YWCA obtained free time on WCSC in the summer of 1953. Anticipating the *Brown* school desegregation decision, she used her shows to "prepare a favorable climate in our community for the Supreme Court decision."[47] Of course, the rise of "massive resistance" to the civil rights movement in the mid-1950s serves as ample reminder that these sorts of efforts failed to produce a universal change of southern white hearts or habits. There was little eagerness to implement the Supreme Court's desegregation rulings in southern schools or any other aspects of southern life. Even so, the voices of southern white racial progressivism, timorous and dissembling though they often were, formed an important part of the intellectual and political milieu of the period. They helped to define the ideological and moral zeitgeist within which the modern civil rights movement emerged, shaping both the evolution of black protest and the complex pattern of white southern responses to those protests—responses that ranged from brutal defiance through grudging acquiescence to active support.

In 1945 Nina Howell Starr of Winter Park, Florida, wrote to SRC executive director Guy Johnson, urging him to "consider radio, rather than pamphlets for the popularizing of the Council's material." Although she acknowledged the expense involved, Starr was adamant about the potential benefits. "It would be more ambitious, far more effective, be a greater public service," she insisted. "Time is on the side of the forces and the inertia we wish to counteract. To depend on pamphlets is a bit horse and buggy-ish in the face of the urgency of issues and stakes." Starr's plans were certainly ambitious. "I have in mind an independent broadcasting station with a full time program, and local stations too, as necessary," Starr explained. "The plan would aim at unity of purpose . . .

through a variety of forms: lectures, news (especially news not handled by most papers and broadcasts), drama, readings, concerts, religious services, discussions, debates, etc." Financing, she suggested, might be found from "one or several of the rich foundations dedicated to educational service," ideally supplemented and perhaps ultimately supplanted by support from local southern communities. Starr added that her ideas were influenced by the plans of Frank Crosswaith and the ILGWU to set up a string of FM stations.[48]

Starr had no doubt that radio was the most effective means to communicate with ordinary black and white southerners. In language suffused with the message of racial improvement and uplift, she recounted her recent experiences visiting a number of black homes in Winter Park. "Everywhere I went the members of the household all seemed to be resting, and most were listening to radio, to soap operas. Few of this group would read pamphlets," she pointed out, "yet, I believe you could win them from soap operas, to the gain of themselves, the community, and the South." White southerners, especially women working at home, could also be targeted much more effectively by a radio propaganda campaign. Since there were "thousands of intelligent women occupied daily in repetitive household tasks which required only a small part of their mental capacities, it seemed inexcusable that radio programs worthy of the balance of their attention were not available to them." Starr's observation "To read a pamphlet one must take 'time out,' while listening to the radio may enhance rather than interrupt much of the day's schedule of many thousands of persons" captured one of radio's major advantages over more visually demanding media.[49]

Guy Johnson needed little persuasion on this matter. A few days after receiving Starr's letter, Johnson wrote to Dr. Justin Miller, president of the National Association of Broadcasters (NAB), congratulating him on the twenty-fifth anniversary of the radio broadcasting industry. Johnson wrote that "radio has already become the greatest single force for enlightening American public opinion and molding the American spirit." Moreover, he clearly grasped the medium's potential for promoting the SRC's program. The Council, he added, "as an organization devoted to the promotion of tolerance and understanding between races in the South, is particularly aware of the tremendous good which radio has done and can do in behalf of interracial good will and understanding."[50]

It was one thing to appreciate, as Nina Howell Starr and Guy Johnson did, the potential of radio to assist the SRC; it was quite another to find the Council steady exposure on southern radio. Fed up with scrambling for occasional slots on all too few friendly stations, in 1947 the Atlanta-based SRC approached nearby WSB with a proposal for a regular SRC-sponsored program to be called *New South Radio Forum*. The suggestion was for a monthly thirty-minute show. Each broadcast would feature a moderator and two guest speakers and culminate in a plenary discussion involving members of the audience. The SRC suggested that once a month WSB might substitute this program for NBC's *University of Chicago Round Table*, although the format for *New South Radio Forum* was actually modeled more closely on NBC's other leading discussion show, *America's Town Meeting of the Air*. The SRC believed that "such a program has great possibilities for raising the level of social and political intelligence in the South."[51]

It was indicative of the Council's early caution that its "Tentative Memorandum" to WSB suggested only one possible discussion topic with any specifically racial dimension: "Is the White Primary Good or Bad?" In the wake of the 1944 *Smith v. Allwright* decision outlawing this instrument of white supremacy, the question should have been moot. Yet it was still too controversial for WSB. As delicate negotiations with the station proceeded, the suggestion was quietly dropped. In May 1947 the SRC offered a new selection of possible program topics: "Does the South Need Federal Aid to Education?" "Will Stronger Labor Unions Help the South?" "Will King Cotton Be Dethroned?" and "Freight Rate Equalization." While a frank discussion of any of these themes might conceivably have involved ruminations on the impact of Jim Crow, none announced itself as a conspicuously "race" program. And none of the proposed guests for these SRC shows was black.[52]

This was a quite deliberate strategy. The SRC felt that both WSB and its principally white audience would initially be deeply hostile to any show that foregrounded racial matters. An internal SRC memorandum stated, "It is extremely important [that] the 'Southern Roundtable' gain the confidence of WSB, the listening audience, and the press. . . . Extremely controversial topics dealing with race will probably be reserved until the series is well under way and has gained support of a wide listening audience."[53] Despite such reassurances, WSB deferred making a decision on the show until the fall of 1947, when it finally decided that such a program was simply too hot to handle. Although frustrated in its efforts to get a regular berth on WSB, the SRC was more successful in its bid to cosponsor an edition of NBC's *Town Meeting* from the Mosque Auditorium in Richmond, Virginia. Broadcast on November 8, 1949, the show included both the CIO's Southern Organizing Drive director Van Bittner and black Houston editor Carter Wesley and was devoted to the question "How Can the South Get Fair Employment?"[54]

Its southern orientation notwithstanding, the lack of regular opportunities for the SRC on local stations, coupled with a desire to put the case of southern racial moderates to the nation as a whole, meant that the Council was happy to publicize its work through network shows like *Town Meeting*. On other occasions it collaborated with sympathetic individuals who already had a slot on the radio. One such useful conduit for SRC views, and for those of other racially progressive groups within the broader southern conference movement, was Dr. Homer

Price Rainey, former president of the University of Texas. In October 1945 Rainey gave six "Problems of the South" talks as part of a radio series called *Religion in Life*. Half a dozen Texas stations, including KTRH-Houston and KTBC-Austin, carried these shows. Rainey's talks covered topics like regional health care, when he noted that "the lack of doctors is especially acute in the Negro field," and voting rights in the South, when he applauded the outlawing of the white primary as an important step toward the democratization of the region's politics.[55]

Rainey was especially indebted to the SRC, however, in the two talks he devoted specifically to race problems in the South, and for the final show in the series, in which he articulated his "program for the South." The first show on race relations emphasized the economic damage inflicted by Jim Crow. Maintaining dual systems of public amenities was expensive and wasteful, he argued, depressing the earning and spending power of both races, much to the detriment of the region's economic growth. This was an argument the SRC repeatedly presented to southern business and political leaders, and Rainey acknowledged that much of his data came straight from the SRC's publication "A Factual Survey of America's Major Race Problem." Rainey turned to the SRC for ideas as well as facts. His intellectual debt was apparent when he read out substantial portions of a statement by sociologist Howard Odum, then president of the SRC. Rainey repeated Odum's call for the South to address its "vast injustices" while pleading with an increasingly concerned nation—by which he really meant federal government—to give it time to do so. This was a classic statement of the SRC's position before the 1950s and of many southern white racial progressives for a good deal longer. It recognized the existence of racial discrimination and undemocratic practices in the South and charged white southerners with the responsibility of rectifying that record. At the same time, it begged for national understanding of the peculiar historical and cultural baggage that precluded all but the most gradual adjustments in racial arrangements and made concerted federal action to secure racial justice unacceptable.

Rainey's second program on race relations also covered familiar SRC ground. He dismissed fears that if African Americans were enfranchised there would be a return to the mythical bad old days of a Black Reconstruction after the Civil War. He scoffed at white notions of excessive black criminality and lack of intelligence. He even confronted white fears that agitation for civil rights was but a prelude to widespread fraternization and intermarriage between the races. Rainey assured listeners that "Negro leaders themselves strongly deny that they have any desires for invading the social life or the institutional life of white people. All they want is justice and not social intermingling." Rainey concluded his final broadcast by endorsing former SCHW president Frank Porter Graham's "program for the South." In this credo, Graham and Rainey called for a wide range of progressive economic, political, and social reforms, including abolition of the poll tax, "equal suffrage rights of all citizens," minimum wage laws, the creation of major southern research universities, and improved educational and health care provisions in the region.

Toward a New Era

In 1945 Homer Rainey's broadcasts were about as bold on racial matters as one could hear from a white southerner. A decade later, however, the center of ideological gravity among southern white racial liberals had shifted toward a more clear-cut rejection of Jim Crow, even if debates over timing and methods continued. Those debates intensified as the South's self-declared racial moderates faced up to the Supreme Court's school desegregation decisions and the birth of black direct-action protests in the region. Although white racial progressives often accepted the goals of federal court action and black civil disobedience, many harbored grave doubts about whether such measures could produce peaceful and lasting change in the region's racial practices. The SRC's own position was evident from the advice it gave to celebrated journalist Edward P. Morgan. In the mid-1950s Morgan frequently turned to the Council for guidance on how to understand and report the rapidly unfolding events in the region. In the immediate aftermath of the first *Brown* decision in May 1954, Morgan had even included a recorded statement from the SRC's executive secretary George Mitchell on his CBS program. Amid talk of widespread closures of public schools to avoid desegregation, Mitchell stressed the South's need to preserve its commitment to public education and urged calm compliance with the Supreme Court's integration ruling.[56]

In August 1955, Morgan—by this time on ABC—broadcast an open letter to Senators Walter George and Richard Russell of Georgia, calling on them to abandon their resistance to the Supreme Court's rulings and support the orderly desegregation of their state's public schools.[57] When George and Russell emerged as stalwarts of massive resistance, Morgan again turned to George Mitchell for advice. In March 1956, just days after the Southern Manifesto announced the implacable opposition of most southern senators and congressmen to federally mandated desegregation, Morgan admitted to Mitchell that he had a "great feeling of impotence and inadequacy in trying to comment intelligently and with some purpose and effect on the subject." He fired off a salvo of questions about the racial situation to the SRC: Should the president say more on the subject? Was there any way to encourage southern industrialists to support integration on economic grounds? Was the Department of Justice doing enough to enforce compliance with *Brown*? How significant was the growth of the White Citizens' Councils? Was there really a Silent South of white racial moderates who could be encouraged to comply? Morgan confessed to Mitchell that he was "groping" to identify an "approach that will encourage progress without being recklessly provocative." This pretty much summed up the SRC's own dilemma as it sought peaceful but prompt desegregation. Mitchell wrote back at considerable length, helping to shape Morgan's editorials calling for congressional bipartisanship on the race issue, condemning the extremism of the White Citizens' Councils, and urging President Eisenhower to stress that, despite the vagueness of the Supreme Court's "all deliberate speed" mandate, the South was still required to start desegregating its public schools.[58]

Perhaps even more portentous for the future of the civil rights movement in the South was the exchange between Morgan and the SRC on the significance of the Montgomery bus boycott, which had started in December 1955. Morgan asked Mitchell if he felt "that the passive resistance in Montgomery might conceivably spread throughout the South as the best answer to the extremists." Mitchell replied in somewhat florid terms that he "would expect that the spirit of that general idea will not long hence bring about a situation in which it will be found that Negro people can no longer be got to work on the old diet of scorn." Economic leverage, as well as the self-respect it engendered among the protesters themselves, was one of the great advantages of the nonviolent direct-action tactics employed in Montgomery. Southern employers would soon find themselves having to treat their black workforce with more respect or lose their custom and labor. These economic realities, Mitchell argued with some prescience, would ultimately usher in real changes in the region's racial arrangements. As businessmen felt the pinch of black demands for dignity and equality, "here and there people will be willing to pay the price and in those towns there will be peace and growth. And it won't be so very long before the word will spread that that's what you do."[59]

This was heartening news for Morgan, who had invested a good deal of hope in the power of nonviolent direct action to achieve peaceful and precipitous change. Indeed, Morgan was one of the first broadcast journalists of national repute to comment on the Montgomery protest. In February 1956, shortly after the mass arrest of the boycott's clerical leadership, Morgan told his audience that he would "respectfully suggest to the civic leaders of Montgomery, Alabama, that if they can find the time they would be doing themselves and the nation a service to bone up a little on what they may have forgotten about the recent history of India." Grasping the Gandhian turn the boycott had taken, Morgan reminded those listeners whose recent Indian history was a little shaky that repeated jailings by the British had not halted the struggle of Gandhi and his followers for independence. In truth, there was still a patina of patronization around Morgan's romantic presentation of a "natural" disposition toward nonviolence among southern blacks. Nevertheless, he was quick to disparage the sexual para-

noia at the rotten heart of white resistance to desegregation and to see the Montgomery bus boycott as "a show of passive resistance that may well become a key
symbol in another struggle for independence." Black protest against Jim Crow in
the South, Morgan told his listeners, "is not a sinister conspiracy of black hordes
to impress a pagan supremacy on genteel citizens of lighter skin. It is not a
swaggering ultimatum, bloodshot with passion as so many seem to fear, that a
Negro shall marry your sister. It is the insistence, springing from the innards of
some of the gentlest souls God ever fashioned, to choose their own seat on a
municipal bus, to travel afoot or on horseback, in a Cadillac convertible or to stay
at home."[60]

Ed Morgan's network editorials were not the only radio broadcasts on the bus
boycott that stressed the protesters' commitment to nonviolence. In early 1956
Clarence Pickett of the AFSC also presented a brief report from the city. Originally founded by Quakers in World War I to offer conscientious objectors an
alternative to military service, the Philadelphia-based organization had quickly
developed a keen interest in racial matters. In the mid-1920s it had established
an Interracial Division, which was superseded in the mid-1940s by a Race Relations Division and in 1950 by a Community Relations Division. Through these
divisions and an extensive network of formal and informal links with other progressive forces, the AFSC quietly played an invaluable part in promoting racial
justice and interracial understanding.[61] Arguably, however, the AFSC's most significant contribution to the civil rights struggle was in the realm of ideas. In
accordance with its pacifist beliefs, years before the wave of bus boycotts, sit-ins,
and freedom rides that became synonymous in the public mind with the southern civil rights movement, the AFSC had vigorously encouraged the use of nonviolent direct-action tactics to dramatize and ultimately remedy social and racial
injustice. Indeed, the Committee boasted close ties to most of the major theore-
ticians and exponents of nonviolent protest in the freedom struggle, including
A. J. Muste, Glenn Smiley, and Bob Moses, while Bayard Rustin, James Lawson,
and Martin Luther King Jr. were among the many who visited India to study
Gandhian techniques under the Committee's auspices.[62]

Skilled though it was in fostering personal contacts and exchanges of information among Gandhians, the AFSC had made only sporadic use of radio between the wars. In the 1940s, however, the Committee decided to make more
use of the medium to promote education, dialogue, tolerance, and reconciliation
in the racial arena. Some of the results were decidedly local in both origin and
intended audience. In November 1946, for example, the southeastern area office, based in High Point, North Carolina, launched a weekly *Education for Peace*
series on nearby WBIG-Greensboro. The shows covered a typical range of AFSC
concerns, including the threat of nuclear war and the problems of refugees. The
series also featured a discussion of "peacemaking in the local community,"

which addressed the issue of racial intolerance and misunderstanding in North Carolina.[63]

Other AFSC radio programs that addressed southern racial iniquities were directed toward national—and sometimes specifically northern—audiences. In 1947 the Committee prepared a broadcast for the long-running *New World A-Coming* radio series on WMCA–New York that dramatized the events of the Journey of Reconciliation conducted by the Fellowship of Reconciliation (FOR) to test the South's compliance with the Supreme Court's *Morgan* ruling against segregation on interstate transportation.[64] Among the ten shows the AFSC produced on WFLN-Philadelphia in 1949 was one dedicated to the Committee's Applicant Preparation Program. Billed as an "adventure in human relations," this program sought to help African American job applicants secure employment in "nontraditional" occupations usually reserved for whites. Another segment of a WFLN program, revealingly titled "An Experiment in Goodwill," described an integrated work camp run by the AFSC in Georgia.[65]

The AFSC had a more significant opportunity to promote its race relations work in November 1949, when the Committee's radio director George Loft arranged for Clarence Pickett and his colleague Erroll Elliot to appear on CBS's popular *Church of the Air* program. While Elliot focused on the historical development of Quakerism, Pickett used the past to emphasize the contemporary relevance of Quaker beliefs to those seeking a more harmonious and just world. "One hundred fifty years ago John Woolman, one of the most consistent Quakers this country has produced, refused to eat meals in homes where food was prepared by slaves," Pickett told listeners. "He did what he could to heal the wounds of the slave, but he saw the corrosive and hardening results of slaveholding on the slaveholder. And he never rested until he had done all he could to awaken in the man who profited by slave labor a willingness to release his slaves." The moral for modern Americans was clear enough. It was every right-thinking citizen's duty not only to condemn racial bigotry and injustice but also to take positive steps to educate the bigots as to the error of their ways. "I believe it is safe to say," Pickett concluded, "based on his success, that if a small percentage of the Christians of his day had followed this course, there would never have been a Civil War. And the Negro minority problem might well have hardly existed."[66] Unfortunately, fewer people heard this message than Loft and the AFSC hoped. About seventy-five stations usually carried *Church of the Air,* including thirteen southern affiliates. No southern stations accepted the show when Pickett and Elliot appeared. This blackout offered mute testimony to the AFSC's reputation for unequivocally opposing Jim Crow at a time when many southern progressives were still hedging their bets.[67] Yet, more generally, the AFSC's experience reflected the recurring problems faced by racial progressives of all stripes as they tried to get meaningful discussions of racism, segregation, and disenfranchisement onto southern radio during the decades before the emergence of the mass civil rights movement.

The AFSC was disappointed by its experiences with *Church of the Air* and frustrated by an unsuccessful attempt to get a regular weekly show on KYW-Philadelphia. The Committee's interest in radio consequently dwindled in the early 1950s, only to revive later in the decade under the guidance of a man called Edwin T. Randall with his Friendly World Broadcasting project. It was no coincidence that Randall's broadcasts echoed the AFSC's emphasis on nonviolence as the key to peaceful and durable racial change in the South. Such broadcasts helped to create the sense throughout America that not only was the battle for black rights incontrovertibly just, it was being waged by eminently justifiable means. Indeed, as the next chapter explains, long before the advent of mass activism in the South, radio played an important role in preparing both whites and African Americans to appreciate the value of a revolutionary protest strategy that bore the crucial stamp of respectability.

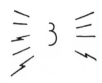

Respectability, Religion, and Rhythm and Blues on Black-Oriented Radio

Man will learn, one of these days, maybe a thousand or
ten thousand or even a million years hence, that there
is more power in an ounce of love than there is power in a
ton of dynamite—the former preserves, the latter destroys.
Rev. William Holmes Borders, WAGA-Atlanta, 1941

Enunciating Respectability

The African American quest for respect on radio—as in American life more generally—was inextricably bound up with efforts to show whites that blacks were worthy of that respect and the citizenship rights that should accompany it. Consequently, the careful cultivation of images of traditional respectability was a hallmark of early African American efforts to use the medium to advance the race. This tendency took a variety of forms, including a good deal of praise for black announcers who exhibited standard American diction as opposed to a distinctively black vernacular style. In 1947 *Ebony* noted that few black deejays "can be identified as Negro on air." The magazine explained how African American announcers could find better opportunities in the industry by adopting "middle-American" language and intonation and thereby endorsing mainstream middle-class social values. The "discovery that a voice has no color has opened new vistas to Negroes in radio," *Ebony* reported. "Disc Jockeys have demonstrated once again that race is only skin deep."[1]

The *Ebony* article serves as a useful corrective to the simplistic way in which most writers on black radio, rhythm and blues, and early rock and roll music have routinely portrayed all black deejays as flamboyant motormouth virtuosos who jive-talked their way through their shows in the distinctive argot of the black streets. In fact, this style of broadcasting became widely popular only in the late 1940s, following the phenomenal success of Mississippi-born Al Benson at WGES in Chicago. Initially far more common among black announcers was the staid, basically raceless, mid-American broadcasting style pioneered by Jack Cooper in the late 1920s and early 1930s on WCAP-Washington and then on WSBC-Chicago. After Benson's breakthrough, the market appeal of black-oriented shows certainly became more closely linked to the identifiably black patter of African American deejays, as well as to the thrilling rhythm and blues platters they spun. Yet the black community was neither monolithic nor one-dimensional in its listening habits, and the full-throttle Bensonite and more demure Cooperite announcing traditions continued to coexist. There was room on black-oriented radio schedules for both kinds of deejays, and many listeners tuned in happily to both.

Nevertheless, in the 1940s and early 1950s, civil rights organizations like the NUL and the NAACP and other boosters of black respectability like the Johnson Publishing Company responsible for *Tan, Jet,* and *Ebony* magazines often demonstrated a marked preference for the more refined Cooperite brand of black radio announcing. In 1953, for example, the NAACP hailed Willa Mae Richardson as "the most influential and active Negro woman in the city of Waycross, Georgia," mainly because of her weekly appearances as host of a community-oriented news show on WAYX. The Association was careful to praise not only Richardson's exemplary commitment to many worthy local church, charitable, and educational initiatives in the black community but also her "diction, and the soft, clear tone of her voice."[2]

Clearly there was an awful lot at stake in the mastery of "correct" English on air. In Houston, Texas, deejay "Joltin' Joe" Howard attributed his own employment at black-oriented stations KNUZ and KYOK in the late 1940s and early 1950s to his "excellent diction." In 1954 that same quality secured Howard a job outside black-oriented radio at WAKE, a general-market station in Atlanta geared to white audiences.[3] Although uncommon, this kind of breakthrough only served to reinforce the prevailing sense that black respectability was linked to upward social and economic mobility. Standard diction could provide a vehicle for escaping the confines of purely black success and open up the opportunities for mainstream success. Paradoxically, however, there was also much to be gained in economic, cultural, and psychological terms from the creative manipulation and disassembling of standard speech by black deejays. The underlying tension between these two impulses was an important feature of the ways in which black-oriented radio in the South interacted with the nascent civil rights movement of the late 1940s and 1950s.

Susan Douglas has dissected the social, political, and racial implications of being able to use and knowingly abuse standard American English on air. The malapropisms and out-of-control syntax of *Amos 'n' Andy,* for example, provided much of the humor in that hugely popular show. Yet this was not wholly a case of whites laughing at faux blacks as they wrestled with the complexities of language. Indeed, Douglas suggests that irrespective of race many Depression-era Americans—particularly men—could easily identify and even empathize with the way that Amos and Andy struggled to comprehend their world and articulate a coherent response to its many problems. Nevertheless, because Amos and Andy were "black," their linguistic ineptitude fused with pervasive white notions that African Americans were innately less intelligent than whites. For white listeners, the twosome's tongue-twisted befuddlement was always at some level symbolic of deeper black mental inadequacies.[4]

Yet even this does not exhaust the complexities of the show, its multiple meanings, or its influence. *Amos 'n' Andy* also mesmerized white audiences with the rapid cut-and-thrust of its dialogue and its use of a beguiling "black" dialect that seemed to replace the regular rules of polite conversation with an altogether more fluid, liberating, and captivating model. This was part of a much broader phenomenon. Many of the most successful radio broadcasters of the interwar years, particularly those like Jack Benny, George Burns and Gracie Allen, and Joe Penner who pioneered radio comedy, flourished because of their ability to bend language to their wit and whim. These broadcasters ground puns to within an inch of their comic lives and spent hours trying to coax double, triple, and even quadruple meanings from commonplace words and phrases. Because radio required the creation of a new auditory world devoid of visual stimuli, its stars had to do more than just master new methods of vocal projection and breath control. They needed to sharpen their wordplay and develop distinctive, instantly recognizable, on-air personalities—hence the evolution of the catchphrases and idiosyncratic monikers at the heart of the medium. These strategies and devices were necessary to grab the attention and stir the imaginations of listeners; they helped to lay the auditory foundations for the make-believe world that broadcasters and their audiences created together.

Ironically, but for the racism within the industry—and it was a huge and tragic "but"—black announcers might have enjoyed a competitive edge in early radio and capitalized on the medium's thirst for gifted wordsmiths.[5] In the black community, oral facility was certainly highly prized, not just as a vehicle and site of entertainment but also as a means to secure recognition and status. Black locutionary geniuses, seasoned by the verbal duels of the dozens and the epic incantations of the toasts, were well equipped to take advantage of radio's need for deft weavers of vivid wordscapes.

To some extent, of course, this is what happened after 1947, when black-oriented radio started to spread throughout the South and beyond. By the early 1950s there were large numbers of Bensonite black deejays on the air, boasting a remarkable range of fanciful sobriquets and catchphrases, and entrancing audiences of both races with their larger-than-life personalities and verbal virtuosity. If *Amos 'n' Andy* had whetted white appetites for black vernacular speech on the air, a new generation of southern whites heard black deejays like "Jockey Jack" Gibson, Vernon "Poppa Stoppa" Winslow, Hal Jackson, Maurice "Hot Rod" Hulbert, and Louisville Lou as hip masters and mistresses of language, not as its victims. Sure, they used slang and bent the rules of grammar promoted by teachers and parents. But that was as much a part of the thrill for these white eavesdroppers as the way that the latest rhythm and blues records by Hank Ballard and the Midnighters, or the Drifters, or Lloyd Price, broke the lyrical and musical rules of Tin Pan Alley pop.

If there was plenty of visceral pleasure to be derived from the sheer verbal facility of these deejays, there was also a buzz to be got from complicity in what was a symbolic act of rebellion against accepted social, cultural, and racial norms. Accepted rules of language and speech always embody and help to perpetuate prevailing hierarchies of power in any society. Black rhythm and blues deejays and their white disciples, like the comedians who had built radio comedy on verbal deviance in the interwar years, mocked the established order of things in America. For whites, mostly young and often southern, as for many African Americans, enthusiasm for these deejays could serve as a marker of difference, of forced or adopted, total or partial, alienation from the mainstream of American society and its values.

Many African Americans delighted in the vernacular skills of the more flamboyant maestros of the microphone, recognizing them as part of a venerable black oral tradition whose singular style signified a proud refusal to defer to putatively "white" measures of excellence in American culture. Yet by no means all felt so enamored of the rise of the Bensonite tendency among black broadcasters. Or, at least, regardless of how they personally felt about the cavalier approach some deejays took to conventional syntax and pronunciation, many middle-class African Americans and activists had reservations about whether these deejays were projecting the images most likely to help advance the cause of black civil rights. This was a time when the NAACP and others were desperate to stir white sympathy for racial reform, not only by appealing to America's democratic creed, constitutional law, and simple morality, but also by showing just how respectable, cultivated, and refined African Americans could be. Little surprise, then, that some wondered if a black voice scatting "Great googly-moogly, that was the Swallows with 'It Ain't the Meat, It's the Motion'" was the best way to dispel pernicious racial stereotypes that encompassed notions of both black childishness and predatory sexuality.

It was within this context of an abiding concern about black broadcasting propriety that the NAACP's emphasis on Willa Mae Richardson's educational background makes sense. The *Crisis* article on Richardson was at pains to point out that she was a graduate of Bethune-Cookman College in Daytona, Florida, and that she continued to prize education as a vehicle of black progress, serving as president of the Bailey Street Parent-Teacher Association in Waycross. Richardson's credentials confirmed *Ebony* magazine's observation that many of the first generation of self-consciously refined and erudite African American radio announcers were college educated, if not actually college teachers.[6]

While this was a national trend, it is striking just how many southern black educators found their way onto the airwaves, hosting, writing, or guesting on pioneering radio shows dedicated to African American history and news. Ambrose Caliver, the creator of *Freedom's People,* was a former high school teacher and the first black dean of Fisk University in Nashville.[7] Nat D. Williams continued to teach at Booker T. Washington High School in Memphis while becoming an institution among black broadcasters on WDIA, where his schoolteacher colleague Gerry Brown also found an announcing job. Revealingly, Williams, whose *Brown America Speaks* program was as close as WDIA came to providing a regular discussion forum for civil rights issues in the late 1940s and early 1950s, was frequently chided by members of his black audience when he assumed a more exuberant jive-talking persona for his rhythm and blues shows.[8] In New Orleans, educator O.C.W. Taylor served as the South's first "director of Negro programming" at WNOE, where he also hosted the station's Hadacol-sponsored *Talent Hour and Jamboree* show.[9] Elsewhere in the Crescent City, WBOK's first black appointment was Xavier University graduate and Green Junior High School teacher Peter Clark, who joined as a sports announcer and public relations director in 1953.[10] Mississippi educator Jerome W. Stampley presented a weekly showcase for black accomplishments on WQBC-Jackson that featured uplifting and eminently reputable classical, semiclassical, and spiritual music from the Alcorn, Jackson State, and Tougaloo College choirs. According to fellow Mississippi radio pioneer Bruce Payne, Stampley's show was "well respected for the quality of culture and entertainment it presented."[11]

Some of these educators actually used radio to protest the inadequacy of black educational provisions in the segregated South. In December 1940, for example, Paine College historian J. W. Brown appeared on WRDW-Augusta both to praise African Americans and to condemn the pitiful lack of educational and employment opportunities for southern blacks.[12] Two months earlier Birmingham supervisor of Negro schools Carol Hayes had appeared on *Wings Over Jordan,* arguing that "the advancement of the Negro in the South . . . can be brought about best through adequate education." Although the tone of Hayes's brief speech was cautious and conciliatory, he did condemn the standard of segregated educational facilities on behalf of the "large number of Negroes who are making the best of their present opportunities, but who are courteously and orderly asking for more." Like many of the era's white racial progressives, Hayes hoped to rouse a Silent South of moderates to oppose blatant racial inequalities in the region. Thus, he appealed to the patriotic sentiment, the moral and religious conscience, and the civic concerns of white southerners as he urged them to help to make "democracy in education a reality by providing for every boy and girl, regardless of race, an equal opportunity to develop fully the individual talents which God, our common father, gave all children." Hayes accepted the gradualist argument that this "goal cannot be reached in a day. It is necessarily a slow and gradual process." Nevertheless, in questioning the quality of separate black public education, if not at this point segregation itself, he had alighted upon the issue that would be at the center of the NAACP's postwar assault on Jim Crow.[13]

The marked presence of African American educators on radio in the South made a good deal of sense. Not only were they able to project the desired air of respectability, erudition, and cultivation, but southern black colleges were also among the first African American institutions to recognize the potential of the medium to contribute to racial progress in the region. In 1928 J. L. Peacock, president of the historically black Shaw University in Raleigh, North Carolina, had written to the Federal Radio Commission (precursor of the FCC) supporting a request from the Durham Life Insurance Company for an increase in wattage for its nonprofit WPTF outlet. The station had broadcast discussion programs and entertainment from Shaw that Peacock—writing "as one deeply interested in the cultural development of our people through radio service"—noted had "been commented on most favorably." Peacock felt that radio could serve not only to inform and educate southern blacks but also, by eradicating crude racial stereotypes, to convince whites that African Americans were worthy of full citizenship rights.[14]

At one level this was part of a general trend in early radio. From its inception as a means of mass communication, many had viewed radio as a vehicle for education and cultural uplift. The ferocious debates of the 1920s and early 1930s over how the medium should be regulated and financed were closely linked to fears that overdependence on advertising revenue would encourage an inferior brand of mass-appeal programming and undermine the medium's capacity to enlighten and educate its listeners. Indeed, one consequence of the triumph of the forces of commercialism was that the number of licenses issued to and held by educational establishments for nonprofit stations had dropped precipitously. Of the 202 licenses granted to educational institutions between 1921 and 1936, only thirty-eight were still in effect in January 1936.[15]

Within the contracting universe of educational broadcasting, it is especially significant that southern black colleges remained so keen to exploit radio for self-promotion and racial advancement. In planning their own radio station, officials at the Tuskegee Institute, for example, could "think of nothing else which would be so effective in making Tuskegee intimately and favorably known to the people of the South." Yet they appreciated that broadcasts from the Institute could also serve broader practical, cultural, and political goals. Radio would provide the Institute with "a means of going direct to a great many Negroes who are now inaccesable [sic] to us with broadcasts of information about agriculture, home economics, health, business, and other matters of great importance to the race." Tuskegee had always looked somewhat askance at the popularity of jazz and its accompanying dance styles, and even at the gospel music that fused sacred messages with the sounds of blues and jazz. Its radio station, therefore, would serve as a bastion of what it considered more respectable and refined forms of African American music. It would rescue "the wonderful spirituals from the hands of jazz-minded, so-called entertainers who have done so much of late to commercialise, degrade and cheapen them." The possibilities of using the medium to improve race relations, meanwhile, were "practically limitless." The station "would have inestimable value also by, at frequent intervals, specifically entering the field of interracial propaganda. It would make available to untold multitudes the addresses of the many speakers of national note who appear from the Tuskegee platform. Musical programs could be interspersed with significant bits of information about Negro history and achievement—the sort of thing which will greatly contribute to a more appreciative attitude on the part of white people."[16]

In late 1943 the NUL's *Opportunity* journal noted that Fisk, Howard, and Atlanta Universities, alongside the all-female Bennett College in Greensboro, North Carolina, were among the other southern black institutions making a concerted effort in the radio field.[17] The Bennett experiment was especially revealing. During the 1940–41 academic year the school coproduced a show called *Gwen's Folks* with WBIG-Greensboro, a CBS affiliate that agreed to air the shows as part of its sustaining—noncommercial—public service programming. *Gwen's Folks* comprised a series of dramatizations in which members of the eponymous Gwen's family were confronted with a range of practical problems: "Bringing Up Junior," "Investing Money," "Making Low-Income Diets." Each week they were rescued from disaster either by Junior's teacher or by Gwen herself, who was a student at Bennett and drew upon the lessons she had learned in such classes as "Foods, Clothing, Consumer Education" or "Family Life Education." These shows, beamed to both black and white listeners in "elementary schools, high schools and colleges within a 50-mile radius of Greensboro," carefully portrayed the benefits of education while at the same time confirming to skeptical whites both the willingness and the capacity of African Americans to learn and act responsibly.[18]

With the outbreak of war, Bennett College's radio broadcasts followed a familiar pattern: African Americans on air simultaneously sought to raise black morale, demonstrate black commitment to the ideals for which America professed to be fighting, and point out how continued racism and discrimination mocked those ideals. Bennett's *Americans, Too, Who Have Achieved* series, for example, highlighted African American contributions to American history. It covered some of the same ground as the black episode in the Office of Education's series *Americans All, Immigrants All* (and as NBC's *Freedom's People*, which had originally been titled *We, Too, Are American*). The *Bennett College Goes-on-the-Air for National Defense* series not only celebrated black patriotism but also, through installments like "The Need for Racial Tolerance," allowed commentary on racial matters under the guise of promoting wartime unity and cooperation.[19]

The Bennett-WBIG initiative also offered rare instruction for African American women in the technical skills of radio production, as well as allowing the students to write and announce. Thus it challenged certain gender as well as racial expectations relating to employment practices within both the industry and the region. In general, however, Bennett's use of radio enshrined African American claims to be thoroughly conventional, respectable, and responsible citizens whose social, moral, and gender values accorded perfectly with those of mainstream America. Once whites were convinced of this fact, so the logic went, surely they would no longer treat African Americans as inferior and second-class citizens? As John Turner noted in *Opportunity*, the Bennett broadcasts were intended to illustrate "that the alleged intellectual differences between the white and colored groups are actually non-existent when opportunity has been equal; second that all Negroes are *not* the same." As a result of the broadcasts, Turner also observed, "Expressions of surprise and wonderment have been received from white friends over the excellent enunciation, diction, and program content of these radio programs."[20]

The Bennett College shows were not the only broadcasts to incorporate positive representations of African American women into a broader commitment to African American respectability on the air. In 1943, for example, Ann Tanneyhill's annual vocational campaign for the NUL had focused on African American women workers. Hoping both to publicize the role of these women in the labor force and to increase training and employment opportunities for other black women, she contributed a script on the subject to CBS's series *The Spirit of '43*. Tanneyhill's "Heroines in Bronze" included historical accounts of the lives of such women as Sojourner Truth, Harriet Tubman, and the black nurses who served in World War I. It also featured contemporary figures like educator and National Youth Administration executive Mary McLeod Bethune, who urged greater employment of black women in the effort to win World War II. Throughout, the show portrayed African American women with dignity and respect, revealing them as intelligent, courageous, and reliable citizens and workers, far removed from the Aunt Jemima and Sapphire stereotypes—the one docile and compliant, the other lascivious and conniving—that dominated popular culture and white racial consciousness.[21]

African American women also introduced a variety of cookery and domestic science shows on southern radio stations. Once more, these shows enshrined middle-class ideals of the patriarchal nuclear family and of conventional male and female roles as breadwinner-protector and homemaker-nurturer respectively. Yet while many African Americans endorsed and pursued these middle-class norms, they were not merely imitating white mores. They were also endorsing moral, social, and gender values vigorously promoted within their own communities by black churches, colleges, business leagues, women's clubs, fraternal organizations, and other institutions. And although the roots of respectability in the black community were inextricably linked to their equivalent in bourgeois white society, the particular forms and implications of that respectability in the black community were very distinctive.

While the "politics of respectability," as Evelyn Brooks Higginbotham has described this phenomenon, yoked middle-class and elite African Americans together irrespective of gender, black women clearly had an especially important role in extending its reach across class lines. As Higginbotham has explained, middle-class and elite black women hoped to "earn their people a measure of esteem from white America" by securing "the black lower classes's psychological allegiance to temperance, industriousness, thrift, refined manners, and Victorian sexual morals."[22] Such goals were only imperfectly realized, and class tensions clearly persisted among African American women of different social and economic standing, just as they endured within the black community at large. Nevertheless, as Victoria Wolcott has neatly summarized, "there is evidence . . . that aspects of the uplift ideology expressed by middle-class elites resonated strongly with the preexisting values of poorer African American women." Respectability "reflected more than simply bourgeois Victorian ideology; it was a foundation of African American women's survival strategies and self-definition irrespective of class." It is certainly useful to see the general concern with black respectability on radio and the more specific example of black women's dignified appearances on domestic science programs as part of a drive toward conspicuous respectability in which black women took a leading role. It was a drive that many imbued with enormous potential for advancing the cause of racial justice.[23]

Domestic science shows on radio were a genuinely biracial and national phenomenon from radio's earliest days, but they became even more common after the advent of television. As advertisers soon became aware, the consequence of widespread television ownership in the late 1940s and early 1950s was not to kill off radio listening. Rather, it was to shift the main site of radio listening from family living rooms into kitchens—traditionally a woman's domain. In 1951 an estimated 77 percent of radio listening in homes that also had televisions involved "secondary sets" located outside the living room, with half of all radio listening taking place in the kitchen. For individual stations and networks like CBS, the housewife-consumer became a vital niche market and a major hook for advertisers. As a mid-1950s CBS sales pitch described, the sounds of radio could "follow housewives everywhere." Radio did not require the undivided attention of its listeners: it could "reach housewives *while they are engaged in routine house-making activities.*"[24]

If radio executives clearly recognized the commercial wisdom of programming to female consumers, it made even more sense to target African American women in the South during the daytime, since they were potentially double consumers. Black women often listened to the radio while doing housework both in their own homes and as domestics in white homes, where they were frequently responsible for making household purchases. KWEM in Memphis had first blazed this particular trail with its *Listen Ladies* show. However, it was Willa Monroe's *Tan Town Homemaker's Show,* aired between nine and ten every weekday morning on WDIA from 1949, that revealed the true commercial potential of such fare. Monroe's show was one of the first on the station to secure a major national sponsor, Procter & Gamble, alongside support from several local Memphis businesses. Featuring mellow music, recipes, and news culled from the black society pages, Monroe's show attracted more than 40 percent of Memphis's daytime radio audience—a figure that indicated not only that a fair few men were listening but also that the show had garnered a significant white audience.[25] Elsewhere in the region, dozens of similar domestic shows flourished from the late 1940s into the early 1960s, serving up much the same blend of cooking instructions, child-rearing advice, marital counseling, fashion and beauty tips, and a smattering of church and social news. Carolyn Shaw's *Kitchen Time* on WOKJ-Jackson was the prelude to her successful career as a deejay. Louise Fletcher introduced *A Woman Speaks* on WSOK-Nashville. Alice Wyre hosted *Home Executive* on WERD-Atlanta. Laura Lane, Delores Estelle, and Sister Bessie Griffith each had homemaker shows on WMRY–New Orleans, as did R. J. Pope at WJLD-Birmingham and Leola Dyson at WRAP-Norfolk.[26]

These shows proudly affirmed traditional family values and gender roles, thereby helping to perpetuate the sort of assumptions and stereotypes that had long constrained women of all races. Nonetheless, they represented a considerable improvement over the portrayal of African American women in earlier cookery and homemaker shows. In the late 1920s and early 1930s, the Quaker Oats company had used its Aunt Jemima trademark character in an NBC show featuring minstrel dialect, "coon songs," spirituals, and the sort of good old-fashioned cooking that only a life of dark leisure on the idyllic plantations of the Old South could have produced. Shortly afterwards, CBS's syndicated *National Radio Home-Makers Club* also ran a series on "plantation cooking" sponsored by

FIGURE 4. R. J. Pope at WJLD-Birmingham was one of dozens of African American women who presented "homemaker" shows on southern radio from the late 1940s. Courtesy of Friedman/Four Octaves.

Brer Rabbit Molasses. Here the old-fashioned cooking methods and folk beliefs of a crudely drawn black "mammy" from New Orleans were ridiculed and contrasted with the healthier, more scientific modern methods of the white hostess, Ida Bailey Allen.[27] In this context, women such as Willa Monroe at least offered positive images of southern African American women as bright, informed, and responsible homemakers. This was important at a time when notions of middle-class respectability, domestic orthodoxy, and rising black consumerism were coming together as both vehicles and indices of black advance toward full citizenship.[28]

There was another, more oblique but still significant, level at which these kinds of shows may have helped to prepare the ground for the mass freedom struggle of the late 1950s and 1960s. Historians of women's social activism have long appreciated that one of the foundations for any such activism was the consolidation of what is sometimes termed a collective "female consciousness." This consciousness flowed, in Nancy Cott's words, "from their shared sense of obligation to preserve and nourish life. . . . [It] was rooted not in feminist rejection of the traditional sexual division of labor, but rather in women's *acceptance* of the division of labor by sex." Under various circumstances, this female consciousness could find expression in either left- or right-wing politics, in progressive or conservative social activism. Historically, as Cott admits, this pervasive female sense of self, place, and responsibility within the existing social order has tended to promote stasis rather than change. Nevertheless, the point is that female consciousness—as opposed to *feminist* consciousness, with which it may or may not coincide in specific cases—has always been critical in propelling women toward social activism of all stripes. As Cott puts it, "If the history of black and working-class women's community lives and public actions has not lined up with the feminist equal rights tradition, that is largely because their self-assertions seem to have derived from the sense of family or community membership."[29]

In other words, many women became political or social activists, not primarily to challenge established gender roles—although, paradoxically, their very activism may have done so—but rather to fulfill those roles in a broader public arena. They entered public life with a shared cluster of ideas about women's special responsibilities and with a desire to discharge them for the good of society as a whole. In this context, the participation of African American women on domestic radio shows both reflected and reinscribed the scope of female duties within the black community. And it was the acceptance of a special responsibility for the nourishment, well-being, and respectability of their households, their families, and ultimately the wider black community that motivated many African American women to play such a prominent role in the mass nonviolent direct-action campaigns of the southern civil rights movement. There was nothing contradictory about a veneration of traditional domestic ideals and passionate civil rights activism for somebody like Willa Monroe, who became a prominent member of the Memphis NAACP and often promoted its work on air.[30]

Preachers and Profits, Prophets and Protest

From the moment in 1924 when Rev. Samuel Crouch of the Wayside Church of God in Christ in Fort Worth, Texas, took to the airwaves, radio station owners, sponsors, and advertisers in the South had been keenly aware of the commercial potential of black religious programming. In this broadcasting tradition, sacred and sometimes secular messages from preachers and their guests were woven into programs that depended heavily on the power of gospel music to pull in their audiences. By the late 1940s, Rev. T. M. Chambers could boast 150,000 listeners for his show on KXLR–Little Rock. Elder Solomon Michaux, whose *Radio Church of God* shows were originally carried in the 1930s by WJSV in Washington, D.C., could be heard across much of the nation on CBS. Rev. John

Goodgame claimed audiences of up to 750,000 for his Birmingham-based radio ministry. In the spring of 1949, *Ebony* magazine reported that African American radio preachers enjoyed a weekly audience of some seven million souls and reached "more Americans of both races than any other group of Negroes in any communications medium."[31]

The biracialism of the audience noted by *Ebony* was crucial in shaping the political content and tone of much black religious broadcasting in the deep and border South. Rev. Singleton Robert Chambers estimated that two-thirds of his Kansas City and Little Rock radio audience of 200,000 was white, while Rev. Seymour Marcus Weaver claimed much the same proportion for his airborne ministry on Houston's KNUZ and KATL.[32] Although some of these white listeners may have been hostile, the fact that they kept tuning in suggests that the vast majority were appreciative and supportive. Indeed, many southern whites appear to have seen African American religious broadcasts as a relatively harmless means to foster better race relations within the context of segregation through an emphasis on Christian love, brotherhood, and understanding. The earnest, if rather patronizing, response of one white Virginia woman to the decision to broadcast black church services on WRVA-Richmond was typical. Gladys Musgrove admitted that, somewhat to her surprise, she thoroughly enjoyed the services and commended the station for its "generous and broadminded gesture which should do much for better race relations." WRVA's manager-president Walter Bishop agreed that "these broadcasts should contribute to improved race relations."[33]

Given both the appeal of religious programs within the black community and their potential for reaching whites, it was not surprising that some African American activist-preachers—and some of their more racially progressive white colleagues—should use the religious airwaves to dramatize southern racial injustices and even agitate for change. It is important not to exaggerate either the extent of this practice or the radicalism of those who dared to speak out against the operation of Jim Crow in the South on radio. Just as the degree of formal political engagement in the struggle for desegregation among pulpit-bound black preachers ranged from negligible to zealous, so there was a great deal of variation in the extent to which individual radio preachers espoused social and political equality in the South. In Miami, for instance, Archbishop Ernest Leopold Peterson reckoned that most of the whites tuned to his weekly WMBM program actually thought he was white himself. Although Peterson's broadcasts may have provided important spiritual succor and at least one kind of social amalgam for Miami's black community, his radio sermons were essentially apolitical, devoid of any condemnations of Jim Crow or any exhortations to protest.[34]

Even those preachers who did endorse efforts to secure earthly deliverance from segregation and disenfranchisement often felt compelled to deliver messages on air that were very tentative. Or their racial militancy was encoded in the preacher's particular choice of scriptural texts, the ways in which they were explicated, and the rhetorical cadences and emotional dynamics of the sermons. In a sense, this was just a variant of the strategies adopted by many southern black preachers, whether they appeared on the radio or not. By selecting certain biblical passages—such as those affirming the equality of all before God—even some of the most outwardly conservative black clergymen preached what educator-activist Rev. Benjamin Mays termed "a revolution, but in disguise."[35] Of course, for many of the black clergy who did appear on the radio, the need to conceal from white listeners any untoward militancy was greater than for pulpit-bound preachers who usually performed to exclusively black congregations.

Despite these constraints and the basic caution of many southern black clergymen, the handful of dedicated radio preacher-activists in the South could sometimes get away with rather more forthright racial commentary than could their secular radio colleagues. One important factor here was that, unlike most southern black radio personalities, preachers were rarely station employees and were, therefore, not wholly dependent on radio for their livelihoods. Most southern stations required preachers to pay for their airtime in a variation on the brokerage system of broadcast financing that dominated the early years of black-oriented radio. At WUST in Washington, for example, Sunday preachers were the only group of broadcasters that the station actually required to purchase their own airtime. WUST was keen to cash in on the fact that these preachers were scrambling for the most popular and profitable time slots in the weekly schedule and would pay top dollar for the privilege. This quasi-independence from the station's core financial and programming structure hardly gave southern black radio preachers a totally free hand to say anything they wanted to say about white racism and discrimination. Nevertheless, the nature of their relationship to the stations gave those of the clergy who dared to speak out against Jim Crow a mite more room for maneuver.[36]

The southern station owners and managers who agreed to carry black religious programs faced one perpetual problem: they could never be entirely sure what topics might come up in the course of a minister's live sermon. Ultimately, however, simple commercial calculations ensured that many southern radio stations were willing to take that chance. Moreover, it is evident that black radio preachers repeatedly found space to make a variety of bold and tentative, general and specific, national and local condemnations of racial prejudice and discrimination, while at the same time replenishing their community's sense of pride, purposefulness, and destiny. Indeed, at its most radical, black religious broadcasting provided the forum for some of the most trenchant discussions of race relations and civil rights issues heard on black-oriented radio in the South prior to the emergence of a mass southern movement. As *Ebony* reported in 1949,

"Militancy is often the theme of many Negro radio ministers who use their air-time to blast racial intolerance."[37]

In truth, much of the overt ministerial militancy to which *Ebony* was referring took place in the North. In Chicago, for example, deejay Norman Spaulding suggested that postwar civil rights activism was "spearheaded by young pastors who gained their popularity from radio broadcasts." Chicago was a city where radio preachers were frequently "the most radical and consistent protesters against racial and political injustices."[38] In the more daunting atmosphere of the Jim Crow South, much of what passed for militancy among black radio preachers before the late 1950s followed the gradualist contours of white progressive thought and veered toward a latter-day accommodationism. It took the form of heartfelt condemnations of the inadequate social, economic, and educational provisions for blacks under Jim Crow, coupled with morally rooted appeals to whites to equalize the segregated system. Rev. H. C. Carswell, speaking on WTOC-Savannah in the fall of 1940, captured the universalist essence of many black radio sermons when he asked his listeners to "encourage the churches of all communities to cooperate with the entire world in saving all people . . . [and to] work for fellowship and unity for all mankind."[39]

For many southern radio preachers like Carswell, a sort of militant gradualism, mainly centered on an eagerness to cooperate with progressive southern whites, was the key to racial change, not direct-action protests, legal campaigns, or federal intervention. Some stuck firm to this approach even as the pace of black protest quickened in the later 1950s. As will be described in chapter 8, Rev. J. Nathaniel Tross at WBT-Charlotte honed this brand of militant gradualism to perfection on air. Tross was far from unique, however; his blend of supplication and petition was commonplace among southern radio clergymen until well into the 1960s. Another radio minister in this mold was Kenneth Harold Johnson. Sometimes hailed—along with about a dozen or so other candidates—as the "first Negro commentator below the Mason-Dixon line," Johnson presented a fifteen-minute *Creed, Color and Cooperation* show on WKY–Oklahoma City each Sunday morning. According to WKY's white program director, Johnson preferred to concentrate not so much on "what should be done but rather what has been done" on the racial front. The program was resolutely celebratory and conservative, not combative and confrontational. In the mid-1940s, for example, Johnson attacked A. Philip Randolph's call for a boycott of the draft until the military was desegregated. He also campaigned successfully against Governor Roy B. Turner's pioneering appointment of an African American to a public relations post at Langston University, arguing that the man was a second-rate candidate. Not surprisingly, perhaps, many of Johnson's 1,800 fan letters a week were from appreciative white listeners who saw him as restraining, rather than galvanizing, local black agitation against Jim Crow.[40]

FIGURE 5. During twenty-five years on WBT-Charlotte, Rev. Dr. J. S. Nathaniel Tross (second from left) promoted interracial understanding and black respectability as the key to racial progress in the South. Courtesy of James Peeler.

If caution was the watchword among avowed gradualists like Tross, Johnson, and Miami's Bishop Peterson, other southern radio preachers were rather more militant. These clerics used their airtime to expose, denounce, and—among those working at the more courageous edges of prudence—occasionally encourage direct challenges to Jim Crow. The career of Bishop Smallwood E. Williams in Washington, D.C., offers a good example of the complex blend of proselytizing zeal, personal ambition, and communal obligation that encouraged some preachers to use radio in their pursuit of social and racial justice. Born in Lynchburg, Virginia, Williams arrived in Washington from Columbus, Ohio, in September 1927 with little more to his name than five dollars, a quick wit, and a powerful faith. He started his ministry in a secondhand tent with a congregation of just fifteen souls. Half a century later, Williams was preaching in a $3 million temple and leading a 100,000–strong Pentecostal Bible Way Church Worldwide organization that was worth an estimated $25 million in Washington alone.[41]

Williams immersed himself in all facets of the black community's life. Evaluating Bible Way's long record of public service—as demonstrated, for example, in the construction of apartment complexes for low-income families near the church's base on New Jersey Avenue—the *Washingtonian* magazine concluded that Williams "may be Washington's most influential clergyman, evangelist, and practitioner of pulpit activism, social and economic."[42] Integral to Williams's social concerns was his opposition to segregation and racial discrimination in the nation's capital. "Too often the churches would not speak out against the blatant evils of racism and injustice," the bishop recalled. "They did not get involved in the fight to change things." It was an accusation that few could level at Williams. In March 1952, two years before the first *Brown* decision ended the District's dual public school system, the preacher had fought unsuccessfully to enroll his son at the all-white Wheatley School. Four years later, in the first meaningful election that Washington's residents were able to participate in since their disenfranchisement in the 1880s, Williams helped to organize African American voters during the local Democratic presidential primary.[43]

Bishop Williams's talents as a religious leader and social activist would no doubt have ensured his popularity and prestige without any help from radio. Indeed, he had been preaching in the District for fourteen years before his radio career began. Nevertheless, Williams's weekly services, carried on WINX from 1941 and continuing on the black-oriented WOOK from 1947, undoubtedly exposed many more Washingtonians to his gifts and expanded his congregation. Within two years of his starting at WOOK, *Ebony* estimated that Williams's sermons enjoyed an audience of approximately 500,000 listeners every week.[44] In one sense, Williams's radio career assisted his civil rights activities, regardless of the actual content of his broadcasts. Insofar as they increased his own popularity, prestige, and influence, Williams's appearances furthered any efforts to recruit black community support for his struggle against the racial status quo. In fact, civil rights became a prominent theme in many of Williams's broadcasts at WOOK. When the Virginia Theological Seminary and College awarded him an honorary doctorate of divinity in 1950, it specifically cited the campaign that he had been waging on air against segregation in Washington.[45]

Williams's personal battle against separate schools in D.C. was a case in point. At the height of his 1952 campaign, the bishop devoted one broadcast to a scathing attack upon District School Board member Robert Faulkner, who had publicly defended the sanctity of the segregated school system. In calling for Faulkner's resignation, Williams gave full vent to his and his listeners' indignation:

> Mr. Faulkner has blatantly exposed a retrogressive and reactionary mind in the fact that he lacks an adequate concept and appreciation of the need of modern educational facilities and equipment. . . . He seems to be so very deficient in a sense of social justice which is so necessary in a just and fair

administration of the Board of Education of our public schools of the District of Columbia. We doubt seriously that he has any contribution to make whatever to the total or permanent solution of the public school problem.[46]

By no means were all of Williams's broadcasts so overtly engaged with traditional civil rights issues. The preacher had the spiritual as well as the temporal needs of his flock to take care of, and many of his sermons were more obviously geared to matters of faith and morality. Yet even here, racial politics were never too far away. Williams's sermons frequently sought to yoke categorical denunciations of racism with attempts to inspire a sense of pride and self-confidence among his listeners. Convinced of the righteousness of the black cause and committed to the notion of a deliverance that must be actively worked for and not passively awaited, Williams believed that a new black consciousness was the key to motivating his flock to join the battle against Jim Crow. "I told them that their ship was sure to come in. It was a message of inspiration," recalled the bishop. "I told them not to worry about white segregationists because their arms were too short to box with God."[47]

In 1965, reflecting on a broadcasting career that had spanned nearly a quarter of a century, Williams expressed a keen appreciation of how black-oriented radio had served both himself and the African American citizenry of Washington:

> [The fact that] when I first sought broadcast time some twenty-five years ago, only WOOK was willing to provide broadcast time for our religious programs on a regular and full basis is indicative of the importance of a Radio Station which serves the needs of the local Negro community. Religious life is the most important part of the life of American Negroes and what is true of the whole country is true of the Negro in the Washington, D.C. area. The churches have been a central point not only in developing and improving the status of the American Negro, but have also been a vital point in the fight for civil rights. The religious community needs an outlet through radio to reach the hundreds of thousands of American Negroes and Station WOOK fulfils that need in Washington.[48]

In Atlanta, preachers such as Martin Luther "Daddy" King Sr. at Ebenezer Baptist Church, Harold Bearden at Big Bethel Baptist Church, and Benjamin Mays at Morehouse College were part of a long tradition of social activism among the city's black clergy. The city was also the site of several of the region's boldest religious broadcasting initiatives. In early 1940, Daddy King was among the members of the Atlanta Baptist Ministers Union who formed a special Public Service by Radio Committee. Chaired by Rev. Samuel Pettagrue of West Hunter Street Baptist Church, the Committee was dedicated to securing "the opportunity for colored ministers to broadcast their services over local radio stations."[49] One of its first accomplishments in the summer of 1940 was to secure time for a thirty-minute religious show called *Chariot Wheels,* which aired on WSB-Atlanta every Sunday at 10:30 p.m. and was eventually syndicated to stations in thirty-nine states. This breakthrough followed some sixteen months of unsuccessful petitioning for a regular spot by various black preachers. The final breakthrough, however, probably depended less on the preachers' campaign than on a change of ownership at WSB, where the strict racial and regional orthodoxy of the original owners had been reflected in its "Welcome South Brother" tag and its penchant for country music. Also important were the public support of leading white minister Rev. Louis D. Newton and a firm undertaking from Pettagrue that all speeches on the program would be "inspirational, non-political, non-commercial and non-racial."[50]

Here in microcosm was the dilemma faced by African American activists, whether church-based or secular, in their quest to maximize the political potential of radio in the South. Indeed, the production of *Chariot Wheels* exemplified a problem faced by the entire freedom struggle. No matter how resourceful, determined, or innovative African Americans were in their pursuit of racial justice and equal opportunities, the basic configuration of economic and political power in the broadcasting industry, as in America more generally, meant that they ultimately had to persuade, shame, or cajole significant elements in the white community to support—or at least acquiesce in—their demands. If and when it came, that acquiescence was often tardy and grudging. Moreover, it tended to be piecemeal, accompanied by a whole host of white provisos designed to diminish the impact of any black gains on white privileges. In Atlanta in 1940, whites had no intention of sanctioning a weekly radio show run by activist black preachers without assurances that a censorship committee would vet "all songs, sermons and addresses used on the programme" to ensure that they were apolitical and noncontroversial.[51] Pettagrue and the other black members of the censorship committee naturally resented such restrictions. They even tested the limits of their apolitical brief a little—for example, by pointedly introducing the show's musical selections as songs that had helped sustain "sorely persecuted blacks in the dark days that tried men's souls" and by inviting Almita Robinson of Atlanta's NUL chapter to appear. Nevertheless, the censorship committee and close scrutiny by the station's management ensured that although *Chariot Wheels* became an institution in black Atlanta, relatively few overtly political, let alone militant, voices were ever heard on the show.[52]

One member of the *Chariot Wheels* censorship committee was Rev. William Holmes Borders. Born the son of an ambitious and upwardly mobile country preacher in Bibb County, Georgia, Borders was a graduate of Morehouse College and Garrett Theological Seminary in Illinois. In November 1937 he returned to Georgia from his first pastorate in Evanston, Illinois, and took over the pulpit at the imposing but struggling Wheat Street Baptist Church on Atlanta's Auburn Avenue.[53] Immediately earning a reputation as a mesmerizing speaker, Borders quickly reversed the dwindling attendances at his church and, with the Wheat Street pews overflowing, joined the clamor to get *Chariot Wheels* on the air as a means to extend his ministry. In less than a year, however, Borders had become deeply frustrated with the show and its preemptive censorship regime. In early 1941 he launched his own radio program on WAGA. Subsequently he also broadcast on the state-owned WGST before moving to WERD shortly after its purchase by Jesse Blayton in October 1949.[54]

From the start of his radio ministry, Borders stood out as one of the most influential and outspoken of all southern radio preachers. Like many others, he recognized the unique opportunities presented by American participation in World War II to expose racial injustice and agitate for change. At a time when hundreds of thousands of African Americans were leaving the South in order to escape the naked racism of the Jim Crow system and find work in the war industries of the North, one of his earliest radio sermons asked: "Should the Negro Leave the South?" The address skillfully fused patriotic support for America's war effort with a stern admonishment that Jim Crow was also an enemy to be fought, not fled. "The opposition of segregation will produce tougher character, taller Christians, better citizens, a greater race," Borders insisted. "I cast my vote with those who feel called upon to dig in, grapple with the problem, knowing that the future is mortgaged to God, democracy, and Christianity."[55] In other radio sermons, he repeatedly railed against low wages, inferior housing conditions, inadequate job training, second-class educational establishments, lax law enforcement, and the lack of recreational facilities for Atlanta's black citizens. Moreover, Borders pulled few punches when it came to condemning whites for their racial arrogance, hypocrisy, and ultimate responsibility for perpetuating the racial oppression that undercut America's democratic pretensions. In "All Blood Is Red," originally broadcast in June 1941, Borders punctured white affectations of superiority by declaring, "No race has a monopoly on any virtue." And his message that "the rugged fact that 'All Blood Is Red' blows asunder the position of racial or national superiority" had a special wartime resonance at a time when the Red Cross still segregated blood supplies.[56]

In one of his most famous sermons, "Some Negro Contributions to American Civilization," which first aired on WAGA in February 1942 and was rebroadcast nationwide in January 1943 on *Wings Over Jordan*, Borders celebrated the black contribution to American history and concluded with a rousing poem of black pride and solidarity, "I Am Somebody." Borders again used the wartime context to emphasize black patriotism and commitment to American ideals. "You recall that the Negro has spilled blood in every war of the U.S., that this democracy might not perish from the earth," he explained.[57] Clearly these messages were aimed at a biracial radio audience. Indeed, there were some weeks when whites comprised a majority of the preacher's radio audience. Consequently, Borders's sermons sought to inspire black self-respect and commitment to the struggle for civil rights while encouraging whites to support black aspirations in the name of God and country. "After the war, let us, black man and white man, build in Atlanta a city for God," he urged his listeners. "But don't wait till then to help my people. We need your help now."[58]

Borders's credibility and the effectiveness of his militant ministry among blacks—particularly young blacks—were helped by the fact that he literally practiced what he preached on air. A lifetime member of the NAACP, Borders had consistently supported legal challenges to the operation and then the very existence of Jim Crow. Like many other preachers, Borders stressed the need for black communication with progressive elements within Atlanta's white civic leadership. Yet he also engaged in direct-action protests, taking to the streets to confront white supremacists and racial discrimination in a number of important campaigns. As a result, the students who launched Atlanta's 1960 sit-in campaign hailed Borders as a pioneer of organized black protest in the city, citing his efforts to bring to justice the lynchers of four African Americans in Monroe, Georgia, in 1945, his role in the campaign to secure—and empower—black policemen in Atlanta, his consistent support for voter registration efforts, and his leadership role in a 1957 campaign against bus segregation in Atlanta.[59]

What was especially interesting about the relationship between Borders's radio ministry and his conspicuous involvement with the Atlanta civil rights movement was his essentially Gandhian prescription for effecting social change. In early 1957 Borders led the Triple L Movement first to the front of Atlanta's buses and then, in a classic Gandhian tactic, into the city jail after their arrest for violating the city's segregation ordinance. The three L's stood for Life, Love, and Liberation. This trinity embodied Borders's longstanding belief in the life-affirming and revolutionary potential of nonviolent protest and of loving one's oppressors.[60] Too realistic and politically savvy to believe that displays of African American love and forgiveness toward whites would alone transform the South, Borders had always sought to weld respect for the common bonds that united all humankind to the sort of direct-action protest necessary to expose and correct racial injustice. This was the core of the Gandhian philosophy for social change that Martin Luther King Jr. and other southern civil rights leaders would subsequently adopt and adapt to their own purposes.

Like many educated African American activists, Borders had closely followed news of Gandhi's campaigns against the British Empire in India during the 1940s. In the early 1950s that fascination had deepened when Borders and his wife used the gift of a round-the-world trip from his Wheat Street congregation to visit India and meet with some of the Mahatma's followers.[61] This meant that when the pace of racial protest in Atlanta quickened in the late 1950s and accelerated again in the early 1960s with the emergence of the Atlanta Student Movement, Borders was able to understand, endorse, and exert some measure of influence on the dynamic new protest forces in the black community. Having gone on air to announce in 1960, "I am for the sit-ins, the marching. There is a time when the good they perform cannot be accomplished by other means," he also "lectured to the marchers on the meaning of non-violence as practiced by Gandhi."[62] Sometimes, he admitted, he struggled to contain the impatience and legitimate anger of young black protesters. Yet he constantly tried "to whet their appetite to read more of Gandhi's writings," always remembering the Mahatma's warning that had guided his own ministry and activism for more than a decade: "One day the black races will rise like the avenging Attila against their white oppressors, unless someone presents to them the weapons of satygrahi [sic]," by which Borders meant nonviolent resistance.[63]

Another progressive radio preacher-activist with marked Gandhian leanings was Rev. Kelly Miller Smith. In the late 1950s Smith emerged as a pioneer of nonviolent direct-action tactics in Nashville, Tennessee, where he greatly influenced the coterie of students who graduated from the Nashville Student Movement to occupy key positions in the fledgling SNCC. In the late 1940s, however, Smith was still a pastor at Mt. Heroden Baptist Church in Vicksburg, Mississippi, where he broadcast regularly on local stations WQBC and WVIM. Smith recognized that the steady secularization of black life in the first half of the twentieth century had reduced the absolute centrality of the church in the lives of many black southerners. After the war, this was particularly true in the rapidly urbanizing South, and even more particularly among a younger generation of African Americans whose attention was increasingly drawn by a whole range of popular culture and entertainment forms. Embedding their preaching within exhilarating gospel music shows was both a shrewd commercial exercise for southern radio preachers and a genuine attempt to compete with the expanding world of secular mass entertainment for the hearts, minds, and money of the black community. Just as Atlanta's *Chariot Wheels* had been hailed by Samuel Pettagrue as "tonic to those who never go to church," so Smith's Mississippi radio sermons were specifically "designed to administer unto the religious needs of those who would perhaps be otherwise unreached."[64]

At the heart of Kelly Miller Smith's radio ministry was the classic social gospel notion that Christianity demanded the active pursuit of social justice. Not surprisingly, Amos was Smith's favorite Old Testament prophet and rhetorical touchstone, just as he would be for Martin Luther King. "We need to hear anew the words of the prophet of social righteousness," Smith insisted in a sermon entitled "The Kingdom of God: Its Meaning," where he foreshadowed many of King's speeches by invoking Amos's injunction "Let justice run down as waters and righteousness as a mighty stream." Justice, Smith insisted, could not be denied indefinitely: "Let it ring in the ears of the rulers of the nations of the world. Let it rest upon the hearts of the local, state and national legislators of America."[65]

There was more to Smith's preaching than powerful rhetorical appeals for justice. He also offered a biting critique of American racial intolerance, linking it to Cold War anxieties about the state of the nation's democratic credentials. In "I Want to Be a Christian," Smith explicitly compared Klansmen and communists, denouncing both as un-Christian and un-American. "A good Christian could never be a communist," he maintained. "The same is true of the underworld hate-peddling organizations that are now rendering anew the spots and blemishes on this amazing America of ours. No good Christian could take active part in any organization that peddles hate against groups, whether minority or majority."[66] In "The Story of Jesus," Christ was enlisted into the contemporary struggle for African American rights and depicted for white edification as a model of racial tolerance. "When he came in contact with persons of different national and racial backgrounds there was no prejudice to blur his vision or restrain his helping hand," Smith explained. The message was clear: to be a good American and a good Christian was to renounce racial prejudice and support African American civil rights.[67]

Preaching these sorts of messages anywhere in Dixie was a dangerous undertaking. More than once, the Klan had dynamited Rev. Borders's Atlanta church. In Mississippi, Smith's outspokenness on the air might have seemed almost suicidal. Concerned members of his own congregation would sometimes remind him of the risks involved. "I've had members come to me . . . who would remind me of the fact that a Negro physician was once tarred and feathered . . . after I'd make a statement on the radio or something. But I never got into any trouble about it." Indeed, Smith was somewhat mystified at what he got away with. "We used to say a lot of things which were considered dangerous in those days, but . . . I never got into any trouble about it. I never understood it." In some ways, however, Smith knew the reason perfectly well. Without underestimating his courage in speaking out as boldly as he did, most of Smith's sermons followed Benjamin Mays's typology, whereby messages of hope, deliverance, and even discreet calls to action were encoded in gospel readings and homilies that would have been very familiar and, on the surface, relatively unthreatening to most white southerners. "They didn't censor my sermons," Smith admitted, "but one of the guys asked me one time . . . 'Now do you have any hot issues in this message?' I said 'Yeah I do.' He said 'What are they?' I said '*Sin.*' And I went on and talked about the race problem in terms of sin." According to Smith, this enabled him to evade any censorship by the radio stations: he was "talking about sin. You can't say a preacher can't talk about sin."[68]

While Smith urged white southerners to follow Christ's example and support racial justice, he was not so naive to believe that they would willingly or easily surrender the privileges of white supremacy. Like William Holmes Borders, he appreciated that African American freedom would not come without struggle. Accordingly, he urged blacks to take responsibility for their own deliverance. In a sermon broadcast during Negro History Week, entitled "God's Answer: The Negro in History," Smith celebrated black contributions to American life and culture. Alongside such messages of racial pride and achievement, however, was a more militant rallying cry urging blacks to join what Smith saw as a diverse battle for black rights being waged across the whole spectrum of American social, legal, political, religious, and cultural life. Citing a variegated crop of contemporary black activists and artists—from NAACP lawyer Charles Houston through politicians like Adam Clayton Powell to activist-entertainers like Paul Robeson—Smith insisted that this was a moment of great opportunity for African Americans to seize the initiative in their struggle. "To view the present situation is to discover that we are marching," he insisted, conjuring up an image of an unstoppable tide of mass black protest with God on its side. "To the person who has always insisted that the Negro is inferior, say that we are marching. To the despondent member of our own group who feels that we are backward say 'We're marching.' . . . We must face the future with hope and courage."[69]

Smith's radio sermons did not dwell on the specifics of how this black protest might be organized. Nevertheless, there were clear references to the Christian ethics that he felt should inform black activism and even some tantalizing clues about the nature of the tactics that might be used. "The way of Christ is the way of peace," he insisted in one address. This was no call for passivity in the face of oppression; rather it was an appeal for a militant strain of Christian pacifism that would seek out and confront racial intolerance and injustice wherever it lurked. "It is a peace that destroys the group prejudice which makes a mockery of our so-called American Democracy and American Christianity."[70]

This was close to the ideas of *satyagraha* (soul force) and *agape* (understanding, creative and redemptive love for all men) that underpinned Gandhian non-violent direct-action tactics. It certainly may have been more than a coincidence that Howard Thurman and Mordecai Johnson, both of whom had visited India to study the Mahatma's methods, were the only two theologians Smith mentioned in his roll call of black activists in the "God's Answer" sermon. This was, after all, an era in which the search for a "black Gandhi"—or at least an exploration of the applicability of some of the Mahatma's ideas to the African American situation—became widespread among those with an interest in civil rights. The March on Washington Movement spearheaded by A. Philip Randolph, the early experiments with sit-ins by the Congress of Racial Equality (CORE), the AFSC's sponsorship of nonviolent workshops and visits to India by leading pacifists, and the FOR's 1947 Journey of Reconciliation all reflected and stimulated growing interest in the use of Gandhian tactics in the African American freedom struggle.

African American interest in Gandhi was initially most pronounced among a relatively small, well-educated, and highly politicized vanguard of black intellectuals and activists. Radio, however, may have provided an important mechanism for conveying at least the gist of Gandhi's protest philosophy to a much broader African American audience in the South and beyond. Of course, radio preachers were not the only sources of information on Gandhian protest tactics and their compatibility with African American Christianity available to the black masses. Some elements in the black press, some of the more politically engaged faculty at black schools and colleges, visiting speakers and publications from India itself, as well as some of the more militant occupants of the southern black pulpit, all contributed to the same educational process. Nevertheless, with African American literacy levels relatively low and the black press in the South frequently muzzled or hypercautious, with many black schools timid on racial matters for fear of losing white-controlled funding and black colleges attracting only a restricted elite clientele, and with formal church attendance in decline after World War II, radio had certain potential advantages in exposing black southerners to Gandhian strategies for social change.[71]

It was in this context that the radio sermons of Kelly Miller Smith, William Holmes Borders, and others may have helped to prepare the ground for a genuinely mass nonviolent southern civil rights movement. From at least the end of World War II, southern radio stations had promoted broadly Gandhian ideas to a wider constituency than newspapers, educators, or pulpit-bound ministers could ever hope to reach. This helped to extend the range of acceptable ideas and protest strategies available both to black leaders and to the black rank and file— a crucial contribution to the development of the freedom struggle. Because of the potency of the nonviolent movement of the 1950s and 1960s, there has sometimes been a tendency to assume that the mass of black southerners had some kind of natural predilection for this tactic. In fact, nonviolent direct action was but one of a repertoire of possible responses to Jim Crow and disenfranchisement that ranged from violent rebellion to the most passive kind of "fingers-crossed" accommodation. For a nonviolent movement to emerge, sufficient numbers of black southerners had to be taught about the revolutionary potential of nonviolence and persuaded that it fitted their cultural and spiritual traditions as well as their practical needs. In other words, Gandhian tactics had to be integrated into the worlds of African American protest politics and a distinctive brand of Christianity in which deliverance was a key theme.

Martin Luther King Jr. alluded to this very synthesis in 1960 when he asserted that "Christ furnished the spirit while Gandhi furnished the method" for the movement.[72] Bayard Rustin, perhaps the most important of King's many early mentors in the use of nonviolence, similarly appreciated that for southern participants in the movement this fusion of ideologies was essential. The starting point, Rustin stressed, was a belief in "Christian-based non-violence" onto which were grafted "the practical strategies and tactics Gandhism had adopted."[73] Such Christian-based nonviolence was also at the heart of Kelly Miller Smith's radio messages. The way of Christ, the way of peaceful protest to disarm and redeem one's enemy through the power of love and the steady insistence that justice must be served, was the rock on which the southern civil rights movement's hybrid brand of Christianized Gandhism was built.

Given their biracial popularity, these African American radio preachers may also have helped to familiarize some whites with Gandhian ideas, stressing their eminent respectability, reducing their alien overtones, and incorporating them into a framework of Judeo-Christian ethics that most white Americans, at least notionally, endorsed. Several nationally and biracially popular progressive white radio preachers, notably Walter Maier, Harry Emerson Fosdick, and his student Ralph Sockman, were also important in this respect. On the *Lutheran Hour,* for example, a show that regularly attracted millions of black and white listeners to Mutual and then CBS during the 1930s and 1940s, Maier taught that race was irrelevant to God and that racial prejudice was un-Christian.[74] While calling for a change of heart and an end to racist practices, some preachers even urged government intervention to protect minority rights from those whites who were unwilling or slow to change their practices. With a weekly audience of two million at the zenith of his NBC career, Fosdick in particular was highly influential. A dedicated pacifist and member of the NAACP Committee of 100 ("Dedicated to the Creation of an America of Justice and Equality for Our Negro Fellow Citizens"), Fosdick broadcast syndicated weekly sermons from New York's Riverside Church. The broadcasts caused much consternation among the white southerners he frequently berated for their racism. One incensed North Carolina businessman wrote to the preacher insisting that despite his and the NAACP's meddling, southern race relations were much better than in the North and "wondering why you are showing more interest in solving the racial problems of the South, many miles away, than you are in solving them in your own 'home town.'"[75] Not only did Fosdick call for an immediate end to segregation as the most egregious example of racial injustice in the nation, he was also one of the first to raise the possibility that an American variant on Gandhian nonviolence might help to secure that goal. He eventually became a founding member of the Committee for Nonviolent Integration around the time of the Montgomery bus boycott.[76]

Ultimately, it is impossible to quantify with real precision the impact of politically engaged radio preachers on the origins and early trajectory of the modern civil rights struggle. Evidence of how their broadcasts were consumed and interpreted by friend and foe alike remains elusive. Nevertheless, the barbs directed against Harry Fosdick and the bombs meant for William Holmes Borders suggest that at least some white segregationists saw them as a serious threat to the racial status quo. Moreover, there was even a certain latent radicalism, a kind of transformational imperative, in the messages of preachers whose racial attitudes had little in common with those of Fosdick or Borders. The idea that human beings were mired in sin and needed conversion in order to get right with God and fulfill His purpose was at the heart of the evangelical Christianity preached with particular zeal in the South. The call for individuals to transform themselves from a state of imperfection frequently fused with the drive to transform a wicked and sinful world into a virtuous one. Of course, among white southerners, this theological perspective rarely translated into a desire to rid the region of Jim Crow. Nonetheless, in the midst of a socially stratified region where the dominant racial discourse proclaimed the permanence of segregation, black inferiority, and white supremacy, evangelical Christianity provided a space where radical change, personal and collective transformation, was viewed as desirable and empowering.

In all likelihood few—if any—black southerners were ever converted into nonviolent warriors simply by hearing latent or manifest Gandhian messages in the sermons of radio preachers. And yet, it is not insignificant that as an Atlanta teenager Martin Luther King Jr. regularly tuned to the broadcasts of Borders, Fosdick, and Sockman. Radio was one of the first institutions to expose King to ways of conceptualizing the problem of racial injustice that were not drawn from his immediate, somewhat fundamentalist, southern Baptist background. Indeed, he was so enamored of hearing Fosdick and Sockman that he made a special study of their work while a student at Crozer Theological Seminary in Pennsylvania. The intellectual and rhetorical imprint of these progressive radio preachers—alongside influences from the black folk pulpit and many other black and white authorities—can be found everywhere in King's own sermons, speeches, and writings. Just as important, King knew that he was not alone in falling under the influence of these preachers: literally millions of Americans listened to national radio pulpits each week. Consequently, when King emerged as a public civil rights leader, he chose to weave the very words of Fosdick, Sockman, and Borders, as well as the broad sentiments they expressed, into the patchwork of his own rhetoric. In so doing, he was manipulating sentiments and phrases that would immediately strike a familiar, reassuring, and authoritative chord among those who had heard those men preach about transcendent love, interracial tolerance and goodwill, and the power of nonviolence. In the 1950s and 1960s, millions would hear and respond to King as he advanced much the same message, in much the same language.[77]

Perhaps even more compelling evidence for the impact of religious radio on the southern freedom struggle is the story of how a radio sermon set one young Alabamian on the path to the forefront of the nonviolent campaign to destroy Jim Crow. In the mid-1950s the future SNCC chairman and distinguished Georgia congressman John Lewis was still a schoolboy, living with his family in Troy in Alabama's rural Pike County. The Lewises were keen radio fans. On weekdays there was little time for listening, since family members were either working the fields or attending school. Weeknights and Saturday evenings were different, and the Lewis family gathered to listen to WLAC from Nashville. WLAC was home to John Richbourg, Hoss Allen, and Gene Nobles, three of the finest white rhythm and blues deejays in the South—although the Lewis family was at least as interested in the station's country music fare. On Sundays, however, their modest house in Carter's Quarters was alive with the gospel sounds and sermons carried by WRMA. This was a black-oriented station based in Montgomery that in 1953 was hailed by *Color* magazine as one of the leading forces for black progress in that city.[78]

One Sunday in early 1955, John Lewis tuned in to hear the morning services. The sermon that day was entitled "Paul's Letter to American Christians." It was delivered by a new young pastor at Montgomery's Dexter Avenue Baptist Church named Martin Luther King Jr. In his address, King transformed Paul's exasperated letter to the leaders of the early church at Corinth into a ringing indictment of Christian complacency in the face of racial discrimination in the United States, especially in the South. The climax of the sermon was a rousing call for all Christians, black and white, to join the battle against Jim Crow in the name of Christ, brotherhood, national unity, and justice. "Americans, I must urge you to be rid of every aspect of segregation. Segregation is a blatant denial of the unity which we have in Christ," King preached. "It scars the soul and degrades the personality. It inflicts the segregated with a false sense of inferiority, while confirming the segregator in a false estimate of his own superiority. It destroys community and makes brotherhood impossible. The underlying philosophy of Christianity is diametrically opposed to the underlying philosophy of racial segregation."[79]

As Lewis recalled, this was "*before*—before the Montgomery Bus Boycott . . . and some of the things that he said sorta stuck with me."[80] The broadcast had simultaneously heightened Lewis's smoldering resentment against Jim Crow and alerted him to an intriguing new voice of Christian-based resistance. "This was the first time I had ever heard something I would soon learn was called the social gospel—taking the teachings of the Bible and applying them to the earthbound problems and issues confronting a community and a society. I was on fire with the words I was hearing. . . . This young preacher was giving voice to everything I'd been feeling and fighting to figure out for years."[81] As Lewis explained, in retrospect his commitment to a lifetime of civil rights activism was that day "sparked by the voice of a man named Martin Luther King"—a voice he initially heard over a southern black-oriented radio station one Sunday morning.[82] When that voice surfaced again during the Montgomery bus boycott, this time with the language of Gandhian tactics grafted onto its Christian skeleton, Lewis was already primed and "took some particular note."[83]

In the final analysis, perhaps the most one can reasonably claim for the contribution of radio preachers during this period is that they played a more significant role in preparing ordinary black southerners to participate in a massive campaign of civil disobedience and nonviolent protest than historians of the early civil rights movement have previously recognized. Undoubtedly they helped to familiarize audiences of both races, in the South and in the nation as a whole, with the rationale, vocabularies, and tactics of Gandhian protest by presenting these through the prism of Christian pacifism. This was crucial to the successes of the 1950s and 1960s, when black demands were articulated and the movement's tactics legitimized by placing them firmly in the triple contexts of American civic ideals, middle-class respectability, and Judeo-Christian morality.

To the Brink of a Revolution

Taken together, the three chapters in part 1 illustrate how various racially progressive black and white broadcasters used radio to promote a diverse range of options for racial change in the South before mass protest emerged in the region. Although hampered by a myriad of logistical, ideological, financial, political, bureaucratic, and even violent constraints, these racial progressives had considerable success in using the airways to expand both the range and the intensity of public debate about segregation and disenfranchisement. Radio thus contributed to an important, if still tentative, shift in prevailing white popular and governmental attitudes toward black rights and, in particular, toward southern racial practices. It helped to create an environment in which increasing numbers of people came to view Jim Crow as an indefensible affront to America's democratic ideals and their own consciences.

Ultimately, however, radio's greatest contribution to the coming of the mass civil rights movement of the late 1950s and 1960s may have been in the cultural arena. Black-oriented radio, secular and sacred, was a vital force for sustaining black identity, self-respect, and communal solidarity. It would certainly be an error to judge the influence of radio on southern race relations during this period solely by the yardstick of how much it inspired formal political activism or carried strident messages denouncing Jim Crow. A broader, more flexible definition of what actually constitutes "politics" is necessary in order to assess radio's contribution to the origins and trajectory of the freedom struggle. Black-oriented radio's major strength was as an entertainment medium, working within a cultural context where African American entertainment was a highly politicized vehicle for survival and resistance. A 1950 Fisk University survey of radio listening habits among Nashville blacks clearly revealed as much. Although only a quarter of those surveyed said that they listened to radio specifically for "educational" purposes, the report concluded that many more respondents felt "that they get an 'education' from programs designed for entertainment."[84] Certainly some of the most explicit political messages found on either black-oriented or general-market radio were embedded within programs designed primarily as entertainment, *Wings Over Jordan* being a prime example. "Stations will not permit discussion of 'Negro rights' unless such topics are so intertwined with entertainment as to make the former very secondary," complained educator-activist L. D. Reddick in 1944.[85]

This situation was neither as negative as Reddick suggested nor entirely attributable to white station owners, managers, and sponsors, terrified about the consequences of allowing open discussions of racial politics on air. For one thing, civil rights advocates could usually sneak far more trenchant discussions of the southern racial situation onto shows billed as entertainment than onto heavily scrutinized public affairs programs and educational forums. Moreover, as the Fisk survey suggested, while some black leaders like Reddick may have seen the entertainment that invariably accompanied radio shows about racial matters as a frivolous distraction from the serious matters in hand, the African American masses had rather different ideas about how and why they listened to radio, and about what they expected to find there. They were definitely well used to extracting political messages and psychological nourishment from their leisure. In 1953 one broadcasting executive told *Sponsor* magazine that radio was easily the most important medium of both education and entertainment among black southerners, without ever quite capturing just how closely these two functions overlapped. "In the South, they read few newspapers, magazines, or books as compared with the time they spend with radio. Negroes get their information, their entertainment and their educational gains from radio and every survey has shown this."[86]

African American culture on southern radio helped to stimulate the sort of revolution in consciousness that was critical to organized mass protest. Yet African American entertainment on air could also help the black cause in other ways. In the late 1940s Georgia's segregationist governor Herman Talmadge warned Zenas Sears, then a deejay and program manager at the state-operated station WGST-Atlanta, to reject any requests to air NAACP announcements. The governor did, however, deem a few black gospel, jazz, and rhythm and blues shows acceptable.[87] Ironically, Talmadge may have been worrying about the wrong sort of programming. From the earliest days of radio, when Ethel Waters and Bessie Smith, Louis Armstrong and Duke Ellington, Cab Calloway and other black artists slipped through the mesh of prejudice and discrimination to take their place on the airwaves, the sounds of African American music had evaded many of the legal, habitual, geographic, and even psychological barriers that separated the races, even in the South. As Susan Douglas has neatly put it, "African-American music crept into white culture and white subjectivity, and this was critically important for the enlivening of American music and for the long, slow struggle out of Jim Crow America."[88]

This complex process of interracial cultural exchange, theft, homage, cross-dressing, and parody accelerated and became more pervasive after World War II as the spread of black-oriented radio created greater possibilities for whites to find black music and culture on the air. Insofar as rhythm and blues music on black-oriented stations began to attract a loyal following of young white southerners, it threatened to erode some of the traditional barriers between the races. Of course, this white love of black music did not always translate into anything resembling genuine acceptance of black equality. Whites had always been perfectly capable of admiring black skill, even genius, in the worlds of entertainment and sport without necessarily abandoning notions of white superiority or the privileges of a racial caste system. Yet if rock and roll was hardly the vehicle for racial integration that its detractors feared and some of its supporters hoped, it nonetheless encouraged a new, more ambiguous attitude toward racial differences among some southern fans.[89] The shared patterns of musical creativity and consumption made possible by radio's ability to transcend the formal spatial segregation of Jim Crow brought with them at least the potential to disrupt traditional racial beliefs and practices. This vital cultural work helped to create the climate of hope in which the mass civil rights activism of the 1960s blossomed. When it did, radio was once more close to the heart of the story.

PART 2

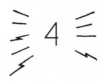

A Dixie Dilemma

Racially Progressive Radio in the Age of Massive Resistance

We could do anything we wanted.
Richard Stamz, WGES-Chicago

A Mass Movement Begins

On February 1, 1960, four African American students in Greensboro, North Carolina, launched a sit-in at the segregated lunch counter of the local Woolworth's. This was not the first time the sit-in tactic had been used, but the Greensboro demonstrations sparked an unprecedented chain reaction across the South. The protest announced the birth of a new era of genuinely mass non-violent direct-action protests that had been foreshadowed by earlier campaigns against segregated buses in Montgomery, Tallahassee, Atlanta, Birmingham, and other southern cities. Within weeks there were dozens of similar protests—usually with students, overwhelmingly black but sometimes white, in the vanguard. In April 1960, at a meeting at Shaw University in Raleigh, this youthful energy was channeled into the founding of SNCC, a new organization that would help to transform the pattern of race relations in the South and the nation.

The basic story of the southern civil rights movement is the subject of a vast and increasingly sophisticated literature and needs only brief rehearsal here.[1] Inspired by the students' example, established organizations such as CORE and the Southern Christian Leadership Conference (SCLC) were spurred into mass activism in the form of freedom rides, voter registration drives, and campaigns of civil disobedience against segregated public facilities all across the South. Although the NAACP generally eschewed these direct-action protests, it maintained a vigorous legal assault on Jim Crow. Even some southern white liberal organizations were rejuvenated by the rising tide of African American activism. The SRC, for example, had struggled to find a coherent and effective response to the *Brown* decision and the wave of massive resistance that had followed the Supreme Court's desegregation rulings. In the early 1960s, however, the SRC played a significant role in the campaign for black voting rights by administering the Voter Education Project (VEP).

In addition to such nationally and regionally prominent organizations, literally hundreds of local groups and individuals provided the foot soldiers and grassroots leadership for the mass mobilizations that became the hallmark of the civil rights movement during the first half of the 1960s. Those protests and the resolute, sometimes brutal, white resistance they encountered helped to persuade many white Americans to support the speedy abolition of Jim Crow. By the summer of 1963, the cumulative effect of hundreds of campaigns, growing popular sympathy for the basic democratic goals of the freedom struggle, and widespread concern about the impact of Jim Crow and racist violence on America's international reputation provoked a new level of federal interest in addressing the civil rights issue. After the passage of the largely toothless, if psychologically significant, Civil Rights Acts of 1957 and 1960—the first such legislation since Reconstruction—the Civil Rights Act of 1964 and the following year's Voting Rights Act reflected the triumph of a remarkable popular uprising. By mid-decade statutory segregation and disenfranchisement in the South were dead.

During this phase of the freedom struggle, radio continued to provide America's advertisers and sponsors with a uniquely effective means to reach a black consumer market that was worth some $27 billion in 1963. The steady expansion of the black economy alone was sufficient explanation for the continuing growth of black-oriented radio. By 1963 there were over eight hundred black-oriented stations, a more than threefold increase since 1953. Much of this growth took place in the South, where 78.2 percent of black households owned a radio by 1960—about 20 percent more than owned a television.[2] Given this level of audience penetration, many individuals and organizations continued to use the medium to further the struggle for black freedom and equality in the American South. The six chapters in part 2 examine different aspects of the relationship between radio and the southern civil rights movement from the late 1950s to the mid-1960s. Collectively, they reveal the significance of attempts by civil rights groups, individual activists, and sympathetic broadcasters to use radio to support and report the southern freedom struggle.

Although television and the print media were vitally important in promoting northern white and federal support for the attack on Jim Crow, movement workers also appreciated the unique potential of radio to help fashion favorable national attitudes toward the southern struggle. Indeed, the rise of massive resistance to desegregation meant that for a while it became harder than ever before to get racially progressive messages onto southern stations. This chapter describes both the enduring obstacles to pro–civil rights broadcasting within the South during the decade or so after *Brown* and the movement's efforts to use radio to encourage sympathy from blacks and whites beyond Dixie.

Southern Radio Faces Massive Resistance

In the early 1960s, Bogalusa was a city of 23,000 souls located in northeast Louisiana, just across the Pearl River from Mississippi. The proximity to Mississippi was more than a mere matter of geography: like much of the Magnolia State, Bogalusa was considered one of the most dangerous places in the Deep South for civil rights workers. According to historian Adam Fairclough, "By 1965 it boasted the largest and most powerful Klan organization in Louisiana, committed to perpetuating segregation through harassment, boycotts, beatings and murder."[3] It was the sort of place where federal court orders and legislation made little difference to traditional racial arrangements. Even after the Civil Rights Act of 1964, there were scant signs of desegregation. Despite the Voting Rights Act of 1965, few African Americans dared to register to vote. Ultimately, the sheer intractability and brutality of racial oppression in the city gave rise to a distinctively militant movement, with a local chapter of the Deacons for Defense offering armed protection against the mix of violence and intimidation routinely meted out to visiting civil rights workers and local activists.

One victim of those terror tactics was Ralph Blumberg, the white owner-operator of radio station WBOX. A St. Louis native who had come to Bogalusa from WABB-Mobile in 1961, Blumberg was an unlikely target for the wrath of the Klan. During his four years in Bogalusa he had exhibited no particular sympathy for the civil rights movement. His station had no connection to either the movement or the local black community: WBOX played nothing but country music and rarely editorialized on anything, let alone civil rights. Nevertheless, Blumberg's story illustrates the enormous pressure to adhere to a strict segregationist line that the forces of massive resistance were able to exert on southern broadcasters.

Ralph Blumberg's problems began in January 1965. One of several community leaders concerned about the economic effects of the rapidly deteriorating racial situation in Bogalusa, Blumberg cosponsored an invitation to liberal Arkansas congressman Brooks Hays to address an interracial meeting at St. Matthews Episcopal Church. Word got out that Hays planned to speak about the need for the South to comply with the previous summer's Civil Rights Act outlawing segregation in public accommodations. This did not go down well with influential elements in Bogalusa's civic and business leadership, while the local chapter of the Original Ku Klux Klan of Louisiana objected so vehemently that the engagement was canceled. Those who had supported the initiative were denounced as race traitors. "They said we wanted to integrate everything in town, which was just not true," Blumberg complained.[4]

In theory, one of the good things about owning a radio station in this situation was that Blumberg could go on air to explain himself to the people of Bogalusa. Unfortunately, however, his first WBOX editorial only made matters worse. Although he never endorsed integration, Blumberg made the mistake of advocating open discussion of the racial situation and urged his listeners, in a barely veiled reference to the Klan, to "fight the fear that hangs over this town like a plague." In response, Mayor Jesse Cutrer denounced Blumberg's speech as "a calculated attempt to further blacken our city's good name." Feeling its own honor especially besmirched, the Klan launched a ruthless campaign against the station and anyone associated with it.[5] Not content with reducing the number of sponsors for WBOX shows from seventy-five to just seven in only two months, vigilantes also smashed Blumberg's car windows, drove nails into his tires, and left a phone message with his wife warning that he had "signed his death warrant." Nightriders even fired shots into the station's transmitter hut, prompting WBOX's petrified engineer to resign. As the harassment intensified, Blumberg sent his wife and children back to St. Louis and moved out of the family home into a trailer on the edge of town. When the owner of the building from which WBOX broadcast summarily evicted Blumberg, presumably under pressure from the Klan, the plucky Blumberg still refused to quit. He continued to broadcast from his trailer home.[6]

By this time the Klan vendetta against WBOX had become an unlikely cause célèbre among both civil rights activists and those who valued freedom of speech. Lazar Emanuel, president of two New Jersey radio stations, telegraphed the NAB urging both "immediate strong counter actions in forms of cash grants to keep WBOX on the air" and a "resolution condemning flagrant denial of radio's right to freedom of expression."[7] A CORE worker explained the ambivalent nature of his own sympathy for WBOX: "Blumberg was never particularly an integrationist, and WBOX is not an integrationist station of any sort. But if it went under now, it would be a major victory for the Klan."[8]

Despite such expressions of support, by July Blumberg was down to just four regular sponsors. Three of these were national companies: Pearl Beer, BC Headache Preparations, and Esso Oil Products. The fourth was Lott and Sons Sales and Service, a local Honda motorbike dealership and repair shop owned by Bob Lott. A tattooed mechanic with impeccable southern credentials and a fondness for mild profanity whenever emphasizing a point, Lott was the only Bogalusa merchant to defy the Klan and continue advertising with WBOX. In explaining his loyalty, Lott drew in equal measure upon venerable southern notions of masculine honor and more universal principles of good business practice. "Hell, if I started letting people tell me who I could advertise with they might suddenly decide they don't like the Japanese or something—and most of my products are made by the Japanese," Lott explained. Although he was quick to add that "this don't mean I like this integration business" and denounce the federal government as "unreasonable," he was adamant that, having built his own business from nothing, he was damn well going to run it however he chose. This may not have been a giant leap forward for racial tolerance, but there were some signs of hope here. Not only did Lott grant kudos to the decidedly non-WASP Japanese for making great motorbikes, but in his mind economic considerations clearly trumped any casual allegiance to the Klan's overzealous racial correctness. This was a lesson that the movement learned early. One of its major strategies was to pressure southern civic and business leaders into accepting change by making the preservation of Jim Crow too costly, both in terms of the economically ruinous civil disorder that often accompanied mass demonstrations and through the withholding of black dollars from firms that refused to desegregate.[9]

While Blumberg admitted that the loyalty of Bob Lott "sort of restores my faith," it hardly generated enough revenue to save his station. Despite donations from various individuals and organizations within the broadcasting industry— and from a group of sympathetic New York merchants who paid for one hundred commercials, each consisting entirely of the preamble to the U.S. Constitution—Blumberg was eventually compelled to abandon his station. As he wryly observed, "We came here four years ago from Mobile to play country music and we're still playing it. And you know, I bet that 90 percent of the Klansmen are still listening."[10] Soon after he left town to take a job as a reporter at WCBS-TV in New York.[11]

The persecution of Ralph Blumberg and the ruin of his radio station after such a modest gesture toward racial change exemplified the perils confronting those seeking to get racially progressive messages onto southern radio in the late 1950s and early 1960s. Although it had never been easy to get southern stations to accept pro–civil rights broadcasts or even open discussions of race relations, the rise of the movement and the campaign of massive resistance that greeted it often made the situation even more daunting. Naked violence and other forms of intimidation directed against broadcasters considered sympathetic to the movement were certainly not unique to Bogalusa. In 1959, for example, segregationists in Manning, South Carolina, disabled the transmitter at WFIG rather than let the station air a speech by the NAACP's Roy Wilkins.[12] In this environment, even on the rare occasions when stations were willing to offer an opportunity to promote the struggle or denounce white racists, black leaders were sometimes simply too fearful to take full advantage. Movement sympathizer Curtis Welborne of WPNC-Plymouth in North Carolina complained to Elbert Jean of the Committee of Southern Churchmen, "We have attempted several times to get our local ministers to record simple messages deploring hate and inciting

FIGURE 6. During the late 1950s and early 1960s, militant segregationists such as John Kaspar often found it easier than civil
rights workers to gain exposure on southern radio stations like
WSB-Atlanta. Courtesy of *Baltimore News American* Photo Collection, University of Maryland, College Park.

love—without condemning any group specifically, although we have made no
attempt to censor that out either—and have failed utterly."[13]

With jobs and personal security at stake, only the bravest, most foolhardy, or
most cunning of southern deejays and announcers tended to align themselves
publicly with the civil rights movement. African American broadcasters in the
region felt particularly embattled. They may have had much riding on the success of the movement, but they were also the most vulnerable to physical and
economic reprisals for any signs of racial militancy. As a crucial part of the cultural apparatus that held the southern black community together and as tireless
promoters of black culture, pride, and identity, many of these black broadcasters
were already doing invaluable work for the movement. Nevertheless, before the

mid-1960s relatively few went so far as to promote civil rights protests on air or even to voice their own support for desegregation in public. Atlanta activist and radio personality Rev. Donald Vails probably got it about right when he explained that, just as in the late 1950s and early 1960s "a lot of the black community in Atlanta did not openly protest," so it was with "the deejays: some of them were very militant. Others wouldn't touch it."[14]

Regardless of the ever-present threat of segregationist violence, the single most compelling incentive for southern stations and their staffs to steer a racially conservative path was still the threat of lost revenue from disgruntled sponsors, advertisers, and white listeners. While this was an especially salient factor in the case of general-market stations, the trade magazine *Sponsor* reassured nervous potential advertisers that even at black-oriented radio stations, "Real controversy is usually avoided." This was "primarily because station operators don't want to frighten off advertisers—assuming," it added pointedly, "they have a crusading zeal in the first place."[15] With a few notable exceptions such as Zenas Sears at WAOK-Atlanta, Francis Fitzgerald at WGIV-Charlotte, and Phil Meltzer at WOKS-Columbus, Georgia, the white owners and managers involved in southern radio seldom exhibited any signs of this crusading zeal.

This was even true in a border state like Maryland. Deejay Del Shields remembered the almost hysterical reaction at black-oriented WEBB-Baltimore when he allowed a scheduled thirty-second newscast to overrun: "The manager came through the door and snatched the copy out of my hand and said, 'You will not educate these niggers at my expense. From now on there will be no news.'"[16] Farther south, the restrictions were even tighter. At WGOK-Mobile, Irene Johnson was one of a whole host of "Miss Mandys" who presented women's programs and hawked Maxwell House coffee, Crisco oil, and Martha White flour on the OK chain of black-oriented stations. Like Del Shields, Johnson blamed white ownership for her inability to speak openly in support of the movement. "We could not be as outspoken as some could, because we worked for a white chain," she explained.[17]

At WDIA in Memphis even the fiercely combative Martha Jean "the Queen" Steinberg accepted that no matter how much black deejays and announcers like herself approved of the fledgling movement, they really "couldn't raise too much sand, because most of us had to go back to white-owned radio stations who would have kicked our butts off the air." According to Steinberg, WDIA's owners John Pepper and Bert Ferguson simply "didn't care anything about us. No reflection. They just didn't care."[18] While the station's peerless community-oriented programs, both on and off the air, continued—raising thousands of dollars for local charities, sponsoring blood drives, creating little-league baseball teams, advertising educational and employment opportunities, and on one celebrated occasion even helping to trace a missing set of false teeth—WDIA usually kept the formal civil rights movement at arm's length. Nat Williams's *Brown America Speaks* may have been a pioneering African American current affairs program, but Williams still had to title his discussion of the first *Brown* decision "Should the Negro Ease Up in His Push for Integration," exemplifying the caution with which WDIA handled civil rights issues in the 1950s. "We think we're doing enough," explained co-owner Bert Ferguson, "and we'd rather move ahead as we've been moving in race relations than get involved in that."[19]

Little changed after WDIA joined the Sonderling chain of black-oriented stations in 1957, with Ferguson, the "southern aristocrat" as Steinberg called him, staying on as executive vice president and general manager. Nat Williams's daughter Natolyn remembered, "During the times when they were having the sit-ins a lot . . . and black kids were trying to get into Memphis State," *Brown America Speaks* "talked about those kinds of topics and subjects." However, her father's enthusiasm for the protests was much more evident in his columns for the black-owned *Memphis Tri-State Defender* newspaper than on his radio shows. The station's decision to begin regular editorials in June 1961 promised more opportunity for comment on the burgeoning movement, but it was several more years before these slots were used to express unequivocal support for direct-action protests or desegregation.[20] In the meantime, however, ingenious and sympathetic WDIA announcers found more subtle ways to indicate their approval of the movement. Local NAACP leader Maxine Smith recalled how newsman Ford Nelson would avoid personally commenting on the rights or wrongs of the freedom struggle, but then would "just ask a question—an open-ended question—and let you say everything you want! Those are the kind of tricks of the trade."[21]

Such subterfuge aside, WDIA's Rick Taylor appreciated that it was not until the movement itself created a sense of its own legitimacy, not just within the southern black community but also farther afield, that the station relaxed some of its constraints. According to Taylor, "WDIA did eventually reach a plateau, a posture where it began to actively advocate integration . . . but it would not be correct to say that it also had forged ahead in that area as a pioneer." Once it "saw what other stations were doing across the nation," WDIA took up the gauntlet and supported the movement "like no other station in Memphis."[22] In the early 1960s, however, WDIA's most conspicuous involvement with formal civil rights activism in Memphis came when the local NAACP picketed the station's Starlight Revue and other fund-raising events because they were held at the municipally owned Crump Stadium—one of many examples of Jim Crow in the city that the Association had pledged to attack. "We were trying to raise the consciousness of people," recalled Maxine Smith, but the station "didn't seem to have any sensitivity to the problem."[23] There were similar reservations about the station's *Workers Wanted* employment slot. This service relied heavily on information from such bastions of segregation as the Tennessee Department of Employment and the Tri-State Farm Labor Office in order to advertise a succession of stereotypically black job opportunities for cooks, farm hands, and maids. As Memphis historian Laurie Beth Green has summarized, this was a paradoxical moment when "WDIA's services and events further cemented listener loyalty, but circulated contradictory messages about white supremacy and Black pride."[24]

Two other factors combined to intensify scrutiny of what was broadcast on southern radio, especially black-oriented radio. The first factor was the interracial popularity of rhythm and blues music and its rock and roll offspring. The success of rock and roll exacerbated anxieties about the role radio might play in rending the fabric of racial segregation in the South. The same White Citizens' Councils and Ku Klux Klan groups at the heart of massive resistance were also at the forefront of the southern campaign against rock and roll. Some segregationist zealots, like Asa Carter in Alabama, even maintained that the music was an NAACP plot specifically designed to encourage integration. Its visceral rhythms and sexually explicit lyrics, Carter insisted, threatened to reduce "white girls and boys . . . to the level of the animal," expose them to the temptations of miscegenation, and thus contribute to the triumph of a degenerate, mongrel race.[25]

Since many young white southerners had originally become hooked on African American music by secretly listening to black-oriented shows on stations like WDIA and WHQB in Memphis, WLAC-Nashville, WGIV-Charlotte, WAOK-Atlanta, and KCOH-Houston, this racially transgressive capability alone justified closer examination of what was being said, as well as what was being played, on southern radio. "It was all right so long as blacks were listening," recalled King Records producer Ralph Bass. After the mid-1950s, however, a blend of racialized moral outrage against rock and roll, anxiety about the rise of African American protests, and fear of reprisals by the forces of massive resistance made station owners, managers, and program directors much more sensitive to anyone or anything that might be facilitating the challenge to Jim Crow. Bass observed that "if you had a black station you figured you gotta be twice as cool as the other cats, so they were screening everything."[26]

A second factor encouraging greater executive control over the conduct and connections of radio station staff was the fallout from congressional hearings into illegal "play-for-pay" deals between record companies, distributors, and deejays. In the wake of the 1960 payola hearings, new FCC codes placed much greater responsibility on station owners and management to monitor the conduct of their employees. While the intent of this legislation was to make sure that deejays were not favoring the products of selected record or publishing companies in return for kickbacks, it had the more general effect of increasing executive scrutiny of staff behavior both on and off air. Staff at black-oriented stations felt this shift especially keenly, since they were considered particularly vulnerable to payola. In part, this susceptibility was a consequence of the fact that the black-oriented stations devoted so much of their schedules to recorded music. It also reflected the low wages routinely paid to black deejays, many of whom relied on payola payments simply to survive.[27]

The new FCC rulings undoubtedly reduced payola opportunities. By requiring management to accept greater accountability for station programming, they also hastened the trend away from the brokerage system of financing black-oriented radio whereby deejays paid the stations for blocs of airtime and then "sublet" them to advertisers. Although the brokerage system was never quite so ubiquitous in the South as elsewhere, whenever and wherever it operated it tended to give deejays a modicum of independence from direct managerial control. In the 1960s, while the charismatic "personality deejays" who dominated black radio were allowed more freedom than their colleagues at heavily formatted Top Forty stations—not least because their improvisational skills at the microphone remained an important part of their commercial appeal—that latitude rarely extended to allowing endorsements of the civil rights movement on air.

In general, the extra scrutiny resulting from the FCC's new guidelines simply added one more obstacle to conspicuous support for the freedom struggle on southern radio, especially from black-oriented facilities. It was no coincidence, therefore, that the two most militant black voices regularly heard on radio in the South during the late 1950s and early 1960s emanated from outside the country. The Black Muslims' weekly *Muhammad Speaks* shows covered much of the United States, thanks to a 250,000–watt transmitter at XERF in northern Mexico. The proto–black power *Radio Free Dixie* programs produced by North Carolina's controversial NAACP leader and armed-self-reliance advocate Robert Williams were beamed in from Cuba. These shows were exceptional. Nevertheless, despite myriad difficulties a resourceful movement did manage to secure important assistance from southern radio even at the height of massive resistance. Before turning to that theme, however, it is important to consider how radio continued to help shape national attitudes toward the southern civil rights struggle and the quest for racial justice in the region. By helping to publicize the goals and methods of the early movement beyond Dixie, radio contributed to a national process of legitimization that by 1965 had persuaded even some southern stations to allow pro–civil rights programming.

Northern Radio and the Southern Movement

Given the obstacles to racially progressive programming in the South, it was inevitable that some of the most important radio broadcasting at the zenith of the southern civil rights movement should appear on stations or networks based outside the region. Although it is beyond the scope of this book to discuss the matter at any length, black-oriented radio stations beyond the South reported just about every major event in the southern campaign and many of the more obscure ones with a partisan passion and candor that was rarely possible in Dixie. To take just two big-city examples, WLIB–New York and WDAS-Philadelphia offered especially impressive on-the-spot coverage and editorial comment. The Novik brothers sent WLIB reporters to Montgomery to cover the bus boycott and in February 1956 dispatched Jimmy Hicks of the *Pittsburgh Courier* to report on events in Tuscaloosa where Autherine Lucy's attempt to desegregate the University of Alabama failed in the face of white mob violence.[28] In the fall of 1957 the station issued "Reports from Little Rock" every hour, while WDAS-Philadelphia stuck with the Little Rock desegregation story long after the mobs had disappeared from outside Central High School and most of the image-hungry television reporters had left. This sympathetic northern radio coverage contrasted dramatically with radio treatment of the crisis in Little Rock itself, where the leading local black-oriented station, KOKY, assiduously avoided civil rights issues. Seven years later, KOKY manager Eddie Phelan was still justifying his station's policy of refusing to endorse the movement. "By serving the black community as an entertainment and news medium and not committing ourselves in the controversial problems, we can serve best. When you choose one side you alienate people."[29]

In 1961 WLIB set up live interviews with freedom riders as they braved the fists and fire bombs of Klansmen in Alabama, and subsequently got a remarkable interview with CORE director and freedom rider James Farmer from his jail cell in Jackson, Mississippi. "We just called up the prison and asked for him," remembered station boss Harry Novik. "They said they'd have to go three flights up to get him. We waited."[30] The following year WDAS editorialized against the imprisonment of Martin Luther King and other civil rights workers in Albany, Georgia, joining "the Negroes of Georgia in mourning the death of Justice, and offering free mourning buttons to our listeners to be worn until these fighters are released." The station called for the mayor of Philadelphia to declare Sunday, July 22, 1962, "Mourn the Death of Freedom Day," and more than ten thousand people signed a petition against the Albany jailings.[31]

Much of this coverage depended on the actions of committed personnel at the individual stations. WLIB had the Novik brothers at the helm, while in Georgie "the Man with the Goods" Woods WDAS could boast one of black radio's most conspicuous activist deejays.[32] In addition to stimulating local protests against racial discrimination in Philadelphia—including a successful 1963 boycott that ensured local rival WIBG hired more black announcers—Woods and WDAS were consistent supporters and reporters of the southern freedom struggle.[33] His own formal affiliations were with the NAACP, which he served as a local vice president and Freedom Fund Committee treasurer. Yet Woods quickly recognized the significance of the new southern-based movement dominated by the SCLC and SNCC. Although perpetually disappointed by the lack of commitment to civil rights activities shown by most of his fellow black deejays—"basically they were clowns; they didn't do anything. Basically, they didn't get involved in demonstrations"—his own record of activism was impressive. In 1965, for example, Woods responded to Martin Luther King's call to join the Selma demonstrations by flying to Alabama, where he used his connections in the music business to organize a celebrity concert that benefited both SNCC and the SCLC.[34]

Woods's level of personal involvement in southern protest activities was unusual among northern deejays. Movement workers were certainly sensitive to the distinction between those stations that allowed civil rights groups airtime to publicize their programs or appeal for financial support and those stations and individuals such as Woods who actively participated in or even organized their own campaigns for racial justice. Still, by 1963 Woods and WDAS were part of an important informal network of black deejays and black-oriented stations around the nation that regularly made themselves available to movement representatives and, in particular, to SCLC president Martin Luther King. Hal Jackson and Jocko Henderson at WLIB, Mary Mason at WDAS's main Philly rival WHAT, Maurice "Hot Rod" Hulbert at WITH-Baltimore and later at WHAT, Purvis Spann, Herb Kent, and Wesley South at WVON-Chicago, and Larry Dean Faulkner and the transplanted Martha Jean Steinberg at WCHB-Inkster/Detroit formed the heart of this network in the North. According to Mary Mason, Dr. King "knew that the black community and black people were his strength and he knew that he could get his message across through black radio."[35]

Beyond the proselytizing strengths of northern radio, movement workers were also aware of its capacity to raise vital funds. When Marion Barry went to Washington, D.C., to raise money for SNCC in 1962, he headed straight for local black-oriented radio stations WOOK and WUST, recognizing that radio offered the quickest route to both black ears and black wallets.[36] This was common practice. In a 1965 tour on behalf of CORE's work in Mississippi, Richard Tinsley personally visited WABQ and WJMO in Cleveland, WJLB and WCHB in Detroit, and WAAF-Chicago, and received from each station a commitment to work on "a continuous fund raising program." Representatives from WVON and the veteran labor station WCFL in Chicago were also "interested in contributing money or their efforts for fund raising."[37] Each of the major civil rights organizations sought, with varying degrees of success, such help. In Detroit, black-oriented WCHB's Dollars for Democracy campaign in 1961 raised more than $1,000 to aid poor black sharecroppers targeted for voter registration efforts in Tennessee.[38] Announcer Eddie Castleberry recalled that during his time at WABQ-Cleveland and WVKO-Columbus in Ohio he "did a lot of fund-raising for Dr.

FIGURE 7. A former announcer at WEDR and WJLD in Birmingham and WMBM-Miami, Eddie Castleberry helped to raise funds for Martin Luther King at Ohio stations WABQ-Cleveland and WVKO-Columbus in the 1960s. Courtesy of Archives of African American Music and Culture, Indiana University.

King," although he candidly confessed, "That was more or less my contribution to the civil rights movement."[39] Sometimes raising funds overlapped with recruiting efforts. In December 1963, for example, WVON-Chicago conducted a Radio-thon intended to add twenty thousand members to the local NAACP rolls. More directly relevant to the southern campaign, Martin Luther King publicly acknowledged that WVON's Purvis Spann had generated crucial money for the 1964 Mississippi Freedom Summer, while by 1966 WHAT in Philadelphia had raised nearly $20,000 for King and the SCLC.[40] In the late 1950s and early 1960s, many other black-oriented stations made similar efforts, contributing modest but valuable amounts to a southern movement that was always strapped for cash.

African Americans were not the only people listening to black-oriented radio in the North during the 1950s and 1960s. Many northern whites—particularly young ones—often tuned in to black-oriented stations. In its bid to shift public opinion and ultimately create a more just and tolerant society, it suited the movement that young whites often heard about the campaign for racial equality from their favorite deejays in between records by black artists they adored. In fact, for obvious tactical and ideological reasons, the movement was always eager to gain access to white listeners via radio. The early movement saw its mission as an attempt to redeem the democratic promise and equalitarian soul of America, not just to secure African American civil rights. Certainly Martin Luther King—the one movement figure with sufficient prestige to command regular time on general-market as well as black-oriented radio—saw his appearances on the two broadcasting formats as serving complementary, but not identical, purposes. On black-oriented radio, the need for a mass movement against Jim Crow and a more general challenge to the evils of racism in America could be taken as given. Thus King tended to concentrate on promoting black solidarity, persuading the skeptical or impatient of the efficacy of nonviolent tactics, and encouraging black moral, practical, and financial support for the southern campaign. In his guest appearances on general-market stations, however, King spent more time simply describing the brutal, unconstitutional, and immoral nature of the oppression African Americans faced in the South. This he hoped would convince white listeners that it was essential to keep up the pressure for change, both on southern authorities and on the federal government, through mass direct-action protests.

This agenda was very apparent during a May 1964 news conference at the powerful 50,000-watt station WINS–New York. A reporter asked King whether he envisaged further protests in the South if the civil rights bill then before Congress passed. King reiterated that he was committed to destroying "the one thing that brings about a great deal of humiliation in the Negro community, mainly the denial of access to public accommodations." Reminding listeners that in the past the South had never shown much respect for federal laws designed to end discrimination, he conceded that further demonstrations were indeed likely. King warned that "some communities in Alabama, Mississippi, and maybe some of the other states, will resist. They will not comply immediately. . . . These are the places where we will have to work in a very determined manner to see that they comply." The protests, he explained, would be "localized in the sense that they will be dealing with public accommodations in the particular communities." King announced that, beyond the question of desegregating public accommodations in the South, "much of our work will be centered around the right to vote." He also confirmed that, once formal segregation and disenfranchisement in the South were taken care of, "I will have to do more work in the North than I have in the past." It would be fanciful to suggest that every white listener who heard this broadcast became a convert to the black cause in general or to King's strategy in particular. Nevertheless, those who listened in would have had a much better insight into the rationale for the SCLC's subsequent campaigns in St. Augustine, Selma, and Chicago, where public accommodations, the vote, and discriminatory real estate practices respectively were the principal targets. In this way, radio could help deepen popular understanding of what was at stake in the freedom struggle.[41]

Radio Networks and the Power of Nonviolence

The successes of the early southern civil rights movement, of which King was such a conspicuous part, depended heavily upon the use of nonviolent direct-action tactics. These tactics served the practical needs of a people confronted by the overwhelming legal, political, economic, and police power of the white South and ensured that the movement occupied the moral high ground whenever it faced the more savage expressions of white supremacy. As a result, those within the movement who worked with the print and electronic media, and those within the media who wished to help the black cause, repeatedly stressed the nonviolent aspect of the southern campaign and contrasted it with the violence of segregationist resistance. This was certainly the formula for most network radio coverage of the early campaigns in the South.

By the time a genuinely mass movement emerged in the early 1960s, the commercial networks CBS, NBC, ABC, and Mutual were no longer the dominant forces in radio that they had been during previous decades. Between 1947 and 1955, the proportion of radio stations that were network affiliates had declined from 97 percent to just 30 percent. In the late 1940s and early 1950s, drama shows and news broadcasts had been the most popular programs distributed by these networks. Later in the decade, however, as many of the best dramas, soap operas, and variety shows moved over to television, news became the single most important part of network radio operations. This shift within the industry occurred just as the movement in the South hit its stride. Civil rights workers were the beneficiaries of revamped and increasingly professional and sophisticated network radio newsrooms, often staffed by dynamic and sympathetic young reporters such as Dan Rather who were eager to make a name for themselves—if only to earn a stab at television.[42]

The relationship between national radio and television coverage of the early movement was complex and, in the main, complementary rather than strictly competitive. The images of southern civil rights confrontations beamed by the television networks into living rooms across America and around the globe undeniably had a particularly intense emotional impact on those who saw them, revealing in graphic detail the injustice, hatred, and brutality that characterized Jim Crow. Yet network radio reporters also did sterling work in spreading news of the southern civil rights struggle to a national audience. Like their television counterparts, they helped to educate Americans beyond the South about the freedom struggle and emphasized the legitimacy of the tactics by which it was being waged. Alongside other media, radio helped to promote the mix of public outrage and sympathy that stirred demands for change in the South and ultimately compelled greater federal action on civil rights. As Columbia University journalism professor William Wood put it, "Suddenly men and women all over the country were as close as across the street to the crucible of revolution. Whites everywhere were awakened and shaken up."[43]

Just as important as the commercial radio networks in publicizing the movement's widespread, if by no means universal, adoption of nonviolent direct-action tactics were the programs made by the independent Pacifica network and by the Riverside Church's WRVR facility in New York. The *New York Times*'s media critic Jack Gould described WRVR's six hours of programming on the 1963 Birmingham campaign, tellingly entitled *Birmingham: A Testament of Nonviolence*, as "not only a first class journalistic coup but . . . a remarkable social document for the ear. . . . The effectiveness of the WRVR coverage lay in the station's determination to let the events speak for themselves." The broadcasts were full of the sounds of "terror and hysteria in the street, the forbidding raucousness of police bullhorns and the chilling shrill of sirens," presenting "a graphic picture of crisis which the imagination of the listener filled out." There was also a disturbing recording of a Klan cross-burning rally that took place the day before the bombing of the Gaston Motel where the leaders of the Birmingham civil rights movement regularly met. As Gould wrote, "The remarks of the speakers constituted their own vivid editorial on white extremism." At the emotional heart of the programs was the contrast between these hooded apostles of ignorance, hatred, and violence and the image of Martin Luther King, the apostle of understanding, love, and peace, "telling his followers that the policy of nonviolence should not be breached under any provocation."[44]

Pacifica also earned praise from Jack Gould for its coverage of the Birmingham campaign in two programs made by its New York outlet WBAI. The shows blended the "actuality radio" style of the WRVR broadcasts with more traditional radio techniques in which a narrator described the action and conducted postevent interviews.[45] Like WRVR, Pacifica consistently stressed the importance of nonviolence, not just in its coverage of Birmingham but also in the extensive treatment of the southern movement produced by its three flagship

FM stations—KPFA-Berkeley, KPFK–Los Angeles, and WBAI—and distributed for use by other stations around the nation. Incorporated in 1946, the left-leaning Pacifica Foundation with its commitment to pacifism and social-justice issues had long been a vocal opponent of racial inequities and a proponent of nonviolent protest to expose and eradicate them. The Foundation's initial mission statement had envisioned a socially responsible radio network that would "engage in any activity that shall contribute to a lasting understanding between nations and between the individuals of all nations, races, creeds, and colors."[46] Moreover, there was always a special commitment at Pacifica to airing "minority points of view which seldom receive a hearing on radio" and to emphasizing "the basic ethical realities in human relations which underlie all public problems of peace and freedom."[47]

Given this agenda, Pacifica was excited when a nonviolent movement for racial justice emerged in the South. In late 1959 and early 1960, for example, it cooperated with the Highlander Folk School on a program dealing with the history of the School and its current work. At the core of the show was an examination of the Citizenship School program that promoted political education and voter registration among disenfranchised African Americans. First aired on KPFA on May 31, 1960, and repeated on WBAI on June 17, the broadcast featured interviews with Highlander founder Myles Horton and leading figures in the South Carolina Sea Islands Citizenship School initiative, including Septima Clark, Esau Jenkins, and Bernice Robinson. Even more compelling listening were excerpts from the vindictive "public nuisance" hearings brought against Highlander by its segregationist enemies and the recordings of an adult citizenship class. This program was a fine example of how Pacifica's broadcasts carefully dissected various aspects of movement culture and presented them in an emotionally engaging and intellectually challenging way. Pacifica's relationship with Highlander continued to flourish throughout the 1960s, with Horton appearing regularly to update listeners on his work and the School's battles with southern authorities.[48]

One of Pacifica's most important shows about the movement in the South was a two-hour documentary called "After the Silent Generation." The program placed the sit-in movement and the newly formed SNCC within the broader context of a rising tide of socially constructive student activism that also embraced free-speech and peace issues. With its passion for participatory democracy and community mobilization, SNCC had quickly become the embodiment of nonviolent protest at Pacifica.[49] Members of the organization regularly appeared to explain their goals and methods, as did other devotees of direct action. In the midst of the 1961 freedom rides, for example, Elsa Knight Thompson, the indomitable head of public affairs at KPFA, interviewed veteran pacifist James

Farmer. The following year Rosa Parks was the focus of a profile on the move-ment's putative origins in Montgomery, while in 1964 Fannie Lou Hamer's life served as the vehicle for a documentary on the Mississippi Freedom Summer.[50]

Two traits distinguished these Pacifica broadcasts from many others devoted to the early southern civil rights campaign. The first was their intellectual and analytical rigor. Although there was overwhelming sympathy for the freedom struggle at the network, these programs were produced by people deeply en-gaged with the practical and ethical questions raised by grassroots organizing and nonviolent protest. Consequently, platitudes and casual assumptions sel-dom passed unchallenged. The second distinctive aspect of the Pacifica civil rights programs was the sheer amount of time the independent network was able to devote to them. A 1963 interview with the SCLC's Wyatt T. Walker on the Birmingham campaign lasted more than an hour. The following August, Donald Wolfe broadcast the whole of an important article by the SRC's executive director Leslie Dunbar titled "The Changing Mind of the South," originally published in the *Journal of Politics*.[51]

Pacifica, much like the Riverside Church's WRVR, enjoyed several advan-tages in maintaining this extensive and insightful movement coverage. Whereas the owners, managers, and sponsors of commercial networks and individual stations often agonized over how—or whether—to address civil rights issues, those who ran Pacifica and WRVR had no such qualms. Staff often saw them-selves as participants in, as well as chroniclers of, the movement. Moreover, Pacifica relied heavily on listener subscriptions. This meant that it was bank-rolled by the same kind of people who worked for the network, and there was rarely any audience opposition to in-depth coverage of the most important social topic of the era. As Jack Gould observed, WRVR and Pacifica demonstrated "one of the major advantages of non-commercial radio. The availability of extended time free from assorted commercial pressures does lead to both depth of treat-ment and outspokenness seldom available elsewhere on the dial." Gould went even further, arguing that radio had some distinct advantages over television in reporting on the racial revolution spreading across the South. "The relatively modest economic demands of radio production make it possible for such sta-tions to do things and go places that in television would be financially out of the question." Although he appreciated that "television inevitably pre-empts public attention in news coverage," Gould maintained that the best radio stations could "give the visual medium a run for its money . . . [in] incisive and substantial reporting."[52]

Gould had a point. Television coverage thrived on the visual and visceral. Its stock-in-trade was the emotionally charged scene that presented major moral issues in simple, dramatic, and often highly persuasive terms. When in March 1965 network television showed state troopers firing tear gas at peaceful marchers in Selma, beating them with clubs as they sought to escape, and rampaging through the midst of fallen and fleeing bodies on horseback, nobody watching was left in much doubt as to how the forces good and evil were arrayed in Alabama. Yet the visual medium's hunger for these sorts of dramatic images meant that it seemed somehow less effective when dealing with less visually arresting, but still critical, stories and ideas relating to the freedom struggle. Indeed, television's voracious appetite for vivid on-screen confrontations and violence partly explained why it lost interest in relatively peaceful protests such as those in Albany in 1961–62 that lacked the necessary flashpoints.

Radio worked differently. Although it also tried to offer compelling live coverage from movement hotspots, it was not quite as driven as television by the need to capture the immediate moment. It could allow itself more time to present thoughtful analyses of complicated issues. The very act of radio listening required more active, cerebral engagement from audiences than did television viewing. Listening to the radio encouraged audiences to think about the content of news broadcasts and public affairs programming, rather than just react viscerally to the horrors paraded on screen. Of course, in reality most people heard some coverage of the movement on radio and saw some coverage of it on television. The point is that each medium, as well as the magazines and newspapers that offered even deeper analysis, brought something different to public discourse about race relations and the struggle for civil rights in the South.

In the late 1950s and early 1960s, movement workers fully appreciated the positive ways that both WRVR and Pacifica presented their nonviolent credentials to a national constituency and helped to encourage sympathy for the southern freedom struggle. The movement could count the benefits of such coverage in terms of recruits, financial help, and an invaluable sense of camaraderie with national campaigns for free speech, peace, and social justice. Birmingham native Angela Davis recalled that, like many other young black activists, she came to expect support and "less biased coverage" from the Pacifica network than from any other white-run media.[53] To be sure, there were limits to the functional effectiveness of these noncommercial, pro-movement broadcasts. For example, they found precious little exposure in the South. Moreover, WRVR and Pacifica both tended to preach to the converted: to northern audiences of like-minded liberals and radicals who were already broadly convinced that Jim Crow needed to go and that direct-action protest and federal intervention were appropriate mechanisms for hastening its demise. Nevertheless, as the civil rights movement found itself at the center of an upsurge in social activism throughout the nation, so Pacifica in particular provided one kind of bond between diverse groups of activists, helping to integrate them into a loose national network of progressive individuals and organizations.

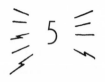

Edwin T. Randall and Friendly World Broadcasting

Radio and White Racial Liberalism in the Age of Mass Protest

Widespread feelings seem to be so high that the use of mass media
[is] ... urgent as one of the few ways to get into homes and hearts
closed to almost any other approach to saying anything.
Olcutt Sanders, AFSC, 1957

Ed Randall and the American Friends Service Committee

While sympathetic radio broadcasts by Pacifica and WRVR rarely found their way onto southern airways in the late 1950s and early 1960s, a number of predominantly white liberal organizations did try to use the medium to ease racial tensions and promote orderly desegregation in the South. Many of the most successful efforts along these lines were the work of a single man, Edwin T. Randall, who managed to get progressive racial messages onto southern radio even at the height of massive resistance. The story of Randall and his Friendly World Broadcasting project, supported at different times by the AFSC, the SRC, and the SCEF, illustrates the nature, strengths, and limitations of white liberal efforts to use radio to promote peaceful racial change in the South from the early 1950s into the very different climate of the late 1960s.

The son of a Methodist minister, Ed Randall was born in Leavenworth, Kansas, on June 30, 1896. As he accompanied his peripatetic father around the country, his education included stints at schools in Tacoma, Pasadena, Oak Park (Illinois), Anderson (Texas), and Seattle, followed by fitful attendance at the University of Oregon, the College of Puget Sound—where his father was founder and president—Princeton, Baker University in Kansas, Willamette University in Oregon, the University of Chicago, and Baylor. After service in the Aviation Section of the Signal Corps during World War I, Randall finally cobbled together enough credits to earn a degree from Northwestern. He worked as a newspaper journalist and a probation officer before embarking on a radio career. Combining his technical training from the military with strong religious convictions, Randall became the national radio director of the Christian Rural Overseas Program. He also hosted popular commercial programs on stations in Minneapolis–St. Paul, Philadelphia, and Worthington, Ohio. It was while working at WFRD-Worthington that he hatched the idea for what later became Friendly World Broadcasting.[1]

In 1950 Randall approached the AFSC about making some programs on its behalf. Respected Ohio Quaker George A. Patterson contacted the Committee urging serious consideration of Randall's offer. Patterson wrote that Randall had "developed a large listening public" on WFRD and was very good at interviewing people. Moreover, Patterson vouched for Randall's special interest in civil rights issues, noting that among the guests he had invited onto his show was the influential Gandhian strategist and sometime AFSC worker Bayard Rustin. Randall "has considerable knowledge of the AFSC and what it has done and what it is trying to do," Patterson continued. "He has discussed on air the FOR and the Federal Employment Practices Commission work of the AFSC and [is] fearless of controversial subjects if a principle is involved."[2] From the AFSC's perspective both the timing of Randall's approach and his attachment to the nonviolent tactics propounded and practiced by Rustin and FOR were especially fortuitous.

Prior to accepting Randall's offer, the AFSC admitted that its "efforts to reach the widest American public through the medium of radio was restricted to informal spot programs" such as occasional guest appearances by Committee staff on established public affairs shows.[3] The AFSC attempted to improve this situation in late 1950 and early 1951, budgeting $10,000 for radio initiatives that included a proposed weekly AFSC news commentary show on KYW-Philadelphia. When this deal collapsed, the AFSC had abandoned its attempts to find a permanent home for its own radio programs.[4] Disillusioned, the Committee slashed its annual radio budget to $2,500 and reassigned radio director George Loft to other duties. At a finance meeting in October 1951 radio was ranked last among the AFSC's budgetary priorities, and public relations director John Kavanaugh conceded, "We have been trying to 'get off the ground' in this field for the last three years, but haven't gotten very far."[5] In the context of the AFSC's frustrations with its own radio experiences, Edwin Randall's offer to produce a regular stream of programs for distribution around the nation seemed like an attractive and inexpensive option.

Initially supported in part by a small Ford Foundation grant to the AFSC, but funded in large measure out of his own pocket, Randall always worked on the proverbial shoestring. During the 1950s, however, he produced literally thousands of five-to-seven-minute taped slots—419 between October 1954 and September 1955 alone—on various topics dear to the AFSC. The format usually consisted of a single commentator of some eminence presenting his or her views on the great social and moral issues of the day. Randall regularly mailed lists of these *Friendly World* programs to stations around the country, sending the recordings themselves to any outlets that expressed an interest in broadcasting them. Randall insisted that these slots should not be used to fulfill a station's sustaining—or free public service—programming requirements, since this might induce stations to hide them away in unpopular time slots. Instead he asked stations to place them into their regular commercial news and public affairs schedules, hoping this would ensure "a favorable audience."[6]

In the 1950s Randall produced dozens of shows relating specifically to southern race relations, as well as many more devoted to the general themes of tolerance and understanding. Among the first programs on the segregation issue to arouse major interest were five short reports by the AFSC's Irene Osborne on the Washington, D.C., school desegregation that had taken place with seemingly little opposition shortly before the first *Brown* decision. Osborne stressed, however, that this was not an overnight triumph but was the result of a long, painstaking exercise in community mobilization and dialogue with the school authorities and other municipal and federal leaders. Osborne noted that she and other AFSC organizers had been patiently working with local community activists "for more than a year before the desegregation program began." These shows were more than mere reportage. They were designed to be educational, inspirational, and exemplary. "We feel that a great deal has been learned that might be helpful and encouraging to others facing the same problems," Randall wrote in his pitch to radio stations considering taking his programs.[7]

Given their subject matter, it was little surprise that few southern stations accepted the chance to broadcast Irene Osborne's description of the way in which black activism had helped to secure the peremptory desegregation of Washington's public schools. Of the twenty-one stations airing the reports, only four were in the South: WTSP–St. Petersburg, Florida; WGAP-Maryville, Tennessee; WDVA-Danville, Virginia; and KFYO-Lubbock, Texas. This was a modest start, but Ed Randall persevered. Over the next few years, as the African American campaign against segregation gathered momentum and massive resistance hardened, his programs enjoyed increasing exposure in the South. By early 1957 Randall was able to report that in the previous two years a total of seventy-seven southern stations had requested at least one tape from him—and fifty-nine had asked for more than one. Moreover, while many of these stations were tiny local outlets, twelve were 50,000-watt powerhouses. Of course, not all of the tapes requested by southern stations pertained directly to race relations. Yet even on this most touchy of subjects there was considerable demand. For example, twenty stations in the South had taken the 1956 report by Clarence Pickett of the

AFSC from Montgomery, including three Alabama stations and WDIA in Memphis.[8]

Even more popular was a broadcast in late 1958 applauding the efforts of two thousand citizens to persuade the governor of Virginia to reopen the public school system in Norfolk, which local authorities had simply closed rather than comply with a court order to integrate. "The Norfolk tape seems to have started a kind of brush fire," Randall wrote excitedly to the SRC's executive director Harold Fleming.[9] As many as 150 southern radio stations may have taken the Norfolk show. White liberal stalwarts Carl and Anne Braden were big fans, writing both to urge SCEF president Jim Dombrowski to support Randall's work and to congratulate Randall himself on a show that they considered "excellent, both in content and arrangement." The Bradens were especially impressed by how Randall brought out the reasonableness and justness of the desegregation struggle by featuring a variety of opinions. Randall interviewed pro-integration community figures like the leader of the Norfolk Ministerial Alliance but also featured white parents who did not necessarily like the idea of integration but preferred it to the prospect of no public schools at all. Randall also gave die-hard segregationists more than enough rope with which to hang themselves. "You let the segregationists have their say, and the contrast between them and the thoughtful and disturbed people who want the schools opened speaks so loudly for itself that no comment is needed. The total effect is one of great impact."[10]

It is easy to see why Randall's productions found an unusual level of acceptance on southern radio. Amid growing militancy on both sides of the racial divide, Randall's programs consistently focused on stories of individual and community reconciliation; they threw the spotlight on calm, responsible leaders, both black and white, who favored dialogue, education, and moral suasion in order to resolve the South's deepening racial crisis. They seemed like a lifeline to embattled white racial moderates driven to silence and impotency by the rise of massive resistance. Thus when Clarence Pickett reported for Randall on the Quaker mission to Montgomery in early 1956, it was "to commend responsible parties on both sides for avoidance of violence in the real and very serious conflict, to talk to both sides and to discover the human values involved." Revealingly, Randall was at pains to assure any southern stations tempted to take Pickett's broadcast that it "very definitely does not represent the approach of a group of northerners undertaking to tell people what to do, but of a group of Christian people seeking to understand a situation in which people on both sides are trying to work out baffling problems in terms of the Christian way of life."[11] In other words, the broadcasts echoed the traditional white emphasis on indigenous southern efforts to promote interracial goodwill and understanding as the keys to civic order and social harmony. Because Randall's messages seemed reassuringly familiar and relatively moderate amid the maelstrom of black protest activity and increasingly violent white resistance, many southern program directors saw fit to use them.

Randall's ability to gain access to southern radio with his AFSC-sponsored programs had much to do with his mastery of the rhetoric of interracial understanding, gradualism, and moderation that continued to characterize southern white racial progressivism. The irony here was that the AFSC was actually far more radical than all but a handful of white southerners when it came to the methods, timetable, and goals of the civil rights struggle. The AFSC supported an immediate end to segregation and disenfranchisement and, although it much preferred persuasion and consent to coerced compliance, the Committee had few problems with the idea of federal action to help rectify such injustices. The AFSC certainly had no objection when Randall invited the NAACP's Washington representative Clarence Mitchell to discuss the urgent need for the federal legislation that became the 1957 Civil Rights Act.[12]

Unlike many southern racial progressives, the AFSC also had no qualms about supporting black direct-action campaigns on the streets of the South to hasten the end of racial discrimination—provided that the demonstrators, like those Clarence Pickett lauded in Montgomery, were nonviolent. Indeed, Randall's programs frequently dwelt on the righteousness, as well as the effectiveness, of nonviolence, helping to extend public approval for the use of the tactic in the pursuit of quintessentially American rights. In 1956, for example, one program had featured English Gandhian Reginald Reynolds; a year later James Bristol, the AFSC's director of peace education, had talked about "the meaning of non-violence as a means of bringing about social change," drawing examples from Montgomery and South Africa.[13]

One of the most attractive features of nonviolence for civil rights activists was its potential for bringing about an end to racial discrimination not by compulsion but by redeeming racist hearts and minds. This was one reason why Randall liked to feature southern converts, even grudging and equivocal ones like Omar Carmichael, the superintendent of schools in Louisville. In 1957 nine southern stations, including the 50,000-watt WSB in Atlanta, took a *Friendly World* show featuring Carmichael's account of school desegregation in Louisville. Although an avowed segregationist, Carmichael had reluctantly accepted the implications of *Brown* and dutifully begun the integration of the school system, thereby providing leadership in what Randall gushed was "one of the most remarkable demonstrations of racial democracy in our history." On air, Carmichael freely confessed his surprise at the ease with which a substantial amount of school integration had already taken place and the fact that black children had not been a disruptive influence in the classroom at all.[14]

With the Klan resurgent and the Citizens' Councils blossoming, Randall was keen to publicize any signs that, beyond a cadre of die-hard segregationists, white racial attitudes were changing. He also hoped to persuade the mass of white southerners to recognize the basic humanity of African Americans, the righteousness of the black struggle, and the disfiguring effects of Jim Crow on the lives of both races. This agenda meant that *Friendly World* sometimes featured influential white racial moderates who were still some way from fully embracing the cause of immediate integration. A good example was the South Carolina gentleman farmer and English professor James McBride Dabbs. Introduced by Randall as a "dyed-in-the cotton six-generation Southerner," Dabbs had become convinced that segregation would have to go, and he joined the SRC, eventually becoming its president in 1957. Nonetheless, Dabbs had serious reservations about the wisdom of the federal government trying to enact immediate desegregation. He believed that ordinary southerners should be persuaded, rather than compelled, to participate willingly in dismantling segregation. As historian John Egerton has put it, Dabbs's "faith was that the rank and file of decent southerners were the real majority, and his aim was to touch them gently, to appeal to their innate sense of fair play." In 1957 Dabbs appeared on one of Randall's programs, denouncing the racist hotheads of massive resistance and appealing to the mass of white southerners to obey their better moral instincts and extend the region's reputation for "courtesy, good manners, and a sense of real values" into the racial arena.[15]

To many black activists and the AFSC, Dabbs's plea for moderation and patience now seemed anachronistic. Although genuinely committed to eventual desegregation, he personified a brand of white gradualism that appeared to be part of the South's racial problem rather than a creed that might secure black equality before the dawn of the next ice age. Dabbs's appearance on Randall's radio program, along with earlier appearances by whites whose progressive credentials were much more dubious, spurred a series of terse exchanges between Randall and the AFSC over the future of the radio project. These exchanges revealed very different conceptions of what radio might realistically contribute to the struggle for racial equality in the South and about who should be the primary targets for *Friendly World* broadcasts.

Aside from Ed Randall, the major participants in this debate were Olcutt Sanders, Alex Morisey, and Barbara Moffett of the AFSC's Community Relations Division.[16] While Moffett and Morisey were suspicious about the content and usefulness of some of Randall's broadcasts, Sanders was greatly impressed with his efforts. Moreover, Sanders sympathized with the logistical problems Randall faced in trying to get airtime for any racial moderates, let alone advocates of immediate desegregation, on southern stations. With this in mind, Sanders wrote to Morisey in January 1957, listing five categories of speakers who "under almost any circumstances . . . would not likely be generally acceptable" on southern radio: "1. Negroes, 2. people identified with integrationist organizations like the NAACP and the Southern Regional Council, 3. people connected with any presently integrated enterprises . . . , 4. people who have come into prominence primarily because they have expressed themselves as whole heartedly in favor of or willing to accept complete integration, 5. people who would be identified as 'carpetbaggers.'" Although Randall actually did manage to feature some NAACP and SRC representatives, Sanders's basic point was well made. There was, he concluded, a "pretty narrow [field] in which we must look for persons who would be useable in the South."

Despite these limitations, Sanders still felt that Randall's radio slots could serve a useful function by featuring southerners like journalists Hodding Carter and Jonathan Daniels "who have stuck their necks out, even a little way." He even provided a list of nine themes that would resonate with southern social and religious traditions and that might therefore pass through the mesh of radio censorship if introduced by respected southern moderates. Acceptable themes included such statements as "The Supreme Court decision is the law of the land and we might as well get used to it" and "the decision is in harmony not only with law but with Christian conscience in an issue which is fundamentally a religious problem and which permits of only one solution in Christian terms" and "distinctions of race in educational, economic, and social life should be made as inoperative as color of hair and eyes."

If there was nothing much for the AFSC to take issue with here, more problematic was the fact that Sanders was willing to feature guests who did not actually favor integration at all, provided that they would publicly "deplore violence and intimidation in any form against the securing by Negroes of the rights which have been declared theirs by law." Like Randall, Sanders felt that at a time when "even the slightest suggestion of an exception to segregation will be inflammatory," such broadcasts were a more realistic possibility. In their minds, the choice was between reaching southern whites in this way—with radio messages that urged calm, obedience to the law, and the need for interracial dialogue and toleration—and not reaching southern whites at all.

Barbara Moffett and Alex Morisey took a very different view. Both fundamentally objected to the presence on AFSC-sponsored radio slots of anyone who, in Sanders's phrase, still took "a position short of full, immediate, and outright integration." In a lengthy memorandum to Sanders after an AFSC staff meeting at Guildford College in North Carolina, Morisey simply stated, "We see no valid reason to help those who would admit on our programs that they do not favor integration even though they deplore violence and intimidation against Negroes." Invoking the name of John Kaspar, who was making a name for himself by stirring up segregationist violence in the South, Morisey concluded: "If we can in conscience support the pro-segregationists then, to carry the idea to an extreme, we would be obligated to provide a forum for John Kaspar or some equally despicable characters."

Morisey and Moffett both felt that Randall and Sanders were too pessimistic in assuming that certain groups or individuals would always be "unacceptable" on southern radio. To hold such a view, Morisey argued, was tantamount to accepting that white southern racial attitudes might never change. "The situation in the South is not static," he insisted, "and those who work in the South or close to the problems of the region do not grant this. If they did then they would be foolhardy to extend themselves on such a hopeless task." Barbara Moffett conveyed similar sentiments from the AFSC staffers who had met at Guildford College: "Perhaps we did not need to set our sights too low and . . . there was real possibility for getting a rather forthright message on some stations." For Morisey and Moffett, the real task confronting those involved with the AFSC's radio project was to try to expand the range of voices deemed acceptable on the southern airways to include those who urged the immediate destruction of Jim Crow.

Not content with urging Ed Randall to feature more radical white southerners on the air, Morisey and Moffett also urged him to pay more attention to the feelings of African Americans at the heart of the freedom struggle. Morisey pointed out that an increasingly mobilized black community was unlikely to take kindly to having cautious southern white moderates with a penchant for temporizing and tokenism paraded as the best hope for racial justice in the region. Indeed, Morisey contended that southern moderates like journalists Hodding Carter and Jonathan Daniels, both of whom Sanders had suggested would make ideal spokesmen on AFSC-sponsored shows, "may not serve our purpose, rather, they may help defeat it." Daniels, he pointed out, "has taken a moderate stand but he asks Negroes to 'voluntary segregate' themselves. This no self-respecting Negro can stomach, as much as he appreciates the Jonathan Daniels as compared with the John Kaspar."

Morisey also believed that the AFSC should feature more African Americans on its radio shows. "One of the grave deficiencies we face is the fact that too little opportunity has been given for Negroes to be heard on the subject of their own aspiration," he complained to Sanders. "The major media of mass communications, controlled almost exclusively by white persons, still effectively denies them this opportunity. Surely the Service Committee can make an effort to right this wrong?" Barbara Moffett agreed. The AFSC, she explained, should help the South to understand the "aims and methods of the NAACP . . . an educational job of highest priority." She urged Randall and Sanders to try to get Roy Wilkins on a program to describe "exactly what the processes are that are used by the

NAACP and what its goals are." She also recommended that they approach Martin Luther King, offering him airtime to "get his message before more people in the South" and, more particularly, to publicize the nonviolent tactics he had deployed so effectively during the Montgomery bus boycott.

Ultimately, Alex Morisey and Barbara Moffett were eager that Randall's broadcasts should accord with the AFSC's best principles concerning racial justice. As Moffett put it, "our role in the South [is] that of a 'stirrer of conscience and advocate,' not primarily that of a reconciler—at least not in the sense of not taking a position. . . . Given this role it would seem that any radio efforts in the South should follow that general concept." The organization rested foursquare on the principle of following the dictates of conscience. This was the source of the AFSC's strength, and Moffett and Morisey could not, in all good conscience, allow that to be negotiated, even if it meant limiting the AFSC's radio guests to avowed integrationists and therefore limiting the Committee's access to the southern airways. "Must we compromise a firm position on race relations to guarantee use of our material on southern stations?" Morisey asked rhetorically. "I think there is a general agreement in the Service Committee that, as much as we regret it, there are certain avenues of communications not open to us because of the ideals we hold." The AFSC's staunch adherence to these ideals made it a formidable ally in the southern freedom struggle. But it also threatened to make life impossible for Edwin Randall and Olcutt Sanders, who complained that the Community Relations Division's principles on who should be allowed on AFSC-sponsored radio were in danger of becoming "so uncompromisingly absolutist that they cannot encompass anyone who would really be acceptable on southern stations."

There was considerable sympathy for Randall's dilemma from others with experience of trying to promote racially progressive broadcasting in the South. Alvin Gaines was a southern Quaker educator who had worked extensively in radio. In August 1957 he wrote to the AFSC's executive secretary Lewis Hoskins to explain that the expectations expressed by Moffett and Morisey were unreasonably high. In an environment where "no representative of the NAACP is likely to breach the wall of rejection built up against that organization in the South," he felt Randall had little alternative but to turn to those southerners who might realistically get a hearing on the region's airways. "True," Gaines admitted, "they might not reflect the finest of Friends' principles," but "they would be southern, carrying their passports in their voices," and "they would be planting doubts in the minds of the segregationalist as to the validity and rightness of segregation the unworthiness of the Negro, etc." Such overtures, Gaines argued, might be especially effective in reaching "the exploited, duped, so-called 'poor white trash' who is the backbone of the segregation forces" and who was therefore most in need of education and enlightenment. "Proper doubt," Gaines insisted, "can often, 'like the fear of the Lord,' be the beginning of wisdom," and radio broadcasts by southern moderates might just sow such seeds of doubt in the minds of poor whites. This, Gaines suggested, was about the best *Friendly World* could hope to accomplish at the present time.[17]

To a greater or lesser extent, variations on these AFSC debates over the use of radio took place in each of the organizations that used radio to promote racial equality in the South during the late 1950s and early 1960s. There was always a tension between the best hopes of reformers for the medium and the realities imposed by the industry's economic structure and the racial views of those who dominated it in the South. By the end of 1957 the tensions between the AFSC's idealism and the realities faced by Ed Randall had become intolerable. When it became apparent that the Ford Foundation would not be renewing the grant from which the AFSC had subsidized Randall's work, it seemed an opportune moment for the Committee to rethink its options.

The Southern Regional Council and Friendly World Broadcasting

In October 1957, Olcutt Sanders issued a press release "to announce a changed relation to radio programs being produced by Ed Randall." Sanders explained that "because of AFSC financial limitations—and to give Ed the greater flexibility that he feels his radio work requires—his programs will continue as his personal undertaking."[18] The split was partial, and more or less amicable aside from a relatively minor spat in 1960 when the AFSC tried to reclaim some broadcasting equipment it claimed it had loaned to Randall but which Randall had in fact purchased out of his own pocket. The AFSC no longer funded Randall or his newly incorporated Friendly World Broadcasting, nor did it participate in program production in any official sense. Nevertheless, Randall continued to accept AFSC ideas for programs and guests, and he regularly put his facilities at the Committee's disposal for AFSC recordings. Periodically he would also approach the Committee for funding, although that hardly made it unique. In dire financial straits after the termination of AFSC funds, Friendly World Broadcasting was largely bankrolled from Randall's own savings, supplemented by modest contributions from the SCEF and from the SRC, which became his most important benefactor and organizational contact.[19]

Again, it is not hard to see why Randall's shows appealed to the SRC. Until it took over administration of the VEP in 1962, the Council had struggled to find an appropriate role within a civil rights movement it broadly welcomed, yet about which it was often apprehensive. Certainly some SRC members still felt that calls for immediate compliance with federal desegregation rulings were counterproductive, and that direct-action campaigns dedicated to the same end were irresponsible. There was a feeling that both tactics played straight into the hands of racial demagogues like George Wallace in Alabama and Ross Barnett in Mississippi who used the racial crisis to raise their own political stock. As they raged against the perils and ignominy of accepting federally imposed integration, these leaders of white supremacy had virtually silenced the voices of moderation in the region, leaving southern politics and much of the region's media largely in the hands of hard-line segregationists and their supporters.

Throughout the late 1950s and early 1960s, the SRC insisted that some of the most important civil rights battles in the region were being fought for the consciences of white would-be racial moderates. This elusive group comprised the mass of decent, law-abiding whites who, although desperately anxious about the implications of desegregation, might be persuaded that it was inevitable and made to appreciate the advantages of accomplishing it in a calm manner. As the SRC saw it, part of its mission was to rouse this latent constituency to stand up against the segregationist zeal of the last-ditch resisters and work for measured, orderly compliance. As late as April 1965, the SRC's executive director Leslie Dunbar was still skeptical about the ultimate efficacy of federal laws in changing the discriminatory patterns of southern race relations if attitudes remained the same. "I grow more and more deeply convinced that the real battle ground is the mind of the American white man, and that we have gone nearly as far as we can get with the belief that by requiring people to alter their behavior patterns we cure the social ills of discrimination."[20] Naturally, African Americans were rather less sanguine about having to wait for a change of southern white hearts before enjoying their constitutional rights. They welcomed the new laws that at least made discriminatory practices illegal.

The SRC's own efforts to win the battle for the southern white mind and move public opinion in more racially tolerant and compliant directions were focused on the publication and distribution of its *New South* journal. A forum for some of the most thoughtful analyses of the southern racial situation to emerge during this period, *New South* reflected the Council's essentially middle-class, educated membership; it had limited popular appeal, and therefore minimal impact, beyond this liberal constituency. As Mercer University professor Joseph Hendricks, who worked with the SRC and the affiliated Georgia Council for Human Relations, recalled, "I think the SRC did more of the hard research trying to see ways that things might move. They were an auxiliary force; they stayed in the background. The intellectual component of what we might [call] liberalism in the South."[21]

Radio exposure offered the SRC the prospect of influencing a much broader cross-section of southern opinion than the more academic, racially progressive readership of *New South*. Yet, as Leslie Dunbar admitted, in the late 1950s and early 1960s, while the Council was extremely adept at producing a flood of reports and pamphlets and dutifully issued regular press releases to local newspapers, it was clueless about how best to approach the electronic media. "We just didn't know how to get into TV. . . . We did our best to get coverage on some of the news reports; now and then you cashed in. We kept talking about doing radio and I don't think we ever did." While SRC staff members made periodic appearances on sympathetic stations like WAOK in Atlanta and even took the opportunity on WSFM-Birmingham to rebut accusations that the Council had been infiltrated by communists, Ed Randall's shows provided an opportunity for more systematic use of the medium at minimal expense.[22]

With the SRC providing intermittent but significant financial support from the late 1950s until the mid-1960s, Ed Randall made thousands of short programs each year, covering just about all the major events and trends in the southern civil rights movement. There were broadcasts from Little Rock, attacks on housing discrimination, and reports on the lunch counter sit-in movement that spread across the South from Greensboro in the spring of 1960. He also produced a longer—fifteen-minute—weekly program called *This Is a Friendly World*, which dealt mostly with "people from other countries and Americans who have visited other countries."[23] In his signature five-to-seven minute spots, however, there was little change in content from the kinds of programs about southern racial reconciliation that he had been making since the early 1950s. The main difference was that, once freed from the AFSC's exacting scrutiny, Randall did not need to agonize quite so much about whether his participants were unimpeachable champions of immediate desegregation. Again, this dovetailed much more easily with the SRC's essential pragmatism, where a concern to promote dialogue with all interested parties usually took precedence over doctrinaire proscriptions.

In one extreme example of this new latitude, in 1961 Randall allowed notorious Georgia segregationist Lester Maddox, then chairman of GUTS (Georgians Unwilling to Surrender), to participate in a discussion with Dr. Heywood Hill, an Atlanta physician and educator deeply committed to desegregating the city. Randall held that this would produce "a fair and impartial presentation of the issues." Shortly afterwards, however, Randall, who had first covered the bitter struggle over Atlanta's schools in 1960, showed where his real sympathies lay. In "A City Changes Its Mind" he reported: "'The Queen City of the South' has firmly determined to open its schools with the degree of desegregation required by law—and without violence!" Randall proclaimed that "the die-hard segregationists are a defeated and inconsiderable minority, who are not likely to offer any effective resistance to the orderly process of education in Atlanta."[24]

Randall's confidence in the value of exemplary stories like this was clear when he revisited the school desegregation saga in Norfolk in August 1960. Three years earlier John J. Brubaker, the superintendent of schools, had closed the city's public school system for six months rather than accept integration. In

1960, however, the newly retired Brubaker went on *Friendly World* to discuss "the unmixed tragedy of closed schools" and to marvel at "the startling facts about the actual acceptance of legal de-segregation" once Norfolk schools had been forced to reopen.[25] Randall was disappointed that only "six or eight stations" in Louisiana aired the Brubaker tapes, since he had specially targeted that state for distribution while New Orleans was embroiled in a similar school crisis. Nevertheless, the SRC's Harold Fleming reassured him that the broadcasts had been "useful in other places that have still to begin desegregation."[26]

In 1962 Friendly World Broadcasting, funded by a $4,000 grant from the SRC, added a new program to its portfolio. In May Randall launched a weekly fifteen-minute show directed at Alabama audiences called *A Yankee in the Heart of Dixie*. The shows were "mostly about the people of the state" and by no means all about racial matters. Many focused on local folklore and cultural events in Alabama. Moreover, Randall, who continued to live in Wallingford, Pennsylvania, was careful to stress that as the eponymous Yankee he was "not there to tell anybody anything, but to learn, to be instructed, to be enlightened." Despite such disclaimers, Randall sought to promote democratic sentiments and good fellowship and to allay the fears of communist subversion that he felt curtailed open discussion of just about every important social issue in the state. Within six months the show had found a berth on fifty-three Alabama stations in some thirty-seven towns and cities.[27]

The program, Randall explained, was "based upon the very firm conviction that people all want to be better than they are and that there are qualities of the divine in every human heart. . . . It is saying to the people who are asked to suspect their neighbors, 'All right. Let's just take a close look at the neighbors and make up our own minds.'" Randall also took the opportunity presented by his new program to articulate the ways in which he believed radio operated on its audiences. "We are also helped by the strange fact that people listening to a well designed radio program somehow feel themselves not only listeners but also, in some odd way, participants. This is the element in this gift we have from God which we have never really understood or used with more than marginal adequacy."[28]

After two decades of socially engaged, religiously rooted broadcasting, it says something about the elusiveness of radio's power that Randall was still trying to fathom the complex ways in which his broadcasts actually affected his listeners. Clearly he felt that racially enlightened radio programs really could help to create, or incorporate people into, a more racially enlightened community. Yet evidence about the impact of Ed Randall's broadcasts is inevitably fragmentary and largely anecdotal. Randall himself recognized that "this is a question to which there is no conclusive answer. It is all guess work." He often resorted to his own sort of "plausible inference" argument. Since his shows appeared on commercial radio stations that were desperate not to lose listeners, he argued that their continued presence meant that they were at least holding their listeners' attention.[29]

Slightly more substantively, Randall was encouraged by feedback from stations that used his programs and from activists engaged in the movement. In August 1956 Joe Long, news director at WNOX-Knoxville, wrote to say that comments on the broadcast about the Montgomery bus boycott had "varied," but that he was generally surprised by its "unusual acceptance in our listening area (six states) and practically all comment has been favorable." Although Long felt that his area was "not plagued by a really extreme attitude on segregation," he looked forward to any further material on desegregation that Randall might be able to supply as it would "be an effective tool in implimenting this transition with a minimum of fuss."[30]

Similar encomiums appeared throughout the 1950s and early 1960s. WFAI-Fayetteville, North Carolina, considered the "interviews with James Dabbs most extraordinary and timely" and urged that "they should be distributed more widely." WAMD-Aberdeen, Maryland, reported "gratifying" comments from its listeners about the same broadcast. Randall was certainly convinced that the original 1958 story on the campaign to reopen Norfolk's schools had significantly influenced events elsewhere in Virginia. Although he had "found it peculiarly difficult to persuade any of the Norfolk stations to use the material," he explained to Harold Fleming that the program "was used elsewhere, notably by WRVA, the 50,000 watt CBS station at Richmond," which declared it "the best thing you've ever done." Moreover, Randall noted that in Richmond, "within a week of the broadcast, both newspapers reversed their positions on massive resistance." If the causal connection here was less simple than Randall implied, at least he had synchronicity on his side. More important, Harold Fleming seemed convinced of the worth of Randall's shows.[31]

The fact that cash-strapped groups like the SRC and SCEF endorsed and financially supported his work from the late 1950s until 1967 suggests that they felt there was some practical value in the broadcasts. Jim Dombrowski was convinced that Randall's shows offered a "unique opportunity to reach people through [the] grass-roots," while his SCEF colleague Don Stephens was incredulous that Barbara Moffett and the AFSC had withdrawn their backing for Randall's work in late 1957. "That lady has never appreciated the important role radio can play in reaching millions of folk with important messages which printed matter and personal contacts can never do," Stephens wrote to Harold Fleming.[32] Fleming himself began a regular correspondence with Randall, even suggesting subjects for *Friendly World* programs, just as Jim Dombrowski had come up with the idea for the original Norfolk schools crisis program and used SCEF funds to help finance it.[33] In the mid-1960s, just a few years after the SRC had helped to fund *A Yankee in the Heart of Dixie,* Fleming wrote simply that "the work of FWB generally has been very helpful." In a letter of endorsement for one of Randall's numerous grant applications, Fleming concluded that the SRC was "convinced the service makes a real contribution."[34]

If nothing else, Randall had increased the SRC's appreciation of radio's potential to move southern opinion. In 1963 a Council handbook on how to prepare southern communities for desegregation featured lengthy instructions on how to utilize local radio. Author Florence Robin advised: "If a station's editorial policy is favorable to you, offer to supply background materials to support their editorials. If it has broadcast hostile editorials, request time on one of their editorial broadcasts for your point of view to be presented." Robin pointed out: "Many local radio stations have community calendars which announce meetings of civil and fraternal groups. Don't neglect these calendars when you have your own meetings." Even more perceptively, Robin explained that radio and its deejays could have a particular impact on young southerners—the generation that would be responsible for the future of the region. "Don't neglect an appeal to young people and students," she urged. "Write to all disk jockeys asking them to talk to their young listeners about good behavior when schools desegregate. An appeal from a disk jockey may carry more weight than one from a school principal."[35]

The SRC's interest in and support of Friendly World Broadcasting continued into the late 1960s, but by 1966 it was becoming increasingly hard-pressed for money itself. Ever ambitious, Randall expanded his *A Yankee in the Heart of Dixie* from Alabama into Mississippi. But the SRC had no funds to spare, and a $30,000 grant from Auburn University that had largely sustained Friendly World Broadcasting for two years was just about exhausted. There was a brief respite when Leslie Dunbar, who had worked with Randall in the early 1960s before succeeding Harold Fleming as SRC executive director and subsequently taking up a post at the Field Foundation in New York, helped to secure a $5,000 Foundation grant. Although by the end of 1966 the indefatigable Randall appeared daily on sixty-nine stations in Mississippi and Alabama, the formal relationship between Friendly World Broadcasting and the SRC was effectively over. Of course, by that time, so was the civil rights phase of the ongoing African American freedom struggle in the South.[36]

Black-Oriented Radio and
the Southern Civil Rights Movement

*We have long been aware of the potential radio
has for reaching large numbers of people quickly.*
Julian Bond, SNCC, 1964

A Strange but Exemplary Case: WOKS-Columbus, Georgia

During the late 1950s and early 1960s just about every organization involved in the southern civil rights struggle coveted media attention, not least from the radio. Although they often had to settle for more exposure on northern stations and networks than in the South, most found at least the occasional friendly berth on the region's airways. As this chapter explains, sometimes that access came about because of the resourcefulness of movement workers who forced their messages onto the air, even at stations where the management would much rather have avoided broadcasting on the racial situation. Sometimes the movement got practical help or positive coverage from southern radio because individuals working at particular stations felt sympathetic toward the black cause. Sometimes—and these were the best of times—these two scenarios overlapped. Activists naturally gravitated toward stations where there were already signs of support for the movement and tried to nudge them in the direction of an even bolder commitment; meanwhile, the most sympathetic staff at those same stations were often searching for more effective ways to express their support for the movement.

Ultimately, the civil rights movement accepted help from southern radio in whatever shape and form it came. And it did come in some decidedly odd shapes and deeply ambiguous forms. Much of the assistance came from black-oriented stations, but there was nothing simple, linear, or predictable about the relationship between such outlets and the freedom struggle. This was a world where there were few unalloyed heroes and where contingency, chance, and commercial calculations often explained as much about the extent of a station's support for the movement as did any principled commitment to racial equality. Moreover, as the next four chapters demonstrate, it was also a world where local circumstances critically shaped the relationship between specific radio stations and the development of the freedom struggle in particular locales.

Typically atypical in this respect was the story of WOKS, a black-oriented station that principally served Columbus, Georgia, although its studio and transmitter were located just across the Alabama border in Phenix City. By December 1962, when Phil Meltzer officially became the new owner of WOKS, he was in the throes of such a protracted alcoholic binge that he "never bothered to ask what the programming was." In fact, he did not even visit his new facility until the following summer. When he eventually did make the trip down from New York, Meltzer was astonished by what he found. "We came up to this shack and there was WOKS in all its glory. I'd bought a black station in Columbus, Georgia. I didn't know what the hell I was doing, because I was drunk. . . . I look at that station and I think, 'Shit, I gotta get out of this!' . . . I've never had a black radio station. I know nothing except WDIA made a lot of money in Memphis." None of this augured especially well for the prospects of WOKS becoming a major supporter of African American rights in a city that had been rather laggardly in organizing effective challenges to Jim Crow.[1]

Meltzer was a native New Yorker from a theater background who had made a small fortune as founder of Radio Concepts Incorporated, a company that produced radio jingles and advertisements. Before his alcohol problem led to his removal from the Radio Concepts board of directors, Meltzer already had a sizeable interest in a number of radio stations located in St. Paul, New Orleans, Tulsa, St. Louis, and Pompano Beach, Florida. At a loss for something better to do with his substantial compensation, in September 1962 he put down $8,000 toward the purchase of WOKS, adding another $10,500 at the closing in December. Meltzer's primary motivation was that he had heard that the station had recently been supplied with brand-new broadcasting equipment and was therefore seriously undervalued at a total asking price of $120,000.[2]

By the time Meltzer turned up to inspect his new acquisition in July 1963, Bobby Hill, an NAACP youth leader, had also arrived in Columbus. Despite indifference and even hostility from much of the black adult leadership in Columbus, Hill had succeeded in rousing the town's black students to challenge segregation at various municipal facilities, notably the Bradley Memorial Library. On July 5, 1963, seven black activists had been denied library cards, prompting a wave of black protests and picketing outside the library itself and at the offices of the Muscogee County School Board that ran it. Over the next ten days, demonstrations at the library, the school board, and segregated recreational facilities across the city escalated steadily, punctuated by occasional outbursts of fighting.

On July 15 an agreement negotiated by adult leaders and the city authorities to halt the protests was rejected by the NAACP Youth Council, and the demonstrations resumed the following day. On his first drive through Columbus, Meltzer had seen one of these protests and inquired what was going on. A movement leader, probably Bobby Hill,[3] told him: "We're going to integrate that library, one way or the other." A naive Meltzer was astonished that this sort of thing was even still an issue. "I said, 'Integrate the library?' It seemed just so ridiculous." Meltzer promised to do what he could to help. "I was a liberal Jew from New York . . . so the decision was not that hard to make."[4]

Meltzer bolted down some whisky and went to introduce himself to the mayor of Columbus, Ed Johnson. "He looked like a pig," Meltzer recalled somewhat uncharitably. "He had big cheeks and a red nose." Instead of the cozy pleasantries Johnson expected from the new businessman in town, Meltzer launched into a liquor-fueled attack on the administration's refusal to negotiate with the protesters. He reminded the mayor of the proximity of the local air force base at Fort Benning, and the way that federal power had recently been used to end Governor George Wallace's schoolhouse-door stand against desegregation at the University of Alabama. "Do you want to be up against the wall like George Wallace?" Meltzer asked. "Now when are you going to integrate that library?"[5]

Throughout his meeting with Johnson, Meltzer was bluffing. Nevertheless, he did feel he had one potential trump card up his sleeve. He thought he might be able to use WOKS to get young black protesters off the streets, and this gave him some leverage with the mayor. "Listen, Mayor Johnson," he said. "You got a whole crowd out there that could be a riot in ten minutes, or maybe I could stop it and send them all home." At one level, this smacked of compromise and an effort to forestall protest. Yet, at another level, Meltzer and Johnson both recognized that it was politically difficult for the mayor to announce that he was even considering integrating the library while the demonstrations still raged. For the white community, such a move would have reeked of cowardly capitulation to black pressure. If the demonstrations stopped, however, Johnson could save at least a little face with his white supporters: he could explain any discussions and concessions in terms of a statesmanlike bid for racial reconciliation and a responsibility to preserve order. By the time Meltzer left the mayor's office, Johnson had apparently agreed to make a firm commitment to desegregating the library if the protests stopped.[6]

Meltzer was unsure whether he could deliver his side of the bargain: "I didn't know if I could clear the crowd from the library." He returned to WOKS, found "Raggedy" Flagg, his most popular deejay, and carefully wrote out the text of the message he wanted him to read out on air. "Mama, get them kids out of the square and go back on home," Flagg told his listeners. Although Meltzer had asked Flagg to deliver the message verbatim, the deejay garnished it with what

Meltzer dismissed as "all kind of gibberish," the vernacular flourishes and rhyming slang that were Flagg's hallmark. There was no mistaking the sentiment, though. Flagg announced that, although there was no fixed timetable yet, there was an agreement with the city that "the library will be integrated or, man, we will go out there in force and WE will integrate it." According to Meltzer, within half an hour the pickets were gone. The following day, July 18, 1963, all formal protest activities were suspended as movement leaders accepted an unexpected invitation to negotiate the city's desegregation plans with the mayor. Four days later the city commission announced the creation of a biracial advisory committee—albeit with a membership consisting overwhelmingly of whites and conservative black leaders—and set a date for the integration of the library. On September 2, 1963, the library formally admitted its first black patrons, and a month later the local movie theater also desegregated.[7]

WOKS obviously did not fashion these changes on its own. Rather, it had belatedly weighed in on an ongoing local campaign. Nevertheless, the station's direct involvement in the mechanics of organized protest demonstrated the potential of black-oriented radio and its deejays literally to move sections of the southern black community. Having seen the power of "Raggedy" Flagg over his black listeners, Meltzer "realized I'd bought a political goldmine." Yet events at WOKS following the breakthroughs of 1963 suggested how difficult it could be to extract that political gold when factors beyond the station militated against on-air commitment to the struggle. The creation of a biracial commission and the desegregation of the theater and library were initially isolated and largely token gestures toward abolishing Jim Crow in Columbus. Moreover, once the dynamic Bobby Hill had left town, adult black leadership quickly returned to more cautious, neoaccommodationist tactics in the face of continuing white hostility to genuine desegregation. WOKS struggled to maintain its activist credentials in this atmosphere of stalled black protest and resolute white resistance. After the integration of the library, Klansmen had pelted Meltzer's house with rocks, leading him to reconsider the prudence of publicly aligning WOKS with black insurgency. For several months, he admitted, "I kept the tenor of the station away from politics, except to say who was elected, who was running." To do otherwise "would have been suicidal." Already vilified by many local whites as a dangerous outsider agitator, Meltzer found that his foray into civil rights organizing had left him struggling for sponsors, although one group of Columbus merchants was immediately more sympathetic. "The Jews in the community very quietly kept me in action," Meltzer recalled.[8]

In a pattern replicated throughout most of the South, the situation for WOKS and Meltzer improved as the decade wore on. An unlikely friendship with Allen Woodall, the owner of nearby station WDAK, helped. A true-blooded southerner who had loyally named his broadcasting company Big Johnny Reb, Woodall held racial views very different from Meltzer's own. However, the two men liked each other and, as long as they avoided racial matters and talked business, they got along fine. "Somehow . . . Allen took the pressure off," Meltzer acknowledged. "He told everybody to lay off, and they laid off. It was that simple. I mean, there were people that still didn't like that Jew from New York, but I wasn't going to get killed." Things got even better as the economic potential of black consumers became more apparent to white businessmen. In 1964 Meltzer persuaded the manager of the newly integrated J. C. Penney store to start advertising on his station. When sales rocketed, other store owners began to use WOKS to target the black market. This encouraged a more adventurous attitude toward black-oriented news on WOKS. "Once the merchants started moving in, then if you did anything negative to the black community, you were fighting the white community, because it was all dollars." Gradually Meltzer began to increase the amount of news programming and "special editorials outlining the issues and all progress made" on the racial front. By early 1964 WOKS had begun to offer free time to the "acknowledged leadership . . . to discuss everything from voter registration to local problems of integration." Two years later when, in the midst of a costly divorce and a continuing battle with the bottle, Meltzer decided to dump WOKS, he felt that the station "could say what we wanted to on the air, we could talk about the good things in the community."[9]

Movement Initiatives on Southern Radio

In Columbus, local NAACP activists had made little effort to solicit the help of WOKS. Their relationship to the station was more reactive than proactive. This was not always the case. The NAACP and other civil rights organizations did attempt, with varying degrees of sophistication and success, to harness the power of black-oriented radio to their pursuit of racial justice during the heyday of mass protest in the South. Indeed, the different ways in which the NAACP, the NUL, SNCC, CORE, and the SCLC conceptualized and developed their relationship to the medium embodied their different approaches to the freedom struggle.

The late 1950s and early 1960s were a difficult time for the NAACP in the South. The Association often had to surrender headlines, members, and funding to groups that pursued more militant direct-action tactics. Nevertheless, NAACP lawyers, organizers, and rank-and-file members endured their fair share of the repression that greeted the rise of the civil rights movement, prosecuted many of the most important legal cases of the era, and even dabbled—especially at the local level—in direct-action campaigns against segregation and for the vote. Similarly, although the Association attempted nothing as ambitious as its *Walter White Show* experiment of the early 1950s, it continued to use radio to publicize and conduct its work both nationally and, despite occupying a place close to Satan's right hand in the segregationists' vision of hell, in the South.

In 1959, NAACP state branches throughout the nation were encouraged to court any local radio stations that might take a specially made program celebrating the organization's fiftieth anniversary. The following year, publicity director Henry Lee Moon wrote again to state branch presidents asking them to contact their "local station immediately and reserve a fifteen minute period" for a show featuring baseball legend Jackie Robinson, executive secretary Roy Wilkins, and newly elected NAACP board chairman Robert C. Weaver. "Radio can offer our branch an excellent outlet for telling its story," Moon reminded these local leaders, and stressed how radio could also assist with recruitment efforts and provide a means to counter the waves of anti-NAACP propaganda put out by the forces of massive resistance.[10] That propaganda took its toll, however. In 1960 the Association complained to the FCC that "the great majority of southern stations refuse even to mention the NAACP in news broadcasts, so frightened are the owners of politicians."[11]

The Association's presence on southern radio improved steadily as the 1960s and the movement unfolded, while its on-air messages pushed beyond the traditional NAACP diet of recruitment, education, and fund-raising. In 1963, for example, black-oriented WSOK in Savannah provided airtime for the local NAACP chapter and its offshoot the Chatham County Crusade for Voters in a weekly half-hour show dedicated to voter registration.[12] By 1964 the censorship of southern radio had eased enough for the NAACP to report that 95 percent of the branches seeking airtime on local radio stations were successful.[13] The following year, it even found time on WAOK-Atlanta to launch a scathing attack on the reactionary forces that had tried to undermine its work by accusing it of communist links. Quite ingeniously, the Association invoked FBI director J. Edgar Hoover, the nation's most notorious red-hunter and a constant thorn in the side of the civil rights movement, to vouch for its—and, by extension, the movement's—rejection of communist influences and its commitment to American democratic ideals. Reminding listeners that Hoover in his book *Masters of Deceit* had commended the NAACP for "keeping communists out of the organization," the broadcast reassured them that "the NAACP has no other belief than those set forth in the Bill of Rights and the Constitution."[14]

While the NAACP had to wait until the early 1960s to get much positive southern radio exposure, the NUL enjoyed rather more success in the early years of the mass movement. This was understandable since the NUL remained the most moderate of all the major civil rights organizations. Its presence on radio was simply less contentious than that of either the litigious NAACP or more direct-action-oriented groups like the SCLC and SNCC. A policy statement by Ed Pate, the pioneering black co-owner of KPRS in Kansas City, Missouri, captured the special appeal of the NUL to broadcasters who wished to make a positive gesture toward racial change, yet balked at publicly endorsing those who were taking to the streets and courtrooms to destroy Jim Crow. Arguing that "because Kansas City peacefully, swiftly, and effectively is integrating all its public facilities, we must avoid airing any controversial discussions which might lead to difficulties which are extant in our adjacent state to the South"—meaning Arkansas—Pate admitted with striking candor that he would allow public service announcements only on behalf of "legitimate community organizations that are not controversial." This essentially meant the local NUL, with whom KPRS had cosponsored a lawn beautification program, distributing free grass and flower seeds to all residents interested in sprucing up their gardens. According to Pate, this rather literal exercise in grassroots activism was "particularly significant in 1956 and 1957 because it was the beginning of integrating neighborhoods. Without our saying as much, what we were really doing was preparing our listeners to move into better-kept integrated neighborhoods. We were giving them an awareness of a well-kept lawn and beautiful flowers."[15]

Other stations were similarly enamored of the NUL's resolute gradualism and abiding concern with respectability. At KXLW–St. Louis, for example, an NUL affiliate called the Block Unit Federation had established a weekly show in the late 1950s specifically designed "to discuss and share their plans for clean-up campaigns, improvement of neighborhoods, housing and sanitation, family life, voter registration and general civic betterment projects."[16] Farther south, the going was a little tougher even for the NUL, although by 1961 the local New Orleans chapter had found a regular home on black-oriented WYLD.[17]

Of the newer civil rights organizations, SNCC was the most sensitive to the potential of radio to help promote the freedom struggle. This was partly a generational issue. SNCC was full of young men and women who had grown up listening avidly to radio, either because they did not have much access to television or because they were often indifferent to a medium that catered primarily to white middle-class adults. SNCC's communications department, headed by Julian Bond and Mary King, was quick to develop a relatively coherent strategy for using radio. While the organization appreciated the importance of the print media and television, it recognized that radio had unique characteristics and capabilities.

SNCC's radio plans were greatly enhanced by the installation of a Wide Area Telephone Service (WATS) system at its Atlanta headquarters in 1963. The WATS system offered unlimited long-distance phone calls for a set monthly fee. Among the various purposes they served, the WATS lines enabled the organization to contact hundreds of radio stations across the nation on a daily basis, offering them brief, specially recorded "actualities" from the movement centers of the South.[18] SNCC staff members were explicitly encouraged to be on the lookout for stories that might "get out the story of the Southern movement in more dramatic form than press releases." During the Mississippi Freedom Summer of 1964, SNCC field workers received a manual instructing them how to make their reports, which they regularly filed to headquarters over the WATS lines, more attractive to radio stations.[19] Devoid of much third-party narration or commentary, these actualities consisted of powerful testimony from the very heart of the southern freedom struggle, as in the report on the murder of SNCC volunteer Jon Daniels in Alabama, or the account of police assaults on peaceful demonstrators in Brownsville, Tennessee. On occasion the programs were more educational, even ruminative, helping to explain the philosophies and practical mechanics of the movement's work, as in a report on the campaign to register three hundred new African American voters in Americus, Georgia, during the summer of 1965.[20]

Like all the civil rights organizations seeking to use radio, SNCC was heavily dependent on the goodwill of individual radio stations and networks to get its actualities and other programs onto the air. For many years, that goodwill was at a premium in the South, and in late 1963 SNCC was sufficiently frustrated in its efforts to get access to the southern media that it drew up detailed guidelines for petitioning the FCC. In 1949 the FCC had modified an earlier ban on editorializing, asserting that all broadcasters had "an affirmative duty . . . to encourage and implement the broadcasting of all sides of controversial public issues over their facilities, over and beyond their obligation to make available on demand opportunities for the expression of opposing views." These basic tenets were reaffirmed in the FCC's Fairness Doctrine of July 1963. In the aftermath of this ruling, SNCC workers were taught how to bring complaints and even legal action against stations that refused to offer balanced news coverage of the civil rights movement, or that would not allow movement representatives to present rejoinders to hostile editorials and news items. A lengthy memo assured workers: "The FCC has been very specific in its statement of station responsibilities with regard to editorial attacks. The station must put you or your chosen representative on the air, even if the station would not otherwise do so."[21]

In 1964 CORE's community relations director Marvin Rich issued local chapters with a similar set of guidelines on how to take action against recalcitrant broadcasters who either ignored or sought to discredit the civil rights movement.[22] As elsewhere in the history of the African American freedom struggle, the promise of increased federal support for equal rights—as manifested in the FCC's Fairness Doctrine—had provided an important stimulus to action. Unfortunately, attempts to make the FCC actually rectify or punish breaches of its rules also illustrated a far less positive theme in movement history: the federal government had promised a lot more in theory than it delivered in practice. For many years the FCC proved reluctant to discipline the many southern stations that continued discriminatory practices and systematically denied air-time to pro-movement voices.

Although CORE was less systematic than SNCC in its approach to radio, its field workers also regularly prepared tapes for airing on the radio. Ed Hollander, an indefatigable organizer in Mississippi and Louisiana, spent his first week as a CORE staff member in New York visiting radio stations and encouraging them to take the tapes he intended to send up from the South. Soon after his arrival in Mississippi in late January 1964, this preparation appeared to have paid off when he appeared with fellow activists Dave Dennis and William Worthy to discuss the situation in Canton on WNEW–New York.[23] Thereafter he supplied a stream of interviews and "actualities" for use by news networks and northern stations, always resigned to the fact that "there's no guarantee the stations will play them even when they do get them."[24] Hollander also tried hard to cultivate contacts with local, especially black-oriented, radio stations in the South. While working in Louisiana in 1964, he had some success in getting CORE material onto a number of black-oriented New Orleans stations. Like many other activists, however, Hollander drew a blank when seeking support for the movement on similar stations in Mississippi.[25]

Between the Montgomery bus boycott and his murder in 1968, Martin Luther King Jr. was the most eagerly sought guest on any radio station interested in covering the civil rights movement, regardless of its location or market orientation. Yet the SCLC was actually rather slow to explore the full potential of radio. Paradoxically, the organization's casual approach to using the medium was probably exacerbated by the fact that it shared premises on Atlanta's Auburn Avenue with WERD. Many writers have repeated the story of how, whenever King wished to speak to black Atlanta, he would simply bang on the ceiling or call upstairs for a microphone to be lowered from the window of the WERD studios on the second floor to his window below.[26]

While such stories add romantic luster to the image of black-oriented radio staunchly aiding the movement at every turn, they also suggest why the SCLC was so lackadaisical in developing a systematic and professional approach to radio. Although the SCLC had paid for weekly radio programs in Atlanta in the early 1960s, King's celebrity meant that he could get airtime virtually whenever and wherever he wanted. This was certainly true in the North, where many of the SCLC's fund-raising and educational drives took place. Even in the South, however, black announcers had quickly created an informal network of friendly contacts eager to publicize and support King's work. Beyond his hometown of Atlanta, "Tall Paul" Dudley White at WENN-Birmingham, NAACP activist Louise Fletcher at WSOK-Nashville, and Nat Williams at WDIA eventually became his premier, if far from his only, southern radio contacts.[27]

The enthusiasm for Martin Luther King on black-oriented stations around

FIGURE 8. Nothing better symbolized the intimate relationship between black-oriented radio and the southern civil rights struggle than the fact that WERD and SCLC shared the same building on Atlanta's Auburn Avenue. Courtesy of Archives of African American Music and Culture, Indiana University.

the nation meant that the SCLC initially felt little need to formulate a coherent policy toward radio. The organization's attitude here was part of a broader pattern, whereby it became almost entirely dependent on King's personal charisma, and his unique ability to raise morale, money, and marchers, to define its tactical agenda and to structure its publicity operations. No surprise, then, that when the SCLC did finally consider a proposal that would allow it to use radio more effectively, King was the main attraction. More surprising, perhaps, was that this initiative did not originate at the SCLC or at its black-owned landlord, WERD. It came from Zenas Sears, the white co-owner of WAOK, Atlanta's other black-oriented radio station.

In December 1964 an SCLC executive retreat recommended that the organization "discontinue paying for weekly radio programs" that aired in Atlanta. Shortly afterwards Zenas Sears wrote to SCLC staffer Randolph Blackwell offering to produce a series of free fund-raising and informational shows. In making his offer, Sears reminded the SCLC of the extraordinary influence black-oriented radio enjoyed in the local African American community. "A great many Negroes listen to a radio on a daily basis," he told Blackwell. "On an average week day morning in Atlanta the ratio of radio tune-ins is well over 50% with 85% listening to a Negro programmed station (either WAOK or WERD)." In particular Sears stressed: "Reliable rating services have discovered that Negroes of moderate and low economic means are consistent radio listeners." Although these listeners had limited financial resources, Sears pointed out that they were eager to contribute to the movement and that radio could help coordinate effective fundraising. "I feel that most Civil Rights organizations have neglected the dimes and quarters that they should be receiving from the mass of Negro listeners who want to be part of the drive for equality but have never been told how to contribute," he explained. This oversight could be rectified by a series of regular spot announcements featuring Martin Luther King and concluding with "a Post Office Box number for contributions." In addition to these brief daily slots, WAOK would produce a fifteen-minute show based on King's sermons each Sunday.[28]

Sears had ambitious plans for these SCLC shows. In addition to taking care of all the production, studio, and equipment costs—even down to purchasing the necessary magnetic tape—Sears hoped to place the SCLC programs "on at least 50 radio stations with a potential of 300 stations." While this proved overoptimistic, the weekly Sunday show in particular was a great success. Retitled *Martin Luther King Speaks* in 1967 and subsequently produced independently by the SCLC's Bill Stein in New York, the program was regularly airing by the start of 1968 on eleven major stations around the country, including WOL-Washington, WEBB-Baltimore, WVON-Chicago, WWRL–New York, and WDAS-Philadelphia. In Memphis 175,000 people, mostly African Americans, listened to the show each week on WDIA—this at a time when the circulation of the city's leading black newspaper, the *Memphis Tri-State Defender,* stood at just 15,000. At its peak the show attracted a weekly audience in excess of two million.[29]

WAOK's support for Martin Luther King and the SCLC was just one aspect of the rich and complex history of black-oriented broadcasting in Atlanta. It is certainly instructive to consider in greater detail the story of black radio in a city that could boast the nation's first black-owned radio station and, as home to the SCLC and SNCC, not to mention the SRC, served as an important hub for the entire southern civil rights movement. What emerges is a fascinating tale of engagement and detachment, commitment and evasiveness, caution and militancy as black and white broadcasters sought to cope with the rise of a mass movement for racial justice across the South and the peculiarities of race relations in Atlanta itself.

WERD Up: Black-Owned, Black-Oriented Radio in Atlanta

In the spring of 1949, white Atlanta businessman Robbie Robinson put a proposition to black Atlanta businessman Jesse B. Blayton. Robinson was a major stockholder in the Radio Atlanta consortium that owned a rapidly failing general-market station called WERD. Since nobody in the white business community seemed interested in buying a station that was hemorrhaging money and embroiled in a bitter wrangle over unionization with some of its employees, Robinson decided to overlook racial differences and ask Blayton if he was interested in purchasing WERD. Race aside, Jesse Blayton was in some ways an unlikely choice. An educator and accountant by profession, he had originally come from Oklahoma to Atlanta to teach accountancy at Morehouse College and Atlanta University. Still, there were at least two good reasons why Robinson singled him out as a potential buyer. First, through hard work and a talent for shrewd investment, Blayton had become one of the wealthiest African Americans in Atlanta. Second, he was a leading patron and occasional instructor at the Midway Radio and Television School, where African Americans could learn the technical and managerial skills required to work in the electronic media.[30]

In 1949, having the requisite qualifications and skills did not necessarily mean that African Americans could find jobs in an industry that employed few black announcers and still fewer technical or managerial staff. According to his long-time assistant Willieboyd McNeil "Mack" Saddler, the prospect of being able to provide employment opportunities for at least some Midway graduates was a crucial factor in Blayton's decision to buy WERD. As Saddler recalled, however, most of black Atlanta business and civic elite thought it was a crazy idea. "I actually typed letters to over thirty-five people trying to get them to come in and to invest in this venture. And nobody said yes other than Mr. Blayton's brother."[31] The only other sympathetic response came from Morehouse president and social activist Benjamin Mays, but he was not in a position to offer any financial help. Eventually Blayton had to use his entire personal estate to obtain the license to the first black-owned radio station in the United States. Blayton remained the owner for the next twenty years.

Blayton was an enigmatic, somewhat inscrutable figure. A frugal workaholic, he showed little interest in living the high life enjoyed by others of his wealth and status. According to Mack Saddler, whose husband Al later became station manager at WERD, Blayton cut a strange, sometimes rather disheveled figure among the well-heeled black elite who gravitated to Atlanta's ritzy Sweet Auburn district. There was, however, little doubt about his gifts as an accountant and entrepreneur. When Blayton bought WERD, he was the only black certified public accountant in the state of Georgia, while the BLAMIYA holding company he co-owned with Clayton Yates and Lorrimer Milton controlled a substantial portion of Atlanta's black business. This empire included the Citizens Trust Bank—the first black-owned bank to be included in the Federal Reserve System—which the three partners had bought in 1932, three years after the death of its founder, Heman Perry.[32]

Long after his demise, Heman Perry continued to exert an enormous influence over the way that Jesse Blayton conceived the relationship between his commercial dealings and his social responsibilities. "The umbrella raised by Perry is over all of us," Blayton once remarked on behalf of Atlanta's black business elite. "I would not have thought of risking my entire estate in WERD except for Perry's shadow."[33] Blayton's motives in buying the station revealed the complex mix of personal ambition and communal concern typical of black entrepreneurs during the Jim Crow era and beyond. Like Perry, Blayton was a disciple of Booker T. Washington, heir to the idea that black economic success—not least his own—was both a form of progressive community politics and a vehicle for collective racial advance.

Blayton believed that thriftiness and the creation of powerful black enterprises and financial institutions behind the wall of segregation were the path to black deliverance. "He was always thinking capital, capital, capital," recalled Mack Saddler. He used to argue, "The reason we can't do anything is that we don't have the capital to invest."[34] Throughout his career, Blayton let very little sway him from trying to accumulate more and more of that capital and using it to expand black economic and employment opportunities. In the early 1930s he even had several exchanges of letters with Washington's nemesis, W.E.B. Du Bois, over the merits of this strategy. When Du Bois insisted that "we cannot rescue the Negro race in America merely by saving money and supplying capital. The remedy must be much more thoroughgoing," and began to offer socialistic solutions to a racial problem he increasingly saw rooted in class and economic inequalities, Blayton complained that this "seems to be clearly a communistic doctrine."[35]

Although Du Bois was quick to point out that communism and socialism were not at all the same thing, this did not make his views any more palatable to Blayton. The two men's political and economic philosophies were poles apart—a gulf that partly explained why Blayton joined the NUL rather than the more militant NAACP. Another letter to Du Bois clearly articulated his own educational and economic priorities for African Americans in a manner that would have made both Heman Perry and Booker T. Washington proud. Blayton called for "some honest-to-goodness effort . . . to encourage thrift. . . . I think that Negroes should now pledge themselves and the race that they will conserve a certain percent of their earnings at all times, thus creating within the race sufficient resources to subsidize industries in which Negroes may be employed."[36] Written nineteen years before he bought WERD, this was nonetheless a blueprint for how Blayton would conceive of his radio station. First, it would encourage probity and respectability among African American listeners. Second, it would provide jobs for black graduates of the Midway Radio and Television School. Third, it would ensure that at least some of the advertising revenue generated by black-appeal broadcasting would find its way into black, rather than white, bank accounts.

Blayton's plans for WERD constituted a classic example of how resourceful African American entrepreneurs found a modus vivendi within the confines of a segregated society. Indeed, at a time when direct challenges to Jim Crow often seemed unrealistic, many African Americans welcomed this sort of dynamic accommodation as a positive good. "Our economic well being is of greater significance than the privilege or rights to attend a white school or to associate with the white people on an equal social base," wrote black Tennessee businessman J. T. Bellanfant in the early 1950s. Moreover, Atlanta in general and Blayton in particular offered a vivid example of what could be achieved by maximizing the ambiguous potential for black economic development offered by segregation itself. "I was in Atlanta and was greatly impressed by the large numbers of outstanding and progressive businesses," Bellanfant remarked. "Atlanta is a strictly segregated city. I was in several New England cities where there is not supposed to be any segregation, and I found not one creditable Negro business. The only Negro owned and operated radio station is not in New York, but in Atlanta, Georgia. . . . Segregation had not only given the Negro in the South an opportunity to carve out his industrial and economic destiny, but it has forced him to the fore as the most substantial and economically secure Negro in the world today."[37] Such views were close to Blayton's own. With even archsegregationist Herman Talmadge appearing on WERD to bless his new venture, Blayton personified a willingness to accommodate to Jim Crow that came under increasing fire in the 1950s and 1960s.[38]

Jesse Blayton may have had his economic and political philosophy all worked out, but he had absolutely no idea how to run a radio station. As part of his deal with Robbie Robinson, he had agreed to retain any white staff members who wanted to remain at WERD. At least one person refused to work for a black boss, but engineer Bill Kennedy, announcer Bob Brissendene, and the wisecracking Jewish deejay Herb Gershorn were among those who stayed. The addition of African American deejays Jack Gibson and later Paul E. X. Brown along with program director Ken Knight meant that the station soon had an integrated staff both on and off the air. As Brown explained, this caused problems at the station's original downtown premises. "The station could not stay at 30 Broad Street [because of] the segregation at that time. The owners of the building didn't want any blacks running in and out upstairs." By the time Brown joined the station in 1951, WERD had already relocated to the Old Red Rock Building at the intriguing address of 274½ Auburn Avenue, in the heart of one of the most affluent and culturally exciting black neighborhoods in the nation. The symbolic significance of this move was not lost on WERD's black staff, even if Paul Brown struggled at the time to pinpoint exactly what it might portend: "To have blacks, whites come down on Auburn and work in an integrated staff. That was a good omen for something!" Herb Gershorn recognized that there were certain ironies to this situation. Although proud that he and his white colleagues "pretty much single-handedly desegregated Auburn Avenue," there were uncomfortable moments that reminded them of the limits of this breakthrough. At times Gershorn and other white staff "felt pretty much like the black demonstrators going downtown to the white-only restaurants and holding their demonstrations. I'd go in to get a cup of coffee and a hamburger and the place would pretty well clear out."[39]

Gershorn's analogy was not entirely accurate. He and his colleagues still got served their lunch and nobody tried to beat them up, spit at them, or stub out cigarettes on their necks, as often happened to movement activists during sit-ins. Nevertheless, there were some encouraging signs of changing racial atti-tudes at the station itself—a little experiment in integration held together by the shared desire to make the fledgling station commercially viable. One white em-ployee had initially refused to drink the coffee Ken Knight brought in for his staff each day. Jack Gibson remembered the quiet satisfaction the black staff felt when he finally relented and took a sip. Maybe, they felt, exposure to African Ameri-cans in the workplace, coupled with a shared fondness for good java, might yet wash away centuries of racial suspicion and stereotyping. At the time, it was easy to see such developments as harbingers of more harmonious and equitable race relations in the South.[40]

As for programming, eclecticism and improvisation were initially the order of the day as WERD's staff cobbled together a sunup-to-sundown schedule. As well as spinning the latest jazz and rhythm and blues records, Jack Gibson read ex-cerpts from the black *Atlanta World* newspaper to fill in time. At noon he joined forces with Herb Gershorn for the madcap *Lunch Call* show—another integrated breakthrough. Other popular personalities included the husband-and-wife team of Dave and Mayme Bondu, known as Mr. and Mrs. Swing, and Johnny "Red Hot and Blue" Martin, a white deejay who sounded black and played the hottest "race" hits of the day. During the week, Atlanta schoolteacher and local thespian Raphael McIver presented an uplifting twice-daily show called *Morning Medita-tions,* while on Saturday mornings the station's home economist Gladys Powell joined Ken Knight in presenting the latest domestic and culinary tips.[41]

After a few years of frantic experimentation, WERD settled on a more fixed format. On Sundays the station devoted itself to highly lucrative religious pro-gramming. There were services from local churches, sermons from preachers like Rev. William Holmes Borders of the Wheat Street Baptist Church and Rev.

Harold Bearden at Big Bethel AME, and gospel music programs hosted by "Brother" Esmond Patterson. During the week, early morning and late afternoon sacred shows bracketed an eclectic mixture of popular music programs, local and community news, sportscasts, and public service announcements. By 1955, when the demolition of the Old Red Rock Building meant another move, this time to 330 Auburn Avenue, WERD had established a distinctive broadcasting identity. It was rather more staid in the music it played and a little more sober in its general tone than nearby WAOK, which debuted in 1954. It was the sound of respectable adult black Atlanta, with just enough gestures toward a younger crowd to keep Zenas Sears and his crew on their toes. Moreover, with advertisements and jingles boldly announcing its place as "America's First Negro-Owned and Operated Radio Station," WERD could claim an extraordinary amount of loyalty and goodwill from a proud African American community.[42]

During WERD's first decade, Blayton was extremely wary about allowing any of his staff to voice explicit condemnations of Jim Crow on air. But it was not hard to detect a lurking contempt for segregation and those who enforced it. The sermons by Borders and Bearden were always likely to throw up messages of interracial fellowship or denunciations of racial discrimination as un-Christian. In the late 1950s, for example, Bearden delivered such a venomous broadside against Georgia's segregationist governor Marv Griffin that state troopers raided the station in search of a tape of the preacher's incriminating broadcast. The troopers left empty-handed, as Bearden had made his comments in the course of a live broadcast. Despite the constant threat of this kind of harassment and intimidation, Rev. Donald Vails of Mt. Zion Second Baptist Church remembered that, thanks to their economic independence, radio preachers in Atlanta remained important advocates of black activism into the heart of the civil rights era: "The churches paid for their radio time, so they basically said what they wanted to say. And that was how they got the word out about rallies, marches, protests of all types."[43]

In 1951 a ratings survey placed WERD in joint first place in the Atlanta radio market. The station marked this achievement by taking out an advertisement in *Sponsor* magazine where it archly observed that here at last was a genuine example of "'Separate but equal'—that famous phrase heard but seldom seen."[44] Beyond such ironic commentary, WERD became tentatively involved with various expressions of organized black protest in Atlanta, most obviously in the field of voter registration. For example, the station provided regular airtime to the Atlanta Negro Voters League (ANVL), helping it to maximize the potential of an expanding black electorate in the city. After 1949 the black bloc vote was instrumental in the success of every Atlanta mayor and most of the other elected officials in the city. In the 1953 mayoral race between incumbent Democrat William Hartsfield and his Republican challenger Charles Brown, WERD was especially important in making sure that black votes counted. Since his first election with black support in 1946, Hartsfield had made serious attempts to improve the lot of African Americans within the structure of segregation. Brown, however, had distributed 50,000 notice sheets falsely indicating that the ANVL had endorsed him rather than Hartsfield. Thanks to revelation of the fraud on WERD and a subsequent disclaimer in the *Atlanta World,* the black vote again went to Hartsfield, proving decisive in a narrow victory.[45]

Eager to improve the quantity and quality of news reaching WERD's listeners, in 1950 Blayton hired Dr. William Boyd, a political scientist at Atlanta University and president of the Georgia NAACP, as the station's first news analyst. Three times a week Boyd broadcast a digest of black-oriented news, seldom missing the chance to denounce racism or urge black Atlantans to register to vote. Although Jesse Blayton declined to take *The Walter White Show,* feeling that the NAACP should pay for it or find a sponsor rather than expect WERD to air it as a public service, the station's links with the local NAACP chapter survived Boyd's death in 1956. The following year, local branch president John Calhoun thanked WERD for being "one of our chief supporters," noting how the Association's work was "greatly enhanced by the use of communications media of such effectiveness as yours."[46]

Throughout the 1950s WERD also provided airtime for the local NUL, a resolutely accommodationist branch of which Blayton was a longstanding board member and eventually chairman. Indeed, given the extraordinarily bitter personal rivalries between the NUL and the NAACP in Atlanta during this period, it says something about the unifying potential of black-oriented radio that these two warring organizations could at least coexist on WERD. In the late 1950s the station also began to broadcast the weekly Hungry Club luncheons from the Butler Street YMCA, an important center for philanthropic and political activity among Atlanta's black elite. At these integrated lunches, guest speakers and concerned citizens debated current affairs, including racial issues. The broadcasts from the "Y" also showcased distinguished speakers such as Atlanta University historian Horace Mann Bond, who gave a 1957 lecture titled "Black Power," and the SRC's Harold Fleming, whose topic was "Moral Dilemmas Facing Today's South." The different titles suggested important differences in black and liberal white perspectives as the freedom struggle entered a new phase.[47]

In 1957 Lucille Chambers summed up WERD's contribution to community, city, and region during its first eight years on air. Echoing a familiar theme, she proclaimed, "This station has done more than any other factor to bring about racial understanding in the South." This achievement could be measured, she argued, by the growing integration of the black radio audience into a national consumer market. "Attention has been called to the neglected billion dollar buyers' market and sales have been boosted," Chambers reported. Moreover, the station had done this with the utmost respect for black listeners and consumers. "All programs are first-rate and stereotyped commercials are avoided." Like other pioneering black-oriented stations, the black-owned WERD "proved to white-owned stations in the South that the use of Colored performers in radio was profitable."[48]

This was precisely the sort of patient, gradualist politics organized around economic growth, consumer power, the use of the franchise, and conspicuous displays of respectability with which Jesse Blayton was most comfortable. Yet, following years of accommodation, cautious black activism, and incremental change, the quickening pace of the freedom struggle in the early 1960s and the emergence of a mass black direct-action campaign against segregation represented a major challenge to Blayton and WERD. Some of those closest to the youthful new insurgency in black Atlanta felt that Blayton's attitude was, like that of many entrepreneurs whose businesses had flourished within the racial enclave provided by segregation, lukewarm. *Atlanta World* journalist and some-time WERD newscaster William Fowlkes believed that, while Blayton had never accepted the legtimacy of Jim Crow, he was reluctant to take a conspicuous public stand against it in case it attracted white retribution and ruined his hard-won social and economic position. "He lent support, but didn't speak out. He wasn't very active politically," Fowlkes said. Esmond Patterson, who worked at WERD from 1956 until joining WAOK in 1963, agreed: "He wasn't that type of man. He was a businessman. He was no civil rights worker. He was never involved in that."[49]

The comments by Patterson and Fowlkes reflected a lingering sense that Blayton and WERD should have been more conspicuously supportive of the new wave of African American protest that swept Atlanta and the South in the late 1950s and early 1960s. Yet, according to Mack Saddler, Blayton desperately "wanted the civil rights movement to succeed. He gave it all he could in the way of money and more than he should in terms of free time." Even Esmond Patterson admitted that although "Blayton just was not involved in civil rights," he did "let those that were involved in it be on his station." This in itself was an important contribution to the freedom struggle. While Blayton was reluctant to place his own or his station's editorial imprint on broadcasts that endorsed the new black insurgency, at WERD those on the movement's front line did have consistent access to the airways. For example, Julian Bond recalled that when the Atlanta sit-in movement began in 1960, WERD and WAOK both carried a weekly show, *The Student Movement and You,* made by the Committee on Appeal for Human Rights. The broadcasts "played an immensely helpful role. . . . The ability to get on the air quickly just made all the difference. I wouldn't say that we couldn't have done it without them, but they certainly made it easier to do what we were doing."[50]

Responsiveness to the changing mood of the black community, its primary market, clearly had much to do with the increased, if still muted and often proxy, interest in civil rights activities at WERD. Another factor was that Jesse Blayton Sr. deferred more responsibility for running the station to his son, Jesse Jr., following a serious car crash in the late 1950s. Most WERD employees rued this change in purely business terms, but Jesse Jr.'s greater control may have created scope for a little more politically engaged broadcasting.[51] More important was the appointment of Preston Mobley as WERD's program director. Although the station still preferred to facilitate rather than fashion movement-oriented programming, Mobley broke that pattern by persuading the fledgling SNCC to produce a weekly *Student Voice* show for broadcast on WERD each Sunday.[52]

Mobley was also more comfortable than either of the Blaytons with airing militant viewpoints on the racial situation. By the early 1960s WERD was even carrying the Black Muslims' *Muhammad Speaks* from XERF in Mexico every Sunday at 6:30 a.m.[53] Somewhat closer to the station's ideological heart, in 1961 WERD invited Dr. Arthur Banks to comment on events at the University of Georgia, where riots had greeted the attempt by Hamilton Holmes and Charlayne Hunter to integrate the school. A political science professor at Morehouse College, Banks pulled no punches in describing "one of the blackest weeks in Georgia's history." He tore into some of the most sacred aspects of the white South's self-image, castigating "a whole society marching under the dirty banner of segregation and discrimination, which had mistaken piety for morals, manners for breeding, a shallow religion for a God-anchored brotherhood, and a twisted sociology for an upright sense of civic duty." White leadership in the state, including Governor Ernest Vandiver, had abdicated "its moral and legal duties . . . , its power, its prestige, its reason, into the hands of the lunatic fringe. The Governor of Georgia must be made to assume the moral as well as the political responsibility of his high office—for all the people of Georgia."[54] Although the fear of further civil disorder had more influence on Vandiver's decision to ensure the successful integration of the university, it would have been unthinkable for WERD to air Banks's forthright criticisms half a decade earlier. That it did so indicated growing sympathy for the new spirit that fueled black activism in the early 1960s.

With Mobley's encouragement and the Blaytons' acquiescence, WERD continued to give or sell airtime to all manner of civil rights groups like the ANVL, SNCC, and the SCLC, as well as the NAACP and the NUL. In 1964 WERD joined WSB and WAOK in publicizing Fulton County's Crash Voter Registration Program, orchestrated by the All-Citizens Registration Committee and featuring a broad coalition of local civil rights groups as well as black fraternities and sororities. Waged under the auspices of the VEP and launched in late August, this campaign sought to register as many black voters as possible before the general election on November 3, 1964. It focused on public housing projects where there was a particular concentration of disenfranchised African Americans and "where door to door canvassing is facilitated." Radio was only one of many devices used to publicize the campaign: "newspapers, handbills, placards, and school children's letters to their parents" were also employed. Probably because of budgetary considerations, there were no plans to use television, where coverage was restricted to "just a few flashes" in which newscasters merely "read from a copy of facts submitted to them on radio." At least some of those financial worries were alleviated by the fact that almost all of the radio exposure was free. A report on the voter registration project singled out a thirty-minute program on WERD for special praise in articulating the goals of the campaign to the black masses.[55]

WAOK: White-Owned, Black-Oriented Radio in Atlanta

Although Jesse Blayton remained perennially anxious about aligning himself or his radio station with the rising tide of mass protest in Atlanta, WERD actually had a very creditable and steadily expanding record of politically engaged broadcasting during the late 1950s and early 1960s. Nevertheless, its performance in this regard was modest compared to that of its chief rival, WAOK. In fact, the contribution to the freedom struggle of virtually every other radio station in the South suffered by comparison with WAOK, while there were few owners who could boast the personal commitment to the cause of racial justice demonstrated by one of its owners, Zenas "Daddy" Sears.

A lean, somewhat scrawny, balding and bespectacled figure who, according to his son Chuck, had the forlorn and bookish look of a "lost paleontologist,"[56] Sears nonetheless had a marvelously authoritative, booming radio voice. Like Jesse Blayton, he was an outsider in Atlanta. Unlike Blayton, he was white and from the North. Having struggled to find work as an actor, Sears arrived in Atlanta shortly before World War II to try his luck as an announcer at the tiny WATL radio station. When war broke out, he served in India, broadcasting for the Armed Forces Radio Network to predominantly black troops on the Burma Road. It was there that Sears began to develop an interest in and then a deep passion for black sacred and secular music. After the war he returned to WATL, began mixing rhythm and blues with white pop fare, and was duly dismissed when the station owner caught wind of this willful breach of racial etiquette. Sears then joined the state-owned WGST, broadcasting out of the Georgia Institute of Technology. There he could play whatever music he wanted, just as long as he steered clear of social commentary or messages on behalf of organizations like the NAACP. Before 10 p.m., he tended to stick to mainstream pop music. Late at night, however, the rhythm and blues of Dinah Washington, Louis Jor-

FIGURE 9. Zenas Sears's racial liberalism and passion for black music helped make WAOK one of the most important social and political institutions operating in black Atlanta during the heyday of the southern civil rights movement. Courtesy of Pullen Library, Georgia State University.

dan, Ray Charles, and Chuck Willis dominated his playlists, and he even flirted with more explicit political and racial messages. Ignoring Governor Herman Talmadge's injunction to avoid anything to do with racial issues, Sears recalled doing "all the get-out-the-vote-stuff anyway. Nobody white listened to the radio after the news at ten o'clock. We started at ten-fifteen p.m. and would run as long as we could sell it, which was usually about two a.m." More than just a hugely popular local deejay among black and adventurous young white Atlantans, Sears also became intimately involved with the business of making and selling rhythm and blues music. He served as singer Chuck Willis's manager in the early 1950s, and in 1954 he hosted a classic Ray Charles session at the WGST studios that yielded the seminal protosoul hits "I Got a Woman" and "This Little Light of Mine." Four years later, by which time Sears was at WAOK, he recorded a live Ray Charles show at Atlanta's Herndon Stadium that was released as the classic *Ray Charles in Person* album. A genuine aficionado and promoter of black music, in an era when white cover versions of rhythm and blues records cluttered the pop charts and clogged the pop airways, Sears steadfastly refused to play pale imitations of the music that he loved and did much to popularize among young whites in the Atlanta area.[57]

As Sears's reputation in the local black community rose, so did the levels of white abuse and harassment. In 1954 several years of epithets and threats came to a head, and Sears was asked to leave WGST and take his "nigger" music with him. Joining forces with former WGST advertising salesman Stan Raymond, he returned to his former employer WATL, which had been renamed WAOK and was now under the ownership of Coca-Cola heir James Woodruff. Although Raymond had no interest in black music and by all accounts, including his own, even less interest in the travails of the African American community, Sears convinced him that with WERD restricted to broadcasting during daylight hours, black-oriented programming was still an underdeveloped market niche in Atlanta. Two years later, when James Woodruff decided that it was far too socially embarrassing—maybe even too dangerous—to be associated with a black-oriented radio station, Sears and Raymond and another business partner, Dorothy Lester, raised $500,000 to buy WAOK outright. By 1963 they had paid off the loan and firmly established the station at the heart of black culture and activism in Atlanta.[58]

Despite Zenas Sears's own racial progressivism, WAOK's initial response to the emergence of mass black protest in the South was much like that of WERD. WAOK made its facilities available to activists engaged in the local freedom struggle but was reluctant to take a strong public position in support of desegregation. Sears and Raymond tried to justify this reticence at the end of 1960 on the grounds of both ignorance and expedience. "The management of WAOK, realizing that their community is involved in tremendous social change, does not feel that we are wise enough to make editorial comment at this time," the management told the FCC. "Putting to one side our ability as editorial thinkers, there is always the possibility that a strong stance on such matters as integration, might possibly have the effect of causing trouble in a community that is desperately trying to remain calm during a period of change."[59]

The onset of the student sit-in protests in Atlanta provoked a change in WAOK's policy. "Until that time," the station told the FCC somewhat self-servingly, "[we] felt that little or nothing could be gained by a discussion of public affairs with our listeners, since, for the most part, our listeners had little knowledge or interest in affairs of national or state-wide importance."[60] Clearly the movement was setting the agenda for the station. It was not as if WAOK had suddenly abandoned its emphasis on playing black music and selling airtime to sponsors for top dollar in order to usher its young African American listeners toward direct-action campaigns. Indeed, WAOK was typical of most southern outlets in seeing its primary social role as helping to cool tempers and preserve civic order, not to encourage more protests. As Sears explained, "Following the first student sit-in demonstrations in the Atlanta area and the sudden increase in the manifestation of the Negro's desire for speedy removal of legal segregation, we have felt that frank and open discussion of the problems involved would not only be of interest to the majority of our audience but of value in the preservation of a peaceful atmosphere within the community. . . . we feel that a great deal has been accomplished by the discussion of racial problems using the voices of those most concerned with the situation."[61]

Although initially reluctant to editorialize in favor of desegregation, WAOK did immediately offer airtime to various organizations engaged in direct-action protests to bring about that goal. In the very first days of the Atlanta lunch-counter sit-ins, the station joined WERD in broadcasting *The Student Movement and You* shows free of charge.[62] This was an invaluable service to impecunious young activists who had to pay full price to advertise their Appeal for Human Rights in the city's only black newspaper, the conservative *Atlanta Daily World*. Frustrated by the *World*, which actually condemned the whole sit-in movement in a series of condescending editorials, the students eventually launched an alternative newspaper, the *Atlanta Inquirer*. Before that, however, radio exposure was especially useful. One of the most significant programs was a Sunday afternoon discussion forum on WAOK called *For Your Information*, which provided local community leaders with an opportunity to inform a mass radio audience about the burgeoning movement.[63]

WAOK's public support for the movement intensified in the summer of 1962 when Zenas Sears hired the SCLC's former publicity director Jim Wood as the station's news analyst and editorial commentator.[64] Wood's concern for the success of the movement was obvious, and once he took control of the newsroom the station's public commitment to reporting and facilitating the freedom struggle became even more pronounced. Indeed, although WAOK's allocation of 7.3 percent of its airtime to news reporting appears modest, this represented considerably more time than was available at a northern black-oriented station like WDAS in Philadelphia, where news accounted for only 4.4 percent of the weekly schedule.[65] Just as important as quantity were the quality and effectiveness of these news broadcasts. Not only did WAOK enjoy "use of the full facilities of the United Press International Service" but, much to the chagrin of WERD, it could also boast of being "the exclusive Atlanta outlet for the International Negro News Service," which provided news "every hour, on the hour."[66] Both these news network links enabled WAOK to minimize the risk of relying on local white news sources that were sometimes subject to censorship or distortion whenever racial topics were involved.

Beyond reports on major civil rights events across the South, the WAOK newsroom under Wood's direction regularly publicized the latest conventions, demonstrations, and voter registration drives organized by civil rights groups in

Atlanta. In late 1963, for example, Wood reported on the inaugural meetings of the Atlanta Coordinating Committee, an umbrella organization designed to encourage cooperation among different groups—and different generations—of Atlanta's black leadership that included Vernon Jordan, Jesse Hill, Rodney Cook, Julian Bond, and A. T. Walden on its steering committee.[67] Early the following year, the station inaugurated a Citizens Award Program to honor people in Atlanta who "give time, energy, and ability in various ways towards serving civic, welfare, social and other needs." Leslie Dunbar, then executive director of the SRC, was an early nominee. So, too, was Julian Bond, although he declined the honor, humbly suggesting that SNCC chairman John Lewis was a more worthy candidate, as he "has worked untiringly in the cause of social justice, and would be, I believe, a proper recipient of the WAOK Citizen Award."[68] A month later Sears wrote to SNCC offering WAOK's help in publicizing any recruitment, fund-raising, or other efforts the organization might be about to undertake. "WAOK considers all organizations involved in the 'Civil Rights Movement' as part of a general group to whom we extend the use of our facilities without charge," Sears explained. Although it did not plan to run a formal membership drive, SNCC was "more than happy to take advantage of your kind offer for announcing mass meetings to the general public." By the end of the year, WAOK had joined WERD and WSB in promoting the All-Citizens Registration Committee Crash Voter Registration Program in Fulton County and pledged to air regular SCLC slots, as well as making and distributing Martin Luther King's weekly shows.[69]

Zenas Sears was no saint. There were times when he put family and self-interest ahead of the struggle for racial justice. For years he felt guilty about withdrawing his son Chuck from an Atlanta school that was about to integrate, fearing that it might become embroiled in racial violence. What especially troubled Sears was that, having paid a sizeable annual fee to place Chuck in a private academy, he failed to send him back to his old public school until the end of the school year, even though it had desegregated in the autumn without incident. Yet the fact remains that, for all the enthusiasm of WAOK's black staff members like Jim Wood and activist deejays Ally "Pat" Patrick and Paul E. X. Brown—the latter had transferred from WERD—the station's growing assistance to the movement simply would not have been possible without Sears's support. Nobody appreciated the depth of this commitment to the freedom struggle better than WAOK's co-owner Stan Raymond, with whom Sears often clashed in his efforts to fashion a more racially progressive, politically engaged station. Raymond was highly suspicious of the civil rights movement and alarmed by the extent to which Sears insisted on linking WAOK to it. His nerves were not calmed any when the Klan burned crosses in front of the station in the early 1960s, or by Sears's support for unionization efforts by WAOK's black staff. He was apoplectic when Sears later refused to accept lucrative Coca-Cola ads in a gesture of solidarity with protests against that company's woeful record in hiring and promoting African Americans. Only growing profits, as WAOK overtook WERD as the most popular black-oriented station in Atlanta, kept Raymond's many reservations about Sears's racial politics in check. There was, however, grudging respect for his partner's personal integrity on the race issue. Raymond admitted, "There was no phoniness about Zenas. A lot of people are liberals in name, but he was truly interested in the welfare of the black community."[70]

Movement activists and those who worked for both WERD and WAOK all agreed that civil rights coverage, public service broadcasting, and community service efforts at WAOK were more extensive than at its black-owned rival. Esmond Patterson, who worked for both Blayton and Sears, had no doubts about who had the greater rapport with the black masses in Atlanta. While Blayton remained a rather aloof, distant figure, Patterson recalled how Sears hung out on Auburn and "could come down and shake hands with you, fellowship with you and . . . you'd think, 'He's one of us.'" Julian Bond, who did not even realize Sears was white until he met him at a fund-raising dinner in the early 1960s, speculated that this intense identification with the black community might actually have been a consequence of the station's white ownership. Bond felt that WAOK "probably made an extra effort to be community-oriented because of its white ownership, and didn't want to be accused of . . . exploiting the community."[71]

There was probably some truth to Bond's analysis. Irrespective of Jesse Blayton's caution, WERD had always enjoyed a special, almost mythical, status in the eyes of black Atlantans simply by virtue of its unassailable position as the country's first black-owned radio station. Faced with this sort of grip on the hearts, minds, and dollars of more than 250,000 black Atlantans, Sears needed to work especially hard to establish WAOK's credentials as a legitimate voice for the city's African American community. One way to achieve this goal was to identify the station ever more closely with rising black aspirations and the emerging civil rights movement. Zenas Sears clearly did this very well. Helped by the fact that the station had a more powerful transmitter (5,000 watts as opposed to WERD's 1,000 watts) and unlike its daytime rival was licensed to broadcast twenty-four hours a day, "WAOK was the big station," according to SNCC activist and later Atlanta councilman James Bond. As Donald Vails noted, this was not exclusively a function of its greater public support for the movement. Agreeing that "WERD was not as popular as AOK," with the mass of Atlanta's black listeners, Vails pointed out that "the better deejays were on AOK."[72] Zenas Sears, a rhythm and blues and gospel man through and through, simply had a better feel for the sort of entertainment that would appeal to his black audience and keep advertising rates high. That such commercial calculations always played an important part in Sears's calculations should not detract from his genuine concern about the struggles of his black listeners. Moreover, Sears acted upon that commitment. Not only did he take up formal leadership positions among the city's white racial liberals, serving, for example, as vice-chairman of the Greater Atlanta Council on Human Relations, but he also ensured that WAOK provided a consistently high level of public service to the black community in Atlanta.[73]

Although WAOK was consistently more popular than WERD among black listeners in Atlanta, it is somewhat disingenuous to split hairs about which station offered the greater sustenance to the movement. It does, however, expose the fallacy that African American ownership of a radio station automatically produced much more engaged, socially conscious, and progressive black-oriented broadcasting. In the final analysis, there were many more similarities than differences between the two stations and their interaction with the organized freedom struggle. Indeed, despite their rivalries, SNCC's assistant communications director Mary King has described an almost "fraternal" relationship between SNCC and the two stations when it came to movement matters. "They would take anything we had to give them. . . . the Atlanta black radio stations were almost like a part of our office," she remembered.[74]

Deejay Paul E. X. Brown reiterated this sense of common ground in his assessment of the two stations' contribution to the movement in Atlanta. While the self-congratulatory image of a "city too busy to hate" wilted in the face of periodic outbreaks of racial violence and continued discrimination, Atlanta did generally avoid the major civic disorder that racked many other southern towns in the late 1950s and early 1960s. This was partly a function of the restraining influence of powerful black and white economic interests in the city. It was also partly a function of the relative strength of black political power in Atlanta, even before the Voting Rights Act of 1965. Yet when tensions ran highest and young protesters headed out onto the streets of Atlanta or gathered at the courthouses and voter registration booths to face down the naked power of white supremacy, Brown insisted that it was black-oriented radio that often cooled tempers and reminded the activists that they were in the movement for the long, nonviolent haul. "I think that we had the same voices on radio—both on WERD and on AOK—that championed justice rather than violence and protracted destruction," Brown suggested. Working in tandem with a civil rights leadership in Atlanta that, for all its differences, "was constantly urging on the voter registration thing and the advocacy of just laws," black-oriented radio in the city was a major factor in promoting constructive, rather than destructive, protest. "We had the ability to reach people and get them to show their best side, and as a result of the black radio's ability to get the message out we were saved . . . a lot of internal struggle— physical struggle. Unlike in some other communities, we did not have the destruction and the violence. . . . I contend that much of that was because of the quick response that radio—radio people—could do in this town to get the message out."[75]

Like Paul Brown, Julian Bond placed a lot of emphasis on the immediacy of radio's response to events in evaluating its importance—and not just in Atlanta. With a few conspicuous exceptions, notably the *Atlanta Daily World,* southern black newspapers came out weekly. "But with radio, you're right there, right today—five minutes from now, you're on the air." There was something special about the real-time quality of the broadcasts on black-oriented radio stations that not only conveyed the urgency and drama of events but could sometimes pull people into wanting to be part of the movement. Black-oriented radio was a community institution. The stations were home to trusted and admired deejays and announcers whose broadcasts, although laced with slick commercial pitches, were imbued with a certain moral authority. When black-oriented radio reported on the struggle for black equality and respect or urged practical support for that struggle, its messages carried much the same weight as when preachers made similar pleas from their pulpits—except that the radio audience was a good deal bigger. Deejay Eddie Castleberry put it succinctly: "As any fool can tell you, nobody can get a black audience like a black radio station can. Nobody!"[76] Mary King also invoked this aspect of black-oriented broadcasting's mass appeal when she described SNCC's use of radio in the South as "an ongoing verbal pep rally." SNCC fought hard to get on black-oriented radio in the South precisely because it was such an effective tool for encouraging black unity and promoting enthusiasm for the movement. More than any other medium, King believed that it was radio that let black southerners "know that there were people who were active. . . . the whole thing just built solidarity, and built a conviction that there was something much bigger than any one town or city."[77]

A Partial Thaw

During the late 1950s and early 1960s, most of the groups interested in using radio to promote the southern civil rights movement tended to plow their own furrows, cultivating their own crop of sympathetic stations and individual owners, deejays, and program directors. In early 1964, however, Robert McNamara III founded the Civil Rights Information Service (CRIS) in Chicago as "a central clearing house for news of the civil rights movement in the United States."[78] With financial backing from various civil rights and religious groups like CORE, SNCC, the National Council of Churches (NCC), and the Gandhi Society, CRIS was designed to coordinate and enhance all aspects of media coverage of the freedom struggle. Ambitious in scope, the initiative was not restricted to either radio or the South.[79] Nevertheless, McNamara felt that improving links between the movement and black-oriented radio was the most important contribution CRIS could make to the struggle for racial equality. Recognizing the medium's unique capacity to reach the black masses, McNamara explained: "Presently the gravest need for regular information is among Negroes. . . . As a generally semi-illiterate group their only regular communication medium contact is with radio."[80] The first practical step toward realizing this goal came with the creation of a Civil Rights Network. Each day CRIS staffers in Chicago sifted through the regular stream of phone calls, telegrams, letters, news clippings, and taped actualities sent in from movement workers and press reporters in the South. They then relayed the most newsworthy items via conference calls to the CRIS network of radio stations. Each weekend CRIS produced a more analytical digest of the week's top stories. By May 1964 twenty-one black-oriented stations in eighteen cities had subscribed to the CRIS service, including important southern facilities like WAOK.[81]

Though funding difficulties meant that McNamara's initiative quickly folded, it was highly influential. CRIS was, for example, partly responsible for a change in the NUL's radio strategy, which until the mid-1960s revolved mainly around cultivating links between local chapters and individual stations. In early 1964, receipt of McNamara's prospectus and his request for funds to launch CRIS had rekindled the League's interest in an earlier proposal by Julius Thomas for "a nation-wide series addressed to the Negro community through a selected group of radio stations that beam their programs to the Negro consumer." Although western regional director Henry Talbert's enthusiasm for using soul radio "to reach many persons who would not ordinarily listen to the sophisticated types of programs" smacked of condescension toward the black masses and their cultural predilections, he nonetheless recognized the potential of black-oriented radio's genuinely mass appeal.[82]

Protracted debates within the NUL and its public relations committee about tactical and budgetary priorities meant that it was not until May 1965 that the NUL began to circulate a pair of weekly shows, *The Leaders Speak* and *Civil Rights Roundup*. Both programs were masterminded by Sherwood Ross, the league's assistant public relations director and later news director at WOL-Washington. Ross intended the shows to fulfill three specific goals: to improve the image of the NUL, to educate the African American community about civil rights activities, and to assist the League's local branches in their membership drives. Written by Ross and presented by Pat Connell of WCBS–New York, *Civil Rights Roundup* distilled the week's major civil rights news stories into a fifteen-minute slot. On June 8, 1965, for example, the show reported on the rise of the Deacons for Defense in Louisiana, a strike by black cotton workers in Leland, Mississippi, and Lyndon Johnson's "To Fulfill These Rights" speech at Howard University, in which the president admitted there was still much to be done to ensure that equality of opportunity became a reality in America. "You do not take a person who, for years, has been hobbled by chains and liberate him, bring him up to the starting line of a race and then say 'you are free to compete with all the others,' and still justly believe that you have been completely fair," Johnson said. *The Leaders Speak* programs consisted of interviews by Ross with a range of civil rights leaders. Among those appearing were Whitney Young of the NUL, Cleveland Robinson of the Negro American Labor Council, the NAACP's Roy Wilkins, and the movement's gadfly genius Bayard Rustin.[83]

At their peak in late 1965, about seventy black-oriented stations around the nation took the NUL's syndicated broadcasts. Even more impressive was the extent to which they were now accepted on southern radio stations including WERD and WAOK in Atlanta, WRMA-Montgomery, WLOK-Memphis, WSRC-Durham, WVOL-Nashville, WAUG-Augusta, WENN-Birmingham, WILA-Danville, WDIX-Orangeburg, WRAP and WHIH in Norfolk, and WYLD–New Orleans.[84] Clearly the climate of opinion in the southern broadcasting industry, as in the region and nation more generally, had undergone significant change in the years since *Brown* and Montgomery.

To suggest that the South was a rather different place in 1965 from what it had been a decade earlier is not to imply that racial justice reigned supreme everywhere—or anywhere, for that matter. Nor is it to minimize the difficulties civil rights advocates still sometimes faced in trying to secure radio time. In 1965 the Committee of Southern Churchmen used a $2,000 grant from the United Church of Christ to produce and distribute to southern radio stations twenty taped programs urging racial reconciliation. There were extremely positive responses from some southern stations such as WSNW-Seneca, South Carolina, WCHV-Charlottesville, Virginia, and WPNC-Plymouth, North Carolina, where manager Curtis Welborne gushed that, in the midst of white reluctance to desegregate, "Your programs may well be the answer to our prayers." Other stations, however, remained coldly dismissive, including WAPF-McComb, Mississippi, WIS-Columbia, South Carolina, and WJAY in Mullins, South Carolina, where the manager refused to touch anything with "what looks like a heavy political overtone to the scripts."[85]

Despite such caution and even outright hostility toward racially progressive broadcasting, the movement and its allies had wrought important changes in law, practices, and attitudes in the South that manifested themselves in better access to the southern airways by mid-decade. By 1965, for example, the CORE chapter in Chapel Hill, North Carolina, actually had a regular local radio show, hosted by Charles Miller. Home of the University of North Carolina and a long-time stronghold of southern racial liberalism, Chapel Hill may not have been typical of much of Dixie. Still, at least it was somewhere that would regularly play the tapes that CORE field worker Ed Hollander had conscientiously compiled farther south, including several reports on the movement and the WBOX saga in Bogalusa.[86] The following year *Broadcasting* reported further signs of changing attitudes and policies on southern radio. After a dozen years of black-oriented programming, WSRC-Durham had finally "joined in" the civil rights movement "to a degree." The station's white president James Mayes felt that by airing news reports, editorials, and discussion programs relating to racial matters, covering civil rights conventions, and allowing activists to make announcements of local meetings, the station was "contributing to progress in our area. . . . we can see results happen when we make time available for discussions, etc."[87]

Even in the Deep South there were signs that restrictions on pro–civil rights radio broadcasts, or at least on more comprehensive and balanced reporting, might be easing. CORE strategists in Louisiana in the summer of 1965 were optimistic that "Negro radio stations may be willing to cooperate in publicizing the activities in Jonesboro and could be especially helpful in obtaining donations of building materials" to rebuild burned churches in an area characterized by especially violent white repression and resistance.[88] In Mississippi, where the media situation for the movement was especially bleak, things became noticeably better around mid-decade. Following years of struggling to get any kind of positive message onto the state's airways, Mississippi Freedom Democratic Party (MFDP) chairman Lawrence Guyot recalled that "After 1965 . . . we could buy time on the radio and we could go on and talk."[89]

Several factors contributed to this gradual, uneven, but unmistakable thaw in the icy treatment many southern radio stations had meted out to the civil rights movement. For all the forces conspiring to frustrate movement efforts to use the southern airways effectively, it is important to appreciate that there were always other, countervailing trends working in precisely the opposite direction to encourage greater recognition of, support for, and, on rare occasions, participation in, the freedom struggle by southern broadcasters. By 1964 and 1965 these forces had combined to foster a change in attitudes within the industry toward covering the southern freedom struggle. One obvious factor here was that, as the movement gathered momentum following the sit-ins of 1960, it quickly became the major domestic news story of the era. This made it much more difficult for any credible radio station to ignore. Of course, some southern stations did their best to do just that, while others offered extremely prejudicial news coverage and public service programming designed more to bolster white resistance than to inspire sympathy for civil rights. Nevertheless, by the middle of the decade most southern stations—general-market and black-oriented—felt compelled to cover the civil rights movement. Moreover, as more white southerners began to accept the inevitability and sometimes even the desirability of an end to Jim Crow, southern news and public affairs programming began to reflect this new per-

FIGURE 10. As the southern civil rights movement flourished in the 1960s, stations like KYOK-Houston became much more publicly involved in demonstrations against Jim Crow. Courtesy of Archives of African American Music and Culture, Indiana University.

spective. After the summer of 1963, this trend was accentuated by the likelihood that civil rights groups would invoke the FCC's Fairness Doctrine to challenge any broadcasters who ignored or wantonly distorted news of the southern campaign for racial equality.

Only a few, mostly black-oriented, southern stations actually became flag-waving champions of desegregation and black voting rights. However, by mid-decade most of the region's broadcasters had recovered sufficiently from the initial shock of mass black insurgency and their fear of white supremacist reprisals to relax prohibitions on reports and discussions of the latest developments in the freedom struggle. As the movement steadily dismantled Jim Crow, many southern radio stations gravitated back to the kind of pleas for interracial goodwill, tolerance, and understanding that had characterized the medium's response to racial issues before the emergence of a mass protest campaign. Ed Randall's *Friendly World* shows enjoyed widespread acceptance in the region during the decade or so after *Brown* by sounding precisely this kind of conciliatory note. Similarly, whenever protest came to a particular southern town or city, local radio stations of all formats were often to be heard encouraging interracial dialogue and urging both races to remain calm and law-abiding. This was true even in Bogalusa in the tense summer of 1965 when black demonstrations against the city's increasingly violent defense of a now illegal system of segregation intensified. While WBOX and Ralph Blumberg served as the focal point for white racial extremists, "police officials and civic leaders were broadcasting appeals for law and order five times each hour . . . over a rival station."[90]

Two other factors also help to explain why the movement enjoyed greater access to southern radio by the mid-1960s. The first applied primarily to black-oriented stations. Since the value of the black consumer market continued to grow, and since radio remained the most effective means of selling goods to those consumers, broadcasters were reluctant to alienate that audience by ignoring a phenomenon so dear to its heart and interests. Many executives at black-oriented stations in the South might have preferred to pretend that the civil rights revolution was not happening, but their black listeners clearly felt very differently and had the economic power to make their feelings matter. By mid-decade, according to Eddie Castleberry, black-oriented station owners "had already gotten the idea that it was to their advantage to be connected with the civil rights movement."[91]

Egmont Sonderling had no reputation as a civil rights advocate, but he recognized this universal truth. Shortly after adding WOL-Washington to his stable of black-oriented stations in 1965, Sonderling confirmed what most of his fellow owners already knew: "A Negro radio station has to be involved in the struggle for integration. You cannot operate a radio station and not be involved. This is true of every city. It does not make any difference whether you operate in Washington, in New York, in Memphis, or in St. Louis, or in New Orleans. The same is true everywhere. . . . You must give a voice to the Negro, that is, to the civil rights organizations." True to this credo, within a year of converting WOL to black-oriented programming Sonderling had hired Sherwood Ross, and the NUL, the NAACP, CORE, and SNCC had all secured airtime on the station.[92]

The final factor explaining the expanded opportunities for pro-movement broadcasts on southern radio was simply that the emergence of a viable civil rights campaign had thrown up a new cadre of emboldened individuals and organizations who were actually interested in trying to use the power of southern radio in the campaign for racial justice. The key individuals here were those civil rights workers, deejays, reporters, owners, and managers who repeatedly tested the limits of what was acceptable in terms of civil rights advocacy and movement news coverage on southern radio. Thanks largely to their efforts, coupled with the demands of black listeners for news of the movement, it became much more common to hear opinions broadly supportive of black civil and voting rights. Thus, one of the many indices of the movement's achievements during the decade or so after *Brown* is that it decisively altered prevailing notions of what constituted acceptable broadcasting on racial matters in the South.

This was not true everywhere in the region, as WBOX's Ralph Blumberg had discovered to his cost in Bogalusa. Just as the civil rights movement unfolded differently in every town, city, and state in the South, so the story of southern radio's relationship to the freedom struggle was ultimately different at every station and in every community. As historian J. Mills Thornton has explained, "just as local politics was essential to the creation of southern segregation, so local politics was the crucial factor in creating the circumstances that ended it." With Thornton's formula in mind, the next three chapters examine in detail the intimate and complex links between local radio and changing patterns of protest politics and race relations in three very different southern locales: Birmingham, Charlotte, and the state of Mississippi.[93]

7

WENN's Push Came to Shove

Black-Oriented Radio and the Freedom Struggle in Birmingham

We, as radio announcers or personalities, certainly knew
that if blacks take up arms and go out in the streets and confront
these people with these things, it would have been chaos.
Shelley "the Playboy" Stewart

The Tangled Roots of Black-Oriented Radio in Birmingham

In 1957, three of the twenty-two radio stations in the American South that programmed exclusively for African American audiences were located in and
around the city of Birmingham, Alabama: WJLD, WEDR, and WBCO.[1] There
were good commercial reasons why broadcasters were so interested in the Magic
City and its black inhabitants. In the early 1950s Birmingham's African American consumer market was hailed as the "South's fastest growing," with black
purchasing power reaching $138 million annually by the end of the decade. Ad-
mittedly, there were already signs of the deindustrialization in the mining, steel,
and other heavy industries that would eventually devastate the black working
class in Birmingham, condemning many to inadequate public housing projects
and squalid rental accommodation. Yet this trend was partially offset by the si-
multaneous expansion of a relatively prosperous and ambitious black middle
class. By 1953 more than half of Birmingham's black population owned their
own homes, compared with just 38 percent in the late 1940s. At the same time,
the average annual black family income of $1,849 was the highest in the entire
South; African American families in New Orleans, Atlanta, and Memphis did
next best, but all lagged more than $200 per year behind their Birmingham
counterparts.[2] Ultimately, this burgeoning black income fueled the growth of
black-oriented broadcasting in the Birmingham area after World War II. As a
WBCO sales pitch from the early 1950s put it, "It's a proven fact that the best way

to *sell* the Birmingham area's quarter million Negroes is with ALL-NEGRO radio."[3]

This chapter examines the role of black-oriented stations such as WJLD, WEDR, and WENN—which effectively superseded WBCO in the late 1950s—in the Birmingham freedom struggle. As elsewhere in the South, these stations helped to fashion the new black consciousness, the sense of common identity, pride, and purpose, upon which civil rights activism was predicated. They served as electronic clearinghouses, simultaneously reflecting local needs and showcasing local talent, while linking Birmingham's African American community to broader regional and national trends in culture and politics. During the 1950s and early 1960s, black-oriented stations in Birmingham also offered financial and moral support to the movement, did their best to report it accurately, and occasionally moved beyond such essentially supportive functions to play a crucial role in shaping local protests. The roots of this involvement, however, lay in the history of black-oriented broadcasting in Birmingham from the 1930s.

In early 1959 the station known as WENN was still a small 250-watt facility located in Bessemer, Alabama. Formerly known as WBCO, the station had been purchased the previous year by broadcasting mogul John McLendon, whose southern outlets already included WNLA-Indianola, WOKJ-Jackson, KOKY–Little Rock, and KOKA-Shreveport. Like WBCO, WENN continued to direct "100% of its programming to the Negro population of Bessemer." At the time, however, Bessemer had a total population of just 32,300, while in metropolitan Birmingham the African American population alone numbered more than 236,000. This metropolitan market was where the largest and most lucrative black audience was to be found. Unfortunately for McLendon, the low-wattage transmitter, combined with Birmingham's peculiarly elongated shape and rigidly segregated residential neighborhoods, made it impossible for his station to reach even half of these potential black customers. What WENN needed was a downtown Birmingham site and a much more powerful transmitter. As luck would have it, in May 1959 both became available thanks to events at WEZB, a daytime station based in the nearby suburb of Homewood.[4]

In the early 1950s WEZB was an affiliate of the Mutual Broadcasting Network and concentrated on programming for a general-market audience. In an effort to extend its share of that market, the owners, Dorsey (Gene) Newman and his father, Charles, had acquired FCC permission to build a more powerful 5,000-watt transmitter and open new studios in downtown Birmingham. Yet the Newmans came to believe that the success of WEZB was less dependent on getting a bigger transmitter than on extending its sunup-to-sundown time on air. WENN, John McLendon's tiny black-oriented experiment, had just the sort of full-time operating license the Newmans coveted. With McLendon hankering after a move from Bessemer to a downtown Birmingham site and a more powerful transmitter, the two parties began to discuss the possibility of swapping facilities.

By the summer of 1959, a complicated transfer involving various sorts of compensation to Gene Newman Radio, Inc.—which was effectively downgrading its facility while simultaneously increasing its airtime—had been agreed. McLendon quickly finished work on what had originally been intended as WEZB's new transmitter and relaunched WENN as a daytime 5,000-watt black-oriented station operating out of new studios on 5th Avenue North. The station was now positioned geographically, as well as culturally and spiritually, in the heart of the black Birmingham community, not far from the Gaston Motel owned by black millionaire A. G. Gaston and just a block away from the Sixteenth Street Baptist Church. Both buildings were destined to play a major part in the histories of the station and the civil rights struggle in Birmingham.[5]

If one strain in WENN's lineage reached back to WEZB, an even more important one connected it to the pioneers of black-oriented radio in the Birmingham area. It is unclear precisely when regular black-oriented broadcasting began in Birmingham. Robert Durr, the black publisher and editor of Birmingham's *Weekly Review*, certainly liked to claim the distinction of having blazed this particular trail. In early 1941 he boasted that his daily show *The Negro in the News* on WSGN was "the only one of its kind in the world," with a weekly biracial audience of anything up to 100,000.[6]

Durr's boast notwithstanding, William Blevins had an even better claim to being the first African American to appear regularly on the city's airwaves. Born in Selma in 1895, Blevins came from an affluent black family—especially on his mother's side, where his grandfather, Rev. Howard Johnson, owned around two hundred acres of land. By the time he arrived at Selma University, Blevins already had a reputation as a fine singer of classical and religious music. After graduating, he moved to Birmingham and, following a stint in the army during World War I, returned to work at the Tennessee Coal, Iron and Railroad Company plant. He took jobs in insurance and as a Pullman porter before joining the transportation department of the *Birmingham News*. Blevins was also a devoted member of the Tabernacle Baptist Church, rising to become star soloist with its choir. This musical talent led him into radio.[7]

In December 1932 the manager of WKBC, Evelyn Hicks, put out a call for singers to audition at the station's studios in the basement of Birmingham's plush Tutwiler Hotel. Having checked with Hicks to see if the station operated a color bar—and having been somewhat surprised to find that it did not—Blevins performed the hymn "Have You Had a Kindness Shown—Pass It On." He was immediately recruited for a gospel slot that aired on Saturdays at 1:15 p.m. An instant success with both black and white listeners, Blevins steadily increased his presence on various Birmingham radio stations throughout the 1930s and

1940s before finding a regular spot on WJLD after World War II. Like most radio announcers and performers of the day, Blevins felt obliged to keep his day job at the newspaper. Indeed, for a while the *Birmingham News*—which purchased WKBC from the R. P. Broyles Furniture Company in the late 1930s and somewhat immodestly renamed it WSGN (for "South's Greatest Newspaper")—actually supported his radio career. The paper hired him as coordinator and on-air announcer when it sponsored shows from the Birmingham Municipal Auditorium featuring local and touring black choirs.[8]

The Famous Blue Jay Singers, the Kings of Harmony, and the Sterling Jubilees were all part of the extraordinary profusion of gospel groups hailing from Jefferson County in the two decades on either side of World War II. These groups not only did much to establish the modern gospel quartet vocal tradition in America, they also joined black preachers in the religious vanguard of early black-oriented programming in Birmingham.[9] At a time when African American radio preachers enjoyed a national audience of seven million souls each week, the sort of religious broadcasting pioneered by Blevins also proved the most consistently popular, and therefore lucrative and widespread, type of programming for Birmingham's African Americans.[10]

At WJLD the intimate links between community, church, commerce, and program content were very clear. Sadie Mae Patterson had initiated the station's first regular gospel show in 1943, barely a year after WJLD had debuted from the Gray Hotel in downtown Bessemer relying on sponsorship from the Davenport and Harris Funeral Home. When, in 1944, prominent local white businessmen George Johnston Jr. and his father, George Sr., who had wide-ranging interests in real estate, investment banking, cemeteries, mining, clothing manufacture, and retail, bought WJLD from its founder J. Leslie Doss for $106,000, the station immediately began to sell more airtime to local gospel quartets at the rate of $15 for thirty minutes. White deejay Truman Puckett was quick to spot this trend and follow the cash. In the mid-1940s he ditched his country music show in favor of a twice-daily gospel program. Puckett remained a fixture at WJLD for more than two decades, during which time the station moved studios several times, first to the third floor of Bessemer City Hall and then in 1947 into the suburb of Fairfield along the Bessemer Super Highway. In 1966 it moved again, to a site in downtown Birmingham at 109 North 19th Street, where it remained until the early 1970s.[11]

Spanning much the same time period was WJLD's close association with the white-owned Epps Jewelry Company, whose owner Taft Epstein had first spotted the commercial potential of black religious programming around the same time that Truman Puckett got profitably sanctified. Beginning in the 1940s, Epps had sponsored broadcasts by Rev. W. A. Clark and Deacon Richmond Davis from St. Peter's Primitive Baptist Church. During the 1950s and early 1960s, many other

Birmingham ministers also broadcast regularly—usually, but not exclusively, on Sundays. One of the most charismatic was Rev. John Goodgame, the aptly named ex–baseball star who could sometimes be heard offering up both prayers and sales pitches for the Birmingham Black Barons baseball team on WVOK. Goodgame invariably concluded his sermons with "Well, I'm going to the ball-game" before urging his flock to do likewise. WJLD was also home to both Rev. R. C. Cain, who introduced local church choirs from around Jefferson County, and the hugely popular Rev. Jasper Robey, an activist minister whose Seven-teenth Street AOH Church of God subsequently became one of the major ven-ues for civil rights meetings in the city. Other black announcers, including Willie McKinstry, Roberta Roland, and N. B. Wooding, also introduced live and re-corded gospel music at WJLD.[12]

At WBCO in Bessemer, Rev. E. W. Williams of the First Baptist Church and Rev. Erskine Faush—who spread the word of the Lord and Ziegler's sausages with equal relish—were stalwarts throughout the 1950s.[13] WENN inherited and initially replicated this emphasis on religious radio when it took over from WBCO at 1450 kilocycles on the dial. Indeed, whereas a general-market station like WEZB had devoted only 1 percent of its airtime to such godly fare, in 1961 it comprised 41.9 percent of WENN's schedule. During the 1960s, however, the sacred share of the airways declined dramatically, not just at WENN but at most black-oriented stations in the South. This was part of a general pattern of secular-ization in the black community, as many of the social, political, economic, and cultural functions traditionally the preserve of the black church were transferred to more secular institutions—not least to those associated with popular culture and mass recreational activities. By late 1963 WENN reported that only 6.1 per-cent of its airtime was given to religious broadcasts, whereas 86.3 percent was dedicated to "entertainment." Changing definitions of precisely what comprised "entertainment" and "religious" broadcasting may have accounted for some of this shift. Nevertheless, WENN's willingness to downplay, as well as downgrade, its attention to religious programming reflected a deeper trend within the south-ern African American community, particularly among the young blacks who comprised an important part of the radio audience.[14]

The idea that secular as well as sacred programming might appeal to black audiences was nothing new to the 1960s. Most black-oriented radio stations in the South had always offered a mixed "Bible and blues" format. In the process they had helped to erode distinctions between the sacred and secular spheres of black life that, although real enough, had always been rather more rigid in pious theory than in popular practice. In Birmingham, WJLD was especially innova-tive when it came to secular programming for its black listeners. Perhaps the most influential show in the city immediately after the War was Bob Umbach's *Atomic Boogie Hour,* which first appeared in 1946 as an hour-long experiment in

FIGURE 11. Bob Umbach's *Atomic Boogie Hour* on WJLD was enormously popular with both white and black audiences in Birmingham during the late 1940s and early 1950s. Courtesy of Friedman/Four Octaves.

rhythm and blues radio. According to locally raised deejay Shelley "the Playboy" Stewart, for a while Umbach's show was "the only place that you could hear black [secular] music on the radio." When Umbach left WJLD in 1953—apparently having made the most of the plentiful opportunities for payola at the time— *Atomic Boogie Hour* had become an enormously popular six-hour-a-day feast of the finest rhythm and blues music that black America had to offer. Indeed, the show became such an institution that it even survived Umbach's departure, being hosted briefly by Roy Wood and then by the flamboyant King Porter.[15]

Bob Umbach, like Truman Puckett, was white. So, too, were several more of the most popular deejays among African Americans in Birmingham during the early 1950s. Joe "Duke the Dynamo" Rumore was an ex-marine who had seen action at Okinawa and worked at WMC-Memphis and Birmingham's WVOK before joining WJLD in April 1952. Rumore gleefully mixed pop and hillbilly with what was euphemistically described in the local press as "other type music"—namely, rhythm and blues. The dapper, bespectacled Jack Jackson—a former combat photographer who had taken the first harrowing shots of the liberated Dachau concentration camp—was similarly eclectic in his record selections at WLBS. Jackson played black and white gospel music to the delight of black and white audiences.[16]

The race of the deejays spinning gospel and rhythm and blues recordings on the radio initially appears to have been of relatively little consequence to African Americans in Birmingham. They were simply thrilled to hear their favorite music given exposure after years of neglect by broadcasters. "We didn't think about [it] one way or the other," confessed Eddie Castleberry, a black Birmingham native who joined WEDR in the early 1950s and later moved to WJLD. Like many other southerners of his generation, Castleberry had actually grown up in the 1940s and early 1950s listening not only to the rhythm and blues spun locally by Bob Umbach and Duke Rumore but also to nighttime broadcasts from Nashville. At the mighty WLAC, white deejays John Richbourg, Gene Nobles, and Hoss Allen cast a magical black musical net over much of the continent long after the daytime stations had fallen silent. The motivations of all these pioneering southern white gospel and rhythm and blues deejays were invariably linked to their commercial aspirations as they sought out the underserviced African American radio audience. Yet there was nothing cynical or shallow about their enthusiasm for black music. Deejays like Dewey Phillips in Memphis, Zenas Sears in Atlanta, and the Nashville trinity were fans and aficionados. Castleberry recalled thinking, "My God, them guys—they *know*—they're hip!" In fact, he conceded, so great was their knowledge of and respect for black style, "We thought the guys *were* black."[17]

Nevertheless, according to Shelley Stewart, gratitude that these white deejays were at least playing some black music was always tempered by a lurking resentment that they prospered because of their ability to "act black" on air at a time when opportunities for black broadcasters were extremely limited. According to *Ebony,* none of the sixteen African Americans permanently employed as deejays in the USA in 1947 worked in the Birmingham market. Ed Castleberry certainly noted the community's excitement as the number of black announcers in the city slowly increased, and the special pride that greeted the launch of WEDR in August 1949. Although WJLD had been steadily expanding its commitment to black audiences and its roster of black deejays since the mid-1940s, it did not become entirely black-oriented until late 1954. WEDR, therefore, was the first station in the area that catered specifically to black audiences and boasted an entirely black on-air staff. "We were so glad when the black guys came on the air. We got a whole station and all the guys on it were black . . . that was great. It had a terrific impact," Castleberry remembered.[18]

Significantly, the black deejays at WEDR did not completely reject the idea of playing some white artists on their shows. While Eddie Castleberry was adamant that he would never help "break a white record"—which is to say he would never give exposure to a newly released white version of a song at the expense of giving airtime to an aspiring black one—he was not averse to playing white disks that had already proved popular with his black listeners. Shelley Stewart was an eclectic from the start and became even more so from the mid-1950s when he noticed increasing numbers of teenaged white fans among those writing requests to his *Roll Call* feature on WEDR. "My position was that you could take it all. I would mix the blues with anything. I would play a Sarah Vaughan, I would play Ella Fitzgerald, I would play a Dinah Washington. I would also play the Ray Charles. I would play the Howling Wolf. I would play B. B. King. I would play anything and I would mix it all. . . . I would even put jazz in my presentation. . . . I played Bobby Darin; blacks did like Bobby Darin. As a matter of fact, I played Elvis Presley."[19]

It was this sort of musical miscegenation, coupled with the evident admiration of many southern white youths for black announcers and recording artists, that led some to hail black-oriented programming as a catalyst for, or at least harbinger of, better relations between the races. If this rather naively simplified the complex and often highly ambiguous relationship between white love of African American music and white racial attitudes, Shelley Stewart agreed that at one level black-oriented Birmingham radio, its producers and consumers, had effectively "integrated prior to the so-called political integration thing." Legal and habitual barriers persisted, but "that music community, that radio community . . . began to communicate . . . because of the music . . . and the black radio in the black community being accepted and enjoyed now by the white community." With the ownership and senior management of black radio in Birmingham still firmly in white hands, however, this was a very limited, perilous, and inequitable form of integration. The racial violence that scarred the city in the late 1950s and early 1960s served as a salutary reminder that it would take rather more than youthful biracial enthusiasm for Elvis Presley and Little Richard to bring down Jim Crow.[20]

Building Community: Black Deejays, Black Programming, and Black Respectability

By the mid-1950s several African American deejays had become beloved and influential figures in Birmingham. In addition to Eddie Castleberry, WEDR had boxing champion–cum–blues jockey Perry "Tiger" Thompson, Frank Smart, and Ben Alexander. WJLD boasted "Rack 'Em Back Zack" Allen and Willie McKinstry, who risked the Lord's wrath by adding a rhythm and blues show to his gospel radio résumé. Andrew "Sugar Daddy" Dawkins and Edward "Johnny Jive" McClure were leading lights at WBCO before it morphed into WENN. As the 1960s dawned, with WENN moving downtown and quickly becoming the leading black-oriented station in the market, its top announcers included the charismatic newscaster-turned-deejay "Tall Paul" White, a U.S. Army veteran who joined from nearby, and black-owned, WEUP-Huntsville. Shelley "the Black

Pope" Pope made the same trip, while namesake Shelley Stewart stepped across town from a rapidly failing WEDR. These radio personalities "were superheroes in our neighborhoods," Eddie Castleberry recalled.[21]

The prestige and respect enjoyed by these black announcers was important to the way radio worked to strengthen the bonds of community in black Birmingham. That process was also linked to their, and the medium's, role as a major source of shared news and information. In 1961, for example, WENN carried ten five-minute newscasts each day, half of which dealt with local events. In addition, it ran various public service spots ranging from weather reports and farm news to black sports roundups and announcements of job opportunities, church fêtes, and a variety of civic and club meetings. By the early 1960s WENN was also pioneering a prototype phone-in show called *Opinion Time*, which ran for thirty minutes every Tuesday and enabled listeners to "call in to express opinions on current topics and issues." The station also demonstrated its sense of community responsibility in very practical ways. For example, when fire destroyed Willie Welton's house in 1959, WENN organized food and shelter. It did the same in November 1962 when Mrs. Fannie Shelby's fatherless family of eight children was left homeless after a fire, and again a year later when a blaze left Mrs. Robeytine and her twelve children destitute at a time when her husband was a patient in the Jefferson County TB Sanitarium. This sanitarium, like the Partlow State School for the mentally retarded in Tuscaloosa, regularly received seasonal gifts from the station's Christmas Fund, while WENN's annual Christmas House project distributed toys to needy black children.[22]

Yet for all its communalizing power, black-oriented radio never completely transcended, let alone erased, the class, educational, gender, and generational cleavages among the city's African Americans. Indeed, the differences in microphone style among the deejays and the nature of some of the programming revealed much about those underlying tensions and about the aspirations of the black community as Birmingham began to loom large in the story of the southern civil rights struggle. Many of the black deejays belonged firmly in the flamboyant, motormouthed announcing tradition pioneered by Al Benson. They scatted and jive-talked their way into—and sometimes through—the exhilarating records they played in a way that announced their place within a rich tradition of African American oral performance. For Shelley Stewart, even the adoption of a personalized nickname was an act of linguistic creativity and, insofar as it reflected the construction of a new public persona, a means to psychological empowerment, social prestige, and economic success. "[I] created another personality to hide who I really was, Shelley Stewart. . . . I created a different personality with Shelley 'the Playboy,'" admitted Stewart, who had good reason to want to distance himself from a tragic past.[23]

Stewart was the son of an alcoholic and frequently violent laborer employed by the Tennessee Coal and Iron Company who had somehow scraped together the money to move to the middle-class black neighborhood of Rosedale. In Rosedale the Stewart family was routinely shunned by its better-to-do neighbors. A life already marked by domestic terror deteriorated further when Stewart saw his father kill his mother in a fit of rage. His father's girlfriend moved into the house shortly afterwards, but the grim cycle of poverty and abuse continued. At one point neighbors called in health department officials to inspect traps set in the Stewarts' backyard to catch the rats that were fried for the family's supper. Eventually Stewart ran away from home—apparently just after his drunken father had broken his arm. On the road, he found work as a stable boy before returning to a foster family in Rosedale, where he was able to attend, if somewhat fitfully, to his high school education. A bright if distracted student, Stewart aspired to be a lawyer. His teachers told him to set his black sights lower: maybe a mechanic. Disgusted, he fled north to New York and worked for a while as a house painter before enrolling at the Cambridge School of Broadcasting.[24]

Having completed his course and gained some experience on radio in New York, in 1949 Stewart returned to Birmingham, where he persuaded WEDR's white station manager John Thompson to let him read the station's brief round-up of news from local black high schools. This was an era when the brokerage system still dominated the economics of black-oriented radio, and WJLD was unusual in having a relatively sophisticated sales department, under the management of the fearsome Otis Dodge, that sold airtime to advertisers on behalf of its regular announcers. Stewart, however, was initially left to his own entrepreneurial devices. Shortly after his debut, Shelley Stewart secured the first of his many sponsors when he persuaded the Shift Family Shoe Store that business would improve if it paid him for some on-air sales pitches. It did. Before long Stewart was broadcasting several hours a day and drawing a regular salary of $17.50 a week—although he earned part of that princely sum cleaning the station.[25]

For many deejays, living on these marginal and inherently insecure broadcasting incomes, radio acted as a sort of commercial loss-leader. It provided a showcase for talents that they would later exploit in more lucrative personal appearances at local clubs and theaters. In other words, when they went on air they were often selling themselves and their personalities along with other products: the station itself, Schlitz beer, Lucky Strikes, or the latest Fats Domino record. With competition fierce, these commercial considerations spurred creativity and contributed to the intense quest for a highly distinctive, personalized broadcasting style. Recalling his own attitude to announcing, Stewart "believed that it had to be presented in a manner that it would really motivate you; give you a little pizzazz. So I took the high road of being uptempo, using slang words, creating slang, not rhyming, but creating slang." As he cued records, for instance, he would holler, "Timberrrr! Let it fall!" and then drop the needle onto the spinning disk. According to Stewart, some African American announcers and members of the black Birmingham elite objected to this high-octane vernacular style precisely because it sounded too black, too working-class, too lacking in refinement and respectability at a time of integrationist aspirations and burgeoning middle-class ideals. As Stewart appreciated, there was a paradox here. Some African Americans disavowed his use of black street idioms, fearing that it might encourage black youths to neglect the need for correct diction and therefore send the wrong sorts of signals to whites who still needed to be persuaded that blacks were respectable citizens worthy of full civil and voting rights. Yet many young whites were clearly drawn to black radio in part by the same mysterious, exotic, and slightly risqué elements in Stewart's announcing style, just as they were attracted by similar qualities they detected in the music he played.[26]

Of course, presenting contemporary black music and culture on radio was not just a device for reaching young white southerners; it was the key to black-oriented broadcasting's appeal to African Americans. Yet elsewhere within the spectrum of black-oriented radio, the style and content of the programming reflected less the veneration of a uniquely black vernacular style than the powerful competing appeal of a kind of all-American, quintessentially middle-class respectability: a respectability that functioned as both a vehicle for and an index of the success of the struggle for black equality. Thus the second major school of black announcers, the heirs of the urbane Jack L. Cooper, also prospered in Birmingham. Although by no means resistant to the odd spot of down-home patter, deejays like Eddie Castleberry and Jesse Champion represented an extension of the Cooperite tradition of "refined" African American broadcasting. It was no coincidence that both men were college educated. Castleberry, who graduated from Birmingham's Parker High School and then went to Miles College, modeled his announcing style on Wiley Daniels, a cool, laid-back deejay who at the start of the 1950s was one of WEDR's hottest properties. He was a "smooth-type jock and I didn't use too much jive," Castleberry recalled. "I always tried to be the smooth cat." Sometimes this meant that it took him longer to make an impression on audiences than his more in-your-face colleagues, but by 1954 he was one of the five most popular deejays in the city. Reflecting the heterogeneity of a black audience all too frequently reduced to one-dimensional stereotypes, Castleberry appreciated there was room for all types of announcers on black-oriented radio. "People liked our contrasting styles. They didn't want every guy on the air to be flamboyant."[27]

Jesse Champion's education had taken him briefly to Morehouse College in Atlanta and from there to a music scholarship at Alabama A&M University in

Huntsville. In Birmingham he deejayed and read the news at WJLD while also working as a schoolteacher to make ends meet. His deep, luscious baritone and careful diction made him an attractive proposition for advertisers who were anxious to give a classy veneer to the products they wished to sell—particularly at a time when the advertising industry, under pressure from the NAACP, was seeking to rid the airwaves of offensive racial stereotyping in commercials. Champion's polished tones also helped those like the hustling local car salesman "Big Hearted Eddie" who really did need to try to squeeze every possible ounce of respectability and credibility out of their sales pitches.[28]

The drive toward mainstream middle-class respectability on Birmingham's black radio, coincident as it sometimes was with the airing of ribald rhythm and blues songs that many whites and some blacks found deeply disreputable, was also apparent in the emphasis on black educational needs, achievements, and initiatives. WENN, for example, regularly broadcast free public service announcements and organized appeals on behalf of the United Negro College Fund, and supported the annual American Education Week program by inviting local black schoolchildren to visit its studios. The station made various annual awards to local African American educators and students and sponsored spelling bees at the city's black elementary schools. In 1963 Tall Paul White served as publicity chairman for a Miles College fund-raising appeal, while later the same year the station sought to use its influence with young blacks in a campaign against high school dropouts. This concern with preventing various forms of delinquency among the city's youth also extended to making gifts of new and used records to various black youth clubs, running regular children's picnics, and sponsoring several softball leagues.[29] These well-meaning gestures actually made WENN complicit in the perpetuation of inferior segregated public facilities and services for blacks in Birmingham. Its financial support offered a tacit endorsement of Jim Crow that, paradoxically, may have helped to make it more bearable and thus retarded the emergence of organized mass protest. Nevertheless, WENN's concern with promoting racial progress through educational excellence and conspicuous respectability reflected the dominant strategies of the early civil rights movement.

As part of a related agenda, WENN also celebrated the middle-class ideal of a patriarchal nuclear family, in which conventional male and female roles as breadwinner-protector and homemaker-nurturer respectively were firmly entrenched. Annual "Mother of the Year" and "My Pops Is Tops" awards announced the station's support for traditional gender and family values. In the early 1960s WENN ran Exposition 60, "designed to introduce the Negro homemakers of the Birmingham area to the latest developments and services related to homemaking," and sponsored the annual Negro Homeshow of Birmingham, where all the latest examples of good domestic taste and smart suburban living

FIGURE 12. From 1947 WJLD was an important presence in the lives of the African American communities of Birmingham and Bessemer, where the station was located. Courtesy of Friedman/Four Octaves.

could be seen. It also ran a daily show sponsored by the Birmingham Housewife's League "to educate the housekeeper in new and better methods of household cleaning, food preparation, etc."[30]

Other black-oriented stations in the city did much the same. When WJLD finally converted to an entirely black-oriented format in 1954, it aired an hourlong *Homemakers Club* three mornings a week. The show featured "cooking and household hints, plus fashion news and a morning sermon from one of the local ministers." It was a perfect example of how conventional domesticity was associated with the sort of virtuous living and moral probity that not only accorded with white middle-class values but was also deeply enshrined in the teachings of black churches, schools, and colleges. Subsequent WJLD programs with a similar format included *Luncheon with Lora* and, perhaps the most popular of all, *The Luncheon Show* hosted by Alma Johnson, who would later marry future U.S. secretary of state Colin Powell. Johnson epitomized the sort of female respectability, education, and refinement that black-oriented stations routinely celebrated and that victory in the struggle for equal opportunity promised to make possible for all black women. Billed with suitable professional gravitas as WJLD's "home economist," Johnson was a gifted and attractive product of the black Birmingham elite. Her father was principal of Parker High School, and she graduated from Fisk University with a degree in speech and drama. Her pedigree shaped her elegant radio style. Eschewing the more frenetic approach of many other broadcasters, Johnson oozed intelligence, poise, and charm. She embodied a vision of a brighter future when African Americans might thrive as fully enfranchised citizens in the mainstream of American life. WJLD assured advertisers with "a product of primary interest to women" that Alma Johnson's "smooth program and smooth delivery can do an outstanding job for you."[31] Thus, while black aspirations and the commercial imperatives that drove the broadcasting industry were often at odds, here they were in some sort of ragged harmony, with consumerism yoked to the black bid for respect, equal opportunity, and civil rights.

The steady endorsement of domestic respectability and traditional gender roles on black-oriented radio in Birmingham was riddled with paradoxes. The rhythm and blues music played by the stations sometimes depicted volatile and predatory relationships between the sexes that were anything but the epitome of domestic stability. Moreover, a combination of poverty, the early stages of deindustrialization, and endemic racism meant that the proportion of black women in the workforce, and of black men who were unemployed, underemployed, and/or absent from their families, was considerably higher among Birmingham's African Americans than among its white population. Nevertheless, African Americans generally aspired to and sought to emulate these elusive domestic ideals, viewing them as important markers of racial, economic, and social progress. At the same time, as the modern freedom struggle emerged, African Americans also became bolder and prouder in their embrace of distinctively black cultural and social practices. The southern movement may have been broadly supportive of integration, but civil rights and integration were never synonyms: there were many precious aspects of African American culture that had flourished under segregation and that the black community was anxious to preserve.

This was one example of a tension that coursed through black-oriented radio in the South and largely defined it from the late 1940s until the early 1960s. Excited by the possibilities of gaining access on equal terms to the rewards of the mainstream, yet aware that its market edge depended on the preservation of a discernibly black identity, the medium was characterized by a sort of Du Boisian frisson between the integrationist and nationalistic impulses that have always jostled for position within black consciousness. This tension was further complicated by the preeminence of white owners and managers in the industry. Although just as aware as their African American staff that healthy profits depended on preserving their stations' racial credentials and characteristics, white executives were less than comfortable whenever that distinctiveness manifested itself in support for the local community's gathering challenge to Jim Crow. In Birmingham those tensions came to a head in the late 1950s and early 1960s as a mass movement for civil rights coalesced under the leadership of Rev. Fred Shuttlesworth.

Black-Oriented Radio and the Birmingham Civil Rights Movement

In a 1961 request to the FCC for renewal of its license, WENN formally explained its sense of community responsibility. In the midst of a pledge to "assist in the promotion of worthwhile community projects: to stimulate education . . . to assist in the promotion of charitable causes" was a vague commitment to "promote racial and religious understanding" in the city.[32] Yet as the 1950s slipped into the 1960s, there was little sign at WENN or any of the other black-oriented stations in Birmingham of overt support for the challenges to segregation and disenfranchisement led by Shuttlesworth and his Alabama Christian Movement for Human Rights (ACMHR).

In a sense, this was hardly surprising, given the racial and economic agendas of the whites in positions of power and authority in black-oriented radio. As Shelley Stewart appreciated, their involvement had "nothing to do with race, it was M-O-N-E-Y. . . . You got to realize that blacks were spending money . . . , they were buying homes, they were buying automobiles, they were certainly buying more clothes . . . , they were doing their shopping at grocery stores, they were buying furniture . . . , so ring the cash register, baby."[33] When white entrepreneurs opened black-oriented stations in the South, they were usually careful to emphasize their economic motivations and deny any suggestion that their facilities would be used to encourage or support civil rights activities. This was especially true in Birmingham, where local segregationists had attacked WEDR's transmitter even before the city's first all-black station went on air in 1949. "They knew that something like that could have an influence on the black community, and it was an influence they did not want," remembered Eddie Castleberry.[34] Following owner J. Edward Reynolds's assurance to local whites that WEDR would "stay completely out of politics," restrictions on what deejays could say or do in relation to racial matters were very tight.[35] WEDR announcer Peggy Mitchell and her husband, both well-known NAACP supporters, were actually forced by a combination of threats and gunshots to flee the city.[36] In these circumstances, the closest WEDR got to any real association with formal black community organizing was when it accepted sponsorship from the Birmingham Federation of Colored Women's Clubs for a *Story Hour* show comprising readings by Federation members.[37]

Birmingham's black announcers resented these restrictions and occasionally found covert ways of commenting on or ridiculing the white power structure that imposed them. Shelley Stewart, for instance, made a habit of dedicating Big Mama Thornton's "Hound Dog" to the city's notoriously racist public safety commissioner Eugene "Bull" Connor—who responded by referring to Stewart as "Shelley the Plowboy." Still, these deejays knew precisely where the power to hire and fire resided, and for the most part they bit their talented and persuasive tongues on matters of racial justice and even on fair remuneration for their efforts. Stewart styled himself "something of a renegade" in his dealings with white bosses like Reynolds or his successor as WEDR's owner, Edwin Estes, or longtime station manager John Thompson. "I would say 'yes sir' on one hand, 'hell no' on the other," he recalled. Yet even Stewart conceded that WEDR's black deejays "would talk one thing in the control room as blacks and show our dissatisfaction. But if there was a meeting called with Mr. Estes . . . or whoever was in charge . . . , when they get before the white ownership or the white management, most of the blacks would say, 'Oh, everything is fine.'"[38]

Despite this widespread caution when it came to racial politics on air, as the Birmingham movement gathered momentum under Shuttlesworth and as the forces of massive resistance—the Klan and White Citizens' Councils—rallied to oppose it, black-oriented radio in the city came under even more intense scrutiny. In part this was because Shuttlesworth, with the connivance of sympathetic black deejays, had occasionally managed to slip details of his activities into public service announcement slots. In June 1956, for example, the rally to set up the ACMHR was advertised on air, as were plans the following year to test the integration of the city's transport system in the wake of the Montgomery bus boycott.[39] One deejay who bravely, but injudiciously, decided to announce his support for the bus protest on air was given twenty-four hours to leave town. Shelley Stewart was more discreet, merging his support for the campaign with a call for young blacks to take their schooling seriously. "Get some education," he told his young listeners, for "someday we may want to drive the bus instead of ride in the back of the bus."[40] Another factor in this growing concern about the power and influence of black radio in Birmingham was the local campaign against rock and roll orchestrated by archsegregationist Asa Carter. A former radio announcer who was no stranger to the potential of radio to mobilize mass support, Carter made rock and roll radio one target of his efforts to stop the mongrelization of southern whites to the beat of African American rhythms.[41]

It was in the context of this escalating racial tension that WEDR's transmitter again came under attack. The incident provided a clear insight into the racial views of some of those running black-oriented radio in the South. On the evening of May 17, 1958, the fourth anniversary of the *Brown* decision, WEDR's switchboard was suddenly jammed with complaints from listeners about a fading signal. Stewart phoned Charles Kirkpatrick, the white engineer at the transmitter site up on Red Mountain, to find out what was going on. Kirkpatrick told him that masked Klansmen were in the process of cutting down the antenna tower. When Stewart asked why Kirkpatrick was doing nothing to prevent this vandalism, the engineer explained to the astonished deejay that he could not intervene as he was actually a member of the Klavern leveling the transmitter.[42]

The attack on WEDR's antenna was probably a response to a bold political foray by one of the station's deejays. Perry "Tiger" Thompson had entered the electoral race for lieutenant governor of Alabama. Although his quixotic candidacy was short-lived and he actually left WEDR around this time, such activities intensified segregationist anxieties about the station and its role in the Birmingham movement. A month later, following the discovery of several dead dogs with slashed throats at the transmitter site, Shelley Stewart arrived for work at the WEDR studio to find "KKK-Negger" daubed in blood on the walls, stairwell, and control room door. Station owner Edwin Estes—who Stewart suspected had once had links with the Invisible Empire up in Etowah County, Alabama—publicly denied that Klansmen were responsible for this dyslexic daubing. Disturbed by "at least 25 calls demanding that we go off air," including one the day before the attack threatening "to level the building," Estes tried to reassure Birmingham whites that his black-oriented station still represented no threat to the established racial order. "We stay completely out of controversial issues," he said, echoing his predecessor J. Edward Reynolds's comments of nearly a decade before. "And we do not accept political announcements under any circumstances."[43]

In this repressive atmosphere, black-oriented radio in Birmingham appeared an unlikely source of succor for a mass movement in the city. Yet events in the spring of 1963 offered a striking example of how engaged deejays could occasionally move beyond a supportive or even reporting role to play a significant part in helping to orchestrate the black community's protests. In the wake of setbacks in Albany, Georgia, in 1961–62, Martin Luther King and the SCLC had carefully chosen Birmingham as the site for their next major initiative. The SCLC hoped to capitalize, not only on several years of local protests under the leadership of Fred Shuttlesworth, but also on growing schisms within white Birmingham, where certain factions were embarrassed by the city's reputation for violently defending segregation. King and his advisors were encouraged by the introduction of municipal reforms sponsored by more progressive elements within Birmingham's business community that seemed likely to remove diehard segregationists like Bull Connor from the corridors of power. In fact, Connor challenged the legitimacy of reforms that threatened to oust him from his post as public safety commissioner before he had served out his full elected term. Despite losing a runoff election for mayor to the more polite, if no less committed, segregationist Albert Boutwell on April 2, 1963, Connor and several other commissioners had refused to relinquish power. With two rival administrations grappling for control of the city, Connor was still on the scene when the SCLC officially entered the fray in Birmingham on April 3, 1963, hoping to assist in the struggle to desegregate public facilities, establish equal employment opportunities, and create a biracial commission in the city.

FIGURE 13. Perry "Tiger" Thompson had stints at both WJLD and WEDR in Birmingham. When the former boxer ran for lieutenant governor of Alabama, the Ku Klux Klan responded with a series of attacks on WEDR in the spring of 1958. Courtesy of Friedman/ Four Octaves.

That campaign of marches, picketing, and sit-ins, coupled with a selective-buying campaign against stores that discriminated against black customers and potential employees, severely undermined Easter season profits among downtown merchants and immobilized much of the city's business district for long periods of time. Moreover, largely thanks to Connor's continued presence, graphic images of police violence directed against peaceful protesters appeared regularly on front pages and television newscasts around the nation. Images of snarling German shepherd dogs, of rampant police wielding billy clubs against nonviolent demonstrators, and of flesh-peeling fire hoses dashing young black bodies across the streets were steadily undermining the resolve of many whites in the city to cling to segregation at all costs. They also vividly demonstrated to the nation at large the obscenity of Jim Crow and helped to increase the clamor for decisive government action, not simply to end the disturbances in Birmingham, but also to introduce the more sweeping civil rights legislation that would eventually become the Civil Rights Act of 1964.

The outlines of this story are well known.[44] Movement historians have long appreciated the role that the national television and print media played in dramatizing the moral and constitutional issues at stake in Birmingham, thereby winning widespread sympathy for the black cause. Yet, with the partial exception of journalists Taylor Branch and Diane McWhorter, most writers have ignored the significance of radio in the Birmingham campaign, despite the fact that it was the most important of all the media operating in the local black community—especially among the rank and file, and even more especially among the youth of the city. This preeminence was true both in terms of news coverage of the unfolding events and in terms of radio's contribution to shaping those events. Moreover, radio had a role to play in raising national consciousness about Birmingham, not least through the series of six hour-long documentaries, *Birmingham: A Testament of Violence,* produced by WRVR.[45]

The quality and extent of local black-oriented radio's news coverage of the 1963 protests in Birmingham should not be exaggerated. WENN, the most politicized of all the city's black-oriented stations, still allocated only 3.8 percent of its schedule to news broadcasting, having actually curtailed the number of daily newscasts from ten in 1961 to just seven.[46] Although Tall Paul White was designated WENN's news director, there was nothing akin to an established newsroom there or at any of the city's other black-oriented stations. There were, however, occasional impromptu on-site reports from staff members out in the streets. Rev. Erskine Faush recalled doing a live broadcast, as police broke up one demonstration in April 1963, from a telephone booth on the corner of Kelly Ingram Park, about half a block from the WENN studios. Later, on September 15, the day when Klansmen bombed the Sixteenth Street Baptist Church and murdered four young black girls, Faush ran a microphone out the window at WENN—again located only a block from the scene—to report on the grief and anger brewing among blacks outside. Yet these were exceptional cases. Given the racial climate in Birmingham, it was unlikely that the police or the white segregationist vigilantes who stalked the city would have made life easy for local black reporters trying to cover events firsthand. "We had to get most of our information from the national media. The networks," admitted Faush. In the absence of official station news reporters or newscasters, announcers who were more at home spinning soul records were required to tear off the news releases coming over the wires from the Associated Press and read them out on air at the appointed newsbreaks.[47]

Ironically, however, this "rip and read" approach, and the reliance on the national media for information, may actually have helped black radio announcers to get rather more authoritative and balanced news of the Birmingham protests to their listeners than other local media could manage. Ever since Fred Shuttlesworth had pioneered direct-action tactics in the late 1950s, city authorities had sought, with some success, to impose a local news blackout concerning major civil rights activities.[48] The principal player here was Vincent "Big Daddy" Townsend, the editorial boss at the *Birmingham News*. Townsend also wielded enormous personal power over the *News*-owned WAPI-TV and WAPI radio. He used a good deal of this power to try to keep stories he considered detrimental to Birmingham's image out of the hands of the mass media. While he struggled to suppress national coverage of successive racial crises in the city, his efforts also ensured that Birmingham's own major print and electronic media consistently ignored or buried stories about the city's—indeed, the region's—civil rights protests.

A good example was when the freedom rides of 1961 reached the Magic City. Erskine Faush remembered that when the integrated group of riders pulled into Birmingham's segregated bus station on Mother's Day in April 1961—only to be greeted by a mob of Klansmen granted a fifteen-minute dispensation by Bull Connor to beat up the protesters before his police intervened—their arrival took many in the black Birmingham community by surprise. "Until the bus was attacked, there was no information that the freedom riders were coming," he explained. "The local media didn't carry a whole lot about it." In fact, the only local radio station to feature any live coverage of the riot was WAPI, and that account was truncated when three angry Klansmen chased reporter Clancy Lake to his car. He gamely tried to renew the broadcast from inside his vehicle, but the men smashed the window and Lake fled. Shortly afterwards, Townsend ordered the plug pulled on journalist Howard K. Smith—the only national news reporter on the scene at the time of the bus terminal beatings—when he went to the WAPI television studios to file a report for the CBS *Evening News* program. Later Smith was able to present a radio report to CBS using WAPI facilities, but this was never aired in Birmingham itself. Nevertheless, the brutalization of the riders was a national outrage, and details of the incident eventually found their way onto local black radio newscasts via national wire service and newspaper reports.[49]

Local news coverage of the spring 1963 protests was similarly uneven, for both blacks and whites. Under Townsend's guidance, local television sometimes suspended or censored the network newscasts that were doing much to stir the sympathy of the rest of the nation. Meanwhile, Ralph Abernathy of the SCLC complained to the *New York Times* that he was "not satisfied with the coverage that is being given us in the local press." He noted that the *Birmingham News* and *Birmingham Post-Herald* offered only very limited and often highly skewed coverage of the campaign, its goals, and its tactics, usually hidden away on the back pages.[50] Things were not much better in the conservative pages of the *Birmingham World,* part of a black-owned chain of newspapers founded by C. A. Scott in Atlanta. Managing editor Emory O. Jackson was highly critical of what he called the "upside-downers" of the SCLC and ACMHR and, like many of Birmingham's black elite, remained generally hostile to what he perceived as their recklessly militant campaign.[51] In short, the local print media left most Birmingham residents woefully uninformed about the ongoing crisis in their own city. Yet by continuing to read news reports taken from the national wire services and on occasion from national newspapers, black radio announcers were able to bypass some of the restrictions and distortions associated with locally generated news reports and provide somewhat better coverage of the demonstrations than was available elsewhere in Birmingham's media.

One key to the success of those demonstrations was the movement's capacity to stretch police resources and patience to the breaking point. The aim was to keep Connor and his lieutenants guessing as to precisely when, where, and in what numbers the demonstrators would next appear. As Erskine Faush explained, "Plans were made to disperse certain peoples, not on one side of town, but on several sides of town, so that police forces could not be in all these places at the same time and hold back the crowds." WENN and to a lesser extent WJLD played an important role in making this possible. As demonstrators gathered in various churches around the city early each morning to learn plans for the day's protests, Faush would play the Highway Q.C.s' equalitarian hymn "All Men Are Made by God" as the signal for them to take to the streets. Shelley Stewart—who had moved to WJLD following a dispute with WENN over whether his decision to open a record store constituted a conflict of interest—and Tall Paul White would also play certain songs to move protesters out of the churches and toward their designated downtown destinations. "It could be anything from 'Wade in the Water' to 'Yakety Yak,'" Stewart remembered. Once outside, movement leaders sometimes used walkie-talkies to coordinate the actions of as many as ten separate groups of marchers. WENN's broadcasts of bogus traffic reports also helped protesters to identify exactly where police had blocked the streets in an effort to keep marchers away from city hall or the downtown shopping area. These fake traffic reports quite literally helped the movement to outmaneuver Connor, intensifying his frustration and making more likely the sorts of violent outbursts that served the movement's interests so well.[52]

WENN really came into its own as a force in the Birmingham campaign during what *Newsweek* dubbed the Children's Crusade phase of activism.[53] Despite some initial successes, in particular the publicity generated by the vicious police response to a Palm Sunday march and by King's Good Friday arrest and imprisonment, by late April the Birmingham movement had stalled in the face of local white intransigence, official duplicity, and federal inaction. The sheer courage and tenacity of those at the heart of the initial protests tended to obscure the fact that the majority of Birmingham's African Americans did not participate in the organized movement at all. Despite King's charismatic presence and Shuttlesworth's unquenchable passion for justice, the campaign struggled to attract new recruits willing to go to prison and thereby exert decisive pressure on the city's court and jail system. Moreover, despite a lot of hopeful rhetoric about forging a classless movement in Birmingham, the ACMHR-SCLC alliance continued to face opposition for its confrontational direct-action tactics from the city's conservative black leaders. Some of these leaders, Emory Jackson among them, began to champion the more moderate Rev. J. L. Ware as an alternative figurehead to the combative Shuttlesworth.[54]

In order to revitalize this flagging and increasingly fractious campaign, furnish enough new volunteers for jail, and make sure that there were sufficiently dramatic images to ensure that the national press remained in the city, James Bevel hatched a plan to recruit Birmingham's black schoolchildren for use in the mass demonstrations. In what Glenn Eskew describes as a "make-it-or-break-it gamble," activists distributed fliers in the local black high schools and, beginning on May 2, involved literally hundreds of enthusiastic young volunteers in the official campaign.[55] There was also another mechanism for getting young blacks to join the formal struggle. Bevel immediately understood that black-oriented radio stations and deejays were ideal vehicles for inspiring and organizing Birmingham's black youth.

After meeting with Bevel, Shelley Stewart and Paul White both announced a "hot luncheon" at the Gaston Motel, located just half a block from WENN's studios. The honored guests at this lunch were some of the most influential and popular black student leaders: athletes, beauty queens, and class representatives that the deejays had got to know when appearing at local school dances. Bevel met with this group of about twenty or thirty high school celebrities and church youth leaders and persuaded most of them to begin quietly spreading the word about forthcoming youth workshops and rallies. Partly as a result of this strategy meeting, Bevel found himself talking to growing numbers of students at a series of afternoon meetings at the Sixteenth Street Baptist Church, where he trained a new battalion of nonviolent warriors. Throughout his dealings with these students, Bevel tried to balance an emphasis on discipline and seriousness of purpose with a sense of fun and youthful rebelliousness. Students were sometimes urged not to tell their teachers or parents about what was being planned, partly out of fear that concerned adults might want to prevent the children from confronting Bull Connor and his dogs. Yet this strategy also encouraged a sense of mystery and devilishness about what the students were doing. While nobody was in any doubt that these protests had deadly serious targets—Jim Crow and white supremacy—Bevel's tone and the involvement of the deejays combined to create an atmosphere of generationally defined defiance among the students. There was a mood of roguishness not too different from the spirit with which many youngsters responded to the slightly racy, grammar-bending patter and cheek of somebody like Shelley Stewart on the radio. In many respects, then, popular deejays were the perfect people to exhort the black schoolchildren of Birmingham to do something of which their parents might disapprove.[56]

After this preparatory phase, the children's marches began in earnest, and Stewart on WJLD and White at WENN played an important part. Early on Thursday, May 2, they directed their young fans to the mass meetings and demonstrations by broadcasting coded announcements concerning a "big party" to be held in the city's downtown Kelly Ingram Park, or at one of the local churches. "We good old Baptists knew there wasn't going to be any dance," recalled Larry Russell, a high school participant in the demonstrations. Like most black kids in Birmingham, Russell knew precisely what the deejays meant. Eight hundred of them were absent from school that day. They even knew what to make of Shelley Stewart's curious instruction "Bring your toothbrushes, because lunch will be served." Toothbrushes were in short supply in Birmingham jails, and the children needed reminding that prison was where most of them were headed. Around one in the afternoon, Tall Paul suddenly started audibly shivering on air at WENN. "It's really cold," he declared. The temperature outside was in the eighties. This was the secret signal for the first wave of students to leave the Sixteenth Street Baptist Church and begin their march. That day some six hundred children were arrested, helping to intensify the pressure on the city jails and propel the Birmingham crisis toward its climax.[57]

These black deejays were local idols, charismatic authorities on all manner of important social and cultural issues, who exerted enormous influence over their young fans. As they broadcast their coded messages about movement activities and segued in and out of the latest classic soul recordings by James Brown, the Impressions, or Sam Cooke, the deejays helped to reinforce a powerful sense of solidarity, common purpose, and sheer exhilaration among those who responded to the call to march. Local activist-minister Rev. Abraham Woods came to appreciate the power of radio to move young hearts and bodies. In early April 1963, Woods had led one of the first in a wave of sit-ins at the Britling Cafeteria that heralded the intensification of direct-action protests in Birmingham. As plans for the children's marches coalesced, Woods personally spent much of his time in and out of local black schools trying to encourage students to join the demonstrations that revived the campaign. Unsure whether to allow his own young children to participate, Woods returned home to find that Tall Paul White had made up their minds for them. His three oldest daughters, Ruth, Anita, and Yvonne, were arrested in Kelly Ingram Park on May 2. They were among the many young Africans Americans who followed coded messages aired by the deejays. "You could see the students coming from every direction from high schools and some elementary schools to go to take part in the demonstrations," Woods recalled. The following day the pattern was repeated, with another wave of teenage protesters taking to the streets with the intention of marching down-town. This time Bull Connor, whose policing of the May 2 demonstrations had shown an unusual degree of restraint, finally lost patience, ordered the use of the dogs and fire hoses, and simultaneously convinced much of America that strong federal action on civil rights was an urgent necessity.[58]

Clearly these broadcasts were of some practical, as well as inspirational, value to the movement in Birmingham—not least, as Martin Luther King later ac-knowledged, in helping to keep the official campaign almost entirely nonviolent despite the white provocation that occasionally prompted less temperate re-sponses from incensed black bystanders. Yet even young activists like Larry Russell appreciated that black deejays were hardly free to say whatever they wanted. They still had to air secret messages out of fear of attracting the attention of hostile local whites, or offending sponsors, or running afoul of the station's white owners. "You knew it was coded for the protection of their jobs," Russell recalled. Shelley Stewart, for example, would often report the turnout at a mass meeting retrospectively, because that way "it's news, and he's covered himself. He might add something in a real quick and sly way—'I wonder how many are going to be there Wednesday night?'—and then he'd go into a rap."[59] Off air there was a little more room for maneuver, and the deejays could sometimes be found attending the mass meetings that were so critical to sustaining the morale and momentum of the campaign. Stewart, for example, turned up at a meeting at St. John's Church on May 10, 1963, clutching a stack of records donated by the activist-comedian Dick Gregory to raise money for the cause.[60]

Stewart, whose own recollections of these events sometimes come perilously close to relegating Shuttlesworth and King to the role of bit players in a drama he directed single-handedly from the WJLD studios, insisted that Birmingham's black deejays would have done whatever needed to be done to encourage and sustain the protests. Yet in his more contemplative moments even Stewart rec-ognized that station owners, managers, and sponsors still set very real limits on what black deejays could say or do.[61] They were "not sensitive to what we as black broadcasters felt were the needs of the community," agreed Erskine Faush. They thought it was enough just to keep cranking out nonstop soul music to the black audience. "That's all important," Faush acknowledged, recognizing the way in which black popular culture has served as an important means of social cohe-sion and as an invaluable source of identity and pride in the black community. "Entertainment is great in its own place. But you had no balance. No balance of giving news and information and things of public interest. Things that people wanted to know about. They wanted to be informed; they just had nobody to inform them."[62]

Faush, however, also noted the peculiar circumstances that enabled WENN deejays such as Paul White and himself to play an unusually prominent role in encouraging the organized struggle. "At first we were more or less covering it. And, of course, there were certain limitations and restriction placed by the fact that there was white ownership. However, I do think that perhaps those of us who worked at WENN at the time were more fortunate than perhaps others. . . . There were some stations who imposed a news blackout." For Faush, the fact that WENN had absentee ownership created slightly more space in which to work for the freedom struggle, especially since Mississippi-based owner John McLendon entrusted the day-to-day running of the station to manager Joseph Lackey. According to Faush, Lackey was vital to WENN's unusual level of involvement. On his promotion from assistant station manager, Lackey had taken the bold step of appointing some of his black staff to executive positions—Faush as program director and Paul White as news director. This in itself indicated a somewhat more enlightened racial attitude than many of the other whites involved in black Birmingham radio could boast. He was "more sensitive than his predecessors, and that also is why we could get away with certain things," explained Faush. Without Lackey's judicious turning of a deaf ear and blind eye, WENN's announcers would have had even less scope to get involved.[63]

By contrast, the station manager at WJLD, George Johnston Jr., was also the station owner (along with his mother, Rose). Following the death of his father, George Sr., in 1962, George Jr. exercised a far more decisive influence on the station's everyday affairs than John McLendon did at WENN. Johnston and sales manager Otis Dodge were always extremely careful not to offend the sensibilities of Birmingham's white community, particularly those businessmen who sold goods and services to African Americans on WJLD, by allowing their station to become associated with the local struggle for civil rights. At one point in the early 1960s, local movement activists actually complained to the FCC about WJLD's refusal to sell them airtime for public information slots announcing forthcoming meetings—a service that Lackey allowed WENN to offer the ACMHR and the SCLC free of charge. Even Shelley Stewart acknowledged, "WJLD was more conservative than WENN." There was, he noted, a policy "on the books that said on-air personnel could not get involved in promoting the civil rights movement during [their] broadcasts," although he did his best to ignore it.[64] Fellow deejay Jesse Champion confirmed that at WJLD there was a firm understanding that "you didn't get too deep into it" if you wanted to keep your job. And, as Champion explained, there were very real practical concerns here, too. Until 1966 the WJLD studio was located in the heart of a white district in Bessemer. Not only did this make deejays such as Champion fearful of "what might happen to you as you left the station," but it also meant that WJLD was simply further removed from the heart of the major civil rights activities taking place near WENN's studios in downtown Birmingham.[65]

Notwithstanding Shelley Stewart's surreptitious announcements, by publicly toeing the line and sticking to a trusted formula of music, limited news reporting, and some fairly innocuous community information announcements, WJLD survived the early 1960s with little more than a handful of spiteful phone calls from white segregationists. WENN was not so lucky. Local authorities viewed it as the most politically engaged black-oriented station, and harassment of its staff was commonplace. Police routinely parked across the street from the studio, menacingly pointing their weapons at the large plate-glass windows behind which the deejays worked, never quite able to decide precisely what the station was doing to assist the movement, but convinced nonetheless that it was promoting black activism. At midnight on Saturday, May 11, 1963, a bomb at the nearby Gaston Motel—site of many of the strategy meetings among the civil rights leadership in the city—shattered those same plate-glass windows. The following morning Tall Paul White arrived for work, clambered over the broken glass and rubble into the station, and was promptly arrested for attempted burglary. Although White, at 6' 3½" and 184 pounds, was hardly an inconspicuous or unfamiliar figure to local police, he was still detained for ten hours before being released. According to Faush, this was an attempt both to scare White and to learn more about WENN's links to the movement.[66]

This was neither White's first nor his last brush with Birmingham's law-enforcement agencies. In the midst of the May demonstrations, police arrested him on a spurious charge of driving without a license. Again, this was most likely an attempt to intimidate a man the police were convinced was aiding the movement. In September 1963, White and W. J. Allen, a WENN deejay who introduced the Epps-sponsored *Gospel Hour* on Sunday mornings, were both questioned at inordinate length by FBI agents investigating the Sixteenth Street Baptist Church bombing. White had actually left Birmingham to visit a girlfriend in Montgomery at around six on the morning of the September 15 outrage, but several hours earlier he had spotted a suspicious-looking blue and white car containing several white men in the vicinity of the church. White believed that he had seen the same car cruising the neighborhood several times during the weeks prior to the bombing. On one such occasion he had even jotted down the license number and given it to Ernest Gibson, the manager of the Gaston Motel, who passed it on to the FBI. Five weeks after the bombing, on October 23, Gibson and White again saw the two-tone car in the neighborhood and again informed the FBI. This time the Bureau treated the report more seriously. It transpired that Klansman Thomas Blanton, a close associate of the chief suspect in the case, Robert "Dynamite Bob" Chambliss, owned the car. While nobody was convicted of the crime in the 1960s, when the case was reopened more than a decade later, transcripts of White's 1963 statements to the FBI and his initial cooperation with investigators were important in securing a murder conviction against Chambliss.[67]

The constant specter of the sort of intimidation and harassment suffered by Paul White helps to explain why WENN's support for the movement remained covert. The station's black employees found themselves torn between truly serving the interests of the black community in its struggle for freedom and justice and avoiding the sort of censure and reprisal from elements within the white community that might silence them and their station forever. This tension was further revealed when the station filed its license renewal request with the FCC in late 1963. The renewal process traditionally represented an opportunity for a station to boast of its outstanding public service record in an effort to persuade both the FCC and members of the public, who had the right to inspect the application, that it was conscientiously serving the best interests of its designated audience. Like most stations, WENN usually did this by appending to its application numerous letters of recommendation and endorsement from important community figures and regular listeners. It also routinely listed all the community-oriented aspects of its scheduling, like public service announcements, news slots, and discussion programs, alongside details of its commitment to various charitable organizations and community aid and award schemes. In 1963 the letters of commendation WENN filed with the FCC were plentiful and gushed with praise. They included messages from local black educators—including one from Alma Johnson's father at Parker High School—YMCA directors, and clergymen, all basically thanking the station for its sense of community responsibility. None mentioned WENN's coverage of, or support for, the spring protests. Perhaps there were no such letters. It is unlikely that Lackey, who prepared the submission, would have included them, anyway: that sort of endorsement would only have encouraged more hostile white scrutiny and reprisals.[68]

Certainly the 1963 application's summary of the station's regular and special news coverage scrupulously avoided any mention of the recent civil rights demonstrations. Instead it stressed WENN's responsible coverage of natural disasters (a flood and a severe snowstorm), the Kennedy assassination, and the Sixteenth Street Baptist Church bombing. The latter might have provided an opportunity to raise the subject of the station's attitude toward its audience's struggle against Jim Crow. But Lackey chose another tack. He emphasized that after the outrage the station had worked to provide a "constant flow of information from the public authorities to the citizenry." Thus he portrayed WENN as a loyal and responsible tool of the city's officials in a time of crisis rather than as a radical vehicle through which black challenges to those officials could be organized or even reported. Moreover, in the midst of the downtown chaos, rage, and sporadic black violence that followed the church bombing, WENN had tried its best to keep the black community calm and allow the emergency services to do their work. Although Erskine Faush, in trying to report objectively on the appalling scene, struggled to camouflage his own anger, he "knew there was a great danger of it erupting into greater violence and that the anger and frustration of people who have been battered for so long would erupt and more loss of life would occur. And so I tried also to have a calming effect." The on-air appeals of black deejays like Faush were in all likelihood more effective in restraining the black community, particularly its younger members, than those of the local public officials and church leaders, all of them white, who appeared on Birmingham's television to urge calm on the evening of the bombing.[69]

Elsewhere in the 1963 FCC submission, Lackey carefully noted the responsible and respectable nature of WENN's work in the community and its concern for the local and national commonweal. For example, although the SCLC and the ACMHR were conspicuously missing from the official list of organizations enjoying free public service announcements, most branches of the U.S. armed forces, the U.S. Postal Service, and even Radio Free Europe were included alongside various worthy health, welfare, and educational causes. Similarly, one of the many letters of endorsement in the renewal application was from Floyd Mann, director of the Alabama Department of Public Safety, who expressed his "personal appreciation" for the coverage the station had afforded to his Accident Prevention Program. Lackey also emphasized the regular assistance the station had provided to local police trying to trace missing persons. It was as if, at a time when African Americans were insisting upon their right to civil equality, WENN was determined to portray itself, its staff, and its listeners as paragons of civic virtue and all-American citizenship. In other words, WENN was firmly attuned to the dominant ethos of the early southern movement, when demands for black civil and voting rights were generally couched in the traditional language of American democratic values and constitutional guarantees. At the same time, however, Birmingham's leading black deejays clearly appreciated the need for nonviolent direct-action protests to make a somnambulant nation wake up to the fact that segregation and disenfranchisement in the South were an affront to those civic ideals.

8

Ample and Frequent Moderation

Radio and Race Relations in Charlotte

*Today, it seems increasingly clear that initial token desegregation, rather
than paving the way for future compliance, is becoming a means of
evasion of the law.*
Charlotte-Mecklenburg Council for Human Relations, 1959

Business as Usual in Charlotte

In the autumn of 1957, a Voice of America radio broadcast contrasted the manner of school desegregation in Charlotte, North Carolina, with the chaos that
accompanied the process in Little Rock, Arkansas.[1] Whereas in Little Rock the
integration of Central High School had taken place against a background of
white mob violence and the intervention of federal troops, Charlotte was held up
as a model of how the desegregation of southern education could proceed in a
smooth and orderly fashion. To be sure, Charlotte was one of the first southern
cities to admit black students to previously all-white schools, but this image of
calm and willing compliance with the *Brown* decision was misleading. Dorothy
Counts's brave effort to integrate Charlotte's Harding High School in early September 1957 ended after two weeks of mob protest inspired by the local White
Citizens' Council.[2] Still, it says much about the character of white Charlotte that
there was widespread condemnation of the Council for fomenting the unseemly
disturbances at Harding. Like the local Klan, whose gatherings were forever being broken up by outraged blacks and Lumbee Indians, the Council movement
in Charlotte consistently failed to win mass white support for its direct-action
approach to preserving segregation. Legal maneuvering and token compliance,
not mob violence, were white Charlotte's preferred response to the threat of desegregation.[3]

The Queen City proved a skilled exponent of the sort of "sly resistance" typical
of a state jealous of its reputation for moderation and civility. This approach was

embodied in North Carolina's adoption of the Pearsall Plan for school desegregation—named for the state's former House speaker Thomas J. Pearsall, who chaired the committee that devised it.[4] As implemented by school boards like the one in Charlotte-Mecklenburg County, the Pearsall Plan turned on the idea that a few black students conspicuously placed in a handful of previously all-white schools was a small price to pay to protect the entire school system from further judicial review and greater federal compulsion. Acceptance of the Pearsall Plan confirmed that, while few Charlotte whites were eager to abandon Jim Crow, most prized social stability and economic progress above the strict maintenance of the color line in schools and other public accommodations. Similarly, in the spring of 1963, while Birmingham was embroiled in an economically disastrous struggle to preserve segregation, Charlotte had responded to various initiatives by local African Americans by integrating its public accommodations.

This pattern of forced voluntarism and the "progress under pressure" that it produced was characteristic of white Charlotte's response to demands for black civil rights after World War II.[5] While generalizations are perilous, Charlotte whites at midcentury exhibited an easy, almost mellow, racism, where a quiet confidence in white superiority informed a genuine, if patchy and paternalistic, concern for black welfare and progress in the city. Certainly the majority of the city's white leadership had conceded the inevitability of Jim Crow's demise soon after *Brown* and, rather than waste time and risk civic disorder trying to resist the irresistible, had channeled their efforts into managing the pace, extent, and direction of racial change. Charlotte's businessmen and, in particular, its powerful Chamber of Commerce played a vital role in setting this gradualist agenda and selling it to the white community. So, too, did WBT, a radio station with important links to that business and political elite and a long tradition of promoting moderation on both sides of the racial divide.

Charlotte was a fiercely ambitious New South city and one of the South's leading centers for textile manufacturing, commerce, and banking. After growth spurts in the late nineteenth century and the 1920s, Charlotte had boomed again in the 1940s, thanks mainly to wartime government contracts and the extension of public housing construction programs begun during the New Deal. By 1960 the city had a population of 201,000, slightly more than a quarter of it African American. Of that total population, 4,500 belonged to the influential Chamber of Commerce.[6] The Chamber served as both an expression of and a vehicle for the economic aspirations of the energetic boosters who dominated Charlotte's business and government. Between 1935 and 1975 every mayor of Charlotte owned his own business, and two—Stan Brookshire and John Belk—had previously served as president of the Chamber.[7] When a *Charlotte Observer* editorial asked rhetorically in 1960, "Guess Who's Boss of Our Town?" the predictable answer was "The Chamber of Commerce."[8] So powerful was the grip of these white businessmen on the affairs of the city that liberal North Carolina journalist Harry Golden once quipped that "they would elect Martin King or Malcolm X mayor if somehow one of them could give them a guarantee of no labor union and no minimum wage for laundry workers."[9]

The Chamber was not only the source of most of the city's major business initiatives and civic leadership; it also acted as a moral compass for the white community. A self-styled bastion of enlightened common sense and progressive thought, the Chamber was the chief arbiter of propriety, decency, and respectability in the city. What the Chamber of Commerce decided was the correct response to any given issue invariably determined how Charlotte dealt with that issue. This was certainly true when members of Charlotte's African American community turned to litigation, direct action, and the ballot in an effort to secure justice and equality of opportunity. It was the Chamber of Commerce that largely dictated white Charlotte's generally temperate, if often equivocal and dissembling, response to black insurgency. It was only in the late 1960s and early 1970s, when the Chamber failed to provide such leadership following a federal court order to use busing to complete the integration of the school system, that the mask of white moderation in Charlotte slipped, leaving exposed an ugly reminder of the prejudice that lurked beneath the civility.[10]

In April 1971, when the Supreme Court's ruling in *Swann v. Charlotte-Mecklenburg Board of Education* upheld the busing directive, the new president of the Chamber of Commerce was Charles Crutchfield, president and general manager of the Jefferson Standard Broadcasting Company, owner of both the AM and FM wings of WBT-Charlotte and of WBTV. A veteran of nearly thirty-eight years of broadcasting in the city, Crutchfield presided over the Chamber during a period of acute racial tension, as whites mobilized to resist the full implications of the busing order and Charlotte's African Americans attacked myriad forms of systemic discrimination in housing, employment, and law enforcement. Chapter 10 will describe how, with the Chamber and Charlotte's political leaders reluctant to break their collective silence on the busing issue, Crutchfield used his broadcasting outlets to urge calm, conciliation, and compliance with the Court's decision. This, however, was merely the culmination of the long, complex, and constantly evolving relationship between Crutchfield, WBT, and Charlotte's black and white communities, which this chapter explores.

WBT was not the only radio station to play a significant role in the unfolding of the freedom struggle in Charlotte. While the general-market-oriented WBT never featured more than a smattering of specifically black-oriented programming on its schedules, by the early 1950s half of nearby WGIV's airtime was devoted specifically to black listeners. That proportion increased steadily until, by the turn of the decade, WGIV was almost exclusively black-oriented. But WGIV, like WBT, was initially white-owned and white-managed. And Francis

Fitzgerald, like Charles Crutchfield, found himself in a position of considerable power and influence as racial change came to Charlotte. How these two radio executives responded to the challenges posed by the movement offers important insights into how many southern whites reacted to the freedom struggle. With varying degrees of enthusiasm, alacrity, and trepidation, the conservative Crutchfield and the more liberal Fitzgerald came to recognize—and even insist upon—the legitimacy of African American demands for civil rights and equal political, economic, educational, and social opportunity. Whereas in Birmingham the relationship between the movement and radio was relatively straightforward—the black-oriented stations working hard, if covertly, to support civil rights activities while the white-oriented stations resolutely opposed them—the situation in Charlotte was more complex. Ultimately, despite differences in style, substance, and timetable, WBT and WGIV had a good deal in common as they sought to bring about peaceful racial change in the city. This chapter examines how these two stations helped to define the tenor of race relations and the nature of black activism in Charlotte.

Up a Tree for WBT

Charles Harvey Crutchfield was born in Hope, Arkansas, on July 27, 1912.[11] Educated in the public schools of Spartanburg, South Carolina, he enrolled in 1929 at the city's Wofford College. On his way to class each morning, Crutchfield passed the offices of South Carolina's first radio station, WSPA. Fascinated by the new medium, he rigged up a crystal receiver to hear the station at home and began to pester station owner Virgil Evans for work. Impressed by Crutchfield's persistence and deep baritone voice, Evans eventually relented and launched Crutchfield's career as a broadcaster, initially paying him with a meal voucher for a local restaurant. Shortly afterwards Crutchfield ditched college, got married, and, after a rapid round of hirings and firings at several South and North Carolina stations—"I was young enough to recognize all the mistakes the managers were making and stupid enough to tell them"—arrived at WBT-Charlotte in 1933.[12]

When Crutchfield came to Charlotte, cutting quite a dash with his sharp suits, William Powell mustache, and cocksure attitude, WBT was already more than a decade old. The Colossus of the Carolinas, as it dubbed itself, had begun life in 1920 as experimental station 4XD. In April 1922 the Southern Radio Corporation, a firm that made and sold radio receivers and parts, secured the first commercial broadcasting license in the South, and WBT went on air primarily as a means to advertise the company's radio sets.[13] It was no coincidence that one of its first entertainment programs was a concert of classical music from the Chamber of Commerce Assembly Hall. The ambitious Charlotte business community saw the station as a means to project an image of refinement and progressivism for the city. In October 1922, Clarence Kuester of the Chamber of Commerce gave a series of talks on WBT hyping the "advantages of Charlotte and the glories of North Carolina." Three years later the Chamber persuaded local Buick dealer C. C. Coddington to buy the station for $2,000, pointing out to him that WBT could easily stand for *Watch Buicks Travel*. While Coddington provided the finance, the Chamber retained control of the programming. Generally resisting the earthy delights of jazz or hillbilly music, the station featured what it considered a better class of music and entertainment—the sort of cultured, sophisticated fare that would cast the city in the best possible light.[14]

This uplifting agenda was modified toward the end of the 1920s. As radio set ownership in Charlotte-Mecklenburg County mushroomed from 500 sets in 1922 to 7,902 in 1929, with 72,000 in North Carolina as a whole, commercial advertisers became more interested in using the medium to sell their wares. WBT became not only a vehicle for publicizing the attractions of Charlotte but also a means to promote products like Lucky Strike cigarettes and the services of numerous other sponsors. This shift in commercial emphasis also dictated changes in the programming. The rarified sounds of classical music were largely supplanted by the more populist sounds of hillbilly groups such as Dick Hartman's Crazy Tennessee Ramblers, whose shows were sponsored by Charlotte's own Crazy Water Crystals Company. An affiliation with NBC opened up the station to even more mass-oriented programming. This process was completed in 1929 when C. C. Coddington died and CBS bought the station for $150,000. Although this meant a change in the precise nature of the relationship between WBT and the Charlotte business community, it remained a close one. And it became closer still in 1945 when the Jefferson Standard Life Insurance Company, already owners of WBIG-Greensboro, bought WBT from CBS for $1.5 million. With local businesses providing a substantial portion of the station's advertising revenue, WBT promoted the virtues of hard work, thrift, personal probity, and civic responsibility that formed the bedrock of Charlotte's self-image.[15]

In 1922 an unidentified group of African American musicians had been among the first artists to perform live on WBT from its makeshift studio at the Andrews Music Company store on North Tryon Street.[16] This aside, before Crutchfield's arrival in 1933 the station had paid relatively little attention to African Americans either as performers or as potential listeners—which was hardly surprising, since as late as 1930 only 1 percent of black families in North Carolina owned a radio set.[17] WBT did, however, faithfully reproduce most of the racial stereotypes of the time and place. In the mid-1920s two white comedians in black-voice briefly appeared on the station as the Two Black Crows, predating the huge popularity of *Amos 'n' Andy*, which the station subsequently also carried. Later in the decade Aunt Sally (Mrs. Pasco Powell) went on air reading

Uncle Remus tales in her best faux-Negro dialect. In the 1930s the station featured the popular *Dixie Mammoth Minstrel* show, with Clair Shadwell serving as writer and interlocutor for a slice of happy-go-lucky plantation bliss. Charlie Crutchfield helped to perpetuate this nostalgic Old South ethos at the station. In 1935 he brought eight former Confederate soldiers into the studio and broadcast the famous rebel yell. One veteran got so excited that he jumped to his feet and started screaming "shoot the damn Yankees" into the microphone. Crutchfield was also a great supporter of Grady Cole, WBT's "Mr. Dixie," who for more than thirty years was the station's main attraction and a steadfast defender of southern traditions. Crutchfield even organized the Briarhoppers, a country music group whose sound was rooted deep in the soil of southern white culture.[18]

By chance, shortly after his arrival in Charlotte, Crutchfield became indebted to the local African American community for an unexpected boost to his career. One Sunday afternoon he was assigned to cover a wedding between two ex-slaves at Ben Salem Baptist Church near Pineville. The bride, Martha Kilpatrick, was a sprightly ninety-two-year-old; the cradle-snatching groom, Righteous Lawrence, was ninety-seven. With the station's remote broadcasting equipment crammed into his 1929 Model T Ford, Crutchfield and his engineer made their way to Pineville only to find that the Board of Deacons considered it sacrilegious to broadcast from within the church. Fortunately, Crutchfield was able to persuade one of the deacons to crack open a window in return for a small "consideration." As he later retold the story, "Poorer by two dollars, I climbed a plum tree outside the window—stuck a mike inside, and aired the entire ceremony. Then, I jumped in the car, pulled up to the front steps, jumped out, opened the door, and told the couple that this was the official wedding car." Once he had them inside, Crutchfield was able to interview the happy couple and ask the groom what his plans were. "Well, son," came the memorable reply, "I'm gonna quit running around now and settle down, raise me a big family to take care of me when I get old." The story was picked up by various wire services and gave a considerable fillip to Crutchfield's career.[19]

J. S. Nathaniel Tross and Black Accommodation at the Microphone

There is no reason to believe that the "slave wedding" sparked in Crutchfield any particular interest in Charlotte's black community and its problems. Nevertheless, a few years afterwards, Crutchfield, who became WBT's program director in 1935, was instrumental in bringing the first regular black programming to the station in the person of Rev. Dr. J. S. Nathaniel Tross. Tross was born in British Guiana in 1889 and had studied briefly at Oxford in England before earning a B.A. at Howard University and a doctorate in religious education from the University of Pittsburgh. After attending Western Theological Seminary and securing a variety of jobs from Portland to Pittsburgh, he came to Charlotte in 1932 as pastor at one of the city's AME Zion Churches. There he joined a small but ambitious black professional and business elite that contributed every bit as much as its white counterpart to the character of race relations in Charlotte. On WBT Tross used his time to promote the kind of militant accommodationism that dominated African American responses to Jim Crow in the city until the 1960s.[20]

Soon after his arrival in Charlotte, Tross had outlined his theological and social views in a book entitled *This Thing Called Religion*. Deploring conflict, Tross insisted that "the clash of opinions today is more dangerous than the clash of arms." He maintained that the key to African American progress in the South was not agitation and protest. Instead, blacks should engage in meaningful dialogue about their problems with white leaders and rely on their goodwill and Christian conscience to produce solutions. This sort of gradualism accorded perfectly with the paternalistic attitude of Charlotte's white civic leadership— and with that of a radio station that shared its commitment to civility and conciliation in all matters of social conflict. Here was a black leader that white racial moderates could respect and with whom they could work without feeling the hot breath of a direct challenge to Jim Crow.[21]

Charlie Crutchfield and Nathaniel Tross met in 1939. Crutchfield was instantly impressed by what he saw as Tross's calm, sensible, and constructive approach to improving black conditions and relations between the races. Tross raised the possibility of appearing on WBT and, following a number of test performances, Crutchfield agreed to put him on the air for fifteen minutes each Sunday morning. The show lasted some twenty-five years. There was initially some disquiet among the WBT hierarchy about having an African American commentator at the station, yet Crutchfield was adamant that Tross's show would be good for racial understanding in the city. Years later Crutchfield still struggled to pinpoint precisely when and why this had even become a concern for him. There was no real tradition of racial liberalism in his family. He described his Texas-born father, Charles Crutchfield Sr., as a typical rural southerner, an unthinking victim and exponent of the racial prejudices of his age and region who was more concerned with how to keep blacks in their place than about alleviating conditions behind the veil of segregation. His father, however, had remained in Arkansas to work in the cotton industry when young Charlie and his three older siblings moved with their mother, Fanny, to Spartanburg. His parents were subsequently divorced. This left his mother, another Texas native, as the most likely source of his belief in the shared humanity and dignity of all mankind. She was, he recalled, a woman of strong religious convictions with a keen sense of fair play. Crutchfield followed her lead to become a stalwart of both

the Myers Park Presbyterian Church and Charlotte's broader religious community.[22]

During the decades on either side of World War II, Crutchfield, like many
fledgling racial progressives of his generation, was still some way from translat-
ing his religious faith into anything like a commitment to black social and political equality, let alone support for a concerted campaign to dismantle Jim Crow.
Nevertheless, his basic sense of Christian decency, coupled with a deep respect
for notions of southern good manners, appears to have made him more sensitive than many other whites to egregious examples of racial abuse and discour-
tesy. In the late 1930s, for example, he publicly reprimanded a member of the
Rangers Quartet country group for a racial slur on air. Similarly in the early
1950s, WBT moved quickly to placate local NAACP activist Fred Alexander after
a monologue on the "darkey and mule" by announcer Gil Stamper had offended
black listeners.[23] Certainly Crutchfield had come to appreciate that African
Americans were being treated very badly under segregation. In his somewhat
paternalistic view, not only was this intrinsically unfair but it also represented a
serious abrogation of civic and social responsibility by whites that would lead to
ill feeling and lawlessness.

It was this sense of civic duty, so powerful among Charlotte's business elite,
that persuaded Crutchfield to put Nathaniel Tross on air. In the aftermath of a
1938 report that revealed the high incidence of crime and other antisocial behavior in Charlotte's deprived black neighborhoods, Crutchfield decided that it
would be a useful public service to provide a radio forum where a temperate
black minister could appeal to whites for a better appreciation of, and response
to, black needs. As if to emphasize the point, WBT always aired the show free of
charge, so that Tross never had to worry about securing sponsorship.[24]

Nathaniel Tross used his Sunday morning *Community Crusaders* slot to promote positive images of African Americans and to push for greater interracial
understanding and cooperation in Charlotte. Although he never directly challenged the existence of Jim Crow, he did question how it was administered, complaining about how unequal accommodations severely disadvantaged black
citizens. In January 1941, for example, Tross used his show to highlight the un-
employment, poverty, poor housing, and lack of recreational facilities that contributed to the high crime rates reported among Charlotte blacks. Skillfully playing on the city's progressive self-image, he appealed to the authorities to address
the social and economic causes of this breakdown of law and order. Tross appeared before the city council to urge the recruitment of black policemen to
patrol black neighborhoods and promoted the same cause on his weekly broadcasts. In classic Washingtonian mode, he also appealed to Charlotte blacks to
make every effort to appear worthy of full citizenship rights. "You cannot escape
your civic responsibilities through drink, through dissipation, and licentious liv-

ing; through idleness, wantonness and crimes," he insisted. At the same time, he reminded whites that there would be a price to pay for continued indifference to the black predicament. "What has happened to a community that deprives so large a portion of its population of parks, swimming pools, large playgrounds and other recreational facilities?" he asked. "In such a community, the crusade against crime is hindered rather than helped."[25]

"The effect of the broadcasts was startling," reported the NUL. "Mass meetings, interracial cooperation was solicited, reforms were suggested and, with the help of civic leaders, carried out." Shortly afterwards the city council appointed two special black police officers and a black truant officer to patrol the black neighborhoods. These achievements attracted national attention in 1943 when *Community Crusaders* won an award from the entertainment magazine *Variety* for "fostering racial good-will and understanding." The wartime context here was important. At a time when it was imperative to reinforce national unity in the face of escalating racial tensions, the award citation reeked of patriotism and paternalism. Tross was commended for helping to nullify "the spread of Axis propaganda among susceptible Negroes." At the same time, WBT received another *Variety* honor for "all-round merit in the wartime enlightenment of its listeners."[26]

Even these apparent victories betrayed the major weaknesses of Tross's recipe for racial progress by polite petition. First, it depended on the consent of kind-hearted whites to black requests, and this was not always forthcoming, not even in enlightened Charlotte. Second, it allowed white civic leaders to hone their talent for making token reforms while leaving the framework of Jim Crow intact. Louis Austin, the spunky black editor of the Durham-based *Carolina Times,* clearly saw the problem with Tross and his accommodationist colleagues. "It is a fine gesture to say that Charlotte is one of the few, very few cities of the South giving employment to colored uniform police officers—two of them," he editorialized sarcastically. "But we are forced to ask Dr. J.S.N. Tross and others who claim the honor of this accomplishment if a full measure of service can be expected from these two standard bearers of the law when the only places of recreation for the 40,000 colored citizens of Charlotte are juke joints, speakeasies, and red light districts." The shortcomings of this breakthrough were further illustrated by the fact that the brace of black policemen secured by Tross's efforts not only were unarmed and forbidden to arrest white people but were also ineligible for the civil service pensions available to their higher-paid white colleagues.[27]

As elsewhere in North Carolina, granting limited concessions to blacks within segregation may have forestalled more militant African American challenges to the racial status quo. In Charlotte, the success of Tross and other black moderates in securing rewards from the white authorities through supplication had a chilling effect on black political activism and protest. In the decade or so after World War II, the head of the state branch of the NAACP, Kelly Alexander (Fred's brother), struggled in vain to rouse the black community to concerted action. In a city that had "no unfair or illegal restrictions" on African American political participation, Alexander declared, "the problem was not white road-blocks to black voting, but black apathy."[28]

One partial exception to this general pattern hinted at the potential of black-oriented radio programming to mobilize Charlotte's black voters. In 1949 the Citizens' Committee for Political Action (CCPA), founded by the Alexander brothers and several other black activists, decided to run Bishop Dale for the city council with Rev. J. F. Wertz, pastor of St. Paul's Baptist Church, standing for the school board. Dale, a Texan by birth, was a former Negro League baseball star who had won a measure of celebrity in World War I as the drum major of the first black drum and bugle corps in the United States Army. Thereafter he had found modest economic success in the insurance and real estate businesses. Although, like Wertz, he was eventually roundly beaten, finishing twelfth of thirty-six candidates in the council primary election and twelfth of fourteen in the runoff, the flamboyant Dale had bought time on WBT in an effort to rally African American support.[29]

Dale did not have WBT's airways all to himself during his campaign. Radio schedules were often contested ideological terrain, and WBT was much happier with messages that urged black patience than with ones designed to stir black activism. Nathaniel Tross explicitly denounced the dangerous level of excitement stimulated by Dale's bold bid for public office. Five years later, while congratulating the CCPA for registering 7,000 black voters, Tross still insisted that few of these African Americans were actually ready for the responsibilities of the franchise. "Many Negroes are not sufficiently educated to keep themselves informed on the candidates and issues," he explained. Little wonder, then, that despite years of painstaking work by the CCPA and others, by 1962 less than half the eligible blacks in Charlotte-Mecklenburg County were registered to vote.[30]

If black political activity in Charlotte was limited and tentative, legal paths to black advance were trod with similar caution. While the threat of a lawsuit did eventually bring about the equalization of salaries and conditions of service for Charlotte's handful of black policemen, Kelly Alexander found few converts to the idea that courtroom challenges to both the operation and the constitutionality of Jim Crow in Charlotte might be the best way to secure black progress. "I was attacked by Dr. Tross and other Uncle Toms in the state—the 'safe blacks'—they said I was too far ahead," he recalled.[31] In 1947 James Shepard, president of the North Carolina College for Negroes and an admirer of both Charlie Crutchfield and his station's racial policies, went on WBT specifically to oppose "any recourse to litigation to hasten the ending of discrimination." Shepard had long shared the opinion of many Charlotte whites that the NAACP represented an unwelcome and essentially alien force, interfering in matters that he felt local black leaders like himself were more than capable of sorting out with their white neighbors. Shepard was certainly keen to allay white fears about the nature of black ambitions, appearing on national radio in 1944 to reassure whites everywhere that "Negroes do not seek social equality and have never sought it."[32]

Nathaniel Tross shared both James Shepard's hostility toward the NAACP and his suspicion of local black militancy. He preferred to use his pulpit, the *Charlotte Post* newspaper he founded in 1949, and his radio show to urge probity and patience as blacks prepared themselves to receive the blessings of equal rights from the city's benevolent white leadership. In February 1960 when Charlotte students were inspired by events in Greensboro to conduct a series of lunch counter sit-ins, Tross immediately condemned their protests on air as "ill-conceived." He argued that in a city where black-white communication was so well established, "their reason is not wrong, but their methods are."[33] Throughout the 1960s he remained publicly opposed to direct-action protest of all kinds. He floridly denounced Martin Luther King for thinking that "we can improve a race, or better race relations by threats and abuses, by hostile and caustic challenges, by threatened demonstrations, by grotesque dramatizations and picayunish exhibitionism masquerading in the habiliments of a spurious martyrdom and a cunning and designing messiahship." True to his belief that social stability was a prerequisite for proper dialogue and reconciliation between the races, he accused the publicity-hungry King and his followers of becoming "willing and active participants in organized disobedience to established Law and Order." King's voice, Tross charged, "is a distinct discord in the chorus of interracial goodwill and understanding."[34] Closer to home, he also used the airways to attack Dr. Reginald Hawkins, a black dentist who in the early 1960s was at the forefront of a local direct-action campaign against segregation in Charlotte's hospitals, hotels, restaurants, and theaters. "Now is not the time for dramatizations and the carrying and waving of banners," Tross declared, urging blacks to refrain from joining Hawkins's protests and advising the city authorities to ignore them.[35]

Tross's perennial caution had always drawn criticism from more militant black activists, but these condemnations grew louder in the wake of *Brown*. In late 1957 the Western Conference of his own AME Zion Church issued a resolution criticizing him for "the part he has played in behalf of those who would stave off integration."[36] Such criticisms became even more voluble in the 1960s, as the direct-action phase of the southern freedom struggle took hold in Charlotte. During the first Charlotte student sit-ins, Tross was vilified in the pages of the *Crusader,* a newsletter founded by Robert Williams, the maverick civil rights leader from North Carolina's Union County. Tross, the paper railed, "is the white man's 'darkie' version of the voice of Dixie. He lurks in the shadows of the white supremacists and cries 'patience! patience! My black brothers wait, wait do not be hasty, the southern man is your friend!'"[37] The nadir came when students from Johnson C. Smith University, after hearing Tross's radio denunciation of their sit-ins, hanged him in effigy outside their college gates.[38]

In the years before the emergence of a mass movement, Tross's accommodationism, his careful courting of influential whites, and his stress upon the shared interests of blacks and whites in economic progress and social stability had secured genuine improvements in the services for the city's black population during the darkest days of Jim Crow. Moreover, his staunch moderation had undoubtedly ensured his continued presence on WBT. By the early 1960s, however, Tross was falling out of step with the new mood of assertiveness and dynamism in the black community. His radio messages criticizing the "new Negro leadership" for "advancing at too dizzy a pace for our masses" and counseling "the urgent necessity for patience, tolerance, endurance, intelligent thinking and Christian goodwill" rang hollow in the face of continuing white prevarication and "sly resistance." By mid-decade, his insistence that blacks should eschew "acrimonious agitations" and instead seek respect and concessions from whites by "rugged discipline through strict attention to our speech and attitude in public and private" sounded demeaning to a community boldly demanding equal rights in the courts and on the streets. His 1965 crusade on WBT to establish a Southern Association for Racial Goodwill and Understanding (SARGU) was doomed to failure—especially as it coincided with one of Charlotte's relatively rare lapses into white vigilante violence. In November 1965 the Klan bombed the homes of the city's four most prominent black leaders: Kelly and Fred Alexander, Reginald Hawkins, and NAACP attorney Julius Chambers. The stillborn SARGU, a monthly biracial forum to analyze and propose solutions to racial problems based on "the friendship and understanding that exists between white and black in the South," was really Tross's last, decidedly muted, hurrah. By the time of his death in 1971, he was viewed as a largely irrelevant anachronism among the city's black leadership.[39]

Nathaniel Tross's long radio career illustrated that black-oriented radio programming in the South was not always the place to find unequivocal denunciations of white racism or rousing calls to mass black activism. Perhaps predictably, while his stock with Charlotte's African Americans declined steadily after the mid-1950s, it rose in inverse proportion among the city's white population. Confronted and confounded by the new militancy of the black community and troubled by signs of a mounting federal commitment to desegregating the South, Charlotte's whites felt less confident than usual of their ability to manage racial affairs in what they still saw as "their" city. In the gathering storm of black protest, Tross seemed like a reassuring eyelet of calm—a black leader who continued to argue that progress for his race would come, not as a consequence of agitation in the streets, but as a gift from well-intentioned whites. Having dubbed him the Ambassador of Goodwill and presented him with an automobile for his services to the community in 1950, Charlotte's white leaders continued to praise Tross. Many of them joined him on air during a Brotherhood Week in February 1964 to celebrate his first twenty-five years of responsible broadcasting. The following year it was the Chamber of Commerce that decided to publish Tross's WBT sermon "Racial Good-Will and Understanding," hoping that his scheme for SARGU would indeed help them to manage modest adjustments in racial arrangements "without vitriolic and vituperative outside interferences—without denunciations and ill-considered pressures."[40]

Charles Crutchfield and WBT Confront Racial Change in a Cold-War Climate

During his many years on WBT, Nathaniel Tross had no greater supporter than Charlie Crutchfield. It was "the best program we had," Crutchfield enthused. "He didn't preach, but he talked and he talked sense." On Tross's death in 1971, Crutchfield declared "that no man in this community made greater contributions to the cause of good race relations and brotherhood than he did." It is not difficult to see why the two men got along. Like Tross, Crutchfield genuinely hoped that honest dialogue would forestall open conflict and promote progress for both races. Moreover, Crutchfield, who at the time of Jefferson Standard Life's purchase of WBT in 1945 had become the youngest manager of a 50,000–watt station in the country, repeatedly allowed his station to serve as the site of such dialogue. Immediately after the war, for instance, WBT promoted a series of Race Relations Sundays, which brought representatives of both races together under the umbrella of Christian fellowship and good faith.[41] The station also made more practical efforts to improve the lot of Charlotte's black community. In late 1946 Crutchfield discovered that a project to build a new black YMCA/YWCA was some $78,000 short of its funding target of $250,000. In January 1947 he authorized an entire week of programming dedicated to raising the missing cash. For twenty hours a day every show on WBT, from Grady Cole's 5 a.m. farm program to the *Dancing Party* that closed down the station at 1 a.m., featured a pitch for the campaign.[42]

This apparently magnanimous gesture, in helping to fund the building of a segregated facility for the city's black population, spoke volumes about the agenda of many southern racial moderates at this time. Six years later, on the eve of the *Brown* decision that finally put an end to the legal fantasy that "separate" facilities for the races could ever be truly "equal," even the most liberal forces in Charlotte were still tiptoeing awkwardly around the whole segregation issue. A sympathetic 1953 report on the status of blacks prepared by the Charlotte Committee on Public Affairs insisted that it was "not concerned with the political question of segregation or non-segregation." Instead the Committee concluded that "the most basic need of the Negroes in Charlotte right now is not so much the right to sit on the same bus seat with the whites, as it is to supply their children with better housing, better health facilities, better dental care, better schooling, and a better hope for the future."[43] Progress within a segregated system was still what many white moderates had in mind for their darker and none-too-proximate neighbors until *Brown* and black activism combined to move the goalposts.

Somehow Charlie Crutchfield had got ahead of the pack here; ahead certainly of Nathaniel Tross. During the decade after World War II, he came to accept the need not to reform but to abolish Jim Crow. Again, there was no nice neat epiphany on Crutchfield's tortuous road to greater democratic and racial enlightenment. It was probably a consequence of his growing involvement with America's propaganda efforts against communism at the height of the Cold War. Whatever Crutchfield's credentials as a racial progressive, he was a staunch conservative on most other social, cultural, economic, and political matters. This was reflected in the way that he and his station warmed to the task of keeping America and the free world safe from the perils of communism. Under Crutchfield's guidance, WBT became one of the stations responsible for producing the Voice of America programs that beamed celebrations of American lifestyles, economics, and political practices to audiences across Europe.[44] In 1951 he spent four months on a State Department "special radio mission" to Greece, where his brief was to improve radio coverage in the hinterlands of that country and establish a series of powerful transmitters capable of extending the reach of Voice of America far beyond the Iron Curtain.[45]

The Greece mission was not the last time Crutchfield was formally enlisted into America's Cold War effort. In 1953 he was appointed to the Radio Advisory Committee of the State Department's International Information Administration.[46] Three years later he joined a small group of businessmen on a goodwill trip to Moscow. During this visit Crutchfield frequently absconded from the official tour party to take secret photographs of Soviet broadcasting and industrial facilities for the CIA. He also compiled a confidential report describing his impressions of Russia's economic conditions and of its citizens' morale and loyalty to the communist regime.[47] In 1962 the State Department sent him to Berlin to monitor the effectiveness of Radio Free Europe, which had been set up on the western side of the Berlin Wall to "counter the falsities that appear daily in ... the East German Government radio and television agencies."[48] By this time, WBT had also institutionalized its own contribution to the domestic fight against communism with its *Radio Moscow* programs. Introduced in 1959, the weekly show was written and produced by Alan Newcombe and Rupert Gillette with the intention of exposing the latest examples of Soviet aggression, subversion, and disinformation. In 1960, the show was nationally syndicated, prompting a glowing encomium for WBT's "marvellous and patriotic endeavor" from South Carolina Representative Robert Hemphill. Hemphill told Congress: "This station and its employees under the able guidance of Mr. Charles H. Crutchfield ... have engaged in a program of education so necessary to the survival of America. ... I salute this magnificent effort."[49]

The connection between Crutchfield's vigorous Cold War activity and his growing conviction that Jim Crow must eventually go was clear. Racial segregation and disenfranchisement—as African American leaders frequently pointed out—provided much grist for the Soviet propaganda mill. Crutchfield appreciated that the chances of winning the hearts and minds of newly independent, nonaligned, nonwhite nations, or even of those already under communist control, were much reduced while legalized racial discrimination was part of the American social and political landscape. Moving beyond a concern for the mere technicalities of covering the globe with pro-American broadcasts, in 1952 Crutchfield wrote to a number of senators, including segregationist stalwarts Richard Russell of Georgia and Harry Byrd of Virginia, about the content of such programming. The language was typically evasive, but it does not take too much creative reading to detect Crutchfield's growing unease with the damage he felt Jim Crow was inflicting on the nation's Cold War aims. For years, he argued, America had "made the mistake of trying to 'educate' the rest of the world to our way of life" with considerable arrogance and little regard for the "cultural and spiritual beliefs and customs of the people we are trying to befriend." The crucial thing America had to do in order to "win the confidence and respect of millions of people in the Arab and Oriental world," Crutchfield suggested, was to "show these people . . . that we are sincere" in proclaiming a commitment to an inclusive notion of democracy, freedom, and international friendship that transcended differences of color, custom, and creed. "Once we have convinced them of our sincerity or our interest in them as individuals and as nations . . . then and only then will we be in a position to convince them of the dangers of Communism."[50]

If this call for tolerance of difference represented less a great leap forward than a shaky stumble in the vague direction of racial justice, there is little doubt that Crutchfield had come to believe that America must put its own racial house in order if it wished to preserve any credibility as leader of the free world. There were other indications that Crutchfield and WBT were subtly preparing their white listeners to cope with the traumatic birth of a more integrated, democratic South. In 1952 a lavish publication commemorating the station's thirtieth anniversary had conspicuously failed to include a picture of Nathaniel Tross alongside other WBT regulars. Instead, a couple of black janitors were featured.[51] Two years later, however, the station produced another promotional pamphlet, titled "Power for the People," in which Tross appeared next to the white Presbyterian radio preacher Lawrence Stell. Even more striking, the cover of the pamphlet featured a cutout through which one could see a crowd scene representing WBT's "people." An African American man was extremely prominent in the section of the crowd visible through the cutout. On opening the cover the whole gathering was revealed as completely, almost excessively, integrated. Here was an image of WBT's black and white consumers mingling together on an equal footing, just as they sometimes did in the ethereal and essentially democratic community of the airwaves—and just as they might someday in Charlotte's schools and public accommodations.[52]

By the time of *Brown*, Charlie Crutchfield had also begun to acknowledge something like a moral imperative to end segregation, not only out of Cold War expediency but also on the simple and unanswerable grounds that it was wrong. WBT had even offered a few tentative "editorials" along those lines "long before there was any attempt to integrate in this area at all."[53] Crutchfield, who in 1953 had been promoted to executive vice president of the Jefferson Standard Broadcasting Corporation while retaining his role as general manager at WBT, was not alone in his views. In 1950 journalist C. A. "Pete" McKnight had editorialized in the *Charlotte News* that "segregation, as an abstract principle, cannot be defended by any intellectually or spiritually honest person."[54] However, McKnight feared that the violence and social rupture accompanying desegregation would be so severe as to render it a Pyrrhic victory. Once Crutchfield had accepted the inevitability and desirability of an end to Jim Crow, his principal concern was to try to avoid such an apocalyptic scenario unfolding in Charlotte. WBT therefore gave relatively little credence or airtime to the die-hard segregationists who battled to preserve absolute segregation at all costs. Instead it continued to encourage dialogue between the races and featured those black and white community leaders who responded to *Brown* in a sane, responsible, and law-abiding manner. The die was cast, Jim Crow was doomed, and militant responses on all sides were to be discouraged. What Charlotte needed was cool and calm deliberation on how best to manage the inescapable end of segregation.

Crutchfield's attitude was apparent when the Supreme Court handed down its historic decision on school segregation in May 1954. He was in New Orleans at the time, but immediately arranged for his friend and sometime neighbor (and longtime fan of the Briarhoppers) Billy Graham to record a radio speech in which the celebrated evangelist tried to allay the worst white fears surrounding integration. Graham urged dutiful—if not necessarily immediate—compliance with what was now the law of the land. Edited into thirty-second, one-minute, and five-minute portions at WBT, the tape was widely distributed to radio stations around the South, where it may have had some influence in reassuring anxious whites and restraining all but a few from resorting to violent resistance.[55]

In North Carolina the initial white reaction to the *Brown* decision was one of concern but hardly panic. It was widely believed that a variety of legal and political maneuverings would enable the region to circumvent the ruling, especially as the Supreme Court had set no timetable for desegregation. The second *Brown* decision in May 1955 raised white anxieties, but the Court's instruction to integrate with "all deliberate speed" was not exactly precise, while the decision to entrust plans for implementation to local southern school boards, most of whom were vehemently opposed to desegregation, was disingenuous. By the time African American parents wishing their students to attend previously segregated schools began to seek legal redress against continuing prevarication and obstruction, thereby ratcheting up white anxieties a notch further, North Carolina's white authorities had already formulated their response.[56]

In August 1954, Governor William Umstead had created a committee under Thomas Pearsall to investigate school desegregation options in the light of the *Brown* decision. Following Umstead's death in November, the committee's report was presented to his successor Luther Hodges in late December 1954. The report essentially sought to preserve the maximum amount of segregation compatible with the state's reputation for moderation and respect for the law. A second Pearsall committee report in April 1956 explained the exact mechanism for executing this juggling act. At the heart of the new report was a legal rationale and constitutional framework for adopting a voluntary or "freedom of choice" strategy that Governor Hodges had first explained to the North Carolina public in an August 1955 radio and television broadcast. Calling for "the continuance of separate schools for the races on an entirely voluntary basis," Hodges argued that this "voluntarism" provided the best way to satisfy the demands of *Brown* with a minimum of social disruption—by which he meant a minimum of real change.[57]

The second Pearsall committee report was considerably more conservative than the first. While the initial report had declined to recommend school closures or the use of private school tuition grants for white students as a means to avoid compliance with *Brown*, the April 1956 report called for constitutional amendments that would allow the payment of tuition fees to parents who did not wish their children to attend integrated schools. It also accepted the possibility of public school closures in the face of threatened desegregation, as long as the decision to close was made by means of a local referendum. This package of recommendations, the Pearsall Plan, was approved by the North Carolina General Assembly in July 1956. It was then turned over to the electorate for ratification in a statewide referendum scheduled for September.

The future of white resistance and the black freedom struggle in North Carolina was at stake in this referendum. Although the Pearsall Plan was more moderate than many of the schemes emerging from neighboring states, it still represented an unmistakable stiffening of white resistance from the previous year. However, it also represented a strenuous effort to keep that resistance within the boundaries of constitutionalism and the political process, rather than surrender it to the more incendiary and intemperate segregationists, whose stock had risen in tandem with white anxieties and black activism after the second *Brown* decision. Although many white North Carolinians eventually supported the Pearsall Plan simply because they saw it as an effective way of preserving a great measure of segregation, some of its most vociferous opponents were actually die-hard segregationists, the last-ditchers who refused to countenance any recognition of the legitimacy of the Supreme Court's rulings, however token. Meanwhile, many of the state's white racial moderates were in something of a quandary. Given the incontrovertible fact that the majority of whites in North Carolina wanted to preserve as much segregation as possible, white racial progressives had little option but to support a plan that was largely dedicated to evading, or at best substantially delaying, widespread integration. The alternative was to risk empowering those factions who demanded more drastic measures to preserve absolute segregation. Consequently, most racial moderates worked to secure a referendum victory for the Pearsall Plan. Nobody did this more effectively than Charlie Crutchfield.

In early August 1956, Crutchfield was appointed to the Governor's Committee for Public School Amendment, chaired by High Point newspaper editor Holt McPherson. Crutchfield's task as chairman of the Television and Radio Committee was "to help inform the public of the details of the legislation."[58] In effect, he had to sell the Pearsall Plan to the voters of North Carolina ahead of the September 8 referendum. This he did by asking the 125 or so radio stations and the dozen television facilities in the state to carry announcements and speeches by Luther Hodges, Thomas Pearsall, and other advocates of the Plan. Not all the radio stations that Crutchfield approached accepted the invitation to air the pro-Pearsall speeches. Some simply wanted to steer clear of the segregation debate; others cited FCC regulations about the need to provide equal time to all sides on controversial issues. "Since the Pearsall plan is a controversial measure WRFC would like to remain as we always have. Neutral," wrote Steve Woodson from his Reidsville radio station. "We intend to aid in a '*get out the vote*' campaign as we always do. BUT TO SPEAK OUT AS PARTISAN is against our better judgement."[59]

Some radio stations like WBUY-Lexington, WDNC-Durham, and WSOC-Charlotte accepted the Committee's materials but pledged to "seek out any organized opposition and offer them equal opportunity over our station," as WSOC's manager Earl Gluck put it.[60] WPTF-Raleigh took its responsibilities in this regard especially seriously. On the successive nights of September 3–7 it aired a series of five radio forums on the proposed amendment, each featuring an advocate and an opponent of the Plan. Guests included Pearsall himself, who debated with a Mrs. J. Z. Watkins. On another occasion State Treasurer Edwin Gill went head-to-head with veteran liberal journalist Mark Etheridge, who clearly saw the Plan as a delaying tactic and spoke up for much greater compliance.[61]

Most North Carolina radio and television stations, however, welcomed the chance to air speeches in support of the Plan without agonizing overlong about the need to offer airtime to its opponents. "We do not feel that it is incumbent upon us to seek out opponents of the Pearsall plan and ram free time down their throats," Jerry Elliot of WCBT–Roanoke Rapids informed Crutchfield. Of course, Elliot explained, "if we are presented with a request for free time, we shall be forced to give it," but only *"if we are shown the person or organization demanding it is responsible, in good faith and otherwise has a right to it."* And that, he assured Crutchfield, would be a tall order, since the radio station reserved "the right to lable crackpots crackpots (even if it's only in our own mind so we can't be sued frivolously by a crackpot for slander)."[62]

That the Pearsall Plan enshrined the mood of restrained but obdurate white resistance in North Carolina was evident from the attitude of some of the radio stations that accepted the Committee's broadcasts. "It is my opinion," wrote James B. Petty, manager of WLTC-Gastonia and a self-professed colonel in the Confederate Air Force, "that any station manager who does not go along with it [the Plan] is nothing but a 'damnyankee.' Put us down for whatever spots and programs are available."[63] Many of these programs pandered to the South's sense of sectional grievance against insensitive and unwarranted outside interference in its racial affairs. When state treasurer Edwin Gill appeared on WPTF-Raleigh to promote the Plan, he was in no doubt as to where the blame for the region's current difficulties lay. Gill urged North Carolinians to support "a sincere and practical answer to the present crisis in education created by the segregation decisions of the Supreme Court of the United States. . . . In rendering this decision the Court ignored the deeply imbedded customs and traditions under which our splendid system of schools had been developed. In so doing, the Supreme Court has placed in jeopardy the fine relationships that have existed between our races and has created a fertile field for the stirring up of friction, distrust and misunderstanding."[64]

Elsewhere, last-minute amendments to the texts of announcements advocating the Plan revealed the desire to preserve an aura of compliance around a measure that many whites actually embraced as a mode of defiance. Crutchfield, together with Committee chair Holt McPherson and information officer Ralph

Howland, agreed that the merits of the Plan should be explained, not in terms of preserving or destroying segregation in education, but as the only viable means of keeping the public school system operating peacefully in the face of the Supreme Court's rash decisions. Crutchfield's initial request to the state's radio stations to carry pro–Pearsall Plan broadcasts was certainly expressed in these terms. The success of the Plan was, he insisted, "a matter of grave concern for all those of us who are interested in the preservation of our public schools." In the same vein, the draft text of a spot that originally assured North Carolinians that a vote in favor of the proposed amendment would help "preserve Segregation in our public schools" was revised to read that a yes vote would "help Governor Hodges preserve our public school program." Another revision removed a reference to the amendment as a device "whereby racial segregation will be preserved in our schools," stressing instead that it was "the future"—rather than the nature—"of public school education in North Carolina" that was at stake.[65]

Ultimately, it is impossible to quantify how much radio contributed to the overwhelming popular endorsement of the constitutional amendment enacting the Pearsall Plan on September 8, 1956. The related television and newspaper campaigns were also important in publicizing the issues. Yet at least one rurally based North Carolina radio executive felt that these other media were less effective. William Moore of WHED-Washington reckoned that before radio picked up the issue "80% of the people in Beaufort County actually [did] not understand the plan fully. The newspapers are always preaching how they serve their communities but it is our opinion that they have sadly neglected their duty in informing the public on this issue." Charlie Crutchfield himself had presided over the arrival of television in Charlotte when WBTV went on air in 1951. He had closely monitored the steady expansion of its reach and influence. Yet he was by no means convinced that at the end of the 1950s television had any more authority in these sorts of matters in the South, particularly in the rural, black-belt South, than radio. Indeed, Crutchfield's loyalties and preferences sometimes sneaked out when he referred to himself as the chairman of "Radio and TV" for the Governor's Committee, reversing the word order of his official designation.[66]

What is indisputable is that radio was part of an effective propaganda campaign whereby Crutchfield and others sold the Pearsall Plan to white North Carolina. The consequences of this achievement were complex. In the short term, the Pearsall Plan cut the rug from beneath the more radical proponents of massive resistance, providing a polite, mannered, and apparently legal means of dealing with the *Brown* decisions. In this sense it may have diminished the amount of violence and social disorder in the state. This was a major part of Crutchfield's agenda. Yet the Pearsall Plan had also substituted tokenism for genuine strides toward integration. This helped to sustain dangerous white hopes that they might yet evade the full implications of *Brown* while frustrating North Carolina blacks. Thus the Pearsall Plan set the context for the campaign against token desegregation in education and beyond that dominated the freedom struggle in Charlotte in the 1960s.

WBT and the Desegregation of Charlotte

The 1950s ended with barely half a dozen black students attending previously white schools in Charlotte and most of the city's public accommodations still segregated. It did not take a genius to predict that integration and race relations more generally would loom large among the concerns of Charlotte's black and white citizens during the new decade.[67] This was reflected by the choice of topic for WBT's *Project '60* show in November 1959. With moderator Clyde MacLean chairing, the program focused on "the current state of race relations in the South." Guests included staunch segregationists Thomas Waring, who edited the *Charleston News and Courier* in South Carolina, and Beverley I. Lake, the former assistant attorney general for North Carolina and one of the state's most zealous massive resisters. Arguing on the side of full compliance with the *Brown* decisions were Harry Golden and Dr. Charles Satchell Morris, a Massachusetts-born, Virginia-reared black educator then teaching at Benedict College in Columbia, South Carolina.[68]

Originally scheduled for an hour, the live show lasted twice that long, with telephone lines opened up to callers for the last forty minutes. Carried aloft on WBT's 50,000 watts of clear-channel power, the *Project '60* "integration versus segregation" debate reached audiences from Maine to Florida. The *Pittsburgh Courier* hailed the straight-talking Morris—whose ad-libbed speech was subsequently published by Benedict College—as a hero to be ranked alongside W.E.B. Du Bois, William Holmes Borders, Martin Luther King (Jr. and Sr.), and Fred Shuttlesworth. The paper also saluted WBT and the three white executives most closely involved with the show, Ned Burgess, Jim Davis, and Virgil Evans—Crutchfield's old boss from his early days at WSPA-Spartanburg—"for having the courage to sponsor the program, with free speech unfettered." As a WBT statement pointed out, however, the station did not wish to align itself formally with either side in this debate. Rather, it sought to "present as fairly and accurately as possible both sides of controversial questions . . . to encourage the public to examine the problem of segregation vs. integration. It was the feeling of WBT that in many quarters only one side of the issue had been presented." Again, this was hardly an unequivocal endorsement of immediate desegregation. Nevertheless, the manner in which WBT sat on the fence at least allowed those in the South who did support such a policy rare exposure in the mass media. The station helped to maintain a climate of reasoned discussion rather than hysterical reaction among anxious whites.[69]

A few years later, in the spring of 1963, WBT finally tumbled off that fence and began to editorialize for the complete and immediate desegregation of public accommodations in Charlotte. Privately, Charlie Crutchfield had been moving toward this position for more than a decade. Yet public endorsement of integration still entailed considerable personal and professional risk. As Crutchfield recalled, local white businessmen like "Mike Kinsey . . . who was a big theater man and a great friend of mine, was furious with me; he couldn't believe that I would 'ruin' his theater crowd by allowing blacks to come in, particularly to sit anywhere they wanted to. . . . I made a lot of enemies with these editorials. But I'm very proud of them. I think we were right; I know we were right."[70]

Crutchfield's conviction that "segregation was wrong and had been wrong at the beginning. Schools, restaurants, buses, everything" mingled with more pragmatic civic and commercial motives as he threw the weight of WBT radio and television behind moves to desegregate the city.[71] Escalating African American activism undoubtedly played a part in this shift. After the Johnson C. Smith University sit-ins of 1960 there had been sporadic, relatively low-key, direct-action protests, notably those in 1961 that succeeded in desegregating the restaurants in two downtown department stores. In April 1963, however, Dr. Reginald Hawkins had begun to organize further demonstrations against the continued exclusion of blacks from most of the city's hotels, restaurants, and theaters. Hawkins realized that the local business community's perennial concern about the impact of any mass protests on the city's image and economic prospects was especially heightened that spring. Charlotte was hosting the North Carolina World Trade Fair and was very much in the commercial shop window. A series of token gestures and unkept promises from the city council had persuaded Hawkins to call off his first planned demonstrations, but by late May 1963 he was preparing to march again.[72]

It was at this time that Mayor Stan Brookshire intervened. Recognizing where real power in Charlotte lay, Brookshire asked the Chamber of Commerce to try to secure from its members a firm commitment to desegregate. On May 23 the Chamber agreed to a resolution that all local businesses "be opened immediately to all customers without regard to race, creed, or color."[73] Over the next few months the more progressive elements within the Chamber worked alongside Brookshire to secure compliance with the resolution. By early June about a third of the city's restaurants had integrated. Most of the others followed shortly afterwards, especially once the influential Frank Sherrill agreed to desegregate his popular S&W Cafeteria.[74] In other southern cities where hard-line segregationists had more leverage, such as in Birmingham, similar Chamber of Commerce resolutions were simply ignored, necessitating further black protests that were often met with mass arrests and white violence. In Charlotte, however, Brookshire and the Chamber had both greater will and more influence than the local hard-core segregationists; they were able to ensure widespread compliance while preserving civic order.[75]

By this time Charlie Crutchfield was an important member of the Chamber of Commerce, and he used WBT to support the Chamber's desegregation initiative in a series of editorials. These regular sixty-second broadcasts were carefully scripted to present peaceful, voluntary desegregation as in keeping with Charlotte's reputation for decency and common sense. They were also tailored to counter hard-line segregationist accusations that the Chamber had capitulated to black pressure. At the same time they sought to calm white fears about what removing racial barriers in public accommodations might actually mean in practice. An editorial on May 27, 1963, was typical. It commended the Chamber for "asking that all business establishments in the city serving the public serve all the public" and recounted the observations of the manager of a recently desegregated restaurant that "the number of Negroes who have used this dining room since then is so small and so well-behaved that only the most prejudiced of persons could take offense at their presence." The message was clear, if complex and laced with a good deal of realism about the fact that, even if the downtown did desegregate, white prejudice was not going to disappear overnight. African Americans were "not especially anxious to eat at the same places as whites," the editorial explained, but understandably they wanted recognition of their right to do so if they wished. Just as important, the editorial reassured skeptical whites deluded by years of ignorance and racist propaganda that, if they did encounter blacks in integrated facilities, they would be pleasantly surprised by how well they behaved.[76]

The editorial went on to endorse the Chamber's call to desegregate by suggesting that "if the recommendation is acted upon, it will cut the ground from under the more extreme integrationists." This was an allusion to black leaders like Reginald Hawkins who were prepared to engage in direct action, rather than interminable negotiations, in an effort to end segregation. Revealingly, WBT refused to blame Charlotte's African Americans for wanting to hasten the pace of change. Instead the editorial insisted that it was the white community's responsibility to do the right thing in order to make street demonstrations unnecessary and leaders like Hawkins irrelevant: "In every case where the white people of a community have shown a disposition to be reasonable, the Negroes have also been reasonable."[77] Two days later another editorial reassured white listeners that the "action of the Charlotte Chamber was not the result of a court order nor a reaction to mass picketing"—although, in truth, the specter of Hawkins's marches had been a crucial factor. Rather, the editorial explained, it was an expression of the city's faith that "any friction can be removed by forbearance on both sides, and by an orderly approach for a common purpose." This editorial was particularly outraged by Hawkins's accusation that "Charlotte is just as sinful as Birmingham." WBT vehemently rejected the comparison with a city that had become a byword for intolerance: "That is not true! Charlotte is much further along the way to solution of its problems, and her local leadership is far more enlightened."[78]

For the rest of the decade, WBT's editorials held up a remarkable mirror to white Charlotte's efforts to come to terms with the civil rights revolution and the subsequent emergence of black power. Most of these editorials were written by Rupert Gillette and read by Alan Newcombe, the two men responsible for the *Radio Moscow* shows. However, the subject matter and general viewpoint to be expressed were usually determined in advance by an editorial board, which subsequently reviewed Gillette's draft copy. Each editorial—there were usually three or four a week—was broadcast four times daily on WBT's AM, FM, and television outlets. Although, like most of the editorial board, Charles Crutchfield occasionally took issue with the substance of one of the slots, few editorials were not personally approved by him before they aired.[79]

Perhaps the most striking aspect of WBT's editorials was their steady quest for evenhandedness, even if that goal sometimes sat awkwardly with the station's basic conservatism and occasionally reactionary politics. WBT never entirely abandoned its quintessentially southern hostility to the idea of federal intervention to regulate racial matters or its conviction that many African American leaders were pressing too militantly for too much change too soon. For example, direct-action protests in pursuit of black civil and voting rights were routinely attacked as unnecessarily confrontational and counterproductive. An editorial on August 27, 1963, roundly condemned the March on Washington as an irresponsibly dangerous enterprise "that is the opposite of orderly, democratic government—mass demonstrations in an effort to influence Congress by intimidation." WBT feared that the march might well produce a riot in the nation's capital. Nevertheless, after the event had passed off peacefully, WBT dutifully aired a reassessment based around a highly critical letter from listener Jacqueline G. Bayer, who had accused the station of being "hypocritical and petty" in its coverage. In particular, Bayer condemned WBT for its readiness to blame Martin Luther King and his followers for the white violence that their peaceful demonstrations sometimes attracted.[80]

More locally, on May 21, 1964, WBT vehemently denounced Reginald Hawkins's plans to picket the Charlotte YMCA, which had refused him membership. As ever, WBT sought to defuse civic disorder and promote constructive dialogue. It urged Hawkins to take his grievances to the central board of the "Y" or to the Mayor's Committee on Race Relations, which was designed to mediate just such disputes. It then crassly suggested that Hawkins might prefer to join the traditionally black McCrorey YMCA anyway. Yet even in the midst of its criticisms and insensitivity, the editorial still affirmed that Hawkins's complaint was essentially justified. Five days later, WBT actually turned over an entire editorial to Hawkins, who stated his position with eloquent simplicity. The picketing, he said, was "to dramatize to the Christians of this nation that there are still YMCAs that practice racial discrimination and segregation against fellow Christian Negro YMCA members."[81]

Throughout late 1963 and 1964 WBT somewhat grudgingly accepted the need for comprehensive civil rights legislation, but it opposed the specifics of a bill it felt "puts too many powers in the hands of Federal officials, and takes away rights from both Negroes and whites."[82] It was a similar story with voting rights legislation. In March 1965 a series of editorials denounced what WBT saw as Martin Luther King's cynical attempts to intimidate the government into speedy passage of a voting rights bill by courting white violence in Selma, and darkly hinted that King may have fallen under the sway of left-wing extremists. Yet the editorials were even more condemnatory of Alabama governor George Wallace and the white law-enforcement officers in Selma who failed to prevent—and actually perpetrated—much of the violence. In the end, extremism on both sides was the real problem, and the station suggested: "Both King and Wallace would make a great contribution by getting out of the streets and into the courts." As for the 1965 Voting Rights Act itself, WBT again had problems with the particulars. It objected to the extension of federal authority over the conduct of local elections, but also to the provision that suspended the use of literacy tests only in states where less than half the voters had gone to the polls in the previous election and where African Americans constituted more than 20 percent of the population. "If a literacy test is used, it should be the same for everyone." It was the discriminatory nature of this ruling, avowedly made in the interests of equalizing voting rights, that jarred at WBT.[83]

Francis Fitzgerald and WGIV: A Black-Oriented Rival

WBT was not the only Charlotte radio station editorializing on racial issues in the 1960s. In order to hear views on the freedom struggle that were closer to those of the majority of the city's African American population, it was necessary to retune to 1600 khz on the AM dial, the home of WGIV. The irony was that those editorials were written by Francis Fitzgerald, an extraordinary white man who had launched the station soon after World War II. In September 1946 the Publix Broadcasting Service of Charlotte, Inc., filed a request with the FCC to open a new radio station. The initial application made no mention of serving the African American community in Charlotte. Instead it emphasized the need for a fourth general-market station with an affiliation to the Mutual network in a city where the existing stations, WBT, WAYS, and WSOC were already wedded to CBS, ABC, and NBC respectively. Within a few years, however, WGIV—which finally debuted in December 1947—was devoting much of its airtime to black-oriented programs and Francis Fitzgerald, the chief stockholder and general manager of Publix Broadcasting, had emerged as one of the most influential figures in the development of black-oriented radio in the postwar South.[84]

Francis Marion Fitzgerald was just a couple of years younger than his fellow radio pioneer, friend, and competitor Charlie Crutchfield. Born on August 30, 1914, into a Catholic family in Augusta, Georgia, Fitzgerald had studied briefly at Duke before transferring to Furman University, where he completed a Bachelor of Science degree. While at Furman, Fitzgerald had worked part-time as an announcer for WSPA-Spartanburg—the same station that had given Crutchfield his first break in broadcasting. After graduation, a brief stint at WIS-Columbia was followed by a longer stay at WCSC-Charleston, where Fitzgerald rose to the position of program director. In 1939 Fitzgerald swapped Charleston and broadcasting for Charlotte and bottling, becoming vice president of the Royal Crown Cola plant. While retaining that position, in 1941 he resumed his radio career and joined WSOC-Charlotte as a promotions manager. During the war Fitzgerald served as a communications officer in the United States Naval Reserve, afterwards becoming general manager of WORD in Spartanburg, although his residence, wife, and young daughter remained in Charlotte. He was still working at WORD when he and two other radio veterans—J. Law Epps, a former sales representative and programmer at WSPA, and T. C. Brandon, the assistant chief engineer at WSOC—decided to form Publix Broadcasting and start a station nearer to Fitzgerald's family in Charlotte.[85]

Twenty years after launching WGIV, Francis Fitzgerald recalled: "My father told me years ago if I was ever to make a success of anything, I must find a definite need, fill it, and fill it well."[86] Like many other ambitious southern broadcasters in the years after World War II, Fitzgerald saw just such a "definite need" among Charlotte's African American community. WGIV exploited the fact that the established stations in Charlotte spent relatively little time programming specifically for a burgeoning black audience. The decision to focus on this neglected market sector also offered the fledgling station a certain extra leverage when it sought FCC permission to upgrade its facilities. By the early 1950s this had become a matter of some urgency. Founded as an impoverished 1000–watt sunup-to-sundown station, WGIV had initially relied on a temperamental old transmitter bought cheaply from the local highway patrol. According to engineer Sam "Bill" Lineburger, the unit had actually blown up within hours of the station's grand opening and thereafter had to be literally kick-started. "We stayed on the air by complying with a sign placed on the gear reading, 'KICK HERE,'" he recalled. Lineburger and his colleagues routinely had to walk on the tops of soft drink crates placed on the floor of WGIV's first studio in order to avoid being electrocuted when the control room flooded after heavy rain.[87] By October 1951, however, the station had done well enough to move to better accommodations and was seeking a modest extension to its allocated broadcasting hours. Revealingly, Francis Fitzgerald appealed to the FCC for permission to sign on at 6:30 a.m. all year round on the grounds that it would allow the station "to continue service to the tremendously large Negro audience, both rural and urban." Fitzgerald proudly informed FCC Secretary T. J. Slowie that WGIV was "the only station in this area which programs exclusively to the Negro from 6:30 until 7:45 a.m. each day."[88]

The following year, after a protracted period of legal and financial restructuring, Francis Fitzgerald became the majority stockholder and president of the Charlotte Radio and Television Corporation, the new owner of WGIV.[89] As general manager and treasurer, Fitzgerald continued to control the day-to-day running of the station he now effectively owned, using that power to steadily increase WGIV's commitment to black-oriented broadcasting. As on many southern stations in the 1950s and early 1960s, the transition from an eclectic but primarily white-oriented format to largely black-oriented programming was a gradual affair. Indeed, until around 1962 WGIV's programming mix defied easy racial or generic categorizations. Tin Pan Alley pop, gospel, rhythm and blues, country, rock and roll, news, weather, sports, and public information programs all jostled for time on the schedules. "You played whatever you felt like playing, whatever you wanted to play, whatever your audience wanted to hear is what you played," remembered black deejay "Chattie Hattie" Leeper. This eclecticism helped to ensure that WGIV captured a substantial slice of the young white audience in Charlotte—especially as the major radio station in the area, WBT, had steered clear of the scandalous new vogue for rock and roll. WGIV, as Leeper noted, "was primarily geared to the black community, but we had a lot of white listeners, because we played a mixture of the music."[90]

Not only were WGIV's playlists and audiences integrated, but from 1948 when Fitzgerald hired Eugene "Genial Gene" Potts, so was its staff. A graduate of Johnson C. Smith University and a member of one of Charlotte's most prominent black families, Potts was an erudite former schoolteacher and principal and sometime insurance salesman, with a rare gift for rhyming patter. Having worked part-time at the station while still a high school student, Hattie Leeper joined full-time in 1951 following her own graduation from Johnson C. Smith. At first she helped Potts and other announcers by compiling news, weather, and traffic bulletins. Before long she was given her own music and talk show, *Hattie's Houseparty*, which aired twice daily at 10 a.m. and 1 p.m. and was sponsored by the Martha White Flour Company. For more than two decades, Leeper fronted a variety of shows on WGIV, becoming one of the station's most commercially successful and respected personalities. Other important black hires soon followed, with Ray Gooding and gospel deejay and newsman William Sanders join-

FIGURE 14. WGIV deejay "Genial Gene" Potts was an important community leader in Charlotte as well as a master of rhymed reason. Courtesy of Archives of African American Music and Culture, Indiana University.

ing Potts and Leeper on air. At a time when black technical staff were extremely rare, Fitzgerald also hired Uriah Gooding, a graduate of DeVry Technical Institute in Chicago, as one of the first black radio engineers in the country. Moreover, Fitzgerald took the unusual step of placing several of these African Americans in important executive positions on the staff. Potts, for example, served as director of public affairs, while Hattie Leeper was appointed women's affairs director.[91]

During the 1950s and early 1960s, WGIV's white and black announcers had much in common in terms of style and presentation. This was true of both the cool, self-consciously refined sophisticates and the high-octane rappers who shared WGIV's airtime. While Gene Potts set the standard for a slick style of patter, it was white deejay "Hot Scott" Hubbs who epitomized the jive-talking rhythm and blues jock. According to Hattie Leeper, Hubbs "sounded exactly like a soul brother" and black fans were invariably astonished to find he was white. "It was an integrated station," observed Leeper. "But the white announcers sounded black, and the black announcers sounded polished." Significantly, Leeper refused to cast this "polish" in terms of the dilution of some black vernacular authenticity. Rather, she saw it as emblematic of a phase in the freedom struggle when many African Americans were anxious to project images of conspicuous respectability in their quest to be treated by white America with respect. In much the same vein, she was even happy to observe the station's formal dress code, which called for all announcers to be properly attired in suits or dresses when on air or making public appearances. "I had good diction. I didn't break verbs. I didn't crack slang. And I didn't show thirty-two teeth. I was never that type of an individual. I mean, it was always a profession that I felt dignified to be in," Leeper explained.[92]

Irrespective of his motivations, Francis Fitzgerald's decision to hire African American staff and to program extensively for blacks was quickly embraced by many African Americans in Charlotte as portending a coming era of racial harmony and progress in the city. In July 1953, for example, St. Paul's Baptist Church, whose activist pastor J. F. Wertz had run unsuccessfully for the local school board in 1949 while Bishop Dale was campaigning for the city council, formally recognized Fitzgerald's contribution to the black community. The church's commendation perfectly captured the blend of altruism, imperfect racial enlightenment, and commercial opportunism that characterized Fitzgerald's conception of his station's purpose. The award was given

In recognition of excellent exemplification of unbiased citizenship and high Christian ideals. Your radio station is the first and only station in Charlotte to allow Negroes of all faiths and creeds to use its facilities indiscriminately in the propagation of their ideas. Your radio station is the first and only station in Charlotte to permit Negroes to use its facilities indiscriminately and continuously for religious broadcasting at the time and hour considered most desirable for religious worship. And for further evidence of your unbiased creed, you gave Charlotte its first Negro "disk jockey"; also, your station holds the unique and outstanding distinction of being the first and only station to employ a Negro woman for regular broadcasting. In a material world, nothing more tangibly expresses brotherhood than to extend respectable and lucrative employment to members of a minority group of people, and to share unselfishly the fruits and substance of your property with a brother without regard to race, color, or creed. Truly your action exemplifies the brotherhood of man and the fatherhood of God.[93]

Obviously, warm praise for white moderates like Fitzgerald made considerable tactical sense for a black community still lacking full civil rights and significant political power. And while Fitzgerald never lost sight of the commercial rationale for programming to African American listeners, he does appear to have been a fairly bold proponent of the kind of racial progressivism that emerged among sections of the white South during the decade after World War II. Certainly Fitzgerald's plaudits for his own leading attraction, deejay Gene Potts, at a November 1953 celebration of Genial Gene's fifth year on air, touched all the right rhetorical bases. "Gene is not only a credit to the Negro race—he is a credit to a truly great America," Fitzgerald insisted, playing off the heightened patriotism of the Cold War era. Not only was Fitzgerald willing to hold up an African American man as a shining example of the best qualities in a "truly great America," but he also offered his own relationship with Potts as a model for future racial comity. Fitzgerald announced, "I don't believe there is anyone who knows Gene better than I do. Gene and I have been through an awful lot together. We've seen the bad times and the good. We've worked closely and in perfect harmony. There's always been a keynote of understanding between us."[94]

Despite their paternalistic undercurrents, such public expressions of white friendship, admiration, and cooperation were of considerable symbolic and psychological importance to the black community. This was, after all, still a time when dialogue with sympathetic and reasonable whites seemed to hold the promise of progress toward equitable treatment and opportunity in a desegregated Charlotte. Furthermore, the close and constructive relationship between Fitzgerald and Potts really did embody WGIV's approach to improving race relations and expanding black opportunity in the city. Of course, the essential power at the station was heavily weighted in Fitzgerald's favor. Nonetheless, rather than quietly exploiting Potts's expertise and heroic status within the black community, Fitzgerald made sure that Potts's importance to WGIV was officially recognized and financially rewarded. In addition to becoming vice president in charge of public affairs at the station, Potts was invited to join the board of directors of WGIV's parent company, the Charlotte Radio and Television Corporation, where he helped to devise an innovative profit-sharing scheme that benefited all the regular staff, black and white.

By the late 1950s, WGIV was well on its way to becoming a wholly black-oriented station, devoting "approximately fifty percent of its time to programming to, for, and by Negroes." In March 1958, barely six months after the White Citizens' Council had hounded Dorothy Counts out of Harding High School, Fitzgerald wrote: "Never before in the history of this area has there been a greater need for positive leadership by setting examples. Race relations through communications to all people will go a long way toward the solution of these problems." Fitzgerald also noted the "national recognition" that WGIV had earned for "its unique approach to racial matters, along with being credited with contributing much to the betterment of race relations in this area." Once again Fitzgerald sought to parlay his station's special attentiveness to the black community into favorable treatment from the FCC. This time he successfully petitioned "for nighttime operation in order to extend this all-important race relations work. . . . In this area of service alone, we feel that an extension of time is most necessary."[95]

Despite Fitzgerald's claims that WGIV had a "unique approach to racial matters," his black-oriented station's attitude toward race relations actually had much in common with that of its notionally more conservative and largely white-oriented neighbor WBT. Both stations stressed the need for tolerance, patience, and dialogue on all sides. Moreover, although WGIV's appeal was primarily to African Americans, Fitzgerald and his staff knew that their ability to reach the ears of some whites in Charlotte was important to the goal of promoting interracial dialogue and ensuring that appeals for racial justice were heard. "WGIV has made a great contribution to Charlotte by pioneering in Race-Relation. . . . You are to be commended for your courage, sincerity and devotion to our American way of life," Thomas Jenkins, pastor of the Statesville Avenue Presbyterian Church, wrote to Fitzgerald in late 1954. "Just today, I visited three business places owned and operated by whites, and their radios were tuned to Genial Gene."[96] Around the same time, Potts comfortably won a contest to choose the city's most popular deejay with a large portion of his votes coming from young white listeners—a phenomenon that one local paper noted "had more than usual meaning against the background of reaction to the Supreme Court decision on segregated schools."[97]

Hattie Leeper agreed that WGIV shared WBT's basic concern to preserve civic order and to discourage extremism on either side of the desegregation issue. In fact, Leeper felt that, while WGIV's black staff were hardly unaware of or personally untouched by racial prejudice and discrimination, their unusual experiences at an integrated station had somewhat insulated them from the rising temperature of black anger against Jim Crow. "We kind of lost touch of the world. . . . We were all one. We all ate together. We all did everything together, the blacks and the whites at the station. We were all like a family. . . . When we heard about a lot of the tension and the things that a lot of the folks were experiencing, it was Greek to us."[98]

Leeper also felt that Charlotte's broader African American community really did believe that the city's white leadership would live up to its carefully nurtured reputation for progressivism; that it would listen to honestly expressed black complaints and exercise decisive leadership to rectify glaring injustices. Such optimism, according to Hattie Leeper, partially explained the belated and relatively limited incidence of direct-action protest in the city. "We didn't have a lot of protests here in Charlotte. We didn't have people taking it to the streets, because we were already a moveable city that was on the go. And we had good leadership.

FIGURE 15. Pioneering WGIV deejay "Chattie Hattie" Leeper exemplified the concern with respectability on black-oriented radio in the South during the 1950s and early 1960s. Courtesy of James Peeler.

We had good role models. We had people that we respected, and we could put a handle on things."[99]

In this environment WGIV's deejays sometimes found themselves using their intimacy with black community leaders and activists, not to encourage or organize protest, but to forewarn city authorities of particular grievances and proposed targets for direct action. For example, as Reginald Hawkins prepared to challenge segregation in the downtown stores in the spring of 1963, WGIV's deejays were among those who contacted Mayor Stan Brookshire to explain the depth of black feeling on the issue and warn him of the likelihood of mass demonstrations. "It wasn't that we were asleep," Leeper explained. "It's just that we were close to our mayor, and we could call him on the telephone and say, 'Look, I'm telling you, now, you'd better listen . . . because they're talking about doing this and such.' And it was quelled."[100] This was much the same approach that Nathaniel Tross had been taking for years; it appeared to make perfect sense in a city where the rhetoric of civility, moderation, and gradualism still held considerable sway over members of both races.

In many respects, then, WBT and WGIV were simultaneously products and architects of the temperate and temporizing mood that typified Charlotte during the decade or so after *Brown*. For all the common ground, however, there were some significant differences in the style and substance of their responses to rising black activism and the prospect of desegregation in the second half of the 1950s and early 1960s. Much of this stemmed from the fact that Francis Fitzgerald and his staff were simply far more comfortable with the new pace, sources, and trajectory of black protest than Charles Crutchfield and WBT. When in the tense aftermath of *Brown* WGIV boldly adopted as its logo a black-and-white handshake and began to advertise itself as "everybody's station," it symbolized Fitzgerald's longstanding commitment to the sort of integration with respect for difference that flourished at his own station. What made this gesture especially noteworthy, of course, was the timing. At the first signs of organized mass black insurgency and federal interventionism—and of the white resistance that greeted them—many self-professed white moderates had fallen mute or quickly distanced themselves from anything that might be construed as an expression of support for desegregation. Fitzgerald not only kept his head above the parapet; he actually increased his station's public commitment to an integrated South.[101]

WBT offered nothing analogous to WGIV's graphic support for desegregation until its editorial campaign in the spring of 1963. With Tross the only black voice regularly heard on the station, WBT lumbered rather uncertainly toward public acceptance of black aspirations, though rarely of the mix of protest and federal intervention by which African Americans sought to fulfill them. Its earnest calls for calm and continued dialogue had often seemed designed to forestall, rather than to encourage, meaningful changes in Charlotte's racial arrangements. WGIV, by contrast, with its roster of popular black on-air personalities, community outreach programs, black-oriented news and public information services, and heavy doses of rhythm and blues, soul, gospel, and other African American music, was positioned much closer to the quickening heartbeat of black Charlotte. The station was unequivocal about the desirability of speedy desegregation. It advocated urgent dialogue simply in order to effect the long overdue dismantling of Jim Crow. It warned city leaders about the very real prospect of mass direct-action campaigns if white tokenism continued, but never questioned the legitimacy of using such tactics if the authorities failed to address black needs.

The cultural resonance of its programming—the actual sound of the deejays and the increasingly soulful, community-oriented content and mood of their shows—did more to establish WGIV's credentials as an institution committed to racial equality than its promotion of any specific social programs or protest activities. But WGIV did sometimes become involved in more direct efforts to

FIGURE 16. When WGIV adopted a black-white handshake as its logo in the mid-1950s, it symbolized a commitment to integration that had been apparent at the station from its birth. Courtesy of James Peeler.

improve the lot of Charlotte's black population. Not surprisingly in a city where business boosterism loomed so large, WGIV had always focused considerable energy on efforts to improve the economic strength and entrepreneurial vigor of the black community. Fitzgerald, for example, was a founder member of the biracial Opportunity Foundation formed in the mid-1950s to improve race relations in Charlotte by expanding economic and educational opportunities for the city's black population. Fitzgerald continued to pursue this agenda as the southern civil rights movement gathered momentum. In 1957 WGIV cosponsored a Business Management Institute at Carver College where Gene Potts served as one of the main conveners. For several years the station also funded a six-week school for African American businessmen in conjunction with the federal Small Business Administration. In 1960 the SBA hailed the WGIV project as "the most successful seminar of its type in the entire United States."[102]

These efforts to stimulate black-owned businesses were part of Fitzgerald's broader commitment to address "the economic problems of the area in such fields as job opportunities, new industry, better wages, and fair employment practices." In January 1962 WGIV collaborated with the North Carolina Employment Security Commission to air a series of daily five-minute *Job Clinic* slots designed to link prospective employees with potential employers. When the commission withdrew its support, WGIV continued the shows anyway. "Better Job Opportunities await the qualified Negroes of the Charlotte area, but prospective employers tell us at WGIV that they do not have any method of finding these people," the station explained. Unemployed workers or those simply seeking better positions were asked to complete a Job Clinic application form stating their skills, qualifications, and experience. The station kept these details on file, hoping to match the applicants to a list of job vacancies gleaned from local employers. The station also took out newspaper advertisements and did a monthly mailing to some five hundred local businesses, encouraging them to hire black staff and informing them how the free Job Clinic service could help them meet their manpower needs. After two months, WGIV proudly announced that the Clinic was "progressing at a rapid pace. Already we have been able to place highly qualified persons in good-paying jobs," suggesting that it was rather easier to find places for skilled or professional black workers than for blue-collar laborers. In the early 1960s the Clinic continued to expand both in size and in scope, even drawing a letter of praise from Attorney General Robert Kennedy. In late July 1963, Kennedy wrote to Fitzgerald expressing interest in "the employment information exchange that you have developed at WGIV" and claiming to be "exploring means of bringing the idea to the attention of others and encouraging them to try it." Describing the Clinic as "an imaginative and valuable contribution toward the solution of one of the Negro's most difficult and fundamental problems in the United States," Kennedy added: "Voluntary steps of this sort by public-spirited individuals like yourself are essential to the solution of the problem."[103]

Educational and voting rights initiatives also formed a major part of WGIV's contribution to black empowerment. Fitzgerald served on the Chamber of Commerce's education committee, while in the early 1950s Gene Potts had worked for the North Carolina Education Committee, albeit at that time working to improve black facilities within a segregated system. Like many black-oriented stations, WGIV was a consistent supporter of United Negro College Fund appeals and offered cash gifts and free airtime to Potts's alma mater, Johnson C. Smith University. On air, Potts would repeatedly stress to his young listeners the importance of getting a good education. His message of uplift and self-improvement no doubt gained extra authority from the fact that in 1960 Potts had become the first black contestant on a network television quiz show when he appeared on *Strike It Rich*.[104] Two years later he rapped, "Get with it, work harder, and make better marks; stop horsing around and going out on silly larks. Respect your teachers and older folks who know, that the *better* your education, the higher you'll go," as part of a four-month Education Booster campaign on WGIV.[105] Similarly constructive was the station's growing commitment to voter registration efforts among African Americans. In the early 1960s the station supported Reginald Hawkins and his Non-Partisan Voter Registration Coordinating Committee. In early 1964 Hawkins wrote to Fitzgerald to thank him for the "fine spots given by you in our last registration drives."[106] In 1965 Fitzgerald himself offered a modest personal contribution to Fred Alexander when the NAACP leader successfully bid to become Charlotte's first black city councilman. WGIV also provided special advertising rates for Alexander's campaign.[107]

Like WBT, WGIV took advantage of a relaxation of FCC regulations concerning editorials in 1963. Francis Fitzgerald assumed considerably more personal responsibility for their content than Charlie Crutchfield did at WBT. "No one else is allowed editorial license at WGIV," the station explained to the FCC. Fitzgerald "makes every decision on issues to be presented." Running for a maximum of ninety seconds, each WGIV "minitorial" was aired at least ten times daily for a minimum of three days.[108] In the main, these spots tended to be slightly more impatient about the pace and extent of racial change than the equivalents on WBT. For example, in 1963 the station praised South Carolina governor Ernest "Fritz" Hollings for his decision to abandon the fight to preserve segregated schooling in the Palmetto State, welcoming his advice to state legislators to "start making progress with dignity." Yet, while saluting Hollings "for his courage and forthrightness," it assailed the governor for spending the best part of the previous four years orchestrating resistance to integration in South Carolina: "He knew this as a truth four years ago; we only wish he had spoken it earlier."[109]

By the late 1950s Francis Fitzgerald had become nationally recognized as a leading figure in black-oriented broadcasting. He had earned the respect and trust of his largely black staff and listeners at a time of great racial upheaval and managed to find an enviable balance between commercial success and community service. It was partly because of this impressive performance that his fellow broadcasters chose him as the first chair of the Negro Radio Association (NRA). Founded in 1960, the NRA comprised mostly white owners of black-oriented stations, indicating where the economic power in radio still resided. Nevertheless, the coming of the civil rights movement and the flourishing black pride and consciousness it brought with it had clearly made an impact on white owners and executives like Egmont Sonderling, John McLendon, and Robert Rounsaville. If for no other reasons than economic ones, these men felt obliged to respond to the steadily growing demands of black listeners and leaders for greater responsiveness to community needs from the stations they patronized. WGIV seemed to offer the ideal model for this. Certainly Fitzgerald echoed his own station's agenda when he explained that the NRA's mission was to "develop and improve Negro programming and to foster and develop public service programming for the benefit of Negro groups" while bringing "to the attention of advertisers the potential of the Negro market."[110]

According to Hattie Leeper, by the mid-1960s the generally convivial and cooperative ethos at WGIV had begun to evaporate in the face of rising black power sentiment. By 1966 there were seven regular black announcers at the station. This included several younger deejays who did not always see eye to eye with Fitzgerald or veterans like Leeper and Gene Potts. Basic resentment that Charlotte's premier black-oriented station was white-owned at all fused with a deepening mistrust of all whites in the radio industry. Tensions mounted steadily until they finally erupted over the issue of unionization. Many of the younger generation felt union membership was essential to protect themselves from the sort of exploitation that was rampant in the broadcasting industry and to attain greater job security. Older staff and management felt just as strongly that a union was unnecessary at WGIV, viewing it as a divisive expression of mistrust at a station where so much had flourished thanks to a rare degree of trust. "We weren't in agreement with it [the union]," Leeper recalled, because Fitzgerald "had given us profit sharing, and we were getting that and we were getting retirement . . . hospitalization. I mean, we had it all." She did, however, have some sympathy for the newcomers, appreciating that precious few other African American broadcasters, especially in the South, had any experience of the sort of progressive and mutually supportive environment that Fitzgerald and his staff had created at WGIV. The newcomers "hadn't been used to having a job where you kind of halfway trusted the president of the station, where you kind of halfway felt comfortable that you were going to be all right, or secure."[111]

Distressed by the changing dynamic at the station and bewildered by the way in which he was suddenly cast in the role of villain by some of his new hires, Fitzgerald battled hard to convince the young militants that a union was unnecessary. Overworked and distraught, he became increasingly unwell. On July 24, 1967, he suffered a massive heart attack and died. He was fifty-three years old. After his death WGIV was sold to the Tracy Corporation of Philadelphia for $370,000.[112] Hattie Leeper "got a nice fat piece of money from profit sharing because I had been there over twenty years." This, she felt, vindicated her faith in Fitzgerald as a man of integrity who really had treated all his staff with equal respect and considerable magnanimity. "We had the kind of visionary owner that included us in his growth, in his climbing the ladder of success," she recalled.[113] Such vision and empathy for the interests of southern blacks were rare among white executives in the black-oriented radio industry of the 1950s and early

FIGURE 17. WGIV's Francis Fitzgerald (right), seen here receiving an award from Rev. J. F. Wertz, was one of the most important figures in the story of black-oriented radio in the South from the late 1940s until his death in 1967. Courtesy of James Peeler.

1960s. It would become rarer still when, in the wake of the civil rights and voting legislation of the mid-1960s, African Americans throughout the South sought to turn statutory equality into genuine equality of treatment and opportunity.

During the two decades that Crutchfield's WBT and Fitzgerald's WGIV shared the airways, they helped to shape important, if limited, changes in racial relations and arrangements in Charlotte. The messages of restraint, orderliness, and interracial goodwill that were the editorial and emotional stock-in-trade at both stations helped to define the ideological and tactical parameters within which challenges to Jim Crow were expected to occur. The direct-action campaigns and rising black impatience of the 1960s seriously tested those boundaries and expectations. Yet both stations, especially WBT, strove hard and with some success to reassert gradualism, negotiation, and—rather more grudgingly—litigation as the appropriate means to improve black conditions in Charlotte. Paradoxically, as well as establishing acceptable strategies for pursuing racial change, these moderating messages helped to establish the limits of publicly sanctioned techniques that whites could use to resist desegregation or otherwise constrain black progress. In other words, they helped to legitimize "sly resistance" while excoriating more violent methods of protecting white supremacy. Other powerful political, economic, and social forces contributed to this process, too. Nonetheless, WBT and WGIV's steady appeal to both races for patience, dialogue, and respect for the law helped Charlotte avoid the bloody confrontations that devastated many other southern cities. Sadly, though, even an earnest commitment to the virtues of gradualism could all too easily facilitate delay and tokenism in the racial arena when what was needed was prompt and radical action to rectify persistent inequalities.

A Telling Silence

Freedom Radio in Mississippi

One of the most pressing problems in Mississippi is the refusal of the mass media of communication to present adequately the Negro point of view to both the white and Negro population of that state.
Rev. Graham R. Hodges, December 1964

The Toughest Nut to Crack

Historians spend a good deal of their time listening for the silences that speak volumes. They are drawn to the absences, the gaps, the lacunae in the historical record that reveal much about configurations of power in the past—and about who controls the way in which that past is represented to succeeding generations. This chapter has something of that character. In the midst of a book primarily dedicated to exploring the ways that radio facilitated the modern African American freedom struggle, it focuses on a state where until the second half of the 1960s precious little airtime was ever devoted to the civil rights movement—unless it was to disavow it.

Mississippi, home to such paragons of white supremacy as Senator James O. Eastland and birthplace of the Citizens' Councils, was the most intransigent of all the southern states in its opposition to black advance. Among movement strategists there was a sense that if they could break white resistance in Mississippi, then Jim Crow in the rest of the South would surely crumble. Thus the movement in Mississippi attained a sort of totemic status for all those seeking a more racially inclusive and just America. For much the same reason, Mississippi also became a notorious rallying ground for last-ditch segregationists, a place where movement efforts were repeatedly met with violence, intimidation, and legal chicanery. Consequently, it also proved consistently more difficult to get racially progressive messages onto the airways in Mississippi than in any other state. This chapter examines both sides of the struggle—the movement's efforts to use radio in Mississippi and segregationists' attempts to retain control of the mass media as an instrument of white supremacy. It also explains how Mississippi became the site for a series of important attacks on racial bias within the media that fundamentally altered the dynamics of American broadcasting.

In 1960 fewer than 2 percent of adult African Americans living in Mississippi were registered to vote.[1] The civil rights workers who strove to change the racial complexion of the state's electoral politics, many of them working under the auspices of the Voter Education Project, were keenly aware of the potential of radio to assist their efforts. The Council of Federated Organizations (COFO)—the statewide organization that coordinated the voter registration work of various groups in Mississippi—worked hard to establish regular radio exposure and even attempted to create an independent radio station based at Tougaloo College. Unfortunately for the movement, the official and unofficial guardians of white supremacy in Mississippi were equally aware of the capacity of radio and the electronic media more generally to mobilize public opinion. This was especially true of the State Sovereignty Commission (SSC). After its creation in 1956, this powerful and insidious government agency partially funded the Citizens' Council's radio and television programs that preached the gospel of massive resistance across the South.[2]

The SSC's experience in using the mass media to promote its own reactionary agenda probably increased its appreciation of radio's potential to help stimulate black political consciousness and activism. Certainly, as COFO stepped up its campaign to harness the elusive power of Mississippi radio during Freedom Summer in 1964, so the SSC and other state agencies devoted ever more resources to trying to discover and thwart COFO's media plans. At a moment when movement access to radio in many parts of the South appeared to be getting somewhat easier, in Mississippi it became more difficult. The SSC's attempts to disrupt COFO's radio initiatives formed an important aspect of the wider campaign of officially sanctioned surveillance, disinformation, and harassment that made life so difficult for the movement in the Magnolia State.

Veterans of the freedom struggle working in Mississippi during 1964 were hardly surprised to find that few local stations were willing to afford them airtime. Back in 1947 the NAACP had complained to the FCC that the NBC affiliate WFOR-Hattiesburg refused to take any network broadcasts dealing with race relations. A particular source of grievance was the station's rejection of a *University of Chicago Round Table* show on the topic "Our Civil Rights—Are They in Danger?" WFOR's manager C. J. Wright had succinctly explained his rationale for pulling the broadcast: "We are down in the Deep South and you got off on the race question." Case closed.[3] From the mid-1950s, similar complaints had rained in on WJDX-Jackson and its sister television outlet WLBT. Owned by the Lamar Life Insurance Company since its launch in 1929, WJDX had always been a bastion of conservative southern social and racial values. In a fictionalized account of the life of Lucius Q. Lamar set in 1872 but broadcast in 1932, the Mississippi educator and politician grumbled: "States' rights are no more. Mississippi is prostrate under the ruthless rule of unscrupulous whites and ignorant negroes." This jaundiced vision of a Black Reconstruction subsequently became central to the rhetoric of massive resistance. Although the station counted blues singer Mabel Batson among its earliest regular performers, this perspective hardly augured well for the possibility that WJDX would emerge as a champion of civil rights.[4]

By the mid-1950s Fred Beard, the general manager of WJDX and WLBT-TV and a Citizens' Council stalwart, was openly using his facilities to promote massive resistance. Notoriously suspicious of what he considered a dangerously liberal, antisouthern bias in network news and public affairs programming, Beard often simply refused to air "hostile" shows that affronted his and his sponsors' commitment to segregation. In January 1956 WJDX dropped scheduled coverage of the Junior Rose Bowl football game from California because, upon learning that Mississippi's Jones County Junior College team was due to play a team that included black athletes, the Mississippi State Power and Light Company had withdrawn its sponsorship. On the rare occasions that WJDX did take network broadcasts that touched on the racial situation, Beard was careful to preface them with warnings that they represented "an example of the biased, managed Northern news" and urge listeners to "be sure to stay tuned . . . to hear your local newscasts."[5]

Nothing much to do with race ever changed quickly in Mississippi, and in the early 1960s civil rights advocacy on the radio was still rare. In part this reflected the scarcity of any black-oriented programming in the state. There were early experiments in broadcasting for African American listeners at stations like WROX-Clarksdale, WNLA-Indianola, WJXN and WSLI in Jackson, and WQBC and WVIM in Vicksburg. However, it was not until September 17, 1954, that WOKJ-Jackson, the state's first radio facility dedicated wholly to African Americans, debuted. Like WNLA, WOKJ was owned by fledgling southern radio mogul—and future owner of WENN-Birmingham—John McLendon. Located just a block away from Jackson State University, the station flourished with a stellar lineup including preacher and gospel deejay Rev. L. H. Newsome and rhythm and blues jocks Bill Spence, Bill Jackson, Carolyn Blount, Jobie Martin, and the "dean of radio in Mississippi," Bruce Payne. An increase in transmitter power to 50,000 watts meant that WOKJ broadcasts covered much of the state. This was important, since in the early 1960s WOKJ was one of only five stations in Mississippi that exclusively or overwhelmingly programmed for black audiences, the others being WCLD-Cleveland, WROX-Clarksdale, WESY-Greenville, and WQIC-Meridian. Another twenty stations regularly devoted at least some of their airtime to African American listeners. Until the founding of WORV in Hattiesburg in 1969, no Mississippi radio stations were black-owned and all were wary about offering either airtime or public endorsement to the civil rights movement. By contrast, many Mississippi radio stations proudly aligned themselves with the forces of white supremacy.[6]

Death and "Dixie" in Oxford

The fidelity of most Mississippi radio stations to traditional racial views was very apparent during the crisis that enveloped Oxford in the fall of 1962, when James Meredith sought to integrate the University of Mississippi. As that crisis lurched toward its bloody climax on September 30, there were few voices on Mississippi radio urging conciliation, let alone compliance with the federal court order to admit Meredith. Instead white supremacists regularly urged support for a variety of legal and extralegal measures to prevent desegregation. While neither radio nor the media collectively were exactly to blame for the tragic events in Oxford, local radio undoubtedly helped to inflame the passions that erupted into lethal white violence. Even the chief of the FCC's Broadcast Bureau, Kenneth Cox, concluded that some broadcasts might "in effect have contributed to the generation of mobs."[7]

It is worth pausing to consider radio's role in the Ole Miss crisis in some detail, since it illustrates the close ties between commercial radio and massive resistance in Mississippi. It was precisely because of this intimate relationship that the civil rights movement, almost in desperation, began to explore the possibility of setting up alternative radio facilities. The exclusion of African Americans and the neglect of their interests in mainstream political, economic, and educational structures prompted activists in Mississippi to create parallel institutions such as the Mississippi Freedom Democratic Party (MFDP). Similarly, the indifference to African Americans and their interests at most Mississippi radio stations eventually compelled the movement to try to establish an alternative radio network.

During the weeks preceding James Meredith's arrival in Oxford, Fred Beard presented a series of inflammatory editorials on WJDX and WLBT-TV. Deftly manipulating the key rhetorical touchstones of massive resistance, Beard announced on September 12, 1962, that the "very sovereignty of our state is threatened. We have every confidence that our elected and appointed officials will prevent the integration of our schools. Our leaders need the support of all people in strengthening their stand against a government that would take away our rights to conduct our own local affairs." Two days later Beard urged "every true and loyal Mississippian" to stand by Governor Ross Barnett "and say 'never!' . . . The word of the hour, the word of the day, the word of the year is: 'never.'"[8]

Betraying a common sense of southern persecution and embattlement, Beard railed against "the liberal press, radio and television" that "will only give coverage to those who will condemn us for the stand that Mississippi has taken." Beard countered such fabrications by depicting opposition to the desegregation of Ole Miss as part of a noble battle for states' rights—not to mention racial integrity—which had the sympathy of all those right-thinking, white-thinking Americans who opposed government tyranny. "Regardless of what you hear from network radio and television or what you see in the liberal magazines and newspapers from outside of our State, millions of Americans are with us and praying for us," he insisted. "The fight we make here in Mississippi will determine to a great extent whether there is any fight left in any other states."[9] In this scenario, men like Governor Ross Barnett and the trustees of the university were "to be envied by all—for the heroic opportunity that comes to a man only once in his lifetime whereby he can, if necessary, sacrifice his life for his state and, in turn, save his country." This was no backwoods southern spat, then, but part of America's deadly struggle against creeping communism. "If our Nation is to survive the threats of Socialism from within our country, it will survive through the efforts of the Southern States," Beard explained. "The re-establishment of the State Sovereignty is the first step in such a plan."[10]

Beard's effort to cast white Mississippi resistance as a heroic crusade for core American values was given an even more ominous spin by Major General Edwin A. Walker. A nationally renowned Korean War hero and a John Birch Society member, Walker was convinced that most of the media and much of the government were already in pro-communist hands. Walker was still recovering from the trauma of having had to command the troops that secured the integration of Little Rock Central High School in 1957. Comparing his Little Rock experiences with the crisis brewing in Oxford, he declared, "I was on the wrong side. This time I am on the right side and I will be there."[11]

One of Walker's main concerns was that Ross Barnett might not be up to the task of resisting pressure from beyond the state to integrate the university. When Meredith had first attempted to register at Oxford on September 20, Barnett had personally blocked his path to the admissions office. A second registration effort at the Jackson offices of the university's board of trustees on September 25 also failed, as did a third effort at Oxford a day later, when it was Lieutenant Governor Paul Johnson's turn to send back Meredith. Throughout this period of defiance, however, Barnett conducted a series of secret and semisecret negotiations with the Kennedy administration and in particular with an increasingly impatient attorney general Robert Kennedy.[12] Fearing that Barnett might be about to concede defeat after his symbolic show of defiance, or that he would be legally out-maneuvered by the Kennedys, General Walker went on the offensive. On Febru-ary 26 he gave an interview with KWKH-Shreveport, a 50,000-watt Louisiana station whose signal reached deep into Mississippi. Walker called for a more militant approach to maintaining segregation at Ole Miss. He urged all loyal southerners to congregate in Oxford, telling them: "It is time to move . . . when and if the President of the United States commits or uses any troops, federal or state, in Mississippi."[13]

The day after Walker's radio appearance, white supremacists from across the mid-South dutifully began to gather in Oxford. Although he publicly disavowed the use of violence, Walker did nothing to discourage those who brought guns to defend the racial sanctity of Ole Miss. He even began to speak grandiosely of this mustering of southern citizenry as the start of "a national protest against the conspiracy from within." As the crisis in Oxford intensified, there was a growing sense that Governor Barnett was losing control of a situation he had cynically manipulated to enhance his own reputation among Mississippi voters. Thanks largely to Walker's radio plea, reporters began to describe a town awash with pickup trucks, Stars and Bars flags, beer coolers, and hunting rifles.[14]

In the fall of 1957, during the Little Rock crisis, Fred Beard had instructed his staff to play "Dixie" instead of the national anthem on WJDX to express his oppo-sition to Eisenhower's use of federal power to desegregate a southern school. In September 1962, local radio stations WSUH-Oxford, owned by the aptly named Colonel Rebel Radio Company, and WRBC-Jackson followed suit. They stoked the fires of neo-Confederate sentiment by repeatedly playing "Dixie," which con-veniently doubled as the fight song for the Ole Miss Rebels football team. The stations also aired a new song called "Never, No, Never" that declared "to hell with Bobby K" and featured the inspired couplet "Ross's standing like Gibraltar / He shall never falter."[15]

In this deteriorating atmosphere, even some hard-line segregationists be-came alarmed that events were careening toward a disastrous showdown with the federal authorities. One consequence was that William "Billy" Mounger, president of the Lamar Life Insurance Company that still owned both WJDX and WLBT-TV, called a halt to Fred Beard's editorials, fearing that they would ignite an already tinderbox situation. Although no fan of desegregation, Mounger would subsequently appear on both radio and television to promote calm in the immediate aftermath of the riot on September 30. This earned him a letter from Robert Kennedy commending him for his "stand on the difficulties that arose at the University of Mississippi. I know you did not follow the course that you did for the purposes of admiration or appreciation, particularly from somebody out-side your state, but I just wanted you to know how grateful we are to you." Later still, Mounger emerged as an important figure in a small contingent of white

Mississippi business leaders who began to question whether last-ditch resistance to desegregation was really the best way to promote their economic interests.[16]

If, thanks to Mounger, some of the media in Jackson began to tone down their rebel-rousing, it was much too late to reverse the trend toward mobocracy. Elsewhere, radio continued to prime Mississippi's white community for a final showdown with the federal government and the proponents of desegregation. WSLI in Jackson, for example, continued to host the *Citizens' Council Forum* shows cosponsored by the SSC. It admitted to an FCC investigation that throughout the crisis it had "presented only viewpoints in favor of segregation in its discussions of the issue of racial integration."[17] James Meredith himself recalled that by Thursday, September 27, "[t]he radio stations had ceased all regular programming and were devoting full time to reporting the preparations for the coming battle." Consequently, when he and a handful of federal marshals and Department of Justice officials were instructed to drive to Ole Miss from Millington Naval Air Station near Memphis in yet another attempt to register, they were able to listen with growing apprehension to radio coverage of the seething scene a hundred miles away in Oxford. Ross Barnett had secretly agreed to a face-saving plan whereby Meredith would quietly be admitted to the university that afternoon under the protection of about thirty federal marshals, at least one of whom would draw a weapon to show white Mississippians that their brave governor was bowing to ruthless federal power.[18]

On the way to Oxford, Meredith recalled, "Most of the news was about Barnett and his crowd which had grown to enormous proportions." As the tone of these radio reports became more alarming, the car containing Meredith left the convoy at Batesville, about twenty-three miles short of Oxford, and Meredith phoned Washington for further information. It was arguably a lifesaving detour. A frightened Barnett had already called Robert Kennedy to say that with the mob now numbering close to three thousand, many of them armed, he could no longer guarantee Meredith's safety on campus. Kennedy agreed that it would be suicidal to continue the registration effort at this time. The tiny convoy turned around and headed back toward Memphis.[19] As the *Atlanta Constitution* reported, "Many in the crowd carried transistor radios and news that Meredith had canceled the attempt spread rapidly."[20] Amazingly, although Meredith had never come within twenty-five miles of Oxford, at least one station continued to broadcast as if the moment of grim reckoning was at hand and the convoy was still bearing down on campus. According to Meredith, "We listened to the blow-by-blow account of the developing battle on the radio on our way back to Millington. The radio newsmen were not going to miss that extra money, and they kept on reporting. . . . The most amusing report of all came just as we were passing the Peabody Hotel in downtown Memphis. The radio announcer boldly announced that 'the caravan

is now approaching the University of Mississippi.'" Although this was an exceptional case, the same dedication to extracting every drop of emotion and drama
from the crisis made radio complicit in creating the feverish atmosphere in
which the Oxford riot occurred.[21]

The following day, September 28, a federal court of appeals in New Orleans
found Ross Barnett and Paul Johnson guilty of contempt, fined them, and gave
them four days in which to comply with the court order to admit Meredith.
Barnett appeared to have run out of options. The next day, however, the governor
attended a football game at Ole Miss that turned into a rousing celebration of his
opposition to federal authority and to all those who favored integration over traditional southern racial arrangements. Buoyed by this popular endorsement, the
capricious Barnett decided to continue his defiance of the desegregation order.
This was the final straw for the Kennedys, who threatened not only to federalize
the National Guard to secure Meredith's safe admittance but also to expose Barnett's earlier willingness to cut a deal with the administration until the Ole Miss
football rally had strengthened his resolve. Once again Barnett shifted position,
agreeing to a new compromise that called for Meredith to fly down to Oxford
immediately and without public announcement. In the late afternoon of Sunday,
September 30, James Meredith arrived on campus, picked out a room in a deserted dormitory, and, with remarkable cool, began reading for his classes. He
was scheduled to register at 8:00 a.m. the next day.[22]

The disturbances started about an hour after Meredith's arrival, as news that
he had been spirited onto campus spread across Oxford. The mob activity left
Robert Kennedy little alternative but to dispatch an emergency force of some five
hundred federal marshals to supplement the highway patrolmen Barnett had
entrusted with Meredith's safety. Barnett responded to this deployment of federal forces with typical irresponsibility, going on statewide radio to urge Mississippi whites to resist the "oppressive power of the United States."[23] Events
quickly gathered tragic momentum. By the time John Kennedy had finished
reassuring a national television and radio audience that law and federal authority had prevailed in Mississippi and that Meredith was safely installed on campus, angry white mobs in Oxford were already running amok and federal marshals were using tear gas to keep them at bay. However, even rampaging crowds
were preferable to what happened when Edwin Walker arrived and began to
direct sections of the mob to lay siege to parts of the campus.

In the rioting that followed, 160 marshals were injured, 28 of them with gunshot wounds. Two people were killed: a jukebox repairman caught by a stray
bullet and Paul Guilhard, a French reporter working for the London *Daily Sketch*
who had tried to photograph some of the mob as they unpacked their guns.[24]
Several other photographers, including Gordon Yoder, were also attacked. Paul

Crider of the Memphis bureau of the Associated Press suffered gunshot wounds. A student asked reporter Fred Powledge to identify himself and, when he did, proceeded to beat him up.[25] Cub reporter Dan Rather found himself on the wrong end of a National Guardsman's rifle butt as he tried to cover events for network radio, while an outside broadcast radio truck belonging to WMPS-Memphis was overturned and set ablaze.[26] Russell Barrett was an Ole Miss faculty member sympathetic to Meredith's plight who spent much of the night sheltering from tear gas in the university's Peabody Building and listening to radio coverage of the extraordinary events unfolding just yards away from him. According to Barrett, representatives of the media, particularly the sorts of outsiders that Edwin Walker and Fred Beard had demonized, were especially vulnerable during the riot. As Barrett wryly observed, "many of the mob were hardly eager to have their actions recorded for posterity."[27]

For various reasons, the television networks failed to provide much live coverage of the dramatic scenes from the Ole Miss campus on the night of September 30. Some of those reasons were technical. Although the communications satellite Telstar had become operational in July 1962, the networks had no instant access to relay pictures of breaking news. Furthermore, cameramen struggled to get decent images at night without using powerful lights—not an especially practical or desirable option at Ole Miss when journalists were already one object of the mob's wrath. Finally, ABC, NBC, and CBS were already extremely sensitive to the charge that the very presence of television crews could "inflame tension in the South" and encourage mobs to "act-up." Economic considerations also militated against extensive live television coverage. President Kennedy had shifted the proposed time of his statement on the crisis several times during the course of the day before settling on 10 p.m., Eastern Standard Time. This left the networks' schedules, not to mention the nerves of their program directors and sales executives, in tatters, creating enormous pressure to return to regular sponsored programming as quickly as possible. Together these factors help explain why, having dutifully aired the president's ten-minute statement, NBC and ABC television immediately resumed their regular schedules, offering only a brief synopsis of events in Oxford later that night. CBS did present a twenty-minute summary of the background to the crisis and the president's statement before it too returned to commercial programming.[28]

New York Times media correspondent Jack Gould observed that radio, unlike television, "faced comparatively few problems because of the medium's greater flexibility."[29] Network radio not only accommodated the president's speech but also stayed with the story, taking live feeds from Oxford as the violence escalated. Ironically, the only live coverage of the rioting to emanate from the campus itself came from the college's own radio station, WCBH (*We Can Be Heard*), which acted as a kind of electronic Trojan horse by setting up radio feeds to all the networks from its own studios. Sometimes WCBH's student employees went on air themselves, exploiting their ability to move around their own campus and gather information with greater safety than visiting reporters. Sometimes the station simply allowed network journalists to use their facilities to file brief reports. This seems to have happened more because the events offered an irresistible opportunity for Director of Broadcasting Duncan Whiteside and his staff to demonstrate their journalistic and technical prowess than because of any particular commitment to informing the rest of the nation about the violence perpetrated in Oxford in defense of Jim Crow. In any case, the station did consistently provide a forum for some of the calmer voices heard at Ole Miss during the crisis. On the day following the riot, Dean of Students Leston Love requested that students tune in to WCBH, where they could hear guidance about classes and messages urging a quick return to normality. WCBH's competent professionalism during the crisis did not go unnoticed. In 1965 the station won the All-American Award as "the most outstanding collegiate radio station in the nation serving under 5,000 people."[30]

WCBH's more mean-spirited competitors for the All-American Award might have questioned whether the station was strictly eligible. During the Ole Miss crisis and its aftermath, there were far more than five thousand listeners in WCBH's market area. It took that many federal troops just to quell the riot, while a few days later 23,000 troops arrived to swell Oxford's regular population by more than three times. Although the worst of the tension abated in a matter of weeks and the number of troops quickly declined, their continued presence conjured up the sort of collective memories of federally enforced Reconstruction that massive resistance thrived on. Again, radio broadcasts helped to drive home that association. "It is becoming increasingly evident that the federal government today is in the control of unscrupulous men who are following the same path as Hitler and Stalin, to destroy American as a great nation," raged Dr. Horace Villee, pastor of the First Presbyterian Church in Columbus in a sermon carried by local station WCBI a week after the riots. "Truly it was a 'Black Monday' in 1954 when the infamous decision regarding public schools was made by a Supreme Court packed with political stooges; and truly it was a 'Red Sunday' in 1962 when our nation's highest officials turned the peaceful campus of the University of Mississippi into a scene for the disgraceful display of power used unlawfully, and also used unnecessarily, and resulting in two deaths." Broadcasts like this did nothing to ease racial tensions in Mississippi as the movement attempted to break the back of segregation and disenfranchisement in that troubled state.[31]

Challenging the Silence

The Ole Miss crisis confirmed that Mississippi broadcasters were often hostile toward civil rights activities. Despite this gloomy picture, however, there were a few glimmers of hope in the early 1960s that the movement might be able to get more racially progressive messages on the radio, especially if it could persuade federal authorities to act against flagrantly discriminatory broadcasting practices. Some of the first signs that concerted efforts in the radio field might succeed appeared during a generally frustrating campaign to publicize the Reverend R.L.T. Smith's unsuccessful bid for Congress in 1962. In February Smith wrote to the FCC complaining that Fred Beard had refused to sell him airtime to promote his candidacy. Although Smith directed his complaints primarily against WLBT-TV, they also included WJDX and had broad implications for movement access to the electronic media throughout the state. Beard initially defended his position by arguing that, since the congressional primary election was not until June 5, it was too early to be selling Smith airtime for his campaign. Beard pointed out that his stations had not sold slots to any other candidates, either. He also noted the very real possibility of white violence against the station should Smith appear. Lawrence Guyot, who would subsequently become chair of the MFDP, recalled approaching Beard about a possible appearance by Smith: "They said, 'No, we can't sell you time, they'd blow up the station.' That's the mentality we were dealing with." The FCC's Ben Waple contacted Beard about Smith's complaints, but accepted his explanation and concluded that "it does not appear that further action by the Commission is warranted."[32]

As the primary approached, however, Beard continued to refuse Smith airtime. He also offered increasingly lurid and intimidating scenarios of what might happen if Smith ever did appear on the station. Beard warned Smith that he would have to "hire fifty policemen, put a fence all around the grounds of the studio," but that even then, "his body and mine, too, would likely be found in the [Pearl] river . . . right across the street from the studio." Undaunted, in the early spring of 1962 Smith and his staff orchestrated a campaign to persuade the FCC to take action against Beard. In addition to writing to the FCC commissioners, Smith wrote to dozens of potentially sympathetic journalists, politicians, labor leaders, and civil rights activists. Some, like Burke Marshall of the Justice Department, took up the cause and urged the FCC to intervene. In mid-April the FCC responded to this pressure and, according to Smith, "ordered WLBT to sell me one half hour." On April 23 Smith wrote excitedly to Marshall and other supporters thanking them for their help and confirming that the "black-out against my campaign has been broken."[33] Once the threat of firm federal action forced Fred Beard's hand, Smith's access to the local media, especially radio, noticeably improved. On May 4, even WJDX broadcast five one-minute announcements, while Smith also found time on WJXN, WJQS, WSLI, WRBC, and WOKJ.[34]

R.L.T. Smith's fleeting radio exposure in the spring and summer of 1962 was the consequence of a concerted campaign to arouse popular and FCC concern about discriminatory practices in the broadcasting industry. On other occasions, however, pro–civil rights messages on the Mississippi airways were a product of individual conscience and initiative. During the height of the Ole Miss debacle in the fall of 1962, at least one white voice appeared on Mississippi radio denouncing the bigotry that masqueraded as a commitment to states' rights and anticommunism. In a series of three sermons entitled "Not Race but Grace" aired by WSSO, Rev. Robert Walkup, pastor of the First Presbyterian Church in Starkville, echoed Kelly Miller Smith's Mt. Heroden broadcasts of more than a decade earlier. Walkup condemned racial intolerance as fundamentally un-Christian and dismissed "all this talk about the State of Mississippi being sovereign" as *"foolishness!"*[35]

As voter registration efforts gathered momentum, some local radio stations covered the arrival of the northern white students who came to Mississippi in 1963 to work on the Freedom Vote. This was an unofficial mock election for governor and lieutenant governor designed to show the eagerness of African Americans to participate in the democratic process. Clarksdale NAACP leader and COFO president Aaron Henry was the gubernatorial candidate, with Tougaloo College's white chaplain Ed King his running mate. While much of the media coverage about this latest invasion of "outside agitators" was extremely negative, some of the students at least got the chance to appear on local radio to explain why they were there. As Lawrence Guyot recalled, "When the volunteers came to Hattiesburg, Mississippi . . . We got a chance for them to go on radio and talk about the problems of registering, the problems of working in Mississippi, the problems of organizing in Mississippi and those were astounding."[36] Even Fred Beard offered R.L.T. Smith, who served on the state executive board for Henry's campaign, fifteen-minute slots on both WLBT and WJDX, apparently in response to another round of protests to the FCC.[37]

Although the competition was hardly fierce, some of the best coverage of civil rights activities on a Mississippi radio station in the early 1960s came from WONA. A low-powered daytime facility located in Winona and licensed to Southern Electronics Incorporated, WONA was part of the Mid-South Network of stations owned by Robert Evans and headquartered at WELO-Tupelo. When WONA opened in the spring of 1959, its manager was Bob Chisholm, an Alabama native with a journalistic background in both broadcasting and print. Although the station offered no specifically black-oriented programming, Chisholm showed a rare commitment to reporting newsworthy local events in a generally full and fair manner. This included stories about the racial situation. In June 1963, for example, the station carried news of the terrible beatings that Fannie Lou Hamer and other SNCC workers suffered at the hands of police officers and coerced inmates at the county jail following their arrest for trying to use a whites-only restaurant at the Winona bus station.[38]

WONA's sympathetic coverage of the Winona beatings and its regular news of civil rights activities created a good deal of unease among the town's white establishment. Bob Chisholm had already aroused the suspicion of some locals by reporting with unusual candor the accusations that G. S. Galloway, Winona's chief of police, was supplementing his salary with money from the town's parking meters. Local leaders had even summoned station owner Robert Evans to town, urging him to curb his maverick manager's overzealous news operations. In the summer of 1963 these anxieties culminated in a formal complaint to the FCC filed by eighteen city and county officials, including three of the policemen indicted for mistreatment and false arrest in the Winona jail beatings case. WONA, the petitioners insisted, was not serving the public interest. Indeed, in a transparent attempt to conceal the racist coordinates of their own complaint, they claimed that WONA was stirring up racial strife by its irresponsible attention to movement-related news. Others in the Winona community clearly felt differently. More than two thousand local citizens signed a counterpetition in support of the station. Even ex–chief of police Galloway, who had been acquitted of charges relating to the parking meter pilfering, submitted an affidavit stating that "Mr. Chisholm was completely fair in reporting all phases of the controversy between me and the city administration."[39]

In February 1965 the FCC, having "carefully reviewed all the pertinent information," dismissed the charges made against Chisholm and WONA. During the eighteen-month investigation, the station had defiantly broadcast reports from the trials of the men accused—and eventually acquitted—in the Winona jail beatings case. It had also reported extensively, if dispassionately, on Freedom Summer, prompting renewed efforts to run Chisholm out of town, allegedly by members of the police force, in the early hours of July 11, 1964. Bob Chisholm never publicly committed himself or his station to the goals of the civil rights movement. Nevertheless, by repeatedly publicizing movement attacks on Jim Crow and exposing the thuggish behavior of some of those who would defend it, the station offered a quietly subversive message and provided evidence of cracks in the solid wall of white resistance. It was the exposure of those cracks, tiny though they were, that helped to give the local people at the forefront of the freedom struggle the courage to keep on keeping on. These signs of change, or even of the potential for change, indicated that their activism was neither pointless nor suicidal. It was just extraordinarily heroic.[40]

Freedom Summer Radio

While Bob Chisholm was trying to cope with attacks from the white power structure in Winona, the 1964 Freedom Summer project was launched, and hundreds of black and white volunteers again joined the indigenous Mississippi movement. As plans coalesced for the MFDP to challenge the official Mississippi Democratic Party delegation at the national Democratic convention in Atlantic City in August, COFO shifted its focus from voter registration to MFDP recruitment. With an ambitious goal of enrolling 200,000 members, by midJuly it was obvious that the MFDP was seriously behind schedule. Although 80,000 blacks had participated in the 1963 Freedom Vote, barely 21,000 blacks and a handful of whites were on the MFDP books, despite the painstaking efforts of hundreds of volunteers working door-to-door in some of the most forbidding counties in the South.[41] Key project organizer Bob Moses, COFO's communications director Ronald Ridenour, and Emmie Schrader of COFO's Jackson office agreed that radio messages might speed up this work and would be especially useful in arousing interest in the MFDP among poor, mostly black, Mississippians with little access to television or the print media.[42]

In late July, Ridenour and his staff began to visit various Mississippi stations, hoping to persuade them to take spot announcements for the MFDP. Most of these announcements began with a special message from Martin Luther King Jr. urging all the "citizens of Mississippi to stand up for justice and equality and support the new Mississippi Freedom Democratic Party. You can help send a Freedom Delegation to the Democratic National Convention by attending Freedom Democratic Party meetings in your precinct or county."[43] King's all-purpose rallying cry preceded a locally oriented announcement of the times, dates, and locations of forthcoming MFDP precinct meetings. However, some of those preparing these local segments, like summer volunteer Mike Higson who worked with WCAR-Columbus, chose to omit precise details of MFDP meetings from their slots for fear of attracting white reprisals.[44]

The broadcasts urged, "All Democrats . . . to attend, regardless of race, religion, color, or creed. . . . All participants must be registered with the Freedom Democratic party in order to qualify. . . . If you haven't registered as of yet, you may do so now or at the meeting." The slots informed listeners, many of whom were unaware of the mechanics of the political process and party organizing, of the purpose of the precinct meetings. "Resolutions will be presented, delegates will be elected, and the National Democratic Platform and candidates will be endorsed." The announcements also explained how the delegates chosen from precinct meetings would be required to attend county, congressional district, and state conventions in Moss Point, Hattiesburg, and Jackson respectively. The national convention in Atlantic City was the ultimate destination for those chosen as statewide MFDP representatives. The tapes ended with a rousing invocation of the faith in grassroots democracy that characterized southern voter registration campaigns: "All Democrats who want their voice heard in *this* presidential election, who do not want the Goldwater alternative, and who want to support the National Democratic Party's platform and its candidates . . . are urged to attend *their* precinct meetings. Regardless of where you live, you live in a precinct."[45]

As Ridenour discovered, however, it was one thing to prepare these informational broadcasts and even agree to a rate and a timeslot with local radio stations; it was quite another thing to actually get them past the formal and informal barriers of Mississippi white resistance onto the air. On the morning of July 24, 1964, representatives of WMAG-Forrest had agreed to broadcast a series of announcements for the MFDP's Leake County convention in return for a cash payment of $36.80. The ink was barely dry on the agreement when station manager Willie Weems drove over to the COFO offices in Harmony, Mississippi, accompanied by the Scott County deputy sheriff, the Forrest chief of police, and several Leake County law enforcement officers. Weems told the MFDP workers that WMAG would not now air the announcement because local authorities had advised that the broadcasts "would be 'inflammatory' and would 'tend to incite a riot.'"[46]

Other stations were also wary about accepting the MFDP slots. Activist Terry Shaw initially thought he had brokered a deal with Keith Glatzer, manager of WFOR-Hattiesburg, to air twenty-five MFDP announcements. A New Yorker educated at the University of Alabama, Glatzer had come to prominence with his investigative reporting on the Mack Charles Parker lynching in Mississippi for NBC radio in 1958. Yet, although personally sympathetic to the movement, Glatzer was still extremely nervous about associating his station with black insurgency. He consulted with attorneys about the wisdom of taking the MFDP advertisements and was advised that the station should not run them "as political announcements because [the MFDP] are not legally a political party." Indeed, because the MFDP was "not registered with the State of Mississippi," there was a possibility that the station "might be held liable (libel)" for the content or the consequences of any such broadcasts. There was a similar response at WPMP-Pascagoula, where lawyer Karl Wiesenburg urged station manager Walter Smith to reject the MFDP broadcasts on two grounds. First, he doubted "whether the carrying of this advertising would serve the public interest, convenience and necessity requirements" that the FCC demanded of its license holders. Second, he pointed out that Mississippi secretary of state, Heber Ladner, "had declined to register the Mississippi Freedom Democratic Party as an organized party in the State of Mississippi because of its failure to comply with the statutory requirements." Both WPMP and WFOR declined to run the MFDP advertisements pending "final determination of the status of the . . . party by the Secretary of the State of Mississippi."[47]

A dyed-in-the-cotton segregationist, Secretary of State Heber Ladner was one of the least likely people in Mississippi to make such a decision in favor of the MFDP. Indeed, Ladner's refusal to allow the MFDP to register as a political party severely hampered its organizing efforts by making it more vulnerable to police harassment. It also helped to ensure that the MFDP was denied airtime at almost every turn.[48] This was dramatically illustrated when COFO worker Lee Garrett sought airtime at WHNY-McComb. As before, it initially appeared that Garrett had obtained an agreement to broadcast twenty-five announcements, handing over $37.50 to station manager Carol Hines for the service. Garrett gave him a tape of the generic Martin Luther King introductory statement and promised to return the following day with the announcements for local MFDP meetings. As Garrett left to try his luck at nearby WAPF, Hines quipped nervously, "Are you going to be around to help me put out the burning crosses?"[49]

The following day, when Garrett returned to WHNY with the local announcement tape, Hines began to interrogate him about whether the MFDP was a legally recognized political party. As Garrett recalled, "I told him we were trying to become one, but I was not positive if we were or not." He phoned the COFO headquarters in Jackson seeking clarification, but it was pointless. Carol Hines already knew the only opinion that mattered in Mississippi on the question of the MFDP's status. He was brandishing a piece of WHNY notepaper on which was printed an Associated Press release: "Secretary of State Heber Ladner has declined to register the New Freedom Democratic Party as a legal political group qualified to operate in Mississippi." Ladner had determined that "the request from those trying to register the party did not comply with state laws." With some justification, Ladner also believed that the MFDP's purpose in seeking to register as a new party was to push for the "eventual up-rooting of the regular party machinery at the National convention." Carol Hines and WHNY were unwilling to flout the power of the state as it arrayed itself so visibly against the MFDP. He tore up the contract and returned the money.[50] It was the same story at WAPF. This culture of caution, if not outright hostility, at Mississippi radio stations was deeply entrenched. More than a year after Freedom Summer ended, WAPF manager Philip Brady was still rejecting tapes on racial reconciliation prepared by the Committee of Southern Churchmen.[51]

As Ronald Ridenour and his colleagues appreciated, Ladner had the MFDP trapped in a Catch-22 situation. By making it virtually impossible for local stations to accept announcements on behalf of an organization that was not yet formally recognized by the state as a political party, the authorities made it extremely difficult for the MFDP ever to attain that status. As Ridenour explained to Walter Smith of WPMP, Secretary of State Ladner was "perfectly correct when he says that the Freedom Democratic Party is not a political party," since "[n]o political party, or so-called party, can become a political party until it has gone through the process of holding precinct and county meetings." The point, Ridenour insisted, was that the MFDP was in the process of "attempting to fulfill the legal requirements" of a fledgling party by publicizing and holding just such meetings; the refusal of local stations to air either paid advertisements or news stories relating to the formation of the MFDP was seriously and deliberately undermining this effort. Ridenour concluded by reminding Smith that, notwithstanding his lawyer's advice, "the public media's duty is to announce what is of importance to the public, and the formation of any political party is in the interest of the public." Ridenour conveyed the same sentiment to the FCC. "The prevention of the Freedom Democratic Party's announcements was meant as discriminatory," he complained. "I protest this is illegal and unjust and that the public's interest would be met" by the airing of the slots. Although the FCC did nothing to correct the situation in time to assist the 1964 summer project, Ridenour's complaints formed part of a gathering attack on racial prejudice and discrimination within the broadcast media in Mississippi. That attack culminated in serious challenges to several stations and ultimately transformed industry practices.[52]

Despite the many difficulties, some MFDP announcements did find their way onto the radio in 1964 via WGCM-Gulfport, WCAR-Columbus, and the two Vicksburg stations WVIM and WQBC.[53] WOKJ-Jackson also took some announcements, and attracted unwelcome SSC attention shortly after Freedom Summer by advertising a mass meeting at St. Peter's Baptist Church where Charles Evers announced plans for an NAACP boycott of stores that refused to hire African American staff.[54] Nevertheless, for all its contribution to black communal solidarity, pride, and purposefulness, the station offered very modest public support for formal movement activities during Freedom Summer itself. Indeed, in May 1964 WOKJ had flatly refused to air extracts from a speech given by James Farmer on behalf of an MFDP recruitment drive in Sharon, Madison County.[55]

The experiences of Freedom Summer, like those in the R.L.T. Smith campaign and during the Ole Miss crisis, demonstrated the difficulties the movement faced in finding meaningful access to Mississippi radio. That civil rights workers nonetheless kept fighting to secure that access suggests the importance they assigned to the medium. In the mid-1960s, those efforts took two distinct, but overlapping, forms. The first involved an attempt to create an independent radio station—an ambitious plan that prompted new levels of harassment from the SSC. The second involved a concerted legal and publicity campaign to make commercial broadcasters more responsive to the needs and aspirations of the black community in Mississippi.

The Radio Tougaloo Experiment

Tougaloo College was a black institution with an integrated faculty located to the north of Jackson. In the early 1960s it supplied the movement with a steady stream of dedicated activists if not quite the flood often attributed to the college in civil rights folklore.[56] According to Lawrence Guyot, in the summer of 1963 there were already vague discussions among movement workers about the possibility of building a radio antenna at the school.[57] By the spring of 1964, Tougaloo's liberal white president A. D. "Dan" Beittel had expressed guarded interest in the radio station idea, Robert McNamara III of the Civil Rights Information Service was in touch with CORE's publicity director Marvin Rich about plans to build a transmitter, and SNCC's Julian Bond was corresponding with Pacifica president Russell Jorgensen about the possibility of linking a movement station to his network. NBC's Pauline Frederick reported the growing "suggestions that a Radio Free Mississippi may have to be set up to circulate the truth."[58]

As usual, the SSC kept a close watch on these developments. On July 9, 1964, an anonymous informant reported to SSC director Erle Johnston that "the Council of Federated Organizations is setting up a radio communications system. They have applied for a license to construct a radio broadcasting center, but this license has not yet been granted." While the application was pending, the report continued, "COFO is setting up a closed circuit two-way system which will link the office in Jackson with certain schools, certain other offices, and designated automobiles."[59] Although the prospect that COFO might actually be about to launch its own independent radio station was the most alarming aspect of this advisory note, the SSC was also interested in any scheme to improve COFO's internal communications system and therefore the effectiveness of its work. Over the next eighteen months, undercover informants furnished Johnston and his staff with details of COFO's ambitious communications plans.

These reports were undoubtedly useful in enabling the SSC to stay one step ahead of the movement. On July 26 an informant revealed that "a new radio has been installed at the Freedom House in Canton, Mississippi." The radio was identified as a Sonar brand citizens band (CB) device. Ten days later the same informant revealed that the transmitting device was in operation and that "there are three sub stations. They are located in Valley View, Harmony, and Cedar Grove in or near Flora." The last substation, it was noted, was "set in an automobile."[60] By early August, COFO had installed its twentieth CB radio set, greatly enhancing the ability of dispersed groups of workers to communicate and coordinate quickly.[61] As a subsequent SSC report explained, "COFO workers are using two-way radios in their own cars and many of them have been cruising the streets at night which accounts for their being able to show up at the scene of a bombing, as they have in several instances, prior to the arrival of officers." The agent's report ended on a perplexed note. "We were unable to ascertain whether they had citizens band radio or if they had an FCC frequency assigned."[62]

In fact, these were all CB radios, and the SSC had already begun to investigate ways to monitor their use and gain access to private COFO conversations. Not that this was an easy task. In August the SSC had to return two portable receivers to Swan Electronics in Jackson, since the devices had failed to provide effective interception of the CB broadcasts that COFO was now making, not just in Jackson, but across the entire state. Undaunted, Erle Johnston inquired whether a more powerful receiver could be installed in the state capitol building in Jackson to enable the SSC to monitor both COFO's CB exchanges and, if plans for a movement radio network took off, its broadcasts throughout the whole of Mississippi. While the technology was available, it would apparently have required building a large antenna on top of the capitol dome. Whether in the interests of preserving the secrecy of this surveillance or because of some lurking aesthetic sensibility, Johnston decided against asking the Mississippi legislature to add this appendage to the state capitol. Instead he "arranged to purchase two portable units, battery operated, which can be carried in automobiles and tuned in at any time a representative of the Sovereignty Commission is in range (five to ten miles) of any citizens band broadcasting unit." This, Johnston admitted, was part of "an effort to increase our knowledge of the plans and progress of the Council of Federated Organizations."[63]

Late in 1964 COFO learned that its request for a broadcasting license had been rejected by the FCC on the grounds that a political organization could not own a public broadcasting facility. This was deeply ironic, given the lengths to which Mississippi authorities had gone to deny the MFDP official status as a political party. Movement workers decided to resubmit the request through a newly formed, notionally nonpolitical organization called the Radio Tougaloo Association (RTA), sometimes also referred to either as the Tougaloo Radio Association or as the Radio City Tougaloo Association. On January 25, 1965, Erle Johnston learned that the RTA had already begun "to raise money for the proposed radio station" and was "in the process of forming a Board of Directors, to be made up of people over the State, and let them apply for the license."[64] A week later Pacifica Radio's Christopher Koch emerged as president and principal architect of the RTA. "We would really like to see objective reporting on what's going on in Mississippi and the rest of the country made available to the people there," Koch explained to the *New York Times*. RTA executive secretary Frank Millspaugh echoed this point. "Hardly a single existing radio station in Mississippi gives objective coverage and broad news coverage. When civil rights activities are mentioned it's always in negative terms." The *Times* report, which duly found its way into the SSC's voluminous files, also observed that the RTA was conducting workshops in "churches, theaters, fields and homes" throughout Mississippi to inform people about the proposed new station.[65]

The plans for organizing Radio Tougaloo put forward by Koch, Millspaugh and the rest of the RTA executive committee, notably treasurer David Finkelstein and vice president Robert McNamara, closely mirrored the grassroots mobilization strategies associated with COFO in Mississippi and SNCC more generally. With Chris Koch at the helm, this was hardly surprising. A protégé of Pacifica's feisty matriarch Elsa Knight Thompson, Koch had worked at the network's WBAI–New York outlet. He shared both Pacifica's broad commitment to pacifism, free speech, civil rights, and democratic accountability and its veneration of SNCC as the best expression of these ideals.[66]

In Koch's vision, there would not be just one station in Mississippi dedicated to progressive politics, culture, education, and news; there would be a whole slew of community-controlled outlets. The stated purpose of the RTA was to "make available to the people of Mississippi the knowledge, skills and resources necessary for them to establish radio stations that will provide outlets for the creative skills of the community, offer forums for interracial communication, and broadcast fast and objective news coverage of events vitally affecting the community." Echoing the language of both FCC licensing requirements and SNCC's commitment to participatory democracy, Koch declared that "these new radio stations can best broadcast in the public interest and necessity if they are controlled by the communities they serve, and that their governing bodies should therefore be elected by those communities they serve." Koch was anxious to encourage the widest possible participation in this endeavor. Accordingly, he proposed that the area covered by any station should be divided into precincts, much like an electoral district, and that these precincts should then "elect representatives to the governing body of the station." Koch further urged "that an equal vote be given to every Mississippian who joins the station's membership, [and] that the cost of membership be minimal."[67]

In early 1965 the RTA began its work in earnest. It concentrated on raising funds, stimulating community interest in establishing local radio stations, and "disseminating the principles of sound broadcasting practice" to those who were interested. In January and February, RTA workers traversed the highways and byways of Mississippi, setting up a series of local radio workshops from which emerged delegates to a couple of Freedom Radio Assemblies held in Tougaloo and Jackson. At Tougaloo on February 14 there was a good deal of cautious optimism as Koch revealed a list of twenty people, "many of them with specialized knowledge of broadcasting," who had already joined or aided the RTA in a significant way. As well as radio experts, the list included a smattering of celebrities, like comedian Dick Gregory and folk singer Theodore Bikel, along with

Tougaloo's recently removed president Dan Beittel. Koch noted that there were "three full-time staff members in Mississippi engaged in the workshops" and announced, "We have also raised several thousand dollars for the project, much of it provided by the National Council of Churches." Koch concluded, "We are confident at this point, after several months of exploration, that a radio station of the kind described can and must be created in Mississippi." Little did he know that Erle Johnston and the SSC were already taking steps to ensure that the project would never come to fruition, or that he himself would be something of an Achilles heel as the forces of massive resistance mobilized against the whole enterprise.[68]

The SSC was extremely adept in the art of the well-orchestrated anticommunist smear campaign. As soon as Johnston and his staff realized that Radio Tougaloo was connected through Christopher Koch to Pacifica, they decided that the best way to undermine the project was to associate it in the minds of the public and the FCC commissioners with a network that had recently been investigated for alleged subversive activities. In late 1962 the Senate Internal Security Subcommittee (SISS), chaired by that factotum of Mississippi massive resistance James O. Eastland, had initiated an extensive investigation of communist infiltration at Pacifica, leading to formal hearings in January 1963. Although this was not the first time that the network's pacifism and left-liberal leanings had attracted close scrutiny, these investigations were the most exacting and vindictive to date.[69]

If Pacifica's support for the civil rights and peace movements provided reason enough for the likes of Eastland to want to see the network humbled, the immediate catalyst for the 1963 hearings was an interview Christopher Koch had conducted for WBAI in October 1962 with a disaffected former FBI agent called Jack Levine. At a time when J. Edgar Hoover's agents were still poster boys for patriotic opposition to domestic communism, Levine described the Bureau's infiltration and illegal surveillance of what it deemed to be dangerous individuals and organizations (including the NAACP and CORE) through phone taps, mail interceptions, and bugs in homes and workplaces. He even suggested that the whole idea of a communist threat in America had been grossly exaggerated merely to justify the FBI's existence and power. In some communist cells, Levine reported, the majority of dues-paying members were actually FBI agents. Far from presenting the Bureau as the guardian of the American way, Levine's revelations depicted the FBI as a profoundly undemocratic and largely unaccountable private agency dedicated to the whims and greater glory of J. Edgar Hoover.[70]

Needless to say, Hoover, the FBI, and many conservatives were apoplectic at these disclosures. Within months of the Levine-Koch interview, Hoover's friends on the SISS launched a full investigation of Pacifica. With retribution the real motivation, the official pretext was decidedly flimsy, mostly revolving around some old articles in anticommunist newsletters that denounced the network's willingness to allow former and current communists to appear on air. Two weeks of formal hearings revealed no evidence of communist subversion, and no charges were ever filed against the network—although the FCC did subsequently ask Pacifica to administer loyalty oaths to its members, sparking a divisive internal debate about whether to comply.[71] In some ways the official findings of the hearings were irrelevant. This was an era when mere investigation by the SISS was tantamount in some quarters to evidence of communist sympathies: the absence of more concrete proof simply confirmed the low cunning of undercover reds.

Anxious to discredit the RTA, the SSC repeatedly emphasized its links to a Pacifica organization that it consistently painted in the reddest of hues. Its task became much easier when Eastland turned over the complete records of the SISS investigation to Erle Johnston.[72] Mining these files for useful nuggets, the SSC gleefully noted that in the past Pacifica had allocated airtime to the likes of "the late Dr. W.E. DuBois [sic], who renounced his American citizenship in favor of Communism, and to Gus Hall, general secretary of the Communist Party, USA." The SSC investigators also stressed that Joanne Grant, news director at WBAI, had been "identified as a Communist on February 3, 1960, at hearings conducted by the House Un-American Activities Committee." No matter that Grant had no connection to Radio Tougaloo; it was enough that she had worked for Pacifica and so did Chris Koch. There was still plenty of mileage in the venerable red-baiting tactic of guilt by association.[73]

Alongside broad hints of communist ties, the SSC frequently asserted that the Radio Tougaloo project was the idea of outside agitators with no respect for southern traditions and racial mores. The RTA board was especially vulnerable to this criticism. Koch was a New Yorker. So, too, were Frank Millspaugh, director of the Books for Equal Education organization and vice president of the United States Youth Council, and David Finkelstein, a professor at New York's Yeshiva University whose Jewishness and intellectualism made him almost a caricature of the sort of outsider often accused by southern whites of stirring up discontent among the region's black population. Robert McNamara III, the RTA vice president, was from Chicago, where his work with CRIS hardly endeared him to the SSC or the champions of segregation. Even the involvement of the National Council of Churches allowed the SSC to cultivate the idea that the RTA was an imported idea. This was a masterful exercise in disinformation, given how Koch and his board had painstakingly planned to ensure that movement radio in Mississippi would be a genuine community enterprise.

Most of the individuals and organizations involved in the RTA were pilloried in hostile SSC press releases denouncing Radio Tougaloo to audiences in Mississippi and beyond. An editorial in the *Charleston Evening Post* regurgitated SSC propaganda, insisting that communistic "Freedom Radio presents an alarming new concept in American broadcasting. No one, of course, believes that this group of racial zealots is capable of anything like objective reporting. . . . what is envisioned here is a station that will take to the air in behalf of a narrow and inflammatory doctrine that even its authors speak of in terms of revolution." Closer to home, the *Jackson Clarion-Ledger* publicized the comments of Marvin Mathis, manager of WSJC-Magee and president of the Mississippi Broadcasters Association, who claimed his organization had "been unable to find any native Mississippian, black or white," who supported the Radio Tougaloo plans. Mathis said that the project "could only serve two purposes—fatten the personal bank accounts of those soliciting the funds in the states outside of Mississippi . . . and create turmoil and ill-will among the citizens of Mississippi." Mathis added that African Americans in Mississippi were perfectly happy with the service provided by the state's broadcasters, noting that the only 50,000-watt full-time radio facility in the state was black-oriented WOKJ.[74]

In mid-March 1965, Erle Johnston made his most influential public statement on the subject of Radio Tougaloo. In an address to the Lion's Club in Brandon, he stated: "If Radio Tougaloo Association is successful in acquiring a license to establish a station on the Tougaloo campus, it could . . . easily become . . . a communication vehicle for Communists and Communist sympathizers to preach their doctrines of hate and atheism—regardless of claims that the station is only interested in promoting civil rights." The speech was widely reprinted in the region's press. A member of one conservative organization based in Laurel wrote to tell Johnston, "Since reading your report, and to further sound the alarm, we are having 1000 copies of the entire page of the *Clarion-Ledger* printed, hoping to get them into the hands of the Mississippi legislators and other interested and influential people."[75] In fact, the SSC had already primed Mississippi's representatives in Washington to do their utmost to scupper any application the FCC might eventually receive from the RTA or any of its derivatives. Congressman Jamie Whitton assured Erle Johnston: "The Clerk of the Committee on Interstate and Foreign Commerce tells us his friends at the agency are keeping an eye out for the arrival of the application for a radio station at Tougaloo, but it has not yet been received. Just as soon as we hear anything further, I will let you know."[76]

There was no doubt about the reach and effectiveness of the SSC's campaign against the RTA. An SSC report filed in March 1965 described how an unidentified African American woman arriving from Chicago to discuss plans for Radio Tougaloo was already aware "that the State Sovereignty Committee had had a lot to say against Robert McNamara" and that it "was attempting to link the radio station with 'Pacifica' radio stations in California and New York."[77] In an attempt to spare the RTA from the particularly vicious attacks directed against him personally, Chris Koch resigned. His selfless act failed to save the Association. With Koch gone, Erle Johnston gloated, the RTA "has never been able to organize a board of directors or acquire sufficient funds to construct a broadcasting facility."[78]

By the spring of 1965 the RTA was in dire trouble. In June there was a final bid to save the project by pooling RTA resources and personnel with those of another group known as the Mississippi Information Broadcasting Cooperative, chaired by Robert Stenson. Ultimately, however, there was little that the newly dubbed Freedom Radio collective could do to stanch the tidal wave of negative publicity and innuendo flowing from the SSC offices. With this sort of political power and popular opprobrium leveled against it, plans for Radio Tougaloo collapsed.[79]

Johnston and the SSC could not claim all the credit for the demise of the Radio Tougaloo initiative. Irrespective of the chilling effect of the SSC's smear campaign on donations, financing a series of community radio stations within a poverty-stricken state like Mississippi was always going to be problematic. With the project on its last legs, an SSC informant had bluntly stated that "the original plan to get money for the Radio Tougaloo Association from citizens has apparently failed and only organizations such as N.C.C. and C.W.A. [Communications Workers of America] and others known to the Commission are coming through."[80] Nor was it by any means certain that the FCC would ever have licensed such a station if it felt it really was little more than a vehicle for a political organization such as the MFDP.

Equally hard to overcome was the ambivalent attitude of the Tougaloo College administration to the prospect of having a self-professed movement broadcasting facility on campus. For some time the board of trustees had been anxious to distance the college from what in white minds—including those of powerful figures in the Mississippi state legislature—was a perilous association with the civil rights movement. In January 1964 the board had decided it would remove President Beittel. The SSC was delighted and looked forward to the installation of a less bothersome replacement. At a secret meeting with the trustees in April 1964, Erle Johnston announced that Beittel "had inspired such resentment on the part of state officials and legislators that a show-down clash appeared imminent." Johnston added that "if Tougaloo had a good man as president . . . the institution could be restored to its former status as a respected private college."[81]

With two hostile bills already on the floor of the Mississippi legislature that threatened to rescind Tougaloo's charter and accreditation, Dan Beittel was forced into early retirement "in spite of an agreement with the Board for a longer term of service." This "sacrifice," as Beittel termed it, certainly helped to ease the pressure on Tougaloo from the SSC and the state legislature. It also left the board free to pursue a lucrative relationship with Brown University and its CIA-backed president Barnaby Keeney that brought with it the promise of major Ford Foundation funding. Yet, if this deal benefited Tougaloo financially and academically, it did so at the expense of a precipitous withdrawal of formal support for almost all civil rights activities by its administration.[82] In these circumstances it was unlikely that the college would have allowed the proposed radio station to use its land, let alone its name. That slim prospect became even more remote once the SSC began to arouse popular concern about Radio Tougaloo's alleged communist links. When an SSC informant visited the site of the RTA headquarters on Hill Crest Road in mid-March 1965, he discovered that, despite the RTA publicity claiming close cooperation with the Tougaloo authorities, its premises were actually off campus. By the time the informant went back a week later, the site was deserted. By the end of the summer the Radio Tougaloo project was all but dead.[83]

There were enough impediments to make Radio Tougaloo a highly speculative venture even without the SSC's intervention. Yet the movement had made a disconcerting habit of beating the odds posted by the forces of racism and reaction, and the SSC was clearly alarmed at the prospect of an independent movement-oriented radio station emerging in Mississippi. In response, it orchestrated a highly effective operation to destroy whatever meager chance of success there was for Radio Tougaloo. Indeed, there was something chillingly impressive about the whole campaign of infiltration, surveillance, and propaganda that symbolized the enormous obstacles the movement had to overcome in bringing some semblance of racial justice and progressive radio broadcasting to Mississippi.

Losing Battles, Waging Wars

It is tempting to chalk up the collapse of the Radio Tougaloo project as one of a succession of victories for the forces of massive resistance in their battle to preserve white supremacy in Mississippi by keeping racially progressive broadcasting off the air. Yet, in this decidedly hostile and unpromising environment, important strides were made toward ensuring that broadcasters would in future be required to pay more attention to the political, social, and educational interests, as well as the entertainment preferences, of local African American audiences. The sheer level of bias evident in Mississippi's electronic media meant that the state became the focus of attempts by civil rights groups to ensure broadcasters became more respectful of and responsive to the needs of black audiences. The way in which this campaign was conducted, with local and national organizations combining to compel decisive federal intervention, mirrored the basic architecture of the broader southern civil rights movement.

Initial complaints to the FCC about racial discrimination in the Mississippi media tended to focus on the rebel-rousing antics of Fred Beard at WJDX and WLBT-TV. In 1955 the NAACP had joined a group of local black Jacksonians to protest, to a largely uninterested FCC, Beard's refusal to take ABC or NBC network shows relating to civil rights issues.[84] In 1962 the Commission did at least investigate complaints about Beard's handling of R.L.T. Smith's campaign and the Ole Miss crisis. Some commissioners, among them Kenneth Cox, clearly believed that Beard had a case to answer. Yet no formal steps were taken to compel him or his stations to abandon their public commitment to segregation, or to honor the FCC's Fairness Doctrine when dealing with significant public issues.[85]

SNCC and CORE had taken particular heart from the FCC's reaffirmation of the Fairness Doctrine in July 1963, seeing it as a federally endorsed mandate to increase their claims for airtime on southern stations. They drew up detailed guidelines on how to invoke the FCC's rulings in trying to gain access to even the most reactionary stations. In the hope of preventing license renewals at notoriously bigoted stations, they also encouraged staff to file formal complaints with the FCC. There was little reason to believe that the Commission would act decisively in these cases. Nevertheless, as a SNCC memo put it, "Even if the FCC does not refuse to renew a license, it may issue strong warnings to the station about which it has received such complaints."[86]

During 1964, as Freedom Summer unfolded and the electronic media in Mississippi generally ignored or actively obstructed civil rights activities, the United Church of Christ (UCC) led the opposition to the renewal of broadcasting licenses at WJDX and WBLT. Complaints to the FCC were also made against three other Jackson facilities—radio stations WSLI and WRBC, and WJTV, a CBS television affiliate owned by the *Jackson Clarion and Daily News*—as well as against the WCBI radio and television franchise in nearby Columbus. Headquartered in New York, the UCC was a two-million-strong union of the Congregational Christian Churches and the Evangelical and Reformed Church with a traditionally progressive racial attitude, considerable financial resources, and a very dynamic office of communications headed by the Reverend Everett C. Parker. In the early 1960s the UCC's general synod had issued a call for all its churches to be more proactive in pursuit of racial justice. In accordance with this directive, in March 1964 the UCC monitored a week of radio and television broadcasts in Mississippi. Disturbed by the complete absence of black voices or viewpoints on Jackson media outlets notionally serving an area with a 45 percent black population, the UCC had petitioned the FCC on behalf of various local groups for leave to testify in the next round of station license renewal applications. Members of the local UCC chapter, R.L.T. Smith, and Aaron Henry were cosignatories of the petition, which asserted: "The Negro population of the area is deprived of proper enjoyment of the available broadcast frequencies and the entire population, Negro and white, receives a distorted picture of vital issues."[87]

The UCC petition raised critical questions about precisely who was entitled to present evidence to the FCC when it considered license renewal applications. The core issue was the extent to which local people could exercise a measure of control over the radio and television facilities that purported to serve them. Faced by plentiful evidence of gross malpractice and discrimination, in May 1965 the FCC decided by a majority decision to grant WJDX and WLBT a probationary one-year license conditional on good behavior. Kenneth Cox and chairman E. William Henry dissented from this decision on the grounds that, with so much evidence that the stations were not serving the "public interest," the FCC should have held a full public hearing before deciding to renew the license, even if only temporarily. The terms of the probation did require station owners and managers to consult with black community representatives and civil rights workers about whether the programming met the needs of local African American listeners. While this provision seemed to suggest heightened FCC concern about racist media practices, the Commission granted each of the other suspect Mississippi stations full three-year licenses, arguing that they had already taken steps to meet UCC objections.

Even more problematic, the Commission had also evaded the most important principle at stake in the UCC's petition. The FCC rejected the UCC's request to be allowed formal representation in the license renewal procedure, declaring that the local citizens the UCC represented had "no legal standing" in the process. In so doing, it upheld a longstanding FCC policy that only technical and economic concerns, such as signal interference or economic injury to another broadcaster, were sufficient reasons to allow third parties to participate in the licensing procedure. This effectively meant that only other broadcasters had the right to challenge existing licensees. Civil rights activists, many of whom were anxiously awaiting the outcome of the Radio Tougaloo initiative, understood the damaging effect of this policy on efforts to increase the responsiveness of radio to local black needs. As the UCC organized an appeal against the FCC's ruling, other organizations—CORE, SNCC, and the NAACP—joined the clamor for the Commission to broaden the range of the parties allowed to participate in renewal proceedings. They also called for the FCC to take firmer action against stations that manifestly ignored the Fairness Doctrine.[88]

One other party that weighed in against WJDX and WLBT was the local Jackson AFL-CIO office, which maintained that the stations were routinely hostile toward labor activities in the area. A Dick Sanders editorial on WJDX in March 1962, for example, urged the 1,600 employees at the city's biggest company, Storkline, to vote against letting the United Brotherhood of Carpenters and Joiners of America represent them for bargaining purposes. The editorial listed a whole range of alleged financial malpractices by the union's leaders, condemned its basic ineffectiveness, and lavished praise on Storkline for its provision of "life insurance, accident and health insurance, hospital and surgical insurance, and sick benefits." It ended with a call to workers to "reject the union . . . for their benefit and the good of Jackson."[89]

The Jackson AFL-CIO certainly had grounds to accuse WJDX and WBLT of antiunion bias. What was especially revealing about local branch president Claude Ramsay's complaints, however, was the length to which he went to distance himself and his union from the civil rights groups that were protesting the license renewals on racial grounds. "I have further learned that the objection raised by the [United Church of Christ] is that of racial discrimination," Ramsay told the local press. "Please be advised that the objections of the Mississippi AFL-CIO are of a different nature." He labeled as "positively not true" the accusation that he had joined "Negro integration leaders" in condemning the stations. So much for the biracial working-class solidarity that some had hoped would be an important instrument of racial change in the South. Indeed, while there were notable local exceptions to this general pattern, Ramsay's determination to deny any involvement in the struggle for racial justice reflected the limited and equivocal support for African American rights offered by many white unionists in the South during the peak years of mass activism.[90]

In 1966 the Court of Appeals for the District of Columbia under Judge Warren Burger upheld the UCC's case that the FCC had no right to exclude representatives of a station's listening or viewing audience from presenting evidence in a license renewal case that might indicate substantial public dissatisfaction with that station's performance. Burger ruled that "we can see no reason to exclude those with such an obvious and acute concern as the listening audience." As a result, the FCC was compelled to allow UCC testimony in a public hearing on WJDX and WLBT. However, much to the disgust of the UCC and its allies, even after hearing this damning testimony, the FCC still saw fit to renew both stations' licenses.[91]

After another three years gathering still more evidence of racial bias at the radio and television stations, the UCC again appeared before Burger's Court of Appeals, challenging the FCC's decision to renew the license. In his last opinion before becoming chief justice of the Supreme Court, Burger rebuked the FCC for its "scandalous delay" in adjudicating what was a clear case of racial discrimination, concluding that "the administrative conduct reflected in this record is beyond repair." Burger ordered the FCC to cancel the Lamar Life Insurance Company's license and appoint an interim operator, which turned out to be a biracial group called Communication Improvement Inc., led by Rev. Kenneth Dean, the executive director of the Mississippi Council on Human Relations.[92]

The long campaign against discriminatory practices in the Mississippi media broadcasting industry had several important consequences. First, at a purely local level, it helped to create a climate slightly more conducive to racially progressive radio broadcasting in the state. That thaw was slow and tentative, but unmistakable. In the summer of 1965, for example, WOKJ in Jackson began to test the boundaries of acceptable programming in Mississippi by airing the NUL's *The Leaders Speak* and *Civil Rights Roundup* shows.[93] A year later, the same station felt confident enough to present four hours of live—and therefore uncensored—coverage of a rally at Tougaloo College to mark the end of James Meredith's March Against Fear. That march had brought the "black power" slogan to widespread public attention, ushering in a new phase of the African American freedom struggle. Ironically, after years of rejecting appeals for airtime by nonviolent integrationists, in the summer of 1966 WOKJ granted exposure to some people who had little interest in either nonviolence or integration.[94]

Second, the Mississippi media campaign of the mid-1960s had profound national implications for efforts to increase community control over radio and other mass media. Federal recognition of the right of community representatives, as opposed to just other broadcasters, to challenge license renewal applications meant that the number of such challenges rose from two in the period July 1968–June 1969 to 108 during the same period in 1971–72. The overwhelming majority of petitions to deny licenses came from African American groups.[95] While relatively few of these challenges succeeded, they did tend to make broadcasters more responsive to the needs and concerns of their listeners than in the past. As media analyst F. Leslie Smith explained, thanks to the Mississippi cases "the public gained a mechanism to affect programming of a broadcasting station, to ensure that it served the interests of the community. The fact that the public could intervene meant that many licensees not only opened their doors to citizen and audience groups but also listened and negotiated."[96]

Meanwhile, a whole slew of civil rights and media organizations dedicated themselves to increasing the number of black owners, executives, and staff members in radio and television, to improving the quantity and quality of public service broadcasting devoted to black audiences, and to ensuring proper African American representation at the FCC. These overlapping campaigns became hallmarks of the black power era—a time of great ferment in southern radio and race relations.

PART 3

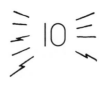

The Quest for Black Power in Southern Radio

The issue is one of white bossism, not only here in Atlanta's WAOK,
but in white-owned, black-oriented radio stations across the country.

SNCC press release, 1967

Ownership, Opportunity, and Service

In 1970 a coalition of eighty-four predominantly African American civic organizations calling itself the Middle Tennessee Coalition for Communications
(MTCC) mounted a campaign against WVOL-Nashville, demanding more employment opportunities for African Americans and improved public service
broadcasting for the black community. Ralph Johnson, president of the Atlanta-
based Rounsaville chain of soul stations that owned WVOL, responded to these
demands at great length. He insisted that the station was doing a good job of
"programming in every respect principally and directly to the needs, interest and
taste of the Black community of Metropolitan Nashville." He also pointed out
that fifteen of the station's twenty-three employees were black. This included
three of the station's six executive personnel, among them WVOL's general manager, Noble V. Blackwell, who was also a vice president and corporate director. In
addition, two of the station's three sales staff and all of its on-air announcers were
black. Johnson insisted that "WVOL has given far more than lip service to the
various fair employment laws and regulations." He declared proudly, "This
meaningful integration has been a trademark of WVOL since it came under the
present ownership in 1956" and emphasized that "the integration of the staff is
not merely at the lower levels, but includes the highest executive levels."[1]

Beyond its hiring record, WVOL could also boast an impressive range of community-oriented news and public affairs programming for African Americans in
Nashville. The station had long presented news of employment opportunities
and run campaigns for "upgraded job offers for Negroes."[2] *On the Line* was a
weekly hour-long show in which "local controversial issues are discussed, the
pros and cons of all subject matters . . . voiced by authoritative civic leaders." *Call
for Action* was a "grass roots community service" program "wherein any Nash-

ville citizen can phone the station and register a complaint or call attention to a specific public need." Even some of the religious programming at the station had a pronounced social gospel feel. *Power for Today* and *All Scripture Is Beneficial* stressed the practical application of biblical teachings in efforts to improve the quality of everyday life. *Know Your Schools* informed listeners about "curriculum, transportation, food service, teacher-parent relations, student activities" in Nashville, while *Educational Motivation* slots urged "teenagers of our community to stay in school." A daily five-minute feature called *Your Social Security* offered advice on "how to get maximum benefits from this Government service." The station even had a passable news-gathering operation "utilizing the fulltime services of one and one-half Newsmen totaling approximately 65 man-hours weekly." Nor did it neglect the kind of consciousness-raising programming that became ubiquitous on black-oriented radio in the late 1960s and early 1970s. WVOL editorialized regularly on "black awareness" matters—including the virtues of the Afro hairstyle and the "appropriate terminology" for African Americans. Three times a day it also broadcast brief *This Is Our Heritage* "vignettes on the historical achievements of the Black man." Although the casually sexist description suggested that WVOL could have spent a little more of its own time reflecting on "appropriate terminology," the show did feature black women, too.[3]

It is hard to imagine what more WVOL could have done to satisfy the MTCC. By almost any index, its record of minority employment and intelligent public service and news programming was better than at most commercial black-oriented radio facilities. Yet WVOL lacked the one thing that groups like the MTCC came to crave above everything else: it was not black owned. "How can a white man know what a black man needs?" deejay-activist Del Shields had asked at the 1964 convention of the National Association of Television and Radio Announcers (NATRA), an organization destined to play a major role in the quest for black power within the broadcasting industry.[4] Shields's question was posed repeatedly during the late 1960s and early 1970s as black activism became increasingly directed toward securing black control over the key institutions and essential circumstances of black social, economic, and political life. Radio was a vital component of that life, and the quest for more black radio station owners and executives accordingly comprised an important aspect of the wider black power impulse. In this context, command of black-oriented radio was simultaneously a valuable prize and a potent weapon in the struggle for black economic and political power. How, and with what success, a diverse range of activists sought to increase black ownership and executive authority in southern radio forms the major theme of this chapter.

The struggle for more black owners, improved job opportunities, and better service in the broadcasting industry was a national, rather than a regional, phenomenon. And it embraced all aspects of the electronic media, not just radio.

Still, southern radio did constitute a special forum for a campaign that took much of its inspiration and many of its tactics from ongoing efforts to bring racist broadcasters to heel in Mississippi. At the same time, the federal government, primarily in the form of the FCC and the Equal Employment Opportunity Commission (EEOC), became simultaneously the most conspicuous target for protests against continued discrimination in the radio industry and the best potential instrument for redressing those inequities. The complex and often fraught relationship between black media activists and these federal authorities forms a second major theme of this chapter.

Underwriting the clamor for more black power in radio were two interlocking assumptions. The first was that black owners would hire more black staff at their stations, especially in executive positions. The second was that black owners and executives would be more conspicuously engaged in community activism and politics—and that they would find a better balance between news, politics, community affairs, and public service broadcasting and the soul music that dominated black-oriented radio. This chapter argues that, while the first assumption often proved correct, the second was more suspect. Although the situation differed from station to station, black-owned and black-managed radio outlets did not necessarily demonstrate any greater commitment to public service broadcasting or community activism than did their white-run counterparts. In fact, most of the black entrepreneurs, managers, and programmers who did secure executive power in radio behaved much like their white counterparts, placing personal interest and economic priorities ahead of narrower racial considerations in their programming decisions.

Black Ownership and Black Employment

There was no doubt that African Americans were historically underrepresented as owners and employees within the radio industry. Black-oriented programming was the industry's biggest commercial success story since the arrival of television. Yet by 1964, when 414 radio stations regularly devoted at least some of their daily programming to black audiences, only 600 of 60,000 employees in the industry were African Americans. Equally damning, only 5 of the 5,500 commercial radio stations operating in America were owned by African Americans.[5] The FCC's 1965 declaration that it supported "maximum diffusion of control of the media of mass communications" had raised some hopes that this situation might be addressed through federal action, but the Commission's policy at this time was more concerned with diversifying ownership to avoid monopolistic practices than with increasing the representation of minorities among those owners.[6]

By 1968, when advertising revenue on the 528 commercial stations featuring regular black-oriented programming topped $35 million per annum, there were still just 8 black-owned stations. At the end of the decade, there were at most 16 black-owned radio facilities among the 7,350 commercial and noncommercial stations in the country. Ten of these black-owned outlets were in the South. These included such "border South" facilities as KPRS in Kansas City, Missouri, co-owned by Andrew "Skip" Carter and Ed Pate, and KWK–St. Louis, whose ownership at the end of the decade was actually being disputed by rival white and black consortia. The ten black-owned southern stations also included two non-commercial outlets owned by historically black colleges: Shaw University's WSHA in Raleigh, North Carolina, and the Hampton Institute's WHOV in Virginia. Of the remaining six black-owned commercial radio stations in the South, singer James Brown owned three: WJBE-Knoxville, WRDW-Augusta, and WEBB-Baltimore—another border South facility. The region's black-owned contingent was completed by the tiny WVOE-Chadbourn, North Carolina, owned by Ralph Vaught; Leroy Garrett's venerable WEUP in Huntsville, Alabama, which after nearly two decades on air continued to survive in a city where less than 10 percent of the population was black; and, perhaps most inspirational of all, WORV-Hattiesburg, the first black-owned station in Mississippi, founded by brothers Vernon and Robert Floyd and Reuben Hughes.[7]

Beyond the ownership issue, for decades there had been steady attempts to expand opportunities and improve the pay, conditions, and promotion prospects for African Americans working in radio on either side of the microphone. These efforts tended to founder on the twin rocks of racism among white executives and economic self-interest (coupled with racism) among rank-and-file white employees who often sought to exclude African Americans from the most desirable positions. Initially there was precious little help for black aspirations from the labor unions most intimately connected to the radio industry. The International Brotherhood of Electrical Workers (IBEW) had at least averred a nondiscriminatory policy since its first involvement in broadcasting in 1926. Until the mid-1960s, however, this policy was largely ignored in the South—and in any case, since the National Labor Relations Act decreed that there could be no union "closed shop" in radio, the stations were not even compelled to hire IBEW workers. The Radio Writers Guild was formed in the late 1930s, but had no black members until admitting a token few in the 1940s. It was an equally daunting picture for black radio performers. The American Federation of Musicians had more white-only locals than any other union in the nation except the railway clerks, while the American Federation of Radio Actors, superseded by ATRA, the Association of Television and Radio Artists, specifically excluded African Americans until World War II. Thereafter it generally disregarded ample evidence of racial inequalities in the profession until 1963, when it began to include clauses against discrimination in its collective bargaining agreements.[8]

While this was a lamentable record, the tentative signs of increased union support for African American workers at the IBEW and ATRA in the early and middle 1960s were given new impetus by several pieces of federal legislation that were themselves largely a consequence of the early civil rights movement. Most important of these were the fair employment provisions under Title VII of the 1964 Civil Rights Act and the creation of the EEOC under the same year's Economic Opportunity Act. Inspired by these developments and the initial promise of Lyndon Johnson's War on Poverty programs, the NUL set up a Broadcast Skills Bank with NBC, ABC, CBS, and the Westinghouse Broadcasting Company, hoping to encourage the recruitment, training, and employment of suitable African American employees. Between March 1966 and March 1967 the number of minority employees at ABC increased by more than 13 percent. The impact of federal initiatives could sometimes be felt more locally in the South. In 1967 the only two jobs created for African Americans as a direct result of a disappointing summer youth employment program run by the Memphis War on Poverty Committee were at WDIA.[9]

In the late 1960s and early 1970s the FCC also began to offer more encouragement to activists working for better black employment opportunities in, and services from, radio. In the summer of 1969, for example, the FCC adopted rules on equal employment opportunities in the broadcasting industry based on those established by the Civil Service Commission. All licensees were required to "avoid discrimination in employment and . . . establish and maintain a continuing program of specific practices designed to assure equal opportunity in all aspects of station employment policy and practice." The new onus on station management to take affirmative steps to demonstrate "their equal employment opportunity programs with respect to significant minority groups" intensified in June 1970 when the FCC made these rules applicable to stations with as few as five employees.[10] At the time of the original 1964 legislation, the EEOC had required proof of positive commitment to equal employment opportunities only from facilities with more than fifty employees. This was amended in 1967 to include stations with more than twenty-five employees, but the new criterion in 1970 meant that virtually every broadcaster in the nation had to demonstrate fair hiring practices in its license renewal applications. Stations with more than one hundred employees also had to file annual reports on their minority recruitment strategies.[11]

These progressive policy adjustments indicated that the FCC was becoming somewhat more receptive to black complaints against broadcasters who failed either to employ, adequately pay, or promote black employees, or who failed to serve the interests of their black listeners in accordance with their licensing provisions. Several factors combined to account for this shift in FCC attitudes. One was the rise of consumer rights advocacy groups, spurred on by Ralph Nader's exposure of the automobile industry's indifference to the safety of its customers. Nader's campaigns helped to create a climate of opinion in which regulatory bodies like the FCC felt increasingly obliged to take seriously the public's complaints about inadequate services from licensees. A more direct influence was Judge Warren Burger's admonishment of the FCC for failing to censure WJDX and WLBT-TV in Jackson despite ample evidence of systematic racial bias and discrimination.

Even more instrumental in changing the ethos at the FCC were two individual commissioners: Nicholas Johnson and Benjamin Hooks. From his appointment in 1966, Nick Johnson supported calls for more socially engaged black-oriented broadcasting and for more African American owners and executives. At a turbulent 1968 NATRA convention in Miami, Johnson told black deejays that simply playing soul music was not enough of a contribution to community empowerment. Recognizing the influence of radio among African Americans, Johnson explained that while "Soul radio is big business, it is also big responsibility. Many institutions try to reach the destitute and alienated millions who seek a richer future in the hearts of our cities. The schools have tried. The Office of Economic Opportunity has tried. Newspapers have tried. But only one institution has consistently succeeded. That is Negro-oriented radio." Calling for more black history, black-oriented news, and community mobilization efforts, as well as for more musical diversity on air, Johnson agreed it was "disgraceful that no more than a handful of the 7,500 radio and television stations in this country are owned by blacks." Some NATRA delegates resented the fact that Johnson appeared to blame the deejays for the relative lack of social engagement on black-oriented radio; as a disgruntled Carleton Coleman put it, deejays "have no control over programming. . . . He should have made this talk to the station owners." Most, however, recognized Johnson's commitment to increasing the number of African Americans in positions where they could decisively affect programming choices. Even Del Shields, president of NATRA during its most militant phase, appreciated Johnson's support. "Nick went back to influence the National Association of Broadcasters and the FCC to put aside X number of dollars for minorities to own stations," Shields recalled. Although limited, the sort of federal assistance advocated by Johnson largely underwrote the modest expansion of black radio ownership during the 1970s.[12]

Benjamin Hooks was no less supportive of expanded black economic opportunity within the industry than was Nick Johnson. But as the first African American to serve on the FCC, Hooks was of considerably more symbolic significance. This is not to suggest that his practical input was negligible. It was no coincidence that shortly after his appointment in 1972, the Commission rededicated itself to enforcing its equal opportunity policies. Following Hooks's lead, chairman Dean Burch announced the FCC's intention to "closely examine diversity profiles at licensees," which prompted James Hulbert, the vice president of the NAB, to gush that "while it may be premature to call [minority employment] a dead issue, it is certainly a dying one." Although Hulbert's optimism proved excessive, from Hooks's arrival until his departure to become chairman of the NAACP in 1977, the FCC became more attentive to racial matters. His presence "heightened the awareness of all of us," remembered Richard Wiley, chairman of the FCC when Hooks bowed out. "It was a big step in the right direction having our own person there," agreed Pluria Marshall, founder of the National Black Media Coalition (NBMC). "We could always call on Ben to discuss things."[13]

The Structures of Struggle

Ben Hooks's appointment to the FCC was the result of a protracted campaign—spearheaded by the UCC, the NAACP, and the Black Efforts for Soul in Television (BEST) organization based in Washington—to get an African American representative onto the Commission. This was a common pattern, wherein the pressure exerted by local and national groups ultimately compelled either the FCC or individual stations to respond to evidence of bias or discrimination within the broadcasting industry. Indeed, what was especially striking in the South was how closely the campaign for more accountable, responsible, and representative radio mirrored the organizational structure of the early civil rights movement, when local, regional, and national forces had combined—sometimes uneasily, occasionally reluctantly—to create pressure for federal action or preemptive local reform.

Although there was a good deal of overlap and fluidity, it is possible to identify three basic types of organization at the forefront of the drive for more black ownership, better employment opportunities, and improved public service from black-oriented radio in the late 1960s and early 1970s. The first type consisted of nationally and regionally prominent organizations for which the radio campaign was just one aspect of a broader struggle for racial justice. The second type of organization tended to be community-based and was formed specifically to target the shortcomings of local broadcasters. The third type of organization emerged from within the media and entertainment world itself. Deploying tactics that included marches, petitions, class-action lawsuits, violence, bribery, intimidation, and the creation of parallel broadcasting institutions, these groups collectively spanned and epitomized the range of black-power-era protest tactics.

As an organization in the first category, SNCC coveted greater access to and control over the most important communication medium operating within the black community, as a means to promote its increasingly nationalistic program for black empowerment. In August 1966, shortly after new chairman Stokely Carmichael had popularized the "black power" slogan during the Meredith march, the organization had reassessed its entire approach to the media. SNCC was increasingly disillusioned with a mainstream print and electronic press that seemed determined to caricature black power as nothing more than an exercise in reverse racism and wanton violence. In a development that paralleled its withdrawal from interracial organizing and shift to a black-only membership, SNCC began to focus more exclusively on mobilizing the black community. Revealingly, however, the organization put little faith in the prospect of fair coverage and support from most black-owned newspapers, which it viewed as hopelessly conservative and conciliatory when the times demanded radical solutions to systemic racial problems. "For the sake of image," SNCC resolved to continue to work with the black press "despite its shortcomings." By contrast with this lackluster commitment, SNCC was extremely enthusiastic about extending its links with black-oriented radio. Since radio was considered "*vital* if we talk about speaking to the Black Community," it was deemed an important focus for SNCC's energies.[14]

The fact that all but a handful of these "vital" stations were white-owned explains the urgency with which SNCC pursued the expansion of black ownership. Indeed, thinking more broadly, as befitted an organization that increasingly expressed national rather than purely regional ambitions, executive secretary James Forman contended that it was the absence of "black control of the means of communication" that enabled black power's opponents to distort the meaning of that term for their own ends. Forman echoed the sentiments of Charles Hamilton, Stokely Carmichael's collaborator on the seminal *Black Power* treatise, who asserted that black "control of a significant portion of the electronic media would be the most important single breakthrough in the black struggle." Control of radio was usually the primary target for such efforts.[15]

Improving contacts with, control over, and service from black-oriented radio was also an objective for other civil rights and black power organizations. In late 1967 and early 1968, the SCLC sought to rationalize and extend its radio operations under the enthusiastic direction of William Stein, with *Martin Luther King Speaks* as the centerpiece of its regular output. Although Stein often stretched SCLC resources close to breaking point, King and his staff understood the value of his efforts. As King told his advisor Stanley Levison in January 1968, "I have talked to so many persons who said they heard me on the radio and although we can't get the TV we can [get] the radio and that is something." The show even remained in syndication after King's murder.[16] Elsewhere, Callis Brown, the community relations director of a CORE organization that was becoming closely identified with a kind of black-capitalism-as-black-power philosophy, actually placed the creation of "a permanent radio show" at the top of his list of priorities, ahead even of publishing a regular newsletter or securing television appearances for CORE leaders.[17] In 1970 the Congress of Afrikan Peoples, an important expression of the black cultural nationalism associated with Maulana Ron Karenga and Imamu Amiri Baraka, spent a good deal of its Atlanta conference discussing practical measures for increasing black control over the black-oriented communications media.[18]

In the second type of organization fighting for better service from the radio industry, and more black representation within it, were community-based groups like the MTCC in Nashville. These often consisted of "organizations of organizations" formed on an ad hoc basis to address racist practices at specific stations, or groups of stations. For example, in 1972 Ted Thornton and Laverne Byrd Smith of the Richmond chapter of the Virginia Council on Human Relations (VCHR) spearheaded the creation of an umbrella organization called the Black Community Coalition (BCC). Chaired by Dwight C. Jones of the Committee of Black Churchmen, the BCC brought together various local groups including the VCHR, the NAACP, the Richmond chapter of the National Association of Black Social Workers, and the Richmond Crusade of Voters, which had been complaining about the media's treatment of African Americans as employees, subjects, and consumers for many years. After attempts to open up constructive dialogue with the management of local stations failed, the BCC petitioned the FCC to deny the license renewal applications of fourteen Richmond radio stations and three television outlets. After a lengthy investigation, in August 1975 the FCC would issue only conditional licenses to five radio stations—WRNL, WEZS, WRQV, and WTVR-AM and -FM—"on the basis of their failure to employ minorities in sufficient numbers and/or implement an affirmative action program that exhibits more than a passive attempt to recruit and employ minorities." The FCC required these stations to increase their meager minority employment levels in all job categories. Meanwhile the Commission refused to renew the licenses of three other radio stations—WXGI and the AM and FM outlets of WIVE—where there were no black staff whatsoever.[19]

The third type of organization involved in the campaign for black power in radio were those with industry credentials and a media background. These included such groups as NATRA, BEST, and the NBMC. The most notorious and for a while the most influential of these organizations was NATRA, which had initially been founded in the 1950s by "Jockey Jack" Gibson as little more than a social club for the handful of pioneering black radio deejays. For years its reputation had rested mainly on its capacity to furnish plentiful supplies of booze, babes, and bribes for the delegates—mostly white—from the recording and broadcasting industries who attended its annual conventions. Inspired by the rise of civil rights agitation, however, at the 1964 NATRA convention in Chicago a self-styled New Breed of highly politicized deejays led by Del Shields and WACQ-Cleveland's Ed Wright tried to shift the focus of attention from prostitutes to protests against white domination of the black-oriented media and recording industries. A year later, in Houston, this New Breed took over the organization's executive committee and ushered in a more militant phase in the struggle for black economic and executive power in radio.[20]

Many of NATRA's first direct-action campaigns targeted black-oriented stations in the South, where wages and conditions were notoriously poor. Shields recalled, "We pulled a number of strikes throughout the South at small radio stations where announcers were getting three or four dollars an hour, or where announcers were not being treated properly. We put pressure on station owners or managers." That pressure sometimes took the intimidating form of mass visitations from sharp-suited, sharp-tongued NATRA personnel. "We would go in there with ten or fifteen strong men, we were the announcers from New York and Chicago, and we would have our attaché cases, and our suit and ties on, and we demanded to have a meeting with the station." According to Shields, southern owners and managers sometimes fired black deejays or reverted to old wage scales and conditions once NATRA's "outside agitators" had left town, but "in general we promoted the health and welfare of the guys."[21]

Adopting the uncompromising rhetoric typical of the black power era, NATRA vehemently denounced white financial and managerial control over most of the nation's black-oriented media. It decried the exploitation and expropriation of black art and culture for white economic gain and, notwithstanding a certain respect for Nick Johnson, castigated the FCC for failing to do more to address racism and the lack of black opportunity in the broadcasting industry. There was much truth in these accusations, yet they were hardly new. Stripped of its nationalistic and occasionally inflammatory rhetoric, NATRA pursued much the same goals of black economic empowerment and expanded employment opportunities that had animated pioneering black radio entrepreneurs such as Jesse Blayton for decades. Indeed, at the core of NATRA's agenda between 1965 and 1968 were plans for the creation of a black school of broadcasting in Wilmington, Delaware, that was not unlike Blayton's own Midway School. By the 1968 NATRA convention in Miami, Del Shields claimed to have raised some $25 million for this project, mostly from record companies with a heavy investment in soul music who recognized the strategic and economic value of black broadcasters in helping to sell their products.[22]

For several years NATRA fought with real verve and imagination for a better deal for African Americans in radio, managing to cultivate links with various strands within the wider freedom struggle. In 1967, for example, the organization had invited both Martin Luther King and SNCC's new chairman H. Rap

Brown to address its annual convention in Atlanta, reflecting its ecumenical approach to the goal of black empowerment. This pragmatism was evident in Shields's own rhetoric. He usually fused passionate demands for more black ownership with pleas for expanded employment opportunities and more socially engaged programming directed at the white owners and executives who dominated the industry and, as Shields realized, were likely to do so for the foreseeable future.[23]

At the following year's Miami convention, a renegade element associated with NATRA transformed this realistic and flexible quest for black power into a sordid exercise in petty gangsterism. For some time before the Miami convention, Del Shields and other executives had been under intense pressure from two distinct sources. On one hand, record company executives and station owners urged NATRA to tone down its increasingly strident demands. On the other hand, what Shields dubbed a Black Mafia was attempting to co-opt NATRA and use it to hold the radio and recording industries to ransom for personal gain.[24]

Between August 14 and 18, 1968, a shadowy group of armed black New Yorkers called the Fair Play Committee (FPC), organized by music industry gadfly Dino "Boom Boom" Woodward and songwriter-producer Johnnie Baylor, terrorized the NATRA convention. According to Shields, this "Black Mafia came through and beat up the members, threatened the members." Many of the white record and radio executives present were forced to leave in the face of occasional physical attacks and ceaseless verbal abuse. Atlantic Records veteran producer and vice president Jerry Wexler was hanged in effigy. Neither NATRA's own leadership nor the black record executives attending the convention were spared. There were rumors that the FPC had made liberal use of baseball bats while demanding job opportunities and what amounted to protection money from former SCLC worker, deejay, and Stax Records vice president Al Bell. It was probably no coincidence that both Woodward and Baylor joined the Stax payroll shortly afterwards. Some believed the FPC had actually kidnapped Del Shields. This was not far from the truth. "They ran me back to New York," he recalled. "I was told to get out of there." Safely back in New York, on August 18 a scared and desperate Shields, who had been reported missing by his own wife, contacted the FBI—hardly the most obvious ally for an African American activist in the late 1960s. Shields explained that he had deliberately "dropped out of sight" to escape harassment by members of the FPC who "effectively took control of NATRA."[25]

Even before Shields called, the FBI had been interested in NATRA and the Miami convention. In part this was a function of the Bureau's hostile surveillance of all black organizations. More specifically, however, it reflected the FBI's knowledge of links between FPC members and various racketeering and prostitution operations. Believing that this group had furnished prostitutes for the

1967 NATRA convention in Atlanta, the Bureau was keen to monitor any similar services to delegates in Miami. The nature and intensity of FBI interest had changed, however, when a shaken Nick Johnson called from Miami. The FCC commissioner explained that FPC members had just threatened him, and that word at the convention was that there were further plans "to cause disruption and demonstrations." A subsequent Bureau investigation revealed the full extent of the violence and intimidation that permeated the convention—as well as confirming a brisk trade in FPC-sponsored prostitutes at the Sheraton Four Ambassadors hotel where it took place. One anonymous representative of the deejays at the premier local black-oriented radio station, WMBM-Miami, told the FBI that the FPC "was using threats of bodily harm if the disk jockeys did not play records recommended by this organization." The informant repeated rumors that Del Shields had been given thirty days to quit NATRA or be killed and explained that most African American deejays believed that the FPC "was trying to take over the country and their aims were masked by claims they were improving Negro opportunity."[26]

Beyond Miami, the FPC attempted to intimidate a number of southern stations. In Birmingham, where "Tall Paul" White was a NATRA stalwart, WENN received a visit from the FPC, demanding protection money and control over what records were played at the station. Manager Joe Lackey immediately contacted the FBI and local police. Although the Bureau did not seem overly interested at the time, Sheriff Mel Bailey apparently located the radicals, riddled the building where they were staying with warning gunfire, and sent them on their way. Tensions at WENN remained high, however, exacerbated by the inescapable fact that whites continued to own and manage the black-oriented facility. Black deejays and white executives at the station often found themselves labeled Uncle Toms and racist exploiters respectively. As the climate worsened, Rev. Erskine Faush even took to coming to work with a pistol. Whereas in 1963 many of WENN's staff had bravely supported the movement, believing that they did so in the service of a great and noble cause, by the early 1970s they were arming themselves against renegade elements within the black community whose radical posturing sometimes hid more cynical profiteering.[27]

Homer Banks, a black Stax songwriter, felt that the violence at Miami and the campaign of extortion that dogged the black-oriented radio and recording industry for a couple of years afterwards were inevitable. After all, he explained, whites had been exploiting black talent and culture for hundreds of years. "It was destined to come, if not at Miami then somewhere else. . . . Blacks made the music, Blacks made the audience, but the ownership was white." This situation was precisely what the New Breed in NATRA had been trying to address. Before he was hounded out of town, Del Shields's own address to the Miami convention had complained that within the recording and radio industries "[t]he black man sings, records, arranges, produces, sells and exposes the records. However . . . he does not enjoy positions and responsibility in management where decisions are made." Few denied that this was the crux of the matter; fewer still believed that the FPC had made the task of improving black ownership levels, executive opportunities, or pay and conditions any easier.[28]

This was an era when white-media and popular paranoia about expressions of black power militancy—especially ones with a hint of real, as well as rhetorical, violence—was reaching fever pitch. It was also a time when widespread white resistance to further legislative or programmatic action in support of African American interests was gathering strength. In this context, the FPC's heavy-handed tactics made it easy for many white executives to dismiss legitimate black complaints as part of an irresponsible campaign to line a few black pockets and exact overdue retribution on all whites involved in black-oriented radio, irrespective of their racial attitudes or attentiveness to black community needs. Psychologically, some African Americans were thrilled to see someone finally "stick it to the Man." Yet nobody, except some FPC members, derived any financial reward from these efforts, and the basic structure of power and opportunity in the industry remained unaltered. Equally damaging, NATRA as a whole was declared guilty by association with the FPC and suffered a critical loss of credibility among blacks and whites in the media and entertainment industries. When Shields had to spend $10,000 of the Association's scarce funds on security for the 1969 convention in Washington, D.C., the organization was clearly in trouble. That same year, many of the New Breed executives abandoned NATRA, which fell under the sway of a more moderate, largely southern faction led by Alvin Dixon.[29]

It is important to emphasize that what happened to NATRA during 1969 represented less the triumph of a new, neoaccommodationist faction over the radicals than a reminder of where the real center of ideological gravity among black deejays had always been. Even at the height of NATRA's real and imagined militancy, southern deejays had comprised an identifiable, if not uniformly, conservative cohort. As tempers flared and fists flew at Miami in 1968, this group had denounced NATRA's executive for spending too much time spouting black power platitudes and invoking fanciful images of an imminent black takeover of the black-oriented media and culture industries. Many southern deejays wanted NATRA to concentrate less on revolutionary posturing and more on expanding black employment opportunities and improving pay and conditions for those already in the broadcasting industry. Some NATRA radicals, including Shields, felt that these deejays were being shortsighted and self-serving. They were failing to grasp, let alone support, the need to challenge the racist structures that underpinned the industry and doomed African Americans to low wages and limited opportunities. By settling for a few more dollars per shift, these deejays were helping to sustain an exploitative industry that ultimately preserved white power and perpetuated black marginality. Nevertheless, most NATRA deejays were willing to try to reconcile their desire for increased black ownership and executive power in the industry with their battle for better wages and conditions irrespective of who paid their salaries.

With the departure of the New Breed, NATRA focused more on problems at specific stations than on the underlying inequities of the entire industry. The goal, as Charlotte deejay "Chattie Hattie" Leeper remembered, was now "to address problems that you have at your station, to address problems going on in your community, and to try to come up with some problem-solving tactics." NATRA, she noted, also revived its original social function, offering an opportunity to "really congregate for a cultural good time. . . . Our ultimate goal was to try to stay focused and try to keep the brothers together in one accord." Thanks in part to the pernicious influence of the FPC, NATRA had managed to foster precious little of this unity between 1967 and 1969. With healing to be done, friendships to be mended, business relationships to be revived, and ideological and tactical differences to be reconciled, it is easy to see why a program stressing black unity, common experiences, and general bonhomie seemed appropriate. Meanwhile, fundamental racial inequities within the industry remained, and by the early 1970s NATRA's president Alvin Dixon was complaining that the organization had once more become "nothing more than a social fraternity." Disillusioned, in 1972 Dixon resigned from NATRA to set up a southern-based alternative called Broadcast and Music Arts, once more dedicated to expanding black economic opportunities within the radio industry. Although esteemed veteran deejay Jack Gibson took over the reins for a while, within a few years NATRA itself was little more than a contentious and contested memory.[30]

A Variegated Crop: Grassroots Southern Media Campaigns

By the mid-1970s the torch of organized black protest within the radio industry had passed from NATRA to a variety of specialist agencies like the Minority and Special Services Division of the NAB and new independent organizations like the Young Black Programmers Coalition, the National Association of Black-Owned Broadcasters, and the Black Music Association. Arguably the most tenacious and effective of these new groups was Pluria Marshall's NBMC, which emerged from Texas to play a conspicuous role in regional and national campaigns for more responsive and responsible black-oriented broadcasting. The history of the NBMC illustrates how the three basic types of group working for more black power in southern radio could interact, sharing ideas, tactics, and memberships.

The roots of the NBMC lay in Pluria Marshall's experiences organizing a local strike for better wages at KYOK-Houston, where he worked as a deejay. Already a veteran of the SCLC's Operation Breadbasket, NATRA, and the Houston-based Black Broadcasters' Coalition, Marshall created the Black Citizens for Media Access in 1971 specifically to challenge the license renewal applications of black-oriented KYOK and KCOH. In a classic example of what was known as the Texarkana Agreement model of black media lobbying and negotiation, Marshall's group agreed to withdraw its complaints to the FCC after the owners of both outlets signed agreements to hire more African Americans, especially in managerial positions. This tactic was named after a 1969 campaign against the license renewal application of television station KTAL-Texarkana, wherein the NAACP and the UCC had agreed to withdraw their objections in return for iron-clad agreements to increase the amount and quality of black-oriented programming and minority employment opportunities at the station. Following his successes in Houston, Marshall was encouraged by William Wright, the founder of BEST, to think about campaigning more broadly, particularly after 1973 when illness forced Wright to curtail his own work. In August 1975 more than one hundred delegates from twenty-two media organizations attended the first formal meeting of the NBMC at the Howard University Law School. Two months later the NBMC was coordinating the work of seventy-one separate local groups intent on improving black representation by and in the media.[31]

Like many of his contemporaries, Pluria Marshall was eager to encourage grassroots activism against racial injustice. Yet he was also adamant that federal authorities needed to play a more positive role in making racial justice and equality of opportunity a lived reality, rather than merely a legislative promise or an elusive dream. By the mid-1970s this was becoming an increasingly unlikely proposition. In a period characterized by "benign neglect" and a partial retreat from progressive federal action in the racial arena, the FCC reversed its ten-year trend toward ever more stringent monitoring of fair employment practices. Over Ben Hooks's objections, in the summer of 1975 the FCC decided to exempt any station with fewer than fifteen full-time staff from the requirement to report on its hiring record and procedures. As the UCC's office of communications pointed out in condemning this decision as "racist and sexist," it effectively removed the hiring practices of 78 percent of American media outlets from regular scrutiny.[32]

Despite such signs of conservative retrenchment, the NBMC had little option but to try to persuade the FCC to address racial discrimination in the media, which it duly did through a spirited campaign of legal petition and propaganda. As long as Ben Hooks was on the Commission, the group had its moments of success. In one typical campaign in Columbia, South Carolina, the organization's local affiliate orchestrated a joint petition from the NAACP, the United Citizens Party, and the South Carolina Community Relations Program urging the FCC to deny a renewal of the licenses of WNOK-AM, -FM and -TV because they had refused to "cease and desist their unfair labor practices."[33]

The kind of class-action suits and petitions favored by the NBMC and exemplified in Columbia and the BCC campaign in Richmond became a common means for local black communities to challenge systemic prejudice and bias in the content and organization of southern radio. This trend was also apparent in Mississippi, where years of dissatisfaction culminated in a 1976 class-action suit against sixty-one radio stations and six television facilities. Organized by Alvin Chambliss's Southern Media Coalition, the petitioners identified four specific cases of impropriety and racial discrimination within the state's media that it wanted the FCC to remedy. First, Jessie R. Williams's three radio stations—WCSA, WKPO, and WJRL—were cited for "racial discrimination and exclusion" in their hiring practices, and for "news suppression, distortion, and news slanting in violation of the Commission's rules." Second, WXXX in Hattiesburg was condemned for having no black employees. The station refuted this accusation, claiming it had employed a black female student in the summer of 1975 and replaced her in early 1976 with Mountie Blackman, an African American woman who was designated public affairs director and entrusted with "putting together a thirty minute public affairs program once a week." Third was an indictment of the unhealthy and possibly illegal concentration of media control in the state. The most conspicuous offenders here were E. O. Roden, who owned WJMI and WOKJ in Jackson, WBIP-Brownsville, and WTUP-Tupelo, and Birney Imes, who supplemented his Columbus newspaper and television holdings with radio stations WELO-Tupelo, WCBI-Columbus, WROX-Clarksdale, WGCM-Gulfport, WNAG-Grenada, and WONA-Winona. "The owners of these stations," the suit claimed, "have shown that the public interest is secondary to monopolistic domination in North-eastern Mississippi." The final and broadest aspect of the suit focused on discrimination in hiring and promotion throughout the state's media. Despite FCC calls for improvements following a 1973 inquiry, three years later the petitioners still found "the top job categories . . . devoid of any real Black presence."[34]

If the substance of these complaints was typical, so was the fact that the suit brought together an extraordinary cross-section of the state's more racially progressive organizations. Indeed, in the midst of the earnest and sometimes rancorous debates over tactics, goals, and priorities that punctuated this phase of the freedom struggle, campaigns for greater black power in the media were occasions where a wide spectrum of black—and some white—activists could still cooperate. Under Al Chambliss's prompting, veteran civil rights groups like the Mississippi Council on Human Relations, the Delta Ministry, and the state branch of the NAACP collaborated with new grassroots media organizations like the Concerned Citizens for Fair Media based in Columbus, the Greenwood Communications Committee, the North Mississippi Coalition for Better Broadcasting, and the Jackson-based Community Coalition for Better Broadcasting. The shared agenda of this coalition was summarized by one of its constituent parts, the Concerned Citizens for Better Communications, which described its goal as "greater involvement for Black citizens in all phases of broadcasting. This includes actively seeking means for improving training, hiring and promotion of Blacks in the media." The organization was also "concerned with the inclusion of Black perspectives in all news, public affairs, sports and other programming."[35]

African American activists dominated most of the campaigns for black power in southern radio. There were, however, some lingering, often ambiguous, but occasionally highly effective examples of interracial cooperation, even at a time when nationalist and separatist strains in black political thought were capturing most of the headlines. This was certainly true of the BCC in Richmond and in the lengthy Mississippi campaign. Similarly, in D.C. in 1966, the biracial Washington Community Broadcast Company (WCBC) had challenged the license renewal application of WOOK, one of the nation's oldest black-oriented stations. Led by former juvenile court judge Marjorie Lawson and with support from celebrated journalist Drew Pearson, local NUL executives William Thompson and Sterling Tucker, and Washington NAACP president Carl Moultrie, the WCBC raised $1.6 million and tried to convince the FCC that it should be allowed to take over WOOK. Owned since 1947 by Richard Eaton, WOOK had once enjoyed a reputation for providing not only fabulous music but also an important forum for black community leaders from nearby Howard University and the local NUL and NAACP chapters. As late as 1965, Carl Moultrie had commended the station for supporting a recent membership drive: "As a result of this special service the NAACP reached more homes and . . . raised by telephone calls and persons coming to the station to turn in memberships, thousands of dollars." Less than a year later, Moultrie was among the WCBC members accusing WOOK of missing "a great opportunity to contribute to the education, the culture, and the aspirations of the community," and instead foisting upon the black community programming that was "far beneath their dignity and educational standards." In 1966 the FCC found nothing wrong with the quality of the service to the black community provided by WOOK. Three years later, however, the station did fall foul of the Commission. In 1969 the WCBC revived its complaints, this time concentrating on financial malpractices and the rumor that some of WOOK's preachers were giving out lottery information and gambling tips disguised as Bible citations. After a lengthy investigation the FCC revoked WOOK's license in 1975, and an appeal by Eaton was finally rejected three years later.[36]

In the summer of 1967, SNCC's Lester McKinnie and H. Rap Brown had initiated similar protests against one of WOOK's great D.C. rivals, the Son-derling-owned WOL. The two men wrote to general manager John Pace com-plaining that "no black person is represented in the hierarchy of your organiza-tion." Adopting the blunderbuss approach that sometimes overwhelmed more carefully calibrated critiques of racism and injustice within the radio industry, McKinnie and Brown told WOL: "your motives are unpatriotic and not good for the good of the DC community. This, of course, has been manifested by your inability to act in a positive fashion by placing black people in positions to control the destiny of their people." A SNCC investigation revealed that there were only eight black employees among twenty-five WOL staff. Five were deejays. None were executives. The probe concluded: "Major money is being pulled from the black community via WOL by black DJs to be used by the white power structure of WOL and the white power structure of business and advertisement for clear green power for itself and nothing for the people whom they get the money from."[37]

With such a catalogue of complaints, SNCC presumed that WOL was ripe for a concerted campaign by black Washingtonians. Revealingly, however, its plans were stymied by the fact that the mass of African American listeners actually liked WOL's soul format (65 percent of DC's black listeners tuned to WOL every day), revered such deejays as Bob "Nighthawk" Terry, and thought that the sta-tion was generally doing a fine job of providing community news, public affairs shows, discussion forums, and public service announcements. *Washington Post* reporter Carl Bernstein believed that "WOL is probably responsible for more 'black consciousness' among Washington's Negroes than Walter Fauntroy, the *Washington Afro-American,* the Free D.C. Movement, Washington SNCC, Julius Hobson and the Le Droit Ramblers all rolled into one. The station represents not the more incendiary aspects of Black Power but rather its theoretical basis, of being Black, the idea of a united Negro community, prideful and fed up with a system Negroes believe perpetuates submission." Indeed, even in the midst of the abuse SNCC hurled at the station, Lester McKinnie gladly arranged WOL airtime for executive secretary James Forman on David Eaton's popular *Speak Up* show, knowing that it offered invaluable access to the black community.[38]

The main problem here was that the principal concerns of most African American listeners and the priorities of those who desperately sought black own-ership of radio stations such as WOL simply did not coincide. It was not as if black southerners were indifferent to the prospects of securing more African American representation and power within the radio industry. It was just that the question of who owned a black-oriented radio station mattered less to most black listeners than the quality of the entertainment and public services the sta-tion provided and the respect it showed their community. Moreover, some African Americans had heard enough of black-owned, black-oriented radio in the South to realize that there really was not much to choose between it and white-owned, black-oriented radio in terms of obedience to commercial imperatives and a generally conservative attitude toward racial politics on air. Indeed, in Atlanta the white-owned WAOK had consistently aired better entertainment and been more politically engaged than WERD, its longtime black-owned rival. Popular recognition of this record meant that, just as SNCC failed to rouse the black masses against WOL, so a similar campaign against WAOK disintegrated in the face of a gracious appreciation of what the station had tried to do for Atlanta's black community.

During the late 1960s WAOK continued to be the most popular black-oriented facility in Atlanta. Nevertheless, the zealously integrationist Zenas Sears had struggled to come to terms with the increased militancy, bolder rhetoric, and more nationalistic ideologies of the black power era. In 1967 the relationship between WAOK and some black activists became severely strained when Sears appointed Jay Dunn as WAOK's new production manager. Dunn was white. Incensed, both the SCLC and SNCC immediately denounced not only the appointment but Sears's whole attitude toward the black listeners who patronized his station. The SCLC's Hosea Williams condemned the lack of black management at WAOK and vilified Sears as "a perfect example of the 'white Jesus' who still believes in the worn-out and false fairy tale that Negroes won't follow Negroes—that white is right and black must and will get back." Williams's criticisms were less true of Sears than of many southern white liberals who continued to think they knew what was best for African Americans, but his comments were symptomatic of a volatile period in the freedom struggle when temperate voices were hard to find. Stokely Carmichael and the man destined to succeed him as SNCC chairman, H. Rap Brown, echoed Williams's sentiments in a series of letters to Sears, who somewhat disarmed his critics by inviting them to meet with him to discuss their grievances. On May 12 Sears announced that an agreement had been reached about music selection policy. However, it was apparent that, beyond recruitment and programming issues, what really vexed SNCC was the fact that WAOK was white-owned.[39]

On May 24, 1967, SNCC organized a picket of the station to protest what it saw as "a clear example of whites controlling the orientation of news and radio programs supposedly geared to the black community." SNCC assured Sears and his partner Stan Raymond that they "have seriously under-estimated the mood of the black community, which now demands that black people control their communities and all enterprises which benefit from and make profit off of our people."[40] Despite this stirring rhetoric, it turned out that about a dozen or so of Atlanta's black community were actually so incensed by this particular example of racial exploitation that they could be bothered to join the formal protests.

SNCC's drive for black economic as well as political and psychological empowerment was surely a sound one. Yet in the tempestuous atmosphere of the late 1960s, as righteous black indignation at continued racial injustice was swelled by growing racial pride, the black power movement frequently failed to sort the wheat of cautious white racial liberalism from the chaff of intractable white racism. This failure was common among the black power leadership, not merely those who set their sights on the radio industry and were dissatisfied by anything less than the installation of black owners at black-owned stations. It is not hard to see why this fiercely nationalistic agenda had emerged. Chastened by the obvious limitations of white racial liberalism and alarmed by the popularity of the racially charged conservatism of George Wallace and Richard Nixon, many black power ideologues and activists had simply written off the possibility of meaningful support from or cooperation with white Americans.

If this retreat into a parochial style of black nationalism was understandable—and in some regards enormously psychologically and culturally empowering—it was also politically naive and ultimately counterproductive. First, it excluded or marginalized virtually all white radicals who supported the struggle for racial justice. Second, it alienated those white racial moderates who, even if endlessly frustrating and equivocating when it came to wholesale assaults on systemic and institutionalized racism, were still potential allies in the quest for black rights and equal opportunities. These whites needed working on and with, not abandoning to the none-too-tender mercies of insurgent racial conservatives. Third, and arguably most damaging, it exacerbated tensions within the freedom struggle itself by encouraging a debilitating blacker-than-thou racial purism. This in turn aggravated tensions between hard-line black nationalists and those, like Martin Luther King, Bayard Rustin, and Jesse Jackson, whose racial pride was unimpeachable but who continued to insist that the pursuit of genuine freedom and justice in America required a ceaseless, often dispiriting, but unavoidable struggle to create progressive interracial alliances.

In the world of black-oriented radio, the logic of black nationalist dogma dictated that any white radio station owner was unacceptable, while any black owner was automatically a good thing—although some radicals did hold that capitalists of any color were equally complicit in the perpetuation of economic exploitation and social injustice. The African American masses seldom saw things so simplistically. Events surrounding WAOK indicated that black southerners, long the victims of crude stereotyping themselves, were often reluctant to tar all southern whites with the same racist brush. Many still nursed a tattered vision of the "beloved community" that had underwritten the early civil rights movement. For a while they appeared much more willing than the black power militants, many of whom had roots outside the region, to give post–Jim Crow white southerners the benefit of the doubt and see exactly how African American fortunes might pan out in a new world with the vote and without formal segregation. All of which is to suggest that in Atlanta, as with the attacks on WVOL in Nashville and on WOL in D.C., SNCC's scattershot had winged the wrong, or at least a deeply ambiguous, target. WAOK was a white-owned, black-oriented radio station that, for all its shortcomings and culpable insensitivity in failing to recruit black executives, had earned the loyalty, respect, and admiration of many in the local black community. In this context, SNCC's 1967 complaints seemed shrill and vindictive and won little African American support.

Rather more successful was a campaign organized three years later by the Community Coalition on Broadcasting (CCB) in Atlanta. The CCB leveled accusations of "gross discrimination" in hiring practices at WAOK and the rest of the city's broadcasters, including WERD, which Jesse Blayton had recently sold to white owners. Both stations immediately appointed African Americans to their boards of directors, while WERD declared that "in deciding what constitutes the tastes, needs, desires and interests of the black community, the views, opinion and leaders which are representative of its members and the authenticity of portrayals of black life, culture and values, the best judge is the black community itself." Whereas in 1967 SNCC had demanded nothing less than the transfer of WAOK's license to black owners, in 1970 the CCB saw little point in such doctrinal absolutism. Like other black media activists, the CCB was adjusting to the realities of the new South—and of American political and economic life more generally—where compromise was a necessary skill and unequivocal and permanent victories were rare. Even though whites retained ownership of WAOK and WERD, the CCB followed the Texarkana Agreement model and withdrew its complaints once core demands for greater communal input into programming choices and more black job opportunities had been met.[41]

The Paradoxes of Black Ownership: A. G. Gaston and WENN-Birmingham

Much of the impetus for the campaign for black power in southern radio came from the understanding that black owners would automatically be more responsive than their white counterparts to black needs, interests, and values. Events in Birmingham in the mid-1970s, however, demonstrated that not all black station owners were especially sensitive to the concerns and beliefs of their primary audiences, while also demonstrating that black business practices were often as ruthless as white ones.

Black radio ownership finally came to Birmingham in 1975, when millionaire A. G. Gaston acquired the license to WENN. Gaston's purchase was initially greeted enthusiastically by the local community and station staff, not least because it brought to an end an extended period of uncertainty at WENN following the death of longtime owner John McLendon in early 1971. Under the provisions

of McLendon's will, all the broadcasting properties owned by his Jomac Corporation were to be sold off as quickly as possible. Accordingly, in May 1971 WENN's
AM and FM outlets were sold for a little over $804,000 to the Hertz Broadcast-
ing Corporation, an Atlanta-based company headed by Louis O. Hertz that already owned two Georgia stations, including WERD. Manager Joe Lackey assured listeners, sponsors, and staff that there would be no format, operational,
or personnel changes at the station because of the new ownership.[42]

The sequence of events between Hertz's purchase of WENN and Gaston's
acquisition of the station four years later was complex and not a little bizarre. Yet
they are worth recounting in detail, since they reveal much about the seamier
side of the competition among black-oriented broadcasters in Birmingham,
about racial attitudes within the city and its broadcasting community, and about
Gaston's own agenda in buying WENN. Shortly after the Hertz Corporation's
takeover, Rev. Robert McKinney, a black Birmingham preacher and sometime
civil rights activist who led the Alabama Economic Action Committee, accused
the station of refusing to sell him advertising spots to publicize his forthcoming
gospel show, "The World of Gospel." McKinney further alleged that WENN's
staff had a policy of refusing to play records by any artists visiting the city unless
the station had a financial stake in promoting their performances. Both accusations constituted possible breaches of FCC regulations and the 1934 Communications Act's provisions concerning discriminatory and unfair commercial practices. In 1973 the FCC initiated an investigation that dragged on for over two
years.[43]

Ironically, in the interim McKinney had withdrawn his original accusations
against WENN. In 1972 he revealed that he had filed his complaints only at the
behest of officials at WJLD, which alongside the newcomer WBUL was WENN's
major rival. According to McKinney, WJLD staff not only had misled him about
the activities of WENN's personnel but had also offered him free advertising for
his shows in return for his cooperation. At WJLD, owner George Johnston Jr.
even admitted that he helped McKinney draft the initial complaint, somewhat
implausibly claiming that he did this as a personal favor, not because it offered
the chance to undermine a powerful competitor. This was pretty damaging evidence, especially as WJLD was already under FCC scrutiny for allowing the
number of women and African Americans it employed to decline between 1971
and 1972. This possible infringement of equal employment opportunity legislation had prompted the FCC to defer the renewal of WJLD's license pending
further investigation. It seems clear that the station had seen the death of
McLendon and the change of ownership at WENN as an opportunity to reclaim
a preeminence in the black market that it had last enjoyed nearly a dozen years
earlier. McKinney—who, in another twist to the tale, actually fled Birmingham
following a conviction for check forgery around the time the FCC hearings

started—seems to have been little more than a gullible and greedy stooge in WJLD's power play. Nevertheless, by bringing both WENN and WJLD under the scrutiny of the FCC, he had opened up the proverbial can of worms and helped to change the history of black-oriented radio in Birmingham.[44]

At the conclusion of its lengthy investigations, the FCC dismissed McKinney's claims that George Johnston had bribed him with free advertising to bring his initial charges against WENN. WJLD's accountant Ann Farley was able to prove that the station had not provided any free advertising spots to McKinney; rather, those spots were paid for—no less mysteriously, perhaps—by the Lawrence Furniture Company. Judge James F. Tierney did find that the Johnston Broadcasting Corporation had violated various laws governing the broadcast of lottery information and had failed to identify the sponsors of record album promotions on the air, thereby raising the specter of payola. The Johnston Corporation was fined $1,000, but its license was renewed.[45]

The FCC also dismissed the claims of discrimination that McKinney had originally leveled against WENN. Far from snubbing the entrepreneurial reverend's "World of Gospel" show, the station had actually broadcast 187 advertisements for it. Despite exoneration on this charge, however, the FCC's investigations ultimately took a far greater toll at WENN than at WJLD. The Commission had unearthed preliminary evidence of serious conflicts of interest between some employees' personal business enterprises and the station's public service commitments. There were also signs of fabricated audience ratings, inflated to enable the station to charge more for its advertising spots. With the loss of his license a real possibility and criminal charges looming, owner Louis Hertz wound up in psychotherapy in Atlanta. His peace and stability of mind were not helped by the fact that he was also mired in serious financial difficulties. Hertz had defaulted on payments of some $700,000 relating to the purchase of the station's broadcasting equipment and the rental of the WENN building at 1428 Fifth Avenue North. On March 1, 1974, the First National Bank of Jackson, Mississippi, acting as trustee for the now defunct Jomac Corporation, filed a request that Hertz Broadcasting be placed in receivership. Four weeks later U.S. District Court Judge James H. Hancock ordered WENN to hand over all its assets to an official receiver, Frank S. Blackford, who was instructed to keep the radio station's AM and FM outlets operating until the FCC could decide whether and under what conditions to renew its license. In the meantime, Louis Hertz was enjoined from any further involvement in the station's affairs.[46]

For most of 1974 and early 1975, uncertainty reigned at WENN. Frank Blackford continued to petition the FCC on Hertz's behalf to renew the station's license. Joe Lackey, meanwhile, began to seek the financial backing that would enable him and other members of the station's staff to buy the facility themselves. After the collapse of a promising deal with John Jefferson III, a prominent white businessman whose family controlled the Birmingham Realty Corporation that owned WENN's rented studios, Lackey approached A. G. Gaston. Initially Lackey was simply looking for a $1.1 million loan, with repayments spread over fifteen years, in order to purchase the station. But during several meetings with Gaston and his chief advisors, Louis J. Willie and Kirkwood Balton, the black millionaire steadily increased his conditions for providing the money. First he asked a 10 percent "finder's fee" for his assistance. Lackey thought this reasonable and agreed to add the money to the total loan. Then Gaston demanded to be an equal partner in the station, holding a 25 percent share along with Lackey, Shelley Stewart, and Erskine Faush. Next, after Lackey had already drawn up the necessary paperwork for the four-way split, Gaston decided that he would furnish the money only if he could become a majority shareholder with a 51 percent stake in the station. Finally, with Lackey and his colleagues still pondering what to do, it was announced that the Booker T. Washington Broadcast Service Inc., owned principally by Gaston and Louis J. Willie, intended to buy the facility outright with a cash payment of $650,000.[47]

Lackey was surprised at this development and more than a little disappointed. Yet his principal concern had always been to ensure the welfare of the staff and the future of the station. Gaston's buyout appeared to guarantee both, and over the next few months Lackey dedicated himself to working out the technical details for the purchase. He liaised between the receiver Frank Blackford, lawyers for the McLendon estate, and representatives of the First National Bank. He also prepared the formal submission to the FCC for a change of ownership. By the middle of December 1975, the FCC had approved the sale and renewed the licenses for both WENN's AM and FM outlets. Two months later Gaston officially assumed control. Black power in the form of black ownership had finally arrived in Birmingham's broadcasting industry. Gaston spoke enthusiastically of how his station would fulfill a real black need in the city. The local media, he insisted, "have been missing a comprehensive look at the real happenings in the black community. The story of progress being made by blacks is a positive one, and not just a continual negative which seems to emanate from much of the media today."[48]

This was precisely what the advocates of a greater black proprietorial and executive presence in southern radio expected to hear from black owners. Stations like WENN would remain important showcases for African American culture but would also display much greater attentiveness to black social, economic, and political needs; they would make a firmer commitment to accurate news reporting and practical efforts to improve black lives. From the midst of chaos and confusion, a new beacon of black hope and opportunity had emerged. A week later, figures from the Audience Research Bureau confirmed WENN's status as the most listened-to station, black-oriented or general-market, in the

FIGURE 18. A hero of WENN's involvement in the 1963 Birmingham civil rights campaign, Tall Paul White counted station manager Joe Lackey among his closest friends and helped to orchestrate the protests against Lackey's dismissal by A. G. Gaston in early 1976. Courtesy of James Peeler.

metropolitan Birmingham area. It claimed more than three times the listeners of its nearest black-oriented rivals.[49]

But then, in what was just about his first official act as the station's owner, Gaston fired Joe Lackey. According to Lackey, the sealed letter Gaston placed in his hand offered no explanation as to why his services were no longer required. It gave no notice and offered no compensation. In that instant the optimism, the racial and moral certainties surrounding the takeover, became clouded. The black deejays at WENN, and soon the black citizens of Birmingham, a community that had seen and suffered so much in the course of a heroic movement for justice and equality, were forced to consider once more the meaning of that struggle and the freedoms for which they had fought. For Joe Lackey, too, the episode raised fundamental questions about the precise nature and extent of changes in racial relations and attitudes within Birmingham.[50]

At 7:32 a.m. on Friday, February 13, 1976, the day following confirmation of Lackey's dismissal, the predominantly black employees at WENN walked off their jobs in protest. Tall Paul White announced the strike on air in a brief but moving statement. An enigmatic, somewhat aloof, but deeply principled man, White had come to count Lackey as perhaps his closest friend and was outraged by Gaston's decision. He bluntly accused the new black owners of racial discrimination and a "gross miscarriage of justice." Speaking on behalf of his fellow deejays, White quietly stated, "We do not raise our voices in protest, rather we silence our voices. There will be no further broadcasting activity by any member of the regular announcing staff of WENN Radio." Shelley Stewart had rejoined WENN from WJLD in 1970 following stints working at KATZ–St. Louis, WAOK-Atlanta, and on the road with soul singer Otis Redding. Stewart explained that after all they had gone through, the WENN deejays simply "would not take an injustice given by a black man, which was A. G. Gaston, against a white man."[51]

Gaston and Willie expressed surprise at their staff's response to Lackey's departure. "We told the employees that the new owner wanted a new head coach and thought we had the right to hire someone else," Willie explained. Gaston claimed that he had actually given Lackey thirty days following the official takeover of the station on February 5 in which to let the new owners know if he wished to stay on. Having not heard from the station manager, Gaston said that he felt perfectly free to hire a replacement, a black station manager named Larry Hayes. Gaston failed to explain to incredulous WENN staffers the arithmetic by which he calculated that February 12 fell thirty days after February 5. It is possible that Gaston's notorious impatience and obstinacy may have been accentuated at this time because he was recovering from injuries sustained during a botched burglary at his home in late January, when he and his wife were assaulted and briefly abducted by a black intruder. Some even speculated that this incident might have been connected in some way to Gaston's impending takeover at WENN, although no evidence of such a link emerged at the trial of his assailant, Charles Lewis Clayborn. Whatever the reason, Gaston categorically refused to discuss Lackey's dismissal with the station staff, as "it might get into a confrontation." Those who had walked out were simply told to consider themselves fired.[52]

As WENN continued to broadcast with a scratch staff, Lackey's supporters organized pickets, not just at the station, but also at many of Gaston's other businesses, including the Citizens Federal Savings & Loan Association, various funeral parlors and cemeteries, drugstores, real estate companies, and the Gaston Motel. On February 18 Erskine Faush led the first of several church rallies in support of Lackey at the Metropolitan AME Zion Church. During the meeting it was announced that the SCLC wished to get involved in the protests on Lackey's behalf—indicating that the organization had moved beyond the rather unconvincing black-power posturing represented by Hosea Williams's attack on Zenas Sears and WAOK nine years earlier. With the conspicuous exception of Emory Jackson's perennially conservative *Birmingham World*, which steadfastly refused to report on the firing of Lackey or the ensuing black protests against Gaston, the press in the city was quick to draw comparisons with the great civil rights mobilizations of 1963. Faush reminded black Birmingham of how, under Lackey's benevolent management, WENN had been "the only radio station in the city that would run announcements of meetings of the protesters." Lackey, Faush said, had "looked beyond this thing called color" and helped to make WENN a "friend to the black community of Birmingham."[53]

Johnny Streeter, another WENN deejay and sometime print journalist, picked up this theme in a series of editorials for the *Birmingham Times*. Streeter reminded readers: "Back during the height of the Civil Rights struggle in 1963 when a white man without a badge, gun and a dog wouldn't dare set foot in an area where bombs were blasting, bricks and bottles were thrown and race relations were at an all-time low, Lackey did. It was through his concern and kindness that many of the black grievances were aired by WENN announcers and were made available to the black community." In another piece, however, Streeter began to unravel the intricacies of the protest, emphasizing that the deejays' support for Lackey was part of a broader concern to protect their own jobs. Gaston's takeover had been accompanied by rumors of mass firings that "brought about a resolution among the employees that if any one person at WENN radio was fired without just cause, everybody else would protest the firing. That firing just happened to be Joe Lackey." Tall Paul White also stressed that "the Joe Lackey matter was not the only [grievance]" behind the decision to walk out. White claimed that the deejays had more than fifty-five other grievances, but the imperious Gaston had refused to hear any of them. Thus for Streeter, White, Faush—and, for that matter, Joe Lackey—the WENN protest ultimately rested less on a perceived racial injustice than on the shared economic interests of workers. A common concern for job security and the desire to resist unfair and arbitrary treatment by a new employer had rendered the race of the first victim of Gaston's caprice irrelevant.[54]

In any event, Lackey himself was deeply moved by the show of solidarity from his colleagues and the genuine outpouring of respect and support from the African American community—particularly given the militant temper of the times and what he recognized as legitimate black aspirations for more power within the industry. He was regularly welcomed into black churches and homes, often with his son, who was intensely proud of the way in which his father was hailed as a hero by the black community. Lackey's wife, however, had an entirely different take on her husband's special relationship with black Birmingham. "One day she just blurted it out," recalled Lackey. She started screaming, "I've never been so embarrassed in my life. It's getting to the point where you have to count on a bunch of niggers to save your job." Years later, Lackey still struggled to come to terms with this sudden revelation of his wife's dogged racism. "It killed me, man. Just killed me. I never knew that she even felt that way." Although Lackey liked to think that his son's attitude was more indicative of a younger generation of Birmingham whites, his wife's reaction served as a sobering reminder of the tenacity of racial prejudice in the city. It was the beginning of the end of Lackey's marriage, and he was divorced a few years later.[55]

WENN, meanwhile, limped rather than leapt forward. Gaston himself took a public mauling as a consequence of the WENN protests, with many questioning the extent of his commitment to the economic and political progress of the black masses, as opposed to the greater glory and wealth of A. G. Gaston. It was revealed that, while he advertised his businesses extensively with the white-owned *Birmingham News,* Gaston spent only $5 to $10 a week with the city's only locally owned black paper, the *Birmingham Times.* In a stinging attack in that paper, W. J. Boyd accused "Mr. Money" of exploiting the black community for years, not least by refusing to pay out full value on burial insurance policies if people declined to allow themselves or their loved ones to be interred in Gaston's own cemeteries. Refuting stories that Gaston buried the indigent for free, Boyd reminded blacks in Birmingham that they "often heard the DJs from both WENN and WJLD soliciting funds from the radio audiences to get enough money to bury people he had at his funeral home." Boyd also condemned Gaston for charging black churches extortionate interest rates on loans and for directing his realty company to build only private housing, rather than low-rent accommodation for the poor.[56]

As for his radio station, under a black management team headed by Kirkwood Balton, the black-owned WENN championed disco and adopted an "urban contemporary" format in an effort to attract a general-market audience. In the process, it compromised something of its special relationship with the black community. Soon it began to lose much of its audience to the veteran WJLD, revitalized by a change of ownership in 1982 when the Johnston family finally sold up to Bob Bell.[57]

By that time Lackey and his WENN crew had also found a new home. During the standoff with Gaston in the early spring of 1976, Lackey's old broadcasting friend Stu Hepburn suggested a possible solution. Hepburn's Crescendo Broadcasting owned a prosperous pop station in Fort Worth called KLOX and a decidedly less successful one in Birmingham called WATV. Hepburn suggested that Lackey simply take his loyal WENN team to WATV, which would overnight become a black-oriented station. Press advertisements urged listeners in quasi-biblical terms to "Come with us to a better place: WATV." On March 31 former WENN stalwarts Tall Paul White, Erskine Faush, Shelley Stewart, Maurice "Thin Man" King, Pat Williams, Johnny Streeter, and former Stax Records president Al Bell were among those who relaunched WATV as a black station. Lackey agreed to serve again as station manager, although he was not initially paid a salary. Indeed, money was very scarce, with little sponsorship and the financial drain of having to broadcast from an expensive suite of rented rooms in the Cabana

Motel. Within a month, however, WATV had found its own premises on Ensley Avenue. Shortly afterwards it boasted the leading share of the black Birmingham radio market, with an average of 12,200 people tuned to the station during every fifteen-minute period. A dozen years later Stewart and Faush bought out the station. Tall Paul White's health was not good throughout this period, and in the midst of various personal crises he drifted in and out of the scene before finally retiring in 1989. Joe Lackey continued to work part-time as an employee of his former staff, mostly attending to the accounts and sales books. He was originally also a part owner of WATV, secretly holding a share of slightly less than 10 percent. "The understanding we have is that this is a hundred-percent wholly black-owned radio station," he explained, slightly embarrassed at the commercially necessary subterfuge. If there was a certain irony that in the mid-1970s WATV proved more appealing to more African Americans in Birmingham than WENN, a station that really was "wholly black-owned," it nonetheless emphasizes one of the main points of this chapter. The relationships among the race of a black-oriented station's owners and managers, its programming style, and its popularity were often more complex than black media activists assumed.[58]

A Capital Ideal; A Shortage of Black Capital

During the late 1960s and early 1970s, the struggle for greater black economic and executive power within the radio industry and for better service to the African American community yielded a mixed crop of tangible achievements, in the South as in the nation as a whole. By the mid-1970s some 80 percent of all the petitions to deny license renewals received by the FCC came from black interest groups. Yet few of these challenges succeeded—only 16 of the 342 filed in 1971–73, for example. This was in part because the FCC, in order to avoid frivolous or malicious requests to deny licenses, set high standards of evidence. Furthermore, the Commission did not feel that the wholesale restructuring of a capitalist industry according to principles of racial justice was part of its brief.[59] Still, the very prospect of public challenges to license holders tended to make stations somewhat more responsive to the programming needs of their listeners and to federal equal employment provisions than in the past. The late 1960s and especially the early 1970s saw the emergence of a new generation of important black radio executives, many of whom were graduates of the School of Communications at Howard University and of that institution's innovative WHUR radio station.

The WHUR experiment started life in 1971 staffed mainly by African American students, with a very eclectic programming schedule reflected in its "360 Degrees: The Black Experience in Sound" slogan and a strong commitment to local community politics and welfare issues. The key figure in nurturing the socially engaged ethos at the fledgling station was manager Phil Watson, a veteran of Pacifica's KPFK outlet in Los Angeles and a fervent supporter of the freedom struggle even in some of its more militant black power manifestations. Watson's radicalism quickly brought him into conflict with Howard's ambitious and conservative president James Cheek. In 1973 Watson was fired and replaced by a succession of more commercially minded managers who gradually changed the sound and the social agenda of the station. With Cheek's encouragement, by mid-decade general manager Tom Jones and a dynamic young sales manager named Cathy Liggins had reoriented the station toward earning the biggest possible market share and generating the maximum advertising revenue. "We're going to try to be No. 1 in town," Jones explained in 1975. "We felt that if we provided a much less collegiate sound on the air we could attract more people who normally listen to commercial stations." This new orientation—"a small compromise to commercialism," Jones called it—was also reflected in employment practices at the station. Whereas it had once been both a training ground for students of broadcasting and a sounding board for college and community opinions, WHUR was now staffed and managed by career professionals whose presence was itself indicative of improved black opportunities in the industry. As the station's early emphasis on community affairs and public service programming receded, its playlists became increasingly predictable in an era of corporate soul and ever tighter black music formats. This black-owned, black-staffed, black-oriented station had become virtually indistinguishable from its white-owned, black-oriented neighbors.[60]

This kind of ambition and philosophy was typical of a new generation of black radio and recording executives who wanted to capitalize on the breakthroughs won by the civil rights and black power movements. Cathy Liggins, known as Cathy Hughes after her marriage, was one of the most impressive and influential figures to come through Howard and WHUR in its formative years. A middle-class native of Omaha, Nebraska, whose father was a certified accountant, Hughes had joined the nascent Howard School of Communications faculty in the early 1970s. After helping to pull in a million dollars in sales revenue and confirming the commercial potential of the station to President Cheek, she succeeded Tom Jones as WHUR's general manager in 1975. Five years later Hughes had raised sufficient funds to buy the old warhorse WOL, which she converted to an all-talk format and moved from its location in the predominantly white Georgetown section of town to the heart of black D.C. around H Street. By the mid-1990s she had created an investment firm called Syndicated Communication to facilitate the purchase of media outlets by African Americans and had expanded her own Radio One Inc. chain to include eight stations, among them WWIN and WERQ in Baltimore and WHTA-FM in Atlanta. By 2003 Radio One was the most successful black-owned chain in the nation, with sixty-six stations, more than two-thirds of them located in the South, valued at around $2 billion. Hughes's commitment to community service never entirely disappeared, yet her stations consistently cut back local news reporting operations in favor of music and talk shows. For example, in 1973 the three black-oriented stations in D.C.— WOL, WOOK, and WHUR—employed twenty-one reporters; thirty years later there were just four reporters shared by two black-oriented stations in the city, and not a single news reporter worked for any of Radio One's four Washington stations. The downgrading of news on Radio One stations was part of a much broader trend among the giant corporate radio chains like Clear Channel that flourished after 1996, when federal legislation removed the limits on the number of stations any company could own in a single market. Insofar as Hughes's programming policies now mirrored those of other, nonminority corporate broadcasters, she had fulfilled one of her main goals. She had always rejected the racial marginalization imposed on black entrepreneurs in the past. "One of the things that I've always aspired towards," Hughes explained, "is I don't want to be the best black, I want to be the best, who happens to be African or African American."[61]

Hughes epitomized the new black entrepreneurs who emerged in the wake of the civil rights movement eager to take their place at the heart of the American media and culture industries, rather than accept restrictions on their careers based on fixed racial categorizations and prejudices. "We're not an ethnic station," Manhattan borough president Percy Sutton had insisted shortly after his Inner City Broadcasting consortium had purchased the black-oriented flagship WBLS/WLIB in New York for between $1.7 and $1.9 million with loans from a federal Minority Enterprise Small Business Investment Company (MESBIC) and the Chemical Bank—which again suggests the tenuous nature of some claims to "black" ownership. Sutton immediately moved his stations out of Harlem to a downtown location. "We're a people station. We want to be in the mainstream of radio," he explained.[62] Most black entrepreneurs, executives, and deejays in the industry found themselves juggling similar impulses, hoping to serve the special needs of the black community while competing for the greater financial rewards of the mainstream.

WBLS/WLIB was a prime northern facility with a price tag to match. But even in the South, decent radio stations were far from cheap. Near the top end of the southern price range, WENN cost A. G. Gaston $650,000 in 1975. Seven years earlier, singer James Brown had paid half a million dollars for the powerful WBBW in Augusta and $75,000 for the smaller WGYW (renamed WJBE) in Knoxville. Building their station from the ground up, in 1969 Reuben Hughes and the brothers Vernon and Robert Floyd spent $60,000 launching the 1,000-watt station WORV-Hattiesburg. To a greater or lesser extent, all of these African American entrepreneurs had become involved in radio for much the same mix of financial, personal, and altruistic reasons. James Brown, for example, saw station ownership as an expression of his faith in the power of black capitalism to promote racial progress. Fired by the "bootstrap mentality" that had helped him rise from dirt-poor roots in South Carolina and Georgia to become a millionaire, and by an unshakable patriotic faith in the capacity of the American system to allow such an apotheosis, Brown was adamant that successful black capitalists like himself had a responsibility to help uplift the entire race. He saw black-owned radio as both an expression of and an instrument for that racial advance.

> First I thought black communities needed radio stations that really served and represented them. . . . Second, I wanted my station to be a media training ground so that black people could do more than just be jocks. I wanted them to learn advertising, programming, and management at all levels. Third, as owner I wanted to be a symbol of the black entrepreneur. All three of these reasons were, to me, part of education. That was real black power.[63]

Of course, few African American consortia or individuals had the capital available to a James Brown or an A. G. Gaston. Indeed, the circumstances whereby the nation's oldest black-owned radio station, WERD, passed into white hands at precisely the moment when there was so much emphasis on trying to increase black ownership demonstrated the problem posed by the chronic shortage of black investment capital. In 1969, having run WERD on a slender and sometimes nonexistent profit margin for several years, Jesse Blayton decided to sell up. Although he fully appreciated WERD's value as a community institution in Atlanta, economics dictated his decision. "I saw it as a medium for bringing together black people—as it *did*. But I thought it might bring them together *economically* as well as socially. It didn't!" Blayton complained. A black syndicate headed by his friends and colleagues Al and Mack Saddler hoped to buy the station, while Chuck Stone, president of the National Conference of Black Power, pleaded with Blayton to wait until a way could be found to keep the station under the control of the black Atlanta community. Instead Blayton chose to sell WERD to the highest bidder, Louis Hertz. To some observers, this action was an act of racial treachery. Yet Blayton was just adhering to his longstanding principle that thrift and sensible business practices were crucial to black progress. He had always sought to reconcile racial and economic, communal and personal agendas. Often these imperatives had coincided. When they did not, Blayton invariably favored hard-nosed commercial calculation and the pursuit of enlightened self-interest over what he considered a self-defeating racial sentimentalism.[64]

With inadequate black capitalization a perpetual problem, one of the most important goals of those who campaigned for the expansion of black radio ownership was to secure more federal start-up funds. Between 1969 and 1983, loans from government-sponsored MESBICs helped to fund the purchase of some 90 percent of all new black-owned communications outlets. Partly as a result, by the end of the 1970s there were some 140 putatively black-owned radio stations in the nation. It had taken twenty years for the number to rise from one in 1949 to barely a dozen commercial stations in 1969. With federal assistance, however, the number of black-owned facilities had increased nearly twelve-fold during the next decade. Much of this increase came late in the 1970s when the Small Business Administration started making significant loans to potential African American owners and the FCC created a Minority Ownership Taskforce. In 1978, for the first time, the Commission introduced measures designed specifically to increase the level of minority media ownership in America. One measure allowed the prospect of minority ownership to be factored into the FCC's calculations when it considered competing bids for a particular broadcasting license. The second, a "distress sale" measure, offered an exemption to an old FCC rule that had prohibited the owners of a station that was in danger of having its license revoked from selling the facility until the FCC's investigations were concluded. This exemption could be claimed only if the station was sold to a minority buyer. A third measure offered lucrative breaks on capital gains tax for broadcasters who agreed to sell their facilities to minority owners.[65] One of the beneficiaries of the FCC's tax break policy was Robert Rounsaville. In 1980, ten years after the MTCC had mobilized to fight for greater community control over WVOL, Rounsaville sold his Nashville soul station to the black-owned Phoenix Communications Group. The irony was that the Phoenix group, dominated by ambitious black entrepreneur Samuel Howard, was actually based in Delaware.[66]

In many respects, the efforts to improve minority ownership levels and increase community influence in the radio industry yielded similarly ambiguous results. For instance, 140 black-owned stations still represented less than 2 percent of the total number of radio stations operating in the U.S. at the end of the 1970s. Moreover, definitions of precisely what constituted a minority-owned station were in constant flux and were eventually revised in 1982 so that owners selling to companies with as little as 20 percent minority participation could apply for special FCC tax breaks. Although loans for minority broadcasters had become somewhat easier to obtain after the mid-1970s, African Americans seldom managed to buy the bigger, more lucrative and prestigious metropolitan stations in the South and had to settle for smaller facilities. Cathy Hughes and Radio One Inc., with its mid-1990s purchases of WKYS-Washington for $35 million and WHTA-Atlanta for $18 million, represented an impressive exception to an enduring national problem. "Half the stations black people own are dogs," Pluria Marshall complained in 1987. Within a decade the deregulation of the airways and the abandonment of vital federal assistance to black ownership initiatives, in the form of distress sale provisions, tax incentives, and restrictions on the number of stations a single owner could have in any market, combined to erode the gains made over the previous twenty-five years. The end of the tax certificate in 1995, Marshall charged, was "just pure, unadulterated racism." As a result of such federal policies, Marshall correctly predicted a steady decline in black ownership from its 1991 peak of 181 stations. Subsequent deregulation simply intensified the concentration of economic power in the radio industry. At the start of the twenty-first century, cookie-cutter music and talk radio schedules and negligible news and current affairs broadcasting were the order of the day at most commercial black-oriented stations.[67]

As in so many other areas of African American life, the story of black-owned radio revealed that the progress generated by the civil rights and black power movements was real, but equivocal. The legislative victories were impressive, but their practical consequences often remained ambiguous, contingent, and in need of constant protection and reaffirmation to prevent recidivism. From the perspective of the mid-1970s, however, the modest expansion of black radio station ownership in the South and the growing attentiveness to local needs and news on air represented major, if limited, achievements of the black power era. These triumphs for black protest and federal action stood as a Janus-faced testament to how much had been achieved by the freedom struggle and to how much work remained to be done to create genuine equality of black opportunity in the region.

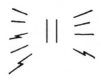

Riots, Respect, and Responsibility

Radio in the New South

WOIC, by virtue of its Negro oriented program format, feels keenly the responsibility of aiding the Negro citizens in its listening area to progress to the fulfillment of their desire to become "first-class" citizens enjoying the benefits and sharing the responsibilities of that citizenship.
WOIC-Columbia, South Carolina, August 1966

W[h]ither the Revolution on Southern Radio?

At the 1969 NATRA convention in Washington, comedian-activist Dick Gregory brought delegates to their feet by telling them, "I have seven black kids and radio has more of an influence on them than I do. I hope you understand what you're doing with your power. . . . You ain't in show business no more, you're in a revolution."[1] Some people took this idea very literally. In October 1974, three armed Black Muslims who had previously been involved in a murderous robbery and shooting spree in downtown Montgomery, Alabama, commandeered radio station WAPX. Arthur Lewis (Arthur X), Reginald Robinson (Malika Shabazz), and Julius Davis (Dawud Baqarah Allah) took two African American staff members hostage: deejay Al Dixon Jr. and secretary Gloria Gilmer. Dixon was the son of the station's operations manager, founder of Broadcast and Music Arts, and former NATRA chairman Alvin Dixon Sr. Before city authorities cut off power to the station, the gunmen had spent an hour broadcasting appeals to local blacks to come "help us in the revolution." Nobody showed up—except two hundred law enforcement officers who surrounded the station and occasionally opened fire. This greatly alarmed the senior Dixon and WAPX's manager, Harold Edwards, who were concerned both about the safety of the hostages and about the fact that police bullets were tearing holes in a building they had only recently had remodeled. Eventually the WAPX siege ended when Dixon Jr. and Gloria Gilmer escaped and, amid a fusillade of tear gas and bullets, their captors surrendered.[2]

Although Alvin Dixon Sr. had criticized the apolitical docility of NATRA in the early 1970s, this was considerably more militancy than he, other black deejays and executives, or the majority of African American listeners wanted at their radio stations. Southern radio certainly never came close to being a vehicle for the kind of revolutionary mobilization that some of the more militant black-power advocates envisioned. There were obvious systemic reasons why this was unlikely. The basic economic and regulatory structure of black-oriented radio had changed only incrementally during the late 1960s and early 1970s. Individual whites and powerful white conglomerates like the Rollins, Rounsaville, Sonderling, Speidel, and United chains continued to dominate the industry, alongside a small cadre of black owners and executives. This broadcasting elite was predictably wary of associating its stations with the most radical, sometimes separatist, and occasionally violent expressions of black power.

Besides the structural and ideological obstacles within the industry, there was another major reason why truly revolutionary broadcasting remained rare on black-oriented stations in the South: black audiences were generally very dubious about the most radical forms of black power ideology. For all their psychological allure, cultural resonance, and sometimes penetrating critiques of American racism, genuinely radical black power organizations like the Revolutionary Action Movement, the Republic of New Afrika, or even the Black Panther Party and the ultranationalistic incarnations of SNCC and CORE had limited appeal to the mass of southern blacks. As African Americans grappled with the practical realities of a post–Jim Crow world, SNCC's Cleveland Sellers summed up the situation in 1974. "The black masses are no longer caught up in the drama and promise of the movement. They are passive; waiting on a viable vision, a new concept of success."[3] Faced by insurgent white conservatism and racial retrenchment, the black masses wanted leadership, direction, a sense of common purpose, and a renewal of faith that justice was attainable. When they had to endure a series of internecine battles between cultural nationalists, revolutionary nationalists, political nationalists, and various other claimants to the black power throne, a flagging interest in mass activism was in danger of waning still further.

This chapter considers how black-oriented radio worked to counteract and partially arrest this trend by helping to maintain a sense of black unity, collective power, and common purpose. While various social, economic, and political forces were conspiring to encourage bitterness, factionalism, and anomie in both the movement and the broader black community, radio helped to sustain the racial pride and self-respect that had always underpinned black resistance and struggle in the South. Much of this was achieved through the promotion and celebration of distinctively black cultural forms on the radio. However, during the black power era, southern stations also began to play a much more conspicuous practical role in local campaigns against racial discrimination and for voter education and mobilization. Thanks to pressure from black activists and, to some extent, the FCC, the era also saw some improvements in the quality of public affairs and news programming for southern black audiences.

These developments helped to create a more militant, if not exactly revolutionary, élan at southern black-oriented stations in the late 1960s and early 1970s. Many stations featured speakers whose bold prescriptions for social, political, and economic change could never have been aired a few years earlier. Of course, allowing more militant black voices on air was not tantamount to expressing support for everything—or anything—they said. Thus, the second major theme of this chapter concerns the ways in which many southern stations sought simultaneously to accommodate, report on, and yet distance themselves from the most extreme and controversial expressions of black power and protest. This intricate dance of embrace and avoidance, encouragement and censure, even at general-market stations such as WBT-Charlotte, was a defining characteristic of radio in the region during the late 1960s and early 1970s.

Soul Power Is Black Power

For African Americans in the South, the black power era was characterized by a blend of rising racial pride, unevenly expanding economic opportunity, increased political power, and deep frustrations about the sluggish pace and palpable limitations of those economic and political gains. Each of these aspects of black life found expression on black-oriented radio. In Atlanta WAOK's *American Heritage* and WERD's *Our Noble Black Heritage* were typical of programs that proudly showcased historical black accomplishments, extending a tradition that had first flourished with a mixture of government, NAACP, and NUL support during World War II. Also building on existing traditions were the many new talk shows and phone-ins that encouraged listener responses to the burning— sometimes literally, in an era of urban unrest—issues of the day. *Family Line* on WAOK simultaneously exploited and encouraged a sense of shared communal identity by inviting listeners to call and discuss current affairs issues on air. WDIA's *Speak Up* was a bolder, post–Jim Crow incarnation of Nat Williams's *Brown America Speaks*. The show provided a forum for the local black community to discuss its continuing struggle for justice and equality of opportunity. Discussion topics ranged from "Is an NAACP Membership Today a Sign of Lack of Militancy?" to "Is Self-help an Answer to the Need to Improve Ghetto and Slum Areas?" and "Is Black Militancy a Help or Hindrance to Black Progress?"[4]

Even in an era when black nationalist and sometimes separatist agendas were highly visible, the traditional interest in using radio to promote interracial cooperation in the South endured. In the early 1970s Aaron Henry launched a show

called *Help Somebody Be Somebody* on the general-market station WKDL-Clarks-
dale. The NAACP and MFDP veteran and longtime campaigner for a more representative media in Mississippi saw this show as a means to encourage black
self-help strategies and political mobilization. Henry also hoped to foster a more
general sense of interracial cooperation in Clarksdale. In language that would
not have been out of place in the decade before *Brown,* he described WKDL's
support as "a clear example of the public spirited desire of us and them to make
sure that Blacks and Whites of Good Will, along with all other citizens of our area
have this opportunity."[5]

Perhaps rather more indicative of the militant ethos on southern black-oriented radio was the way that individual deejays and even entire stations felt more
able—indeed, more compelled—to take public stands against examples of racial
injustice affecting the local African American community. A telling example of
the practical implications occurred at KOKY–Little Rock. In 1964 station manager Eddie Phelan had explicitly forsworn any commentary on racial issues at
KOKY. Four years later, however, the station was at the forefront of a campaign to
get justice in the case of Curtis Ingram, a black prisoner clubbed to death by a
white trusty at the Pulaski County Penal Farm. According to prison officials, the
trusty had acted in self-defense following an attack by Ingram. But KOKY deejay
Bob Broadwater managed to find two witnesses who testified that the trusty had
acted on the orders of one of the guards, without provocation from Ingram. The
state attorney's investigation of the case and the conviction of the trusty on a
manslaughter charge represented a major victory for the black community
against a notoriously brutal and racist penal system. It was also testimony to the
potential of radio to dramatize injustice and create pressure for change.[6]

Like the crusading Bob Broadwater, WDIA's Chris Turner personified a new
generation of irreverent, opinionated, and politicized southern black deejays.
Just twenty-two years old in 1968, Turner openly flaunted his membership in a
Memphis black power organization called the Black Knights—although, in a
good illustration of the perennial tension between militancy and moderation on
radio during this period, he insisted that "we don't do any burning up or anything like that."[7] Hugely popular in the local black community, Turner felt
sufficiently confident to lobby for a black buyout of the Sonderling-owned
WDIA. With dead airtime one of the most heinous offenses any deejay could
commit, he also brazenly broadcast a minute of silence to protest Mayor Henry
Loeb's handling of a black sanitation workers strike. That strike, which eventually drew Martin Luther King to the city and his death, was the subject of extensive coverage and comment by Turner and other WDIA announcers. Indeed, the
station appears to have been important in sustaining community support for the
strike. Historian Laurie Beth Green describes how Minerva Johnican, an "ardent
supporter of the sanitation workers," heard "an appeal for help over WDIA while

driving home from work, which convinced her to go directly to Clayborn Temple for her first mass meeting. The announcement changed her life by convincing her to join the support committee, a step that set her political career in motion."[8]

Chris Turner's condemnations of racial discrimination and appeals for expanded black economic and political power in Memphis sometimes pricked the consciences of his more cautious black colleagues. Deejay Rick Taylor said, "I think in more ways than one he probably made most of us . . . feel maybe a little ashamed of ourselves that we were not doing as much as we could have done." It certainly created a good deal of consternation among WDIA's white managers and executives. Still, Turner's large audiences and high advertising ratings meant that his job was never in serious jeopardy. As Taylor put it, "The bottom line [was] the balance sheet."[9] Just as important, Turner was swimming with the tide of executive opinion at WDIA. His outspokenness took place at a time when engagement with the ongoing freedom struggle and a certain radical chic had become commercially obligatory, not courageously exceptional, on southern black-oriented radio.

Even Bert Ferguson's editorials on WDIA caught something of the militant mood of the times. Ferguson railed against inadequate black educational facilities and teacher-training opportunities in Memphis, supported the federal Operation Headstart initiative, and demanded improved preschool provisions for poor children. On the economic front, he announced that "WDIA believes that all citizens of Memphis and its surrounding area—both Negro and white—should have equal job opportunity," something that he insisted was dependent on genuinely equal access to job training programs. In early 1968 he also declared that WDIA "supported a municipal order that all construction firms, doing work on City jobs in the Public Works Department, must adopt a policy of hiring without regard to race or color." Ferguson was especially proud of WDIA's support for integration in Memphis, taking partial credit for a campaign that finally secured the desegregation of municipal swimming pools in the summer of 1967.

"Community interest," Ferguson insisted, "is the first rule of thumb for WDIA editorials." Yet the way in which the station characterized "community interest" and its resolutely integrationist tone revealed its confidence in the soundness of the American economic and political system and its suspicion of more radical perspectives. "WDIA believes it has a duty to aid the Negro in his search to enter the mainstream of American life," Ferguson editorialized. While WDIA could indulge and support Chris Turner's attacks on black exclusion from or marginalization within the "mainstream of American life," it habitually rejected separatist positions that denied the virtues of integration.[10]

One issue on which most southern station owners, managers, deejays, and listeners agreed by the late 1960s was that radio was in the business of promoting black racial consciousness, pride, and self-respect. As Ferguson wrote, "In a deliberate attempt to boost the Negro's pride in himself and his race, WDIA has stressed prominent figures of American Negro history. Also, we have stressed, whenever possible, achievements of Negroes in current society. Some critics might label such efforts as propaganda. But WDIA's editors believe that the Negro has much to be proud of that he doesn't know about because little is taught in public schools about Negro history. He has the right to know—and to be proud."[11] With a penchant for African-style shirts and clenched-fist black power salutes, Chris Turner regularly paraphrased James Brown's black pride anthem by telling his listeners, "Say it loud, baby. I'm black and sure enough proud of it."[12] There was certainly no attempt to modify his unmistakably black patter on air: like most of the African American announcers who dominated black-oriented radio in the black power era, Turner was delighted to demonstrate his mastery of black vernacular as he spun his soul disks and introduced community news and public information announcements. If the Cooperite tradition of self-consciously "refined" black announcing was not exactly dead, it was far less healthy than the Bensonite brand of black banter.

This was also an era when songs celebrating black identity, solidarity, pride, determination, and self-respect sold millions of copies and were ubiquitous on black-oriented radio. Soul and funk classics like Aretha Franklin's "Respect," the Staples Singers' "Respect Yourself," Johnnie Taylor's "I Am Somebody," and Curtis Mayfield's "Move on Up" competed for airtime with songs of soulful social commentary like Marvin Gaye's "What's Going On," Syl Johnson's "Is It Because I'm Black," the Spinners' "Ghetto Child," and Stevie Wonder's "Living for the City." Of course, long before these kinds of overtly political "message songs" had become so popular, black identity had been expressed on radio through the actual *sounds* of blues, jazz, gospel, rhythm and blues, and soul. By the mid-1960s, the biracial smorgasbord of sounds that had characterized popular music radio in the late 1950s and early 1960s had already been replaced on black-oriented stations—and on black record players—by the gospel-inflected, self-consciously nationalistic sounds of soul music. Now the growing presence of explicitly engaged political songs on station playlists helped to intensify the sense that black-oriented radio was deeply embroiled in the black community's struggles. Irrespective of its capacity to orchestrate protest campaigns or mobilize black voters, the significance of black-oriented radio in the South remained inextricably tied to the music played and the style of its announcers. At its best, the message and the medium fused to create a total package of empowering black-oriented sound.[13]

This blend was a hallmark of the programming at WOL in Washington, D.C. In the early summer of 1966 Sherwood Ross, the NUL's former assistant public relations director and the recently appointed director of public affairs at the

FIGURE 19. In June 1966 former NUL executive Sherwood Ross (left) was covering James Meredith's "March Against Fear" through Mississippi for WOL-Washington, D.C., when the civil rights activist was shot. Courtesy of *Baltimore News American* Photo Collection, University of Maryland, College Park.

Sonderling-owned soul station, had met James Meredith while covering Lyndon Johnson's White House Conference on Civil Rights. Meredith, hero of the Ole Miss integration crisis, revealed his plans for a March Against Fear across Mississippi, and Ross decided to cover the trek from Memphis to Jackson for WOL. On June 6 Ross was with Meredith just outside Hernando, Mississippi, when Meredith was felled by a shotgun blast. Within half an hour, WOL's listeners could hear Ross's eyewitness account of the event.[14]

Later that month, as various civil rights leaders took up the march on behalf of the hospitalized Meredith, Ross expressed WOL's response to the controversial black power slogan that had arisen from the ranks of SNCC workers in Mississippi: "If it means that negro citizens should have a voice and a vote, full opportunities and everything that goes with it, we are *for* 'Black Power,'" he announced. "Negroes must guide their own destinies just as other racial and ethnic groups have done in America." The station was, however, rather less enthusiastic about some of the other connotations of the new rallying cry. Martin Luther King had refused to condemn black power outright and fully supported the drive for black political, economic, and social rights at its core. But he argued that the slogan itself was unfortunate, even counterproductive, as it was doomed to be widely interpreted as intrinsically separatist, antiwhite, and even as an endorsement of armed rebellion. WOL held much the same views. "If 'Black Power' means a separate state without integration, or if it means the use of force, violence and hatred, WOL will stand with Dr. King," Ross explained. Thus, while the station supported many initiatives associated with black power it consistently rejected violent and separatist responses to black oppression. Instead WOL strove to channel the anger and frustration that fueled black power into what it saw as more practical efforts to improve black lives.[15]

WOL's extensive coverage of the Meredith march confirmed the close links between the station and the travails of the African American community in Washington and beyond. The *Washington Star* noted that "Ross's Presence Was No Accident" and described the station's activist credentials and extensive programming on issues such as employment discrimination, poverty, substandard housing, and inadequate educational facilities in some of D.C.'s predominantly black neighborhoods. Notwithstanding SNCC's allegations in its 1967 campaign against the station, WOL did its best, not only to entertain its black listeners but also to attend to the material needs of those who were forced to live, as Ross put it in one broadcast, in the "other Washington—seldom seen by tourists—a monument to poverty, a tangle of slums, a city of sorrows."[16]

WOL was not content to catalog the woes of the black community. It also encouraged listeners to participate in efforts to eradicate or ameliorate those problems. Its War on Slums campaign was a good example of how radio could simultaneously publicize social evils while encouraging the black community to confront them. Ross appealed for local residents to contact him with complaints about the condition of their rented accommodation and the failure of landlords to make necessary repairs. He then forwarded these complaints to the Department of License and Inspection of the District of Columbia for investigation and kept a file of any improvements that were ordered as a result. Any landlord who failed to implement the mandated repairs was named and shamed on air. Rather than wait for listeners to complain or landlords to respond, Ross—dubbed by some the Robin Hood of Sherwood Jungle and widely viewed in the ghetto as "the only honest white man in town"—could even be seen scouring black neighborhoods in his "slummobile" looking for dilapidated accommodation to report.[17]

Back in the WOL studio, Ross rarely minced his words when exposing individual slumlords. "I want this landlord, whose initials are J.N., to know that every slum you own will be reported to District housing officials. Your tenants won't report it, Mr. N., I will," he warned in one broadcast. And to listeners who did complain, he offered the station's power and prestige as protection against possible reprisals. "We will support every single family which is suffering because slum landlords have made their lives unbearable. So I have a message today for every slum landlord in Washington. Don't you ever, I repeat, don't you ever, ever try to evict any family which contacts this radio station." After just eleven weeks of this campaign, investigations of some two hundred complaints revealed more than two thousand housing violations. Within nine months, the number of complaints exceeded one thousand, and local housing inspectors were enjoying an overtime bonanza because of their increased workload.[18]

As at WDIA, the effectiveness of WOL's social activism on the airways was connected to the communalizing power of the soul music—and other soul stylings—that dominated its schedules. The way in which these two crucial aspects of black-oriented radio programming intersected and reinforced each other during the black power era was apparent in the very language Ross used to attack slumlords and motivate black activism on air. "When you hear the sound of Soul Radio coming from their house you better keep your hands off of that family," Ross warned, evoking the image of a WOL-led "Soulvation Army"—as the station liked to characterize its family of listeners—united around the sounds of soul and committed to effective action. "The people who listen to [soul] know their rights under the law," Ross continued. "They know that they are free, free from fear of eviction by slum landlords like you. They know that if you try to pressure them or evict them that you are going to have the power of Washington's Number One Radio Station down on you so fast you won't know which slum to clean up first. When you hear the sound of Soul Music playing you are dealing with a family that's not gonna let you push them around."[19]

Soul music enabled WOL to reach lower-class sections of the African American community in Washington with messages that might otherwise have gone unheard. As Ross explained, "Because WOL is 'The Soul Station,' it has a built-in listenership of the very people who civil rights leaders can't reach. The listener doesn't have to read anything or go to a meeting. He just listens to the music he likes and gets the message along with it."[20] The salient question at stations like WOL was not whether to go with either a music or a news-and-public-affairs programming schedule; it was how to find the appropriate balance between the two modes of programming. Ross and a growing number of activist-announcers at WOL including Soulfinger, Ruddy Runnels "the Tall Tanned Texan," Dewey Hughes, and, most popular of all, Bob "Nighthawk" Terry, simply wanted to en-sure that this emphasis on unity and pride did not become an ego-gratifying end in itself. They wanted to harness such feelings to effective campaigns to eradi-cate the worst material aspects of black inner-city life.

Of course, aside from any moral or philosophical commitment to promoting black pride and social activism, emphasis on these themes also made good eco-nomic sense. Chain owner Egmont Sonderling had acquired WOL only in mid-1965. As a relative newcomer in a black-oriented market long dominated by WUST and WOOK, he had deliberately promoted WOL as a dynamic, hip, and activist alternative to the existing commercial stations. WOL prided itself on be-ing more in tune with the militant spirit of the times and the aroused mood of Washington's black community. Its rapid eclipse of its rivals in the ratings—it earned $1.5 million in its first year of operation and could claim 65 percent of the black market within two years—depended on its capacity to demonstrate an equally intimate understanding of the cultural predilections and the social aspi-rations of its listeners.[21]

This rough alignment of commercial interests, cultural politics, and social activism helped to create an environment where Sherwood Ross and his black colleagues could accurately report on the difficulties facing their listeners and participate openly in efforts to resolve them. Indeed, as WOL became part of the fabric of the lives of many black Washingtonians, it transcended its role as a medium for the expression of black culture to become an integral part of that culture itself. As Ulf Hannerz wrote in his ethnographic study of the Washing-ton ghetto, "Black radio, its programming and its personnel are not simply a faceless component of the ghetto cultural apparatus but a set of individuals and events which also take their place among the things ghetto dwellers know they have in common, the things which serve to define their community."[22] SCLC's Walter Fauntroy made much the same point in 1967. Again Fauntroy empha-sized how WOL's sensitivity to African American cultural tastes and habits—from dress and cuisine, through music and humor, to deportment and speech—was inseparable from its attempts to promote black political, economic, and social progress through education and activism. "There is at WOL this thing about—call them Negro cultural amenities—how you eat chicken, that sort of thing," he observed. "The people identify with that." Noting the commendable lack of condescension WOL showed toward the black lower classes and their tastes, Fauntroy explained, "The station takes people at their threshold and it leads them to other areas of thought. The great appeal is the rhythm and blues music. People tune in to listen to the music and they hear these . . . cultural amenities. They are listening and interested, then they hear about employment and slums and action. This is of tremendous value. We've never had anything like this in Washington before."[23]

Getting Out the Southern Black Vote: The Case of Modjeska Simkins

Exercising the franchise was one means to effect meaningful changes in black lives, and WOL repeatedly urged African Americans to get out and vote. Sherwood Ross even invoked the voter registration work undertaken by the SRC in the Deep South to shame reluctant local residents out of their apathy and into the voting booths:

> Right here, right *here*, in our city, there are thousands of eligible Negroes who haven't bothered to take the time to register. While Southern Negroes are risking their jobs, their homes, their farms, and even their lives to go to the polls—there are people listening to this broadcast now who wouldn't walk one solitary block to cast their ballot.
>
> Well, maybe we need the Southern Regional Council to come up here to Washington to take those people by the hand and show them where to register.
>
> This radio station hopes that this won't be necessary. For in every one of us there is a conscience—and this conscience should tell us that the vote is power—*power* to change our lives, and the lives of our children for the better—*power* to elect the men who *care* about equality and justice for black Americans, too.[24]

The Voting Rights Act of 1965 was arguably the most significant and enduring victory of the southern civil rights movement. In the decade that followed, wherever federal observers and registrars appeared in the South, white attempts to dilute the power of the African American vote by a mixture of intimidation and gerrymandering were just about kept in check. As a result, black voting strength and the number of black elected officials in the region rose rapidly. In 1964, Herculean efforts by the movement had still placed only about 35 percent of eligible southern blacks on the electoral rolls. Five years later, helped in part by the launch of a second VEP in 1966, that proportion had risen to around 65 percent. In a related development, the number of black elected officials in the region rose from barely a hundred in 1965 to 1,185 by 1969. To be sure, many of these black officeholders teetered precariously on the lowest rungs of the political ladder, and the rate of increase would eventually slow and even reverse in the 1980s. Nevertheless, these initial increases in black political power represented a significant and inspirational triumph for the combination of grassroots southern mobilization and federal action.[25]

As in earlier periods in the freedom struggle, painstaking house-to-house recruitment remained the mainstay of black political organizing. In the post–Jim Crow South, however, black-oriented radio was able to play a much more prominent part in some of the campaigns that announced the arrival of a major black presence in the region's politics. As Julian Bond reflected in a 1968 VEP report, "For reaching black voters, radio stations broadcasting to Negro audiences are particularly effective." Certainly, television remained beyond the pocketbooks of many pioneering African American candidates. Athalie Range, who was elected to the city commission in Miami in 1967, remembered using "every medium other than television. TV is too expensive, and we simply did not have that kind of money." In Texas, Barbara Jordan also noted the significance of radio in the 1966 campaign that saw her become the first African American and the first woman elected to the state senate. Contrasting her success in that election with two unsuccessful earlier bids for election to the Texas House of Representatives, she set much store by her decision to ignore television and concentrate on black-oriented radio. "When we got it broken down into districts, we did not put any funds into television, and only into radio for the two Negro stations that we had."[26]

Few southern civil rights leaders were more passionate about encouraging black political participation than South Carolina's veteran activist Modjeska Simkins. From the mid-1960s until the late 1970s—although somewhat more sporadically after 1972—Simkins appeared for fifteen minutes every Wednesday evening on WOIC-Columbia to urge African Americans to straighten up and vote right. The broadcasts were sponsored by the Richland County Citizens Committee (RCCC), an organization that NAACP stalwart Simkins had cofounded in 1944 primarily to register black voters in the county.[27] The RCCC had originally sought a regular radio slot on WOIC precisely because it thought it would be the best means of "properly informing our people on candidates and issues, and for getting a full turnout on election days."[28]

Although she used her broadcasts to encourage attendance at the RCCC's weekly meetings and to discuss a wide variety of social and cultural issues, Simkins focused on the need for blacks to learn how to exercise the franchise effectively. In Simkins's view, the contemporary struggle for power and opportunity in the South was really no different from the struggle African Americans had been waging for centuries. The goal was still black economic and political power. "Don't let anyone get your mind off the real Black Power issue of united effort in spending our dollars and casting our votes to enrich our futures," she told her listeners, yoking together black consumerism and political power. "This is all that the Black Power idea has ever meant since Frederick Douglass mentioned it generations ago." Unable to conceal her contempt for the black and white opportunists she felt were riding the black power slogan to personal celebrity and financial gain, she told WOIC listeners: "Our strategy must be to disregard Negro misleaders and 'hand grease artists' who care nothing for the future of our people."[29]

Simkins's passion for mobilizing the black vote coincided with WOIC's declaration that "as a strong back-up to the cause of good citizenship" it would "endeavor to make even more strenuous efforts than in the past in the area of voter education."[30] The Speidel-owned soul station had long been supportive of this kind of responsible political broadcasting to the African American community. It allowed deejay Charlie Dee to rally black voters on air and openly boasted that "WOIC is unique in that its staff is almost entirely composed of individuals who are active volunteer community workers." Rev. William Bowman, for example, was head of the Columbia NAACP, supervisor of religious programming at WOIC, and host of the *Negro Citizens in the News* show every Sunday. In addition to Simkins and the RCCC, the station also worked with such civic organizations as the League of Women Voters and the Richland County Legislative Delegation, all of whom it felt "make a significant contribution to the cause of civil rights."[31]

Revealingly, WOIC's relatively progressive record on racial issues was not enough to save it from one of the era's many challenges to white-owned, black-oriented radio outlets. In late 1969 the Columbia Citizens Concerned with Improved Broadcasting complained to the FCC that WOIC was denying African Americans adequate employment opportunities. The FCC eventually dismissed the complaint as groundless, but the Columbia Citizens kept up the campaign for better service, more black executive positions, and ultimately black ownership until 1973, when the station was sold to the Nuance Company. In the intervening years WOIC appears to have had little difficulty in retaining the loyalty of many of the more than 250,000 black listeners who resided in its market. This was largely because it continued to offer an attractive blend of soul music, religious broadcasts, news programming, and locally oriented current-affairs shows like the one hosted by Modjeska Simkins.[32]

Simkins's attempts to mobilize the black electorate in Richland County deployed much the same rhetoric as Sherwood Ross used on WOL in D.C. She couched the responsibility to vote in terms of a moral imperative that transcended class, gender, and even generational divisions within the black community. In one of her most affecting radio jeremiads, Simkins solicited the help of the very young in persuading their parents to vote out of a sense of family duty and racial responsibility:

> There are thousands of little boys and girls who are hoping that the world will be better for them when they grow up than it is now for their parents. ... One of the best ways, in fact the best way, is to see that your parents vote in every election. . . . No matter how much you would like to vote, you cannot because you are not old enough. That is your excuse, and it is a good one. Ask your parents and other relatives, and the friends of your family, what is their excuse if they do not register and vote. And don't you give them any rest. You be ashamed if your parents are not registered. You be ashamed if they do not vote, don't let them rest until they have gone to the polls.[33]

In 1966 WOIC had committed itself to "urge our listeners to register and then to vote, but also to instruct them in the use of voting machines, to prepare them for what to expect when they go to the registration office and at the polls when they go to cast their ballots."[34] Indeed, Simkins's radio shows functioned much like an electronic variant on the movement's Citizenship Schools, offering Richland County's newly enfranchised black voters an invaluable guide to the rigors of actually registering and casting their votes. "The use of voting machines is easy, as hundreds of citizens know," Simkins told them, once again fusing the franchise, citizenship, and a deep sense of communal responsibility. "Remember, too, that there are people at the polls to help you; that even if you cannot read or write, but are registered, you can vote; that it can be arranged for someone to come along with a poll manager to assist you." The details of the process were then explained with great thoroughness. "On entering the curtain one sees a red lever or handle at the left, which must be pushed all the way over to the right until a bell rings. Find the names you want to vote for. Pull a little black voting pointer down over each and leave it down. When fully satisfied you have pulled down each pointer over your choices, push the big lever all the way back to the left again. This registers your vote."[35]

Simkins clearly recognized the value of radio as an instrument of political education and organization at a moment when politicians of every persuasion were beginning to recognize the importance of black ballots in local and state elections. The impact of these black votes was much enhanced whenever African Americans voted as a coherent bloc. Indeed, Simkins had to work hard during her WOIC shows to dispel the reputation that South Carolina blacks voted "like sheep" for Democratic Party candidates, as a hostile headline in the *Columbia Record* had suggested.[36] In a spring 1972 broadcast, she announced that the RCCC intended to "emphasize the importance of increased voter registration, and the folly or foolishness of voting like slaves for one party or for certain persons who black misleaders try to grease and push down the throats of black voters."[37] Genuinely concerned to raise the political sophistication of black voters and anxious to end unthinking support for a single party, Simkins even suggested that black voters should contemplate the appeal of some of the state's new breed of Republicans. Her logic was that South Carolina's Republicans would at least have to adopt some genuinely progressive policies toward African Americans to earn their vote, whereas the state's Democratic Party had grown so accustomed to knee-jerk black loyalty that it had stopped paying even lip service to black needs. "The South Carolina Democratic Party has been in power for generations," she complained. "It has a vicious built-in machine that is not sensitive to the needs of the masses. . . . Any benefits blacks have accrued have come from the national party."[38]

The irony of this bid to rid black voters of their reputation for sheeplike allegiance to the Democrats was that Simkins was perfectly happy to take on the role of electoral shepherdess on WOIC. She had no hesitation in recommending precisely which candidates should get the support of Richland County blacks in every upcoming local, state, and national election.[39] Frustration with the treatment of African Americans by the state Democrats had certainly made Simkins sympathetic to anyone who challenged the old guard of white racial conservatives within the party. In one of her very first WOIC shows in March 1965, for example, she urged African Americans to vote for the maverick John Bolt Culbertson, who ran time and time again—with negligible success—against Democratic machine candidates on a pro-labor, pro-welfare, pro–civil rights platform.[40] Simkins consistently supported Culbertson's candidacies, feeling that even in failure his presence had a positive, liberalizing effect upon the state's generally reactionary white politics. In 1968, for example, she credited Culbertson's campaign against Senator Ernest "Fritz" Hollings with the senator's sudden decision to visit some deprived black neighborhoods and personally acquaint himself with the racialized poverty that blighted his state. Unimpressed by this gesture, Simkins asked her listeners, "How much did the announcement by John Bolt Culbertson of his intention to oppose Hollings in the Senate race have to do with the slum parade?"[41]

If Simkins was happy to use her airtime to endorse individuals, her broader mission was simply to encourage local African Americans to exercise their right to vote in an intelligent and effective manner. By using WOIC to explain candidates' positions on issues directly affecting the African American community, and by suggesting coherent voting strategies, Simkins was trying to maximize the potential of the black vote in Richland County and beyond. She was also demonstrating how black-oriented radio might be used to influence the political ideas and activities, as well as the social and cultural lives, of black southerners.

Black Radio News Networks

Modjeska Simkins was no stranger to the unifying and inspirational power of black popular culture. Yet in the late 1960s and early 1970s she was far from convinced that the cause of racial justice was being well served by a growing obsession with certain cosmetic and commercially exploitative expressions of black identity. Simkins had little time for black countercultural gestures, especially if they offended her powerful sense of middle-class propriety and civic virtue, or provided an excuse for the exploitation of the black community in the name of what she saw as a debilitating form of faux Afrocentrism. "Mr. Charlie knows that thousands of blacks are going to sink hundreds of thousands of dollars in way-out clothing that often makes us look like freaks," she warned her listeners. "Charlie makes all of these way-out clothes to charm the silly black market, all these flop hats worn on top of afros that there was never anything like in darkest Africa, and so on."[42]

Many black critics shared Simkins's concerns about the relationship between black-oriented radio's endless paeans to soul style and the quest for black liberation. In a 1970 report prepared for the Race Relations Information Center in Nashville, Bernard Garnett posed one of the central questions of the era when he asked: "Is the broadcasting industry's budding sense of 'blackness' much more than the recognition of black power as a new commercial commodity? Is 'soul,' black radio style, the acceptance of the black man's quest for self-determination or is it a superficial sales slogan?"[43] Many wanted to hear much less soul and more discussion forums, newscasts, and educational programs on the radio. William Wright of BEST complained that the typical white owner of a black-oriented station "gives us 24 hours of 'soul' because it pads his already stuffed pockets and keeps black people ignorant."[44]

These critics had a point, as the proportion of airtime allocated to music on commercial black-oriented stations in the early 1970s ranged between 70 and 90 percent. At the same time, news and public affairs programming on stations geared to the black community accounted for an average of 8 and 5 percent of their schedules respectively. An analysis of more than one hundred radio facilities revealed that the amount of news and public affairs programming was lowest on stations with a wholly black focus or on ones that offered more than twenty-one hours of black-oriented fare each week. In stark terms, the greater the extent of a station's black orientation, the less time it devoted to news.[45]

Quantity aside, the quality and scope of the news and public affairs programming on black-oriented radio increased substantially during the late 1960s and early 1970s. This was due in part to the emergence of a number of black-oriented news networks. In 1954, African American publisher and entrepreneur Leonard Evans had created the first news service specifically for black-oriented radio sta-

FIGURE 20. Like most black-oriented radio stations in the South, WGIV had always tried to provide an effective community news operation. In the late 1960s and early 1970s, however, pressure mounted to increase the quantity and quality of black-oriented radio news. Courtesy of James Peeler.

tions, believing that it could provide more relevant information for black audiences than established news networks like the Associated Press. "This is not a crusade for the intermingling of the races," Evans carefully assured prospective clients for his National Negro Network (NNN) and their sponsors. "We're out to move tonnage, to sell merchandise." It was formed, agreed one subscriber, not as "a social 'cause' but as a business venture to provide advertisers with special access to Negro listeners." Although by 1954 NNN had garnered thirty-five affiliates, a cash crisis led to the collapse of Evans's experiment after little more than a year.[46] Other black-oriented news service initiatives followed. The Keystone Broadcasting System (KBS) established the Keystone Negro Network in 1955. By 1960 it loosely connected some 463 stations, with a potential audience of twelve million African Americans. The same year, the Negro Radio Association, chaired by Francis Fitzgerald from WGIV-Charlotte, also began its short-lived and generally disappointing attempt "to study, foster and develop public service programming for the benefit of Negro groups."[47]

By the time a new wave of black-oriented news networks appeared in the early 1970s, there was much less trepidation about radio coverage of racial problems or of organized protests. Yet the new news networks never lost sight of Leonard Evans's basic commercial agenda. Eugene Jackson, for example, was a Kansas

City–born college-educated engineer who had worked for the corporate giant Colgate-Palmolive before becoming a venture capitalist. Like many of his entre-preneurial black contemporaries, Jackson was convinced that the best way to promote black interests was through the development of economic power. When Jackson, together with industry veterans Sidney Small and Del Rayee, launched the National Black Network (NBN) in 1972 with the aid of a major Bank of America loan, he stressed to his 119 soul station affiliates that effective black news coverage would increase their market share. "No other network can give you our kind of service and profits," he explained. After a sluggish start, when it actually lost some of its affiliates, struggled to attract sponsors, and ran up debts of around $2 million, NBN's fortunes improved. In 1976 the network made more than $2.5 million with its mix of news and public affairs shows, including a digest of newspaper stories (*Black Issues and the Black Press*), a program explor-ing African American links to Africa (*Yesterday, Today, Tomorrow*), and a series hosted by black actors Ossie Davis and Ruby Dee that celebrated black cultural accomplishments.[48]

Even more impressive was the rise of the Sheridan Broadcasting Network. In 1976 Ronald Davenport, the founder of the Sheridan chain of stations, bought a 49 percent stake in the struggling Mutual Black Network (MBN). Originally cre-ated in 1972 to service those black-oriented stations connected to the low-pow-ered Mutual Broadcasting System network, MBN had assembled some marvel-ously committed and gifted black radio newsmen, including Eddie Castleberry and Sheldon Lewis from WPAL-Charleston. But despite its talent, MBN was always in financial difficulty. It was in terminal decline when Davenport inter-vened and renamed the news and public affairs service operation Sheridan Broadcasting Network. By 1978, when Sheridan bought out the remaining 51 percent of MBN, the network had ninety-one affiliates and earned $3 million annually. Thirteen years later Sheridan acquired Eugene Jackson's NBN to create the American Urban Radio Network (AURN). Clearly the drive toward consoli-dation and conglomeration in the modern media was not the prerogative of any one race, but rather a function of modern capitalism. As the only black radio network on air in the early 1990s, AURN had the potential to reach some 90 percent of African Americans with its mix of news, sports, current affairs, talk shows, and black heritage programming.[49]

Noncommercial Community Alternatives

The improvements to news and current affairs coverage made possible by black news networks were welcome. Yet many movement activists still hankered after more socially engaged, community-oriented programming on local stations. To an extent they got their wishes, not on commercial radio outlets but on the public radio stations that emerged in the late 1960s and early 1970s. The catalyst here once again was a combination of local initiatives and federal legislation, in this case the 1967 Public Broadcasting Act. This Act reduced the strict "educational" criteria the FCC had previously applied to noncommercial stations and instead emphasized more broadly defined "public service" criteria when granting licenses. The newly created Corporation for Public Broadcasting (CPB) also offered federal funding to noncommercial stations that employed five or more employees and regularly broadcast for a minimum of eight hours daily. Although these provisions favored bigger, better resourced, and more stable outlets, they nonetheless encouraged the growth of noncommercial FM broadcasting in the South, including several stations associated with historically black colleges and universities. Following the lead of KUCA at the University of Central Arkansas and WSHA at Raleigh's Shaw University, the early 1970s saw the debut of stations such as WCLK at Clark College, Atlanta, WHCJ at Savannah State College, WAMF at Florida A&M University, KGRM at Grambling College in Louisiana, and, of course, WHUR at Howard.[50]

Not all of these college stations were immediately committed to public affairs or news broadcasting, although most did make an effort not to replicate the soul-heavy formats of their commercial neighbors. WSHA, for example, initially went on air at Shaw University with a music format copied from commercial radio, but quickly placed jazz, rather than soul, at the heart of its programming. It then augmented music with a wide range of community-oriented news and educational programming designed, as Shaw's dean of humanities H. B. Caple, put it, to "meet the educational needs of the school and the local community. There seems to me to be an absence of the kind of resources with which our local black citizenry can get the kinds of information that is needed or that is essential to them and that is available to other communities."[51]

Reaffirming ideas that had animated black radio boosters from Jesse Blayton to Del Shields, Caple's colleague Willie High stressed how WSHA helped to extend the technical skills of the students who worked on it and to make them more employable:

> All of us saw the need to have a black, black owned educational non-commercial station, not only for the black community, but . . . because all of those stations in the area that our students had any association with or even listened to were commercial and if they had black persons on the radio station [they] either functioned as a Disc Jockey or they might have been a personality for a special program, but to have free exposure to the airwaves and be able to express themselves before a mass audience we had not had that opportunity.

The students themselves not only used the radio station [WSHA] to help them verbalize orally their concerns, but they learned summary techniques, to be able to edit for air, which was different from the print media, they were able to be exposed to and be more critical of what they heard on the commercial station.[52]

Although Shaw students were generally reckoned to be among some of the most radical of their generation in the South, little of that radicalism found its way onto their station's programming. While black students largely staffed the station and held executive positions within its hierarchy, WSHA's general manager was always a paid professional. The first manager was white faculty member Dr. Betty Czech, whose insistence that all scripts be submitted to her in advance discouraged some of the most radical members of the campus and surrounding community from seeking airtime at all. To some extent this policy was a reflection of Czech's professionalism rather than any particular conservatism. Czech knew that WSHA was essentially bankrolled by foundation gifts and federal grants, including the $250,000 one from the Department of Health, Education, and Welfare with which the station was launched. In theory, the host institution was supposed to provide matching funds, but Shaw seldom managed to stump up more than $2,500 annually. Czech recognized that with external money vital to the station's survival, it was imperative not to alienate would-be benefactors or compromise FCC regulations by inappropriate programming content. Like their commercial counterparts, even public broadcasting stations like WSHA staffed by a new generation of young African Americans had paymasters to satisfy, bosses to appease, and regulations to observe.[53]

While stations such as WSHA continued a tradition of black-oriented broadcasting from southern educational institutions, its neighbor WAFR in Durham and Atlanta's WRFG (Radio Free Georgia) offered different models of noncommercial community radio. Radio Free Georgia started in 1973 as the kind of station that the movement had always hoped Radio Tougaloo might become. As SNCC activist and WRFG stalwart Fay Bellamy explained, "The interest was to start a nonprofit radio station which would allow movement people to have access to mass media, which we did not have at that time." The biracial staff drew heavily from the ranks of SNCC, Students for a Democratic Society, various women's and antiwar organizations, and contributors to the underground magazine *The Great Speckled Bird*. With premises in the integrated Little Five Points area of Atlanta—a sort of southern Haight-Ashbury—the station offered an arresting mix of black consciousness–raising shows and interracial hippie chic. According to Bellamy, there was some rhythm and blues at WRFG, but not too much, since other local stations already filled that niche. Instead WRFG featured an eclectic range of jazz, gospel, and black and white "roots" music, alongside extensive, Pacifica-style news and public affairs programming devoted to universal issues of war, peace, poverty, free speech, and human rights. However, in an era of simmering racial tensions, the presence of an undercover agent provocateur undermined the biracial cooperation that marked the station's early years. Forced off the air amid bitter internal wrangling in the mid-1970s, the station later resurfaced with programming dedicated more exclusively to Atlanta's black community.[54]

While WRFG managed to stay afloat thanks largely to the black listener support available in Atlanta's massive metropolitan market, WAFR in Durham was less fortunate. The station was founded in 1971 by Robert Spruill, Ralph Williams, Robert Chapman, and Obitaye Akinwale (formerly Charles Copeland), a group of enterprising ex-students from North Carolina Central University who had been alarmed by the demise of Durham's major black-oriented commercial station WSRC. Not that they had been especially enamored of the relentless diet of soul music and down-home bonhomie that had dominated WSRC. As Akinwale recalled of his listening experiences while a student at NCCU, "I woke up one morning and turned the radio on. I heard this 'Ya-hoo, I'm a Country boy' kind of thing on . . . and of course that happened throughout my college career." He and his colleagues agreed that they wanted a respite from what they saw as crude, one-dimensional black programming. "I see it as an alternative to the garbage folks are getting on commercial radio," explained cofounder and president Robert Spruill. "We don't feel that advertising should be the major work of a radio station."[55]

Setting up the Community Radio Workshop Inc., the partners initially tried to buy the bankrupt WSRC, but lost out to Duke University. When that bid failed, they secured a $53,000 grant under the provisions of the Educational Broadcasting Act, supplemented it with contributions from the Southern Education Foundation and other philanthropic sources to reach a total of about $60,000, and launched their own public radio station. With guidance from the technical staff at nearby WSHA and the help of a handful of keen if barely competent volunteers, WAFR took to the air in October 1971 at 90.3 on the FM dial. It was the nation's first black-oriented noncommercial radio station not directly affiliated with an educational institution. In its four years on air, the station directed all of its programming toward the black community of Durham, sometimes attracting an audience of 75,000. Fifty percent of the station's schedule comprised music, but again soul constituted only one aspect of a diverse playlist. The rest of the programming was devoted to African American history and culture, religious programming that emphasized "the relevance of religious teachings to everyday living," newscasts that deliberately avoided the mainstream wire services in favor of African American news, and special slots reserved for a variety of local individuals and organizations. A defining feature of the station was its strong commitment to exploring the African links to African American history and culture. This was even apparent in its call letters W(ave)AFR(ica) and a similarly titled weekly news roundup of African affairs. WAFR also aired a good deal of contemporary African music and even taught children rudimentary Swahili in some of its *Saya Wa Toto* (Children's Hour) programs.[56]

Resourceful and passionate though its founders were, the WAFR experiment was short-lived. A critical lack of capital scuppered the station in the mid-1970s. WAFR had always relied on an annual sustaining grant from the CPB, awarded on the assumption that the station would eventually develop an independent funding base. In fact, WAFR found it impossible to raise the necessary funds from the black community in Durham and depended heavily on support from prominent local white-owned businesses like textile giant Burlington and sundry white individuals who served on the station's board of directors. With money scarce, the station occasionally vanished from the airways for hours, even days and weeks on end, simply because it had no money to carry out basic equipment repairs or pay its permanent staff. This unreliability and the lack of independently generated capital made it difficult for WAFR to secure more federal money. The task became impossible as the CPB began to require a minimum of seven full-time paid professional staff and a regular broadcasting schedule of no less than forty-eight hours per week at any station it supported. When the CPB declined to provide a new grant in 1975, the station shut down.

According to Robert Spruill, there were a number of reasons for WAFR's failure to generate sufficient financial support, as opposed to appreciation, from the local black community. He felt that a well-established black elite in Durham often looked upon the young WAFR crew with suspicion. Although Spruill and his colleagues tried gamely to make up the cash shortfall with appeals to the black masses, it was this well-heeled sector of African American society that was really in a position to offer substantial financial aid to the station, and it generally declined to do so. "We were on the outside of even the black establishment and were considered somewhat as outside troublemakers," he explained. Spruill interpreted the failure of WAFR in terms of generational and class divisions in the black community. Yet it is also possible that WAFR was the victim of another kind of cleavage within the southern black community. While earnest, engaged, and committed activists involved with radio—many of them from the same sort of university background as the founders of WAFR—continually strove for more public affairs, heritage programming, community information, and news broadcasting on radio, it was never clear that this type of programming was what the mass of black listeners wanted to hear. At least, it was not what they wanted to hear all or even most of the time. Although deeply sympathetic to WAFR's efforts, even media analyst Paul Vandergrift admitted that "one important lesson can be learned from the funding activities of WAFR ... know your community's feeling about a particular project and their interest in it." The harsh truth was that insufficient numbers of Durham blacks were interested enough in WAFR's innovative programming to rally to save the station.[57]

The fate of WAFR confirmed an important aspect of black-oriented broadcasting in the South. Irrespective of what black power militants or even civil rights moderates might want, black listeners continued to tune to stations where soul music dominated the schedules. While activists often demanded more attention to black economic, political, and social issues on radio, deejays and executives at commercial black-oriented stations simply pointed to continued black patronage and skyrocketing advertising revenue as an endorsement of their programming decisions. "As broadcasters, we don't dictate taste; our listeners do," argued Alan Henry, vice president of the Sonderling chain in 1970. "'Soul' music is what our listeners have shown they prefer, by and large, to other types. The reformists can like what they want, but the listeners dictate the programming."[58]

In fact, as the critic Gilbert Seldes had pointed out in the 1950s, this was a typically glib response by mass media moguls that obscured a more complex reality. "When a broadcaster says, 'We give the people what they want,'" Seldes argued, "the translation should be, 'The people would rather have something than nothing, so we give them something,' and 'The people don't dislike what we give them.'"[59] It is not necessary to take quite such a jaundiced view to appreciate that it was difficult to untangle whether radio stations led or followed popular tastes. The relationship between creating, serving, and manipulating radio audiences was always intricate and never static. Alan Henry's disclaimer aside, although radio stations clearly had a vested commercial interest in catering to established consumer preferences, they also helped to shape those preferences. Radio programmers and personalities had the power—not absolute, not unfettered, but nonetheless significant—to create new tastes and attitudes and change expectations among their audiences. Consequently, black activists constantly complained that black-oriented radio station owners, managers, and personalities could do much more to educate and mobilize, as well as to entertain, their listeners.

Paradoxically, the expansion of public broadcasting dedicated to African American audiences made it easier for commercial radio executives like Alan Henry to justify and continue their emphasis on soul music. After all, they noted, if black audiences really did want to hear more public affairs programming, news reports, and political commentary, there were now a growing number of noncommercial alternatives for them to listen to. Yet commercial black-oriented radio had suffered no discernible loss of market share to this competition. As Henry pointed out, the figures did not lie. Soul radio still had the programming format the majority of African American radio audiences favored for the majority of their listening time.

Alan Henry was neither the first nor the last person to identify this basic truth about the nature of the black radio audience, its preferences and expectations— and the relationship between those patterns and the medium's potential as a political and educational tool. In the late 1980s James Hutchinson, president of the black Inter-Urban group of broadcasters, discovered that his station WYLD– New Orleans lost listeners to white-owned rival WQUE when it tried to increase its news and public affairs programming. To win back its listeners, WYLD had to crank up its musical offerings.[60] More than two decades earlier, prototype black-power leader Robert Williams had recognized the need to leaven his radical radio messages with top-notch jazz, blues, and soul on the *Radio Free Dixie* programs he beamed into the South from Cuba between July 1962 and March 1966. Williams condemned Yankee imperialism, critiqued the capitalist roots of racial oppression in the American South, and praised black protest activities. "*Radio Free Dixie* was meant to be a voice of agitation and prophesy," Williams explained. But it also "played the music, the bitter protest songs, and spoke a biting truth that no other station dared program."[61] He was always careful to maximize the impact of his political messages by combining them with "Afro-American jazz, the blues and good soul music."[62]

Robert Williams's quest for balance in his radio programs revealed a keen sense of the way radio actually functioned within the southern black community. Williams understood that most African Americans tuned to radio in the first instance to be entertained and were likely to recoil from an unrelieved diet of social documentaries, political treatises, news reports, and calls to arms— figurative or literal—if these were not offered within an entertaining context. It was certainly true that the cultural and psychological work done by black-oriented radio in the black power era continued to be as important as any role it played, overt or covert, active or supportive, in organizing the southern masses in their struggle for freedom and justice. The point is that these goals were never mutually exclusive; they were inextricably linked. While the proportions differed from station to station, and were appreciably different at most noncommercial facilities, the most racially progressive, highly politicized, and politically effective black-oriented broadcasting in the South had always taken place to the sounds of music and other forms of popular culture that embodied black pride, self-respect, and communal identity.

Urban Riots on Southern Radio

Throughout the black power era, most southern black-oriented radio stations continued to accept the capacity of the American social, economic, and political system to redress legitimate black grievances. These stations consistently sought to dissuade African Americans from resorting to extralegal activities, violence, or separatism, even as they urged them to push for change within existing legal and political frameworks. Sherwood Ross explained this agenda to Hubert Humphrey in 1966, after the vice president had requested information about WOL's antislum campaign in D.C. "Often," Ross wrote, listeners "were unable to get their landlords on the telephone for two or three years." Following WOL intervention, "Suddenly, they find repairs made. Since many tenants know landlords are violating the law by allowing deficiencies to exist, their confidence in their ability to bring change within the existing legal framework is improved."[63]

This rejection of violence as a legitimate instrument of black protest informed black-oriented radio's response to Martin Luther King's murder on Thursday, April 4, 1968, and the urban disturbance that followed. In Washington several days of burning, looting, and rioting claimed twelve lives, resulted in more than 7,600 arrests, caused estimated property damage of $25 million, and required 10,000 troops to quell.[64] In a pattern replicated throughout the nation, WOL's operations manager Ted Atkins responded to news of King's shooting by immediately dropping all commercials from the station's schedules as a mark of respect while his deejays went on air to appeal for calm.[65] Bob "Nighthawk" Terry called for restraint and urged his listeners to get off the streets and go home out of respect for King. "This is no time to hate," Terry implored in a statement that aired frequently and was widely reprinted in the local press. "Hate won't get you anywhere."[66] A specially recorded appeal by King's colleague Walter Fauntroy and three special editions of David Eaton's *Speak Up* show echoed this message, calling upon the community to respond to the tragedy in the nonviolent spirit of the slain King. In a marathon *Speak Up* session on Saturday, April 6, listeners were encouraged to call the station to express their grief rather than turn to violence.[67]

In another vivid illustration of the way in which the social significance of black-oriented radio intersected with its cultural coordinates, one of WOL's major contributions to efforts to bring the rioting under control was to locate singer James Brown. Responding to personal requests from President Lyndon Johnson and Mayor Walter Washington, station manager John Pace had contacted the singer in New York. On April 6, Brown appeared on Washington's television and radio stations, rapping, "Don't terrorize. Organize. Don't burn. Give the kids a chance to learn." After these general media appeals, Brown went to WOL's studios, where he spent hours answering phone calls and counseling restraint.[68]

During the most acute period of civil unrest in D.C., WOL temporarily increased its news coverage. By its own calculations, the station devoted approximately 50 percent of its airtime to news on the first night of the riots and averaged between fifteen and thirty minutes per hour over the next two days. This included coverage of similar disturbances across the nation. As on many previous occasions during the course of the freedom struggle, commentators like those writing in *Variety* agreed: "In general, radio's speed and mobility were harnessed to good advantage" on the night of the murder. "The radio listener was closer to the scene of breaking news than the tv viewer." WOL, as part of the Sonderling chain, was also able to capitalize on the news-gathering operations of its sister station WDIA in Memphis, the scene of King's murder. The chain would cooperate again for King's funeral in Atlanta, with WAOK taking the lead in a temporary American Freedom Network, hastily created specifically to relay news of the services around the nation.[69]

Closer to home, in the days following King's murder WOL reporter Alan King distinguished himself with a series of dramatic feeds direct from the city's flashpoints. Beyond simply reporting the turbulent events on the streets of the capital's black neighborhoods, the station also tried to help local black residents come to terms with them. WOL announced where to find emergency food, clothing, and shelter and reported details of office and factory closures and disruptions to the transportation system. Coming shortly after the president's National Advisory Commission on Civil Disorders had condemned sensationalist media coverage of the 1967 summer urban riots for contributing to the spread of violence, WOL strove to balance comprehensive reporting of events in D.C. with an effort not to exacerbate tensions in the city. As the station's management later explained, "We had a responsibility to the community to broadcast the news factually, to hold down as many rumors as possible, and to let our listeners know, for the most part, what was happening in the city of Washington and across the country.... At the same time, because of the highly volatile reaction to the news of King's death, we had to assume the role of 'guardian' and not add to the problems that began occurring in the District."[70]

This sense of civic responsibility was usually manifested in the language of reconciliation rather than in actual suppression of news about the riots and rumors of impending black rebellion. Nevertheless, there were occasions when the station did withhold information for what it considered the greater public good. For example, newsmen were not allowed to identify the precise locations from which they were reporting ongoing disturbances, so as to prevent more would-be rioters flocking to the scene.[71] Similarly, WOL decided to censor reports of the press conference held by Stokely Carmichael the morning after King's murder when the incensed black power leader appeared to urge African Americans to take up arms against their oppressors. "When white America killed Dr. King last night, she declared war on us," Carmichael insisted. "We have to retaliate for the deaths of our leaders. The execution for those deaths will not be in the court-rooms. They're going to be in the streets of the United States of America. . . . Black people know that they have to get guns. White America will live to cry since she killed Dr. King last night." Although WOL's Ron Pinkney had recorded the entire press conference, station executives Ted Atkins and John Pace deemed it inappropriate to broadcast Carmichael's comments.[72]

While the generally calming response of WOL to the violence and destruction that erupted in the wake of King's murder was understandable, this was not an exceptional response to the tragic events of April 1968. Rather, it was entirely consistent with the pattern of support for nonviolent black protest strategies that had been evident on both black-oriented and general-market radio stations in the South for decades. Similarly, it reflected the prevailing view at such stations that any black violence, organized or spontaneous, individual or collective, overtly political or conventionally "criminal," was detrimental to black interests. Two years before the King riots, for example, WOL had responded to disturbances among a predominantly black crowd at a fairground in Washington's Glen Echo Park—disturbances that arose because the overcrowded park had closed before some customers could enjoy the rides for which they had already paid—by edito-rializing that "The violence could not have come at a worse time." WOL declared it "a body blow to every civil rights group urging non-violent protests and boy-cotts to help bring home rule to Washington."[73]

WOL was not unusual in being cautious about reporting either provocative rhetoric or actual incidences of black violence. Tom O'Brien, vice president of ABC's Radio Network News, announced his determination to avoid "inflam-matory journalism" and concurred with the news director at WIL–St. Louis who felt that local radio stations risked promoting copycat incidents among "kids running around with transistor radios" even by airing news of disturbances in other cities.[74] KCOH-Houston president Robert Meeker explained his station's policy toward reporting urban riots and the rabble-rousing oratory that often accompanied them. "Our news is screened so that when an individual with trea-sonous motives says 'go out in the street and kill and burn' we do not report this." Jesse Blayton's WERD was another station that routinely suppressed news of black riots. In Danville, Virginia, the site of bitter civil rights struggles through-out the 1960s, WILA hoped to minimize the potential for black violence by pre-paring a tape of moderating messages from black celebrities and civil rights leaders to air in the event of summer rioting.[75]

In Memphis, radio played an especially critical role in reporting and interpret-ing the tragic events of the spring of 1968. WDIA had been closely covering the sanitation workers' strike that brought King to the city in late March. When King arrived, he found an indigenous movement riven by ideological, class, and generational tensions—tensions that were only intensified by covert FBI operations to disrupt black protest in the city. Local black resentment simmered both against the white authorities headed by Mayor Henry Loeb and against what some perceived as King's unwarranted interference in a local campaign. On March 28 King was forced to curtail a march through downtown Memphis when nonviolent discipline broke down and there were serious disturbances. At WDIA, Bert Ferguson was quick to applaud King for abandoning a march that had deteriorated into violence. He urged the entire community to restrain those who were undermining efforts to reduce racial antagonisms in the city. "We do not intend to be Pollyannas at WDIA," he told listeners, "but we still think that racial harmony is desired in our city by both a majority of whites and a majority of Negroes. . . . do everything that you can to influence those around you to obey the law and to act like responsible citizens."[76]

A week later, on the eve of King's death, the station was much more critical of the civil rights leader. King had returned to Memphis to lead another march, eager to prove that nonviolence had not outlived its usefulness as a protest tactic. Ferguson argued that King was being irresponsible and simply inviting more violence:

> Anyone who plans a march through Downtown Memphis, as happened on Thursday, must accept partial responsibility for any resulting violence. . . . It was obvious to any on-looker on Thursday that those who created the violence had little thought of civil rights, as a cause, in their minds. They had sticks in their hands and they decided to break some windows. We believe that the white community has to share the responsibility for the creation of such irresponsible young men. But we also believe that the black community has an equal responsibility to help stop them when they set out to destroy the community.[77]

The next day King was killed. Instantly, reservations about the prudence of King's decision to resume mass marches were set aside. Death transformed King into a paragon of peace and a model of dignified, responsible black protest. Literally within hours radio and television had suppressed criticisms of King's opposition to the Vietnam War, his increasingly radical critique of the intersection of militarism, economic exploitation, and racism in American life, and his refusal to stop protesting injustice in the nation's streets. Instead the electronic media, quickly followed by the mainstream print media, began to portray King as the unimpeachable apostle of nonviolence and integration whose unflinching message of love and racial reconciliation contrasted with the rage, violence, and separatism they associated with black power leaders like Carmichael and H. Rap Brown.

In Memphis, Rev. James Lawson, civil rights leader and one of the foremost proponents of nonviolent direct action, was half-watching television while eating dinner when he heard the announcement that King had been shot. His first reaction was that he must get to WDIA and put out an appeal for calm in the community. As early wire reports announced that King was severely injured but still alive, Lawson recorded the first of several tapes. "Stay calm. Don't listen to rumors. At this moment we only know that he is wounded. Pray. We must adhere to nonviolence. . . . Keep faith in his life and works. We must go on with the struggle." The tape was airing when the station got word that King was dead. Lawson immediately made another tape, another call for restraint. "Since he was dead we should want to honor him by seeking to live out what he lived for and died for," Lawson explained.[78]

With the regular WDIA announcers in shock, Bert Ferguson had taken over reading all the news bulletins. He echoed Lawson's call for local blacks to respect King's own commitment to nonviolence and invoked the influence of the church to check the rising clamor for vengeance and retribution in the black community. "That the deep reservoir of spirituality built into the people of Memphis by years of worship may now take solid hold and restrain all of us from further tragic acts is to be hoped and prayed for," Ferguson intoned. "I implore you . . . pray and wait. Restrain with any power you may possess your own emotions and those of anyone you may influence. We must hold to reason." Similar messages aired on black-oriented radio across the nation. At WGOK in Mobile, Irene Ware was one of those who tried to get people off the streets: "Tell 'em to go in, you know, follow the curfews. And basically that's what we did throughout the day . . . we stayed on with gospel music hoping to tame the wilds." Ex–WDIA deejay Maurice "Hot Rod" Hulbert was working at WITH-Baltimore at the time of the assassination. Gus Harris, head of the Maryland state militia, insisted that Hulbert go on air as disturbances broke out. "They had me on the air talking to our people, trying to quiet them."[79]

It is a moot point how successful these broadcasts were in defusing black anger and reducing the violence and destruction in April 1968. Even James Brown's appearance on WOL had failed to end all the rioting in Washington, while Bert Ferguson admitted that widespread calls for calm on WDIA had not always been heeded in Memphis. "Strangely," Ferguson lamented, King's "passing has already been seized upon by opportunists, apparently blinded by the same force of hate which drove the assassin's bullet into his neck, opportunists who have stolen by looting, destroyed by fire, wounded by angry force. All of these acts, acts of stupidity, would have been strongly opposed by the man whose death somehow has been causing them."[80]

Yet if black-oriented radio was unable to stop the riots, Jack Gibson was among those who insisted that "if it were not for black radio, I imagine more cities in the United States would have been burnt to the ground." Certainly the deluge of commendations and awards received by black-oriented radio stations—among them D.C. outlets WOL, WUST, and WOOK and Memphis stations WDIA, WMCT, and WSM—from law enforcement agencies and civic leaders in recognition of their contribution to restoring order, suggests that these stations had played a significant role in preventing a terrible situation from becoming even worse.[81]

NATRA's Del Shields believed that the impressive way in which black-oriented radio responded to the assassination and the riots actually revealed just how much influence the medium had over the black community—and ensured that its power would be much more closely monitored and controlled in future. Shields, who was on the air at WLIB–New York at the time of King's murder, insisted that although black-oriented radio had been unable to prevent the immediate outburst of violence among some sections of the black community, it nonetheless helped to check its spread and escalation. "All across the country," Shields recalled, "the black disk jockey went to the microphone and talked to his people. . . . It was black radio that doused the incendiary flames across America. . . . We curtailed the riots. Had we not been on, hadn't . . . told the people, 'Don't burn, baby,' and all of that, it would have been worse. And somebody sat up and said, 'Whoa, this is too much. This is too much power. We can't let them have it.'" Paradoxically, according to Shields, it was at this moment of bittersweet triumph that the opportunities for genuinely politicized, socially conscious, community-focused black-oriented commercial radio began to diminish. "Somebody detected that this was too much power. It had to be broken up. So one of the ways to break it up was . . . to get rid of personality radio." Historically, Shields argued, the individual personality deejay, a trusted and respected member of the community, was the key to black radio's power. "Take away the personality of radio and develop it into format," he explained, "and you've got the garbage that you have today."[82]

Stripped of Shields's conspiratorial spin, this rather pessimistic view of black-oriented radio became commonplace after the riots of 1968. Many black commentators felt that changes in black programming formats and the commercial aspirations of owners, managers, and deejays eager for a shot at a more lucrative mainstream radio market combined to reduce the responsiveness of many stations to the real interests of black audiences. "What is black, has an affinity with some twenty million people, and has abdicated its responsibilities for a fast dollar?" asked journalism experts Douglas O'Connor and Gayla Cook. "The answer is black radio." Historian Thomas Blair agreed. Black radio, he argued in 1974, "is both a lucrative form of commercial exploitation and an electronic Trojan horse in the black community."[83]

There was more than a grain of truth in some of these criticisms. In retrospect, however, it is ironic that such complaints were made in the midst of an era when concerted black media campaigns and beneficial federal legislation promoted more politically engaged, informative, and socially responsible black-oriented radio programming than in any era before or since. In any case, the critics were misguided on at least two counts. First, they disregarded what sort of listening fare black audiences traditionally wanted or expected to find on their favorite stations. Once the smoke had cleared over the riot zones, most southern black listeners gravitated back to stations where soul was the staple among a variegated programming crop, and where personality deejays continued to be major attractions. Second, the critics substituted wishful thinking for efforts to deal with the realities of commercial black-oriented radio's political and social agenda. In the unique circumstances of April 1968, radio stations had responded by temporarily increasing their quotient of news and community-affairs programming in an effort to control the behavior of the black masses. In the midst of this crisis, various radicals in the industry and in the broader freedom struggle had caught another tantalizing glimpse of what a truly politicized, progressive, and socially engaged black-oriented radio might accomplish; how it might be used to move minds and hearts and bodies. Yet they generally failed to note how black-oriented radio's response to the crisis confirmed the medium's essential moderation and antipathy to radical political or programming agendas. The medium was steadfastly integrationist and preferred reconciliation to confrontation—although it was increasingly willing to support legalistic or electorally based protests.

This philosophy was clear at WDIA, which quickly began to promote the NAACP's Roy Wilkins as King's successor as putative "leader" of the black freedom struggle. One editorial applauded Wilkins's "positive program to offset any threat of new violence in the months ahead. . . . He still believes that integration into the American mainstream is the Negro's best hope. So do we at WDIA." During the rioting and even more so in the months that followed, other editorials revived gradualist mantras about how interracial goodwill and cooperation would eventually eradicate racial discrimination and redeem the South. Bert Ferguson told listeners that he had spoken with other white businessmen who assured him of their determination "to see to it that the past is pushed aside and that a new day comes to Memphis. We are going to talk to our Negro neighbors. We are going to be fair to them in our hearts and in our actions. Equal opportunity for every person is coming to Memphis and it is going to start in my place of business right now." Ferguson beseeched his exasperated and bitter black listeners not to dismiss this latest round of white promises. "With whatever force my voice can muster, I plead with those who trust me to believe that these are not just promises in the heat of emotion. I listened to these men. I have heard them before. Now . . . they mean business and they mean business for right now. Not sometime in the distant future. You give your white friends a chance. I will stand by my Negro friends and together . . . but only if we stay together . . . we will emerge into a new day."[84]

WBT Confronts Busing and Black Power in Charlotte

It was not only black-oriented radio stations in the South that had to respond to the challenge of urban riots, the growth of black power, and the various social, economic, and political developments that characterized the first decade after the demise of statutory Jim Crow. General-market stations also reflected and helped to shape important changes in race relations and racial consciousness in the region. Events at WBT in Charlotte in the late 1960s and early 1970s dramatized the station's continuing efforts of to navigate a moderate path between black radicalism and what it saw as an equally disturbing trend toward white conservative extremism.

One of the most incendiary issues in Charlotte—and elsewhere—during this era was the use of busing to complete the integration of school systems where desegregation had been stymied by a mixture of white obstructionism and the persistence of racially discrete residential neighborhoods. When the 1964 school year opened, only 3 percent of black students in the Charlotte-Mecklenburg public school system attended integrated schools. In the wake of the Civil Rights Act, which linked federal funding for state education to evidence of desegregation, the situation improved somewhat. Around 10 percent of black children attended integrated schools during the 1965–66 school year. It was clear, however, that this represented at best glacial and grudging progress. Ten African American families represented by NAACP lawyer Julius Chambers sued the Charlotte-Mecklenburg school board, hoping to replace the chicanery of "voluntarism" and "pupil placement" plans with a plan to fully integrate the system. Chambers skillfully maneuvered the cases, consolidated as *Swann*, through various court hearings and appeals processes all the way to the Supreme Court. In April 1971 the Court upheld earlier recommendations—and eventually instructions—by federal judge James McMillan to use busing to overcome the injurious effects of racially segmented residential patterns on the racial mix in Charlotte's schools.[85]

By the time of the *Swann* decision, WBT's Charlie Crutchfield was four months into a year-long term as president of the Charlotte Chamber of Commerce. While the usually influential Chamber was mute and ineffectual during this latest racial crisis, WBT once again emerged as a powerful voice for moderation in the face of seething white anger at Judge McMillan's busing directives. Not that Crutchfield or his station was ever a supporter of the policy itself. WBT had always opposed busing in both principle and practice. As early as May 1964 it had editorialized, "We do not favor gerrymandering school districts. They are just as dishonest as forced segregation or forced integration."[86] It held fast to this basic position throughout the protracted legal wrangling and civic chaos of the late 1960s and early 1970s. When James McMillan issued his initial April 1969 recommendation that the Charlotte-Mecklenburg school board should bus to achieve integration, the station's response was typical. On one hand, WBT expressed sympathy for McMillan. It noted that the Supreme Court's 1968 *Green* decision had put an affirmative responsibility on local school boards to end school segregation even if the causes of that segregation—for example, residential patterns—were not strictly its responsibility. This, one editorial suggested, had left McMillan with little option but to seek the rapid and full integration of Charlotte's schools. On the other hand, WBT made no effort to disguise its exasperation at what it considered to be yet more judge-made law in the racial arena, and it argued that busing was a financially and logistically impossible means to integrate the schools. Despite the objections, however, the editorial ended with one of WBT's typically powerful demands that everyone in Charlotte respect a legally binding court order, no matter how much they disagreed with it. "This station believes very strongly that quality education should be available to all children, but we question the advisability of busing. Nevertheless, if the court's order [*Green*] is to be obeyed, student busing seems inevitable, until such time as housing patterns change. Perhaps it isn't fair, perhaps it isn't sensible, perhaps it isn't worth the problems it will cause. But it is here."[87]

In editorials like this, WBT represented the voice of disappointed and reluctant white realism in Charlotte; it reflected a middle ground of white opinion that was chastened, but at least somewhat changed by the successes of the civil rights movement. By contrast, from the spring of 1969 until early 1970, the Charlotte-Mecklenburg school board clung tenaciously to the sort of sly, quasi-legalistic resistance that typified white North Carolina's response to desegregation. The board asked McMillan for a succession of extensions and then, in August 1969, submitted a new plan that completely ignored the judge's busing recommendations. Instead it tried to shore up the neighborhood school system and freedom-of-choice principles that had long served as bulwarks against meaningful integration. WBT endorsed the board's proposals as sensible in the context of mounting popular anger at McMillan's April recommendations. But it did appreciate that the city's African Americans would be angry, and regretted "that once again, they must be asked to shoulder a heavier burden than the white population on the road to racial equality." Understandably, the black community was not quite so sanguine about being asked once more to be patient while white Charlotte decided precisely when and how it would honor clear legal directives in the racial arena. WBT recognized this and a day later gave Rev. George Leake the chance to reply. One of the most dynamic black leaders to emerge in Charlotte during the second half of 1960s, Leake condemned the "non-empathetic position to the black people [taken,] once again, by our ultra-conservative friends of WBT." He reiterated the guarded enthusiasm of most Charlotte blacks for busing "as a necessary tool to implement desegregation and promote meaningful integration." The ironic tension in Leake's characterization of WBT as both "ultra-conservative" and "friends" perfectly captured a serpentine relationship between the station and the African American community that was always complicated, often ambiguous, and sometimes just plain contradictory.[88]

Judge McMillan rejected the school board's August 1969 plan and did the same to several similarly evasive ones that followed. Frustrated by the board's continued obstructionism and cognizant of the Supreme Court's recent *Alexander* decision—which had finally laid to rest the vague "all deliberate speed" formulation of the second *Brown* decision by calling for the immediate implementation of desegregation plans for schools—McMillan lost patience. In February 1970 he moved beyond making recommendations and ordered the school board to adopt a busing plan for the desegregation of all elementary, junior high, and senior high schools, to be implemented by May 4, 1970.

The white response to McMillan and his decision was overwhelmingly, if not exclusively, hostile. The school board immediately appealed the decision to the Supreme Court and asked the U.S. Fourth Circuit Court of Appeals to stay the introduction of busing pending the Supreme Court's further deliberations on the constitutionality and wider implications of McMillan's decision. Through the summer and early fall of 1970, the board submitted various new proposals in an attempt to avoid busing. McMillan found them all wanting. Meanwhile the incensed suburban whites who formed the vanguard of a massive noncompliance movement in the city formed a militant Concerned Parents Association (CPA). The CPA hoped to resist busing by methods that ranged from petitioning political leaders and school board members to preparing for a white boycott of the public schools should busing actually proceed. McMillan himself was the subject of horrendous abuse and numerous threats. The intensity of the popular white anger unleashed by the judge's busing order far exceeded that created by *Brown*, or by the desegregation of public facilities in 1963. Moreover, in 1963 Mayor Stan Brookshire and the Chamber of Commerce had intervened decisively to encourage calm compliance, whereas in 1970 Mayor John Belk and the Chamber failed to provide similar leadership over busing. As tensions mounted, they remained silent—although, given Belk's hostility to busing, his silence at least avoided giving more encouragement to an increasingly militant white opposition.

In the absence of clear and effective civic leadership, the atmosphere in Charlotte deteriorated steadily, becoming positively poisonous as the new school year approached. That summer the Supreme Court had refused to uphold further stays, leaving the school board no alternative but to prepare cross-city transportation for some 20,000 students. In September 1970, Charlotte nervously opened the most fully integrated urban school system in American history. Having witnessed the turmoil and rising tempers of the previous six months, many observers braced themselves for an unprecedented outbreak of racial violence and disorder in the city.

In fact, there was much less strife than anticipated and much less than in many other cities where widespread busing occurred. There were some scary and ugly moments, to be sure. "No Forced Busing" slogans were daubed on the walls of three schools a few days before opening; six schools were closed on the first day of classes as a result of bomb threats; one school bus actually had its windows broken; and a few months later Julius Chambers's house was bombed. Yet, reprehensible though such acts may have been, they still fell some way short of the cataclysm that many had predicted. Once more, white Charlotte's dogged respect for legal authority, its disdain for extralegal resistance, and its concern to maintain a working public school system at all costs combined to preserve a remarkable measure of law and order in the midst of seething rage and resentment.

With most local politicians and business leaders staying diplomatically or fearfully silent on the busing issue, WBT was again an important factor in promoting this relative restraint. By the time the schools reopened in September 1970, Charlie Crutchfield had solicited a series of one-minute spot announcements from various black and white celebrities—including his old pal Billy Graham—and even from a smattering of bolder local politicians and businessmen. All offered variations on the same theme: "This is the law, the important thing is not whether we like it or not but whether we believe in law and order. Don't blow your cool." These editorials, alongside those of the *Charlotte Observer,* were the most conspicuous and consistent public voices urging compliance with McMillan's orders until the Supreme Court should rule otherwise.[89]

By April 1971, when the *Swann* decision made it clear that no such reversal was going to happen, Charlie Crutchfield had assumed the mantle of president of the Chamber of Commerce. A majority within the Chamber still eschewed taking a formal position on the busing issue for fear of aligning with the "wrong" side. Nevertheless, while the Chamber remained officially silent on what to do about busing, Crutchfield made sure that his radio and television stations took their traditional opinion-making and peacekeeping responsibilities more seriously than ever. It was as if Crutchfield felt obliged to use WBT to compensate for the reluctance, or inability, of the Chamber, the city council, and the mayor's office to offer leadership in the midst of the crisis that threatened to engulf the city.

As usual, WBT condemned extremism on every side of the dispute and urged further dialogue between all interested parties. It was unequivocal in its denunciation of both the CPA's renewed plans for a schools boycott and of the white violence that had greeted the *Swann* decision. In the wake of that ruling, the station lavished praise on Julius Chambers and applauded Chambers's responsible, legalistic approach to racial change. At the same time, it patriotically affirmed the basic soundness of the American social and judicial system that allowed him to adopt those tactics. In this regard WBT shared the same core values and endorsed much the same kind of restraint and respectable protest in addressing racial injustice as did most black-oriented stations in the South. "Many of us are not happy with the results of the Charlotte-Mecklenburg school desegregation case," the editorial admitted.

> But let's hope nobody will fail to acknowledge that the man who led the winning side all the way—Charlotte attorney Julius Chambers—used the courts rather than the streets. . . . Chambers didn't win his case by staging protest marches or demonstrations or riots. He worked within the system. And the system upheld him—all the way to the top. . . . Julius Chambers has shown how it can and should be done. . . . He has proved that the American system works for anyone willing to put it to the test. We hope that this lesson will not be lost on those who are out to destroy it.[90]

Despite Crutchfield's disappointment with the *Swann* decision, WBT accepted it, and even adopted a far more proactive role in promoting orderly compliance in the city. In the summer of 1971 the station sponsored the "Project Hope: A Bridge to Understanding" initiative. This brought together a thousand black and white junior-high and high-school students over a period of eight weeks at Johnson C. Smith University in order to discuss racial issues. The hope was that "when they return to school in September they'll be far better equipped to forestall the kinds of racial disturbances which have racked our community this Spring."[91]

Project Hope met with limited success. There was a serious outbreak of violence at three city high schools when they reopened in the autumn of 1971, leading to their temporary closure and the expulsion of four thousand students. Most of those expelled were African Americans, as were all but two of the seventy-seven students arrested in connection with the disturbances. This racial imbalance added credence to black accusations that there was discrimination in the disciplinary procedures at these newly integrated schools, eventually prompting Judge McMillan to order the school board to prepare new codes of disciplinary practice. Hardly known for soft-pedaling on acts of lawlessness, WBT's editorials nonetheless urged "that charges against students arrested as a result of riots in our schools should be dropped." The station even endorsed the views of its old sparring partner George Leake, who argued in a guest editorial that the unequal burden of arrests, charges, and expulsions smacked of discrimination and would only further alienate an already inflamed and suspicious black community, destroying the chance for the "rational discussion that *leads* to understanding."[92]

Beyond his traditional concern to use WBT to promote understanding, dialogue, and reconciliation across racial lines, there was another reason why Charlie Crutchfield may have felt compelled to support the black community and encourage greater white sympathy for its continuing plight. In May 1971 he found himself at the center of a controversy that very nearly destroyed whatever credibility he had built up over the previous decades as a racial moderate. On the evening of May 26, Crutchfield gave a speech to the Raleigh Chamber of Commerce on the recent proliferation of essentially white "bedroom suburbs" around cities such as Raleigh and Charlotte. Many of these satellite suburbs were now seeking incorporation as separate cities and Crutchfield condemned the trend, arguing that this "white-flight"—in no small part related to white fears about the effects of inner-city busing on their children's schooling—represented a regrettable form of racial resegregation.[93]

Once the formal speech was over, Crutchfield participated in a plenary discussion about the changing face of southern municipal politics, during which the subject of Atlanta came up. In 1969, partly as a consequence of white-flight and a coordinated African American voting campaign, Maynard Jackson had become the city's first black vice-mayor. With African Americans already comprising 52 percent of the Atlanta population, Crutchfield predicted—correctly—that it would soon have a black mayor, a black-controlled city council, and blacks in various other key administrative positions. Charlotte, he suggested, would follow suit if it allowed "bedroom suburbs" to incorporate. Then he dropped his bombshell. "I'm not disparaging the black race, but certainly, as of now, I don't think they are economically or mentally qualified to run a city as big as Atlanta. Maybe in few years they will be."[94]

When an aide pointed out precisely what he had said, Crutchfield immediately recognized that his words were at best ill-chosen, at worst an inexcusable slur on black mental capabilities. Within two minutes Crutchfield returned to the microphone to clarify his remarks. Stressing that it was not his intention to disparage blacks, he explained that he had meant to say, "Due to their educational background at this point in history, they are not ready to run a city." He added that he also felt the same applied to poor whites and members of any race who lacked the necessary education and experience for governing a major city.

FIGURE 21. Charles Crutchfield's experience in southern
radio from the 1930s until the
mid-1970s spanned the period
from the darkest years of Jim
Crow to the birth of the New
South. Like many other southern whites, he sometimes
struggled to come to terms
with the implications of the racial revolution that WBT both
reported and helped to shape
in Charlotte. Courtesy of Library of American Broadcasting, University of Maryland,
College Park.

This attempt at damage limitation did little to stem an outpouring of black condemnation, ironically stimulated by coverage of the speech on WBTV's 11 p.m.
newscast as well as a front-page article in the following morning's *Charlotte Observer*.

On May 27, the day after Crutchfield's remarks, reporter Ben Waters covered
the rising tide of black anger for WBTV's *Early Scene*. Former school board member Rev. Coleman Kerry called Crutchfield's comments an "irresponsible statement . . . and an insult to black citizens," while George Leake complained that it
"sets back and polarizes the community." Crutchfield meanwhile continued to
express his deep regrets both publicly and privately. Waters read out a prepared
statement in which Crutchfield said, "It is regrettable that my remarks in Raleigh last night have apparently offended some of our black citizens. Certainly
nothing could have been further from my intent." Crutchfield insisted that
"blacks, I believe, are as 'mentally qualified' as anybody else, given the same
education, experience, background, and other advantages. What I intended to
say was that blacks, unfortunately, have not had the advantages, by and large,
that others have had." He concluded by returning to a familiar theme, stressing
the need for interracial cooperation and understanding. In the past such messages had been directed primarily at the white community. Now Crutchfield was

appealing at least as much to the black community for indulgence and forgiveness for his lapse. "If our community is to grow and prosper and close the wounds which racial misunderstanding has caused in the past, it is essential that all of us work together, as one people to get the job done."[95]

The same day, Crutchfield also sent an internal memo to the WBT staff, expressing regret that his remarks "have apparently offended some of our staff, as well as some other citizens of Charlotte," and explaining his broader thinking on busing, incorporation, and racial progress in detail. The incorporation of "bedroom suburbs," he repeated, would "set integration back to where it was before the Brown Decision in 1954. . . . If the whites move to the suburbs and lock themselves out of the city through incorporation, this will mean we'll have a predominantly black city in a white perimeter, which, in my judgment, is segregation at its worst."[96]

Crutchfield thought these retractions, apologies, and glosses would end the matter. He was wrong. On May 28 the infuriatingly intrepid reporter Ben Waters was still soliciting reactions to Crutchfield's original remarks for *Early Scene*. Understandably, thrice-elected city councilor Fred Alexander felt personally affronted by the implication that he was not yet competent to participate in city government. Compared to some of the vitriol heaped on Crutchfield, Alexander's response to his long-time associate's predicament was relatively subdued, even sympathetic, but he was deeply disappointed. "It is unfortunate indeed when a person who has done much to improve the plight of the Negro in his community, possibly loses the effectiveness of his efforts, and gets caught up in the crossfire of condemnation, from both Negroes and whites, over the wrong use of words, in attempting to explain one of America's most complex social problems. . . . Such is the position Charles Crutchfield . . . finds himself in. Regardless of how the words came out, I emphatically disagree with what the statement implies, and understand why Negroes feel offended."[97]

Over the next few days, Crutchfield was the recipient of much more public and private criticism. He was even advised to post a guard outside his house in case the mood should turn more ugly. Although he was somewhat contrite, Crutchfield was also bewildered by the way that what he saw as a mere slip of the tongue threatened to negate all his previous work on behalf of better race relations in Charlotte. Yet this was as nothing compared to the anger and sense of betrayal he felt toward some of his own staff, whom he blamed for drawing public attention to his error. After a weekend at the beach, during which he had "a chance to study my Raleigh error and cool off," he admitted, "my cool is slow in coming." Still furious, on June 1 he summoned all the station's white radio and television management to a meeting where he challenged them to justify their decision to let their newsrooms make "a federal case" out of his gaffe. He concluded the meeting with a clear reminder that, irrespective of the distractions of his civic duties and his advancing years, he was still running the station. "There seems to be some misunderstanding as to who's in charge here. I am. And I intend to be until I decide to retire or until I'm retired at age sixty-five. Following this episode, I would like to announce here and now that I have no intentions of retiring early."[98]

As the meeting broke up, Crutchfield instructed those white managers who had African American employees in their departments "to call them in today—this morning if possible—in a group, and discuss this entire matter with them, giving them the facts as outlined here this morning."[99] Crutchfield had initially seemed nonplussed and even a little resentful and suspicious at the passions of the black response to his remarks, feeling that some local leaders were simply using his mistake to draw attention to themselves. However, the indignant response from many of his own black staff had a much greater emotional and intellectual impact. Of all the African Americans in Charlotte, he felt these people should know of his decency, his record of commitment to racial dialogue and progress. Hadn't they applauded when he formally accepted as part of WBT's brief the need to promote "better understanding of the divergence within the black community" and better understanding of the "Black Power and the Black Panther movement"? Or when he set up a Black Advisory Council at the station, or when, with the cooperation of Fred Alexander, he had instituted an in-house training program for "disadvantaged persons" designed to increase minority employment opportunities? These people surely knew that he was well-intentioned toward the black community.[100]

In fact, there were a few expressions of support from African Americans associated with the station. Allegra M. Westbrooks, an acquisitions librarian at the Charlotte and Mecklenburg County Library who served on WBT's Black Advisory Council, wrote "to commend your courage in quickly modifying the recent statement concerning Charlotte's black community." Westbrooks added that "it is good to note that through programs to come, opportunities will be provided to air some of the problems, hopes, aspirations, and talent of the black community. The insistence . . . that the programming be of good quality should help to ease the myth regarding black 'mental capacities.'"[101]

Such messages were the exception. Crutchfield simply could not escape the fact that he had deeply offended his black employees. Frankie Hutton pulled no punches, writing to Crutchfield, "You seem surprised that some members of the staff found your remarks in Raleigh last night offensive. Personally, I was let down tremendously and disappointed that you—a leader would make such a public statement. It was unethical." Even more poignant was the letter from engineer Jan Spence, a man whose loyalty to Crutchfield and the station was never in doubt. "As possibly the longest employed black serving in a technical position with the Jefferson Standard Broadcasting Company, I feel that I would be untrue to my beliefs if I did not express my deep regret over the statement that was made to the Mecklenburg legislators in Raleigh. . . . I've always been proud to be an employee of this firm and I considered my job as important as the next person; I enjoy doing my best for the good of the station. The statement that was made was an insult to me and the black community." A month later, Florence C. Avery was still fuming: "I can't understand nor find any justification for your public attack on the Black man's place in this society. You have personally insulted me and my fellow Black co-workers and many other Blacks here in the city."[102]

The Raleigh incident and the volley of criticism it elicited from African Americans, together with his concerns about busing, appear to have provoked one of Crutchfield's periodic reexaminations of what he might do to improve race relations in Charlotte. There followed an intensification of his commitment to encouraging African American progress through support for black businesses and expanded employment opportunities. To some extent, this reflected Crutchfield's enthusiasm for the sort of black capitalism promoted by the Republican party under Richard Nixon. Indeed, before the Watergate debacle, Crutchfield was a big admirer of Nixon. Certainly, one can trace the tentative beginnings of the Chamber of Commerce's reemergence as a major shaper of racial opinion and policy in Charlotte to Crutchfield's term in office. Without exaggerating what were still quite modest achievements, the Chamber was a rather more racially diverse and progressive body by the time Crutchfield's term expired in January 1972.

Incremental though the achievements may have been, they were a matter of great pride to Crutchfield. When he gave his presidential farewell address, he listed various citywide racial initiatives as his proudest accomplishments. "In a significant expansion of its historical role," he recapped, "the Chamber . . . began a Minority Enterprise Program to assist blacks in setting up and running their own businesses. We established a blue-ribbon Public Education Task Force—involving the total community—to improve quality education in our schools. And we formed a 'Bridge of Hope' Task Force whose purpose is to bring blacks into the mainstream of Chamber and Community life." Soon afterwards he told writer Mary Boger that he felt he "had made his greatest contribution to Charlotte during this electric period. He could see that the danger lay in hysteria and that somehow the people must be calmed and urged to obey the law even when it was not palatable."[103]

Crutchfield had also concluded that the city should take responsibility for reversing the damage caused by its own racially driven urban planning policies. "The major problem of Charlotte today is housing, and this must be attacked with boldness immediately," he told Boger. "We are in danger of doing nothing but building new ghettoes unless we diversify the housing pattern." Over the next few years Crutchfield and WBT pushed for more enlightened planning and development policies, while urging tolerance for busing until the impact of this urban restructuring could be felt. Shortly before his retirement in 1977 Crutchfield admitted publicly, "I even believe history will show Jim McMillan was right in his busing decision. After studying it and looking at the housing patterns, I honestly don't see how he could have made any other decision."[104]

Within WBT itself there were similar slow, limited, but nonetheless significant changes in the racial arena, notably in minority hiring practices, but also in the way that the station consulted the African American community about its programming needs. By mid-decade an Equal Employment Opportunity Program, the heir to the training program devised by Crutchfield and Fred Alexander in 1969, was pursuing "an aggressive policy of recruiting, employing, training and promoting minority and female staff members." Fifteen percent (six out of forty) of the full-time staff at WBT were African Americans—an unusually high proportion for a general-market radio station and considerably higher than at many black-oriented stations in the South. Two of the six black employees were women, and five of them were in professional-level positions.[105] Meanwhile the membership and role of WBT's Black Advisory Council continued to expand. In June 1975 Crutchfield, ever the southern gentleman, waxed lyrical about the genteel ways in which the Advisory Board meetings were conducted and the constructive proposals that emerged from them. "People didn't hesitate to speak their minds and to speak them bluntly," he noted, "but—so far as I could tell—there was absolutely no malice or ill will on the part of anybody, which proves the old adage that 'People can disagree without being disagreeable.'"[106]

Here was Crutchfield returning to ideological home turf, to the belief that sane and civil dialogue was indispensable to the pursuit of racial harmony in the South. If this faith sounded naive and anachronistic amid the inflamed passions and occasionally flaming cities of the black power era, it had nonetheless been at the core of his and WBT's—and arguably the vast majority of southern black-oriented radio stations'—racial politics for some forty years. During that time Crutchfield had seldom failed to listen to the diverse voices emanating from black Charlotte. In fact, his radio station had given a platform to many of them, including some whose views were anathema to his own. Often his preferences for gradualism, negotiation, and consensus had made him much slower to respond to the urgency of black demands than many African Americans would have liked. For years it had certainly blinded him to the need for vigorous federal action to promote meaningful changes in the region's racial arrangements. And yet, as he kept listening, so Charlie Crutchfield had kept learning; his own views on the "race problem" and how to address it underwent countless minor, and a few major, revisions. "I've mellowed. . . . When I was younger, I used to go right down the conservative line, no deviation whatsoever. . . . I've learned over the years that liberals are nice folks, too. I'm not sure I was ever a complete conservative—I believe in helping people who can't help themselves," he explained.[107]

Charlie Crutchfield's experience was typical of many southern whites whose stories have been generally under- or misrepresented in the voluminous literature on the civil rights movement. These were honest, decent, law-abiding, God-fearing, hardworking people whose entire world was threatened and then turned upside down in the years after 1945. Most of them struggled sincerely, anxiously, and with decidedly mixed success to cope with the emergence of black protest, with fundamental challenges to their cherished racial assumptions, with the end of Jim Crow, and with the erosion of many of the privileges they had long enjoyed simply by virtue of being white in a legally sanctioned racial caste system. From the mid-1950s, most white southerners found themselves occupying a position between die-hard segregationists at one end of the ideological spectrum and those who rushed to join the movement at the other end. To a large degree, Crutchfield saw WBT's role in terms of keeping the white and, insofar as WBT could reach them, the black inhabitants of Charlotte out of the clutches of extremist ideas and dangerous fanaticism at either end of that spectrum. The difference between most southerners and Charlie Crutchfield was that Crutchfield ran a radio station: a station whose broadcasts and internal politics embodied and helped to shape the ways that Charlotte tried to cope with the dramatic changes wrought by the civil rights and black power movements.

Conclusion

Radio and the Southern Freedom Struggle

*Radio was ushering in an era when nothing could be put to sleep as it
once had been, an age of motion as well as sound—motion and sound
which could not be controlled. Could not be stopped. Turn it off and it
goes right on. And you can never pick up where you left off.*
Will D. Campbell, Brother to a Dragonfly

Black deejay Jack Gibson once boasted that black-oriented radio was "the thing
that caused the civil rights movement to happen."[1] Of course, no single factor
caused the movement to happen, and the claims made in this book for the importance of radio are a little more modest. The main argument here is that radio
warrants a prominent place among the many social and cultural institutions that
shaped the African American freedom struggle and fashioned important
changes in racial attitudes and arrangements in the South. Viewing the freedom
struggle from the perspective of radio certainly serves as a reminder that the
movement and the transformations it wrought occurred at a number of social
and psychological, political and attitudinal, economic and emotional, legal and
cultural levels. Radio—especially black-oriented radio—often mediated between, or yoked together, these diverse expressions of movement culture and
experience. Radio was a place where black social, economic, political, legal, and
cultural activities intersected, just as they did in the lives of black communities—and just as they did in a freedom struggle that was simultaneously about
legal, political, and economic justice, and about black pride, identity, and self-
respect.

Although radio did not create the southern civil rights movement, it did contribute to its unfolding in several key ways. That contribution took various forms
depending on local circumstances, overarching legal, economic, and technical
factors, and the actions of individuals and organizations in the radio industry, in
the movement, and in the federal government. Amid the constantly evolving and

contingent relationship between radio and the freedom struggle, however, it is possible to discern certain distinctive patterns.

Before the era of mass protest, black activists and sympathetic whites used radio mainly to challenge pejorative images of African Americans and promote a more inclusive vision of American democracy where black civil and voting rights would be respected. Although opportunities to air such racially progressive messages on southern airways were restricted, network radio beyond Dixie helped to prick racial consciences and foment public and governmental concern about Jim Crow. Meanwhile the growth of black-oriented programming in the South, especially after World War II, helped to sustain and reinvigorate a powerful sense of black identity, pride, and purposefulness. This process revealed one of radio's most enduring qualities. Whether it was promoting a sense of national cohesion via the networks or encouraging a more circumscribed sense of local, regional, ethnic, racial, gender, or generational distinctiveness through local stations or niche programming, radio could foster a deep sense of shared experience and common identity among its listeners.

By the 1950s, according to media scholar Michele Hilmes, "Radio became the place where those culturally excluded from television's address could regroup and find a new identity."[2] This was certainly true for black southerners. They flocked to hear programs that proudly featured black secular and sacred cultural forms and offered a smattering of black-oriented news and discussion. Those broadcasts also stressed the importance of conspicuous black respectability in the quest for civil rights while stimulating mass awareness of the nonviolent direct-action protest tactics that could be employed if southern whites remained unwilling to recognize those rights.

Equally significant, some southern radio stations were the sites of tentative experiments in interracialism long before the formal desegregation of southern life began. The piebald playlists and biracial audiences of deejays such as Shelley Stewart and John Richbourg, the integrated staffs at WERD and WGIV, and the messages of interracial cooperation and goodwill broadcast by Nathaniel Tross, the SRC, and Friendly World Broadcasting, all hinted at alternatives to the strict racial separation at the heart of Jim Crow. For southern blacks and white racial progressives, radio offered a model for the kind of world they hoped to create. Indeed, the mass movement of the 1950s and early 1960s attempted to realize and extend the kinds of interracial possibilities that were sometimes evident in the sentiments, sounds, and, to a lesser degree, structure of southern radio. Because it was impossible to segregate the airways, the medium helped to blur, at least a little, the boundaries between different southern identities—racial, gender, generational, urban, rural, and class—that had often appeared immutable. This may even have been the most subversive of all radio's many contributions to

FIGURE 22. During the Jim Crow era, black-oriented radio stations like WGIV had become intimately involved with the people and institutions of the black South, although this sometimes meant supporting segregated facilities like the Queen City Medical Center in Charlotte. "Genial Gene" Potts (right) with Elbert Phillips, owner of the Center. Courtesy of James Peeler.

the movement, since the preservation of fixed social identities is invaluable to maintaining rigid structures of domination and subordination.[3]

Radio's capacity to expand its listeners' mental horizons and posit new social, cultural, and intellectual possibilities was a trait that movement activists consistently coveted and sought to exploit. This was no easy task. In a commercially driven, state regulated, capitalist industry dominated by white men, most radio stations embodied and reproduced—literally broadcast—the social orthodoxies of mainstream America. Radio usually worked to affirm, rather than challenge, dominant ideologies and social structures, including those relating to race. In the South until the later 1960s, this usually meant that radio endorsed segregation and white supremacy. Yet the content and meanings of radio broadcasts always proved difficult for segregationists to control with absolute authority.

There was space on radio for other, contradictory messages—often implicit, occasionally explicit—that called into question conventional attitudes and values. For the movement and its supporters, the medium offered an opportunity to refute the racist dogma on which Jim Crow rested and to promote new, alternative, more equalitarian conceptions of race and race relations. In many ways this book is testament to the resourcefulness of black activists and their allies as they defied the fundamental conservatism of commercial broadcasting and harnessed at least some of radio's latent counterhegemonic potential. There was no master plan here. Rather there was—as in the broader freedom struggle—a good deal of improvisation. Civil rights workers learned through experience the extent to which they could enlist radio in their bid for racial justice. Largely thanks to their efforts and those of black and white sympathizers within the industry, racially progressive radio broadcasts helped to encourage new levels of ideological, moral, and political opposition to the most egregious forms of racial discrimination.

During the late 1950s and early 1960s, radio stations in the South were required for the first time to deal with a mass movement on their own doorsteps, as well as the threat—or promise—of an increasingly active federal government in the racial arena. Some stations tried to ignore the movement. Many general-market stations, such as WJDX in Jackson, strenuously opposed it. Others, including WBT, tried to reconcile white preferences for the racial status quo with a growing recognition that Jim Crow was wrong and doomed. Meanwhile some southern black-oriented stations, such as WAOK in Atlanta, WENN in Birmingham, and WOKS in Columbus, Georgia, chose to support the local civil rights movement in various ways. At their boldest, these stations—and the civil rights organizations that capitalized on their extraordinary prestige in the black community—mobilized black protesters and aspiring black voters in very practical ways. Occasionally, radio crucially affected how civil rights campaigns were organized and how they fared in particular towns and cities. More generally, regardless of where individual stations stood on the civil rights issue, they all reflected and helped to define their community's experiences of the movement and the uncertain dawn of a New South.

With the demise of statutory Jim Crow, the focus of black activism in the South shifted toward extending black political and economic power. Both of these overlapping agendas found expression on black-oriented radio during the late 1960s and early 1970s. Having glimpsed radio's ability to influence opinion and mobilize sections of the black community, many black media analysts and activists lamented that the medium was still not as socially or politically committed as they would like. Their response was to orchestrate a wave of protests against individual stations, soul radio chains, and the FCC, hoping to increase the number of black owners and executives in radio and to improve the public service broadcasting offered to the black community. Largely because of these efforts, attention to black political, social, and economic issues and community news on southern radio was never greater than in this period. Indeed, coupled with the steady, if still uneven, expansion of black economic opportunities within radio, this represented a major accomplishment of the black power era.

Despite these advances, many activists remained disappointed at the levels of communal advocacy and the quality of public affairs broadcasting and news reporting on black-oriented radio, even at the growing number of stations that were under black ownership or management. This lurking sense of disillusionment and underachievement was nothing new to the black power years. It reflected a permanent tension between the movement's desire to make black-oriented radio a highly—or, rather, an overtly—politicized educational and organizational tool and the black audience's insistence that the primary purpose of black-oriented radio stations was to entertain them. In a sense, however, the most remarkable aspect of radio's relationship to the black freedom struggle is the way that it reveals the inadequacy of simple distinctions between entertainment and education, recreation and resistance, and pleasure and politics when examining the structure of the civil rights movement. Radio was simultaneously a commercial enterprise, a disseminator of news and ideas, a forum for competing political and ideological positions, an instrument of mass mobilization, an object of protest, a subject of federal legislation, a repository of diverse cultural, social, and racial values, and a source of entertainment. With all of its complexity and ambiguity, the medium embodied and reproduced the turbulent crosscurrents that defined southern life as Jim Crow came under concerted attack and finally crumbled.

Notes

Abbreviations for archival sources are detailed at the beginning of the bibliography.

Where misspellings and similar errors were encountered, especially in quotes from the often unedited scripts and transcriptions of radio broadcasts, these have been silently corrected.

Introduction: Dials Set to Freedom

1. Chester Laborde, interview with Robin Ward, June 23, 1998; Willis Reed, interview with various interviewers, 1998, both LLMV.

2. WLCS, "Hearings on Applications of Air Waves Inc. and KJAN Broadcasting Co.," files 9527 and 9528, December 7, 1951, box 154, FCC-DOC. See also WLCS, fiche 805, MMBSHC.

3. For more on the Baton Rouge bus boycott, see *New York Times*, June 20, 1953; Morris, *Origins of the Civil Rights Movement*, 17–25; Fairclough, *Race & Democracy*, 156–62.

4. Hilmes, "Rethinking Radio."

5. Savage, *Broadcasting Freedom*. My debt to Savage is especially apparent in chapter 1, although my interests are more southern. The only other significant "movement" treatment of radio is Stephen Walsh's unpublished dissertation, "Black-Oriented Radio."

6. Branch, *Parting the Waters*; McWhorter, *Carry Me Home*.

7. Jackson, *House That Jack Built*; S. Stewart, *The Road South*; George, *Death of Rhythm and Blues*; W. Smith, *Pied Pipers*; Barlow, *Voice Over*; Newman, *Profit and Pride*; G. Williams, *Legendary Pioneers*; Cantor, *Wheelin' on Beale*. There are useful discussions of radio and racial issues in general histories of the medium, such as Barnouw, *History of Broadcasting*, Eberly, *Music in the Air*, and MacDonald, *Don't Touch That Dial!*

8. S. Douglas, *Inventing American Broadcasting* and *Listening In*; Hilmes, *Radio Voices*; Smulyan, *Selling Radio*.

9. For the shifting attitude of television and the print media toward the freedom struggle, see Walker, "A Media-Made Movement?"

10. M. L. King, "Transforming a Neighborhood."

11. Julian Bond, interview with Stephen Walsh, August 17, 1995.

12. A. Meyer, *Black Voices*, 3; Martha Jean Steinberg, interview with Jacquie Gales Webb, June 13, 1995, BR.

13. Haring, "The Negro as Consumer," 21.

14. Sterner, Epstein, Winston, et al., *The Negro's Share*, 330–33; MacDonald, *Don't Touch That Dial!* 157.

15. Waller, *Radio: The Fifth Estate*, 42; *Broadcasting Yearbook, 1957*, 342–44.

16. Yarger, "Don't Touch That Dial," 98; *Sponsor*, July 28, 1952, 78–80; August 24, 1953, 66.

17. Statistics drawn from *Sponsor*, August 24, 1953, 66; July 28, 1952, 78; September 20, 1958, 16. Radio Advertising Bureau, *Radio and the Negro Market*, 5.

18. U.S. Department of Commerce, *U.S. Census of Housing* (1960), vol. 1, part 1, table 26. *Sponsor*, July 28, 1952, 78–80; August 24, 1953, 66. See also Walsh, "Black-Oriented Radio," 36–37.

19. S. Douglas, *Listening In*, 9.

20. Marchand, *Advertising the American Dream*, xix.

21. Smulyan, *Selling Radio*, 78.

22. Kammen, *American Culture, American Tastes*, 18–19. For the triumph of capitalist interests in the 1934 Communications Act, see McChesney, *Telecommunications*.

23. Mrs. Allean Wright, interview with Willie Mae Lee, January 24, 1956, PV.

24. Charles Eagles made a similar point about the inadequate attention paid to white southerners in his survey of movement historiography, "Towards New Histories of the Civil Rights Era," esp. 842–43.

25. C. Sumpter Logan and Theodore A. Braun, "Henderson Pastors' Diary," *New South*, December 1956, 9–12.

26. Hangen, *Redeeming the Dial*; Hall et al., *Like a Family*, 233, 237, 252, 254, 261–62.

27. Angelou, *I Know Why the Caged Bird Sings*, 111–15.

28. J. C. Danley, quoted in Newman, *Profit and Pride*, 98; see also 93–104. James Singleterry, interview with Ray Funk, quoted in Seroff, "On the Battlefield," 66.

29. Morris, *Origins of the Civil Rights Movement*.

30. David Hollinger, "How Wide the Circle of the We?" See also his *Postethnic America*, 131–72.

31. L. Cohen, "Citizens and Consumers." See also her *A Consumer's Republic*. Several other essays in the Daunton and Hinton collection and in Glickman, *Consumer Society*, also influenced my thinking here.

32. Important early efforts to examine the relationship between black consumerism and black civil rights activities include Weems, *Desegregating the Dollar*, and especially L. Cohen, *A Consumers' Republic*, 166–91, 323–31.

33. Hale, *Making Whiteness*, 136. S. Douglas, *Listening In*, 222.

Chapter 1. An Uphill Battle: Network Radio, Local Radio,
and the Roots of Racial Change

1. *Our World*, February 1950, 33.

2. *Broadcasting Yearbook*, 1957, 342–44; *Our World*, November 1955, 40–43.

3. Nat Williams quoted in McKee and Chisenhall, *Beale Black and Blue*, 93.

4. Bert Ferguson, quoted in Cantor, *Wheelin' on Beale*, 22; see also 48–49.

5. J. Edward Reynolds, quoted in "Dream Radio Station," *Newsweek*, September 12, 1949, reprinted in *Negro Digest*, January 1950, 24.

6. Lavarda Durst, interview with William Barlow, n.d., BR. Rothenbuhler and McCourt, "Radio Redefines Itself"; on Durst, see 374–75.

7. Robert Austin Dunlea (owner of WMFD-Wilmington), quoted in Wallace, "Broadcasting in North Carolina," 292–93.

8. Cantor, *Wheelin' on Beale*, 63. Maurice Hulbert, interview with Jacquie Gales Webb, January 24, 1996, BR.

9. *Opportunity*, July 1928, 218.

10. *Opportunity*, Summer 1947, 166–67.

11. *Sponsor*, October 10, 1949, 24–25, 54–55.

12. *Publishers Weekly*, July 5, 1947, 34–35.

13. *Ebony*, December 1947, 44–49; *Opportunity*, Summer 1947, 167.

14. Savage, *Broadcasting Freedom*, 157.

15. Ibid., 160–68.

16. Ibid., 159, 168–77.

17. McChesney, *Telecommunications*, 29; Eberly, *Music in the Air*, 171.

18. *Opportunity*, October 1943, 168–69.

19. For the origins of *Wings Over Jordan*, see *Atlanta Daily World*, July 7, 1940.

20. For the conservatism of the Atlanta Urban League, see Spritzer and Bergmark, *Grace Towns Hamilton*, 136–43.

21. *Atlanta Daily World*, October 11, 1940.

22. Dr. J. E. Walker, "*Wings Over Jordan* Speech," quoted in *Atlanta Daily World*, August 23, 1940.

23. See R. Meyer, "Blacks and Broadcasting," 222; Barlow, *Voice Over*, 27.

24. John F. Royal, memo to Janet MacRorie, May 1, 1935, folder "Music—Restricted Songs," box 245, NBC.

25. Edna Turner, memo to William Burke Miller et al., December 8, 1938, same folder.

26. Miller, memos to Thomas Belviso and to Turner, December 9, 1938, same folder.

27. Turner, memo to Miller, December 12, 1938, same folder.

28. This section relies heavily on the chapter on *Round Table* and *Town Meeting of the Air* in Savage, *Broadcasting Freedom*, 194–242.

29. John Royal, letter to Niles Trammell, June 30, 1939, folder 32, box 73, NBC. Also quoted in Savage, *Broadcasting Freedom*, 197.

30. Savage, *Broadcasting Freedom*, 209–10.

31. Lash, "The Negro and Radio," 177.

32. Savage, *Broadcasting Freedom*, 83.

33. Ibid., 88.

34. Ibid., 90.

35. Ibid.

36. S. Douglas, *Listening In*, 76.

37. Savage, *Broadcasting Freedom*, 199–202.

38. Ibid., 203–6.

39. Ibid., 208–9. William Barlow, apparently following J. Fred Macdonald, claims that *Town Meeting* discussed race and the defense industries in 1942, but according to Savage the proposed show was scrapped. See Barlow, *Voice Over*, 72.

40. Savage, *Broadcasting Freedom*, 210–22.

41. Ibid., 206–22.

42. For more on *Minority Opinion*, see ibid., 189–92.

43. J. Hutton Hyde, "Let's Talk It Over," December 1, 1946, II-A-157, NAACP. For the links between the Cold War and the civil rights movement, see Dudziak, *Cold War Civil Rights*.

44. Savage, *Broadcasting Freedom*, 246.

45. Dates and Barlow, *Split Image*, 187.

46. Shelley Stewart, interview with Brian Ward, October 26, 1995.

47. Savage, *Broadcasting Freedom*, 21–58.

48. Roy Wilkins, "Radio Talk over Station WINX," December 28, 1941, 5–6, II-A-564, NAACP.

49. For details of NAACP involvement in these programs, see Savage, *Broadcasting Freedom*, 38–40, 73, 179, 117–21.

50. Ibid., 106–24 (Milton Starr quote, 119).

51. Elmer Davis, quoted in ibid., 121.

52. Ibid., 122.

53. *Pittsburgh Courier*, February 20, 1943. See also Hilmes, *Radio Voices*, 256.

54. Savage, *Broadcasting Freedom*, 148–53. For the *People's Platform* show, see MacDonald, *Don't Touch That Dial!* 348.

55. Gene Kelly and Frank Sinatra, dialogue from *Songs by Sinatra*, CBS, 1945, on the CD set *Frank Sinatra: In Celebration* (Music Digital, CD 6108, 1997).

56. NAACP Publicity Committee, "Recommendations for Improving the Publicity and Public Relations Work of the NAACP," n.d., II-A-129, NAACP.

57. "Memorandum Re: Action of the Committee on Administration on the Recommendations from the Publicity Committee for Improving the Publicity and Public Relations Work of the NAACP—September 24, 1945," September 27, 1945, II-A-128, NAACP. The best overview of the NAACP's radio initiatives after World War II is in Walsh, "Black-Oriented Radio," 66–92.

58. Press release, June 20, 1947, II-A-33, NAACP. Harry Truman, quoted in *Washington Star*, June 30, 1947. See also Savage, *Broadcasting Freedom*, 224.

59. Ibid., 230–42.

60. Allen Ellender, speaking in "Should We Adopt President Truman's Civil Rights Program?" *University of Chicago Round Table*, February 6, 1949, quoted in Savage, *Broadcasting Freedom*, 233.

61. Raymond Walsh and Arthur Gaith, "Approach to Radio Stations," n.d., II-A-507, NAACP.

62. Jackson, *House That Jack Built*, 73–75.

63. Hope Spingarn, memo to Walter White, November 12, 1946, II-A-157, NAACP; see also memo of December 10, 1946, II-A-128.

64. Harry Novik, letter to Walter White, January 10, 1951, II-A-157, NAACP; White, letter to Eugene Martin, June 3 1952, II-A-544, NAACP. Walsh, "Black-Oriented Radio," 73–78.

65. In his memoir Hal Jackson gives a rather ungracious account of his time at WLIB and his experiences with the Novik brothers (whose surname he, like William Barlow in *Voice Over*, spells incorrectly throughout as "Novick") and seems only dimly aware of the extent of their links to the local NAACP. See *House That Jack Built*, 128–30, 144.

66. WLIB, "Application for Consent to Assignment of Radio Broadcast Station Construction Permit or License," June 21, 1949, part 1, question 11[c], box 207, FCC; Wilkins, "WLIB—tape for April 29, 1950," II-A-564, NAACP.

67. See, for example, Harry Novik, letter to Frank R. Crosswaith, May 15, 1951, folder G18, box 31, FRC.

68. Henry Lee Moon, letter to Harry Novik, February 27, 1953, II-A-544, NAACP.

69. "NAACP Scroll," February 24, 1954, II-A-544, NAACP.

70. Mort Silverman, quoted in Abarbanel and Haley, "New Audience for Radio," 57.

71. Egmont Sonderling, quoted in *Washington Post*, May 7, 1967, 25.

72. Harry Novik, letter to White, January 10, 1951, II-A-157, NAACP; White, letter to Eugene Martin, June 3 1952, II-A-544, NAACP. Transcripts and guest list for *The Walter White Show* can be found in II-A-545, NAACP.

73. White, "WLIB News," December 10, 1953, II-A-545, NAACP.

74. White, "New WLIB and Affiliated Stations," December 18, 1952, II-A-545, NAACP.

75. *New World A-Coming*, May 28, 1944, WMCA. See also Savage, *Broadcasting Freedom*, 246–60; Barlow, *Voice Over*, 78–83.

76. White, letter to Morris Novik, June 11, 1952, II-A-544, NAACP.

77. See, for example, White, letters to Lionel Lindsay and to Clarence Mitchell, February 20, 1953, II-A-544, NAACP.

78. White, letter to Mrs. Freeman, June 27, 1952, II-A-544, NAACP.

79. Morris Novik, letter to Jesse Blayton, June 18, 1952, II-A-544, NAACP.

80. Frank Hubbs, letter to White, January 26, 1953, II-A-158, NAACP.

81. *Baltimore Afro-American*, December 13, 1952; M. W. Day and C. L. Dinkins, letter to H. Calvin Young, January 16, 1953, II-A-499, NAACP. See also Walsh, "Black-Oriented Radio," 87–89.

82. Day and Dinkins, letter to Young, January 16, 1953; Day and Dinkins, letter to FCC, February 4, 1953, II-A-499, NAACP.

83. *Cleveland Call and Post*, March 7, 1953. See also *Memphis Tri-State Defender*, March 14, 1953. Joseph LaCour, letter to Wilkins, March 19, 1953, II-A-499, NAACP.

84. Wilkins, letter to Joseph B. LaCour, March 20, 1953, II-A-499, NAACP.

85. Clarence Mitchell, letter to White, February 17, 1953, II-A-499, NAACP.

86. Wilkins, "WLIB—tape for April 29, 1950," II-A-564, NAACP.

87. For the NAACP campaign against *Amos 'n' Andy*, see Ely, *Adventures of Amos 'n' Andy*, 163–77; Barlow, *Voice Over*, 41–44. For WBT's *Two Black Crows*, see "Pilot of the Airwaves You Seem Like a Friend to Me," n.d., CCG. For *Rufus and Roberta*, see *Cycle: The News of Radio*, May 10, 1953, Special Silver Anniversary Edition for WRBL, in BMLCF.

88. Reddick, "Educational Programs," 384.

89. "Summary of Meeting with Radio Group," March 16, 1948, II-A-128, NAACP.

90. White, memo to Mr. Moon, Mr. Wilkins, Mr. Marshall, and Miss Baxter, June 16, 1948, II-A-507, NAACP.

91. *Broadcasting*, February 28, 1949, 46.

92. *New World A-Coming*, March 12, 1947, WMCA. See also Barlow, *Voice Over*, 81–82.

93. Quoted in *Negro Digest*, July 1950, 19–21.

94. Ibid.

95. *Broadcasting*, July 18, 1949, 73.

96. *Sponsor*, August 17, 1964.

97. *Sponsor*, July 28, 1952, 37, and August 24, 1953, 76; Newman, *Profit and Pride*, 133–35.

98. *Sponsor*, August 14, 1950, 51, and October 10, 1949, 54.

99. *Sponsor*, July 28, 1952, 37, and October 10, 1949, 54.

100. Ben Hooks, interview with Stephen Walsh, August 3, 1995.

Chapter 2. Goodwill Radio: Labor, Liberals,
and the Search for Interracial Understanding

1. L. Cohen, *Making a New Deal*, 129–44.

2. Ibid., 325–33 (Foster quote, 341). For the racial record of CIO locals in the South during the interwar years, see Korstad and Lichtenstein, "Opportunities Found and Lost"; Norrell, "Caste in Steel"; Goldfield, "Race and the CIO."

3. Frank R. Crosswaith, "Radio Address on WEVD," December 15, 1935, folder B56, NLC.

4. Crosswaith, letter to George Field, December 31, 1941, folder E41, box 26, FRC.

5. A. Philip Randolph, quoted in Seabrook, "Black and White Unite," 76.

6. See Crosswaith and Lewis, *Negro and White Labor*, 31–32.

7. "NLC-WEVD Script," February 1, 1941, folder E41, box 26, FRC.

8. Ibid.

9. "NLC-WEVD Script," August 1, 1941, folder E41, box 26, FRC.

10. "NLC-WEVD Script," September 6, 1941, folder E41, box 26, FRC.

11. Crosswaith, "Looking Around and Beyond," March 4, 1939, folder E3, NLC.

12. Crosswaith, letter to Governor of Illinois, June 23, 1936, folder B121, NLC.

13. "NLC-WEVD Script," March 1, 1941, folder E41, box 26, FRC.

14. Field, letter to Crosswaith, October 16, 1941, folder E41, box 26, FRC.

15. Phil Landwehr, letter to Crosswaith, May 19, 1954, folder D52, box 21, FRC.

16. "Provisional Committee for Democracy in Radio," folder 1, box 473, JM. On the ILGWU bid, see *New York Times*, October 9, 1945.

17. "Script of the CIO Broadcast on Action of the District of Columbia Recreation Board," July 19, 1945, II-A-157, NAACP.

18. See Honey, *Southern Labor*, 252–63 (McCrea quote, 254); Green, "Battling the Plantation Mentality," 280–81.

19. Owing to a technicality, the USWA could not be listed on the CIO ballot, but disaffected Mine, Mill workers and USWA loyalists were invited to vote instead for a generic CIO-chartered Local Industrial Union. See Zieger, *The CIO*, 280–82. Hepner, "Union War in Bessemer" (anonymous quote, 13).

20. Zieger, *The CIO*, 282.

21. "Text of Speech by George Baldanzi," October 19, 1946, "Operation Dixie," series VII, CIO.

22. Zieger, "Venture into Unplowed Fields," 168. "Text of Speech by George Baldanzi," October 19, 1946; also Baldanzi, letter and enclosures to Paul Christopher, January 13, 1950, "Operation Dixie," series VII, CIO.

23. Glen, *Highlander*, 38, 114–15, 123.

24. Myles Horton, *Cross Section USA*, CBS, February 22, 1947, HFS; Dwight Cooke, letter to Horton, February 17, 1947, HFS.

25. Horton, *Cross Section, USA*.

26. Zilphia Horton, untitled radio transcript, WQQW-DC, April 19, 1947, HFS.

27. Ibid.

28. R. B. Eleazer, letter to C. W. Hyne, December 10, 1929, series IV, reel 28, CIC.

29. Hyne, letter to W. W. Alexander, December 4, 1929; Hyne, letter to Eleazer, December 18, 1929; "The Utica Jubilee Singers," press release, series IV, reel 28, CIC.

30. Nora Allison Barber, "Some Ways to Promote Better Understanding Between the Races," radio talk, [c. 1936], series VI, reel 39, CIC.

31. Ibid.

32. Marjorie Stanford, "Contributions of the Negro," radio talk, n.d., series VI, reel 39, CIC.

33. George Connor, "Radio Talk," n.d., series VI, reel 39, CIC.

34. Ibid.; from folder 89, reel 1, ASWPL: Alma Chestnut, letter to Atwood Martin, April 8, 1936; Jessie Daniel Ames, letter to Chestnut, April 20, 1936; Leland Bickford, letter to Ames, May 23, 1936; Secretary [Ames], letter to Bickford, May 26, 1936.

35. See note 33.

36. Reed, *Simple Decency*, 15–19; Sosna, *Silent South*, 91–97.

37. Reed, *Simple Decency*, 186.

38. Louise O. Charlton, "Report of Proceedings of the Southern Conference For Human Welfare, Birmingham, November 20–23, 1938," 6, folder 103, box 9, SCHW. James Dombrowski, memo to Director, Archives Division, Tuskegee, June 5, 1981, SCHW File Finding Guide, SCHW. (Somewhat confusingly, the SCHW papers are listed as SCEF papers in the Tuskegee University archives.)

39. Reed, *Simple Decency*, 186; Edmonia W. Grant, memo to board members, January 23, 1948, folder 103, box 9, SCHW.

40. For the campaign against Bilbo, see Dittmer, *Local People*, 1–9.

41. "Answer to Bilbo," August 22, 1946, folder 112, box 10, SCHW.

42. Ibid.

43. Ibid.

44. "Answer to Bilbo," August 29, 1946, folder 103, box 9, SCHW.

45. Sosna, *Silent South*, 117–20, 152–59.

46. "Supreme Court Considers Segregation"; "South of the Future"; see also Sosna, *Silent South*, 155–66. Marion Wright, quoted in *New South*, November 1955, 2.

47. Anna Kelly, quoted in "Highlander Workshop, July 12–August 8, 1953: 'The Supreme Court Decisions and the Public Schools,'" reel 33, HFS.

48. Nina Howell (Mrs. Nathan C.) Starr, letter to Guy Johnson, October 12, 1945, reel 43, SRC.

49. Ibid.

50. Johnson, letter to Dr. Justin Miller, October 18, 1945, reel 58, SRC.

51. SRC Atlanta, "Tentative Memorandum on a Proposal for a New South Radio Forum" to Radio Station WSB, Atlanta, April 2, 1947, reel 58, SRC.

52. Ibid.; SRC Atlanta, memo to Radio Station WSB, Atlanta, May 29, 1947, reel 58, SRC.

53. Memo: "Proposed Roundtable on Southern Problems to be Sponsored by Southern Regional Council on Radio Station WSB, Atlanta," reel 58, SRC.

54. "Proposal For 'Town Meeting of the Air,'" November 8, 1949, reel 58, SRC.

55. Dr. Homer Price Rainey, "Religion in Life: Radio Addresses Presented from October 15 to October 20, 1945," folder 112, box 10, SCHW.

56. Ed Morgan, letter to Dr. [George S.] Mitchell, May 25, 1954, and Mitchell, letter to Morgan, May 31, 1954, reel 1, SRC.

57. *Edward P. Morgan and the News*, ABC, August 2, 1955, reel 1, SRC.

58. Morgan, letter to Mitchell, March 28, 1956, and Mitchell, letter to Morgan, April 4, 1956, reel 1, SRC.

59. Ibid.

60. *Edward P. Morgan and the News*, ABC, February 24, 1956, reel 1, SRC.

61. "Summary of Programs Requested by Southern Stations," 1957, folder "Information Services, Audio Visual Aids, Radio & Television-Correspondence," box "General Administration, 1957—Information Services to International Affairs Seminars of Washington," AFSC.

62. See Walker, "Black Violence and Nonviolence," 22–56.

63. *AFSC: Southeastern Area News*, December 1946, NCC.

64. *New World A-Coming*, November 18, 1947, WMCA, folder "FOR Projects & Co-Sponsorship Journey of Reconciliation, 1947," box 20, series E, FOR.

65. George Loft, memo to Henry Beerits, WFLN broadcasts, September 23, 1949, folder "Radio, WFLN AFSC Series," box "General Administration, 1949—Central Services, Publicity Department," AFSC.

66. Clarence Pickett, "The Quaker Faith: Its Current Significance," address on CBS's *Church of the Air*, November 20, 1949, folder "Radio, Church of the Air Program," box "General Administration, 1949—Central Services, Publicity Department," AFSC.

67. See Loft, memo to Anne Hatfield, October 31, 1949, and George Bliss, letter to Dear Friend, November 1, 1949, folder "Radio, Church of the Air Program," box "General Administration, 1949—Central Services, Publicity Department," AFSC.

Chapter 3. Respectability, Religion, and Rhythm and Blues on Black-Oriented Radio

1. *Ebony*, December 1947, 44.

2. *Crisis*, October 1953, 467.

3. Joe Howard, quoted in W. Smith, *Pied Pipers*, 134.

4. My argument in this section is indebted to Susan Douglas's chapter on early radio comedy in *Listening In*, 100–123.

5. Ibid., 87.

6. *Crisis*, October 1953, 467. See also G. Williams, *Legendary Pioneers*, 15.

7. Savage, *Broadcasting Freedom*, 64.

8. Cantor, *Wheelin' on Beale*, 29, 62–64, 91.

9. Press release, "Radio Negro Talent Hour, 1949–1950," II-A-507, NAACP.

10. *Louisiana Weekly*, July 4, 1953.

11. Quoted in Thompson, *Black Press in Mississippi*, 36.

12. G. Blackwell, "Black-Controlled Media," 76.

13. C. W. Hayes, "Education for Negroes in the South," on *Wings Over Jordan*, October 7, 1940, file 1102.14, BWOF.

14. J. L. Peacock, letter to Federal Radio Commission, January 5, 1928, Legal Series, box 44, Durham Life Insurance, JB.

15. For the debates over advertising on radio, see Smulyan, *Selling Radio*, esp. 65–153 (figures from 130), and McChesney, *Telecommunications*.

16. "Possibilities of Proposed Tuskegee Radio Station," n.d., series 7: Radio, CIC.

17. Lash, "The Negro and Radio," 172–74.

18. John G. Turner, "Radio at Bennett College," *Opportunity*, January 1943, 8–10, 29.

19. Ibid.

20. Ibid., 29.

21. Savage, *Broadcasting Freedom*, 168–77.

22. Higginbotham, *Righteous Discontent*, 14–15.

23. Wolcott, *Remaking Respectability*, 7.

24. See Wang, "The Case of the Radio-Active Housewife" (CBS quotes, 358).

25. For the Memphis "homemaker" shows, see W. Smith, *Pied Pipers*, 126–28; Cantor, *Wheelin' on Beale*, 117–18.

26. Barlow, *Voice Over*, 147–48.

27. Hilmes, *Radio Voices*, 80–81.

28. For more on respectability and the civil rights movement, see Chappell, Hutchinson, and Ward, "Dress Modestly, Neatly."

29. See Cott, "What's in a Name?" 827–28.

30. Green, "Battling the Plantation Mentality," 267.

31. "Top Radio Ministers," *Ebony*, March 1949, 56–61 (quote, 56). Some of the ideas about the significance of radio preachers contained in this chapter initially appeared in Ward and Walker, "'Bringing the Races Closer'?" and were elaborated in Walker, "Black Violence and Nonviolence," 66–84.

32. "Top Radio Ministers," 57, 59, 61.

33. Gladys Musgrove, letter to Walter Bishop, November 30, 1953, and Bishop, letter to Musgrove, December 1, 1953, folder 623, box 65, WRVA.

34. "Top Radio Ministers," 57.

35. Benjamin Mays, quoted in Morris, *Origins of the Civil Rights Movement*, 97.

36. Perry Walders, interview with Stephen Walsh, January 28, 1995.

37. "Top Radio Ministers," 58.

38. Spaulding, "Black-Oriented Radio in Chicago," 169, 181.

39. H. C. Carswell, quoted in *Atlanta Daily World*, September 18, 1940, 2.

40. "Radio Pioneer" (quote from Hoyte Andre, WKY–Oklahoma City program director, 183).

41. This account of Smallwood Williams's radio ministry draws on Walsh, "Black-Oriented Radio," 229–35; Hathaway, "God's Master of Ceremonies"; S. Williams, *This Is My Story*.

42. Hathaway, "God's Master of Ceremonies," 163.

43. Smallwood Williams, quoted in *Washington Post*, July 5, 1991; S. Williams, *This Is My Story*, 97–150; Hathaway, "God's Master of Ceremonies," 164.

44. "Top Radio Ministers," 58.

45. *Washington Afro-American*, October 28, 1950.

46. S. Williams, *This Is My Story*, 147.

47. Williams, quoted in *Washington Post*, June 30, 1991.

48. Williams, letter to E. Carlton Myers Jr., August 18, 1965, United Broadcasting Company Petition to Enlarge the Issues, August 23, 1965, file 15795, vol. 1, box 237, FCC-DOC.

49. *Atlanta Daily World*, February 16 and April 4, 1940.

50. Ibid., July 11, 1940, 1, 6, and December 29, 1940, 5.

51. Ibid.

52. Ibid., July 14, 1940, 4.

53. Biographical information from English, *Prophet of Wheat Street*; Juel Pate Borders-

Benson, "Biographical Sketch: William Holmes Borders," in "Celebration of the Life of William Holmes Borders, Sr.," memorial service program, Wheat Street Baptist Church, Atlanta, November 29, 1993. Copy in possession of author.

54. English, *Prophet of Wheat Street*, 56–59.

55. Quoted in English, *Prophet of Wheat Street*, 57.

56. Borders, "All Blood Is Red," in *Seven Minutes at the "Mike."* See also *Pittsburgh Courier*, June 7, 1941, 15.

57. Borders, "Some Negro Contributions to American Civilization" and "I Am Somebody," both in *Seven Minutes at the "Mike."* See also *Atlanta Daily World*, February 16, 1941.

58. Quoted in English, *Prophet of Wheat Street*, 58.

59. *Atlanta Inquirer*, December 24, 1960, 7. For Borders's civil rights activities, see English, *Prophet of Wheat Street*, chap. 5; Borders, interview with Bernard West, November 29, 1978, box 35, LA.

60. For the broader context of the bus desegregation campaign, see Tuck, *Beyond Atlanta*, 105.

61. English, *Prophet of Wheat Street*, 83.

62. Ibid., 98.

63. Ibid., 156.

64. Rev. Samuel Pettagrue, quoted in *Atlanta Daily World*, July 11, 1960, 6. Kelly Miller Smith, *Microphone Messages: Nine Radio Sermons*, (Vicksburg, Miss., 1949), 1, file 29, box 13, KMS.

65. Ibid., 13 (in sermon "The Kingdom of God: Its Meaning").

66. Ibid., 8 (in sermon "I Want to Be a Christian").

67. Ibid., 3 (in sermon "The Story of Jesus").

68. Kelly Miller Smith, interview with John Britton, December 22, 1967, RB.

69. K. M. Smith, *Microphone Messages*, 29 (in sermon "God's Answer: The Negro in History").

70. Ibid., 3 (in sermon "The Way of Christ").

71. The early embrace of Gandhian ideas, primarily by African American elites, is discussed in Kapur, *Raising Up a Prophet*.

72. M. L. King, "Pilgrimage to Nonviolence" (quote, 38).

73. Bayard Rustin, quoted in Anderson, *Bayard Rustin*, 188.

74. Hangen, "Man of the Hour."

75. Charles Williams, letter to Harry Emerson Fosdick, June 3, 1954, folder "Subject File: Segregation Correspondence, 1954–55," box 9, CP.

76. Anderson, *Bayard Rustin*, 194.

77. Miller, *Voice of Deliverance*, 44–60, 86–100. See also Lischer, *The Preacher King*; Moses, *Revolution of Conscience*.

78. J. Lewis, *Walking with the Wind*, 33. "Station WRMA Spurs New Life in Ole Confederacy," *Color*, December 1953, 49.

79. M. L. King, "Paul's Letter," 142.

80. J. Lewis, quoted in Raines, *My Soul Is Rested*, 73.

81. J. Lewis, *Walking with the Wind*, 56.

82. Ibid., 53.

83. J. Lewis, quoted in Raines, *My Soul Is Rested*, 73.

84. "Radio Listening Habits of Urban Negroes," n.d., Fisk University report, box 61, PV.

85. Reddick, "Educational Programs," 384.

86. *Sponsor*, August 24, 1953, 68.

87. W. Smith, *Pied Pipers*, 65.

88. S. Douglas, *Listening In*, 85.

89. For more on the relationship between rock and roll and white racial attitudes, see Bertrand, *Race, Rock, and Elvis*; Ward, *Just My Soul Responding*, 37–39, 225–52; Chappell, "Hip Like Me."

Chapter 4. A Dixie Dilemma: Racially Progressive Radio in the Age of Massive Resistance

Author's Note: The Stamz quote is from an interview with Sonja Williams, March 29, 1995, BR.

1. Good overviews of the civil rights movement include Lawson, *Running for Freedom*; Cook, *Sweet Land of Liberty*; Fairclough, *Better Day Coming*.

2. U.S. Department of Commerce, *U.S. Census of Housing* (1960), vol. 1, part 1, table 26. *Sponsor*, July 28, 1952, 78–80, and August 24, 1953, 66.

3. Fairclough, *Race & Democracy*, 344–45; for a compelling account of the Bogalusa movement, see 344–80.

4. Ralph Blumberg, quoted in *New York Times*, March 21, 1965. Brooks Hays mistakenly places this incident in 1966; see *Politics Is My Parish*, 239–40.

5. *New York Times*, March 20, 1965.

6. *New York Times*, March 21 and 26, 1965.

7. *New York Times*, March 21, 1965.

8. *New York Times*, April 4, 1965.

9. *New York Times*, July 22, 1965.

10. Ralph Blumberg, quoted in *New York Times*, July 22, 1965.

11. *New York Times*, December 30, 1965.

12. *Lights and Shadows Over the South East Region* (annual report, South East Regional Office, NAACP Atlanta, 1959), 16, in folder 11, box 18, KA; *Baltimore Afro-American*, December 5, 1959, 1–2.

13. Curtis Welborne, letter to Elbert Jean, October 5, 1965, folder 18, special file "Radio Ministry, Radio Tapes (1965–1967)," box 6, WC.

14. Rev. Donald Vails, interview with Jacquie Gales Webb, n.d., BR.

15. *Sponsor*, September 26, 1959, part 2, 48.

16. Del Shields, interview with Sonja Williams, May 9, 1995, BR.

17. Irene [Johnson] Ware, interview with Jacquie Gales Webb, March 14, 1995, BR.

18. Martha Jean Steinberg, interview with Jacquie Gales Webb, June 13, 1995, BR.

19. Bert Ferguson, quoted in Cantor, *Wheelin' on Beale*, 3.

20. Natolyn Williams, interview with Jacquie Gales Webb, January 5, 1996, BR. WDIA, "Application for Renewal of Broadcast Station License," May 18, 1964, exhibit E, box 170, FCC. Walsh, "Black-Oriented Radio," 129.

21. Maxine Smith, interview with Stephen Walsh, August 3, 1995. Walsh, "Black-Oriented Radio," 146–47.

22. Rick Taylor, interview with Stephen Walsh, August 5, 1995.

23. Maxine Smith, quoted in Cantor, *Wheelin' on Beale*, 228.

24. Green, "Battling the Plantation Mentality," 260, 276–78 (quote, 277). See also Cantor, *Wheelin' on Beale*, 217.

25. *Southerner*, March 1956, 5. See also Ward, *Just My Soul Responding*, 95–106.

26. Ralph Bass, quoted in Lydon and Mandel, *Boogie Lightning*, 84.

27. For more on the payola hearings, see Ward, *Just My Soul Responding*, 161–69.

28. Walsh, "Black-Oriented Radio," 101, 114.

29. Ibid., 102–3; Eddie Phelan, quoted in *Arkansas Gazette*, June 14, 1964.

30. Walsh, "Black-Oriented Radio," 101, 114, 140–41; Harry Novik, quoted in *New York Times*, May 27, 1961.

31. Walsh, "Black-Oriented Radio," 128–29.

32. For a celebration of Woods's career, see Spady, *Georgie Woods*, and Georgie Woods, interview with Jacquie Gales Webb, September 15, 1995, BR.

33. Press release, December 6, 1963, II-C-137, NAACP; "Report of Direct Action: Philadelphia Branch NAACP for Year 1963," II-C-137, NAACP. See also *Billboard*, November 30, 1963, 3, and December 7, 1963, 37.

34. Woods interview; Barlow, *Voice Over*, 204–6; Ward, *Just My Soul Responding*, 269.

35. Mary Mason, quoted in Spady, *Georgie Woods*, 183. See also Barlow, *Voice Over*, 209–11; Maurice Hulbert, interview with Jacquie Gales Webb, January 24, 1996, BR.

36. Marion Barry, letter to James Forman, July 21, 1962, A-IV-47, SNCC.

37. Richard Tinsley, letter to Richard Jewett, [February 1965], B-I-13, reel 8, CORE-ADD.

38. *Sponsor*, March 13, 1961, 81.

39. Eddie Castleberry, interview with Jacquie Gales Webb, January 5, 1996, BR.

40. Wesley South, letter to Roy Wilkins, December 5, 1963, III-A-319, NAACP. M. L. King, "Transforming a Neighborhood." *Broadcasting*, November 7, 1966, 73.

41. "The WINS-News Conference: Transcript," May 31, 1964, and Stan Brooks, letter to King, June 1, 1964, series 3, subseries 1, MLK.

42. Eberly, *Music in the Air*, 171, 166; Bliss, *Now the News*, 188–90.

43. Wood, *Electronic Journalism*, 105.

44. *New York Times*, June 10, 1963.

45. Ibid.

46. Pacifica Foundation, "Articles of Incorporation," 1946, cited in Land, *Active Radio*, 41.

47. WBAI, Pacifica Foundation, "The Exacting Ear," 1966, cited in Land, *Active Radio*, 49–50.

48. In "Publicity: Pacifica Foundation Broadcast" file, HFS: Harold Winkler, letter to Myles Horton, November 13, 1959; Horton, letter to Winkler, November 17, 1959; Alice Cobb, letter to Gene Marine, November 30, 1959; Cobb, letters to Winkler, January 9 and May 2, 1960; Elsa Knight Thompson, letter to Horton, June 1, 1960; Gene Bruck, telegram to Highlander Folk School, June 10, 1960; "The Durable Mr. Horton," KPFA, January 14, 1967; "Myles Horton Reports on Highlander Center," KPFA, February 23, 1967.

49. See Land, *Active Radio*, 72.

50. Ibid., 84–85. "The Freedom Ride," 1961, PR; "Rosa Parks: Beginning the Bus Boycott," 1962, PR; "Interview with Fannie Lou Hamer," 1964, PR.

51. "Reverend Wyatt T. Walker: Civil Rights Activist," 1964, PR. Harry Kantor, letter to Leslie Dunbar, June 15, 1964, and Mildred M. Johnson, letter to KPFA, July 23, 1964, reel 59, SRC.

52. *New York Times,* June 10, 1963.

53. Angela Davis, interview with Brian Dooley, April 21, 1997. Copy in possession of author.

Chapter 5. Edwin T. Randall and Friendly World Broadcasting: Radio and White Racial Liberalism in the Age of Mass Protest

1. Edwin Randall, "Who in the World is Edwin T. Randall?" n.d., reel 2, SRC.

2. George A. Patterson, letter to Ray Newton of AFSC, [1950], folder "Radio/Television—General," box "General Administration, 1950—Central Services, Publicity Department," AFSC.

3. *AFSC Annual Report—1947,* 21, AFSC.

4. George Loft, memo to Clarence Pickett, "AFSC Radio Commentator Project," April 3, 1951, folder "Radio/Television—Radio Commentator Project," box "General Administration, 1951—Central Services, Publicity Department," AFSC; *AFSC Bulletin,* June 1951, 9.

5. Lewis Hoskins, memo to Finance Committee, "Recommendations of Program Evaluation Committee," October 22, 1951, and John Kavanaugh, letter to Lucy G. Morgan, October 17, 1951, folder "Radio/Television—General," box "General Administration, 1951—Central Services, Publicity Department," AFSC.

6. "Report on Radio and TV Activity, October 1954–September 1955," October 20, 1955, folder "Information Service, Audio Visual, Radio and Television," box "General Administration, 1955—Information Service (American Section) to Publications," AFSC.

7. "Radio Programs Available on Tape, 5 to 7 Minute Conversations, 1955–, List B," same folder.

8. "Summary of Programs Requested by Southern Stations," 1957, same folder.

9. Randall, letter to Harold Fleming, November 10, 1958, reel 2, SRC.

10. Carl and Anne Braden, letter to Ed [Randall], November 4, 1958, folder 2260, box 115, SCEF. See also Carl and Anne Braden, letter to Jim Dombrowski, November 4, 1958, and Dombrowski, letter to Franz Daniel, [November 1958], same folder.

11. "Clarence Pickett, Visit of Quaker Team to Montgomery, Alabama," folder "Information Services, Radio/Television Work," box "General Administration, 1956—Information Service (News Releases) to International Affairs Seminars of Washington (Seminar Meetings—"Next Steps in US Development Programs")," AFSC.

12. "Radio Programs Available on Tape—1957—List B—5 to 6 Minute Spots: Clarence Mitchell," folder "Information Services, Audio Visual Aids, Radio & Television—Friendly World Series," box "General Administration, 1957—Information Services to International Affairs Seminars of Washington," AFSC.

13. "Radio Programs Available on Tape—1956—List M: Reginald Reynolds, 5 Spots," same folder as note 11. "Radio Programs Available on Tape—1957—List A—5 to 6 Minute Spots: James Bristol," same folder as note 12.

14. "Summary of Programs" as in note 8; "Radio Programs Available on Tape—1956—List O," same folder as note 6.

15. James M. Dabbs, "Radio Programs Available on Tape—1957—List D—5 to 6 Min-

utes Spots," same folder as note 12. Egerton, *Speak Now Against the Day*, 552.

16. The opinions stated by Sanders, Morisey, and Moffett here and in the following eight paragraphs can be found in Olcutt Sanders, memo to Alex Morisey, January 31, 1957, folder "Information Services, Audio Visual Aids, Radio & Television—Correspondence," same box as note 12; Morisey, memo (Radio Programs) to Sanders, February 8, 1957, same folder; Barbara Moffett, memo (Radio Programs) to Sanders, February 8, 1957, same folder.

17. Alvin Gaines, letter to Hoskins, March 4, 1957, same folder as note 12.

18. Sanders, "Proposed Arrangements with Ed Randall," October 2, 1957, same folder.

19. Don Stephens, letter to Josephine Wilkins, November 11, 1958, folder 2260, box 115, SCEF.

20. Leslie Dunbar, "Annual Report of the Executive Director of the SRC," April 1965, reel 219, SRC.

21. Joseph Hendricks, interview with Susan Glisson, May 7, 2002, SRCOH.

22. Leslie Dunbar, interview with Susan Glisson, May 10, 2002, SRCOH. From reel 20, SRC: WSFM editorial, n.d.; interoffice memo to Dunbar, February 21, 1962; Dunbar, letter to WSFM-Birmingham, February 23, 1962; James Melonas, letter to Dunbar, March 16, 1962; Dunbar, letter to Melonas, April 25, 1962.

23. "About Friendly World Broadcasting," [1963?], reel 2, SRC.

24. "Radio Programs Available on Tape—1961—List W" and "Radio Programs Available on Tape—1961—List X," reel 2, SRC.

25. "Special Offer—August 1960: Five 5–7 Minute Spots: John J. Brubaker," reel 2, SRC.

26. Randall, letter to Harold Fleming, October 14, 1960, and Fleming, letter to Randall, October 27, 1960, reel 2, SRC.

27. Randall, "The Exciting Story of 'A Yankee in the Heart of Dixie,'" n.d.; Randall, letter to Paul Rilling, September 26, 1962; Randall, letter to Paul Anthony, January 14, 1966, all on reel 2, SRC.

28. Randall, "Yankee in the Heart of Dixie" and letter to Rilling (see note 27).

29. See note 6.

30. Joe B. Long, letter to Randall, August 21, 1956, same folder as note 11.

31. "Radio Programs Available on Tape—1959—List O," reel 2, SRC; Randall, letter to Fleming, May 18, 1959, reel 2, SRC.

32. Stephens, letter to Fleming, November 25, 1958, reel 2, SRC.

33. See note 19.

34. Fleming, letter to Whom It May Concern, [1964?], reel 2, SRC.

35. Florence Robin, "Transition Without Tragedy: A Community Preparation Handbook," 1963, reel 219, SRC.

36. Randall, letter to Anthony, January 14, 1966, and letter to Dunbar, October 10, 1966; "Yankee in the Heart of Dixie," reel 2, SRC.

Chapter 6. Black-Oriented Radio and the Southern Civil Rights Movement

1. *Broadcasting Yearbook, 1966*, B-38. Philip Meltzer, interview with Brian Ward, November 7, 1998. *Columbus Enquirer*, July 11 and 12, 1963. See also Tuck, *Beyond Atlanta*, 143–45.

2. Meltzer interview. See WOKS, "License Application Transfer," September 1962, box

276, FCC. Ben F. Waple, "Consent to Assignment of Radio Construction Permit or License," November 14, 1962, and "Application for Authority to Construct a New Broadcast Station or Make Changes in an Existing Broadcast Station," December 4, 1962, WOKS, fiche 895, MMBSHC.

3. When interviewed, Phil Meltzer mistakenly thought that CORE led the Columbus campaign and could not recall the name of the movement leader he met, but it is likely that it was Bobby Hill.

4. Meltzer interview. "The Civil Rights Crisis: A Synopsis of Recent Developments," part II (July 26, 1963), reel 219, SRC. For details of the summer 1963 campaign in Columbus, see *Columbus Enquirer*, July 6, 10–13, and 16–20, 1963.

5. Meltzer interview.

6. Meltzer interview.

7. "The Civil Rights Crisis: A Synopsis of Recent Developments," parts II (July 26, 1963), III (September 5, 1963), and IV (December 31, 1963), reel 219, SRC. Meltzer interview.

8. Tuck, *Beyond Atlanta*, 145. Meltzer interview.

9. See note 8. Also, Philip Meltzer, "Policy to Be Pursued Towards Making Time Available for Discussion of Public Issues," January 2, 1964, WOKS, "Application for Renewal of Broadcast Station License," January 2, 1964, exhibit 8, box 276, FCC; "Application for Consent to Transfer of Control of Corporation Holding Radio Broadcast Station Construction Permit of License," February 3, 1966, exhibit 2, box 276, FCC; *Broadcasting Yearbook, 1967*, B-41.

10. Henry Lee Moon, memo "Anniversary Day Radio Program," to branch presidents, January 1960, folder 13, box 19, KA; Moon, letter to branch presidents, January 26, 1960, III-A-252, NAACP.

11. *Jet*, March 10, 1960, 11.

12. WSOK, "Application for Renewal of Broadcast Station License," December 13, 1963, exhibit 7, box 309, FCC.

13. "Publicity Handbook," n.d., III-A-311, NAACP.

14. "NAACP Information Series," note attached to Ruby Hurley, memo to L. Black and Gloster Current, May 27, 1965, II-A-265, NAACP.

15. Ed Pate, "Supplementary Statement of Policy," January 16, 1959, KPRS, "Application for Renewal of Broadcast Station License," January 1959, box 59, FCC.

16. "Your Block Unit Forum of the Air," press release, n.d., folder 1102.2.20, BWOF.

17. *Sponsor*, October 9, 1961, part 2, 12.

18. Mary King, *Freedom Song*, 164, 215–16; Julian Bond, interview with Stephen Walsh, August 17, 1995.

19. "Communications Manual," n.d., 9, A-VII-4, SNCC; Betty Garman, memo to Friends of SNCC, February 5, 1965, C-I-1, SNCC.

20. WATS Reports, July-August 1965, A-VII-4, SNCC.

21. "Radio and Television Programming and Editorializing," n.d., A-VII-1, SNCC; *New York Times*, December 6, 1962.

22. Marvin Rich, memo to CORE chapter leaders, October 6, 1964, part 2, reel 9, CORE.

23. Edward S. Hollander, "Field Report," April 1, 1964, F-III-130, reel 22, CORE-ADD.

24. Hollander, letter to Marcia, May 3, 1964, F-II-130, reel 22, CORE-ADD.

25. Hollander, "Field Report," October 19, 1964, F-III-130, reel 22, CORE-ADD.

26. Jack Gibson, interview with Jacquie Gales Webb, January 7, 1996, BR. This story is repeated in Barlow, *Voice Over*, 208–9; George, *Death of Rhythm and Blues*, 46.

27. "Minutes of SCLC Executive Committee Retreat," November 10–12, 1964, 4, folder 4, box 143, SCLC; "News Media Request," September 12, 1963, folder 10, box 118, SCLC. Barlow, *Voice Over*, 209–11.

28. "Minutes of SCLC Executive Committee Retreat," 4. Zenas Sears, letter to Randolph Blackwell, December 24, same folder.

29. Sears, letter to Blackwell; Tom Offenburger, memo, February 2, 1968, folder 24, box 47, SCLC. Newspaper statistics from the 1968 *Ayer's Directory*.

30. For the story of WERD, see G. Blackwell, "Black-Controlled Media," 121–62. Also "The WERD Story," October 2, 1994, MTR; *Chicago Defender,* September 24 and December 17, 1949; *Pittsburgh Courier,* October 15 and December 17, 1949; *Jet,* June 24, 1954, 60, and October 22, 1959, 58; *Black Radio Exclusive,* June 15, 1979, 12–13.

31. Mack Saddler, quoted in "The WERD Story."

32. Willieboyd "Mack" Saddler, interview with Brian Ward, October 19, 1995. See also Henderson, "Heman E. Perry."

33. Jesse Blayton, quoted in Henderson, "Heman E. Perry," 242. See also 217.

34. Saddler interview.

35. W.E.B. Du Bois, letter to Jesse B. Blayton, July 9, 1930, reel 43, and Blayton, letter to Du Bois, April 22, 1935, reel 30, WEBD.

36. Du Bois, letter to Blayton, April 26, 1935, reel 43; Blayton, letter to Du Bois, June 14, 1930, reel 30, WEBD.

37. J. T. Bellanfant, letter to the *Methodist Challenge,* n.d., folder "Segregation—Clippings, Leaflets, Miscellaneous," box 9, CP.

38. *Pittsburgh Courier,* December 17, 1949.

39. Paul E. X. Brown and Herb Gershorn, quoted in "The WERD Story."

40. Ibid.

41. *Pittsburgh Courier,* December 17, 1949; "The WERD Story."

42. G. Blackwell, "Black-Controlled Media," 140; "The WERD Story."

43. "The WERD Story"; Rev. Donald Vails, interview with Jacquie Gales Webb, n.d., BR.

44. *Sponsor,* August 13, 1951, 75; Walsh, "Black-Oriented Radio," 55.

45. Tuck, *Beyond Atlanta,* 8–9; Blackwell, "Black-Controlled Media," 134–36; Walsh, "Black-Oriented Radio," 85.

46. G. Blackwell, "Black-Controlled Media," 142–43; Morris Novik, letter to Blayton, June 18, 1952, II-A-544, NAACP; John Calhoun, letter to Preston Mobley, August 13, 1957, III-C-27, NAACP. See also Walsh, "Black-Oriented Radio," 81, 84–86, 98.

47. For more on the conservative Atlanta Urban League branch, see Spritzer and Bergmark, *Grace Towns Hamilton,* 136–43. WERD, "Application for Renewal of Broadcast Station License," December 27, 1957, exhibit IV, 14–17, box 121, FCC. Walsh, "Black-Oriented Radio," 99.

48. Chambers, *America's Tenth Man,* 168.

49. William Fowlkes, interview with Brian Ward, October 18, 1995; Esmond Patterson, interview with Brian Ward and Jenny Walker, October 19, 1995.

50. Saddler interview; Fowlkes interview; Patterson interview; Bond-Walsh interview; Walsh, "Black-Oriented Radio," 106.

51. "The WERD Story"; Saddler interview; G. Blackwell, "Black-Controlled Media," 136.

52. (Horace) Julian Bond, letter to Mobley, January 23, 1964, A-VII-I, SNCC.

53. *Muhammad Speaks*, December 30, 1962.

54. Dr. Arthur C. Banks, WERD broadcast, January 15, 1961, transcript in *Atlanta Inquirer*, January 21, 1961.

55. Unsigned handwritten report on All-Citizens Registration Committee, n.d., and "Crash Voter Registration Program, Fulton County—August 31st Through September 14th," reel 183, SRC; *Atlanta Daily World*, September 3, 1964.

56. Chuck Sears, quoted in W. Smith, *Pied Pipers*, 62.

57. W. Smith, *Pied Pipers*, 61–75 (Zenas Sears quote, 65). Lydon, *Ray Charles*, 114, 160–61.

58. WAOK, "Application for Renewal of Broadcast Station License," December 31, 1960, exhibit F, part 1, 1–4, box 135, FCC. *Atlanta Constitution*, March 14, 1984.

59. WAOK, "Application for Renewal," December 31, 1960, exhibit F, part 1, 29.

60. Ibid., 27.

61. Ibid., 27–28.

62. Bond-Walsh interview.

63. James Wood, letter to Zenas Sears, December 1, 1960, WAOK, "Application for Renewal," December 31, 1960, exhibit 17. *Atlanta Inquirer*, January 21, 1961, 5. See also Tuck, *Beyond Atlanta*, 120–21.

64. WAOK, "Application for Renewal of Broadcast Station License," December 29, 1963, exhibit 7, 23, box 415, FCC.

65. WAOK, "Application for Renewal," section IV, question 2(a), December 29, 1963, box 415, FCC; WDAS, "Application for Renewal of Broadcast Station License," April 16, 1963, box 202, FCC. See Walsh, "Black-Oriented Radio," 138.

66. WERD advertisement, *Atlanta Inquirer*, January 21, 1961, 5.

67. "Minutes, Organizational Meeting of the Atlanta Coordinating Committee," November 29, 1963, and "Minutes of Atlanta Coordinating Committee," December 9, 1963, folder 4, box 1, series II.A, RC.

68. Wood, letter to Leslie Dunbar, n.d., reel 59, SRC; Wood, letter to Julian Bond, January 7, 1964, and Bond, letter to Wood, January 14, 1964, A-VII-1, SNCC.

69. Zenas Sears, letter to SNCC, February 7, 1964, and SNCC, letter to Sears, February 11, 1964, A-VII-1, SNCC.

70. Stan Raymond, quoted in W. Smith, *Pied Pipers*, 75. See also 72, 74.

71. Patterson interview. Julian Bond, interview with Brian Ward, March 20, 1996. Bond-Walsh interview. Walsh, "Black-Oriented Radio," 110.

72. Vails interview.

73. James Bond, interview with Brian Ward, October 16, 1995. Ledella Forehand, letter to Rodney Cook, August 10, 1966, folder 3, box 1, Series II.A, RC.

74. Mary King, interview with Stephen Walsh, April 17, 1995; also Bond-Walsh interview; Paul E. X. Brown, interview with Stephen Walsh, March 16, 1995.

75. Brown interview.

76. Bond-Walsh interview. Eddie Castleberry, interview with Jacquie Gales Webb, January 5, 1996, BR.

77. Mary King interview. Walsh, "Black-Oriented Radio," 139–40.

78. Robert McNamara III, letter to Dear Friend, n.d., part 3, reel 2, SCLC-MIC. See also Walsh, "Black-Oriented Radio," 118–20.

79. "Statement of Goals," in Robert McNamara III, "Proposal, Civil Rights Information Service," n.d., part 3, reel 2, SCLC-MIC; "Civil Rights Information Service Financial Statement" and "Gifts Committed to Civil Rights Information Service," attached to Robert McNamara III, letter to Edward Clayton, n.d., same reel.

80. "The Present Status of Civil Rights Information Service," attached to same letter.

81. "The Present State of CRIS," attached to McNamara, letter to Clayton, May 20, 1964, same reel.

82. Julius Thomas, quoted in Guichard Parris, memo to PR Advisory Committee, March 25, 1963, II-V-22, NUL; Minutes of Meeting of Public Relations Committee, March 26, 1963, II-V-22, NUL. Walsh, "Black-Oriented Radio," 120–24.

83. Sherwood Ross, memo to regional directors and local league executive directors, April 19, 1965, II-V-17, NUL; Ross, memo to station managers, May 25, 1965, and memo to regional directors and local league executive directors, June 30, 1965, II-V-15, NUL; script for *Civil Rights Roundup*, June 8, 1965, II-V-46, NUL. Johnson, *Vantage Point*, 166.

84. For the demise of the NUL shows, see Vince Mallardi, letter to Parris, September 27, 1965, and Parris, letter to Mallardi, October 1, 1965, II-V-17, NUL. This incomplete list of stations taking the shows comes from Ross, memo to regional directors et al., June 30, 1965.

85. Will Campbell, letter to Committee of Southern Churchmen members, April 28, 1965, box 2, Will Campbell Correspondence, 1963–1979, K/JYH. From "Special File: Radio Ministry, Radio Tapes (1965–1967)," folder 18, box 6, WC: undated memo; J. A. Gallimore, letter to Elbert Jean, October 7, 1965; Robert Walker, letter to Jean, October 4, 1965; Curtis Welborne, letter to Jean, October 4, 1965; Phillip D. Brady, letter to Jean, October 5, 1965; Frank Harden, letter to Jean, October 5, 1965; James Ramsay, letter to Committee of Southern Churchmen, October 7, 1965.

86. Ed Hollander, letter to Marvin Rich, March 6, 1965, F-III-130, reel 22, CORE-ADD.

87. *Broadcasting*, November 7, 1966, 87–88.

88. Unsigned memo to student volunteers for the Jonesboro Project, part 2, reel 4, CORE.

89. Lawrence Guyot, interview with Brian Ward and Jenny Walker, December 16, 1995.

90. *New York Times*, July 22, 1965. Although the article does not mention the rival station by name, it was probably WISX in Bogalusa.

91. Castleberry interview.

92. Egmont Sonderling, testimony to FCC, *Official Report of Proceedings Before the Federal Communications Commission*, July 11, 1966, 51, file 16533, vol. 2, box 164, FCC-DOC; WOL, "Amendment to Application for Consent to Assignment of Radio Broadcast Station Construction Permit or License," May 7, 1965, exhibit XXI, 2–7, file 16533, vol. 1, box 163, FCC-DOC. For an exhaustive account of Sonderling's takeover of WOL, see Walsh, "Black-Oriented Radio," 240–43, 245, 248–76.

93. Thornton, *Dividing Lines*, 3.

Chapter 7. WENN's Push Came to Shove: Black-Oriented Radio and the Freedom Struggle in Birmingham

1. *Broadcasting Yearbook, 1957*, 342–44.

2. Statistics drawn from "Birmingham: The South's Fastest Growing Market Recog-

nized as One of the Nation's Number 1 Test Markets Gives You a Big Plus," 1954 report, file 1102.2 (Birmingham—Blacks), BWOF. *Sponsor,* August 17, 1964, 34. See also Kelley, *Race Rebels,* 79–84.

3. "WBCO Sells Greater Birmingham's Quarter Million Negroes," [1951?], promotional booklet, LAB.

4. Gene Newman Radio, Inc., letter to Mary Jane Morris, May 26, 1959, and "Explanation of Transaction," exhibit A4, WENN, "Application for Consent to Assignment of Radio Broadcast Station Construction Permit or License," May 7, 1959, box 121, FCC.

5. Ibid.

6. *Birmingham Weekly Review,* January 17, May 2, and October 17, 1941.

7. Christina T. Stewart, "The Big Story," in *Announcer and Radio Artist: William Blevins—The South's First Negro Announcer and Entertainer,* publicity pamphlet, c. 1948. Copy in possession of author.

8. Ibid.; Bob Friedman, *A Short History of WJLD, Fairfield/Birmingham,* n.p., n.d. Copy in possession of author.

9. On Jefferson County gospel, see Seroff, "On the Battlefield."

10. *Ebony,* March 1949, 56–61. *Birmingham World,* August 19, 1949.

11. Friedman, *WJLD;* "Program Schedule Analysis," WJLD, "Application for Renewal of Broadcasting Station License," December 15, 1954, box 141, FCC; "Program Schedule Analysis," WJLD, "Application For Renewal Of Broadcasting Station License," December 12, 1957, box 146, FCC. For George Johnston Sr. and Jr., see "Interests of Applicant Partners," WJLD, "Application for Authorization to Change Location of Transmitter," June 12, 1946, box 190, FCC.

12. Friedman, *WJLD;* "Program Schedule Analysis," WJLD, December 15, 1954, and December 12, 1957 (see note 11). For more on Rev. John Goodgame, see Fullerton, "Striking Out Jim Crow," 87. Use of Jasper Robey's Seventeenth Street AOH Church by the ACMHR is noted in "Program," June 4–6, 1962, and "List of Places Desegregated Because of ACMHR," 1964, files 1102.2.3–4 (ACMHR), BWOF.

13. "WBCO Sells" (see note 3).

14. "Statement of Program Service of Broadcast Applicant," WEZB, "Application for Renewal of Broadcast Station License," March 6, 1958, box 121, FCC; "Statement of Program Service," WENN, "Application for Renewal," January 7, 1961, box 121, FCC; "Statement of Program Service," WENN, "Application for Renewal," December 11, 1963, box 180, FCC.

15. Shelley Stewart, interview with Brian Ward, October 26, 1995.

16. *Birmingham Post-Herald,* April 9 and 12, 1954.

17. Eddie Castleberry, interview with Jacquie Gales Webb, January 5, 1996, BR.

18. Stewart interview. "Disc Jockeys." Castleberry interview. For WJLD's conversion to all-black programming, see *Birmingham Post-Herald,* November 5, 1954.

19. Eddie Castleberry, quoted in G. Williams, *Legendary Pioneers,* 43. Stewart interview.

20. *Our World,* November 1955, 40. Stewart interview.

21. Castleberry interview.

22. "Summary of Public Service Activities of Radio Station WENN Since September 1958," WENN, "Application for Renewal," January 7, 1961, box 121, FCC; "Summary . . . Since January 1961," WENN, "Application for Renewal," December 11, 1963, box 180, FCC.

23. Stewart interview.

24. Stewart interview. See also S. Stewart, *The Road South*, and McWhorter, *Carry Me Home*, 359–60.

25. Stewart interview. Friedman, *WJLD*. Jesse Champion interview with Brian Ward, October 26, 1995. Eddie Castleberry, quoted in G. Williams, *Legendary Pioneers*, 41.

26. Stewart interview.

27. Eddie Castleberry, quoted in G. Williams, *Legendary Pioneers*, 38. *Birmingham Post-Herald*, April 9, 1954.

28. Champion interview. Friedman, *WJLD*.

29. "Statement of Program Service," WENN, January 7, 1961, and December 11, 1963 (see note 14).

30. See note 29.

31. "Program Schedule Analysis," WJLD, December 12, 1957 (see note 11). WJLD, "Alma Johnson," publicity flier, n.d.

32. "Summary of Public Service Activities," WENN, January 7, 1961 (see note 22).

33. Stewart interview.

34. Castleberry interview.

35. J. Edward Reynolds, quoted in "Dream Radio Station," *Newsweek*, September 12, 1949, reprinted in *Negro Digest*, January 1950, 24.

36. Barlow, *Voice Over*, 207.

37. Birmingham Federation of Colored Women's Clubs, "Yearbook, 1952–53," file 24, box 21, JWM.

38. Stewart interview. McWhorter, *Carry Me Home*, 360.

39. Eskew, *But for Birmingham*, 125, 135.

40. *Jet*, October 10, 1957, 43. Shelley Stewart, quoted in McWhorter, *Carry Me Home*, 360.

41. On Asa Carter and the campaign against rock and roll in Alabama, see Ward, *Just My Soul Responding*, 95–105.

42. Stewart interview. *Montgomery Advertiser*, May 30, 1958.

43. Ibid.; *Birmingham News*, May 29, 1958; Stewart interview.

44. For the Birmingham campaign, see Branch, *Parting the Waters*, 725–802; Eskew, *But for Birmingham*; Garrow, *Bearing the Cross*, 231–85; Thornton, *Dividing Lines*, 141–379, 513–31.

45. See Branch, *Parting the Waters*, 755, and McWhorter, *Carry Me Home*, 359–60. *Birmingham: A Testament of Violence*, July 1965, folder 16, box 117, SCLC.

46. WENN, "Application for Renewal," December 11, 1963.

47. Erskine Faush, interview with Lex Gillespie, September 13, 1995, BR. See also Champion interview.

48. Eskew, *But for Birmingham*, 38, 224–25.

49. Faush interview. McWhorter, *Carry Me Home*, 183–84, 207, 209, 214; Thornton, *Dividing Lines*, 248.

50. Ralph Abernathy, quoted in *New York Times*, April 21, 1963; Eskew, *But for Birmingham*, 252.

51. Emory O. Jackson, letter to Anne G. Rutledge, April 12, 1963, EJ; Eskew, *But for Birmingham*, 260–61.

52. Faush interview; Stewart interview; S. Stewart, *The Road South*, 247; Eskew, *But for Birmingham*, 264.

53. *Newsweek*, May 3, 1963.

54. Eskew, *But for Birmingham*, 234–35, 259–61.

55. Ibid., 261–63.

56. McWhorter, *Carry Me Home*, 360.

57. Larry Russell, quoted in Levine, *Freedom's Children*, 101. McWhorter, *Carry Me Home*, 366–67. See also Abraham Woods, interview with Brian Ward and Jenny Walker, October 25, 1995; Joseph Lackey, interview with Brian Ward, October 26, 1995; Stewart interview.

58. Woods interview. Abraham Woods, quoted in Manis, *A Fire You Can't Put Out*, 368; ACMHR, "Program—1964," file 1102.2.4 (ACMHR), BWOF. Eskew, *But for Birmingham*, 217.

59. See M. L. King, "Transforming a Neighborhood"; Larry Russell, quoted in Levine, *Freedom's Children*, 101. Stewart interview. Lackey interview. Woods interview.

60. R. A. Watkins to Jamie Moore, "Report on Meeting of May 10, 1963, held at St. John's Church," May 15, 1963, box 13.5, EC.

61. Stewart interview.

62. Faush interview.

63. Faush interview.

64. Faush interview. S. Stewart, *The Road South*, 240.

65. Champion interview.

66. Faush interview; "Report of FBI Interview with Paul D. White on 19 September 1963," September 24, 1963, folder 10.29 (White, Paul D), BAPD.

67. Ibid. "Federal Bureau of Investigation Report," October 10, 1963, file 1308.1.10, FBI-CB; "Report of FBI Interview with Paul D. White on October 25, 1963," October 31, 1963, file 1308.3.4, FBI-CB; "Report of FBI Interview with W.J. Allen on 26 September 1963," October 2, 1963, file 1308.1.3, FBI-CB. See also Sikora, *Until Justice Rolls Down*, 55–57, 128–29.

68. "Summary . . . Since January 1961," WENN, December 11, 1963 (see note 22).

69. Faush interview. "Unsigned Report on Bombing," 1963, file 1102.4.2, BWOF.

Chapter 8. Ample and Frequent Moderation: Radio and Race Relations in Charlotte

Author's Note: The quote is from a statement by the Charlotte-Mecklenburg Council for Human Relations, "School Board Must Move Toward Full Compliance," *New South*, December 1959, 11.

1. Marion Wright, "Integration and Public Morals," *New South*, November 1957, 7–14.

2. The struggle to desegregate Charlotte's schools is ably told in D. Douglas, *Reading, Writing & Race*, and Gaillard, *The Dream Long Deferred*.

3. For the Lumbees' rout of the Klan, see G. Lewis, "Not So Well Red."

4. For the idea of "sly resistance," see Houghton, "North Carolina Republican Party." Also Chafe, *Civilities and Civil Rights*; D. Douglas, *Reading, Writing & Race*, 28–30, 32–34.

5. The phrase "progress under pressure" is borrowed from Leach, "Progress under Pressure."

6. For Charlotte's economic development, see ibid., 4; D. Douglas, *Reading, Writing & Race*, 50–52; Hanchett, *New South City*.

7. Leach, "Progress under Pressure," 11.

8. *Charlotte Observer*, February 12, 1960.

9. Quoted in Pat Watters, "Charlotte: Special Report," May 1964, reel 220, SRC.

10. D. Douglas, *Reading, Writing & Race*, 183.

11. Biographical information comes from Charles Crutchfield, interview with Brian Ward, November 13, 1995; Crutchfield, interview with Lynn Haessly, January 8, 1986, SOHP; "Charles Crutchfield: Biographical Data," CCG; Crutchfield, interview with David Mays, December 1977, CCG; Sherry Johnson, "Crystal Set Hooked Crutchfield on Broadcasting," n.d., and Lew Powell, "Charles Crutchfield," *Charlotte Observer*, [1977], in "Charles H. Crutchfield," NCCCF. See also Boger, *Charlotte 23*, 70–9.

12. Crutchfield-Ward interview.

13. For the early years of WBT, see WBT, "Colossus of the Carolinas: 30th Anniversary, 1922–1952," 1952, NCC; WBT, "Pilot of the Airwaves You Seem Like a Friend to Me," n.d., CCG; Jarrett, "Broadcasting." Grundy, "From *Il Trovatore*" and "Good People"; Wallace, "Broadcasting in North Carolina."

14. Grundy, "From *Il Trovatore*."

15. Ibid.; Grundy, "Good People." For the sale of WBT to the Jefferson Standard Life Insurance Company, see WBT, "Agreement Between Columbia Broadcasting System and Jefferson Life Insurance Co., Greensboro, NC," April 30, 1945, and "Application for Consent to Assignment of Radio Broadcast Station License," part I, May 18, 1945, and part II, May 12, 1945, folder 2, box 125, FCC.

16. *Charlotte News*, April 12, 1922; Wallace, "Broadcasting in North Carolina," 63.

17. Yarger, "Don't Touch That Dial," 98.

18. WBT, "Pilot of the Airwaves"; Crutchfield-Ward interview. Crutchfield, "Untitled Recollections," n.d., NCC; Jarrett, "Broadcasting," 72.

19. Ibid., 72–73; Crutchfield-Haessly interview; Crutchfield, "Untitled Recollections."

20. *Charlotte Observer*, March 31, 1971; Leach, "Progress under Pressure," 57–68.

21. Tross, *This Thing Called Religion*, 123; Crutchfield-Ward interview; Crutchfield-Haessly interview.

22. Crutchfield-Ward interview; Crutchfield-Haessly interview; "Charles Crutchfield: Biographical Data."

23. Boger, *Charlotte 23*, 71. Fred Alexander, letter to Crutchfield, July 29, 1953, and Larry Walker, letter to Alexander, August 10, 1953, folder 1, box 51, FA.

24. Crutchfield-Ward interview. Lash, "The Negro and Radio," 180.

25. Nathaniel Tross, "Radio Address, WBT," May 18, 1941, cited in Leach, "Progress under Pressure," 62.

26. Lash, "The Negro and Radio," 167, 180. Leach, "Progress under Pressure," 61–62. *Variety*, January 6, 1943.

27. *Carolina Times*, January 3, 1942; Leach, "Progress under Pressure," 61–62.

28. Quoted in *Charlotte Observer*, March 29, 1962; *Charlotte News*, December 23, 1959. See also Leach, "Progress under Pressure," 106–11.

29. For the founding of the CCPA, see "Minutes of Meeting," September 16, 1948, and November 11, 1948, folder 19, box 52, FA; for Bishop Dale, see L. G. Green and Emma Le Maye, "Statement," February 4, 1949, same folder; *Charlotte Observer*, February 22, 1949, and October 16, 1976; *Charlotte News*, April 26, 1949; Hanchett, *New South City*, 327 n. 9.

30. Tross, quoted in *Charlotte News*, April 26, 1949; *Charlotte Post*, March 18, 1954. Voter registration figures in *Charlotte Observer*, March 29, 1962.

31. Quoted in Leach, "Progress under Pressure," 71. See also 61–62.

32. D. Douglas, *Reading, Writing & Race*, 19. See James E. Shepard, letter to Crutchfield,

September 1945, folder "Congratulations Letters 1945," box 1, CCG; Shepard, "Race Relationships in North Carolina," February 17, 1944, box 82, JMB.

33. Nathaniel Tross, quoted in *Charlotte News*, February 12, 1960. Leach, "Progress under Pressure," 65.

34. Tross, "Note," n.d., cited in ibid., 63–64.

35. Nathaniel Tross quoted in *Charlotte News*, March 26, 1962; Leach, "Progress under Pressure," 66–67.

36. *Charlotte Observer*, November 19, 1957; Leach, "Progress under Pressure," 64.

37. *Crusader*, February 13, 1960.

38. *Charlotte News*, February 12, 1960. Leach, "Progress under Pressure," 65.

39. Tross, "Racial Good-Will and Understanding," WBT radio address, [1965?], NCC.

40. Boulware, *Oratory of Negro Leaders*, 278–79. *Charlotte News*, February 21, 1964; Tross, "Brotherhood Week," February 20, 1964, WBT; Leach, "Progress under Pressure," 67. Tross, "Racial Good-Will."

41. Crutchfield-Haessly interview; Crutchfield, "Statement," cited in Leach, "Progress under Pressure," 68. *WBTips*, 1, 2 (March 1951), clippings file "Radio Station WBT, 1922–1979," CM.

42. *Atlanta Daily World*, January 5, 1947.

43. "Preliminary Outline for a Complete Survey on the Status of the Negroes of Charlotte, North Carolina, 1953," January 5, 1953, folder 20, box 52, FA.

44. See *Sponsor*, July 2, 1962, 54, 59.

45. U.S. State Department, "Authorization of Official Travel, 1–10533," June 14, 1951, and "Schedule," n.d., folder "State Department Assignment, 1951," box 1, CCG; Crutchfield, letter to David Sarnoff, August 28, 1951, folder "State Department Assignment, 1951," box 2, CCG.

46. U.S. State Department, press release, [1953], folder "State Department, 1953," box 4, CCG.

47. Crutchfield, "Confidential Report," n.d., folder "Moscow Trip," box 2, CCG. See also Boger, *Charlotte 23*, 73; Powell, "Charles Crutchfield" (see note 11).

48. Crutchfield, notes of interview with Thomas C. Foote (chief of staff, U.S. Command Berlin), October 21, 1962, folder "Radio Free Europe, Oct. 12th–23rd 1962," box 2, CCG.

49. Morton and Rankin, *Making a Difference*, 53; Hemphill, "Statement."

50. Crutchfield, letter to Clyde Hoey, February 22, 1952, folder "State Department Visit, 1951," box 2, CCG. The other recipients of this letter were Senators Lodge, Mundt, Smith, Kefauver, Taft, Russell, and Byrd.

51. WBT, "Colossus of the Carolinas," 1952, NCC.

52. WBT, "Power for the People," 1954, NCC.

53. Crutchfield-Ward interview.

54. C. A. McKnight, "Editorial—Handwriting on the Wall," *Charlotte News*, June 7, 1950, cited in D. Douglas, *Reading, Writing & Race*, 59.

55. Crutchfield-Ward interview. Billy Graham, telegram to Wallace Jorgenson, November 28, 1977. Copy in possession of author.

56. D. Douglas, *Reading, Writing & Race*, 25–49.

57. Luther Hodges, quoted in Edwin Gill, "Radio Address on WPTF-Raleigh," Septem-

ber 6, 1956, folder "Speeches," special file "Governor's Committee for Public School Amendment" (hereafter GCPSA), box 131, LH.

58. Press release, August 7, 1956, folder "Newspaper Releases," GCPSA, box 131, LH.

59. Steve Woodson, letter to Charles H. Crutchfield, August 9, 1956, folder "Governor's Committee on School Amendment," GCPSA, box 131, LH.

60. Greeley N. Hilton (WBUY), letter to Crutchfield, August 9, 1956, and J. Frank Jarman (WDNC), letter to Crutchfield, August 10, 1956, same folder; E. J. Gluck, letter to Crutchfield, August 13, 1956, folder "Publicity," GCPSA, box 131, LH.

61. Graham B. Poyner (WPTF), memo to Phil Ellis, August 29, 1956, folder "Howland," GCPSA, box 131, LH.

62. Jerry Elliot, letter to Crutchfield, August 9, 1956, folder "Governor's Committee on School Amendment," GCPSA, box 131, LH.

63. James B. Petty (WLTC), letter to Charles H. Crutchfield, August 9, 1956, same folder.

64. Edwin Gill, "Radio Address on WPTF-Raleigh," September 6, 1956, folder "Speeches," GCPSA, box 131, LH.

65. Crutchfield, letter to various radio stations, August 8, 1956, folder "Publicity," GCPSA, box 131, LH; transcripts of "TV/Radio Spot for Governor's Committee (30 Seconds)" and "TV/Radio Spot for Governor's Committee (1 Minute)," same folder.

66. William Moore (WHED), letter to Crutchfield, August 9, 1956, folder "Governor's Committee on School Amendment," GCPSA, box 131, LH. Crutchfield-Ward interview.

67. Leach, "Progress under Pressure," 94.

68. *Pittsburgh Courier,* November 21, 1959.

69. Ibid.

70. Crutchfield-Haessly interview.

71. Crutchfield-Haessly interview.

72. See D. Douglas, *Reading, Writing & Race,* 96–103; Leach, "Progress under Pressure," 123–88.

73. D. Douglas, *Reading, Writing & Race,* 98–102.

74. Ibid., 99; Leach, "Progress under Pressure," 176–77.

75. D. Douglas, *Reading, Writing & Race,* 100.

76. WBT editorial, May 27, 1963, WBT.

77. Ibid.

78. WBT editorial, May 29, 1963, WBT.

79. See WBT editorial, June 24, 1964, WBT; also Crutchfield, letter to Ben Waple (acting secretary, FCC), April 30, 1963, folder 7–A, 1963, box 429, FCC.

80. WBT editorial, August 27, 1963, WBT; editorial response, September 30, 1963, WBT.

81. WBT editorial, May 21, 1964, WBT; editorial response, May 26, 1964, WBT.

82. WBT editorial, February 17, 1964 (see also April 22, June 1, and December 21, 1964), WBT.

83. WBT editorials, March 16, March 22, April 7, and June 4, 1965, WBT.

84. WGIV, "Application for New Standard Broadcast Station Construction Permit," September 10, 1946, folder 1, box 122, FCC.

85. Ibid.; *Who's Who in the South and Southwest, 1965–1966.*

86. Francis Fitzgerald, quoted in Jarrett, "Broadcasting," 78.

87. S. K. "Bill" Lineburger, quoted in ibid.

88. Francis M. Fitzgerald, letter to T. J. Slowie, October 4, 1951, folder 2, box 122, FCC.

89. "Narrative Statement," "Minutes of Special Meeting of Board of Directors, Charlotte Radio and Television Corporation," "Changes in Staff," and "Table 1," December 23, 1952, folder 2, box 122, FCC.

90. Hattie Leeper, interview with Sonja Williams, April 22, 1995, BR.

91. Leeper interview. See also Fitzgerald, "Staff of WGIV—Exhibit XVIII," August 1963, folder 4A, box 196, FCC.

92. Leeper interview.

93. "Citation for Award to Francis M. Fitzgerald, from St. Paul's Baptist Church, Charlotte" (signed by J. C. Clemmons and Rev. James F. Wertz), July 1953, in "Program for Genial Gene Day," Charlotte Armory Auditorium, November 22, 1953, 15. Copy in possession of author.

94. Fitzgerald, "What I Know About Gene," in "Program for Genial Gene Day," 7.

95. Fitzgerald, "Additional Program Data: Exhibit VII—Part II," March 1958, folder 4, box 196, FCC.

96. Thos. A. Jenkins, letter to Fitzgerald, December 20, 1954, same folder.

97. Abarbanel and Haley, "New Audience for Radio," 59.

98. Leeper interview.

99. Leeper interview.

100. Leeper interview.

101. Abarbanel and Haley, "New Audience for Radio," 59.

102. Edward Brown (director of Carver College), letter to Fitzgerald, October 22, 1957, and "Exhibit V: Additional Program Data," August 15, 1960, folder 4, box 196, FCC.

103. "Exhibit XXVI—Participation in Economic Life of the Charlotte Area," August 21, 1963, and Robert F. Kennedy, letter to Fitzgerald, July 29, 1963, same folder.

104. *Charlotte Observer,* April 13, 1988.

105. R. P. Perry (president of Johnson C. Smith University), letter to Fitzgerald, May 14, 1962, and H. Liston, letter to Fitzgerald, April 9, 1956, folder 4, box 196, FCC; Eugene Potts, "Education Booster Campaign," February 5–June 1, 1962, folder 4A, box 196, FCC.

106. Dr. R. A. Hawkins, letter to Fitzgerald, February 25, 1964, folder 5, box 475, FCC.

107. For Fitzgerald's support of Fred Alexander, see receipt no. 36, April 8, 1965, and "WGIV Invoice to Fred Alexander," April 19, 1965, folder 31, box 1, FA.

108. Fitzgerald, "WGIV Policy on Editorials and Controversial Issues," August 1963, folder 4A, box 196, FCC.

109. "WGIV Minitorial," folder 4A, box 196, FCC.

110. Fitzgerald, quoted in *New York Times,* August 5, 1960. "The New Negro Radio Association," *Sponsor,* September 26, 1960, 14/52; "NRA: It's Straining to Profile Its Audience," *Sponsor,* October 9, 1961, 15/25.

111. Leeper interview.

112. *Charlotte News,* July 25, 1967; *Charlotte Observer,* February 1, 1974.

113. Leeper interview.

Chapter 9. A Telling Silence: Freedom Radio in Mississippi

Author's Note: The quote from Rev. Graham Hodges appeared in a letter to the *New York Times,* December 31, 1964.

1. Payne, *I've Got the Light of Freedom*, 1.

2. "State Sovereignty Commission Schedule of Payments Made to Citizens Council Forum for the Period July 1, 1960 Through June 30, 1965," folder 9, box 2, EJ; Bill [no last name], letter to Erle Johnston, November 18, 1987, same folder. See also *Jackson Daily News*, August 20, 1961. For the history of the SSC, see Katagiri, *Mississippi State Sovereignty Commission*, and Johnston, *Mississippi's Defiant Years*.

3. C. J. Wright, quoted in "Mississippi Radio Station Cuts Civil Rights Program," December 26, 1947, II-A-157, NAACP. See also Walsh, "Black-Oriented Radio," 191.

4. "Radio Show Script," April 6, 1932, folder 49, box 24, LL; "List of Executives and Regular Staff Employees of Station WJDX, Also Artists and Groups Presenting Regular Programs Over the Station," 1932, folder 50, box 50, LL.

5. George McConnaughey, letter to NAACP, January 13, 1956, and Fred Beard, letter to Mary Jane Morris, December 8, 1955, III-A-265, NAACP. *New South*, January 1956, 11. Beard, quoted in *New York Times*, May 21, 1965.

6. *Jackson Advocate*, April 18–24 and April 25–May 2, 1991. *Broadcasting Yearbook*, 1961–62, B-93–96. See also Thompson, *Black Press in Mississippi*, 56, 78.

7. Cohodas, *The Band Played Dixie*, 75; Kenneth Cox, quoted in *New York Times*, December 6, 1962.

8. Beard, "WJDX-Jackson Editorials," September 12 and 14, 1962, folder 7, box 4, VH.

9. Beard, "WJDX-Jackson Editorial," September 21, 1962, same folder.

10. Beard editorial, quoted in Lord, *Past That Would Not Die*, 150; Beard, "WJDX-Jackson Editorial," September 17, 1962, folder 7, box 4, VH.

11. Edwin A. Walker, quoted in Johnston, *Mississippi's Defiant Years*, 154.

12. Thomas, *Robert Kennedy*, 197–98.

13. Walker, quoted in Lord, *Past That Would Not Die*, 182.

14. Ibid., 184; Johnston, *Mississippi's Defiant Years*, 157–58, 169.

15. Ibid., 387, 157–58; Lord, *Past That Would Not Die*, 174; Thomas, *Robert Kennedy*, 197.

16. Robert Kennedy, letter to William Mounger, November 15, 1962, reprinted in *Jackson Clarion-Ledger*, May 1, 1997.

17. Ben F. Waple, "FCC Memorandum Opinion and Order (FCC 65–435 67809), Re: Applications of Capitol Broadcasting Company for Renewal of Licenses for Standard Station WSLI and Television Station WJTV, Jackson, Mississippi, May 19, 1965," folder 8, box 1, RS.

18. Meredith, *Three Years in Mississippi*, 205–6.

19. Ibid.

20. *Atlanta Constitution*, September 28, 1962.

21. Meredith, *Three Years in Mississippi*, 205–6.

22. Thomas, *Robert Kennedy*, 199.

23. Ross Barnett, quoted in Faragher et al., *Out of Many*, 862.

24. *New York Times*, October 1, 1962.

25. *Atlanta Constitution*, October 1, 1962.

26. Rather, *The Camera Never Blinks*, 79. Hugh Clegg, letter and memo to Charles D. Fair, November 8, 1962, folder "Meredith Case," box 9, VC.

27. Barrett, *Integration at Ole Miss*, 145, also 123–62. Thomas, *Robert Kennedy*, 203.

28. *New York Times*, October 1 and 5, 1962.

29. *New York Times*, October 1, 1962.

30. *Billboard*, March 28, 1964, 44–45; *College Radio*, April 5, 1964, 22; Clegg, letter to Duncan Whiteside, Radio Station Scrapbook, box 8, Academic and Administrative Departments, UMSM. Barrett, *Integration at Ole Miss*, 163.

31. Dr. Horace L. Villee, "Sermon Text," October 7, 1962, folder "Meredith Crisis," box 17, GS.

32. Beard, telegram to Ben Waple, February 1, 1962; Waple, letters to R.L.T. Smith, February 8 and 21, 1962; Smith, letter to Beard, March 22, 1962, all in folder 8, box 1, RS. Lawrence Guyot, interview with Brian Ward and Jenny Walker, December 16, 1995.

33. R.L.T. Smith, letter to Burke Marshall, April 23, 1962, folder 8, box 1, RS (other recipients of Smith's requests for help included Robert F. Kennedy, John F. Kennedy, Medgar Evers, Clarence Mitchell, Roy Wilkins, Hubert Humphrey, James Wechsler, J. Harold Flannery, Eleanor Roosevelt, and Cleveland Robinson); Smith, statement to FCC, attachment F/exhibit 3, June 4, 1964, same folder.

34. P. R. Storm, "WLBT-TV Contract," May 22, 1962; Beard, "WJDX Contract," May 4, 1962; "WOKJ receipt," May 11, 1962; "WJXN Receipt" and "WJQS Receipt," May 24, 1962; "WSLI Contract" and "WRBC Contract," May 28, 1962, all in same folder.

35. Robert H. Walkup, "Not Race but Grace," sermons broadcast September 30–October 7, 1962, in Shriver, *The Unsilent South*, 58–71 (quote, 63).

36. Guyot interview. For the Freedom Vote, see Dittmer, *Local People*, 200–207.

37. R.L.T. Smith, letter to Beard, October 27, 1963, folder 8, box 1, RS.

38. Plans to launch WONA were made in October 1958, but the station did not debut until March 25, 1959. See WONA, fiche 898, MMBSHC. Robert Chisholm, letter to Waple, [August 1964], folder 2 (FCC 1963–1965 [1]), box 1, WONA.

39. "Complaint to FCC," May 20, 1964; Jack Groce and Rupert Ringwold (signatories), "Complaint to FCC," June 25, 1964; Waple, letter to WONA, August 5, 1964; Waple, letter to Ringwold, February 26, 1965; G. S. Galloway, letter to FCC, August 8, 1964; Chisholm, letter to Waple, all in same folder.

40. Waple, letter to Ringwold. WONA, "Trial Reports, #1–10 and Final Report," December 2–10, 1963, folder 3, box 1, WONA; "News Award Taped Exhibit," n.d., folder 1, box 1, WONA.

41. Dittmer, *Local People*, 272–73.

42. Bob Moses and FDP Coordinators, memo to All Field Staff and Voter Registration Volunteers, July 7, 1964, folder 1, box 136, PJ.

43. For the text of King's message, see Karl Wiesenburg, letter to Walter Smith, July 24, 1964, box 21.g, MFDP.

44. Mike Higson, affidavit, August 4, 1964, box 21.g, MFDP.

45. Invoice, Radio Station WGCM-Gulfport, July 24, 1964, and untitled spot announcements, n.d. and July 24, 1964, same box.

46. "Forrest Radio WMAG Unable to Run Spot Announcement of FDP Meetings," n.d.; Willie Weems, "Statement Re: Refusal of Political Advertising," July 24, 1964; receipt from Dorothy Teal, all in same box.

47. "Political Broadcast Agreement With WFOR," July 23, 1964; unsigned affidavit (probably by Terry Shaw), July 24, 1964; Wiesenburg, letters to Walter Smith, July 23 and 24, 1964, all in same box. *Jackson Clarion-Ledger*, July 15, 1986.

48. Johnston, *Mississippi's Defiant Years*, 264.

49. Lee Edward Garrett, affidavit, August 5, 1964, box 21.g, MFDP.

50. Ibid.; Associated Press release, WHNY-McComb, July 27, 1964, same box.

51. See Philip D. Brady, letter to Elbert Jean, October 5, 1965, folder 18 (Special File: Radio Ministry Tapes [1965–1967]), box 6, WC. Will D. Campbell, letter to Committee of Southern Churchmen members, April 28, 1965, box 2, Will Campbell Correspondence, 1963–1979, K/JYH.

52. Ronald Ridenour, letter to [Walter] Smith, July 25, 1964, and Ridenour, letter to FCC, n.d., box 21.g, MFDP.

53. WGCM-Gulfport, "Agreement with COFO," July 24, 1964, and untitled document on Vicksburg radio, n.d., box 21.g, MFDP; unsigned report, October 13, 1964, folder 5, box 136, PJ.

54. Ibid.

55. Edward Hollander, "Field Report," October 19, 1964, F-III-130, reel 22, CORE-ADD.

56. Dittmer, *Local People*, 225–26.

57. Guyot interview.

58. Robert McNamara, letter to Marvin Rich, July 23, 1964, series 5:145, reel 27, CORE. Julian Bond, letter to Russell F. Jorgensen, April 22, 1964, A-VII-1, SNCC. "NBC Newscast," May 25, 1964, ID 3-74-2-29-1-1-1, folder "Radio Tougaloo," SC.

59. Erle Johnston Jr., memo re COFO Radio Broadcast, July 9, 1964, folder 8, box 141, PJ.

60. Unsigned report, July 26, 1964, folder 1, box 136, PJ.

61. Unsigned report, August 5, 1964, folder 2, box 136, PJ.

62. "General Report to Mississippi State Sovereignty Commission: Reference—McComb Violence," October 8, 1964, folder 5, box 136, PJ.

63. Director, State Sovereignty Commission, memos, August 14 and September 28, 1964, folder 4, box 136, PJ.

64. Unsigned report, January 25, 1965, folder 1, box 137, PJ.

65. Christopher Koch and Frank Millspaugh, quoted in *New York Times*, January 31, 1965.

66. Land, *Active Radio*, 72.

67. Koch, Open Letter, n.d., folder "Tougaloo Radio Association," box 48, DM.

68. "Freedom Radio News," June 15, 1965, folder 595 (Freedom Radio News), box 11, EK. Koch, Open Letter, n.d., and "Association Members, Supporters, and Advisors," n.d., folder "Tougaloo Radio Association," box 48, DM.

69. Land, *Active Radio*, 74–81; Lasar, *Pacifica Radio*, 190–213.

70. Lasar, *Pacifica Radio*, 192.

71. Land, *Active Radio*, 76.

72. Johnston, *Mississippi's Defiant Years*, 302.

73. Untitled report (Radio Tougaloo Association), n.d, folder 3, box 137, PJ.

74. *Charleston Evening Post*, February 9, 1965. Marvin Mathis, quoted in *Jackson Clarion-Ledger*, May 3, 1965.

75. "Press Release: Erle Johnston's Brandon speech," March 11, 1965, ID 99-139-0-21-1/2/3-1-1, folder "Radio Tougaloo," SC; Mrs. C. M. Combest, letter to Johnston, March 17, 1965, ID 3-74B-0-34-1-1-1, and Johnston, letter to Combest, March 23, 1965, ID 3-74B-0-35-1-1-1, same folder.

76. Jamie L. Whitton, letter to Johnston, n.d., ID 3-74B-0-11-1-1-1, same folder.

77. "Special Report," March 9, 10, 11, 1965, folder 3, box 137, PJ.

78. Johnston, "Report on Mississippi Delta Ministry," to Bryant George, February 28, 1966, folder 6, box 142, PJ.

79. "Freedom Radio News," June 15, 1965, folder 595 (Freedom Radio News), box 11, EK.

80. Unsigned memo, March 15, 1965, folder 3, box 137, PJ.

81. Johnston, memo to Tougaloo College Trustees, April 24, 1964, ID 3-74-2-16-1-1-1, folder "Radio Tougaloo," SC.

82. A. D. Beittel, memo to Board of Trustees of Tougaloo College, May 29, 1964, folder "Memo to Board of Trustees," AB. See also Dittmer, *Local People*, 234–36; Johnston, *Mississippi's Defiant Years*, 301–2.

83. Unsigned reports, March 15 and 20, 1965, folder 3, box 137, PJ.

84. McConnaughey to NAACP; Beard to Morris (see note 6). For the campaign against racial discrimination in the Mississippi media, see Head, Sterling, and Schofield, *Broadcasting in America*, 298; Phelps, "The Office of Communication," 43–80; Fife, "FCC Policy on Minority Ownership," 108–24; Cole and Oettinger, *Reluctant Regulators*, 204–6; Johnston, *Mississippi's Defiant Years*, 387–94.

85. *New York Times*, December 6, 1962.

86. SNCC, "Radio and Television Programming and Editorializing," n.d., A-VII-1, SNCC; Rich, memo on FCC Fairness Doctrine to CORE chapter leaders, October 6, 1964, part 2, reel 9, CORE.

87. *New York Times*, April 16, 1964.

88. Head, Sterling, and Schofield, *Broadcasting in America*, 298; Barnouw, *History of Broadcasting*, 3:240; *New York Times*, May 21 and June 11, 1965.

89. Dick Sanders, "WLBT-WJDX Editorial," March 21, 1962, A-VIII-127, SNCC.

90. *Jackson Clarion-Ledger*, April 27 and May 28, 1964.

91. Judge Warren Burger, quoted in Cole and Oettinger, *Reluctant Regulators*, 204.

92. Ibid., 206; Head, Sterling, and Schofield, *Broadcasting in America*, 298.

93. Sherwood Ross, memo to regional directors and local league executive directors, June 30 1965, II-V-15, NUL.

94. WOKJ, "Application for Renewal of Broadcast Station License," February 27, 1967, exhibit B, part 5, box 30, FCC.

95. Cole and Oettinger, *Reluctant Regulators*, 205–6.

96. F. L. Smith, *Perspectives on Radio and Television*, 350–51.

Chapter 10. The Quest for Black Power in Southern Radio

1. Ralph B. Johnson, letter to Avon N. Williams, July 20, 1970, file 15, box 97, KMS.

2. *New York Times*, November 11, 1968.

3. See note 1.

4. Del Shields, quoted in *Broadcasting*, August 31, 1964, 60.

5. *Broadcasting*, August 31, 1964, 60–62.

6. FCC, "Policy Statement on Comparative Broadcast Hearings," *Public Notice*, 1, FCC, 2d, 393 (1965).

7. Figures drawn from *New York Times*, November 11, 1968, and Ferretti, "White Captivity of Black Radio," 88–91.

8. R. Meyer, "Blacks and Broadcasting," 217; Gould, *Black Workers*, 126–27; Barlow,

Voice Over, 28.

9. *Broadcasting*, August 31, 1964, 60–62; R. Meyer, "Blacks and Broadcasting," 216, 218. Pam Coe, memo to files re: interview with Washington Butler, May 8, 1968, folder "Memphis Exploration, 1968," box "Civil Rights Division, 1968, Administration," AFSC.

10. Legal Department, NAB, memo to membership, June 1970, folder "Memoranda," NAB.

11. NAB, memos to management, July 1967 and July 1968, same folder.

12. Nicholas Johnson, "Soul Music Is Not Enough," speech to annual convention of NATRA, Miami, August 17, 1968. Copy in possession of author. *New York Times*, November 11, 1968. Del Shields, interview with Sonja Williams, May 9, 1995, BR.

13. Dean Burch and James Hulbert, quoted in *Broadcasting*, September 25, 1972, 27; Richard Wiley and Pluria Marshall, quoted in *Broadcasting*, July 25, 1977, 24.

14. "Report of the Communications Section of the Atlanta Office," August 1, 1966, A-VII-4, SNCC.

15. Forman, *Making of Black Revolutionaries*, 459. Hamilton, "Blacks and Mass Media," 226.

16. William S. Stein, memo re: *Martin Luther King Speaks*, March 12, 1968, and "*Martin Luther King Speaks*—Job Description for Producer," n.d., folder 24, box 47, SCLC. Martin Luther King, telephone conversation with Stanley Levison, January 12, 1968, reel 7, FBI-MLK; Bill Rutherford, telephone conversation with Levison, May 19, 1968, reel 8, FBI-MLK.

17. Callis N. Brown, memo to Floyd B. McKissick, January 10, 1968, E-III-10, reel 12, CORE-ADD.

18. Baraka, *African Congress*, 451–57.

19. FCC, "Memorandum Opinion and Order," August 1, 1975, folder 4, box 7, CB; Theodore E. Thornton, memos to John Whiting, n.d., and to David Wilborn, March 25, 1971, folder 7 (Conference on Media Relations, 1971), box 1, CB; "Minutes of the Media Relations Committee Meeting, Richmond Council on Human Relations," May 4, 1971, same folder; affidavits of Theodore E. Thornton, Laverne Byrd Smith, and Dwight C. Jones, August 31, 1972, folder 1 (WTVR), box 7, CB. Dr. Laverne Byrd Smith, interview with Brian Ward, February 27, 2003. See also *Jet*, September 28, 1972, 16. *National Black Media Coalition Newsletter*, September 1975, 3–4, folder X:A:2013, box 119, AH.

20. *Broadcasting*, August 31, 1964, 60–62. *New York Times*, August 10, 1967. See also Martha Jean Steinberg, interview with Jacquie Gales Webb, June 13, 1995, BR. The story of NATRA (called NARA before the addition of black television announcers to its membership in 1965) has been told with varying degrees of accuracy and sophistication in Barlow, *Voice Over*, 219–25, 248–49; Guralnick, *Sweet Soul Music*, 381–85; George, *Death of Rhythm and Blues*, 111–15; Wexler and Ritz, *Rhythm and the Blues*, 227–29; Picardie and Wade, *Atlantic and the Godfathers*, 161–65; Ward, *Just My Soul Responding*, 288, 432–36.

21. Del Shields, interview with Sonja Williams, May 9, 1975, BR.

22. Shields interview.

23. *Jet*, August 10, 1967, 56–60.

24. Shields interview.

25. Memo to director and Miami, subject: National Association of Television and Radio Announcers, August 19, 1968, file 166–3866, FBI-NATRA. Shields interview.

26. Report, New York Office, November 21, 1968, field office file 166–2134, 5–6, and

memo from New York to director and Miami, August 17, 1968, field office file 166–2134, FBI-NATRA. Because many of the names in these FBI documents have been redacted, my identifications of some of the individuals described in these reports are based on compelling circumstantial evidence and corroborating detail.

27. Joe Lackey, interview with Brian Ward, October 26, 1995; Shelley Stewart, interview with Brian Ward, October 26, 1995.

28. Homer Banks, quoted in Guralnick, *Sweet Soul Music*, 383–84. Del Shields, quoted in *Broadcasting*, August 24, 1968, 1, 66.

29. Shields interview. Barlow, *Voice Over*, 224.

30. Hattie Leeper, interview with Sonja Williams, April 22, 1995, BR. Alvin Dixon, quoted in *Jet*, October 5, 1972, 21–22.

31. *National Black Media Coalition Newsletter*, September 1975, 3–4, folder X:A:2013, box 119, AH. Pluria Marshall, quoted in Barlow, *Voice Over*, 250–53. Phelps, "The Office of Communication," 56. See also Merritt, "Pressure Group in Broadcasting," 44–125; "Pluria Marshall: A Man with a Mission," *Black Radio Exclusive*, November 6, 1987, 9. Heiss, "Texarkana Agreement."

32. UCC Office of Communications, press release, August 18, 1975, folder 6, box 5, CB.

33. "Comments of National Black Media Coalition on Proposed FCC Equal Employment Opportunity Policies for Broadcast Licensees (Docket #20550)," October 13, 1975, and Robert Valder, letter and enclosures to Vincent Mullins, October 31, 1975, folder 11, CB.

34. Alvin O. Chambliss, "Petition to Deny and to Intervene, or in the Alternative, Revocation of Broadcast Licenses for Racially Discriminatory Employment Practices and Petition to Prevent Continuing Violations of the Communications Act and Other Commission Policies and Rules," May 1, 1976, folder X:B:2046, box 120, AH; Charles Saunders, letter to Mullins, January 20, 1976, included in "Initial Decision of Administrative Law, Judge James F. Tierney," April 1, 1976, same folder.

35. Chambliss, "Petition" (see note 34).

36. Drew Pearson, quoted in *Washington Post*, September 1, 1966, and June 24, 1969. *Washington Star*, September 12, 1975, and January 23, 1978. Carl H. Moultrie, letter to E. Carlton Myers Jr., August 19, 1965, United Broadcasting Company Petition to Enlarge the Issues, August 23, 1965, file 15795, vol. 1, box 237, FCC-DOC. For the story of WOOK in the late 1960s and early 1970s, see Walsh, "Black-Oriented Radio," 220–35, 276–78.

37. Lester McKinnie and H. Rap Brown, letter to John Pace, July 3, 1967, and "WOL Radio," n.d., C-I-143, SNCC. See also Walsh, "Black-Oriented Radio," 279–81.

38. *Washington Post*, Sunday, May 7, 1967. McKinnie, letter to James Forman, November 23, 1967, C-I-56, SNCC.

39. "Hosea Williams Says," *Atlanta Voice*, May 7, 1967; Zenas Sears, letter to Stokely Carmichael, May 5, 1967, and Sears, letter to H. Rap Brown, C-I-143, SNCC. Walsh, "Black-Oriented Radio," 197–98.

40. "SNCC News Release," May 24, 1967, C-I-143, SNCC.

41. *Broadcasting*, January 12, 1970, 44, and April 6, 1970, 66, 68.

42. *Birmingham Post-Herald*, May 6, 1971.

43. Details of McKinney's claims and the FCC's investigations can be found in the *Birmingham News*, December 6, 1974, and the *Birmingham Post-Herald*, March 28, 1974, and April 16 and December 16, 1975.

44. *Birmingham Post-Herald*, May 2, 1973, and April 16, 1975; *Birmingham News*, December 6, 1974.

45. *Birmingham Post-Herald*, May 2, 1973; *Birmingham News*, December 6, 1974.

46. *Birmingham Post-Herald*, March 28, 1974; *Birmingham News*, March 2, 1974.

47. Lackey interview.

48. A. G. Gaston, quoted in *Birmingham News*, February 15, 1976.

49. See *Birmingham Times*, February, 12–14, 1976.

50. Lackey interview.

51. *Birmingham News*, February 13 and 19, 1976; *Birmingham Post-Herald*, February 14, 1976. Stewart interview. S. Stewart, *The Road South*, 255–90.

52. A. G. Gaston, quoted in *Birmingham Post-Herald*, February 14, 1976; *Birmingham Times*, February 19, 1976. For the Gaston kidnapping case and the subsequent trial and conviction of Charles Clayborn, see *Birmingham News*, January 24, 1976; *Birmingham World*, January 31, 1976; *Birmingham Post-Herald*, February 19 and 20, May 26 and 28, and July 11, 1976.

53. Erskine Faush, quoted in *Birmingham Post-Herald*, February 18, 1976.

54. John Streeter, editorials, *Birmingham Times*, February 19 and 26, 1976. Paul Dudley White ("Tall Paul" White), letter in *Birmingham Times*, March 11, 1976.

55. Lackey interview.

56. Jesse Lewis, editorial, *Birmingham Times*, February 26, 1976; W. J. Boyd, open letter, *Birmingham Times*, March 25, 1976.

57. Lackey interview; Friedman, *WJLD*.

58. *Creations Magazine* 1, no. 1, (1977), copy in BWOF. Lackey interview; Stewart interview; *Birmingham News*, March 20, 1976.

59. Cole and Oettinger, *Reluctant Regulators*, 205–6.

60. Tom Jones, quoted in *Washington Post*, January 26, 1975. For more on WHUR, see Barlow, *Voice Over*, 236–41, 272–75; George, *Death of Rhythm and Blues*, 131–35; Walsh, "Black-Oriented Radio," 282–84.

61. Cathy Hughes, interview with Jacquie Gales Webb, February 24, 1995, BR. Barlow, *Voice Over*, 271–78. *Washington Post*, February 5, 2003; *Black Commentator* 44 (May 29, 2003), http://www.blackcommentator.com/44/44_cover_pr.html (accessed May 29, 2003).

62. Percy Sutton, quoted in Alston, "Black-Owned Radio," 21. The cost of WBLS/WLIB differed in various sources. See *Amsterdam News*, July 17, 1971; *Jet*, July 13, 1972, 98.

63. Brown, *James Brown*, 178. *Jet*, July 31, 1969, 47.

64. Jesse Blayton, quoted in G. Blackwell, "Black-Controlled Media," 157. Willieboyd "Mack" Saddler, interview with Brian Ward, October 19, 1995.

65. J. Blackwell, *The Black Community*, 233–35; Barlow, *Voice Over*, 252–53. Bush and Martin, "FCC's Minority Ownership Policies." *New York Times*, May 31, 1994.

66. Alan Roy Dynner, letter to James L. Oyster, April 21, 1980, and Vincent A. Pepper, letter to William Tricarico, May 6, 1980, WVOL, box 28, FCC.

67. Pluria Marshall, quoted in *Wall Street Journal*, September 23, 1987, and in Barlow, *Voice Over*, 278. See also Alston, "Black-Owned Radio," 205; Bogart, "Black Is Often White"; Soley and Hough, "Black Ownership."

Chapter 11. Riots, Respect, and Responsibility: Radio in the New South

1. Quoted in *Broadcasting*, August 24, 1969, 44.

2. *Montgomery Advertiser*, October 13–16, 1974.

3. Sellers, *River of No Return*, 253–54.

4. WAOK, "Application for Renewal of Broadcast Station License," December 12, 1966, exhibit 5, box 415, FCC. Walsh, "Black-Oriented Radio," 169–70.

5. Help Somebody Be Somebody, Inc., press release, June 1, 1973, folder X:A:2011, and Ms. L. Pruett Pemberton, letter to Robert J. McIntosh, May 14, 1974, folder X:A:2012, box 119, AH; "Application to Incorporate Help Somebody Be Somebody Inc.," January 1973, and application to FCC, July 2, 1973, folder X:B:2047, box 120, AH.

6. *Arkansas Gazette*, August 10, 1968; Kirk, *Redefining the Color Line*, 179–80.

7. Chris Turner, quoted in *New York Times*, November 11, 1968.

8. Green, "Battling the Plantation Mentality," 281.

9. Rick Taylor, interview with Stephen Walsh, August 5, 1995. See also Walsh, "Black-Oriented Radio," 173–74.

10. Bert Ferguson, "The Story of WDIA's Editorial Program," [c. March 1968], folder 64, container 8, SWSC.

11. Ibid.

12. Chris Turner, quoted in *New York Times*, November 11, 1968.

13. For more on the politicization of soul in the late 1960s and early 1970s, see Ward, *Just My Soul Responding*, 345–69.

14. *Washington Post*, June 7, 1966; *Washington Star*, June 7 and 8, 1966 (clippings in WOL exhibit 11, part VI, file 16533, FCC-DOC).

15. WOL editorial, "Black Power," June 25–30, 1966, WOL exhibit 11, part V, file 16533, FCC-DOC.

16. WOL editorial, "Progress and Poverty," May 26–29, 1966, same exhibit; *Washington Star*, June 8, 1966. For more on WOL, see Walsh, "Black-Oriented Radio," 240–76, 278–81.

17. *Washington Post*, May 7, 1967.

18. Ibid.; WOL editorial, "Eviction Notice: War on Slums Broadcast," October 14, 1966, WOL "Application for Renewal of Broadcast Station License," July 1, 1969, exhibit 16D, box 36, FCC.

19. Ibid.

20. Sherwood Ross, quoted in *Washington Post*, May 7, 1967.

21. Ibid.

22. Hannerz, *Soulside*, 156; see also 151–55.

23. Walter Fauntroy, quoted in *Washington Post*, May 7, 1967.

24. WOL editorial, "Vote," n.d., WOL exhibit 11, part V, file 16533, FCC-DOC. See also Walsh, "Black-Oriented Radio," 256.

25. Lawson, *Black Ballots*, 331, and *Running for Freedom*, 203.

26. Julian Bond, "Black Candidates: Southern Campaign Experiences," VEP Commissioned Study, 1968 (Athalie Range and Barbara Jordan quotes, 34 and 31), folder 1 (Mississippi Council on Human Relations), LT.

27. RCCC radio program, March 29, 1972, topical file "Richland County Citizens Committee, Feb–May, 1972," MS.

28. A. P. Williams and Adam Stewart, open letter, September 24, 1966, topical file "Richland County Citizens Committee, 1966," MS.

29. RCCC radio program, December 7, 1966, same file.

30. WOIC, "Application for Renewal of Broadcast Station License," August 1, 1966, exhibit 1–B, box 35, FCC.

31. For Charlie Dee's help in getting out the black vote, see RCCC radio program, November 15, 1966, same file as note 28. WOIC, "Application for Renewal," August 1, 1966, exhibits 1–A, 1–B.

32. For the campaign against WOIC and its owners, see Ferretti, "White Captivity of Black Radio," 94; WOIC, fiche 893, MMBSHC.

33. RCCC radio program, September 28, 1966, same file as note 28.

34. WOIC, "Application for Renewal," August 1, 1966, exhibit 1–B.

35. RCCC radio program, June 7, 1976, topical file "Richland County Citizens Committee, 1974–9," MS.

36. *Columbia Record*, November 17, 1966, cited in RCCC radio program, November 30, 1966, same file as note 28.

37. See note 27.

38. RCCC radio program, October 29, 1974, topical file "Richland County Citizens Committee, 1973–4," MS.

39. RCCC radio programs, September 28, 1966, May 20, 1970, and June 2, 1976, topical files "Richland County Citizens Committee" for 1966, 1970, and 1974–79 respectively, MS.

40. RCCC radio program, March 11, 1965, topical file "Richland County Citizens Committee, 1965," MS.

41. RCCC radio program, January 24, 1968, topical file "Richland County Citizens Committee, 1968," MS. See Lamis, *The Two-Party South*, 67.

42. RCCC radio program, February 3, 1972, same file as note 27.

43. Garnett, *How Soulful Is "Soul" Radio?* 2.

44. William Wright, quoted in ibid., 2.

45. Vandergrift, "Comparison of Two Approaches," 21–23. See also Haralambos, *Right On*, 93; Dates and Barlow, *Split Image*, 221; Surlin, "Black-Oriented Radio's Service," 552.

46. Leonard Evans, quoted in *Newsweek*, January 18, 1954, 51; Reggie Scheubel, quoted in *New York Post*, December 30, 1953. See also Barlow, *Voice Over*, 130–31.

47. Ibid., 131–32 (quote, 131). Francis Fitzgerald, quoted in *Sponsor*, September 26, 1960, 14, 52.

48. Eugene Jackson, quoted in *New York Times*, March 19, 1972. See also James B. Cheek, letter to Jackson, June 2, 1972, and "National Black Network Press Release," March 20, 1972, files "Radio" files, SCCF. *Jet*, May 18, 1972, 46. Barlow, *Voice Over*, 253–55.

49. Ibid., 255–59.

50. Ibid., 280–84.

51. H. B. Caple, quoted in Vandergrift, "Comparison of Two Approaches," 28. See also Barlow, *Voice Over*, 281.

52. Mrs. Willie High, quoted in Vandergrift, "Comparison of Two Approaches," 27–28.

53. Ibid., 34, 37–43.

54. Fay Bellamy, interview with Brian Ward, October 18, 1995. Barlow, *Voice Over*, 288–89.

55. Obitaye Akinwale, quoted in Vandergrift, "Comparison of Two Approaches," 47; Robert Spruill, quoted in *Durham Morning Herald*, May 7, 1972, and September 14, 1971.

56. This account of the life and death of WAFR is drawn from Vandergrift, "Comparison of Two Approaches," 45–64; Barlow, *Voice Over*, 286–87; H. Smith, "Educational Broadcasting," 136–38.

57. Vandergrift, "Comparison of Two Approaches," 49, 58–61 (Spruill quote, 58).

58. Alan Henry, quoted in Garnett, *"Soul" Radio*, 15.

59. Gilbert Seldes, "Notes from a Traveler," *Saturday Review of Literature*, March 20, 1954, 24, cited in Kammen, *American Culture, American Tastes*, 45.

60. *Wall Street Journal*, September 23, 1987.

61. Robert F. Williams, foreword to "Radio Free Dixie," unpublished manuscript, folder "Oct–Nov 1966," box 1, RW.

62. Williams, quoted in R. Cohen, *Black Crusader*, 210–11.

63. Sherwood Ross, letter to Hubert Humphrey, October 26, 1966, WOL, "Application for Renewal," July 1, 1969, exhibit 16D, box 36, FCC.

64. Gilbert et al., *Ten Blocks*, 119.

65. "WOL's Coverage of Events Surrounding the Assassination of Rev. Dr. Martin Luther King, Jr.," WOL, "Application for Renewal," July 1, 1969, exhibit 16B, box 6, FCC (hereafter "WOL's Coverage").

66. Gilbert et al., *Ten Blocks*, 17; "WOL's Coverage," 5.

67. "WOL's Coverage," 3, 11–14.

68. "WOL's Coverage," 8–9, 11, 18. Brown, *James Brown*, 188–89.

69. "WOL's Coverage," 3, 6–13, 16–17. *Variety*, April 17, 1968, 30, 50.

70. Walsh, "Black-Oriented Radio," 272. "WOL's Coverage," 4–5. *Report of the National Advisory Commission on Civil Disorders*, 362–89.

71. "WOL's Coverage," 4–5.

72. Stokely Carmichael, quoted in Gilbert et al., *Ten Blocks*, 60–61; "WOL's Coverage," 7.

73. WOL editorial, "The Glen Echo Riot," May 30, 1966, WOL exhibit 11, part 2, file 16533, FCC-DOC. *Washington Post*, April 12 and 13, 1966.

74. *Variety*, April 10, 1968, 30/52.

75. Robert Meeker, quoted in *New York Times*, November 11, 1968. *Billboard*, June 29, 1968, 18/30.

76. WDIA editorial, March 29 1968, SWSC.

77. WDIA editorial, April 3, 1968, SWSC.

78. James Lawson, quoted in Beifuss, *At the River I Stand*, 296, 301.

79. WDIA editorial, April 4 1968, SWSC. Irene Ware, interview with Jacquie Gales Webb, March 14, 1995, BR; Maurice Hulbert, interview with Jacquie Gales Webb, January 24, 1996, BR.

80. WDIA editorial, April 5, 1968 (see also April 9), SWSC.

81. Jack Gibson, interview with Jacquie Gales Webb, January 7, 1996, BR. On awards and commendations for radio's coverage of the riots, see *Broadcasting*, April 15, 1968, 25–26; *Billboard*, April 20, 1968, 74.

82. Del Shields, interview with Sonja Williams, May 9, 1995, BR.

83. O'Connor and Cook, "Black Radio," 233; Blair, *Retreat to the Ghetto*, 140.

84. WDIA editorials, April 19 and 6, 1968, SWSC.

85. For the Charlotte busing crisis, see D. Douglas, *Reading, Writing & Race*, 107–244; Gaillard, *The Dream Long Deferred*, 39–171; Leach, "Progress under Pressure," 81–105.

86. WBT editorial, May 13, 1964, WBT.

87. WBT editorial, April 28, 1969, WBT.

88. WBT editorials, August 6/7 and 8/11, 1969, WBT.

89. Charles Crutchfield, interview with Brian Ward, November 13, 1995. Crutchfield, quoted in Boger, *Charlotte 23*, 77.

90. WBT editorial, May 25, 1971, WBT.

91. WBT editorial, June 4, 1971, WBT.

92. WBT editorial, November 17, 1971, WBT.

93. Crutchfield, quoted in *Charlotte Observer*, May 27, 1971.

94. Ibid.

95. WBTV, Ben Waters/*Early Scene* script, May 27, 1971, folder "Raleigh Chamber Meeting 5/26/71" (hereafter RCM), box 26, CC.

96. Crutchfield, memo to staff, May 27, 1971, folder RCM, box 26, CC.

97. WBTV, Ben Waters/*Early Scene* script, May 28, 1971, and John Edgerton, memo to Crutchfield, Nov 29, 1971, folder RCM, box 26, CC. Fred Alexander, handwritten statement, n.d., folder 17, box 54, FA.

98. "Remarks By Charles Crutchfield," Tuesday, June 1, 1971, 10 a.m., folder RCM, box 26, CC.

99. Ibid.

100. WBT, "Application for Renewal of a Broadcast Station License," 1969, folder 7–B, box 429, FCC. Crutchfield, letter to Alexander, January 3, 1969, folder 29, box 18, FA.

101. Allegra M. Westbrooks, letter to Crutchfield, May 31, 1971, folder RCM, box 26, CC.

102. Frankie Hutton, memo to Crutchfield, [May 27, 1971]; Jan Spence, memo to Crutchfield, May 31, 1971; Florence Avery, letter to Crutchfield, June 27, 1971, same folder.

103. Crutchfield, "Farewell Speech," January 11, 1972, folder "Remarks," box 27, CC. Boger, *Charlotte 23*, 77.

104. Ibid, 78; Crutchfield, quoted in *Charlotte Observer*, [1977], "Crutchfield, Charles Harvey," card 1 [00766], NCCCF.

105. The percentage of black staff at WBT-TV (10.2 percent) was somewhat lower than at the radio station, although the absolute number was greater, with 13 black staff out of 128 employees at the TV station. See Tommi L. Jones, memo to Crutchfield, July 28, 1975, folder "Minority Training Program, 1975," box 34, CC; Crutchfield, letter to Alexander, January 3, 1969, folder 29, box 18, FA.

106. Crutchfield, letter to members of Black Advisory Board, June 25, 1975, miscellaneous folder "Black Advisory Board," box 34, CC.

107. Crutchfield, quoted in *Charlotte Observer*, [1977], NCCCF.

Conclusion: Radio and the Southern Freedom Struggle

1. Jack Gibson, interview with Jacquie Gales Webb, January 7, 1996, BR.

2. Hilmes, "Rethinking Radio," 4.

3. See Bhabha, *The Location of Culture*, 66.

Bibliography

Manuscript Collections

AB   A. D. Beittel Papers, L. Zenobia Coleman Library Archives, Tougaloo Col-
            lege, Tougaloo, Mississippi.
AFSC   American Friends Service Committee Papers, AFSC Archives, Philadel-
            phia.
AH   Aaron Edd Henry Papers, L. Zenobia Coleman Library Archives, Tougaloo
            College, Tougaloo, Mississippi.
ASWPL   Association of Southern Women for the Prevention of Lynching Papers,
            microfilm collection, George A. Smathers Library (West), University of
            Florida, Gainesville.
BAPD   Birmingham (Alabama) Police Department Surveillance Files, 1947–80,
            Birmingham Public Library Department of Archives and Manuscripts,
            Birmingham.
BMLCF   Clippings file, Bradley Memorial Library, Columbus, Georgia.
BR   Telling It Like It Was: Black Radio Collection, Archives of African Ameri-
            can Music and Culture, Smith Research Center, Indiana University,
            Bloomington.
BWOF   *Birmingham World* Office Files, Birmingham Public Library Department
            of Archives and Manuscripts, Birmingham.
CB   Papers of Collie Burton, Special Collection and Archives, James Branch
            Cabell Library, Virginia Commonwealth University, Richmond.
CC   Charles H. Crutchfield Papers, Manuscript Division, Southern Historical
            Collection, Wilson Library, University of North Carolina, Chapel Hill.
CCG   Charles Crutchfield Gift, Library of American Broadcasting, University of
            Maryland, College Park.
CIC   Commission on Interracial Cooperation Papers, microfilm collection,
            George A. Smathers Library (West), University of Florida, Gainesville.
CIO   CIO Organizing Committee Papers, microfilm collection, George A.
            Smathers Library (West), University of Florida, Gainesville.
CM   Charlotte-Mecklenburg Collection, Wilson Library, University of North
            Carolina, Chapel Hill.
CORE   Congress of Racial Equality Papers, 1941–67, microfilm collection,
            George A. Smathers Library (West), University of Florida, Gainesville.

CORE-ADD   Congress of Racial Equality Papers, addendum 1944–68, microfilm collection, George A. Smathers Library (West), University of Florida, Gainesville.

CP   Clarence H. Poe Papers, North Carolina State Archives, Division of Archives and History, Raleigh.

DM   Delta Ministry Records, Martin Luther King Center for Nonviolent Social Change, Atlanta.

EC   Eugene "Bull" Connor Papers, Birmingham Public Library Department of Archives and Manuscripts, Birmingham.

EJ   Erle Johnston Papers, McCain Library and Archives, University of Southern Mississippi, Hattiesburg.

EK   Ed King Papers, L. Zenobia Coleman Library Archives, Tougaloo College, Tougaloo, Mississippi.

FA   Fred D. Alexander Papers, Special Collections, J. Murray Atkins Library, University of North Carolina, Charlotte.

FBI-CB   FBI, Sixteenth Street Baptist Church Bombing Investigation files, Birmingham Public Library Department of Archives and Manuscripts, Birmingham.

FBI-MLK   FBI, Martin Luther King Jr. file: part 2, King-Levison file, microfilm collection, Alderman Library, University of Virginia, Charlottesville.

FBI-NATRA   FBI, National Association of Television and Radio Announcers file, no. 66–3866, Federal Bureau of Information, Washington, D.C.

FCC   Federal Communications Commission License Renewal Files, National Archives II, College Park, Maryland.

FCC-DOC   Federal Communications Commission Docketed Case Files, National Archives II, College Park, Maryland.

FOR   Papers of the Fellowship of Reconciliation, Swarthmore College Peace Collection, Swarthmore College, Swarthmore, Pennsylvania.

FRC   Personal Papers of Frank R. Crosswaith, Negro Labor Committee Records Group, microfilm collection, Robinson Library, University of Newcastle upon Tyne, U.K.

GS   George Street Collection, Department of Archives and Special Collections, J. D. Williams Library, University of Mississippi, Oxford.

HFS   Highlander Folk School Papers, microfilm collection, University of Nottingham, U.K.

JB   Josiah William Bailey Papers, Special Collections Division, William R. Perkins Library, Duke University, Durham, North Carolina.

JM   J. B. Matthews Papers, Special Collections Division, William R. Perkins Library, Duke University, Durham, North Carolina.

JMB   J. Melville Broughton Papers, North Carolina State Archives, Division of Archives and History, Raleigh.

JWM   James W. Morgan Papers, Birmingham Public Library Department of Archives and Manuscripts, Birmingham.

KA   Kelly M. Alexander Papers, Special Collections, J. Murray Atkins Library, University of North Carolina, Charlotte.

K/JYH   Katallagete/James Y. Holloway Collection, Department of Archives and

	Special Collections, J. D. Williams Library, University of Mississippi, Oxford.
KMS	Kelly Miller Smith Papers, Special Collections, Jean and Alexander Heard Library, Vanderbilt University, Nashville.
LA	Living Atlanta Collection, Auburn Avenue Research Center, Atlanta.
LAB	Library of American Broadcasting, University of Maryland, College Park.
LH	Luther P. Hodges Papers, North Carolina State Archives, Division of Archives and History, Raleigh.
LL	Lamar Life Insurance Company Records, Mississippi Department of Archives and History, Jackson.
LLMV	Louisiana and Lower Mississippi Valley Collections, Louisiana State University Libraries, Louisiana State University, Baton Rouge.
LT	Lucy Turnball Collection, Department of Archives and Special Collections, J. D. Williams Library, University of Mississippi, Oxford.
MFDP	Mississippi Freedom Democratic Party Papers, Martin Luther King Center for Nonviolent Social Change, Atlanta.
MLK	Martin Luther King Papers, Martin Luther King Center for Nonviolent Social Change, Atlanta.
MMBSHC	Mass Media Bureau Station History Cards, microfiche, Federal Communications Commission Information Reference Center, Washington, D.C.
MS	Modjeska Monteith Simkins Papers, Modern Political Collections, South Caroliniana Collections, University of South Carolina, Columbia.
MTR	Museum of Television and Radio, New York.
NAACP	National Association for the Advancement of Colored People Papers, Manuscript Division, Library of Congress, Washington, D.C.
NAB	National Association of Broadcasters Papers, 1965–75, Special Collections Division, William R. Perkins Library, Duke University, Durham, North Carolina.
NBC	NBC History Files, Motion Picture, Broadcasting and Recorded Sound Division, Library of Congress, Washington, D.C.
NCC	North Carolina Collection, Wilson Library, University of North Carolina, Chapel Hill.
NCCCF	North Carolina Collection clippings file, 1976–89, Wilson Library, University of North Carolina, Chapel Hill.
NLC	Negro Labor Committee Papers, Negro Labor Committee Records Group, microfilm collection, Robinson Library, University of Newcastle upon Tyne, U.K.
NUL	National Urban League Papers, Manuscript Division, Library of Congress, Washington, D.C.
PJ	Paul B. Johnson Family Papers, McCain Library and Archives, University of Southern Mississippi, Hattiesburg.
PR	Pacifica Radio Archive, Hollywood, California.
PV	Preston Valien Papers, Amistad Research Center, Tulane University, New Orleans.
RB	Ralph J. Bunche Oral History Collection, Moorland-Spingarn Research Center, Howard University, Washington, D.C.

RC   Rodney M. Cook Papers, Richard Russell Library, University of Georgia, Athens.

RS   R.L.T. Smith Papers, L. Zenobia Coleman Library Archives, Tougaloo College, Tougaloo, Mississippi.

RW   Robert F. Williams Papers, Bentley Historical Library, University of Michigan, Ann Arbor.

SC   Sovereignty Commission Records, Mississippi Department of Archives and History, Jackson.

SCCF   Clippings files, Schomburg Center for Research in Black Culture, New York.

SCEF   Southern Conference Educational Fund Papers, Tuskegee University Archives, Tuskegee, Alabama.

SCHW   Southern Conference for Human Welfare, Tuskegee University Archives, Tuskegee, Alabama.

SCLC   Southern Christian Leadership Conference Papers, Martin Luther King Center for Nonviolent Social Change, Atlanta.

SCLC-MIC   Southern Christian Leadership Conference Papers, microfilm collection, George A. Smathers Library (West), University of Florida, Gainesville.

SNCC   Student Nonviolent Coordinating Committee Papers, Manuscript Division, Library of Congress, Washington, D.C.

SOHP   Southern Oral History Program, Southern Historical Collection, Wilson Library, University of North Carolina, Chapel Hill.

SRC   Southern Regional Council Papers, 1944–68, microfilm collection, George A. Smathers Library (West), University of Florida, Gainesville.

SRCOH   Southern Regional Council Collection, Samuel Proctor Oral History Program, University of Florida, Gainesville.

SWSC   The 1968 Sanitation Workers' Strike Collection, Memphis Multi-Media Archival Project, Mississippi Valley Historical Collection, Ned R. McWherter Library, University of Memphis, Memphis.

UMSM   University of Mississippi Small Manuscripts Collection: Academic and Administrative Departments, Department of Archives and Special Collections, J. D. Williams Library, University of Mississippi, Oxford.

VC   Vice Chancellor's Collection, Department of Archives and Special Collections, J. D. Williams Library, University of Mississippi, Oxford.

VH   Verner Holmes Collection, Department of Archives and Special Collections, J. D. Williams Library, University of Mississippi, Oxford.

WBT   WBT Editorials Collection, North Carolina Collection, Wilson Library, University of North Carolina, Chapel Hill.

WC   Will D. Campbell Papers, McCain Library and Archives, University of Southern Mississippi, Hattiesburg.

WEBD   W.E.B. Du Bois Papers, microfilm collection, George A. Smathers Library (West), University of Florida, Gainesville.

WMCA   WMCA Collection, Mass Communications Research Center, State Historical Society, University of Wisconsin, Madison.

WONA   WONA (Winona, Mississippi) Radio Station Records, Mississippi Department of Archives and History, Jackson.

WRVA WRVA Radio Collection, Special Collections, Alderman Library, University of Virginia, Charlottesville.

Newspapers, Magazines, and Periodicals

Amsterdam News, 1971
Arkansas Gazette, 1964, 1968
Atlanta Constitution, 1962, 1984
Atlanta Daily World, 1940–75
Atlanta Inquirer, 1960–61
Baltimore Afro-American, 1952, 1959
Billboard, 1963–64, 1968
Birmingham News, 1956–76
Birmingham Post-Herald, 1944–76, 1982
Birmingham Times, 1976
Birmingham Weekly Review, 1941
Birmingham World, 1949, 1976
Black Commentator (www.blackcommentator.com), 2003
Black Radio Exclusive, 1979, 1987
Broadcasting, 1934–77
Broadcasting Yearbook, 1957–66
Carolina Times, 1942
Charleston Evening Post, 1965
Charlotte News, 1922, 1945–67
Charlotte Observer, 1949–76, 1988
Charlotte Post, 1954
Chicago Defender, 1949
Color, 1953
Columbus Enquirer, 1963
Crisis, 1945–76
Crusader, 1960
Durham Morning Herald, 1971–72
Ebony, 1947–76
Jackson Advocate, 1991
Jackson Clarion-Ledger, 1964–65, 1986, 1997
Jackson Daily News, 1961
Jet, 1954–76
Louisiana Weekly, 1953
Montgomery Advertiser, 1958, 1974
Muhammad Speaks, 1958–64
Negro Digest, 1950
New South, 1949–68
New York Post, 1953
New York Times, 1945–76, 1994
Newsweek, 1949, 1954, 1963
Opportunity, 1928–47
Our World, 1950, 1955

Pittsburgh Courier, 1941, 1943, 1949, 1959

Publisher's Weekly, 1947

Southerner, 1956

Sponsor, 1949–64

Variety, 1940–76

Wall Street Journal, 1987

Washington Post, 1966–76, 2003

Washington Star, 1947, 1966–78

Books, Articles, and Dissertations

Abarbanel, Albert, and Alex Haley. "A New Audience for Radio." *Harper's*, February 1956, 57–59.

Alston, Ronald. "Black-Owned Radio: Taking to the Airwaves in a Hurry." *Black Enterprise*, July 1978, 20–25.

Anderson, Jervis. *Bayard Rustin: Troubles I've Seen—A Biography*. New York: Harper Collins, 1997.

Angelou, Maya. *I Know Why the Caged Bird Sings*. 1970. New York: Bantam, 1983.

Ayer's Directory of Newspapers and Periodicals 1968. Philadelphia: N. W. Ayer and Son, 1968.

Baraka, Imamu Amiri [LeRoi Jones], ed. *African Congress: A Documentary History of the First Modern Pan-African Congress*. New York: Morrow, 1972.

Barlow, William. *Voice Over: The Making of Black Radio*. Philadelphia: Temple University Press, 1999.

Barnouw, Erik. *A History of Broadcasting in the United States*. 3 vols. New York: Oxford University Press, 1966–70.

Barrett, Russell H. *Integration at Ole Miss*. Chicago: Quadrangle, 1965.

Beifuss, Joan Turner. *At the River I Stand: Memphis, the 1968 Strike, and Martin Luther King*. Memphis: B&W Books, 1985.

Bertrand, Michael T. *Race, Rock, and Elvis*. Urbana: University of Illinois Press, 2000.

Bhabha, Homi K. *The Location of Culture*. London: Routledge, 1994.

Blackwell, Gloria. "Black-Controlled Media in Atlanta, 1960–1970: The Burden of the Message and the Struggle for Survival." Ph.D. diss., Emory University, 1973.

Blackwell, James. *The Black Community: Diversity and Unity*. 2d ed. New York: Harper and Row, 1985.

Blair, Thomas L. *Retreat to the Ghetto: The End of a Dream?* New York: Hill and Wang, 1977.

Bliss, Edward, Jr. *Now the News: The Story of Broadcast Journalism*. New York: Columbia University Press, 1991.

Bogart, Leo. "Black Is Often White." *Mediascope* 3, no. 11 (1978): 53–56.

Boger, Mary Snead. *Charlotte 23*. Bassett, Va.: Bassett, 1972.

Borders, William Holmes. *Seven Minutes at the "Mike" in the Deep South*. Atlanta: B. F. Logan Press, 1943.

Boulware, Marcus H. *The Oratory of Negro Leaders: 1900–1968*. Westport, Conn.: Negro Universities Press, 1969.

Branch, Taylor. *Parting the Waters: America in the King Years, 1954–63*. New York: Simon and Schuster, 1988.

Brown, James, with Bruce Tucker. *James Brown, the Godfather of Soul.* New York, Macmillan, 1986.

Bush, Antoinette Cook, and Marc S. Martin. "The FCC's Minority Ownership Policies from Broadcasting to PCS." *Federal Communications Law Journal* 48 (1996): 423–46.

Campbell, Will D. *Brother to a Dragonfly.* New York: Seabury, 1977.

Cantor, Louis. *Wheelin' on Beale: How WDIA-Memphis Became the Nation's First All-Black Radio Station and Created the Sound That Changed America.* New York: Pharos, 1992.

Chafe, William H. *Civilities and Civil Rights: Greensboro, North Carolina, and the Black Struggle for Freedom.* New York: Oxford University Press, 1980.

Chambers, Lucille Arcola, ed. *America's Tenth Man: A Pictorial Review of One-Tenth of a Nation.* New York: Twayne, 1957.

Chappell, David. "Hip Like Me: Racial Cross-Dressing in Pop Music Before Elvis." In *Media, Culture, and the Modern African American Freedom Struggle,* edited by Brian Ward, 104–21. Gainesville: University Press of Florida, 2001.

Chappell, Marisa, Jenny Hutchinson, and Brian Ward. "'Dress Modestly, Neatly . . . as if Going to Church': Respectability, Class, and Gender in the Montgomery Bus Boycott and the Early Civil Rights Movement." In *Gender in the Civil Rights Movement,* edited by Peter J. Ling and Sharon Monteith, 69–100. New York: Garland, 1999.

Cohen, Lizabeth. *Making a New Deal: Industrial Workers in Chicago, 1919–1939.* Cambridge: Cambridge University Press, 1990.

———. "Citizens and Consumers in the United States in the Century of Mass Consumption." In *The Politics of Consumption: Material Culture and Citizenship in Europe and America,* edited by Martin Daunton and Matthew Hinton, 203–22. New York: Oxford University Press, 2001.

———. *A Consumers' Republic: The Politics of Mass Consumption in Postwar America.* New York: Knopf, 2003.

Cohen, R. C. *Black Crusader: A Biography of Robert Franklin Williams.* Secaucus, N.J.: Lyle Stuart, 1972.

Cohodas, Nadine. *The Band Played Dixie: Race and the Liberal Conscience at Ole Miss.* New York: Free Press, 1997.

Cole, Barry, and Mal Oettinger. *Reluctant Regulators: The FCC and the Broadcast Audience.* Reading, Mass.: Addison-Wesley, 1978.

Cook, Robert. *Sweet Land of Liberty? The African-American Struggle for Civil Rights in the Twentieth Century.* New York: Longman, 1999.

Cott, Nancy F. "What's in a Name? The Limits of 'Social Feminism'; or, Expanding the Vocabulary of Women's History." *Journal of American History* 76, no. 3 (1989): 809–29.

Crosswaith, Frank R., and Alfred Baker Lewis. *Negro and White Labor Unite for True Freedom.* 2d ed. New York: Negro Labor News Service, 1940.

Dates, Jannette L., and William Barlow, eds. *Split Image: African Americans in the Mass Media.* Washington, D.C.: Howard University Press, 1990.

Daunton, Martin, and Matthew Hinton, eds. *The Politics of Consumption: Material Culture and Citizenship in Europe and America.* New York: Oxford University Press, 2001.

Davis, Thulani. *1959: A Novel.* London: Hamish Hamilton, 1992.

Dittmer, John. *Local People: The Struggle for Civil Rights in Mississippi.* Urbana: University of Illinois Press, 1994.

Douglas, Davison M. *Reading, Writing & Race: The Desegregation of the Charlotte Schools.* Chapel Hill: University of North Carolina Press, 1995.

Douglas, Susan J. *Inventing American Broadcasting, 1899–1922.* Baltimore: Johns Hopkins University Press, 1987.

———. *Listening In: Radio and the American Imagination from Amos 'n' Andy and Edward R. Murrow to Wolfman Jack and Howard Stern.* New York: Times Books, 1999.

Dudziak, Mary L. *Cold War Civil Rights: Race and the Image of American Democracy.* Princeton: Princeton University Press, 2000.

Durr, Clifford J. "What Is Happening to Radio Broadcasting?" *Consumer Reports,* July 1945, 186–91.

Eagles, Charles W. "Towards New Histories of the Civil Rights Era." *Journal of Southern History* 66, no. 4 (2000): 815–48.

Eberly, Philip K. *Music in the Air: America's Changing Tastes in Popular Music, 1920–1980.* New York: Hastings House, 1982.

Egerton, John. *Speak Now Against the Day: The Generation Before the Civil Rights Movement in the South.* Chapel Hill: University of North Carolina Press, 1994.

Ely, Melvin Patrick. *The Adventures of Amos 'n' Andy: A Social History of an American Phenomenon.* New York: Free Press, 1991.

English, James W. *The Prophet of Wheat Street: The Story of William Holmes Borders, a Man Who Refused to Fail.* Elgin, Ill.: D. C. Cook, 1973.

Eskew, Glenn T. *But for Birmingham: The Local and National Movements in the Civil Rights Struggle.* Chapel Hill: University of North Carolina Press, 1997.

———, ed. *Labor in the Modern South.* Athens: University of Georgia Press, 2001.

Fairclough, Adam. *Race & Democracy: The Civil Rights Struggle in Louisiana, 1915–1972.* Athens: University of Georgia Press, 1995.

———. *Better Day Coming: Blacks and Equality, 1890–2000.* New York: Viking, 2001.

Faragher, John Mack, et al. *Out of Many: A History of the American People.* Volume C: *Since 1900.* Upper Saddle River, N.J.: Prentice Hall, 2000.

Federal Communications Commission. "Policy Statement on Comparative Broadcast Hearings." *Public Notice,* 1 FCC. 2d, 393 (1965).

Ferretti, Fred. "The White Captivity of Black Radio." 1970. In *Our Troubled Press: Ten Years of the Columbia Journalism Review,* edited by Alfred Balk and James Boylan, 87–97. Boston: Little, Brown, 1971.

Fife, Marilyn Diane. "FCC Policy on Minority Ownership in Broadcasting: A Political Systems Analysis of Regulatory Policy Making." Ph.D. diss., Stanford University, 1984.

Forman, James. *The Making of Black Revolutionaries: A Personal Account.* New York: Macmillan, 1972.

Fullerton, Christopher Dean. "Striking Out Jim Crow: The Birmingham Black Barons." Master's thesis, University of Mississippi, 1994.

Gaillard, Frye. *The Dream Long Deferred.* Chapel Hill: University of North Carolina Press, 1988.

Gaines, Kevin K. *Uplifting the Race: Black Leadership, Politics, and Culture in the Twentieth Century.* Chapel Hill: University of North Carolina Press, 1996.

Garnett, Bernard. *How Soulful Is "Soul" Radio?* Nashville: Race Relations Information Center, 1970.

Garrow, David J. *Bearing the Cross: Martin Luther King, Jr., and the Southern Christian Leadership Conference*. New York: Morrow, 1986.

Gatewood, Willard B. *Aristocrats of Color: The Black Elite, 1880–1920*. Bloomington: Indiana University Press, 1990.

George, Nelson. *The Death of Rhythm and Blues*. New York: Pantheon, 1988.

Gilbert, Ben W., et al. *Ten Blocks from the White House: Anatomy of the Washington Riots of 1968*. New York: Praeger, 1968.

Glen, John M. *Highlander: No Ordinary School*. 2d ed. Knoxville: University of Tennessee Press, 1996.

Glickman, Lawrence B., ed. *Consumer Society in American History: A Reader*. Ithaca, N.Y.: Cornell University Press, 1999.

Goldfield, Michael. "Race and the CIO: The Possibilities for Racial Egalitarianism during the 1930s and 1940s." *International Labor and Working-Class History* 44 (fall 1993): 1–32.

Gould, W. B. *Black Workers in White Unions: Job Discrimination in the United States*. Ithaca, N.Y.: Cornell University Press, 1977.

Green, Laurie Beth. "Battling the Plantation Mentality: Consciousness, Culture, and the Politics of Race, Class, and Gender in Memphis, 1940–1968." Ph.D. diss., University of Chicago, 1999.

Grundy, Pamela. "From *Il Trovatore* to the Crazy Mountineers: The Rise and Fall of Elevated Culture on WBT-Charlotte, 1922–1930." *Southern Cultures* 1, no. 1 (1994): 51–74.

———. "'We Always Tried to Be Good People': Respectability, Crazy Water Crystals, and Hillbilly Music on the Air, 1933–1935." *Journal of American History* 81, no. 4 (1995): 1591–1620.

Guralnick, Peter. *Sweet Soul Music: Rhythm and Blues and the Southern Dream of Freedom*. New York: Harper and Row, 1986.

Hale, Grace Elizabeth. *Making Whiteness: The Culture of Segregation in the South, 1890–1940*. New York: Pantheon, 1998.

Hall, Jacquelyn Dowd, et al. *Like a Family: The Making of a Southern Cotton Mill World*. New York: Norton, 1987.

Hamilton, Charles. "Blacks and Mass Media." 1971. In *Issues and Trends in Afro-American Journalism*, edited by James S. Tinney and Justine J. Rector, 225–31. Lanham, Md.: University Press of America, 1980.

Hanchett, Thomas W. *Sorting Out the New South City: Race, Class, and Urban Development in Charlotte, 1875–1975*. Chapel Hill: University of North Carolina Press, 1998.

Hangen, Tona J. "Man of the Hour: Walter A. Meier and Religion by Radio on the *Lutheran Hour*." In *Radio Reader: Essays in the Cultural History of Radio*, edited by Michele Hilmes and Jason Loviglio, 113–34. New York: Routledge, 2002.

———. *Redeeming the Dial: Radio, Religion & Popular Culture in America*. Chapel Hill: University of North Carolina Press, 2002.

Hannerz, Ulf. *Soulside: Inquiries into Ghetto Culture and Community*. New York: Columbia University Press, 1969.

Haralambos, Michael. *Right On: From Blues to Soul in Black America*. New York: Drake, 1975.

Haring, H. A. "The Negro as Consumer." *Advertising & Selling*, September 3, 1930, 21.

Hathaway, Paul R. "God's Master of Ceremonies." *Washingtonian*, September 1981, 162–66.

Hays, Brooks. *Politics Is My Parish*. Baton Rouge: Louisiana State University Press, 1981.

Head, Sidney W., Christopher H. Sterling, and Lemuel B. Schofield. 2d ed., brief version. *Broadcasting in America: A Survey of Electronic Media*. Boston: Houghton Mifflin, 1996.

Heiss, Robert. "The Texarkana Agreement as a Model Strategy for Citizen Participation in FCC Licence Renewals." *Harvard Journal on Legislation* 7 (May 1970): 627–43.

Hemphill, Robert. "Statement." *Congressional Record*, May 25, 1960, 11115–16.

Henderson, Alexa Benson. "Heman E. Perry and Black Enterprise in Atlanta, 1908–1925." *Business History Review* 61 (summer 1987): 216–42.

Hepner, Arthur W. "Union War in Bessemer." *Reporter* 1, no. 6 (1949): 12–15.

Higginbotham, Evelyn Brooks. *Righteous Discontent: The Women's Movement in the Black Baptist Church, 1880–1920*. Cambridge: Harvard University Press, 1993.

Hilmes, Michele. *Radio Voices: American Broadcasting, 1922–1952*. Minneapolis: University of Minnesota Press, 1997.

———. "Rethinking Radio." In *Radio Reader: Essays in the Cultural History of Radio*, edited by Michele Hilmes and Jason Loviglio, 1–19. New York: Routledge, 2002.

Hollinger, David A. "How Wide the Circle of the We? American Intellectuals and the Problem of the Ethnos Since World War II." *American Historical Review* 98 (April 1993): 317–37.

———. *Postethnic America: Beyond Multiculturalism*. New York: Basic Books, 1995.

Honey, Michael K. *Southern Labor and Black Civil Rights: Organizing Memphis Workers*. Urbana: University of Illinois Press, 1993.

Houghton, Jonathan T. Y. "The North Carolina Republican Party: From Reconstruction to the Radical Right." Ph.D. diss., University of North Carolina at Chapel Hill, 1993.

Jackson, Hal, with James Haskins. *The House That Jack Built: My Life Story as a Trailblazer in Broadcasting and Entertainment*. New York: Amistad, 2001.

Jarrett, C. Scott. "Broadcasting." In *Charlotte & Mecklenburg Co. Today*, edited by Malcolm Donald Coe, 71–79. Charlotte, N.C.: Crabtree Press, 1967.

Johnson, Lyndon B. *Vantage Point: Perspectives of the Presidency 1963–1969*. New York: Holt, Rinehart and Winston, 1971.

Johnston, Erle. *Mississippi's Defiant Years, 1953–1973: An Interpretive Documentary with Personal Experiences*. Forest, Miss.: Lake Harbor, 1990.

Kammen, Michael. *American Culture, American Tastes: Social Change and the 20th Century*. New York: Knopf, 1999.

Kapur, Sudarshan. *Raising Up a Prophet: The African-American Encounter with Gandhi*. Boston: Beacon Press, 1992.

Katagiri, Yasuhiro. *The Mississippi State Sovereignty Commission: Civil Rights and States' Rights*. Jackson: University Press of Mississippi, 2001.

Kelley, Robin D. G. *Race Rebels: Culture, Politics, and the Black Working Class*. New York: Free Press, 1994.

King, Martin Luther, Jr. "Pilgrimage to Nonviolence." 1960. In *A Testament of Hope: The Essential Writings of Martin Luther King, Jr.*, edited by James Melvin Washington, 35–42. New York: Harper and Row, 1986.

———. "Paul's Letter to American Christians." In *Strength to Love*, 137–45. New York: Harper and Row, 1963.

————. "Transforming a Neighborhood into a Brotherhood." *Jack the Rapper* 13, no. 666 (1989): 1.

King, Mary. *Freedom Song: A Personal History of the 1960s Civil Rights Movement.* New York: Morrow, 1987.

Kirk, John A. *Redefining the Color Line: Black Activism in Little Rock, Arkansas, 1940–1970.* Gainesville: University Press of Florida, 2002.

Korstad, Robert Rodgers, and Nelson Lichtenstein. "Opportunities Found and Lost: Labor, Radicals, and the Early Civil Rights Movement." *Journal of American History* 75 (1988): 786–811.

Kratt, Mary Norton. *Charlotte, Spirit of the New South.* Tulsa: Continental Heritage Press, 1980.

Lamis, Alexander P. *The Two-Party South.* New York: Oxford University Press, 1984.

Land, Jeff. *Active Radio: Pacifica's Brash Experiment.* Minneapolis: University of Minnesota, 1999.

Lasar, Matthew. *Pacifica Radio: The Rise of an Alternative Network.* Philadelphia: Temple University Press, 1999.

Lash, John S. "The Negro and Radio." 1943. In *Issues and Trends in Afro-American Journalism,* edited by James S. Tinney and Justine J. Rector, 167–81. Lanham, Md.: University Press of America, 1980.

Lawson, Steven F. *Black Ballots: Voting Rights in the South, 1944–1969.* New York: Columbia University Press, 1976.

————. *Running for Freedom: Civil Rights and Black Politics in America Since 1941.* New York: McGraw-Hill, 1991.

Leach, Damaria Etta Brown. "Progress under Pressure: Changes in Charlotte Race Relations, 1955–1965." Master's thesis, University of North Carolina, 1976.

Levine, Ellen, ed. *Freedom's Children: Young Civil Rights Activists Tell Their Own Stories.* New York: Putnam, 1993.

Lewis, George. "Not So Well Red: Native Americans in the Southern Civil Rights Movement Reconsidered." *Borderlines: Studies in American Culture* 3, no. 4 (1996): 362–76.

Lewis, John, with Michael D'Orso. *Walking with the Wind: A Memoir of the Movement.* New York: Simon and Schuster, 1998.

Lischer, Richard. *The Preacher King: Martin Luther King, Jr. and the Word That Moved America.* New York: Oxford University Press, 1995.

Lord, Walter. *The Past That Would Not Die.* New York: Harper and Row, 1965.

Lydon, Michael. *Ray Charles: Man and Music.* New York: Riverhead, 1998.

Lydon, Michael, and Ellen Mandel. *Boogie Lightning: How Music Became Electric.* New York: Dial, 1974.

MacDonald, J. Fred. *Don't Touch That Dial! Radio Programming in American Life, 1920–1960.* Chicago: Nelson-Hall, 1979.

Manis, Andrew M. *A Fire You Can't Put Out: The Civil Rights Life of Birmingham's Reverend Fred Shuttlesworth.* Tuscaloosa: University of Alabama Press, 1999.

Marchand, Roland. *Advertising the American Dream: Making Way for Modernity, 1920–1940.* Berkeley and Los Angeles: University of California Press, 1985.

McChesney, Robert W. *Telecommunications, Mass Media, and Democracy: The Battle for the Control of U.S. Broadcasting, 1928–1935.* Oxford: Oxford University Press, 1993.

McKee, Margaret, and Fred Chisenhall. *Beale Black and Blue: Life and Music on Black America's Main Street.* Baton Rouge: Louisiana State University Press, 1981.

McWhorter, Diane. *Carry Me Home: Birmingham, Alabama—the Climactic Battle of the Civil Rights Revolution.* New York: Simon and Schuster, 2001.

Meredith, James. *Three Years in Mississippi.* Bloomington: Indiana University Press, 1966.

Merritt, Bishetta Dionne. "A Historical-Critical Study of a Pressure Group in Broadcasting—Black Efforts for Soul in Television." Ph.D. diss., Ohio State University, 1974.

Meyer, Anthony J. *Black Voices and Format Regulations: A Study in Black-Oriented Radio.* Stanford: ERIC Clearinghouse, 1971.

Meyer, Richard J. "Blacks and Broadcasting." In *Broadcasting and Bargaining: Labor Relations in Radio and Television,* edited by Allen E. Koenig, 203–27. Madison: University of Wisconsin, 1970.

Miller, Keith D. *Voice of Deliverance: The Language of Martin Luther King, Jr., and Its Sources.* New York: Free Press, 1992.

Morris, Aldon D. *The Origins of the Civil Rights Movement: Black Communities Organizing for Change.* New York: Free Press, 1984.

Morton, Hugh M., and Edward L. Rankin Jr. *Making a Difference in North Carolina.* Raleigh: Lightworks, 1988.

Moses, Greg. *Revolution of Conscience: Martin Luther King, Jr., and the Philosophy of Nonviolence.* New York: Guilford Press, 1997.

Newman, Mark. *Entrepreneurs of Profit and Pride: From Black-Appeal to Radio Soul.* New York: Praeger, 1988.

Norrell, Robert J. "Caste in Steel: Jim Crow Careers in Birmingham, Alabama." *Journal of American History* 73 (December 1986): 669–94.

O'Connor, Douglas, and Gayla Cook. "Black Radio: The 'Soul' Sellout." 1973. In *Issues and Trends in Afro-American Journalism,* edited by James S. Tinney and Justine J. Rector, 233–46. Lanham, Md.: University Press of America, 1980.

Payne, Charles M. *I've Got the Light of Freedom: The Organizing Tradition and the Mississippi Freedom Struggle.* Berkeley and Los Angeles: University of California Press, 1995.

Phelps, Ernest Edward. "The Office of Communication: The Participant Advocate—Its Function as a Broadcast Citizen Group, March 1964 to March 1971." Ph.D. diss., Ohio State University, 1971.

Picardie, Justine, and Dorothy Wade. *Atlantic and the Godfathers of Rock and Roll.* London: Fourth Estate, 1993.

Radio Advertising Bureau. *Radio and the Negro Market.* New York: Radio Advertising Bureau, 1957.

"Radio Pioneer." n.d. In *Issues and Trends in Afro-American Journalism,* edited by James S. Tinney and Justine J. Rector, 183–86. Lanham, Md.: University Press of America, 1980.

Raines, Howell. *My Soul Is Rested: Movement Days in the Deep South Remembered.* New York: Putnam, 1977.

Rather, Dan, with Mickey Herskowitz. *The Camera Never Blinks.* New York: Morrow, 1977.

Reddick, L. D. "Educational Programs for the Improvement of Race Relations: Motion Pictures, Radio, the Press and Libraries." *Journal of Negro Education* 13 (summer 1944): 367–89.

Reed, Linda. *Simple Decency & Common Sense: The Southern Conference Movement, 1938–1963*. Bloomington: Indiana University Press, 1991.

Report of the National Advisory Commission on Civil Disorders. New York: Bantam, 1968.

Rothenbuhler, Eric W., and Tom McCourt. "Radio Redefines Itself, 1947–1962." In *Radio Reader: Essays in the Cultural History of Radio*, edited by Michele Hilmes and Jason Loviglio, 367–87. New York: Routledge, 2002.

Savage, Barbara Dianne. *Broadcasting Freedom: Radio, War and the Politics of Race, 1938–1948*. Chapel Hill: University of North Carolina Press, 1999.

Seabrook, John. "Black and White Unite: The Career of Frank R. Crosswaith." Ph.D. diss., Rutgers University, 1980.

Sellers, Cleveland. *River of No Return: The Autobiography of a Black Militant and the Life and Death of SNCC*. New York: Morrow, 1973.

Seroff, Doug. "On the Battlefield: Gospel Quartets in Jefferson County, Alabama." In *Repercussions: A Celebration of African-American Music*, edited by Geoffrey Haydon and Dennis Marks, 30–53. London: Century, 1985.

Shriver, Donald W., Jr., ed. *The Unsilent South: Prophetic Preaching in Racial Crisis*. Richmond: John Knox, 1965.

Sikora, Frank. *Until Justice Rolls Down: The Birmingham Church Bombing Case*. Tuscaloosa: University of Alabama Press, 1991.

Smith, F. Leslie. *Perspectives on Radio and Television: Telecommunication in the United States*. 3d ed. New York: Harper and Row, 1990.

Smith, Harry Kenneth. "The Development of Educational Broadcasting in North Carolina, 1922 to 1972." Master's thesis, University of North Carolina, 1972.

Smith, Wes. *The Pied Pipers of Rock 'n' Roll: Radio Deejays of the 50s and 60s*. Marietta, Ga.: Longstreet, 1989.

Smulyan, Susan. *Selling Radio: The Commercialization of American Broadcasting, 1920–1934*. Washington D.C.: Smithsonian Institution Press, 1994.

Soley, Lawrence, and George Hough. "Black Ownership of Commercial Radio Stations: An Economic Evaluation." *Journal of Broadcasting* 22 (fall 1978): 455–67.

Sosna, Morton. *In Search of the Silent South: Southern Liberals and the Race Issue*. New York: Columbia University Press, 1977.

Spady, James G. *Georgie Woods: I'm Only a Man: The Life Story of a Mass Communicator, Promoter, Civil Rights Activist*. Philadelphia: Snack-Pac, 1992.

Spaulding, Norman. "History of Black-Oriented Radio in Chicago, 1929–1963." Ph.D. diss., University of Illinois at Urbana-Champaign, 1981.

Spritzer, Lorraine Nelson, and Jean B. Bergmark. *Grace Towns Hamilton and the Politics of Southern Change*. Athens: University of Georgia Press, 1997.

Sterner, Richard, Leonore A. Epstein, Ellen Winston, et al. *The Negro's Share: A Study of Income, Consumption, Housing and Public Assistance*. New York: Harper and Brothers, 1943.

Stewart, Shelley, with Nathan Hale Turner Jr. *The Road South: A Memoir*. New York: Warner, 2002.

Surlin, Stuart. "Black-Oriented Radio's Service to the Community." *Journalism Quarterly* 50 (autumn 1973): 556–60.

Thomas, Evan. *Robert Kennedy: His Life*. New York: Simon and Schuster, 2000.

Thompson, Julius E. *The Black Press in Mississippi 1865–1985*. Gainesville: University Press of Florida, 1993.

Thornton, J. Mills, III. *Dividing Lines: Municipal Politics and the Struggle for Civil Rights in Montgomery, Birmingham, and Selma*. Tuscaloosa: University of Alabama Press, 2002.

Tinney, James S., and Justine J. Rector, eds. *Issues and Trends in Afro-American Journalism*. Lanham, Md.: University Press of America, 1980.

Tross, J. S. Nathaniel. *This Thing Called Religion*. Charlotte, N.C.: AME Zion Church, 1934.

Tuck, Stephen G. N. *Beyond Atlanta: The Struggle for Racial Equality in Georgia, 1940–1980*. Athens: University of Georgia Press, 2001.

U.S. Department of Commerce. Bureau of Census. *U.S. Census of Housing*. Washington, D.C.: U.S. Government Printing Office, 1960.

Vandergrift, Paul F. "Comparison of Two Approaches to Public/Non-Commercial Radio in Raleigh, Durham, and Chapel Hill, North Carolina." Ph.D. diss., University of North Carolina, 1977.

Walker, Jenny. "Black Violence and Nonviolence in the Civil Rights and Black Power Movements." Ph.D. diss., University of Newcastle upon Tyne, 2000.

———. "A Media-Made Movement? Black Violence and Nonviolence in the Historiography of the Civil Rights Movement." In *Media, Culture, and the Modern African American Freedom Struggle*, edited by Brian Ward, 41–66. Gainesville: University Press of Florida, 2001.

Wallace, Wesley Herndon. "The Development of Broadcasting in North Carolina, 1922–48." Ph.D. diss., Duke University, 1962.

Waller, Judith C. *Radio: The Fifth Estate*. Boston: Houghton Mifflin, 1946.

Walsh, Stephen Roy James. "Black-Oriented Radio and the Campaign for Civil Rights in the United States, 1945–1975." Ph.D. diss., University of Newcastle upon Tyne, 1997.

Wang, Jennifer Hyland. "The Case of the Radio-Active Housewife: Relocating Radio in the Age of Television." In *Radio Reader: Essays in the Cultural History of Radio*, edited by Michele Hilmes and Jason Loviglio, 343–66. New York: Routledge, 2002.

Ward, Brian. *Just My Soul Responding: Rhythm and Blues, Black Consciousness, and Race Relations*. Berkeley and Los Angeles: University of California Press, 1998.

———, ed. *Media, Culture, and the Modern African American Freedom Struggle*. Gainesville: University Press of Florida, 2001.

Ward, Brian, and Jenny Walker. "'Bringing the Races Closer'?: Black-Oriented Radio in the South and the Civil Rights Movement." In *Dixie Debates: Perspectives on Southern Cultures*, edited by Richard H. King and Helen Taylor, 130–49. New York: New York University Press, 1996.

Weems, Robert E., Jr. *Desegregating the Dollar: African American Consumerism in the Twentieth Century*. New York: New York University Press, 1998.

Wexler, Jerry, and David Ritz. *Rhythm and the Blues: A Life in American Music*. New York: Knopf, 1993.

Who's Who in the South and Southwest, 1965–1966. Chicago, Marquis, 1965.

Williams, Gilbert A. *Legendary Pioneers of Black Radio*. Westport, Conn.: Praeger, 1998.

Williams, Smallwood. *This Is My Story: A Significant Life Story: The Autobiography of Smallwood Edmond Williams*. Washington, D.C.: William Willoughby, 1981.

Wolcott, Victoria W. *Remaking Respectability: African American Women in Interwar Detroit*. Chapel Hill: University of North Carolina Press, 2001.

Wood, William A. *Electronic Journalism.* New York: Columbia University Press, 1967.

Yarger, Lisa. "Don't Touch That Dial: Carolina Radio Since the 1920s." *Southern Cultures* 5, no. 2 (summer 1999): 96–99.

Zieger, Robert H. *The CIO, 1935–1955.* Chapel Hill: University of North Carolina Press, 1995.

————. "A Venture into Unplowed Fields: Daniel Powell and CIO Political Action in the Postwar South." In *Labor in the Modern South,* edited by Glenn T. Eskew, 158–81. Athens: University of Georgia Press, 2001.

————, ed. *Organized Labor in the Twentieth-Century South.* Knoxville: University of Tennessee Press, 1991.

Index

Page references in italics refer to illustrations.

Brian Ward teaches American history at the University of Florida. His publications include the award-winning *Just My Soul Responding: Rhythm and Blues, Black Consciousness, and Race Relations* (1998) and, as volume editor, *Media, Culture, and the Modern African American Freedom Struggle* (2001).